AN INTRODUCTION TO
FILM GENRES

W. W. Norton & Company, Inc. also publishes

Looking at Movies: An Introduction to Film, Fourth Edition
Richard Barsam and Dave Monahan

Writing About Movies, Third Edition
Karen Gocsik, Richard Barsam, and Dave Monahan

Film Analysis: A Norton Reader, Second Edition
Jeffrey Geiger and R. L. Rutsky, eds.

Engaging Cinema
Bill Nichols

A History of Narrative Film, Fourth Edition
David A. Cook

American Film: A History
Jon Lewis

AN INTRODUCTION TO FILM GENRES

Lester Friedman
Hobart and William Smith Colleges

David Desser
University of Illinois at Urbana–Champaign

Sarah Kozloff
Vassar College

Martha P. Nochimson
Film and Media Critic

Stephen Prince
Virginia Tech

W. W. NORTON & COMPANY
New York · London

W. W. Norton & Company has been independent since its founding in 1923, when William Warder Norton and Mary D. Herter Norton first published lectures delivered at the People's Institute, the adult education division of New York City's Cooper Union. The firm soon expanded their program beyond the Institute, publishing books by celebrated academics from America and abroad. By mid-century, the two major pillars of Norton's publishing program—trade books and college texts—were firmly established. In the 1950s, the Norton family transferred control of the company to its employees, and today—with a staff of four hundred and a comparable number of trade, college, and professional titles published each year—W. W. Norton & Company stands as the largest and oldest publishing house owned wholly by its employees.

The text of this book is composed in Legacy Serif Std Book with the display set in Intro Book

Composition and page layout by Brad Walrod/Kenoza Type, Inc.
File management: Devon Zahn
Art file conversion: Jay's Publishers Services
Manufacturing by Courier—Westford, MA

Editor: Peter Simon
Senior project editor: Thomas Foley
Associate production director, college: Benjamin Reynolds
Copy editor: David Sutter
Book design: Lisa Buckley
Associate design director: Hope Miller Goodell
Managing editor, college: Marian Johnson
Marketing manager, film: Kimberly Bowers
Photography director: Trish Marx
Assistant editor: Quynh Do

Library of Congress Cataloging-in-Publication Data
Friedman, Lester D.
  An introduction to film genres / Lester Friedman, David Desser, Sarah Kozloff, Martha Nochimson, Stephen Prince.—First edition.
    pages cm
  Includes bibliographical references and index.
  ISBN 978-0-393-93019-1 (pbk.)
  1. Film genres.   I. Desser, David.   II. Kozloff, Sarah.   III. Nochimson, Martha.
IV. Prince, Stephen, 1955–   V. Title.
  PN1995.F744 2013
  791.43′6—dc23   2013016115

W. W. Norton & Company, Inc., 500 Fifth Avenue, New York, NY 10110
wwnorton.com
W. W. Norton & Company Ltd., Castle House, 75/76 Wells Street, London W1T 3QT
1 2 3 4 5 6 7 8 9 0

Contents

Preface

THE APPEARANCE OF A TEXTBOOK about film genres might seem a quaint artifact in the digital age, a dusty adjunct to the demise of the film industry, which has been predicted many times since at least the middle of the twentieth century. In the 1950s and 1960s, social commentators declared that viewers' easy access to hours of free television programming would bury an industry dependent on screening its productions in movie theaters. Then they predicted that the flood of VHS tapes (in the 1970s and '80s), DVDs (in the 1990s), and streaming video (in the late 2000s), coupled with the ever-more-sophisticated home theater systems that developed alongside these media, would snuff out the public's desire for large-screen excursions, eradicating a viewer's need to venture farther afield than the well-stocked refrigerator in the nearby kitchen. Now, social pundits anticipate new media delivering the final blow to "legacy" media, including traditional studio-produced cinema. They foresee a future in which the hypnotic Internet converges with portable digital devices to alter the movie business permanently, relegating movie theaters to sepia-tinted relics of a bygone era.

All of these claims contain some essential truths. Each technological innovation has revolutionized the multiple modes and systems by which we do business, create productions, receive information, access entertainment, and interact with other people: TV viewing and re-playable discs are massively popular, the Internet is an omnipresent force, and a dazzling array of portable new digital devices seems to appear almost weekly, making it ever easier for us to watch movies anywhere and at any time we choose.

What few envisaged, however, was that all of these technological developments, initially thought to hammer the final nail in the coffin of the cinema industry, have actually contributed to its evolution and continued growth. Far from being shrouded with cobwebs and relegated to the dustbin of history, the experience of seeing a film on a large screen continues to entice patrons into the darkness. To the surprise of cinema's obituary writers, movie theater attendance actually *increased* in 2012, reaching 1.36 billion tickets sold, up from 1.2 billion in 2011. Clearly, a large audience is still willing to drive to the local multiplex or art house cinema.

However, these positive trends veil dramatic changes in the way that audience members view and share movies, which will significantly impact future movie theater attendance figures. By the end of 2013, for example, film distributors will no longer dispense 35mm movies; instead, they will offer their products exclusively on hard drives, thus requiring theaters to install expensive digital cinema technology. This will improve the visual and sound quality of the films, but it will also force many independent theaters that cannot afford such upgrades out of business. In addition, a generation of young viewers increasingly watches movies within the flexible boundaries of portable technology—on laptops, tablets, and even smart phones—rather than actually "going to the movies." The current trends toward multipurpose devices that can transfer digital materials from one platform to another, toward increased viewer interaction with media productions, and toward meeting the consumer's demand to watch productions at a convenient time and place will fundamentally alter how, when, where, and even if film continues to be a vital art form.

How does a traditional approach to cinema, like genre—the oldest categorization system used by producers, distributors, and consumers to examine and to classify almost all realms of creative works—relate to this brave new world of technology and the changing viewing habits of audiences? Film historian Robert Sickels contends that "contemporarily, genre is more important in the industry than perhaps at any other point in its history.... As film moves increasingly into the digital age, genre films have as strong a presence as they ever have had in the American cinema."[1] Sickels argues that the increasing prevalence of sequels and remakes that characterize contemporary Hollywood filmmaking, as

---

[1] *American Film in the Digital Age* (Westport, Conn: Praeger Publishers), 2010, pp. 74, 76.

well as the need for familiar tropes that can capture a large audience, generate a ravenous need for easily identifiable movies, especially in the digital era where the competition for our attention and money has become more heated than ever before.

An Introduction to Film Genres highlights for students and general readers the continuing importance of film genres as a whole, and the particular qualities of thirteen individual genres that have historically dominated Hollywood movies. This book grew out of its authors' collective experiences over many decades of teaching courses centered on or about genre. Although a vast body of creative, inspiring, and valuable scholarship on film genres in general and individual genres specifically remains available, we all felt that no single text brought the study of film genre to undergraduates in an easily manageable form, and in an accessible voice that specifically addressed their needs. Our task, therefore, was to incorporate the best of what has been written over the years about these popular genres, rather than offering startlingly new interpretations. Our goal was to be both summative and creative—we drew together a wide range of complex ideas and historical trends, integrated these with a visual consciousness, and strove to illuminate a broad spectrum of genres while remaining conscious of our target audience.

To best accomplish this, we agreed to give each chapter a similar structure. Following a brief introduction of the specific genre, each chapter includes (1) a historical overview of the genre's evolution; (2) a discussion of recurrent typologies, themes, and theories related to that genre; (3) an analysis of the genre's relevant iconography; (4) a close reading of one significant movie within the genre or an in-depth consideration of one aspect of a few movies within the genre; and (5) a series of questions to stimulate classroom discussion. We have also included a number of frame grabs within every chapter to illustrate specific points and highlight significant films within the genre. Each frame grab includes a succinct paragraph that explains the importance of the particular visual image, stressing key points elaborated in the text.

This simple structure and approach—consistently applied to all of its chapters even as each chapter speaks in the distinctive voice of the particular author who wrote it—gives *An Introduction to Film Genres* something akin to the familiar and pleasantly predictable feel of the best genre films themselves. We hope this structure will make the experience of reading about and studying film genres an enjoyable one. More importantly, we hope that it will make the intriguing history of genre movies and the exciting theories about them as memorable as they possibly can be.

Lester Friedman
David Desser
Sarah Kozloff
Martha P. Nochimson
Stephen Prince
June, 2013

Acknowledgments

LESTER FRIEDMAN would like to express his personal gratitude to his co-authors. One could not have asked for a more knowledgeable and congenial group of exceptional film scholars to work with in preparing this volume. He appreciates their time, energy, enthusiasm, and patience as this book wound its way to publication.

Martha Nochimson would like to thank David Chase, creator of the *The Sopranos*; Terry Winter, creator of *Boardwalk Empire*; and *Boardwalk Empire* writers Howard Korder and Steve Kornacki for hours of good conversation about the gangster genre. She would also like to thank the countless colleagues and collaborators during the years she spent writing for American television soap operas (1984–1990), who helped shape her thinking about how fantasy and suspense work in the mass media.

All of the contributors to this volume would like to thank their students, whose feedback and passion in our courses have been inspiring and invaluable.

We would also like to acknowledge the dedicated staff at W. W. Norton & Company, Inc., who provided advice, support, encouragement, expertise, and good humor during this book's long gestation period: our editor, Peter Simon; assistant editors Quynh Do and Conor Sullivan; senior project editor Thom Foley; copy editor David Sutter; production director Benjamin Reynolds; art director Debra Morton-Hoyt; design director Rubina Yeh; photo director Trish Marx; and photo researcher Michael Fodera, among others whose names go unmentioned here but whose efforts we deeply appreciate.

Finally, we all join the publisher in thanking the reviewers of early drafts of our chapters, all of whom were anonymous to us during the process of writing and editing this book, but whom we are very pleased to finally be able to acknowledge by name: Lucy Bucknell (Johns Hopkins University), Jose Capino (University of Illinois, Urbana-Champaign), George Grella (University of Rochester), Gino Moliterno (Australian National University), Phillip Novak (LeMoyne College), Matthew Powers (New York University), and Michele Schreiber (Emory University). Thank you all.

AN INTRODUCTION TO
FILM GENRES

Introduction

But I don't go to the movies much. If you've seen one you've seen them all.
  —*Kathy Selden to Don Lockwood,* Singin' in the Rain

Every text participates in one or several genres, there is no genreless text; there is always a genre or genres.
  —*Jacques Derrida,* "The Law of Genre"

DESPITE ITS ENDURING POPULARITY and widespread usage, genre's seemingly solid definitions and practical utilities slip through our outstretched fingers when we try to pin the concept down too rigidly. This fluidity should be no surprise. Many classification systems that organize large numbers of items often prove quite ambiguous upon deeper reflection. Think for a moment about categorizing elements and experiences in our daily lives, such as grouping stores by their traditional designations. CVS and Walgreens, for example, are commonly referred to as drug stores, but their shelves are stocked with groceries, cosmetics, magazines, candies, household appliances, bug sprays, lightbulbs, and a host of other, nonpharmaceutical items. Similarly, grocery stores like Wegmans and Tops contain sections filled with the same over-the-counter medications found in CVS and Walgreens, and often have a 24-hour pharmacy as well. Film genres often skid and slide into each other in much the same way.

For a classic instance of this fluidity in cinema history, take *Citizen Kane* (1941), considered by many the finest American movie ever made. Is this compelling story of Charles Foster Kane's life a *melodrama* or a *reporter* story? Does the obsessive search for "Rosebud" make it a *mystery* or a *detective* story? Is its tale of incalculable wealth and ruthless capitalism the stuff of the *social problem* movie or a *crime* film? What about all those *film noir* flourishes? How do we classify Orson Welles's visual style and production values: experimental, independent, or mainstream? Is the final product a studio fabrication designed for popular consumption or an antistudio anomaly intended for art-house enthusiasts?

To cite a more contemporary example, how should we categorize the waves of costumed superheroes soaring into our cineplexes to rescue the world from their malevolent archenemies? Should the ever-expanding iterations of Superman, Batman, Iron Man, Captain America, the Hulk, Thor, Spider-Man, the X-Men, and a slew of other extraordinary beings be separated from each other and spliced into traditional categories—say the *disaster* or the *fantasy* or the *science-fiction* film genres? Or should we unite them to form a new genre of their own: the *superhero* films, or the *comic book* adaptations, or even the *mutant* movies? One could name a seemingly endless series of similar examples that illustrate the complexities and dichotomies of genre formation. Such issues remain troubling, but they do not diminish the continuing significance of genre's pivotal role in American film history. To gain a fuller understanding of how this concept functions within the production, distribution, reception, and analysis of cinema, we need to fit pieces of the genre puzzle together to form a coherent picture by examining its history, scrutinizing the construction of categories, exploring various approaches to studying it, and moving beyond the screen.

Genre History

First, we need some historical perspective. Genre remains the oldest categorization system used by producers, distributors, and consumers to examine and to classify almost all realms of creative works. The foundations of genre construction stretch as far back as Aristotle's formal differentiation among the various internal properties of imitative modes (epic, lyric, and dramatic poetry) in his *Poetics* (335 BCE). In 1603, Polonius's loquacious recitation of specific types of plays in Shakespeare's *Hamlet* (II, ii) seems, at least to modern ears, like a parodic listing of theater genres; and Alexander Pope's "Essay on Criticism" (1711) provides a witty take on eighteenth-century rules and conventions of poetic creation. In more modern times, Austin Warren and René Wellek's *Theory of Literature* (1948) argued that literary works should be grouped on the basis of their "outer form" (structural and formal elements) and "inner form" (attitude, tone, purpose), a strategy Ed Buscombe revived in the 1970s by adapting those terms to define film genres. Moving to a broader, more all-encompassing concept, Northrop Frye's archetypal approach in *Anatomy of Criticism* (1957) attempted to uncover and then to categorize literary works by their underlying narrative patterns and mythic structure.

Although contemporary scholars and popular critics such as Rick Altman, Wheeler Winston Dixon, John Frow, Barry Keith Grant, Raphaelle Moine, Thomas Schatz, and Andrew Tudor continue to spar vigorously over various aspects of genre study, neither academia nor the public has abandoned the fundamental methodology of genre. For example, Roger Ebert's website contains "A Guide to Film Noir Genre." Explaining his rating system, he wrote: "In the early days of my career I said I rated a movie according to its 'generic expectations,' whatever that meant. It might translate like this: '...If a director is clearly trying to make a particular kind of movie, and his audiences are looking for a particular kind of movie, part of my job is judging how close he came to achieving his purpose.'"[1] Thus, sustained efforts to conceptualize, understand, and utilize genres remain a vibrant, central preoccupation of media creators, audiences, critics, scholars, and exhibitors alike.

Despite its long history, critical consensus rarely exists about even the most basic issues concerning genre, such as how to define the very concept itself. From the beginning, disparate voices have asserted opposing claims about the uses and misuses of genre. Each faction seeks to build a sturdy philosophy that can withstand the disputes waged regarding genre studies from one century to the next. With blueprints from the past as guideposts, the traditionalists stress adherence to formal doctrines of practice and layers of conventions contoured by artists over time, a practice epitomized by the rigid aesthetic rules demanded by eighteenth-century British neoclassicists. Modern critics advocating this position believe that genre works should remain firmly embedded within clearly defined narrative and/or spatial boundaries, utilize easily identifiable character types, and fit clearly inside long-established

---

[1] Roger Ebert, *Roger Ebert's Journal* (blog), "You Give Out Too Many Stars." *Chicago Sun-Times*, September 14, 2008. www.rogerebert.com/rogers-journal/you-give-out-too-many-stars.

categories. Their aesthetic standard rests on the concept of "mimesis," a term that originally meant to imitate nature but later came to denote attempts to emulate the master writers of the classical Greek and Roman periods. When applied to film production, this model necessitated the use of recurring narrative patterns, conventional characters, and recognizable iconography derived from Hollywood's "classical" film period during the studio era (1936–1970).

Those who rebuke traditionalists for imposing inflexible edicts, formulaic principles, repetitive patterns, and clichéd narratives construct a starkly different philosophy. These scholars admire works that shatter conventional rules and reject comfortable standards within any particular genre's traditions. Derived from the rebellious attitudes of the nineteenth-century Romantics, twentieth-century poet Ezra Pound's exhortation to "Make it New!" exemplifies this position, as does his definition of art in *How I Began* (1913): "A work of Art which is not a beginning, an invention, a discovery, is of little worth." This perspective glorifies inspired originality and characterizes the true artist as one who generates something unexpected, innovative, and imaginative. It sees the customs venerated by the neoclassicists not as blueprints but as shackles that thwart the flowering of individual talent and obstruct our appreciation of unique art works. Those who espouse these ideals brand predictable productions with their ultimate insult: "generic." Such unremitting, often vociferous debates spotlight the inherent tension between those who revere tradition and those who worship originality, a clash of fundamental aesthetic principles that flows across almost all the mediums of expression and reemerges in most every era. As demonstrated throughout this book, many of American cinema's best genre films successfully negotiate a passage between the neoclassical and Romantic ideals. Indeed, the productions of mainstream cinema in the United States can be aptly characterized as a continual process of convergence, both in form and content, between repetition and variation, formula and innovation, and commercially popular conventions and novel deviations.

The average moviegoer, however, rarely considers such disputes over the form and content of genres. Viewers who recognize specific genre categories bring to the movie theater basic expectations about what they will see on the screen; many arrive with a sense of that genre's history or, at the very least, recollections of particular films they liked or disliked within that genre. As such, they can be delighted (or horrified) when a filmmaker offers them differences in visual style, narrative patterns, and expected characterizations. As the film scholars David Bordwell and Kristin Thompson put it, "Audiences expect the genre film to offer something familiar but also demand fresh variations on it."[2] This easily stated principle belies the fact that no formula exists for producers to calculate the balance between one and the other. Too many repetitive elements pile up clichés that may bore viewers; too many departures from generic expectations may confuse, frustrate, or even irritate them.

Thus, genre films inevitably become amalgamated productions replicating some recognizable structures and conventions from the past while simultaneously incorporating inventiveness and originality that speaks to the present. In other words, filmmakers working within broad and distinguishable genre configurations reconceptualize a familiar pattern by infusing it with their particular worldview, as well as elements from the historical period they inhabit. Therefore, a literary classic such as Jane Austen's *Emma* (1815) can be transformed into a Beverly Hills high-school story to become *Clueless* (1995) and Austen's lily-white English characters can morph into black American teenagers. Similarly, though in quite a different emotional and visual pitch, *Inglourious Basterds* (2009) can incorporate, satirize, and often invert many of the typical conventions of the combat film, even providing an alternative ending to Hitler's reign of terror and ultimately to World War II, while concurrently staying within the expected boundaries of the genre.

Who Creates Genres?

With this brief history as context, we can now move on to another section of the puzzle and ask some basic questions: How are genres formed? How do they develop? Who (or what) determines them? Of course, no single answer solves these fundamental riddles. No single piece fits snugly into the puzzle. Instead, genres arise out of the composite and recurrent interaction of three main sources of meaning: 1) creators, 2) texts, and 3) audiences. In its most basic form, the diagram below illustrates the intrinsic interconnections among these three.

---

[2] David Bordwell and Kristin Thompson, *Film Art: An Introduction*, 7th ed. (New York: McGraw-Hill, 2004), 111.

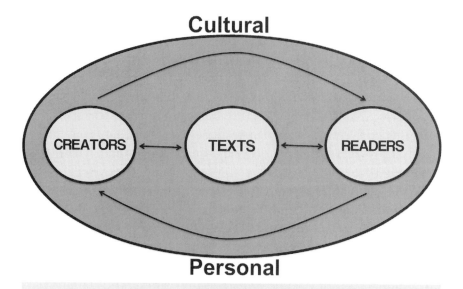

Cultural

CREATORS ←→ TEXTS ←→ READERS

Personal

The Generation of Meanings This diagram demonstrates the constant interactions among creators, texts, and readers. These dynamic interfaces generate multiple meanings that can change over time and vary with differences in audience demographics. Culture always surrounds and affects these three factors in the construction of meanings. Artists cannot avoid being considerably influenced by events, both social and personal, that surround them, and the same holds true for readers. From a contemporary perspective, a viewer's ability to see movies at any time on a variety of different platforms drastically alters the screening experience and radically redefines the relationship among creators, texts, and readers. These three factors are never static, and the result of their interdependence upon each other creates meanings.

In the diagram above, the terms "creators," "texts," and "readers" are specified as plurals to accent the multiplicities contained within each designation. 1) *Creators.* Filmmaking is an inherently collaborative process. Though directors often decide essential questions required to generate a cinema text, their collaborators inevitably provide crucial advice, assistance, inspiration, designs, and technical skills. Such important contributions affect and can even considerably alter the evolution and final shape of a work. After all, Oscars are awarded each year in far more categories than just Best Director, and lengthy end credits display the large and small contributions a host of people make to every movie. Therefore, there are many creators for each film. 2) *Texts.* Similarly, all texts contain manifold meanings that exist simultaneously within the same collection of screen images and dialogue. Images and words always contain both denotative and connotative substance and, consequently, their import shifts over time along with changing historical circumstances and cultural perspectives. Additionally, images and words can carry various (sometimes quite dissimilar) emotional valances for different people that leave open the potentiality for a wide range of responses. 3) *Readers.* Finally, audiences are not monolithic entities whose members automatically share a single point of view. While viewers can be encouraged—some would say manipulated—to read a particular film in a certain way, or to admire one character and despise another, they don't mechanically march together in compliant intellectual and/or emotional lockstep. Instead, individual audience members bring their own biological, sociological, and psychological profiles to every screening, forming pockets of personal agreement, disagreement, and negotiation not necessarily similar to those of other audience members. Creators, texts, and readers always influence each other to some degree, and the arrows that connect these three illustrate their intrinsic attachments to and interdependence on one another.

An even larger circle called "cultural" encompasses these three smaller units. For the purpose of a straightforward representation, this far-reaching and somewhat vague term includes everything from current events, prevailing ideologies, the state of film technology, available delivery platforms, distribution strategies, and anything else that affects the creators, the texts, and the readers as participants within the world they inhabit. Artists never labor in a cultural vacuum and cannot avoid being influenced by events, both social and personal, that surround them. Great works may transcend their times, but they are always part of them as well. For example, comparing the levels of violence and overt sexual content in modern movies, like Brian De Palma's *Scarface* (1983), with those the studios made during the Hays Code era (1930–1968), like Howard Hawks's *Scarface* (1932), speaks as much about the state of society and censorship as it does about the individual sensibility of visual artists. Similarly, the accessibility of technical tools strongly influences productions: *Jaws* would have been dramatically different if Steven Spielberg had access to sophisticated computer-generated imagery, instead of having to rely on a mechanical shark. A viewer's ability to see movies at any time on a variety of different platforms drastically alters the screening experience and radically redefines the relationship of readers to each other. Finally, the "Personal" elements that creators bring to the artistic process play an important role in generating meanings, including: age, gender, sexual orientation, race, personality, and other individual traits.

Keep in mind, this admittedly basic schema of creators, texts, readers, and culture as we traverse the topographies of genre theories, since most of the critical approaches focus on one of the circles and, in doing so, sometimes miss the indispensable linkages so important for mapping the entire terrain.

Approaches to Genre Study

With the history and creation pieces of the genre puzzle in place, we can now consider various approaches to studying these film categories. Because both readers and authors view every genre movie with a history of reading and interpreting previous ones, no one film exists in total isolation from the past. Thus, all films are by their very nature intertextual. This term, in its most uncomplicated and oversimplified sense, has come to mean that every text is shaped by our experiences and understandings of other texts, both past and present. This process between old and new works affects a text's creation, production, and reception. It can be overt, as in a direct allusion from one text to another—Sergio Leone's use of Monument Valley as a geographic backdrop in *Once Upon a Time in the West* (1968) makes an explicit reference to the famous Westerns that John Ford filmed there—or indirect, in that texts we have previously read automatically mediate our responses to those we are currently reading. In addition to creation, production, and reception, intertextuality directly influences economic decisions, particularly distribution strategies and marketing campaigns. In a wide variety of ways and across different mediums, advertisements directly invite viewers to replicate the pleasure they received from previous movies in the same genre. Posters promoting *Raiders of the Lost Ark* (1981) contained tag lines such as "The Return of the Great Adventure" and "From the Creators of *Jaws* and *Star Wars*," invoking both genre expectations and previously popular movies from Spielberg and George Lucas. Similarly, posters promoting *You've Got Mail* (1998) hailed it as "the best romantic comedy of the year" and prominently featured Meg Ryan and Tom Hanks. The image of these two stars together immediately recalls their hit movie of five years earlier, *Sleepless in Seattle* (1993). "If you loved that one," the posters implicitly claim, "you will love this one. So buy a ticket."

Because contemporary movies continually invoke memories and conventions of preceding movies, intertextuality becomes a pervasive ingredient in all filmmaking and viewing, an elemental building block in the processes of genre production, distribution, reception, and study. The constant process of repetition and variation bespeaks an intimate and ongoing conversation between films of the past and current movies today. Consciously or not, viewers' minds are stuffed with remembrances of past films, so neither authors nor readers can escape intertextual influences. In this sense, all genre films become visual palimpsests: traces of older films remain within the frames of newer ones. These dialogues between the cinema that was and the cinema that is do not necessarily confine themselves within the same genre; they often disregard boundaries, migrate among formats, and transgress lines of critical demarcation. Filmmakers continually amalgamate narrative and iconographic elements from various sources, ultimately forging genre movies into malleable hybrids that rarely reside exclusively in just one category. As theoretician Jacques Derrida says in the epigraph at the start of this introduction, "Every text participates in one or several genres."

Examples of these intertextual hybrids abound: *Blade Runner* (1982), a noir detective movie that sets its action in the Los Angeles of 2019; *Back to the Future III* (1990), a fantasy film that takes its protagonist from the 1950s back to Hollywood's Old West; *The Rocky Horror Picture Show* (1975), a musical featuring a Dr. Frankensteinian transvestite; *Paint Your Wagon* (1969), a musical Western with tough guys Clint Eastwood and Lee Marvin both singing; *Prizzi's Honor* (1985), a crime movie with the plotline of a screwball comedy; *Outland* (1981), a science-fiction movie that replays the classic Western *High Noon* (1952) on one of Jupiter's moons; *(500) Days of Summer* (2009), a romantic comedy featuring a dancing and singing interlude; *Inglourious Basterds* (2009), a World War II combat movie that mimics the visual conventions of a spaghetti Western; and *The King's Speech* (2010), a biopic that details historical events. The list is almost endless. In fact, hybridization was as common in earlier eras of film history as it is today, as film scholar Geoff King convincingly argues, citing *Casablanca* (1942) as his prime example. Hollywood films have always mixed genres to reach a wider range of filmgoers. In so doing, they fuse together characteristic elements and conventions from different genres.

An understanding of genre's intertextuality and hybridization does not invalidate its significance in the creation, production, reception, criticism, and distribution of cinematic art. It simply means genre categories should not straitjacket our understanding of the multiple possibilities within texts. Think, for a moment, about Spielberg, considered by many

Genre Films as Intertextual Hybrids Contemporary movies invoke memories of their predecessors, either via direct allusion or by means of style and structure. An essential building block in the production, distribution, reception, and study of genre movies, intertextuality references the constant process of repetition and variation that creates an ongoing conversation between films of the past and current movies today. Filmmakers habitually amalgamate narrative and iconographic elements from various sources, ultimately forging genre movies into intertextual hybrids that rarely reside exclusively in just one category. *Blade Runner* (1982), a murky detective movie that harkens back to the 1940s, is set in a futuristic Los Angeles and illustrates the fusion of characteristic elements and conventions from the science fiction, detective, romance, and film noir genres. This intertextual and hybrid nature of genre movies allows filmmakers to incorporate deeper layers into their creations and provides insight into how and why genre movies strike resonant chords within their audiences.

critics and movie buffs as the most accomplished action/adventure film director of his generation. Yet even his thrills-and-chills movies, such as *Jaws* (1975), *Indiana Jones and the Last Crusade* (1989), and *Jurassic Park* (1993), center around makeshift family structures threatened by outside forces: a rogue shark, dastardly Nazis, and genetically engineered dinosaurs. Their narrative structures all spring from the protagonist's need to reconstitute the "family" while battling antagonists that seek to destroy those he loves. From this perspective, then, Spielberg's films become essentially melodramas, their core dilemmas revolving around domestic instability and resolved by reconstituting a fractured social structure. Yet to see the consistent melodramatic focal points in Spielberg's movies complements, rather than competes with the more traditional ways in which we situate his films within the action/adventure genre. This is another reason why genre study remains a viable methodology for media scholars, as it reveals the deeper layers that filmmakers have incorporated into their creations, providing insight into how and why movies strike resonant chords deep within us.

GENRES AS CULTURAL MYTHS. One widely held genre theory conceptualizes recurring narratives as a series of communal myths that reiterate important cultural stories, offer a set of fundamental archetypes, and provide a sense of ritual missing in secular society. Historically, communal myths attempt to recapitulate a particular idea or aspect of culture in order to express and perhaps resolve painful conflicts from the past. These narratives, therefore, condense and distill a society's collective fantasies, aspirations, obsessions, and anxieties. As such, standard characters within these myths traditionally embody particular sets of values that either affirm or clash with accepted social practice. From the advent of mechanically reproduced, widely disseminated, and shared mass media in the late nineteenth century, genre movies have been the modern equivalents of ancient myths that encapsulated—and sometimes challenged—social values and identities. Thus, the relationships among a great number of films compiled over time formulate genre categories and conventions that are able to adjust themselves to either conform with or militate against any given era's prevailing cultural perspectives.

As a paradigmatic example of this mythic/genre approach, the Western tells of the American frontier experience, a series of defining events that many historians feel make American history unique and that helped to forge our national identity. From the earliest silent films to the latest multimillion-dollar productions, these retellings of the western myth reflect assorted, sometimes contradictory versions of historically based events, some that actually occurred and some that are fictitious. How many Billy the Kids, Wyatt Earps, and Jessie Jameses have shot up American movie screens? How often have swinging doors opened to reveal smoke-filled saloons alive with the tinkling of tinny pianos, the slap of cards on wooden tables, and the clink of whiskey bottles against shot glasses? Depending on its originality and point of view, a Western can sustain or alter our evaluations of the events it depicts and, by extension, our cultural narratives as well. Think how the status of Native Americans in Westerns has evolved from that of the savage enemy to that of the noble warrior. On a more general level, critics generally agree that Westerns depict the conflict between the individual's connection to or alienation from the evolution of society, exemplified by the alteration of the wilderness by the onset of civilization.

Yet the dearth of Westerns produced over the last decade or so, despite the critical success of *Unforgiven* (1992), the remakes of *3:10 to Yuma* (2007) and *True Grit* (2010), the laconic *Appaloosa* (2008), and the

Genre Films as Cultural Myths Genre movies serve as communal myths that encapsulate important cultural stories, offer a set of fundamental archetypes, and provide a sense of ritual missing in secular society. They distill a society's collective fantasies, aspirations, obsessions, and anxieties, while their standard characters embody particular sets of values that may be in conflict with each other. The Western, for example, retells the defining American frontier experience for different generations, either sustaining or altering this cultural narrative. By visiting and revisiting crucial narratives and settings that define American culture, genre films either reaffirm the status quo or offer fresh perspectives. *Pat Garrett & Billy the Kid* (1973), directed by Sam Peckinpah, draws upon one of the most famous legends of the American West, but infuses this familiar tale with new meaning by combining contemporary musical icons such as Kris Kristofferson, Rita Coolidge, and Bob Dylan, with actors from the classical days of Hollywood Westerns, such as Chill Willis, Katy Jurado, Jack Elam, Slim Pickens, and Barry Sullivan.

ultraviolent *Django Unchained* (2012), indicates that this once-pervasive cultural myth is no longer popular, no longer evocative or even relevant to contemporary audiences. Ironically, some of its most cherished tropes have morphed into other genres, particularly science fiction: consider *Star Trek*, with Captain Kirk as a Western-like hero, Mr. Spock as his faithful, Tonto-like sidekick, and Bones as the grumpy country doctor exploring, with the rest of the crew, "the final frontier" while facing savage aliens that fill the role of hostile Indians. (Since Gene Roddenberry was, before *Star Trek*, the head writer of the TV series *Have Gun, Will Travel* (1957–1963) and called his science-fiction creation "a wagon train to the stars," such a reading would have biographical validity as well.) But the frontier experience that once launched thousands of movies now seems like an antiquated, at times even racist, set of hackneyed dichotomies. For modern viewers, Westerns have become moth-eaten sweaters Dad once wore with pride but that his sons only occasionally take out of the closet for sentimental reasons.

Despite the demise of the Western, what ideological functions does the cinematic replication of cultural myths in genre films fulfill? Some scholars consider genres films simplistic and reactionary productions that actually thwart social change. For these critics, genre films merely reproduce socially acceptable stories that lull audiences into believing that the status quo represents the way society naturally evolved and, indeed, should always be. As such, genre films function as entertaining opiates that replicate, disseminate, and reinforce the dominant ideology of any given culture; sanctioning a particular point of view as correct and normal, while totally ignoring divergent positions or consigning them to the periphery. Genre films, these detractors contend, rarely engage seriously with social or political issues even when they purport to; instead, they habitually reinforce mainstream values by turning important cultural problems into backdrops for romantic love stories, proffering one-dimensional solutions to complex issues, and eliciting emotional responses instead of substantive actions.

Some critics, on the other hand, believe that the genre-as-myth formulation can lead to positive social changes or at least to discussions, perhaps obliquely, of important contemporary issues (despite genre films often being set in past or future eras). By visiting and revisiting crucial narratives that define American culture, they argue, genre films offer the possibility of fresh perspectives that can change entrenched attitudes once deemed normative, fixed, and certain. During the 1970s, for example, a host of films deconstructed traditional genre patterns, including Westerns, police dramas, detective movies, horror films, melodramas, musicals, and combat films. *McCabe and Mrs. Miller* (1971) reconceptualized the onset of American civilization, *The French Connection* (1971) presented police officers that were as repugnant as their criminal counterparts, *Five Easy Pieces* (1970) offered a male melodrama, *Little Big Man* (1970) deconstructed the cavalry mythos, *The Exorcist* (1973) revealed the horror of parenting, *Chinatown* (1974) portrayed the private eye failing to triumph over evil, *Saturday Night Fever* (1977) exposed the urban grit behind the disco glitz, and *Apocalypse Now* (1979) depicted a psychedelic Vietnam War. Such demythologizing challenges hallowed traditions woven deeply into the fabric of our social and personal tapestries, encouraging audience members to meditate on conventional cultural beliefs and narratives. Of course, genre parodies, such as *Blazing Saddles* (1974), *Scary Movie* (2000), and *Tropic Thunder* (2008), forthrightly ridicule genre conventions and, in so doing, cast doubts on our trusting acceptance of their clichés and fundamental ideological assumptions.

GENRES AS CULTURAL MEMORIES. Genre films can function as cultural memories as well as cultural myths. Though the two are intimately entwined, films that function as memories usually style themselves as realistic, though often wrapped in fictional disguises, while myths partake of broader archetypes and narratives less overtly tied to everyday events. Cultural memories, therefore, accrue some of their power from being ostensibly based on actual events, although they may treat them with a wide range of fictional devices. For example, most films about World War II are cultural memories rather than myths. Even a fanciful movie like *Kelly's Heroes* (1970), about a ragtag group of GIs who sneak behind enemy lines in search of Nazi gold, leaves us wondering if something like that sorta-coulda-mighta happened. Similarly, many Westerns base their narratives, no matter how far removed from historical accuracy, on actual occurrences, like the gunfight at the O.K. Corral, Custer's last stand, and the Lincoln County range war. Conversely, horror and science-fiction films such as *Frankenstein* (1931) and *Star Wars* (1977) deal more in myths. While we know these events never occurred, mythic films often depend on creating a patina of reality to lull viewers into thinking scientists might actually be creating monsters or that Darth Vader is breathing heavily down their necks. Crossovers, however, do occur quite regularly. Clint Eastwood's Western figures clearly partake of mythic stature, personifying a hypermasculinity meant to enfold American manhood within a large-than-life serape. Conversely, Eastwood's embodiment of Inspector Callahan in the Dirty Harry series, while equally macho, strives to be taken as far more realistic, though his story is no more factual than that of his Western counterparts.

Technology provides many ways to produce and share cultural memories, and visual images play a dominant role in constructing both personal and communal recollections. But this is slippery territory. Scientists now believe what artists have always known: memories constantly get revised and rewritten. Like digitized imagery, they are never stable and easily altered. Neuroscientists call this process "reconsolidation": our memories of past events are altered by other experiences that have

Genre Films as Cultural Memories Our age of mechanical and digital reproduction allows readily attainable images of the past to be easily recorded, expertly redesigned, and rapidly disseminated for popular consumption. Because of their longevity, repetitions, variations, and conventions, genre works are important building blocks in constructing these cultural memories, particularly those that accrue their power from being ostensibly based on actual events. These "prosthetic memories" are widely circulated, technologically generated memories that becomes as important a part of a person's sense of identity as actual lived experiences. As such, genre films form a repository of communal memories and continue to play a central role in the negotiation and codification of historical events in American culture. For example, the exploits of real-life criminals are romanticized and transformed into the escapades of rebellious 1960s outsiders in *Bonnie and Clyde* (1967).

occurred since, which then modify—by revision and adjustment—our original mental images, transforming them into new memories. Thus, our memories are always part imagination. But what happens to our cultural memories when media mixes the messages? Does the Beatles' song "Revolution" lose its rebellious power when it fuels a Nike commercial? How does seeing Marlon Brando wearing his outlaw biker's outfit from *The Wild One* (1953) while shilling for MasterCard affect our cultural memories? "What're you rebelling against, Johnny?" "Whadddya got" is the famous question and answer in *The Wild One*; should it now be, "Just go get that credit card!" Finally, what to make of Bob Dylan, the embodiment of an antiestablishment outsider, slinking around in a Victoria's Secret commercial ("Angels in Venice") while "Love Sick" plays on the sound track? Seeing these figures and hearing these songs in such unexpected juxtapositions unavoidably alters our original memories and inevitably conditions our future responses. Such cultural clashes roughly shuffle and shift memories, both personal and cultural, providing new associative contexts that change their meanings—at least until they are reconsolidated once again.

How might this idea of reconsolidation work in relation to genre production, reception, and study? Because of their longevity, repetitions, variations, and conventions, genre works are often cited by critics as important building blocks in constructing our cultural memories. The current surge of so-called memoirs that flood the literary landscape aptly demonstrates that personal memory is a catacomb of edited perceptions, justifications, affirmations, lies, explanations, truths, recollections, and inaccuracies mediated by a present self explaining past actions. Penned five years later or earlier, the same memoirist would no doubt write a different book about the same events, for memories are always evolving, forever reconsolidating. The movies we construct about our lives are rarely accurate portrayals of what actually happened. The same is true about genre films in the service of cultural memories. The historical variations on genre narratives and conventions tell us more about the time in which the film was made than about the era in which it is ostensibly set.

GENRES AS RITUALS. A story told once disappears into the shrouds of time; it is the retelling over and over again that can transform narratives into culturally significant rituals. The fact that only certain genres survive and that audiences respond to repeated viewings of them leads some critics to believe that these repetitive acts of showing and watching fulfill basic human needs to recount and revisit influential episodes, be they historical or fanciful. That audiences return to particular configurations of elements decade after decade aptly demonstrates that these combinations continue to resonate. Some critics roughly equate watching genre films with religious ceremonies, noting that each activity offers the participant dependability, comfort, and familiarity.

Rituals, religious or otherwise, also perform a social function: they build communities by gathering together people who share similar values, tastes, and points of view. Genre films can serve a comparable purpose. To take an obvious example, numerous fan sites on the web invite the sharing of cinema passions: the Yahoo directory alone contains almost two thousand sites devoted to classic Hollywood genres such as horror, science fiction, Westerns, martial arts, and film noir. If you have

Genres as Rituals The telling and retelling of similar stories over and over again can transform narratives into culturally significant rituals. The fact that only certain genres survive and that audiences respond to repeated viewings of these formulas and conventions suggests that repetitive acts of showing and watching fulfill basic human needs to recount and revisit influential narratives. That audiences continually return to particular configurations of dramatic elements aptly demonstrates that these combinations offer them dependability, comfort, and familiarity. Such organizing rituals also perform a social function; they build communities by gathering together people who share similar values, tastes, and points of view. Film genres achieve status through ritual repetitions over time, and as such, can become the collective expression of a particular era and, overall, of the American consciousness. *The Maltese Falcon* (1941), for example, initiated a cycle featuring the hard-boiled detective, the duplicitous femme fatale, and the competition for a valuable object, a pattern that sustains the crime genre to this day.

a particular interest in a specific type of film, you can find a like-minded community on the Internet ready to welcome you. Because film genres achieve mythic status through ritual repetitions over time, they become the collective expression of a particular era and, overall, of the American consciousness.

GENRE FILMS AND INDIVIDUAL ARTISTS. In the short history that began this introduction, I noted the tension between those who viewed genre conventions as prototypes to emulate and those who rejected them as cliché-ridden straitjackets. Yet, critical emphasis on the individual auteur and genre study can inhabit common ground. *Chinatown* is simultaneously an important film in the collective work of Roman Polanski and in the history of film noir. Certainly, genre expectations

Genre Films and Individual Artists Individual artists have a long history of working within genres. For example, *Chinatown* (1974) is simultaneously an important film in the overall film legacy of Roman Polanski as well as in the ongoing history of film noir detective movies. While genre filmmaking offers certain restraints, these parameters can actually enable communication by constructing new edifices upon an established foundation. Visual artists can assert their personalities by using genre conventions as loose guidelines rather than as strict rules and can stamp personal themes and artistry upon a particular set of cinematic traditions. Genre films can also provide filmmakers with the camouflage of predictable entertainment that permits them to delve into taboo subjects, frightening realities, and dark nightmares. Genre narratives, conventions, and iconography, therefore, do not obliterate the role of the auteur, but rather situate a filmmaker within a long tradition of film history that he/she remains free to embrace, modify, or attack. Genre study and auteurism, therefore, can complement each other to illuminate the same movie.

may limit an artist's sense of total freedom, but all creators, no matter their discipline, work in a historical tradition bound by some rules and conventions. To use literary critic Harold Bloom's term, an "anxiety of influence" pervades all the arts, as contemporary practitioners revere or reject, respect or revamp, the work of their predecessors and the traditions they endorsed. This tension between new and old is palpable and omnipresent in genre works because their formulations seek a balance between the similarities that align the current piece with the previous works and the differences that define it as unique.

While genre filmmaking involves certain restraints, some critics claim it actually enables communication by permitting the construction of new edifices upon an established foundation; in other words, an understanding of genre works demands previous knowledge that allows viewers to absorb new information and meaning. From this perspective, visual artists can assert their personalities by using genre conventions as loose guidelines rather than as strict rules. In fact, the ability to stamp personal themes and visual artistry upon a particular genre, as Alfred Hitchcock did with the thriller and Sam Peckinpah did with the Western, clearly demonstrates that genre and individual genius can cohabit the same text.

Equally important, genre films can provide filmmakers with the camouflage of predictable, amusing entertainment that permits them to delve into sensitive or disturbing material that might otherwise prove inadvisable or even downright dangerous. Under the protective cover of genre, they can examine taboo subjects, frightening realities, and dark nightmares. In this case, genre narratives, conventions, and iconography provide concealment for those authors clever enough to use them as valuable tools rather than seeing them as imprisoning bars. For example, most critics agree that many science-fiction films deal with racism under the pretext of human-meets-alien narratives, much as John Ford explores the same theme using Western tropes in *The Searchers* (1956). Genre study and auteurism, therefore, can complement each other to illuminate the same movie. To employ genre criticism does not totally obliterate the role of the auteur; rather, it recognizes individual genius and situates a filmmaker within a long tradition, one that he/she remains free to embrace, modify, or attack. Perhaps ironically, a genre can throw a spotlight on the uniqueness of a particular auteur: when many filmmakers work within similar parameters, the strengths and weaknesses of each can be perceived even more clearly.

Genre: Beyond the Screen

Now that we have fit the pieces of the genre puzzle—history, creation, and approaches—into their places, we can investigate elements beyond the screen that make significant contributions to the formation of genres.

GENRE AND AUDIENCES. Over the decades, the various protocols of genre have conditioned audiences to recognize their themes and formats; in turn, the patronage and preferences of viewers have influenced genre practices, making spectators active participants in determining the contours and evolution of genre production and history. Knowledgeable readers of genre texts commonly anticipate the appearance of certain images, conventions, and narrative cues regularly associated with the type of film they are screening. Satisfying these "fields of references" (to use critic Robert Warshow's famous term) provides part of the pleasure audiences receive from watching genre movies. Such familiarity also permits unexpected and innovative variations on the traditions to deepen the experience, since those who value the genre can recognize and appreciate (or reject) these deviations.

This process of expectation and fulfillment forms a social compact, a tacit agreement between authors working within generic traditions and those viewing them, to fulfill their obligations to each other. As film scholar Thomas Schatz points out, this "dynamic process of exchange" creates a "reciprocal relation" between creators and their audiences, as well as a "built-in feedback" circuit that encourages producers to recycle successful narratives, conventions, and visual styles. Thus, viewers are empowered by the knowledge of genre. It allows them a deeper understanding of the text that, even for the uninitiated or nonexpert, gives them ways to talk about it beyond simple restatement, personal opinion, or summary.

While accepting that a social compact incorporating expectations and fulfillments exists between creators and readers of genre texts, theories that see audience members as responding more or less the same way to genre narratives ignore the individual complexity of those who compose the group. While still aware of genre conventions, every viewer brings a particular combination of psychological, sociological, and biological traits to the screening of a film. In her classic essay "Visual Pleasure and Narrative Cinema" (1975), Laura Mulvey sharply differentiates between the perspectives of the male and female spectator, posing questions about how gender influences both "the gaze" and reception. Other scholars introduce similar questions about the racial, social, sexual orientation, and ideological identifications that divide viewers. Also, individuals may present different aspects of their personality depending on who they are with and their circumstances at that point in time. Do you act the same with your parents as you do with your friends or roommates? Probably not, since we each emphasize different aspects of ourselves at different times and to different audiences.

Clearly, then, we each carry multiple points of view to any film screening. This basic fact precludes an audience from sharing any monolithic reading on any given evening, much less across a diverse nation like the United States. Sometimes even the content of a film itself can create an inner conflict between our own varied, personal viewpoints, since each of us is composed of many different selves. Take, as an example of this dilemma, the situation of a Native American watching one of John

Ford's early cavalry films. These movies depict Indians as bloodthirsty savages with no apparent motivation for attacking peaceful wagon trains, raiding civilized forts, scalping brave settlers, or raping white women. If a contemporary Native American viewer identifies with the Native Americans on the screen, then he/she would seem to be endorsing slaughter and cruelty. If they sympathize with John Wayne and the rest of the Seventh Cavalry, however, then they appear to be siding with people who killed their ancestors. So, in a broad sense, the Native American moviegoer is forced to choose between either accepting the narrative

Genre and Audiences The conventions of genre filmmaking condition audiences to recognize the themes and formats of genre films; in turn, the knowledge and patronage of viewers makes them active participants in determining the contours and evolution of genre production. Such familiarity with genre formulations permits unexpected and innovative variations on the traditions to deepen the viewing experience, since those who value the genre can recognize and appreciate (or reject) these deviations. This process of expectation and fulfillment forms a social compact, a tacit agreement between authors working within generic traditions and those viewing them, to fulfill their obligations to each other. While accepting that a social compact incorporating expectations and fulfillments exists between creators and readers of genre texts, we each carry multiple points of view to any film screening that militate against any monolithic reading by an audience. Individual differences among viewers inevitably change their attitudes over time and this evolution predictably affects responses to a movie. A film like *Saturday Night Fever* (1977) captures the mood and feeling of a particular time period but may seem quaint, or even humorous, to more recent viewers.

that Native Americans brutally obstructed the civilizing of America or of rejecting the frontier ethos regarded by some as the foundational event in our national history.

Another aspect to take into account is that individual audience members inevitably change their attitudes over time and this evolution predictably affects how he/she responds to a movie. When I first saw *Five Easy Pieces* in 1970, I cheered, like the rest of the college-age audience, when Bobby Dupea (Jack Nicholson) angrily sweeps the dishes off the diner table after being refused his simple request for an order of toast. To many during that time, his defiant act summed up an attitude toward heedless authority, a romantic rebelliousness that characterized an alienated generation during a tumultuous period in American history. Now, when I teach this film as part of my class on Seventies Cinema, I respond totally differently to that sequence. It seems a small, almost petty, reaction from a callous man unaccountably wasting his life, a flare-up that speaks primarily to his self-indulgence and contains little historical resonance or power. More important, I wonder why this highly educated man takes out his personal frustration on a blue-collar worker, a waitress who is no doubt tired, has had her fill of demanding customers, wants to go home, and fears losing her job if she fails to enforce the management's rules. Ego, not ideology, triggers Bobby Dupea's emotional eruption, an outburst arising from a hollowness that generates his own psychological problems rather than from the current social situation. The images have not changed from 1970 to 2013, but I have. Being a father, a husband, and a teacher in the twenty-first century has reframed my viewing positions and modified how I respond to images from my past. Such permutations make viewing films an evolving, active experience rather than one solidified into permanence. The role of the audience is always a crucial element in the creation, distribution, and reception of genre works. Readers don't assume a passive role, but rather one that strategically influences receptions of the text.

The vital set of interconnections at the beginning of this introduction never really ceases: to survive, the industry needs audience members to financially support the type of genre filmmaking that has, in the past, provided pleasure and ticket sales. To do so, it encourages filmmakers to create new genre texts that will be distributed to generate profits. At this point, one might reasonably ask the chicken-or-the-egg question: is it audience cravings that impel the production of genre works or is it genre works that craft audience cravings? In other words, does the audience drive the industry or the does the industry drive the audience? How the cycle started now seems irrelevant. Though genres existed in other art forms, most obviously literature, before the advent of cinema, the desire to produce, show, and see certain genre narratives and conventions was integral to the development of this infant art form. The important thing to recognize is its unyielding grip on Hollywood filmmaking.

GENRE AND ECONOMICS. Some genre commentators downplay the connections among genre, myth, and ritual to focus on the economic aspects of production, analyzing these films more as commodities than as examples of artistic achievement or communal expressions. Cinema creation on every level remains, at best, an uneasy compromise and, at worst, a bitter clash between art and commerce. As has been the case throughout Hollywood's history, perhaps most tragically exemplified in the career of Orson Welles, even great filmmakers whose works consistently lose money eventually don't get to make movies. Staking millions of dollars on two hours of celluloid is always risky business, and those who provide the funding seek every possible way to hedge their bets against the vagaries of the marketplace. For film backers to reap profits, audiences must be willing to pay to watch movies, whatever the venue and format. One way to entice viewers to open their wallets is to offer them a way to repeat experiences they previously found pleasurable or associate with fond memories. Thus, as many critics have noted, films within the tradition of popular genres afford backers a sense (or at least an illusion) of economic predictability. If consumers bought tickets to this type of movie before, they may well do so again, given the right combination of stars and clever packaging. While some critics analyze myths and cultural rituals, others concentrate on how and why genre films may provide broad avenues of profit.

During the classical era of Hollywood filmmaking, this notion of repeated pleasures spurring ticket sales combined with the practical aspects of film production to make genre movies seem financially prudent investments. Indeed, genre films formed the foundation of classical Hollywood. Studios, structured rather like factories despite their level of cinematic artistry, produced movies in an analogous fashion, with various segments of the lot functioning like stops along an assembly line. The standardized nature of their system, with the built-in economy of reusing standing sets, costumes, plots, and stars currently under contract, strongly encouraged studios to produce genre movies that were recognizable to large segments of the audience. In this economic approach to genre, then, films are seen primarily as providing narrative templates that have proved successful in the past and that allow studios to make use of their current assets (recycled props, sets, costumes, and casts and crews already under contract), delivering both a potential audience and a substantial monetary savings. Modern producers attempt to insure their investments to an ever-greater degree; instead of merely recycling genres, they generate numerous sequels, a rare occurrence in the studio days. For example, there was no *Gone with the Wind II: The Rhett and Scarlett Chronicles.*

GENRE AND NEW MEDIA. The numerous screens that dominate the physical and cultural landscape of modern society visibly signal the ascendancy of the so-called New Media. The transformations New Media has fostered between technology and its users have dramatically altered the relationships among authors, texts, and readers, and have raised a series of questions about the production, distribution, and reception of all types of media in the digital age, including genre works. According to New Media scholar Henry Jenkins, the contemporary era is experiencing a "cultural convergence." More than just a series of technological innovations, this rapidly expanding process of convergence is drastically altering both the production and consumption of media. Jenkins speculates on his blog that popular-culture fans are actively building new genres. He dissects how "both the commercial and grassroots expansion of narrative universes contribute to a new mode of storytelling ...which gets put together differently by each individual consumer as well as processed collectively by social networks and online knowledge communities."[3] On the most basic level, New Media is revising the customary roles and status of everyone engaged in creating, distributing, and viewing films, if not the fundamental nature, of both past and present imagemaking. This explosion of technological innovations has spawned a fluid social environment saturated with media and media devices. As such, the traditional ways we receive information and entertainment, the systems we employ to communicate with each other, and the ways we derive enjoyment now arrive and depart via a startling array of new formats delivered by a series of diverse apparatuses. Such revo-

---

[3] Henry Jenkins, www.henryjenkins.org.

lutionary shifts inspire not only an array of philosophical questions about the role media does and should play in society, but also pragmatic concerns about shifting economic responses and industrial patterns.

Several hallmarks distinguish this world of New Media technology from its predecessors, including increased portability, greater agency, pervasive networking, increased interactivity, and perpetual instability. Put simply, viewers now have the power to see almost anything they want at any time, as well as to actively engage with what they see while simultaneously talking with others. A recent innovation allows a viewer to tweet responses to a movie while watching it; those responses then scroll across the screen in a text bar, allowing everyone watching the same film to see the comments, weigh in on them, and add their own opinions about the movie. Such options blur the lines of demarcation between aesthetic experiences and our everyday existence. While still sitting at our desks, we can go anywhere, be anyone, and do most anything. Yet, these digitized images are unstable and easily manipulated in ways that past generations could never imagine. A readily available program like Photoshop, for example, can spin straw into gold, or at least make us think that is what we see.

All of this affects filmmaking on every imaginable level. New Media scholar Lev Manovich contends that digital composing, combining images within the frame to create an illusion, will ultimately replace traditional editing, a process of relating one frame to another, as the most important tool for filmmakers. If he is correct, then the prevailing notion of montage, the way images are juxtaposed with each other to create meanings, will change considerably in this modern age of computer-generated images and digital editing. In conversations with my colleague, Leah Shafer, she often asks what it portends for exhibition practices when viewing habits shift from the theater to the subway platform. Since genre classification is, at least in part, a tool for facilitating the sale of art objects to the consumer, these developments should be read as industrial shifts operating under narrative cinema's ageless need for commercial success. Clearly, these temporal and spatial disjunctions, as they evolve more fully over time, will change the way that creators, distributors, and readers all think about and utilize narrative productions.

Add to these considerations the provocative issue of how the Internet reflects and refracts genre thinking. When we order or view a film online, algorithms gather data and draw conclusions about the types of movies we want to see. This results in messages along the lines of, "If you liked movie *x*, then you might like movie *y* as well." Currently, 60 percent of Netflix's rentals result from its recommender system's suggestions. According to its designer, Robert Bell at AT&T Labs, the recommender system groups movies together "using the nearest neighbor method, which associates movies with others a person has rated highly." He cites *Saving Private Ryan* (1998) and how its "nearest neighbor" might be a war movie or another Spielberg film. "Because the selection factors are based on algorithms," continues Bell, "action movies would be grouped together, as would romances."[4] Interestingly, then, this technology of taste classifies movies contained within the Netflix catalog via identifiable characteristics, using genres as a large delimiting boundary; but it also makes the consumer's personal preferences an integral part of the categorization process. The traditional study of genre relies heavily on identifying patterns of similarity, but these new classificatory systems reject patterns of content and substitute them with patterns of collections. As such, it may work as a marketing device but it fails to coax viewers out of their comfort zones.

The ever-widening range of technological developments provides seemingly endless opportunities for recycling past texts and thus placing them in direct juxtaposition with new iterations of the same genre, and sometimes even the same movie. Rick Altman sees this contemporary world of cinema as a kind of Jurassic Park where genre movies from different eras exist simultaneously and where new genres can crosspollinate with old ones. Now, Dracula can shake hands with Michael Myers. Even remakes can occupy the same time zone. We can board the *3:10 to Yuma* either in 1957 or in 2007 or compare John Wayne (1969) to Jeff Bridges (2010) as Rooster Cogburn in *True Grit*. Such possibilities transform the past into the present and, in turn, form a genre landscape that simultaneously and often seamlessly blends the historical with the contemporary. It allows a modern consciousness to contemplate older perspectives on similar subject matters and, on a broader scale, makes genre movies from an earlier era a distinctive part of modernity, allowing a continual rearticulation and reevaluation of their significance, influence, power, attraction, and worth.

---

[4] Annalee Newitz, "Movie Tips from Your Robot Overlords." *Washington Post*, August 3, 2009, B2.

Genre and New Media The transformations that New Media has fostered between technology and its users have dramatically altered the relationships among authors, texts, and readers in the digital age. The ever-widening range of technological developments provides seemingly endless opportunities for recycling past texts and thus placing them in direct juxtaposition with new iterations of the same genre, and sometimes even the same movie. For example, the most recent version of *The Great Gatsby* (2013) can be juxtaposed with formulations of the same narrative from 1926, 1949, 1974, and 2000 (TV version), and viewers can compare and contrast the performances of actors in each of these visualizations of the famous novel. Such possibilities transform the past into the present and form a genre landscape that simultaneously blends the historical with the contemporary. It allows a modern consciousness to contemplate older perspectives on similar subjects and makes genre movies from an earlier era a distinctive part of modernity, allowing a continual reevaluation of their significance, influence, power, attraction, and worth.

Conclusion

Genres can be a tease. Like the femme fatale in a film noir, they capture our attention by presenting themselves as one thing and then, unexpectedly, often turning out to be quite something else. We are enticed into thinking we recognize what is about to happen and then are either disappointed or delighted when something unforeseen transpires. Despite its acknowledged importance in the creation, distribution, and reception of filmmaking, its lengthy history as a series of categories and critical tools, and the various approaches designed to illuminate and define it, genre remains a thorny subject. Yet some things are clear. All genre works are inherently intertextual and, by their very nature, hybrids to one degree or another. In this sense, genre works are necessarily self-conscious of their histories, conventions, characterizations, and iconographies.

Genres are assemblages of ingredients that offer visual and auditory frameworks of style and meaning, a collection of conventional options and innovative opportunities. Like all narrative stories, genre movies attempt to make sense of our world and, in turn, influence how we look at our surroundings. They structure experiences within a delicate balance of traditions and modifications, allowing creators to express personal points of view through entertainment vehicles, and for viewers to receive them through their own personal lenses. Over the last century or so of American cinema history, the interplay between producers, distributors, scholars, and viewers has created the generally accepted boundaries of what constitutes various genre categories, though overlaps and disagreements abound.

This does not mean genres are static entities. Quite the contrary, they are fluid, open-ended, and responsive to social conditions. All the components that constitute genres are always in play, always available for revisiting and revising. As such, genres provide a series of renegotiations with societal issues and even cultural foundations. Take, for example, the American obsession with violence. One might effectively chart the varying attitudes toward violence over the course of the last decade or so by exploring that issue in particular genres, most notably Western, combat, and crime films. Similarly, the changing roles of women and ethnic groups in American society are reflected in various genres over the decades, particularly melodramas and romantic and slapstick comedies. Differing attitudes toward technology appear in the science-fiction, social problem, and horror genres. And, of course, sex appears in every genre, but the display of the human body reveals much about our cultural mores. It should come as no surprise, therefore, that genre films, even loosely defined, have been the mainstay of mainstream American filmmaking.

Kathy Selden, from *Singin' in the Rain* (1952), was partially right when she said, "If you've seen one, you've seen them all." Hollywood films do often resemble each other. Genre films seem as familiar to us as our family members at a crowded Thanksgiving dinner. We want to spend some time with kindly Uncle George, listen to the stories of funny Aunt Norma, but avoid our annoying little cousin Stuart. But Kathy Selden failed to see the vital differences that characterize the most significant genre movies. Her very own musical, *Singin' in the Rain*, offers a paradigmatic example of that elusive blend of convention and invention that characterizes the art of genre filmmaking. Unlike Lena Lamont, Kathy's rival in the picture, the best genre movies have a powerful voice and need not rely on someone behind the curtain to please an audience. They can make us laugh and make us cry. They can inspire us to be better people and reveal the deepest fissures in the human psyche. At their best, like good art in any medium, genre movies both entertain and enlighten us. They whisk us off to galaxies far, far away or take us deep into the bloody killing fields of Rwanda. Genres emerge and endure because they meet a series of artistic, commercial, and audience needs. They fill a cultural role that has existed from the early days of recorded time to the present day: the human need to tell and retell, to hear and rehear, stories that move and teach us about ourselves and the world around us. They bring to life characters with whom we can identify with in ways that engage our heads, our hearts, and our imaginations. Who knows? They might even teach us how to sing in the rain.

Lester Friedman

QUESTIONS FOR DISCUSSION

1. In what ways do you classify the world surrounding you? How do you make distinctions between what fits into what category? Are there hybrids? In a similar manner, do you think the classification of films is useful and, if so, in what ways?

2. Do you choose which movies to see by referring to genres at all? If so, what genres do you prefer and why? Do you see any parts of your personality that draw you to particular genres? How does who you are affect how you relate to certain genres?

3. Take an older movie and a more contemporary film from the same genre. Compare and contrast them in terms of conventions, such as characterizations, narrative structures, iconography, and other characteristic elements. How does the time period of the earlier film make it different from the later version in the same field?

4. Genre works are inherently intertextual. Explore this issue in greater depth by looking at how a current genre movie recalls earlier ones. List the various allusions you find, both specific references and more general connections.

5. Which of the critical approaches to genre seem most relevant to you? Pick one and explore it in depth, citing specific films and demonstrating how they relate to the selection theory.

6. The relationship between genre and New Media is being revised every day as new technologies continuously change our viewing habits and approaches to genre study. Select one new form of seeing genre films and discuss how it changes our perception of that movie.

FOR FURTHER READING

Altman, Rick. "Cinema and Genre." In *The Oxford History of World Cinema*, edited by G. Nowell-Smith, 276–85. Oxford: Oxford University Press, 1998.

————. *Film/Genre*. London: British Film Institute, 1999.

Bazin, Andrew. "The Evolution of the Western." In *Movies and Methods: An Anthology*, edited by Bill Nichols, 150–57. Berkeley: University of California Press, 1976.

Bordwell, David, and Kristin Thompson. *Film Art: An Introduction*. 7th ed. New York: McGraw-Hill, 2004.

Braudy, Leo. "Genre: The Conventions of Connection." In *Film Theory and Criticism: Introductory Readings*, 5th ed., edited by Leo Braudy and Marshall Cohen, 613–29. New York: Oxford University Press, 1999.

Browne, Nick, ed. *Refiguring American Film Genres: Theory and History*. Los Angeles: University of California Press, 1998.

Carr, David. *The Night of the Gun*. New York: Simon & Schuster, 2008.

Collins, Jim. "Genericity in the Nineties: Eclectic Irony and New Sincerity." In *Film Theory Goes to the Movies*, edited by Jim Collins, Hilary Radner, and Ava Preacher Collins, 242–63. New York: Routledge, 1993.

Corrigan, Timothy, and Patricia White. *The Film Experience: An Introduction*, 289. Boston: St. Martin's Press, 2004.

Dixon, Wheeler Winston, ed. *Film Genre 2000: New Critical Essays*. Albany: State University of New York Press, 2000.

Frow, John. *Genre*, 10. London: Routledge, 2006.

Gorry, G. Anthony. "Empathy in the Virtual World." *Chronicle of Higher Education* 56, no. 2 (September 4, 2009): B10–12.

Grant, Barry Keith. *Film Genre: From Iconography to Ideology*. London: Wallflower Press, 2007.

Jenkins, Henry. *Convergence Culture: Where Old and New Media Collide*. New York: New York University Press, 2006.

————. *Textual Poachers: Television Fans and Participatory Culture*. London: Routledge, 1992.

Johnson, Steven. "The Science of *Eternal Sunshine*." Slate.com, March 22, 2004. www.slate.com/articles/arts/brave_new_world/2004/03/the_science_of_eternal_sunshine.html.

King, Geoff. *New Hollywood Cinema: An Introduction*. New York: Columbia University Press, 2002.

Langford, Barry. *Film Genre: Hollywood and Beyond*. Edinburgh: Edinburgh University Press, 2005.

Manovich, Lev. *The Language of New Media*. Boston: MIT Press, 2002.

Moine, Raphaelle. *Cinema Genre*. Translated by Alistar Fox and Hilary Radner. Oxford: Blackwell Publishing, 2008.

Mulvey, Laura. "Visual Pleasure and Narrative Cinema." *Screen* 16:3, Autumn 1975. 6–18.

Neale, Steve. *Genre and Hollywood*. London: Routledge, 2000.

Newitz, Annalee. "Movie Tips from Your Robot Overlords." *Washington Post*, August 3, 2009, B2.

Qvortrup, Lars, ed. *Virtual Space: Spatiality in Virtually Inhabited 3D Worlds*. London: Springer, 2002.

Schatz, Thomas. *Hollywood Genres: Formulas, Filmmaking, and the Studio System*. Philadelphia: Temple University Press, 1981.

Sturken, Marita. *Tangled Memories: The Vietnam War, the AIDS Epidemic and the Politics of Remembering*. Berkeley: University of California Press, 1997.

Tudor, Andrew. "Genre and Critical Methodology." In *Movies and Methods: An Anthology*, edited by Bill Nichols, 118–26. Berkeley: University of California Press, 1976.

Warshow, Robert. "Movie Chronicle: The Westerner." In *Film Theory and Criticism: Introductory Readings*, 5th ed., edited by Leo Braudy and Marshall Cohen, 654–67. New York: Oxford University Press, 1999.

Wood, Robin. "Ideology, Genre, Auteur." In *Film Theory and Criticism: Introductory Readings*, 5th ed., edited by Leo Braudy and Marshall Cohen, 668–78. New York: Oxford University Press, 1999.

Wright, Judith Hess. "Genre Films and the Status Quo." In *Film Genre Reader II*, edited by Barry Keith Grant, 41–49. Austin: University of Texas Press, 1995.

The Gold Rush (1925)

Slapstick Comedy

BEFORE ELVIS PRESLEY shook his hips or Michael Jackson moonwalked, Charlie Chaplin twirled his cane and jauntily ambled into cultural immortality. It is hard to imagine that in the days before television and the Internet a movie star could become the most recognizable person in the world. Indeed, in the 1920s no one in any arena—music, art, literature, politics—equaled Chaplin's fame. His celebrity continues to this very day, more than three decades after his death and five since he last appeared in a major film role: just the mere image of a bowler hat, cane, ill-fitting coat, and large shoes unmistakably calls the name of Chaplin to mind.

Although no one in the 1920s equaled Chaplin's global celebrity, another comic actor came close to his box-office clout and international film stardom: Harold Lloyd. Lloyd had both a quintessentially American and a universally appealing stardom. Even Chaplin couldn't boast of being a fashion icon, whereas Lloyd's glasses became very much in vogue—even in Japan, one had only to ask for "Roido" frames at the optician's shop to receive a replica of Lloyd's glasses, the most recognizable feature of his costume. Buster Keaton, not nearly the celebrity that Chaplin was or quite the box-office king that Lloyd became, was a highly successful star and director of comedies. He was ultimately acclaimed as one of the finest directors of the 1920s. Extremely influential in Europe, he became a favorite of the art-cinema surrealist filmmakers, Luis Buñuel in particular.

These film stars, whose major contribution to the art and craft of cinema was to make people laugh, remain among the most famous and respected film artists in cinema history.

Chaplin, Keaton, and Lloyd grew out of the comic traditions of vaudeville and the minstrel shows. Their influences stretch all the way back to Aristophanes and then progress through the commedia dell'arte of Renaissance Italy on to Shakespeare.

The term usually applied to their brand of comedy—the kind practiced by most comic actors of the 1910s and '20s—is slapstick. The name derives from the twinned sticks or boards of the commedia, a sound effect tool that made a slapping sound when an actor was to be struck on stage. Over time, the slapstick became an integral part of the clown tradition in the circus, well known to Chaplin, Keaton, and Lloyd. Critics commonly refer to the great comic movie stars of this period as the "silent clowns," who used the physicality of earlier comic traditions but without the actual sound of the slapsticks. Certainly with their imperviousness to physical pain and their existence in a world that defies common logic and physical laws, along with their ability to capture the basic humanity that resides in people everywhere, Chaplin, Keaton, and Lloyd (and the lesser-known actors inspired by them) were participating in timeless comic traditions. This cinematic tradition, however, was threatened by the arrival of sound. As comedy became dialogue-centered and the dominant mode switched from physical to romantic, slapstick would become governed mostly by comic violence and simple pratfalls.

This chapter argues, following the lead of critic Alan Dale, that although slapstick comedy enjoyed its golden age in the silent era, it was by no means dead after the arrival of sound. Dale posits something called "verbal slapstick"—dialogue performed at breakneck speed—but we will go beyond even that, referring more universally to dialogue that is playfully insulting and filled with puns, double entendres, and other sorts of word play. This not only allows us to link the clown tradition of the silent era with the comics of Hollywood's classical period (1930–1970), but to see physical comedy as encompassing the realm of verbal dexterity. With this definitional expansion in mind, we can answer the question of what happened to that line of comedy pioneered by the likes of Chaplin, Keaton, and Lloyd when the movies learned to talk. For some, the occasional anomalous highlight notwithstanding—the Marx Brothers, W. C. Fields, Jerry Lewis—the glory days of slapstick comedy faded into celluloid memories. Such critics and fans of silent comedy find it heretical to extend this comic tradition into the modern era of John Belushi, Jim Carrey, Adam Sandler, Jason Biggs, Will Ferrell, and Steve Carell. Such traditionalists find it sacrilegious to postulate continuity from

The Freshman (1925) to *Animal House* (1978); from *The Immigrant* (1917) to *American Pie* (1999) or *The 40-Year-Old Virgin* (2005); from *Safety Last* (1923) to *The Waterboy* (1998); or from *The General* (1926) to *Anchorman* (2004). But making the connection is not a value judgment; one need not defend *American Pie* as the artistic equal of *The Immigrant* or claim that the Police Academy series captures an audience's ambivalence about modernity, domesticity, and authority as successfully as Mack Sennett's knockabout antics with his Keystone Kops. It is, rather, a question of genre—in particular, the path along which the great tradition of slapstick migrated and how more modern films such as *Animal House, The Waterboy,* and *American Pie* participate in a timeless tradition of laughter.

History

In conceptualizing the history, theory, and iconography of this genre, there is one major difference to consider from most others in this volume. Whereas central figures arise in the history of any genre—Fred Astaire and Ginger Rogers in the musical, John Wayne in the Western—most do not depend on individual stars or directors for their generic identity. In conceptualizing slapstick comedy, however, one cannot possibly imagine it other than as almost solely the product of the cinematic figures on screen, identifiable by name, by persona, and by physicality. This fact is undeniably true of films from the silent era through the 1960s, but is also largely, though less exclusively, true of the contemporary era as well. Referring to the period from 1930 to 1970 or so, critics have come to call this reliance on the centrality of the performers and the consistency of their persona "comedian comedy," but it also seems applicable to many post-classical figures.

Unlike the great romantic comedies and their close cousin, the musical, however, women represent a relatively insignificant force in slapstick comedy, except as objects of male narrative drives and desires. In the annals of film comedy, no woman can be compared to Chaplin, Keaton, or Lloyd or to later figures like Jerry Lewis and more contemporary stars like Eddie Murphy, Jim Carrey, and Adam Sandler. There are no female comedy teams on the order of Laurel and Hardy, the Three Stooges, Abbott and Costello, or Martin and Lewis; no sisters exist on a par with the Marx Brothers. Although there have certainly been talented actresses who could wring a laugh out of a pratfall, a sly look, or a devilish bit of business—Katharine Hepburn slogging through the stream in *Bringing Up Baby* (1938); Irene Dunne vamping Cary Grant's date in *The Awful Truth* (1937); the withering looks Barbara Stanwyck gives Henry Fonda in *The Lady Eve* (1941); the air of complete innocence Cameron Diaz projects with the special "mousse" in her hair in *There's Something About Mary* (1998)—viewers rightly don't think of these talented, beautiful women in the same way they do the male screen clowns. Only Mabel Normand in the 1910s and Mae West in the early 1930s achieved comparable stardom in physical comedy—although they were not devoted to athletic pratfalls or modest self-effacement. In the world of television at least one woman would enter the pantheon of great screen clowns: Lucille Ball and her antics in *I Love Lucy* (1951–1957). A minor star in the cinema, she remains the queen of the small screen. Yet slapstick, for the most part, has been a male-dominated genre.

Slapstick comedy from the 1910s until well into the 1950s was not exclusively sustained by feature films, but also by shorts. In fact, a school of thought makes a convincing case that slapstick comedy was never better than in the short form: that Chaplin was at his strongest in his Mutual period [e.g., *The Pawnshop* (1916), *Easy Street* (1917)], that Laurel and Hardy have no feature to compare to any number of their shorts [*The Music Box* (1932), *Towed in a Hole* (1932), *Busy Bodies* (1933)]; or that the Three Stooges in their heyday never made a feature as good as *You Nazty Spy!* (1940). As the short film disappeared, physical comedy naturally morphed into acceptable long-form modes, and it did so quite well, but at the cost of abandoning pure, unadulterated, knockabout mayhem.

The lack of synchronized sound, the brief running times, and the sheer physicality that defined early movies ensured that slapstick comedy was born at the dawn of the new medium. The Lumière Brothers' *L'arroseur arrosé* (*The Sprinkler Sprinkled*, 1895), for instance, showcases nothing other than a bit of monkey business as a young boy causes a gardener to wet himself with a hose, demonstrating the cinema's ability to capture life in its more humorous (if staged) modes. As film historian Tom Gunning points out, this short, deceptively simple film gave birth to a series of films revolving around a gag or bit of mischief, typically inaugurated by a young rascal.[1] Such films predominated in

---

[1] Tom Gunning. "Crazy Machines in the Garden of Forking Paths: Mischief Gags and the Origins of American Film Comedy," in *Classical Hollywood Comedy*, eds. Kristine Brunovska Karnick and Henry Jenkins. (New York and London: Routledge, 1995), 89.

the early days of cinema around the 1890s–1900s. Magician-turned-filmmaker Georges Méliès included plenty of knockabout in his fantasy films of this period, but if someone got hit with a pie in the face or a kick smack on the bottom he was more likely to disappear in a puff of smoke rather than do a slow burn. The so-called "chase films" of the twentieth century's first decade brought a bit more narrative complexity to the single-shot, single-gag comic film—chase films taking both comic and melodramatic turns. The French comedian Max Linder discovered the basics of character-centered comedy at the same time. Late in the decade, the prolific director D. W. Griffith at Biograph often turned to comedy but more often allowed his young assistant Mack Sennett to tackle the comedy subjects [e.g., *The Joke on the Joker* and *Pants and Pansies* (1912)].

A true slapstick comedy genre emerged in the summer of 1912 when Sennett became a partner in the newly formed Keystone Film Company. Given Griffith's low opinion of comedy, Sennett had been confined to the split-reel (five to six minutes) format at Biograph. At Keystone, he lengthened the films to one reel, then two, and even occasionally to feature length, such as *Tillie's Punctured Romance* (1914), perhaps the longest American film made up to that time. Sennett took to the role of actor-director-producer-entrepreneur-studio head as no one before ever had, both stamping the Hollywood company with his own personality and nurturing the greatest array of comic talent the cinema would see for quite some time. Keystone released nearly six hundred films in its merely seven years of existence, and the comedy troupe Sennett assembled remains unsurpassed. Though its most famous alum was Charlie Chaplin, Keystone also nurtured Fatty Arbuckle, Mabel Normand, Marie Dressler, Gloria Swanson, Ben Turpin, Chester Conklin, and, though for only a brief time, Harry Langdon and Harold Lloyd. Sennett also allowed his performers the opportunity to create coherent personae, often naming the films after his leading players to encourage an association between star and character. Thus, *Mabel's Nerve*, *Mabel's Busy Day*, *Mabel's New Job* (all 1914), and *Wished on Mabel* (1915), among many others, feature the beauteous and talented Mabel Normand; *Fatty Joins the Force*, *Fatty's Flirtation* (both 1913), *Fatty's Finish* (1914), and *Fatty's Chance Acquaintance* (1915) star the portly, but nimble Fatty Arbuckle. This idea was extended when the two teamed up for *Fatty and Mabel's Simple Life*; *Mabel, Fatty and the Law* (both 1915); *Fatty and Mabel Adrift* (1916), and others.

Sennett's working methods were typical of pre-classical cinema, before the studio system demanded that scripts and coherent production schedules be approved prior to shooting. Sennett took advantage of local events and worried about constructing a story only afterward, as in such films as *Kid Auto Races at Venice* (1914) and *Fatty and Mabel at the San Diego Exposition* (1915). In this way, the Keystone films also provide a priceless documentary look of Southern California at the beginning of its transformation from sleepy backwater to the center of the entertainment industry. They also capture some of the speed, dynamism, and newfound freedom in the transition from traditional American small-town life to urban modernity. Most of all, Sennett produced films that centered on timeless slapstick comic devices, from pratfalls to pie throwing to complex chase scenes. Although Sennett favored films about domestic life, some of his output displays a darker tone, exemplified by the surprisingly mean-spirited characters played by Chaplin and Normand in *Tillie's Punctured Romance*. Many of Sennett's films mock authority via the incompetent Keystone Kops, a troupe that was so popular that it became an iconic representation of the studio itself. Sennett's understanding of audiences and the nature of comedy rendered these clowns indelible figures in cinema history.

Among the comic actors who became stars while working with Sennett, none were bigger than Charlie Chaplin. He remained with Sennett for only one year (1914) and in that time did not fully develop the coherent persona with which he is forever associated, although he did find most of the accoutrements of the Little Tramp character in the vast Sennett props department. Chaplin played a variety of roles (including director) and types while honing his craft. Yet within that single year at Keystone, Chaplin appeared in thirty-five films—an indication of the speed with which they were produced, certainly, but more important, a clear sign of Chaplin's embracing this unique chance to learn, experiment, and grow as a film actor and director. By the end of his time with Sennett, Chaplin was a major star.

This success induced the Essanay Company to woo him away from Keystone. Appropriately enough, Chaplin's first film at Essanay was titled *His New Job* (1915) and found him wreaking havoc at a movie studio. The roaring success of the fifteen films he made there was testimony to Chaplin's ability to move screen comedy into another dimension. At Essanay, he also first utilized the screen presence of the ethereal Edna Purviance, whose beauty and charm would be a constant foil for

Chaplin's shy, awkward, and love-smitten Tramp for years to come. (Indeed, she appears in virtually every Chaplin film until her retirement in 1923.) But the most important event in his time at Essanay was the filming of his short *The Tramp* (1915), which indelibly etched Chaplin into audiences' hearts and minds forever. The film tells the story of a hobo who rescues a farm woman from other hoboes. She repays him by offering him a job on the farm. Although he proves to be a poor farm-hand, the hobo does fall in love with the woman. But when her husband returns to the farm, the tramp must go on his sad, but jaunty way.

Chaplin himself continued on his jaunty way, leaving Essanay for the Mutual Film Company in 1916, where he gained complete creative control over his films. He used his year or so at Mutual to perfect his cinematic skills, taking longer to produce his films (approximately one per month), injecting more character into the Tramp figure and more pathos into his films overall. From *The Floorwalker* (May 1916) to *The Adventurer* (October 1917), Chaplin's Mutual films represent one of the most artistically and commercially potent series of movies ever made. Chaplin relies almost exclusively on the Tramp costume (bowler hat, cane, tight coat, baggy pants, floppy shoes) and keeps the interior core of the Tramp character (mischievous yet sentimental, optimistic yet filled with a sense of pathos) throughout the dozen Mutual masterpieces. In some of the films, sheer comedy is the main point, with *The Rink* (1916) a particular highlight, featuring Chaplin's performing spectacular stunts on roller skates. At the opposite end of the comic spectrum are films like *Easy Street* (1917), a deceptively grim look at urban poverty and its attendant social problems, and *The Immigrant* (1917), a similarly down-beat (but hilarious) look at how unwelcoming American shores can be to those without money.

A move to First National proved less artistically important, save for films like *Shoulder Arms* (1918), *Sunnyside* (1919), and especially *The Kid* (1921). This latter film reveals Chaplin at his best, along with an emerg-ing weakness—his tendency toward not just sentiment, but sentimental-ity. *The Kid* is essentially an old-fashioned, neo-Dickensian melodrama leavened by frequent scenes of inspired comedy. The story, of an unwed mother who tries to place her child in the care of a wealthy man only to have the youngster end up with the Tramp instead, plays like a slightly lighter version of *Oliver Twist*. Only when Chaplin plays the piece for humor—some gentle, such as the way the Tramp retrofits his slum apart-ment for the needs of a baby, some more biting, such as the depictions of the brutality of ghetto life—is the mood more in keeping with his earlier, funnier films. Indeed, such was Chaplin's attraction to melodramatic expression that his first film for the newly formed United Artists studios was an outright melodrama—*A Woman of Paris* (1923), in which he has only a walk-on part, with top billing going to Edna Purviance.

To be sure, one could hardly argue with both the artistic and box-office success of *The Gold Rush* (1925). Filled with classic moments—from the spectacular opening shot of prospectors making their way up the treacherous mountainside, to the famous boiling of boots to ward off starvation, to the "Oceana Roll" performed by Charlie in his imagination on a sad New Year's Eve—the film is one of the highlights of world cinema.

Chaplin believed the coming of sound in 1927 would prove anathema to the image of the Tramp character. His universality was aided precisely by the fact that he did not speak—no accent to betray national origin or social class or to get in the way of the immediacy of the visual image. His first "sound" film, made in 1931, avoids dialogue of any type, though it does include synchronized music. *City Lights*, the story of a tramp who raises money to restore the sight of a blind flower girl, resembles *The Kid* in its bittersweet ending and stands as another tribute to Chaplin's ability to draw both laughter and tears from an audience.

Chaplin's next film would avoid his melodramatic impulses and certainly brings much more of the new technology to bear; appropriately enough for a film about technology and its attendant dehumanization.

The Gold Rush (1925) Among the most graceful figures ever to emerge in the cinema, Charlie Chaplin set a standard for slapstick film comedy that has never been equaled. A recognizable figure even today and by people who may never have seen an actual film of his, his Little Tramp character fashioned a pathos that was less a function of plot than a recognition of the essential ambiguity and sadness of the human condition. What he can do with just two forks and rolls of bread is matched by the pathos of the situation—a brilliant comic performance of the "Oceana Roll" that takes place only in his imagination, unseen by the woman he loves.

Modern Times (1936) borrows liberally from the French comedy *À nous la liberté* (René Clair, 1931)—a film itself highly influenced by Chaplin. Chaplin spent years on the film, working on complex gags and tinkering with the effects. The use of the Tramp figure is especially piquant for the way this Everyman comes to stand in for the little people who are mere cogs in the machine: dehumanized by meaningless labor, by imperious bosses, by the criminal justice system, and generally, by large, social forces.

Modern Times essentially marked the last appearance of the Tramp character. There is something of him in the little barber of *The Great Dictator* (1940), though the film is better remembered for Chaplin's uncanny and rather frightening rendition of an Adolf Hitler–like dictator, especially the gruesomely graceful scene of the mad leader tripping the light fantastic with a globe. A speech at film's end for tolerance and peace obviously had no impact on larger world events. For many, this film marks the end of Chaplin's influential cinematic artistry.

Another Keystone alum to go on to greater heights was Fatty Arbuckle. He left Sennett's employ in 1917 to form a partnership with Joseph M. Schenck, the New York–based Comique Film Studio. With a pudgy baby face and surprising grace despite his bulk, Arbuckle was a gifted slapstick comedian. His films are characterized by off-the-cuff working methods learned from Sennett and an ability to improvise around a setting, as seen in films like *Coney Island* (1917), *The Bell Boy* (1918), *The Cook* (1918), *The Garage* (1920), and many others. But what Arbuckle is perhaps best known for, besides a scandal that effectively ended his career, is the fact that he gave Buster Keaton his start in movies in 1917.

Striking off on his own in 1920, set up by Schenck in his own Los Angeles studio, Buster Keaton made a string of shorts that, taken together, demonstrate an unprecedented combination of spectacular stunts, complex gags, mechanical ingenuity, and cinematic perspicacity. Yet when he turned to feature films, his works demonstrate a command of cinematic structure equally unmatched. Unlike Chaplin's works, Keaton's features are not merely episodic in structure, moving from gag to gag with only minimal plot development. Instead, they are models of tight construction, the gags integrated into the character and setting, often so integral to the plot that, unlike favored moments in *The Kid* or *The Gold Rush*, they cannot be coherently excerpted. Indeed, if Keaton had a weakness as a comic, it was his being more concerned with the complexities of gags, stunts, and mechanics than with getting his audience to laugh.

Keaton used his short films to experiment with his craft. When he turned to features in 1923, he had a firm foundation of gag and cinematic structures. He has a pure chase sequence in *Cops* (1922), for example, and later reworks the basic idea of a lone figure being pursued by hundreds in his feature-length *Seven Chances* (1925). He replays the water-borne adventure *The Boat* (1921) on an epic scale in *The Navigator* (1924). The comic Western is tried in *The Paleface* (1922) and then again in the feature *Go West* (1925). Keaton's interest in mechanical and electrical engineering is manifest in films like *One Week* (1920), *The Scarecrow* (1920), *The Electric House* (1922), and even more famously in *The General* and *Steamboat Bill, Jr.* (1928). Pure cinema seems his goal in both *The Playhouse* (1921) and *Sherlock Jr.* (1924). Keaton was little given to social reflection or analysis, and today, a film like *Seven Chances* is almost unwatchable for the casual racism it betrays, reproducing the hoariest stereotypes in its use of black characters, especially the dim-witted, slow-footed servant chasing after Keaton—played by a white actor in blackface.

Harold Lloyd had a lengthy apprenticeship in the short form, but his reputation rests firmly in features. Lloyd often portrayed a young man ready to make his mark on the world—and completely ill-equipped to do so, a veritable innocent abroad. Yet what he lacks in sophistication, he makes up for in pluck and energy; many of his films climax in stunts and chases, Lloyd's character finally getting to unleash the comic energy he has kept bundled up all along. Conquering his fears and capturing a criminal in *Grandma's Boy* (1922); climbing ever higher in *Safety Last*; using every conveyance imaginable to reach his lady love in *Girl Shy* (1924); the heroic run for glory on the football field in *The Freshman*; the violent fight that finishes *The Kid Brother* (1927); the streetcar hurtling through New York City in *Speedy* (1928)—these typify Lloyd's comically inventive thrill rides. Like Chaplin, he could inject pathos into his films—his humiliation at the hands of the spoiled rich kids in *The Freshman* is quite affecting—but he is always rewarded by the object of his affection (in the features portrayed first by Mildred Davis, whom he married in 1923, and then by Jobyna Ralston). It is almost impossible not to side with Lloyd's characters, usually named Harold to foster a close association between star and persona. But the only real autobiographical connection between star and character was a commitment to hard work and entertainment, both of which paid off handsomely for him.

Though little remembered today, there was a fourth major silent clown: Harry Langdon. He was forty years old before he made his first film in 1924—a half decade or more older than the comedians with whom he is usually associated. But the Langdon character acts even younger than the postadolescent Keaton and Lloyd, probably due to his baby face and pasty complexion, his boy-in-a-man's-body demeanor emphasized by his trademark too-small jacket. A veteran of both the circus and vaudeville, Langdon was brought to the movies by Mack Sennett, who in turn entrusted him to the care of his gag writer Frank Capra, who would go on to direct him in one of his finest features, *The Strong Man* (1926). Langdon's infantile persona is perhaps as unsettling as it is humorous. In *Long Pants* (1927), he has been kept in a kind of perpetual boyhood as symbolized by the forced wearing of short pants but is finally allowed to don the title garments. When he does, he reveals himself to be completely unprepared for the world around him, inappropriately lusting after a fast and loose woman and ignoring the sweet, virginal young woman his mother has selected for him. The sight of the forty-three-year-old man just out of short pants and riding a bicycle to impress a worldly, glamorous woman will strike one as either disturbing or absurd and maybe a little of both.

The three great clowns of the 1920s—Chaplin, Keaton, and Lloyd—had relatively little success in talkies, but two acts triumphed when they found their voice. Stan Laurel was Charlie Chaplin's understudy in the Fred Karno music hall troupe and, like Chaplin, he tried his hand at silent comedy. He made his film debut in 1917 and labored long and hard for a decade with minor success in the comic-crazed Jazz Age. Eventually he landed in the lap of Hal Roach, who had done a great deal to shepherd Lloyd to stardom. But Lloyd struck out on his own in 1923 and Roach needed another major star. Laurel, though it was not immediately apparent, proved to be his savior, but only after he teamed up with another veteran comic actor working for Roach, the portly Oliver Hardy.

Hardy, who began in films in 1914 as Babe Hardy, started working with Laurel in 1927 with *Hats Off*—a precursor to their classic *The Music Box* (1932), and in which they play "Stan" and "Ollie." By the end of 1928 Roach understood what he had in the well-matched pair, and they would go on to make two dozen silent shorts together. But when they turned to sound in the "all-talking" year of 1929 with *Unaccustomed As We Are*, they became even more successful. Though it was perhaps inevitable that they would make the occasional feature film, their first being *Pardon Us* (1931) and their best *Sons of the Desert* (1933), their forte was the short. Sound added a lot to their two lovable-losers personae, incompetent at every job and, when married, invariably henpecked by harridan wives. Stan's vaguely British accent and high-pitched tenor and Ollie's dulcet Southern baritone proved as complementary as the thin versus round bodies they respectively possessed.

Their comic masterpiece is *The Music Box*, in which the boys struggle mightily and foolishly to deliver a piano up a monumental flight of stairs, though other films such as *Beau Hunks* (1931), a Foreign Legion adventure spoof; *Scram!* (1932), a classic farce; and *Busy Bodies* (1933), in which the boys are disastrously employed at a saw mill, show off their comic timing and basic human foibles to good effect.

The other silent clown who could thank his lucky stars for sound was W. C. Fields. He made his best-remembered films at Universal, including the decidedly mean-spirited, anti–middle-class comedies *The Bank Dick* (1940) and *Never Give a Sucker an Even Break* (1941). In these films he also lampoons the alcohol consumption that gave him his famously misshapen nose and would contribute to his death at the age of sixty-six in 1946, making jokes like asking a bartender in *The Bank Dick* if he had come in the previous night and spent a twenty-dollar bill; and, when told that he had, replying: "What a load off my mind. I thought I'd lost it"; and in *Never Give a Sucker an Even Break*, when told that "someday you'll drown in a vat of whiskey," he exclaims, "Drown in a vat of whiskey? Death, where is thy sting?" At Universal, Fields worked with Mae West in their only film together, *My Little Chickadee* (1940), which takes good advantage of their characters, such as the reversal when Fields says, "Why don't you come up and see me sometime?" to which West replies, "Yeah, yeah, I'll do that, my little chickadee." West's notorious sexuality is also present in the film when someone proclaims, "Spring is the time for love," and she wonders in return, "What's the matter with the rest of the year?"

The teaming of Fields and West marked a kind of reunion in that both had been major stars at Paramount in the early 1930s. West's tenure as a major star at the studio was somewhat short-lived. Her powerfully transgressive comedy was based on her outrageously sexualized persona—an exaggerated hourglass figure and sexual innuendos (that

She Done Him Wrong (1933) "Why don't you come up sometime and see me?" This memorable line from *She Done Him Wrong* is as often misquoted as the unsaid "Play it Again, Sam" from *Casablanca* (1942), with people invariably moving "sometime" to the end of the line (as W. C. Fields does in *My Little Chickadee* [1940]). But whatever the exact phrasing, in Mae West's innuendo-filled delivery (here directed toward Cary Grant), it can still set off sexual sparks. A unique figure in film history (pun intended), West was a rarity as a woman screenwriter and star. Unfortunately, the invigorated Hays Office under the auspices of the Production Code Administration took the heart out of West's brand of forthright humor. When it became impossible for the bawdy, Brooklyn-born comedienne with the exaggerated hourglass figure to wonder, "Is that a pistol in your pocket, or are you just glad to see me?" her stardom slowly faded away into the stuff of legend.

weren't always just innuendos!). That she was also the screenwriter of her best films only made her that much more powerful and unique. But the revitalized Production Code of 1934 cut the heart out of West's brand of comedy as Hollywood settled in for a long period of tamer entertainment. But until the Code put the kibosh on her outrageous flouting of sexual codes of conduct, she made a handful of memorable films, including *She Done Him Wrong* (1933) and *I'm No Angel* (1933). *She Done Him Wrong*, nominated for an Academy Award for Best Picture, retains the distinction of being the shortest film ever nominated in that category. But what it lacks in running time it makes up for in wit and wisdom. Sparkling dialogue and pithy one-liners such as the unforgettable, "When women go wrong, men go right after them," are delivered in West's inimitable style. Although she commanded one of the highest salaries of any female star of the period, the Production Code and a shift to more traditional romantic comedies brought her glory days to an end.

Also at Paramount, the Marx Brothers brought their infectious, anarchic humor to the movies. The Marxes were already a well-known Broadway comedy troupe when they completed their first feature, *The Cocoanuts* (1929), an adaptation of their stage hit with book by George S. Kaufman and Morrie Ryskind and music and lyrics by Irving Berlin.

The Marx Brothers were tailor-made for the new medium of sound, with Groucho's snappy banter and one-liners, Chico's outrageous puns, and Harpo's noisy silence—he does not speak but manages to create more aural havoc than any figure in film history. Their films unabashedly take on sacred cows in ways not seen since the Keystone Kops. *The Cocoanuts* satirizes the Florida land boom and its attendant hucksterism; *Animal Crackers* (1930) punctures the pretensions of high society; *Monkey Business* (1931) takes on gangsters and cruise ships; *Horse Feathers* (1932) examines the world of universities and big-time college football; and *Duck Soup* (1933) tackles politics, corruption, and war. Untamed ethnic humor also abounds. In *The Cocoanuts*, for example, when Groucho tells Chico that "all along the river, those are the levees," Chico asks, "That's the Jewish neighborhood?" and Groucho replies, "We'll pass over that." In *Animal Crackers*, when Chico asks a man posing as a member of high society, "When did you get to be Roscoe Chandler?" insisting that he is actually Abie the Fish Peddler, Chandler demands to know, "When did you get to be Italian?" In *Duck Soup* the Brothers restage the Negro spiritual "Heav'n Heav'n" and its famous lyric "All God's children got shoes," changing it to "All God's children got guns." The end of their five-picture deal with Paramount sent the brothers packing into the willing, if less adventuresome, arms of MGM, where studio executives made the Marxes ensemble players, much as they had Buster Keaton more than half a decade earlier. Though their first two films at their new home, *A Night at the Opera* (1935) and *A Day at the Races* (1937), have their famous moments, and their frequent costar Margaret Dumont is her usual unflappable self, many aficionados of all things Marxian prize the Paramount pictures above all others.

Comedy teams that combined physical and verbal slapstick ruled the roost from the 1930s through the mid-1950s. Marx Brothers imitators like the Ritz Brothers—Al, Harry, and Jimmy—had a nice run as supporting players until the trio called it quits in 1943; Bert Wheeler and Robert Woolsey gave Laurel and Hardy a run for their money until Woolsey's death in 1938. One slapstick comedy team that did survive the 1930s well into the 1950s is the Three Stooges. Moe Howard, Larry Fine, and Jerry (Curly) Howard began, like many clowns of the silver screen, in vaudeville. Moe, the creative and business leader of the group, and Larry, who began his show business career as a violinist, appeared in nearly two hundred films as two-thirds of the Stooges. Curly, the performer most fondly recalled of the group, appeared in almost a hundred films until a stroke in 1946 ended his run with the trio. He died six years later at only forty-eight years of age. He was replaced by his brother Shemp, who was actually the oldest of the three Howard (né Horwitz) boys. Shemp made seventy-seven films as part of the trio from 1946 to 1955, when he suddenly passed away at age sixty.

The Three Stooges took their cue from Laurel and Hardy in terms of portraying characters who are totally incompetent and whose physical and mental defects serve only to escalate every situation from bad to worse. They are far more violent in their behavior, however, and perhaps their most memorable feature is the constant hitting, slapping, and eye-poking they inflict on each other. Their films often are genre spoofs, such as *We Want Our Mummy* (1939) and the 3-D horror film *Spooks* (1953), although mostly they just put the boys into some generic situation and let them wreak havoc. Classic examples include *Termites of 1938*, with the trio as exterminators; *Violent Is the Word for Curly* (1938), in which they pose as college professors; *Oily to Bed, Oily to Rise* (1939), wherein the boys discover oil on a kindly widow's property; and *From Nurse to Worse* (1940), in which the trio attempt some insurance fraud. The popularity of their shorts was such that the Stooges also made propaganda films in favor of the war effort. *You Nazty Spy!* was the first film to satirize the Nazi regime, predating Chaplin's *The Great Dictator* by eleven months. A sequel of sorts was released the following year, *I'll Never Heil Again* (1941). One reason the Three Stooges remain well remembered is that their preferred medium, the short film, made an easy transition to television. Columbia Pictures, their studio from 1934 to 1957, was an early advocate of selling films to the competitor medium.

Thus, generations of boys knew how to protect themselves from pokes in the eye or bonks on the head and imitate the "nyuk, nyuk" and barking sounds made famous by Curly.

Another slapstick comedy team of the classical era who retained their fame due to television was the vaudeville and burlesque duo Bud Abbott and Lou Costello. Following a successful career in feature films in the 1940s, they took their act to television with the half-hour situation comedy *The Abbott and Costello Show*, which ran from 1952 to 1953. They made their film debut in 1940 with *One Night in the Tropics*, but hit it big in leading roles with the armed services–themed *Buck Privates* and its sequel, *In the Navy* (both 1941). Though their characters were not called Abbott and Costello, they kept a consistent format of Abbott being the straight man/con man with Costello as the dim-witted, funny, and sweet one. Oddly, a number of their films, such as *Abbott and Costello in Hollywood* (1945) and *Abbott and Costello Meet Frankenstein* (1948), use their names in the titles though the characters they play have different monikers, demonstrating the popularity of the duo as a brand name. Their comedy was primarily verbal slapstick, never involving the physical punishment Laurel and Hardy would deliberately or accidentally mete out to each other, never even remotely approaching the shock and awe the Stooges could bring.

Yet for all the popularity of Laurel and Hardy, Abbott and Costello, and the Three Stooges, none approached the commercial success of the two nightclub performers Dean Martin and Jerry Lewis. In *My Friend Irma* (1949), based on a popular radio series, they virtually steal the film out from under its putative leads. Producer Hal Wallis knew what he had in the pairing of the popular duo and quickly produced a sequel in *My Friend Irma Goes West* (1950) with the same major cast, except that Martin and Lewis had more substantial roles. Dino croons, Jerry clowns, and movie stars were born. An astonishing fourteen more films followed until their partnership dissolved in 1956. They were not only the most successful comedy team of the era—they were the biggest box-office draws of that time. Beginning with *That's My Boy* (1951), most of their films rely on the pattern of Martin as straight man/romantic figure/crooner, Lewis as slapstick clown/juvenile/physical comic. There was something of a father-son/older brother–younger brother dynamic and even a strongly homosocial bonding between the two men. Martin appears bigger, more physically imposing, though in fact Lewis was slightly taller. Martin called Lewis "the kid" or "the boy" despite a mere nine-year age difference. But their films continually emphasize the physical, emotional, and sexual differences between the two.

Yet Lewis is always the real star, just as offscreen he was the creative force behind the team. Martin is usually likeable enough, playing straight man to Lewis's clown, but in some instances he comes off as something of a villain, ill-treating not his romantic opposite but his partner, as in their classic *The Stooge* (1952), loosely based on the duo's nightclub act. Lewis had already demonstrated his ability as a physical comedian as well as a creative force in these years, which would keep him in good stead when the pair split up. If Lewis is better remembered today for his films as writer, director, and star, it is predicated on his ability to function in these roles as no one since Charlie Chaplin and Buster Keaton had. But to ignore his work with the easy-going and affable Dean Martin is to forget what an important artist he was for a decade before he became the most successful solo clown in the immediate postclassical era (see Pomerance).

Lewis's solo career began with the fairly tame *The Delicate Delinquent* (1957), but he hit his comic slapstick stride with *Rock-a-Bye Baby* (1958), in which he plays a babysitter to triplets in this remake of the Preston Sturges classic *The Miracle of Morgan's Creek* (1944). Lewis's essential incompetence delivers the comedy, his sweetness a touch of Chaplinesque pathos. He made his directorial debut with *The Bellboy* (1960) and would go on to direct himself in nine more comic films through the rest of the 1960s into 1970. The masterpiece of this period is certainly *The Nutty Professor* (1963), with Lewis portraying both a nerdy scientist and an arrogant nightclub singer as a variation of Dr. Jekyll and Mr. Hyde. Lewis termed his comic alter ego "the Idiot" in recognition of the poor guy's near-complete incompetence. But he was always a sympathetic character, one whom audiences could root for if not always admire or identify with due to his sheer ineptitude. Films like *Cinderfella* (1960), *The Errand Boy* (1961), and *The Patsy* (1964) put the Idiot through his paces as the klutz who can do nothing right except keep a gentle and optimistic disposition in the face of the cruelty of his fellow man.

We would be remiss, at this point, if we did not acknowledge the work of Frank Tashlin, one of the directors who helped guide Martin and Lewis in a couple of their films and Lewis in his solo career. Tashlin, with his background in animation (working on the classic Looney Tunes cartoons), brought a sensibility to the screen little seen in a generation. He also contributed to the career of the often underrated Bob

Hope and brought to the fore the "mammary madness" of comedienne Jayne Mansfield. Tashlin himself has rather faded from view, but his influence on the cartoon-oriented works that followed is still apparent.

Meanwhile, as Lewis's movie career petered out, another comic appeared on the cinematic scene, one deeply influenced by both Groucho and Hope (a comic who may be said to straddle the slapstick and satirical traditions) with his own persona developed on the stand-up comedy circuit. Woody Allen began as a gag writer and then became a screenwriter. He launched his film career as the writer, director, and star of *Take the Money and Run* (1969), a faux documentary that casts Allen as a total nebbish, a loser in every way. He utilized this basic characterization in a handful of films, each more assured than the last, in particular *Sleeper* (1973), which uses a science-fiction structure for some good-natured satire and romantic buffoonery, and *Love and Death* (1975), a film that evokes Tolstoy and Dostoevsky as well as Sergei Eisenstein and Ingmar Bergman. Allen shows himself capable of delivering comic one-liners with all the slyness of Groucho and of taking more than a pratfall or two in addition. Yet in a pattern that would be repeated by later comics, once he achieved a substantial level of success, Allen often abandoned the slapstick model in favor of outright dramas, serio-comedies, or fluffy romances, with the occasional postmodern meditation.

As Allen was turning his attention to more serious comedies, director John Landis was assembling a cast of little-known actors to produce one of the most surprising successes of the 1970s in *National Lampoon's Animal House*. This college-set comedy would prove as influential as Chaplin's slapstick brand had been sixty years earlier, setting a tone of youthful anarchy that eventually morphed into the teen sex comedies so popular subsequently. *Animal House* revels in rebellion, in poking fun at those on the inside while making heroes of the lovable losers, slackers, and clowns who make up the comic fraternity of Delta House. The authority figures harken back to the Keystone Kops in their bumbling incompetence, while the young heroes invoke the Marx Brothers. Along the way, it made a movie star of John Belushi. His Bluto Blutarsky is a study in comic mayhem, a satyr like Harpo Marx, but with an appetite like Shakespeare's Falstaff. The film maintains a sense of innocence, perhaps owing to its being set in 1962—a time before the killing of President John Kennedy and the Vietnam War cast a pall over the country. Landis and Belushi teamed up again in 1980 for *The Blues Brothers*, an expansion of the musical sketches Belushi and costar Dan Aykroyd developed for the late-night TV sensation *Saturday Night Live*. As successful as the film was commercially, it reveals a problem that many comedies of the 1980s would succumb to in their zeal to out-slapstick each other: excess. Compare, for example, how little mayhem and destruction Keaton and Lloyd relied upon in their famous chase scenes with the absurdity and overkill of what is virtually a demolition derby in a shopping mall in the climax of *The Blues Brothers*.

Set like *Animal House* in the more innocent past (here it's 1954), *Porky's* (1982) reveals itself to be anything but innocent as its horny teenage boys spy on the girls in their locker room, torment their teachers, and hope to catch a glimpse of the "talent" on view in the sleazy nightclub that gives the film its title. When the boys are humiliated and thrown out of the club, they vow revenge. For all of the apparent influence of *Animal House*, this is the film that gave life to the "gross-out" genre, or what critic William Paul calls "animal comedy." *Porky's*, as Paul notes,

Animal House (1978) Perhaps no comic film in the entire sound era has had more impact than *Animal House*. Certainly one of the most successful film comedies ever made—fairly low budget, its box-office take achieved blockbuster proportions—it gave rise to an entire subgenre of comedy, variously termed "animal comedy" and "gross-out comedy." Though college had been a popular setting for comedy films before, now college and high school became an arena for sex, drugs, drinking, rock and roll, and youthful rebellion—accurate reflections of life, perhaps, but little seen in the movies up to that time. An engaging cast led by John Belushi in his big-screen debut and an anarchic spirit make the film impossible to dislike—unless perhaps you are a college or university administrator.

"upped the stakes on raunchiness in adolescent comedies."[2] Its connection to the slapstick tradition is a lot closer than many of the teen sex comedies to follow in that the film is intimately concerned with the body and its vicissitudes. Indeed it is less about sex than physical expression, sex being the excuse, as it were, for the body humor.

One film in the slapstick tradition of body humor that owes a clear debt to *Porky's* is *American Pie* (1999). Though it achieved a new level in raunchiness, it had none of the meanness of *Porky's*. Instead, it concerned a group of rather average, mostly likeable teenage boys with a healthy interest in what teenage boys are usually interested in: girls and the promise of sex they might deliver. The boys vow to lose their virginity before they graduate from high school, but in the slapstick tradition of clown-incompetence they seem unlikely to achieve their salacious goal. The senior prom becomes the ticking clock of their desires. The essential sweetness of the film is carried both by its boyish star Jason Biggs and Eugene Levy who plays his good-hearted, if somewhat befuddled father. The boys approach their task with all the pluck of Harold Lloyd and luck turns out to be on their side, as well. Though, of course, more sexually explicit and with heroines much more inspired by the feminist movement than the demure damsels of yore, the physical humor, the body comedy, predominates. For many, *American Pie* was on the order of a film of the previous year, *There's Something About Mary* (1998), in which Ben Stiller shows himself a worthy successor to the lovable losers of slapstick clown comedy, although the film possesses a cynicism and meanness little apparent before *Porky's* and more akin to W. C. Fields's misanthrope than to Charlie Chaplin's sentimentality. *American Pie*, however, retains not just charm but a romanticism that would not have been out of place in the world of Keaton and Lloyd—absent the sex and the notoriety of the pie itself.

What the short film had been to the silent clowns of the 1920s, *Saturday Night Live*, or *SNL*, as it is affectionately known, became for a new generation of screen comedians. Besides Belushi and Aykroyd, the alumni list of *SNL* includes a who's who of contemporary clown comedy, with Chevy Chase, Bill Murray, Eddie Murphy, Adam Sandler, Billy Crystal, Rob Schneider, Mike Myers, Dana Carvey, Chris Rock, Will Ferrell, and Kristen Wiig turning post-1980s motion picture comedy into

---

[2] William Paul, *Laughing Screaming: Modern Hollywood Horror and Comedy* (New York: Columbia University Press, 1994): 116.

an *SNL* alumni reunion. Murray came to embody the slacker, though he plays a complete comic idiot in *Caddyshack* (1980), being consistently outwitted by a gopher. Films like *Stripes* (1981), *Ghostbusters* (1984), *What About Bob?* (1991), and *Groundhog Day* (1993) better capture his deadpan humor and slacker mentality. Eddie Murphy, meanwhile, made the transition to film stardom with the action film *48 Hours* (1982) and then turn to action comedies with the wildly successful Beverly Hills Cop series (1984–1994). He moved to more pure slapstick with the big-budget remake of *The Nutty Professor* (1996). Where Jerry Lewis's nutty professor was a hopeless nerd, Murphy's Sherman Klump is vastly overweight, insecure, shy, and retiring. Under what seems a literal ton of makeup, Murphy remains almost unrecognizable, a feat he plays upon when he also incarnates four others of the Klump family in the form of Grandma, Ma, Pa, and Brother Klump. He is also, of course, his own evil alter ego, named, as in the Lewis original, Buddy Love. Murphy plays Buddy Love as a more obnoxious version of himself. Murphy played in a variety of comic styles, but his *Nutty Professor* and a 2000 sequel are highlights in a career in which the comic was a major star for two decades.

SNL alum Adam Sandler also emerged as a major comic star in the slapstick clown tradition with his early films *Billy Madison* (1995) and *Happy Gilmore* (1996), his persona very much the juvenile in both senses of the term. In the former film, he must return to grade school; the sight of this overgrown child trying to fit behind the desk of an elementary school classroom conjures images of Harry Langdon and his short pants. In *Happy Gilmore*, his short-fused hockey player must learn to control himself in the more sedate world of golf—the taming of the anarchic comic spirit to conform to social norms. Lots of physical humor reminiscent of the Three Stooges shows up here, as it does in the sports-themed *The Waterboy*. But rather quickly Sandler softened his image and tried for a more adult persona with *Big Daddy* (1998), in which he finds himself wanting to adopt a child who has been thrust into his life. He then totally displaced the slapstick clown image when he worked with cult director Paul Thomas Anderson in the cerebral *Punch-Drunk Love* (2002). Yet Sandler hasn't entirely abandoned the slapstick tradition, as films like *Mr. Deeds* (2002), a remake of the classic Frank Capra screwball comedy *Mr. Deeds Goes to Town* (1936), and *Anger Management* (2003) duly attest with their segments of pure physical humor. The same is true of *Jack and Jill* (2011), in which he plays a dual role as

Billy Madison (1995) It is possible to see Adam Sandler's early films as taking a harder edge to the man-child persona that was the specialty of Harry Langdon during slapstick comedy's golden age of the 1920s. Where Langdon is sweet and innocent, more childlike than childish, Sandler is angry, ill-tempered, and immature. He eventually softened this persona, but he rose to stardom on the strength of films like *Billy Madison*, in which he plays a kind of post-Belushi slob without the sweetness, at least through most of the film. In this story of a man-boy among actual boys, Sandler brings the "dumb-and-dumber" humor popularized by Jim Carrey and Jeff Daniels to his own starmaking vehicle.

twins, one of whom is a woman. Most of the pratfalls and comic violence are performed by and directed at this female incarnation. Kristen Wiig, meanwhile, would speak up for real ladies in *Knocked Up* (2007), *Whip It* (2009), and her breakthrough film—which seemed something of a breakthrough for women everywhere—*Bridesmaids* (2011).

Outside of the *SNL* roster, but from the small-screen hit *In Living Color* (1990-1994), Jim Carrey emerged as the most important slapstick star since Jerry Lewis. Though he didn't have quite the total creative control of Lewis in his solo phase, the force of his personality certainly make his films his own, such as the breakthrough *The Mask* (1994). The film's spirit and special effects link it more closely with the classic Warner Bros. cartoon shorts of the 1940s, with surrealistic transformations impossible in live-action cinema. Another Jekyll-and-Hyde structure, like *The Nutty Professor*—here, the mild-mannered bank clerk is transformed into a raging id—allows Carrey to show off his rapid-fire delivery and talent for mimicry. *Dumb and Dumber* (1994) solidified his box-office appeal, amplified by the success of *Ace Ventura: Pet Detective* (1994) and *Ace Ventura: When Nature Calls* (1995).

As the likes of Eddie Murphy, Adam Sandler, and Jim Carrey have largely abandoned their clown personae, writer-director Judd Apatow has stepped into the fray with his simultaneously sweet and sexy comedies featuring a new style of man-child. In *The 40-Year-Old Virgin* and *Knocked Up* he offers up quasi-romances with unlikely heroes. Though he relies on a kind of stock company (Paul Rudd, Jason Segal, Seth Rogen, Leslie Mann) he doesn't rely on a star persona; rather, he relies on a consistent type, a lovable loser or a slacker who needs to make only minor changes of lifestyle and attitude to win the day. The focus is on the male body, though instead of performing incredible stunts and physical gags, the body is a rather inappropriate one for the typical Hollywood romance.

The stunt tradition itself was taken up in mainstream Hollywood cinema when Jackie Chan—who had an aborted run at American film stardom in the 1980s—began a successful career outside Hong Kong with both the Rush Hour series (1998–2007) and the duology of *Shanghai Noon* (2000) and *Shanghai Knights* (2003). Chan was clearly working in the tradition of Buster Keaton, with an athleticism and disregard for his own safety unseen since the diminutive silent comic's height of popularity. Yet Hollywood felt the need to use Chan in action genres (the police thriller and the Western) and to pair him with established American actors (Chris Tucker, Owen Wilson), both of which worked to segment Chan's transcendentally imaginative gags and stunt work from the overall arc of the films. Moreover, Chan was in his midforties when his Hollywood stardom arrived—still capable of inventive acrobatics, but certainly past his prime. For his true Keaton-like genius, one must return to his Hong Kong films of the late 1970s through the early 1990s.

Typologies, Themes, and Theories

Jerry Lewis once said, "The premise of all comedy is a man in trouble, the little guy against the big guy." The size differential between the 5′5″ Charlie Chaplin and his villains was always one he wished to exaggerate, for instance casting the 6′5″ Eric Campbell opposite himself in virtually all of the Mutual films. The 6′2″ Mack Swain is the foil for the diminutive clown in *The Gold Rush*. The similarly proportioned Buster Keaton used his lack of height to his comic advantage not only by using larger actors opposite himself but often by casting women of similar height to himself as his female leads. Oddly enough, Woody Allen also measures 5′5″, as did Harpo Marx before him (Groucho managed only another couple of inches). Eddie Murphy is a mere 5′9″. One could develop a theory of comedy based solely on physical stature, but that would discount the 5′10″ Harold Lloyd and Adam Sandler, along with the 6-foot Jerry Lewis and the 6′1″ Jim Carrey. To be sure, the comics who were short of stature did play upon their physical disadvantage, but it was always more a matter of their being slightly at odds with the world rather than with the tape measure. The "trouble" is not so much, then, the little guy against the big guy unless we understand this metaphorically as well as literally. For Lewis also realized, as Mack Sennett and Chaplin did so well before him, that the big guy was authority, reason, social decorum, and the forces of repression—anyone or anything that tries to make little guys of us all. In Keaton's case, the very universe itself, all of the forces of nature, seem to conspire against him, from raging rivers to thundering cyclones—a man in trouble indeed!

Chaplin understood that the clown could never fit into society. That is the ultimate pathos of the Tramp. Keaton and Lloyd begin as outsiders, but bend the universe with their indomitable will. W. C. Fields and the Marx Brothers had too much sense and cynicism to want to fit into the society. Fields is inside, but wants out; the Marxes are on the outside and want to stay that way. Mae West, too, wants things her way, and her dominating sexuality makes her unsuitable for any notion of normal American, male-dominated society. Lewis's persona seems desperate to want to fit in but, unlike Keaton's and Lloyd's, can only imagine the world accommodating his difference. In his early, slapstick-oriented films, Allen also knew that he could not fit in and this was, as in *Sleeper* and *Love and Death* especially, the fault of the world. For Carrey and Sandler, the world was basically all right and they are the ones who cannot—and, they acknowledge, should not—fit into it. The world could use a Bluto Blutarsky to keep the rest of us from becoming a bit too staid and stolid. This insider-outsider dialectic is one of the ways that slapstick comedy differs from romantic comedy. In romantic comedy, the formation of the couple rests on their ability to make society conform to their beliefs, but the society must be one worthy of the couple. Whether there are social or personal impediments to the formation or re-formation of the couple, the world in which they live must be one in which they similarly wish to dwell. In the slapstick tradition, the clown

Safety Last (1923) For many years the knock against Harold Lloyd from the critical establishment was that he possessed little sense of social criticism or cynicism; that he was entirely too optimistic and boy-next-door. Maybe those are weaknesses, but from the standpoint of both commercial success and the ability to capture the spirit of the times and the essence of a nation, Lloyd's comic ability still seems positively uncanny. A gifted physical comedian and a gagman par excellence, Lloyd can still offer up as many laughs as any comedian in film history—and still tell us something about the culture and the nation in which he thrived. Climbing the skyscraper in *Safety Last* is both a metaphor for his eternal striving and can-do attitude and the epitome of the comedy of thrills Lloyd provided.

must stand just outside society and society must be the worse for being unable to accommodate him.

Yet another way slapstick comedy differentiates itself from romantic comedy rests on the nature of the comic hero. The fun of romantic comedy is seeing two equally matched, often glamorous stars engage in witty repartee in elegant settings. The obstacles to their love may include romantic rivals but usually revolve around their own inner problems. Yet the audience never doubts the suitability of the couple and their eventual union. In a sense, the slapstick comedy presents the audience with a hero who is manifestly *unsuitable* to the role of lover; that is to say, he is a most unsuitable suitor. Chaplin's Tramp, of course, presents the clearest index of this, and even when the union does occur it seems a gift on the part of the woman. Good examples, if sentimental ones, occur at the end of *The Kid* and *City Lights*, where it is clear that however noble and kindhearted the Tramp is, he is not a candidate for a romantic happily-everafter. Keaton and Lloyd tend to allow their characters a happy ending, but it is a matter of their proving themselves through physical challenges and not of their innate romantic qualities. Whatever else they are, these slapstick figures are hardly suave, sophisticated, and socially adept. As for Harry Langdon, his doughy, baby face and diminutive size make him a particularly unsuitable paramour, especially when cast against strapping athletic women, such as the comic villainess played by Gertrude Astor in *The Strong Man*—an ironic title, given Langdon's persona. More to the point, Langdon emerges as a suitable romantic partner for Priscilla Bonner's Mary Brown largely because she is blind—a motif Chaplin later took up, and milked for its pathos, in *City Lights*.

The unromantic nature of clown comedy in the classical era is particularly notable, for this was the age of the great screwball comedies. In the transitional period between silents and sound, figures like W. C. Fields and the Marx Brothers went about their anarchic ways, rejecting conventional plots, which included romantic coupling. They were all, in any case, hardly suitable objects of desire, but their films had them actively rejecting all traces of romance—in Fields's case, he was pitted opposite shrewish wives, such as in the short *The Barber Shop* (1933), and in the case of the Marx Brothers, Harpo is a satyr-like lecher, Chico is completely asexual (something of an in-joke as he was a notorious womanizer offscreen), and Groucho actively engages in sending a constant barrage of one-liners against the redoubtable Margaret Dumont. As screwball comedy began to dominate the genre in the wake of *It Happened One Night* (1934), the Marx Brothers were relegated to being part of an ensemble, with the romances providing the impetus for the plots. Fields's films took on a positively antiromantic quality, finding family life a nightmare requiring escape from an unending series of harridans, spoiled children, and mean little dogs.

The same unromantic qualities are manifest in more contemporary clown comedies where the comic possesses characteristics that would certainly disqualify him from the witty world of screwball comedies. Woody Allen's frail, cowardly, hopelessly neurotic alter ego often comes up short when juxtaposed with more conventionally handsome and suave romantic rivals as in *Love and Death* and even in later films like *Crimes and Misdemeanors* (1989). Adam Sandler's alter-ego figures in *Billy Madison* and *Happy Gilmore* are childish, petulant, ill-tempered slobs; Jim Carrey is a nightmare of bad hair and rubber-faced mugging in the Ace Ventura films. Steve Carell's forty-year-old virgin in the film of that title seems needlessly oversensitive and withdrawn, while the whole premise of *Knocked Up* is that Seth Rogen is, for a number of reasons (lack of conventional physical attractiveness; total lack of ambition and drive), a completely inappropriate partner for the lovely Katherine Heigl. When not childlike or childish, the male figures are adolescent in both senses of the term: either teenage boys incapable of acting like grown-ups but with very grown-up desires, or grown-ups acting immaturely.

To acknowledge the very unromantic nature of the male protagonist, the animal or gross-out comedies that began in the 1970s devalue romance in favor of sex; the protagonist's sexual conquest only occasionally translates into romance thereafter, as in the American Pie series. Otherwise, in films like *Animal House* and *Porky's* the goal is bodily satisfaction, not seeking and finding a soulmate, especially among the clown figures. Bluto is the lovable paradigm here: the clown who is outside the normal world in his appearance, appetites, liminality, and magical abilities. (A jokey coda insists that he gets the gorgeous blonde and becomes a United States senator.) In fact, what separates *Animal House* from the gross-out comedies that followed is precisely the charming disruptiveness of the boys of Delta House.

***American Pie* (1999)** In an era when the teen-sex comedy was king, *American Pie* became the court jester, with box-office sales and sequels unmatched since the subgenre first emerged. Ironically, its MPAA R-rating should have prevented much of its target audience from seeing the film unless accompanied by a parent or guardian. And most parents were not likely to take his or her youngster to this sex-filled extravaganza, which featured Jason Biggs, here finding a new and surprising use of good old American apple pie. And yet, as is often the case, there was a little bit of heart and soul to the shenanigans of a group of sex-starved high-school boys whose biggest fear was that they would enter college as virgins and be confined to special dorms for people just like them.

Inserting the comedian into film genres entirely inappropriate to his persona best demonstrates the disruptiveness and antiromance of comedian comedy. Buster Keaton's films are essentially adventure stories: *Our Hospitality, The Navigator, The General,* and *Steamboat Bill, Jr.* Keaton's athleticism and singular imagination enable him to prove himself a worthy hero, but he is no Douglas Fairbanks. He acknowledges that he is not suited for traditional heroic roles in *The Three Ages* and *Go West* (1926), both genre spoofs. Woody Allen follows a pattern similar to Keaton's in genre comedies like the science fiction *Sleeper* and the war epic *Love and Death.* These aren't genre spoofs like *Take the Money and Run* and *Bananas* (1971). Rather, they are comedies that take the genre elements reasonably seriously and put in a protagonist so obviously ill fitted to take on the hero's role.

The antiromantic qualities of the comedian are also indicated by the frequent use of such motifs as cross-dressing (Arbuckle in *The Butcher Boy* [1917]; Bob Hope in *The Princess and the Pirate* [1944]; Allen's taking

***The Nutty Professor* (1963)** The nerd figure, not so named at the time, became the alter ego of Jerry Lewis, who famously if ungenerously called him "The Idiot." Professor Julius Kelp, the nutty professor of the title, is not an idiot, however, but a poor schlemiel who is picked on by his colleagues and students. He sets out to change his image and in so doing unleashes an alter ego, Buddy Love, who is everything he is not, including mean and nasty. For all of Buddy's manly attributes and self-confidence the lovely Miss Purdy (Stella Stevens) prefers the nerd. But is this wish fulfillment on the part of the unromantic geek, the comic clown whose laughter cannot hide the tears?

***The Nutty Professor* (1996)** The makeup used by star Eddie Murphy to transform himself into the overweight Sherman Klump is nothing short of astounding. A lowering of his voice completes the change. He also transforms himself into almost his entire family—grandmother, mother, father, brother—for a hilariously true-to-life dinner-table scene. Yet it is in the morphing of the character Klump via the Jekyll-and-Hyde motif into the evil twin Buddy Love that is the film's greatest joke. For if Jerry Lewis partly implied that his dark side was Dean Martin (though those in the know knew better), Murphy makes the joke more obviously on himself, when his doppelgänger is clearly a facet of Eddie Murphy. Perhaps no remake in film history is a more loving tribute to an original, while extending it for more contemporary audiences.

on the role of Blanche DuBois at one point during *Sleeper*; Steve Martin's channeling Barbara Stanwyck's role in a mash-up of *Double Indemnity* [1944] in a scene in *Dead Men Don't Wear Plaid* [1982] or being inhabited, for that matter, by Lily Tomlin in *All of Me* [1984]; Adam Sandler in *Jack and Jill*); or the playing of multiple roles that destabilize the protagonist's masculine identity (Jerry Lewis in *The Nutty Professor*, *The Family Jewels* [1965], and *Three on a Couch* [1966]; Eddie Murphy in his Nutty Professor films). The instability of the comedian's identity is a function of his insecurity, his sense that he is not manly enough and is thus uncomfortable with himself and within his own body. This is also made manifest by the adolescent nature of the hero, which makes him not just an unsuitable romantic partner but very much a work-in-progress. The adolescent, by definition, struggles with identity and with a growing sense of the body's changes. A profound discomfort with his own body and an inability to control it—seen everywhere from the animal-like noises and movements of the Three Stooges' Curly to the hemming and hawing, looking away, and extreme shyness that characterize Jerry Lewis, to the overcompensation or crudity of the slapstick adolescent comedies—give further meaning to the idea of slapstick as a most unromantic genre.

Yet clearly one of the most trenchant ways that the slapstick tradition rejects romance is through the use of comic teams. These teams clearly have a homosocial component to them, necessitated by the very continuity of the teaming—no individual member of the team can go off into the sunset of wedded domestic bliss lest the team be broken up. Critic Molly Haskell has gone so far as to claim that the male comedy duo—Laurel and Hardy, Abbott and Costello, Martin and Lewis— excludes heterosexual romance in favor of a near-homosexual coupling, a marriage of opposites, such as thin/fat, short/tall, straight man/comic. The homosocial nature of the comic duo brings with it the feminization of at least one of the members of the team. One thinks of Laurel's crying jags; the often-hysterical reactions of Lou Costello similarly come to mind as feminizing features. But nowhere is this clearer than in the Martin-Lewis combo. Though Lewis is often infantilized or juvenilized compared with Martin, he is just as frequently feminized. In *Living It Up* (1954), the team's remake version of *Nothing Sacred* (1937), Lewis takes on the role originally played by Carole Lombard. The neediness that Lewis's character often expresses for Martin's goes beyond a big brother– little brother or father-son relationship, drifting more clearly toward romance. *Jumping Jacks* (1952) concludes with a kind of embrace between Martin and Lewis that is more typical, as Krutnik notes, of the ending of conventional romantic comedies (Karnick and Jenkins 38).

Iconography

The most obvious of the icons of slapstick comedy is the pratfall. Though many characters are subject to falling down, the protagonist handles it best. It is the oldest of the slapstick icons and the most clichéd: think of slipping on a banana peel. Chevy Chase made the old-fashioned pratfall his signature move in his *SNL* introductions and comic impersonation of President Gerald Ford, and he took the tool into the movies, especially in the National Lampoon Vacation series. All of the silent clowns took their comic spills, Keaton especially, even to the point of breaking his leg during production of *The Electric House* in 1920. (He later

***Steamboat Bill, Jr.* (1928)** Buster Keaton's weakness as a commercial filmmaker was his willingness to sacrifice the laugh in favor of a "wow" so subtle that by the time one realizes what he has accomplished the film has moved on and left one behind. His interest in the creative possibilities of the motion picture apparatus itself set him apart from all of his comic contemporaries and brought him closer to the European avant-garde of the 1920s. There was also something of the civil and mechanical engineer in Keaton: witness in this moment from *Steamboat Bill, Jr.* how the wall is about to fall on him and seems likely to kill him instantly. Yet note the window, which will, in fact, provide a small window of opportunity, some few inches square, for his survival.

returned to *The Electric House*, releasing the film as we know it today in 1922). More seriously, he fractured a vertebra in his neck during a stunt for *Sherlock Jr.* For Laurel and Hardy and Jerry Lewis, the pratfall was a function of their physical incompetence. Lewis, especially, made this a major characteristic of "The Idiot" in films like *The Disorderly Orderly, Cinderfella,* and *The Family Jewels.* Jim Carrey in the Ace Ventura films performs impossible stunts (aided by special effects) that other characters in the film react to with terror but which he accepts as an integral part of his off-beat world.

One of the most notable features of slapstick comedy, but one often overlooked amid the pratfalls, exaggerated violence, comic inversions, and sheer anarchy, is the breadth of the comic's imagination. The clowns function as *bricoleurs* (creative and imaginative tinkerers), adapting and transforming objects from one use to another in surprising and, of course, humorous ways. No one was better at this than Chaplin, but it is an ability demonstrated by Keaton, Lloyd, the Marx Brothers, Jerry

Lewis, and in many films of the contemporary era. The transformation of the athleticism of the silent era into the more gross bodily functions of modern times finds an analogous treatment of transformation gags. Some are so outrageous that they have become indelibly entrenched in the cultural memory, such as the near-cannibalism and the "Oceana Roll" scenes in *The Gold Rush*. By any standards such moments as the transformation of ejaculate into hair gel in *There's Something About Mary* or a pie into a substitute for the female sexual organ in *American Pie* remain in memory not just for their outrageousness but for the principle of transformation they highlight.

Of course, the transformation gag is a staple of silent comedy. The cleverness of the comic mind must be visually demonstrated. But it also stems from the clown's need to remake his world, for in a universe where you don't fit in, where things will go invariably wrong, necessity is the mother of invention. In *The Kid*, because the Tramp has no funds to outfit a baby nursery, a sheet becomes a hammock for the child to sleep in; a glove on the end of a teakettle becomes a nipple for a baby bottle; and a wicker chair has part of its seat cut out for a potty. A boot becomes a steak and shoelaces strands of spaghetti; and two forks and rolls become legs and feet in *The Gold Rush*. In Keaton's *The Boat*, a bathtub becomes a lifeboat (but still a bathtub after all at the end when the little boy pulls the drain plug); the shelves and compartments of a doughnut case becomes a baseball scoreboard, with little bits of the treat removed to make numbers in Lloyd's *Speedy*.

Jackie Chan is the modern master of the transformation gag, turning household items into occasions for inventive stunts, where umbrellas and chairs become swords, refrigerator doors act as shields, and bicycles are put to more uses than perhaps even Chaplin or Keaton could have imagined. Indeed, it is likely that Chan's use of props in his Hollywood films was what most impressed critics and audiences little familiar with his Hong Kong work.

But transformation gags may also be extended to verbal slapstick, which is to say the use of puns, mispronunciation, and malapropism. The masters of these were the Marx Brothers—Chico's whole shtick, after all, involved the misunderstanding and mangling of English in his outrageous and politically incorrect Italian accent. One book devoted to the Marx Brothers' verbal humor is even titled *Why a Duck?*, from the routine in *The Cocoanuts* in which Chico misunderstands "viaduct" for "why a duck." Even more famous than this is the routine in *A Night at*

Duck Soup (1933) Often acclaimed as the Marx Brothers' finest film, *Duck Soup* marked the end of their career at Paramount Studios. What is hard to believe is that even at a studio known for its sophistication and daring, the film is a lightning-fast series of puns, sight gags, and philosophical musings, along with an undisguised political rancor. The film is among the darkest indictments of political corruption and the ideology of warfare ever produced in classical Hollywood, even pre-Code Hollywood. Not content to castigate Europe for its interminable series of wars started at the drop of a hat, even the Untied States has its patriotism punctured by the anarchic brothers with the U.S. military uniforms worn by Groucho throughout the film indicating the history of American wars.

the Opera in which Groucho is trying to get Chico to sign an agreement. At one point he explains that there is a "sanity clause" in every contract, but Chico knows better: "You can't fool me. There ain't no Sanity Clause [Santa Claus]." Groucho didn't always need Chico for the puns in their films, either, as in *Monkey Business*, when, to a woman's comment "I don't like this innuendo," Groucho replies "That's what I always say: 'Love flies out the door when money comes innuendo.'"

The most famous of all verbal transformation gags is surely Abbott and Costello's beloved "Who's on First?" sketch. A variation on numerous vaudeville and movie patter routines involving verbal twists and turns that were especially effective with nonnative English speakers who often experienced such confusion learning their new language, "Who's on First?" had been used by the team for years before they introduced it in their film debut, *One Night in the Tropics*, though its fullest incarnation is from *The Naughty Nineties* (1945), and it is this version that can be seen on video at the National Baseball Hall of Fame in Cooperstown, New York. Its transformative principle involves the use of common interrogatives and other phrases to substitute for the names of the players on a baseball team. When Abbott explains that "Who's on first, What's on second, I Don't Know is on third..." he is repeatedly interrupted by Costello's frustrated exclamation, "That's what I want to find out!" Abbott continues to insist on the same litany of names, and Costello is equally insistent that his partner is not telling him what he wants to know. It becomes funny also by the principle, discussed below, of repetition: the longer Bud keeps trying to explain that Who is the name of the man playing first base and What is the name of the man on second, the more frustrated Lou gets. At one point the exchange is fast and furious, the timing just as important as the repetition of the transformation:

> *Costello:* Well, then, who's on first?
> *Abbott:* Yes.
> *Costello:* I mean the fellow's name.
> *Abbott:* Who.
> *Costello:* The guy on first.
> *Abbott:* Who.
> *Costello:* The first baseman.
> *Abbott:* Who.
> *Costello:* The guy playing...
> *Abbott:* Who is on first!
> *Costello:* I'm asking you who's on first.
> *Abbott:* That's the man's name.
> *Costello:* That's (whose) name?
> *Abbott:* Yes.
> *Costello:* Well, go ahead and tell me.
> *Abbott:* That's it.
> *Costello:* That's who?
> *Abbott:* Yes.

At another point, Costello asks "What's the name of the guy playing first," only to be told that "No, What is on second." And on it goes, Costello never quite getting it.

A variation on puns and verbal transformation is the reliable double entendre, and slapstick comedy is no stranger to that strategy; Mae West, of course, made it a specialty. In *She Done Him Wrong*, she is asked if she ever met a man who could make her happy. Her reply: "Sure, lots of times." In *I'm No Angel* we learn from Mae, "When I'm good I'm very good, but when I'm bad, I'm better." A simple but effective innuendo comes by way of Woody Allen in *Sleeper*. When his character, Miles, is threatened with brainwashing, he exclaims: "Not my brain! It's my second favorite organ!" Working on the idea that more contemporary comedy is a bit grosser than classical works, in *Ace Ventura: Pet Detective*, Jim Carrey keeps with the theme of pets by replying to a woman who asked, "You really love animals, don't you?" with "If it gets cold enough." Even W. C. Fields got in on that act. When told by a waitress in *Never Give a Sucker an Even Break* that "there's something awfully big about you," he replies, "Thank you, dear, thank you, dear, thank you...." And amid Groucho's insults and sly asides, we find this gem in *Animal Crackers*: "Signor Ravelli's first selection will be 'Somewhere My Love Lies Sleeping' with a male chorus."

Still, at the heart of slapstick comedy is the physical gag, and the heart of the gag is the principle of repetition. If something is funny once, it gets progressively funnier with each iteration, as long as there is also some variation. It can be as simple as slipping on a banana peel, then standing up and slipping again. Take the following repetition gags from *Sleeper*. Miles comes upon a field of genetically engineered fruit and vegetables. Among the scientific wonders is a giant banana. Eventually that banana is peeled, and only someone new to the experience of film comedy would not anticipate the inevitable slippage. (Anticipation is another important comic principle.) Sure enough, when the police spot Miles and give chase, they slip on the giant peel, not once, but again and again. Gags must also have what is called a "topper." Here it is that Miles also slips on the peel. Or another gag and topper: The police possess a large, futuristic cannon. The first time they attempt to fire it, it fizzles. So when we see the cannon again, we can expect it not to work. And that is the case, except it doesn't work in an even more spectacular way, by nearly blowing up. A third attempt to use the cannon results in nothing happening at all, while the fourth time is the charm—it works! But the topper is that precisely by working, it enables Miles to escape when the rocket it launches punctures his spacesuit, which propels him across a wide lake.

The Music Box (1932) Sisyphus, the mythical king compelled to roll a rock up a hill only to see it repeatedly roll back down, has nothing on Stan Laurel and Oliver Hardy in this, their most perfect of comic shorts. Relying on the principle of repetition—pushing the piano up the stairs over and over with each attempt getting ever-closer yet each time something new going wrong—it tops the gag when the boys actually reach the top only to be told that there is a road around the back and therefore they didn't need to use the stairs. So sure enough they take the piano back down the stairs to use the road! Whether this says something profound about the human condition or just reveals the comic genius of these two classic clowns may be up to the viewer, but it's a gag that lives in the hearts and minds of film fans of all ages and times.

Keaton was the master of the repetition gag in the golden age. In *Sherlock Jr.*, at the end of his shift at a movie theater the young protagonist diligently sweeps the trash into a large pile. He finds a dollar bill and is very pleased about it. But when an old woman gives him a sob story about losing a dollar he hands it over. When an attractive young lady comes by a few moments later and gives him a sob story about losing a dollar, he hands her one of his own. Then when a tough-looking guy walks over to him, Keaton doesn't even wait to hear his tale, but simply takes out a dollar bill. Funny—but that's not the gag's conclusion. Instead, the guy waves him off derisively, pokes around the trash pile and comes out with a big wallet full of cash. The Marx Brothers, too, knew the value of the repetition gag. A small example from *Duck Soup* suffices: President Firefly (Groucho) has a motorcycle and sidecar as his official vehicle; Pinky (Harpo) is his driver. The first time Firefly gets into the sidecar and tells his driver to go, Pinky and the motorcycle take off without him. Thereafter we anticipate each new iteration of the gag. Firefly finally catches on and sits in the driver's seat. Of course, now the sidecar, with Pinky sitting in it, takes off without him.

Repetition gags can also be verbal. Each time W. C. Fields goes to the door and opens it in *The Fatal Glass of Beer* (1933), he exclaims, "And it ain't a fit night out for man nor beast." He then gets what is obviously a puff of hand-tossed snow in his face. What at first seems an innocuous throwaway becomes, by the sheer number of times it occurs, the most memorable feature of this classic short.

From film to film, we expect the comic to perform these kinds of stunts, deliver certain kind of gags, make the jokes and faces, and wear the silly makeup. Within the classical era, the use of a star with a specific persona and humor has been termed "comedian comedy." Comedian comedy, as defined by film scholar Steve Seidman, takes the star vehicle further than other genres, even the musical, where the star is a transtextual phenomenon, not just a character. The star in comedian comedy (it is virtually always a "he") stands apart from the narrative: he is able to joke about the plot, as when Groucho notes in *The Big Store* (1941) that "I told you in the first reel he was a crook." The comic may be part of a process of breaking down the narrative. He may engage in direct address to the camera, such as Groucho telling members of the audience that he has to remain while Chico performs a piano solo, but they are welcome to get up for a few minutes, or moving closer to the camera to proclaim that he will now have a "strange interlude" in *Animal Crackers*; in *Annie Hall* (1977), Woody Allen's Alvy Singer asks the audience to verify that Annie said "wife" not "life." The star may make fun of his costars as real-life people or simply engage in behavior and dialogue inappropriate either to the ostensible genre of the film or to Hollywood narrative films in general.

Such strategies are possible only in comedian comedy. The line between star and character must be extremely thin, while the comic's persona must be fairly well set. This is one reason that W. C. Fields's Universal films are now more respected and better known than his Paramount work. His persona was either not so consistent in his earlier films or he was cast in character roles as an actor, not a star persona. But in the Universal films, all of which he scripted, he wrote precisely for the persona he most wished to put forth and which was so successful. Curiously, comedian comedy no longer has much of a presence. For all of the vehicles that carried Jim Carrey, Eddie Murphy, and Adam Sandler to

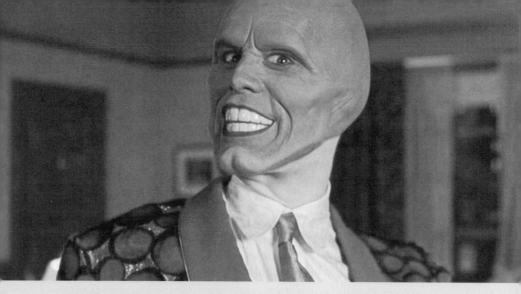

The Mask (1994) Stanley Ipkiss, the mild-mannered bank clerk played by Jim Carrey in one of his two star-making performances of 1994, spends a lot of his sad and lonely time watching cartoons on television. This is not only appropriate for this character, an awkward and timid man-child who develops a powerful alter ego, but also an acknowledgment that the film itself is as close in spirit to Heckel and Jeckel as it is to Jekyll and Hyde. The titular mask transforms the milquetoast bank clerk into a madcap mad hatter of a party animal whose verbal dexterity is matched by a physical dexterity possible only in the realm of the surreal world of animation, with clear and clever influences from the lunatic minds of the Loony Tunes creators of the Warner Bros. stable. With insults aplenty and mind-blowing special effects on view, Bugs Bunny would be proud to call the character of the Mask a close cousin.

stardom, there is relatively little of the playfulness between comedian and audience, few knowing winks, few diegetic ruptures. It may be that the breakdown of genre itself is responsible for the inability of films to carry the worldview that classical genres so importantly managed to do. Or it may be that for all of the gross-out comedy and sexual explicitness of our coarse times, films are, for all that, a bit more conservative, at least when it comes to slapstick comedy. Mack Sennett retains a radical spirit; the Marx Brothers their anarchic nature; Mae West her sexual outrageousness; and Chaplin, Keaton, and Lloyd a physical grace and power to bend the universe to their demands. Still, Eddie Murphy, Adam Sandler, Ben Stiller, Jim Carrey, Jackie Chan, and the Judd Apatow ensemble present a vision of life's possibilities that finds room for the little guy to win against the forces of nature and society that conspire to keep him down. Pluck, luck, and sheer will can still win the day and the damsel.

Hollywood Shuffle

It is likely that audiences unfamiliar with the portrayal of African Americans in earlier days of American cinema will not appreciate the rich significance of the term "Hollywood Shuffle," which gives a 1987 comedy by Robert Townsend its title. The title of Townsend's sweet but caustic comedy refers to a particular kind of shuffling gait associated with the racist imagery of African Americans as portrayed in Hollywood films from its beginning all the way through, it might be argued, the 1950s. The persistence of stereotypes and the remnants of racism certainly meant that at the time of the film's production, most adult Americans and certainly all African-American audience members would understand what Townsend was referring to with this ironic, multipronged title as they watched the film. Hollywood shuffle combines the elements of visual humor, verbal slapstick, puns, and double entendre characteristic of classical sound comedy but has them serve a very specific sociopolitical goal. For this is a film simultaneously about a young black man, Bobby, trying to make it in the American film industry (Hollywood) who must go along to get along—go along with the limited and limiting stereotypes that confine African-American actors—and a film that reveals through parody and deft social commentary just what those stereotypes are and some of their debilitating effects.

Townsend delivers perhaps both the funniest and most biting moments in the film some fourteen minutes in, a fantasy of Bobby's as he awaits his first audition. A fellow actor has told him not to take a degrading role, not to be a "butler or a slave." A dolly-in to a contemplative Bobby is then accompanied by drum beats. We then see a group of escaped slaves crawling through the woods. First a black woman exhorts her male counterparts to continue on their journey: "I kills anybody . . . who stands in the ways of freedom." The use of the exaggerated Hollywood slave dialect lends the serious topic a comic tone. Next, a black man crawls to the top of a lookout and is soon joined by the beautiful Lydia, Bobby's girlfriend outside of his fantasies, who says, "Mandingo, I's go anywhere with you!" Then an anachronistically stereotyped woman with plaited hair captured by white ribbons exclaims, "Oh, Mandingo, I's love you!" Mandingo replies, "I love you, too, Bessie Willie

Robert Townsend as Jasper can't quite understand the concept of "the promised land."

Mae." Then a white woman with curly blond hair tells him, in a heavy Southern accent, "Mandingo, I can't go back there. I love you, too!" Mandingo replies, "Missy Ann, what about your kinfolk?" They kiss, he helps her up and they run off down the road, leaving the two black women to fend for themselves. The next shot cuts to Bobby himself, carrying a butler's tray, moving slowly with a dumbfounded expression on his face. He exclaims, "I don't know why we's leavin' Massa's house. He been good to us." Another slave asks him, "Jasper, don't you want freedom? We goin' to the promised land, the promised land." Jasper replies, "The promised land? Cleveland?" "No, the promised land!" Jasper: "Baltimore?" Shortly thereafter, we hear someone call "Cut!" and Bobby breaks character and into an upper-class British accent. It turns out what we have just seen is a promo for the Black Acting School, which teaches its students (through the use of white teachers) how to "act black." As the commercial comes to an end, Townsend delivers the kicker—the school's phone number appears on screen drawn with highly racist imagery.

There is much to unpack in these few minutes. Some of the humor is very accessible, some more in need of certain background information, while other aspects seem geared more toward black audiences. There is a comment about "light-skinned or yellow blacks" being unsuitable for playing those kinds of roles; this refers both to the fear the white community has of dark-skinned black men and to the "colorism" of black people, who have internalized the values of mainstream white society wherein lighter skin tone is more beautiful and thus preferable. (Even the films of the great black pioneering director Oscar Micheaux typically equate light skin with physical desirability and darker skin with criminality.) The male slave who loves the two black women but who is also loved by a white woman and goes off with her, plays on the stereotype of the oversexed black male and his irresistible attraction for white women. Calling him Mandingo is a direct reference to the 1975 exploitation film written and directed by white men, featuring heavy-weight boxing champ Ken Norton in the role of a slave named Mede, a member of the Mandingo people. Townsend uses the name Mandingo, then, to recall the film and its blatant portrayals of sexual stereotypes. In 1987, *Mandingo* still retained a good deal of its notoriety; today it is justly forgotten. It is likely, alternatively, that Mandingo's calling his white lover Missy Ann is a joke intended for black audiences. Derived from the character played by Sandy Duncan in the TV sensation *Roots* (1977), Missy Ann(e) came to define any white woman who seemed sympathetic but who was actually condescending, haughty, and untrustworthy.

More subtly, Bobby's incarnation of a slave butler recalls, in his speech and general demeanor, the classical-era actor Stepin Fetchit (né Lincoln Perry) who was both the most successful black actor in the 1930s and a highly controversial one. Appearing in dozens of films and earning millions of dollars, he was often condemned for the image he

The pun here on "black actor" is subtle—of course he is a "black" actor, but he is also someone who "acts black."

Black Actor
ROBERT TAYLOR

The Black Acting School is significantly populated by an all-white faculty.

projected as lazy, slow, and shiftless. Whether audiences in 1987 were familiar with Stepin Fetchit is open to question, but the image he created, for better or for worse (and most critics, especially black critics, feel the latter), has retained its power. Yet this seemingly slow-witted slave points to a profound truth: there is no real promised land. His fellow runaway slave keeps insisting they are running off to the Promised Land, but Jasper's question if it is Cleveland, Baltimore, or Minnesota indicates that for blacks in America, the Promised Land was always a vague concept, a nowhere place.

When Bobby breaks character to become Robert, we note that he is identified as a "black actor." On one level, it is obvious that he is a "black actor," which is to say, an actor who is black. But the double meaning here is that he is an actor who *acts* black; and the point of the Black Acting School is precisely to teach actors who are black to act black. Thus it is noteworthy that the instructors are white, since the creation of the stereotypes that pervade popular media are the creation of white people, just as the film-within-the-film, *Jivetime Jimmy's Revenge*, is the product of a writer, a producer, and a director who are white. Bobby's British accent in his guise as Robert further elaborates on the difference between being an actor who is black and an actor acting black. Indeed, in the commercial we see black actors who are not yet proficient at acting black, a more subtle indication that there is nothing essential, nothing natural, about acting and walking "black"—these are pop-culture creations that continue to live on in contemporary media.

Another important fantasy of Bobby's involves the discrepancy between a white critical establishment and ordinary black audiences. After a basketball game Bobby and his friends sit down and relax as his friends wish Bobby luck on his casting call. They hope he gets the role and that the film is a hit. Bobby says he just hopes the critics like it. This inspires two of his friends to start talking about critics who are obviously, if unnamed, Gene Siskel and Roger Ebert and their movie-review shows popular at the time: *Sneak Previews* and *At the Movies*. His friends exclaim, "They need some real brothers critiquin' the movies." This leads to Bobby's fantasy of two black men hosting a movie-review TV show, which he imagines is called *Sneakin' in the Movies*. Speed and Tyrone sneak into movies around town and report back on which films are worth paying for. Their first film is an *Amadeus*-like costume film, *Amadeus Meets Salieri*. Tyrone's complaint is that he doesn't like movies whose titles he can't pronounce. (He pronounces the latter name "Salerious.") The next film is *Chicago Jones and the Temple of Doom*. Tyrone says he liked the first two Chicago Jones and the Temple of Doom films (as if all three had the same title), but he couldn't believe this one. Speed disagrees and thinks it was plausible. Their disagreement leads to a lot of trash-talking and a near fight. Next comes the new movie by Dirty Larry (not featuring Dirty Larry, but "by" him, as if the character were the director). This clip

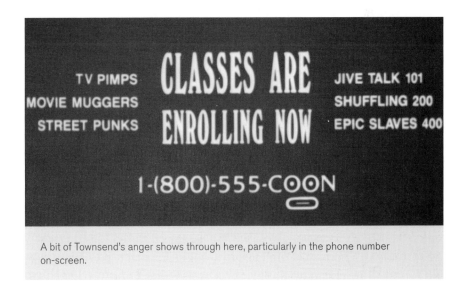

A bit of Townsend's anger shows through here, particularly in the phone number on-screen.

is the comically broadest yet in that the street gang of hostage-takers Larry confronts (a Latino and two black men) is clearly incompetent, not to mention baldly stereotyped. When Larry tells them to drop their guns, one gang member says, "Whatchou say honky, sucker, pig-head, jive-turkey fool?" Again, the two critics don't like the film based on their desire for realism—they simply can't accept three guys with guns losing out to one; and they sneer at the line "Make my day" (the famous line from the Dirty Harry movie *Sudden Impact* [1983]). Finally, there is *Attack of the Street Pimps*, in which we see women dressed stereotypically as hookers on the run from a group of men dressed stereotypically as pimps and coded as zombies. The two critics love the film. Tyrone proclaims that it could really happen and that "the director captured the essence of street life.... The dude in the yellow suit looks like a dude around the corner from my house; that's what's so horrifying about it."

In looking deeper into this sequence, the first thing we notice is that the films the two critics do not like are those with what might be called not simply white characters but a white milieu. The first, the *Amadeus* spoof, with its high European culture, is obviously quite far from any notion of street-level black experience. This is not to say African Americans may not participate in such cultural pursuits, though it is unlikely that Tyrone, a high-school dropout, is one of them. Rather, the point is that this kind of film, as well as *Chicago Jones* (an obvious reference to the Indiana Jones series), typically excludes black people and, in the latter case, uses Third World countries as exotic settings for its white characters. By the same token, the Dirty Larry film villainizes its ethnic Latino and black characters and posits a lone white man who can outthink and outshoot three men of color. Only the pimp-zombie movie—hilariously absurd on the face of it—appeals to their sense of "realism," which is to say their direct, lived experience. Black audiences have made many a mainstream Hollywood film a hit, but this often requires reading against the grain or allowing oneself to participate in a process of buying into stereotyping and negative images.

A sustained fantasy sequence finds Bobby interrupted at home with Lydia by his grandmother, who sits between them on the couch as they watch television, a Sam Ace detective show starring "Devon Townsend." This is a spoof of hard-boiled detective films (Sam Ace being an obvious reference to Sam Spade of *The Maltese Falcon* fame), titled *Death of a Breakdancer*. The film is replete with tough-guy voice-over narration, black-and-white cinematography, and a mysterious dame who hires Sam

The application of Jheri curl seems a particular in-joke directed mostly at African-American audiences.

to investigate a murder case. Yet the 1940s look of the film is anachronistic, since the case Sam is on is the killing of a breakdancer in contemporary Los Angeles. Sam soon learns that a prime suspect in the killing of Cookiehead Jenkins is Jheri Curl, who "hated Cookiehead like he was an Afro." The use of film-noir style makes *Death of a Breakdancer* a "black noir"—something of a pun, since "noir" means black. But virtually no classic noir ever featured a black man. It is the "Jheri Curl" reference and the transformation of Keenen Ivory Wayans's hair when his activator is taken from him by Sam that is the most Afro-centric, so to speak, moment in the film.

Jheri curl was a kind of hair treatment found in the ethnic hair care section of supermarkets and drugstores. The relaxed curls and lustrous shine was a style popular in the 1980s, an alternative to straightened hair and the Afro. In addition to relaxing the tight curls of black hair, it required the use of a spray activator to keep the hair moist. The character Jheri Curl is constantly spraying his hair; when his activator is taken by Bobby, his hair immediately transforms into other stereotyped images of black hair—a wild Afro and very tight, short curls. Whether or not white audiences (who had no reason to shop in the ethnic hair care section) are generally familiar with the ins and outs of the Jheri curl is unknown, but to black audiences the in-joke of naming a character for a hair treatment would have been unmistakable, as would have been the exaggerated comedy of his constant spraying with the activator.

In bed, toward the film's end, Bobby imagines playing roles like King Lear, Superman, and Rambo, which becomes "Rambro: First Young Blood." This is to say, that he wants to do classical theater—theater which does belong now to African Americans as much as to white people; comic book–hero films (which, ironically, became even more popular a couple of decades later but which still find black men in short supply); and blockbuster action spectaculars—perhaps the only genre in which black men have thrived, a welcome change, no doubt, to Robert Townsend, whose deft satire and slapstick sensibilities in *Hollywood Shuffle* have thus been redeemed.

David Desser

QUESTIONS FOR DISCUSSION

1. It is perhaps understandable that there were no women slapstick clowns in the silent era, given that the opportunities for women in that period were highly constrained and ideologically restrictive. But in our feminist and postfeminist age, why do you suppose women haven't emerged as major comic stars in the slapstick tradition?

2. Why has television proved more hospitable to female slapstick or nonromantic stars than the cinema? Think of Lucille Ball, Mary Tyler Moore, Valerie Harper, and Roseanne Barr, who dominated the sitcoms of their eras with clown comedy of a decidedly unconventional sort.

3. Given the success, fame, and lasting impact of the likes of Chaplin, Keaton, Lloyd, Fields, the Marx Brothers, Bob Hope, and Jerry Lewis, why have so many contemporary clown-comics, like Woody Allen, Steve Martin, Jim Carrey, Eddie Murphy, Adam Sandler, and Ben Stiller, rather quickly turned away from the slapstick orientation of their early careers to more conventional roles in romantic comedy or toward quirky auteurist or independent cinema?

4. Given that such stars as Woody Allen, Adam Sandler, and Ben Stiller have emerged as suitable objects of romantic attraction in the contemporary age, can we say that images of masculinity common to the romantic comedy have shifted significantly? Even when they have kept some of their insecurities, flaws, and neuroses, these stars have attained a status as "serious" comic performers capable of winning the hearts of attractive

women—not in spite of but arguably because of these once-disgraced traits.

5. Hong Kong's Jackie Chan emerged as one of the most popular stars in the world starting in the 1980s, largely on the strength of his stunt-filled martial arts comedies. He also demonstrated a mastery of the transformation gag. He was clearly a direct descendent of the clown tradition of slapstick comedy. Yet when he came to Hollywood he was typically paired with an American actor and his films transformed into "buddy comedies," thus deemphasizing Chan's singular stardom. Why do you suppose Hollywood could not imagine him in the kind of films made famous by Chaplin, Keaton, and Lloyd?

FOR FURTHER READING

Dale, Alan S. *Comedy Is a Man in Trouble: Slapstick in American Movies.* Minneapolis: University of Minnesota Press, 2001.

Horton, Andrew, ed. *Comedy/Cinema/Theory.* Berkeley and Los Angeles: University of California Press, 1991.

Jenkins, Henry. *What Made Pistachio Nuts: Early Sound Comedy and the Vaudeville Aesthetic.* New York: Columbia University Press, 1992.

Karnick, Kristine Brunovska, and Henry Jenkins, eds. *Classical Hollywood Comedy.* New York and London: Routledge, 1995.

Kerr, Walter. *The Silent Clowns.* New York: Knopf, 1975.

King, Geoff. *Film Comedy.* London: Wallflower Press, 2002.

Krutnik, Frank. "A Spanner in the Works? Genre, Narrative and the Hollywood Comedian." In Karnick and Jenkins, 17–38.

Mast, Gerald. *The Comic Mind: Comedy and the Movies.* 2nd edition. Chicago: University of Chicago Press, 1979.

Pomerance, Murray, ed. *Enfant Terrible: Jerry Lewis in American Film.* New York: New York University Press, 2002.

Seidman, Steve. *Comedian Comedy: A Tradition in Hollywood.* Ann Arbor, MI: UMI Research Press, 1981.

Les Misérables (2012)

Melodrama

"CHEESY." "CORNY." "CHEAP." Such negative associations unfairly stigmatize the spectrum of films commonly labeled as melodramas. A particular animus crops up again and again. A popular website, Rotten Tomatoes, says of *I Am Sam* (2001): "Not only does the manipulative *I Am Sam* oversimplify a complex issue, it drowns it in treacle." The same site quotes a reviewer panning a similar film: "*Martian Child* [2007] wants to make us cry. It nearly made me gag. This is an exercise in shameless and inept emotional manipulation." (As if other movies avoid emotional manipulation, or are more skilled at it, or at the very least, *more ashamed*.) Interestingly, on Rotten Tomatoes both films appear to be quite popular with average viewers.

Historically, popular melodramas addressed mass audiences, as opposed to the educated social classes, and were linked with sentimentality and femininity. These lingering connotations account for the widespread disdain expressed by many scholars and critics for these films. Certainly, inept melodramas stoop to cheesiness. But the clumsy use of story materials threatens any film that relies more on mundane formulas and insincerity than creativity and heartfelt emotion. At their best, melodramas strive for the sublime (in the sense that the Romantic poets and painters used the word, as connected to the highest realms of human feeling or exaltation), and when they succeed, they provide an unparalleled experience of emotional plentitude. Even when they fail overall, such movies often furnish audiences with memorable scenes and unforgettable moments.

The term "melodrama" refers to three overlapping but still distinct categories: a mode, a type of theatrical play, and a film genre.

First, melodrama may refer to a "mode," an overarching narrative approach on the same level as tragedy, comedy, and realism. "Modes" are larger and more amorphous than genres; they embody a generalized tone—perhaps a philosophical approach—about living in this world. Traditionally, comedies see everyone as loveable fools, and life as absurd; tragedies perceive kings and rulers as noble but flawed, their fates unchangeable. Melodramas, however, depict the world as sharply divided into good and evil, with the suffering virtuous people deserving of pathos and admiration. Whereas tragedies concentrate on the nobility and the fate of kingdoms, melodramas focus on the lower gentry or middle classes, and particularly on the destinies of families and lovers. Unlike realism, with its emphasis on plausibility and the prosaic—on shoe polish and cabbage soup—the melodramatic mode features an exciting, sensational universe saturated with meaning, action, and coincidence. Here, every gesture, object, and sentence pulsates with significance: the ring you wear denotes your lineage, and the aged servant turns out to be your father in disguise. Nothing is downplayed: storms rage; winds howl; waterfalls crash; hearts shatter; characters sink to their knees; women faint. Comparative literature scholar Peter Brooks characterizes melodrama as the mode "of excess." Novelists like Dickens, Balzac, and Hugo gravitate toward melodrama in *A Tale of Two Cities*, *Le Père Goriot*, and *Les Misérables*—so does Baz Luhrmann in movies such as *Romeo + Juliet* (1996) and *Moulin Rouge!* (2001).

Melodrama as a mode takes its name and distinctive qualities from a type of French theater that began in the late eighteenth century. *Mélo-drames*, plays with music (and without speech), were dramatic performances that appeared around the time of the French Revolution in the 1780s. Soon incorporating dialogue and spreading from France throughout Europe and to the United States in the nineteenth century, these plays proved enormously popular with middle- and lower-class audiences living in urban centers. In particular, the plays focused on themes relevant to their audiences' anxieties about the rapidly modernizing social fabric: recognizing and coping with injustice, locating innocence, and balancing monetary and familial claims. Peter Brooks argues that, beneath the often-crowded surface action, the plays actually staged a search for applicable moral codes in confusing and increasingly post-sacred societies.

The sensational plays of Pixérécourt in France, Holcroft in England, and countless imitators incorporated spectacles of impressive scenery and theatrical effects, including blinding snowstorms, huge pirate ships, fierce battles, daring swordfights, baying hounds, and stomping horses. These plays didn't try to be realistic or plausible—coincidences abound, and impossible things happen in every scene. Fundamentally, the stories were meant to overwhelm their audiences' emotions with giant ladlings of astonishing events. While these plays are rarely performed today, we see their like in librettos that form the basis for nineteenth-century operas (poor Butterfly! poor Mimì! poor Carmen!) and in the second-longest-running Broadway show of all time, *Les Misérables*, taken from Victor Hugo's melodramatic novel.

The nineteenth-century American stage gravitated toward the-atrical melodrama like metal filings to a magnet. Sometimes it took Shakespeare's plays and bowdlerized them into melodramas, often it simply stole European works, but by the mid- to late-1800s American

Mission: Impossible III (2006) Everyone categorizes *Mission: Impossible III* as an action film, but the melodramatic mode underlies its plot and creates its appeal. Ethan Hunt (Tom Cruise), the hero seeking to expose the villain and his secret collaborators and to reestablish moral order, has been captured by his nemesis Owen Davian (Philip Seymour Hoffman). This prolonged torture scene pictured above—reminiscent of equally painful and emotionally-charged scenes in James Bond films in which 007 is tortured or in peril—works to make this superstrong hero a *victim*, which activates our pity and emotional investment. Moreover, the method of torturing Ethan here links the film even more closely to melo-drama: Davian is threatening to shoot a woman Ethan believes to be his bride; thus the crisis revolves around a situation completely analogous to the archetypal threat of the innocent heroine tied to the railroad tracks with the locomotive bearing down upon her.

dramatists were creating their own native stories dealing with American themes. *Uncle Tom's Cabin*, adapted for the stage by George Aiken from Harriet Beecher Stowe's 1852 novel, stressed the pathos of the separation of mother and child, the injustice of slavery, and the sadness of death, becoming the biggest blockbuster success in the history of American theater. *The Poor of New York* (1857), adapted and localized by the Irish playwright Dion Boucicault, stressed reversals of fortune in America's largest metropolis during the financial panics of 1837 and 1857, while David Belasco's *The Heart of Maryland* (1895) told a story of love and betrayal set during the Civil War, and his *Girl of the Golden West* (1905) celebrated the frontier. All American melodramas offered exciting stage effects, nationalist sentiments, lessons in democracy, and moral parables.

Third, melodrama has become the name of a film genre. The invention of silent film overlapped with the decline of American stage melodramas, and many film historians have ascribed silent-film narratives, themes, and acting to these stage models. During the era of early cinema, trade journals routinely referred to nearly all films as melodramas-with-a-hyphen, e.g., "western-melodramas," "crime-melodramas," "war-melodramas," "romantic-melodramas." These industry labels made sense because nearly all films employed the tropes and techniques of theatrical melodramas and, more broadly, the mind-set of the melodramatic mode. Over the years, however, "Western" became a genre designation of its own, and "melodrama" was dropped from the name. Yet the magnetic force field of melodrama still pulls all American films in its direction. In "Melodrama Revised," film scholar Linda Williams convincingly argues, "Melodrama is a peculiarly democratic and American form that seeks dramatic revelation of moral and emotional truths through a dialectic of pathos and action. It is the foundation of the classical Hollywood movie."[1]

Certain films were left behind, uncategorized, when Westerns, gangster films, combat films, and horror films (movies primarily addressed to *male* viewers) spun off into separately recognized genres. Many of the "leftover" films were adaptations of stage melodramas or melodramatic novels and/or stories featuring female protagonists. When genre theory advanced to become one of the dominant strains of film studies,

---

[1] Linda Williams, "Melodrama Revised," in *Refiguring American Film Genres: History and Theory*, edited by Nick Browne (Berkeley: University of California Press, 1998): 42.

Titanic (1997) Made on a budget of $200 million, at the time the most ever spent on a movie, *Titanic* exemplifies the major contemporary melodrama. The most financially successful film ever, earning $600.8 million at the box office, Titanic developed into a cultural phenomenon that captured the attention of the American public. It includes scenes of exciting action and spectacle, as did stage melodramas, yet its central story concerns the separation of two lovers (Kate Winslet and Leonardo DiCaprio). Just as the iceberg halved the historic vessel, so the film split the viewing public in two: those who found the story incredibly moving and those who found the film's heightened emotionality cloying and embarrassing.

feminist scholars recognized similarities among 1) silent melodramas; 2) those films Hollywood producers literally named "women's films," e.g., films produced during the studio years featuring major women stars, designed to lure female audiences to the theaters; and 3) a 1950s cluster of films centering on family and community. Over the decades, academics have debated whether yoking these disparate groups under one label actually crystallized a film genre or, as Russell Merritt vehemently argues, simply provided a catch-all term for discussing films hitherto left orphaned from our genre canons. In my opinion, the connections between the different cycles are strong enough to justify linking them under a single rubric, and the term "melodrama" (despite its unwieldy tripartite meaning) remains preferable to alternative designations such as "woman's films," "tearjerkers," and "weepies," all of which are too narrow and belittling, or "dramas" or "romances," which are too broad, and fail to capture the films' emotional tenor.

Currently, when speaking of melodrama as a film genre, then, one refers to *films centering on personal relationships—whether friendship, romance, or family dynamics—that seek to elicit spectator sympathy for the films' protagonists and tell their stories in a heightened style that may include spectacular effects, implausible coincidence, plot twists, and a clear dichotomy between good and evil.*

Melodramas privilege intimate connections imperiled in a changing, hostile world. Physical or emotional separation and death constantly threaten various characters within the narrative; melodramas activate and then assuage viewers' primal separation anxieties, which, say some theorists, underlie the basic emotional responses viewers have to film. Most of all, melodramas elicit intense emotions, particularly pathos. When you think melodrama, think *Titanic* (1997).

History

Throughout the decades, film melodramas morphed into whatever best responded to changing social conditions and varying cultural mores. Melodramas appeared at the founding of the cinema. The British short, *Rescued by Rover* (1905), in which a baby is stolen from a nurse by a gypsy and rescued by the loyal family dog, who finds the baby and then goes back to fetch the father, still charms today. Edwin S. Porter, a pioneer in American silent cinema, directed *Rescued from an Eagle's Nest* (1908), in which the soon-to-be famous D. W. Griffith plays a father who rescues his child from a (very fake-looking) bird of prey.

When Griffith started directing later that year for the Biograph Company, he imbued his short films with the tropes of stage melodrama in which he had been trained. For instance, in *The Lonely Villa* (1909), burglars threaten a mother and her young daughters, successively breaking through locked doors into their home as the father rushes back to save them. (Such breathtaking last-minute rescues became the hallmark of a cycle of immensely popular melodrama serials, including *The Perils of Pauline*, *The Exploits of Elaine*, and *The Hazards of Helen*, all of which started in 1914.) Some of Griffith's silent features, such as *Way Down East* (1920), about a young girl who is tricked into a fake marriage and bears an illegitimate child before finding her true love, were adapted from previously successful stage melodramas. Nevertheless, whatever source material he used, all of Griffith's features serve as classic examples of the melodramatic genre.

Yet Griffith's movies were hardly unique. The world-famous silent-film star Mary Pickford excelled in melodrama. In *Stella Maris* (1918), for example, she plays dual roles, a disabled rich girl and a forlorn, abused orphan. A decade later, in *Sparrows* (1926), she again plays an orphan, Molly, the eldest child of a group held prisoner by a magnificently evil orphanage director, Mr. Grimes (Gustav von Seyffertitz), who not only mistreats and starves his charges but also kidnaps babies from rich families for ransom. To rescue a darling toddler Mr. Grimes is going to murder, Molly leads the children on a daring nighttime escape through a swamp that threatens them with both quicksand and hungry alligators. Whereas Pickford generally responded to her persecution with spunky defiance, the other leading lady of the silent era, Lillian Gish, often played more pitiful maidens. In *Broken Blossoms* (1919) and *The Wind* (1928), Gish's tribulations drive her to hysterics and madness.

By the Roaring Twenties—the Jazz Age—adaptations of nineteenth-century melodramas seemed passé. The 1927 Broadway musical play *Show Boat* includes an affectionate parody of old-fashioned melodrama, a parody emphasized in the 1951 film version when Gaylord Ravenal (Howard Keel) first overhears Magnolia (Kathryn Grayson) rehearsing these absurd lines from the parodic *Tempest and Sunshine*:

> Oh sir! Is there no mercy in your evil soul? No kindness in your ugly heart? Oh sir, what manner of foul jackal are you? Coming into our humble home, rich as you are, yet reeking of the carrion of the flesh-pots. Oh sir, I plead with you on bended knee, from the torn and wretched heart of a mother, stop giving my little daughter diamonds and go home to your wife!

In *The Decline of Sentiment: American Film of the 1920s*, Lea Jacobs traces the increasing impatience with and condescension toward melodrama manifested in film reviews and the rise in popularity of naturalism/realism and sophisticated comedy. But the disdain of the elites did not hamper millions from adoring Charlie Chaplin's films, in which heart-wrenching melodrama is leavened by comedy. The narrative skeleton of *The Kid* (1921) is classic melodrama, as Chaplin was well aware; he starts the film with an intertitle: "A picture with a smile—*and perhaps, a tear*" [my emphasis]. Chaplin, in his usual role, plays the Tramp, who discovers a baby boy abandoned by his unwed mother. He raises the child as his own, and the two live happily on meager earnings, derived mostly from the boy's breaking windows with rocks, after which the Tramp coincidentally saunters by with glazing materials. However, when meddling child welfare agencies discover this unconventional household, they remove the child, leading to a climactic last-minute rescue as the Tramp runs over rooftops to reunite with his adopted son. Such tugging at the heartstrings also occurs in *The Gold Rush* (1925) and, especially, in

The Kid (1921) Charlie Chaplin was a world-famous comic icon. We think of his feature films as comedies, but they are also melodramas. In *The Kid*, meddling officials seek to tear the child (Jackie Coogan) away from his foster father, but after an exciting chase, the Tramp manages to rescue him. *The Kid* ends on a happy note, with the Tramp, the child, and the child's mother united. Melodramas do not have to end with separation or death, but they do have to activate our pathos.

City Lights (1931), in which the reunion between the now-sighted flower seller and the Tramp, who paid for her operation with years in prison, has entranced generations of filmgoers.

During the silent era, cultural elites' attitudes toward melodramas were inconsistent. Although they sneered at American melodramas, when émigré directors F. W. Murnau and Victor Sjöström adapted melodramatic material with European artistic sensibility, critics changed their tune. *Sunrise* (1927) and *The Wind* (1928) were critical successes, and history textbooks still see them as the apogee of silent cinema. Even today, critics more readily accept melodrama in foreign films. Foreign, exotic, and historic settings somehow seem more hospitable to high romance and exalted feelings than prosaic, contemporary American environments, which we know too well.

When sound emerged at the end of the 1920s, film actors had to leave behind the broad, rather histrionic melodramatic postures perfected during the silent era and adopt more understated and realistic tropes of performance. Characters became more individualized—it would no longer do to call the heroine "The Girl" or "The Little Dear One" or "The Kid." Moreover, as the country fell into the trough of the Depression, melodramas tackled more contemporaneous cultural issues that menaced America's stability. The threats, therefore, stemmed not from dastardly villains, capricious weather, urbanization, or infernal machines, but from harsh social conditions and poverty.

In the 1930s and 1940s, two prevalent subgenres of melodrama emerged. In the "fallen woman" subgenre, a woman suffers because she has succumbed to out-of-wedlock sex. *Back Street* (1932), *Shanghai Express* (1932), *Anna Karenina* (1935), *Camille* (1936), and countless less-famous titles focus on the pathos of a woman's fall. These films highlight the delirious pleasures of forbidden sexual liaisons, including the consuming passion and the material benefits. Audiences relish the beautiful gowns Marguerite (Greta Garbo) wears as a courtesan in *Camille* and the world-weary sophistication, outrageous furs, and bold independence that mark Shanghai Lily (Marlene Dietrich) in *Shanghai Express*. Yet industry regulations insisted on showing that sexual dalliance led to misery; loose women always paid the ultimate price of sin: unhappiness and disgrace, if not death. The moral strictures of the era were so tight that in William Wyler's *Jezebel* (1938), Julie (Bette Davis) must suffer just because she flaunted her sexuality (by wearing a red dress) and disobeyed her fiancé. She endures bitter humiliation, years of abandonment, and ultimately goes off to her death.

The second prevalent subgenre, the maternal melodrama, rehearses the pain of losing a child. This subgenre flourished as America moved toward smaller families but still faced a high infant mortality rate. Typically in these stories, the child is ripped from the female protagonist who has slipped from the moral high ground due to socially unacceptable behavior. She may lose her child because she cheats on her husband (in *Madame X*, filmed three times—1929, 1937, and 1966), because she prostitutes herself to earn the money to afford life-saving medical intervention for her husband (in *Blonde Venus* [1932]), or because she had a one-night stand with a soldier off to war and cannot raise the child as an unwed mother (*The Old Maid* [1939] and *To Each His Own* [1946]). In *Mildred Pierce* (1945), Mildred (Joan Crawford) loses her younger daughter to illness because she has been inattentive and self-absorbed in her career and her love life.

In *Stella Dallas* (1937), the title character suffers the loss of her beloved daughter simply because she is too lower class and uncouth. Stella (Barbara Stanwyck), a laboring man's daughter, manages to snag an upper-class husband, Stephen Dallas (John Boles). Shortly after the birth of

Christopher Strong (1933) *Christopher Strong* was directed by one of the few female studio directors, Dorothy Arzner. Katharine Hepburn plays Lady Cynthia Darrington, an aviatrix, a woman of courage, accomplishment, and independence, modeled after Amelia Earhart, a role that fit comfortably with her star persona. Yet she falls in love and has an affair with Christopher Strong (Colin Clive), a married man. He cannot leave his family; she cannot live without him. He does not want her to fly; she cannot bear life grounded. Like so many protagonists of the fallen-woman cycle, the heroine—the woman who loves not wisely but too well—must die to escape her predicaments and atone for her sexual transgressions.

their daughter, Laurel, the marriage founders, and they divorce, with Stephen moving to New York City. Though Stella and Laurel are very close, the girl suffers from her mother's déclassé behavior and tasteless dress. Ultimately, Stella realizes that the teenage Laurel (Anne Shirley) would have more opportunities if she lived with her remarried father and his refined second wife. To send Laurel away, Stella pretends that she doesn't want her anymore. Years later, on the night of Laurel's wedding—the film's climax—the kind and wise stepmother deliberately opens the mansion's curtains to let onlookers peer in; Stella stands crying in the rain, a literal outsider watching her daughter get married. Stella is finally chased away by a policeman. Newspaper reviews of 1937 term the movie "a rousing weep festival," and note "a good cry may be had by all." Seven decades later, it is still impossible to watch with completely dry eyes.

During the 1940s, when men were overseas fighting World War II, Hollywood put great emphasis on major female stars such as Bette Davis, Joan Fontaine, Greer Garson, Joan Crawford, and Ingrid Bergman. Their films, directed by such premier exponents as Alfred Hitchcock, George Cukor, and William Wyler, became prestige properties, commanding high budgets, beautiful cinematography, and less formulaic narratives. The romantic longings typical of the woman's film reach their culmination in *Letter from an Unknown Woman* (1948), directed by the émigré director Max Ophüls and starring Joan Fontaine and Louis Jourdan. As a young teenager in turn-of-the-century Vienna, Lisa falls in love with her neighbor, Stefan, a concert pianist. She unrequitedly adores him all her life. An inveterate, callous womanizer, Stefan does not recognize the eighteen-year-old Lisa as his neighbor during the short, dreamlike affair he has with her, leaving her pregnant. Worse yet, ten years later, when she goes to him to confess her life-long obsession, he doesn't know her at all: Stefan slips into his practiced seduction routine—now revealed to Lisa as prosaic and insincere—as if this were their very first meeting. Only when she writes him from her tubercular deathbed does he fully understand their story and realize the complete and enduring love he threw away. Sobered by reading Lisa's letter, Stefan commits suicide by fighting a duel with her husband that he knows he will lose.

If an American director had made *Letter from an Unknown Woman*, Lisa's glorious *amour fou* might have been ascribed to a father fixation or an unloving mother. Throughout the twentieth century and intensifying after World War II, Hollywood—following American society as a whole—became fascinated with Freudian models of individual psychology. Popular Freudianism saturated mass culture with advice columns, books, and magazine articles. Whereas melodrama had previously employed stock characters with little psychological depth, the genre now rushed to embrace this new and seemingly more scientific and nuanced understanding of psyches. Presaged by *Now, Voyager* (1942), in which Bette Davis plays a loveless, dowdy, shy spinster set free by her psychiatrist, the late 1940s saw a series of films focused on women beset by psychological demons.

The screens of the 1950s—those years of supposed domestic contentment but actual quiet desperation—were dominated by what critics now call "family melodramas," films tracing the trials of various family

Rebel Without a Cause (1955) *Rebel* is a famous wide-screen, color, family melodrama from the 1950s, particularly noteworthy for making James Dean a star. Jim Stark (James Dean), an unhappy teenager, ascribes his difficulties to his family's dynamics: his mother is domineering and his father (Jim Backus) a milquetoast. Director Nicholas Ray visualizes Mr. Stark's weakness in this scene by dressing him in a floral apron. The other teens in the film, Judy (Natalie Wood) and Pluto (Sal Mineo), also have inattentive parents and troubled family lives. Thus, the film epitomizes the trend in 1950s Hollywood toward Freudian explanations of family dysfunction causing personal unhappiness.

members and friends in a small town or community. While the problems on display have significant social components, the major strains are psychosexual neuroses: accordingly, character types include fathers who don't love their sons, or mothers who love their sons too much; mothers whose frigidity or sexuality disturbs their daughters, or daughters whose sexuality disturbs their parents; daughters with crushes on their mother's beau, or (step)fathers who desire their daughters; husbands who are impotent or closet homosexuals, or wives who are nymphomaniacs. Insecurities, compulsions, and alcoholism abound, while dark pasts or devastating secrets haunt everyone. Although the acting is more subtle and individualized, ultimately, the mechanical repetitions of pseudo-Freudian psychology reduce these characters to formulaic patterns, basically creating stock figures who do not show that much more depth or plausibility than the traditional figures in silent film melodramas (This same shallow Freudianism appears in other genres during this time. See Hitchcock's *Spellbound* [1945] and *Psycho* [1960].)

The majority of 1950s family melodramas offer vibrant color and widescreen productions because the studios hoped that these visual pleasures and "racy" topics would lure viewers away from their new televisions with free programming. These movies tend to be long and epic in scope, cluttered with numerous subplots. In addition to Nicholas Ray, Vincente Minnelli [*Some Came Running* (1958) and *Home from the*

Hill (1960)] specialized in family melodramas. *Picnic* (1955), *Peyton Place* (1957), *The Long, Hot Summer* (1958), and *Splendor in the Grass* (1961) demonstrate that the cycle spread to other directors and studios as well.

However, many critics consider Douglas Sirk, who directed a series of films for Universal in the late 1950s, the master of family melodrama, for his works *Magnificent Obsession* (1954), *All That Heaven Allows* (1955), *Written on the Wind* (1956), and *Imitation of Life* (1959). These texts fascinate scholars because their tone is so ambiguous. Sirk had been involved in Marxist theater movements in Germany in the 1930s; in interviews he has stated that he deliberately designed these Universal melodramas to be ironic. Certainly, his films remain a puzzle. Universal marketed them "straight," as touching melodramas: the tag line for *Magnificent Obsession* is "The story of a woman's need for a man that will become one of the great emotional thrills of your lifetime!" Yet Rock Hudson, Jane Wyman, and Lana Turner—who were the biggest stars under contract at Universal at the time—give stilted performances; they have little of the passion and star charisma of the great melodrama stars of the 1940s. Is their stiltedness due to a lack of skill or a deliberate ploy on the part of the director? The overwhelming music, the carefully composed mise-en-scènes, and the overheated, byzantine plots cause such disorientation and even bewilderment that viewers rarely know whether to laugh or cry. Although many viewers now see Sirk's films as camp, other present-day viewers still respond empathetically—witness the blogger who wrote on IMDB about *Imitation of Life*:

> I have seen this movie a countless number of times and know the dialogue by heart. Each time I watch it, I say, "I'm not going to cry this time." Sometimes I almost make it, but then Mahalia Jackson starts to sing and I lose it.... To me the most heart-wrenching scene is where Annie visits Sarah Jane in her hotel room. She says, "I want to hold you my arms one more time. Just like you were my baby." I puddle up just writing about it.

Is this viewer a naïve dupe of Hollywood conventions, or is the film genuinely pathetic and ambiguously critical?

By the mid-1960s, melodrama per se was practically exiled from American screens. College students and teenagers dominated audience demographics rather than the women moviegoers of earlier decades, and these groups were less open to the genre's themes and sentimentality. The years of youth rebellion from 1965 to 1975 were particularly

All That Heaven Allows (1955) Douglas Sirk, a German director who immigrated to the United States, is famous for a cycle of melodramas he made for Universal in the 1950s. *All That Heaven Allows* dramatizes the complications that ensue when Cary (Jane Wyman), an upper-class, middle-aged widow, falls in love with her younger gardener, Ron (Rock Hudson). The deer that appears on cue smack in the middle of this picture window at the end serves as a metaphor for the more natural life Cary will have if she breaks with her social set and follows her heart to marry Ron, who recently has been injured/emasculated by a gunshot wound. But this deer is so silly and blatant— should the viewer laugh? And if you laugh, are you laughing at the deer, the movie, the convention of excess in melodrama, or the conceit that one can or would want to live like Thoreau in 1950s America? Sirk's reputation as a left-wing director allied with Brechtian theater creates contradictions that place the spectator on uneasier footing than is typical with traditional melodramas.

inhospitable. In *From Reverence to Rape: The Treatment of Women in the Movies* (1974), Molly Haskell points out that the films appearing around her were mostly buddy movies about men, exhibiting a virulent misogyny. Women stars, family issues, love stories, or tears were so rare that thoroughly mediocre melodramas such as *Love Story* (1970), about a young couple who meet as students at Harvard and are deeply in love until the wife dies of brain cancer, and the TV movie *Brian's Song* (1971), about the rare interracial friendship of professional football players Gale Sayers and Brian Piccolo, who dies of cancer, garnered wide attention and large audiences.

Contemporary melodrama has not received nearly the attention it deserves. The genre has not died; it is hidden in plain sight. Classic chestnuts have been remade: *Brief Encounter* (1945) became *Falling in Love* (1984); *Stella Dallas* was recast as *Stella* (1990) with Bette Midler. Also, television "Movies of the Week" often follow the formula of conventional melodrama. Contemporary cable channels, such as *Lifetime*— "for women," specialize in this genre. In general, however, melodramas have morphed into configurations more acceptable in an era when "Cynic" is everyone's middle name. New topics and anxieties have come to the fore. To defend itself from disdain, "new melodrama" has adopted certain types of camouflage.

One way contemporary melodramas seek critical respectability is by concentrating on *male* protagonists. In earlier decades, many of the novelists whose works were adapted into melodramas were female, and in the majority of the women's films, the male characters were pale figures, because the production budgets were devoted to the famous female lead. In new melodrama, however, many of the writers of the original material are male and more stress is placed on male characters. A male witness, Stingo, narrates the adaptation of William Styron's *Sophie's Choice* (1982); although Sophie's past provides the central mystery, equal stress is laid on him. *The Bridges of Madison County* (1995), *The Horse Whisperer* (1998), *Message in a Bottle* (1999), *A Walk to Remember* (2002), and *The Notebook* (2004) all come from novels written by men, and all give at least equal weight to their male stars. Current representatives of the therapy subgenre feature *men* who seek help; *Ordinary People* (1980) tells the story of a teenage boy who seeks psychiatric assistance to deal with his brother's death; in *Prince of Tides* (1991) and *Good Will Hunting* (1997), men are freed from childhood traumas by their psychiatrists. *Kramer vs. Kramer* (1979) and *I Am Sam* are *paternal* melodramas: in each, the father-child bond is imperiled until the last reel. *Field of Dreams* (1989) is really about a son's search for his lost father, and the magical moment when that father appears and invites Ray (Kevin Costner) to play catch causes many a viewer to swallow a lump in his or her throat. Gay-themed movies, such as *Brokeback Mountain* (2005), ponder the heartbreak of doomed love between two men.

A second strategy to win contemporary acceptance recasts the villain. In our health-conscious age, nothing shivers the soul as much as a bad prognosis. New melodrama has concentrated time and again on illness and untimely death: *Terms of Endearment* (1983), *Steel Magnolias* (1989), *Lorenzo's Oil* (1992), *Boys on the Side* (1995), *Marvin's Room* (1996)—written by a screenwriter/playwright dying of AIDS—*Stepmom* (1998), *Dying Young* (1991), and *Seven Pounds* (2008) prompt audience members to scrounge for tissues. In each case, a character is struck down too young, and viewers grieve for the character and face their own mortality from the safety of the fictional remove.

More recent melodramas have also worked to position themselves

***One True Thing* (1998)** Meryl Streep is dying of cancer in this film, an example of a new melodrama made palatable to modern audiences because the villain is *illness* rather than an evil headmaster of an orphanage. However, *One True Thing* still concentrates on the familial relations typified by earlier melodramas. Universal Studios' press book quotes the director, Carl Franklin: "I read the script on a plane and I just couldn't stop crying. I was deeply moved not only by the characters but because here was a screen-play that really delved into the primary relationship between men and women, mothers and daughters, fathers and daughters—the relationships that are so fundamental to contemporary life and who we are."

not as low-culture bathos but as high-culture art. Auteurist, low-budget, independent films by Woody Allen, John Sayles, and Sam Mendes are accepted as "serious" films, aimed at elite audiences. Some of these, such as *Hannah and Her Sisters* (1986), *Passion Fish* (1992), and *American Beauty* (1999) are "quieter" than traditional melodramas, and they are particularly likely to end unhappily or inconclusively (as a mark of their realism and artistic ambition). But as Linda Williams argues, realism doesn't subvert a melodramatic core; it works "in the service" of melodrama to help audiences suspend disbelief.

Finally, we should realize that many high-budget, prestige adaptations of respected novels in recent years could be categorized as melodramas. Such adaptations have always been a major strand of the genre, including all of the versions of *The Scarlet Letter, Anna Karenina,* or *Wuthering Heights. Doctor Zhivago* (1965) was one of the most prominent films of the 1960s. Though they do not advertise themselves as melodramas, *The French Lieutenant's Woman* (1981), *Out of Africa* (1985), *The Age* of *Innocence* (1993), *The English Patient* (1996), *Cold Mountain* (2003), *The Constant Gardener* (2005), and *Atonement* (2007) continue this tradition. Far from being cheap or cheesy formulaic tripe, these movies garner esteem and awards. Contemporary stories of doomed love often "get away" with their heightened emotionality by setting the action in the past—preferably in a foreign country—so that contemporary audiences can more readily suspend disbelief and accept the conventions and pleasures of emotional excess.

To imagine a time when melodramas disappear totally from our screens is to imagine audiences that are no longer interested in identifying with characters and no longer interested in stories about personal relationships. This genre is permanently ingrained in American cinema.

Typologies, Themes, and Theories

The climax of *Peyton Place* (1957) occurs in a courtroom. Selena Cross (Hope Lange) is on trial for murdering her stepfather, Lucas (Arthur Kennedy). She claims self-defense but won't explain either why she killed him or why she hid the body afterward. However, viewers know what only one witness in the room, Dr. Swain (Lloyd Nolan), knows—that Selena is not telling the whole truth because a year earlier Lucas had raped and impregnated her. Dr. Swain aborted the baby and forced Lucas to leave town. When Lucas returned he attacked Selena again, and she beat him to death in fear and fury. However, she will not admit the mitigating circumstances because she doesn't want her boyfriend to know her sordid history. At the climax of the trial, Dr. Swain bursts out with the truth and pulls Lucas's written confession out of hiding. The boyfriend, of course, still loves Selena, and the townspeople, whose gossip and scorn Selena so feared, rally around her.

Let's use this scene from a totally conventional movie in the middle of the genre's history as a pedal point to enumerate many of the most common themes of melodramas.

SEX. First, the story hinges, as many American melodramas do, on sex. Except for the subgenres dealing with illness and parental issues, these films fixate on sexual matters: they rehearse endlessly the conflicts between desire and morality, virginity and experience, love and lust, frustration and satisfaction, actions and consequences. Perhaps melodrama attained such dominance on American screens because of our puritanical history and the seemingly continual culture wars over all expressions of sexuality in our media. Moreover, as we all know, sex sells a movie. Even post-1980, when sex itself is not presented as an unforgivable sin, melodramas obsess over the one category of sexual liaison that is still taboo: illicit affairs that threaten to break up marriages and families. Thus, in *The Horse Whisperer* and *The Bridges of Madison County*, the love affairs are doomed from the start because one of the pair owes allegiance to a family.

CLASS. In *Peyton Place*, Lucas, who works as a school janitor and lives in a shack literally on the other side of the tracks, has been driven to drink because of his poverty in a town of plenty. He justifies his rape of Selena to himself because he feels he never obtained anything he wanted in his life. Class conflict comes up repeatedly in this genre, often intertwined with sex. In *Way Down East*, the aristocratic man from the city tricks and seduces the poor country girl. In other films—*Stella Dallas*, *All That Heaven Allows*, *Love Story*, *Titanic*, and *The Notebook*—the barriers between the lovers stem from their belonging to different social classes. The ideological tenet that "all you need is love" is repeatedly and compulsively put to the test in melodrama.

GOOD VERSUS EVIL. Lucas is the scapegoat in *Peyton Place*, the figure of evil. Most melodramas include such a figure, an obvious throwback to theatrical precursors. In cinematic melodramas, which gesture more toward realism and plausible character psychology, each character has his/her reasons, but stereotyping continues. As Linda Williams points out, Americans seem incapable of thinking about race in terms that are not polarized. Racial minorities are often portrayed as heartbreakingly innocent victims, such as the noble savage or the tragic mulatto, or, conversely, as the scheming Oriental or lecherous "buck." The good characters suffer all sorts of tribulations but never slip from the moral high ground. Our sympathies align with the good, and we are taught to hate the evil-doer.

YEARNING FOR THE PLACE OF INNOCENCE. Selena's best friend, Allison, narrates *Peyton Place*. Allison begins the film by talking about the significance of the seasons in this small New England town. At the end, with Selena reincorporated into the community, Allison says that the

Peyton Place (1957) The poster for *Peyton Place*, based on the hugely popular and controversial 1956 novel by Grace Metalious, emphasizes the film's sexual content and its suitability only for adult audiences. Such racy content, along with CinemaScope, helped woo viewers away from their television sets in the 1950s. While earlier melodramas were just as concerned with illicit sexual relations, the advertisement explicitly calls attention to the film's more overt treatment of these themes. *Peyton Place* became such an archetypal melodrama that it was turned into a popular soap opera that ran on television from 1964 to 1969 and launched the careers of Mia Farrow and Ryan O'Neal. Obvious connections exist between soap operas and melodramas.

town has reached the "season of love." Melodramas repeatedly express a yearning for some other time and place, a space of innocence. In *Wuthering Heights*, Heathcliff (Laurence Olivier) and Cathy (Merle Oberon) recall their youth on Penistone Crag. In *Random Harvest* (1942), Charles (Ronald Colman) finally recovers from his amnesia and recognizes the love of his life (Greer Garson) when he returns to the flower-bedecked cottage where they lived long ago. Traditional melodramas frequently contrast the sinful city with the rural utopia, but the bucolic setting is not essential in itself. Sometimes these places are not even on a map but occur at an earlier point in time. Many melodramas linger on flashbacks of the romanticized past. This nostalgia for another time and better place represents a deep longing for a reversal of the coming of sin and homeless exile in a cruel and confusing world—to use biblical imagery, a prelapsarian Garden of Eden, or to use psychological terms, the time of infancy, when one lived secure in one's mother's love and total care.

RECOGNITION. *Peyton Place* hinges on the public recognition of the suffering and innocence of one character by others, knowledge the viewer possesses. In stage melodramas, characters spoke directly to the audience in "asides," making sure we knew their real motives. Similarly, *we* know in *The Kid* that the boy's real mother, having come to do charity work in the slum, is sitting right behind him on a step; *we* know in *Magnificent Obsession* that Bob Merrick (Rock Hudson), who is indirectly responsible for the death of Helen's (Jane Wyman) husband, has atoned for his dissolute past and devoted his life to loving and helping her, but she—blinded in an accident that Bob is also responsible for—doesn't know the identity of the man with whom she is falling in love. The climax of the majority of melodramas revolves around a private recognition and/or public acknowledgment of something the viewer has been bursting to shout at the screen. "She's your mother, you nitwit!" "She's your wife!" "He's your illegitimate son!" "She did this to protect you!" "Don't you recognize Lisa as your true love?" By the end of the film, secrets must be expressed and gaps in knowledge filled in for all concerned.

SELF-SACRIFICE. In *Peyton Place*, Selena is willing to go to jail rather than speak the truth. In *An Affair to Remember*, a car runs over Terry McKay (Deborah Kerr) while she is en route to meet Nickie Ferrante (Cary Grant) on the top of the Empire State Building. The accident disables her. Terry prefers letting Nickie think her unfaithful to saddling him with a wife in a wheelchair. This kind of self-sacrifice is *de rigueur* in melodramas. "Waiting—always waiting—in the shadows of the back streets...longing for the man she loves...asking nothing, receiving nothing—yet content to sacrifice all for him. Why?" reads the tagline for the 1932 version of *Back Street*. Melodramas stress not only the protagonists' suffering but their *noble* suffering, as Annie Johnson (Juanita Moore) suffers in *Imitation of Life* (1959). For the most part, melodramas embrace a Christian—perhaps, given that Catholic censors drafted and enforced the industry Production Code regulating screen content, specifically a *Catholic*—virtue of self-sacrificial suffering as purifying and ennobling. Intriguingly, however, the films frequently show the sacrifice to be misplaced and unwanted. Nickie is damaged, embittered, and angered by Terry's noble gesture; she was mistaken to hide her disability from a man willing to accept it and still love her. Selena sacrifices to conceal her sordid history from her boyfriend and the townsfolk, all of whom ultimately prove more forgiving than she expected.

FORGIVENESS. The only personal trait that comes close to being as lauded in melodramas as self-abnegation is another preeminent Christian virtue: forgiveness. Helen forgives Bob in *Magnificent Obsession*. In *The Letter* (1940), Robert (Herbert Marshall) forgives his wife, Leslie (Bette Davis), even though she is a liar, an adulteress, and a murderer. Those who don't forgive, those who are judgmental, become villains. In *Way Down East*, Squire Bartlett (Burr McIntosh) is unjust to throw Anna Moore (Lillian Gish) out of his house into a snowstorm when he discovers she is not chaste; in *Brokeback Mountain*, it is vicious homophobes who are condemned, not homosexuality. When one considers that so many other American genres revolve around revenge/vengeance, the primacy of forgiveness in melodrama is both remarkable and pro-social.

THE MORAL LESSON. On the stand in *Peyton Place*, Dr. Swain chastises his fellow townspeople for their lack of attentiveness to Lucas's poverty and blasts the town gossips' censorious small-mindedness. (Note that in this case the lesson leans more toward social liberalism than conservative ideology.) Like all genre films, melodramas often function as cultural problem-solving devices. They teach viewers about self-sacrifice and forgiveness, about charity, equality (sometimes across class, sometimes across race or ethnicity), and fidelity. Griffith starts *Way Down East* with a title pleading for men to be monogamous. We may shudder at his pretentious

***Sparrows* (1926)** This film takes its title from a gospel hymn that reassures us that God pays attention to every sparrow. In this scene, a baby dies in Molly's (Mary Pickford) arms. In her dream, the barn door dissolves and Jesus comes to take the infant. *Sparrows* is merely more explicit about a Christian ideology than most American melodramas; Christian themes animate many of the films in less overt ways through their emphasis on the nobility of suffering and the blessedness of forgiveness. See, for instance, *Les Misérables* (2012).

prose and dismiss the relentless emphasis on chastity throughout the genre as old-fashioned and constricting. Still, in a confusing world where traditional patterns of life have been disrupted, where technology alters the fabric of daily life on an ongoing basis, where institutions and authority figures are unmasked in their incompetence or venality, melodramas seek to reestablish a moral code based on virtue. This urge toward moral clarity explains why the melodramatic mode underlies social-problem films; it also clarifies why some scholars see this genre as conservative while others perceive it as expressing a liberal ideology.

In academic discussions, the great debates about melodrama, which have primarily been conducted through the lens of psychoanalytic theory, run thus: how much self-sacrifice do the films advocate, and how much do they depict as unnecessary masochism and/or the cruel sadism of an elitist, white, patriarchal society? Is having mass audiences empathize with minority characters' plights belittling or socially progressive? Do the films promote the sexual double standard that men may sow their wild oats but an unchaste woman must suffer, or do they condemn these hypocritical canards? Do melodramas indoctrinate viewers in traditional, conservative social values or awaken their anger and resistance?

If the films are as sexist and conservative as many of them appear, why do many women viewers find enjoyment in them? Could this be because so many other genres center on male protagonists that any representation of women is better than none? Do family melodramas enforce conventional gender roles for men or show up their limitations? To these established questions I would add: what about contemporary male viewers? Legions of men must appreciate this genre; after all, male filmmakers made the classic melodramas. Do post-1980 male viewers secretly enjoy melodramas but find it just too embarrassing to admit because they fear to seem effeminate? Or does the genre truly offend their sense of decorum and taste?

Obviously, the answers to these questions depend on which film is under discussion and which viewer is decoding it. Even more complicating, the answers often depend on which part of the movie one stresses: the part where the protagonist breaks free of some social convention, or the part where he or she suffers for this transgression. Some movies—not only Sirk's—purposely deconstruct themselves and invite oppositional readings. For instance, lines of dialogue in *Jezebel* encourage one to read the film not as a condemnation of Julie but as a rebuke to a social system that holds women in such straitjackets. As Julie says, "This is 1852! Not the Dark Ages. Girls don't have to simper around in white just because they're not married." However, let's not make the mistake of privileging only the "ironic" melodramas. Too many scholars have focused on Sirk and his followers—Todd Haynes, Rainer Werner Fassbinder, and

***Stella Dallas* (1937)** This is a key text for scholars of melodrama. The end, when Stella (Barbara Stanwyck) watches her daughter (Anne Shirley) get married from the sidewalk outside a picture window, has been much discussed in the critical literature. Scholars debate why we cry at the end, and the extent to which Stella, smiling through her tears while watching her daughter's wedding as an outcast in the rain, is a model of women viewers watching the film.

Pedro Almodóvar—claiming that their self-consciousness saves the genre from itself by making the sentimentality of standard melodramas absurd. The majority of melodramas are quite sincere in their over-the-top emotional tenor, and we need to study (and enjoy) them on their own terms. If the films weren't excessive, we would label them differently, perhaps as re ic dramas.

Iconography

Some films you watch, others you feel.
–Tagline of Ordinary People

How do melodramas break our hearts? What formal qualities create this tone of heightened emotionality? Music is key. Reliance on music is buried deep in the genre's ancestry. Many films thematize music by making one of the characters a musician of some sort. Hollywood melodramas rely heavily on their lush musical scoring: these are the films for which some c he great studio composers, such as Max Steiner, Franz Waxman, an Iugo Friedhofer, wrote their most luscious scores. New melodramas not only rely on offscreen scoring but also incorporate theme songs that have become emblematic of the films' romanticism: think of "Lara's Theme" from *Doctor Zhivago*, "The Way We Were" from the 1973 movie of the same title, "My Heart Will Go On" from *Titanic*, and "I Will Always Love You" from *The Bodyguard* (1992).

Second, from stage melodramas onward, the genre has been characterized by a distinctive time scheme. Melodramas employ delaying tactics to stretch out the climactic scene until the last possible moment of tension. In *Homeward Bound: The Incredible Journey* (1993), a story of two dogs and a cat separated from their family, the animals travel across country to be reunited with their owners. The younger dog and cat emerge to receive a joyous welcome, but when Shadow, the elderly golden retriever fails to appear, the father sadly tells the son that Shadow must have b   o frail to survive the trip. *Finally*, just as the viewers too have l   hadow arrives. Similarly, in *Way Down East*, David Bartlett (thelmess) arrives just in time to save Anna from going ove   all. In *Johnny Belinda* (1948), Stella McCormick (Jan Sterling) sp   : truth in the courtroom just in time to save Belinda (Jane Wyman, .om conviction.

However, in *The English Patient*, Count Laszlo de Almásy (Ralph Fiennes) fights the desert and the army's bureaucracy to try to get help back to Katharine Clifton (Kristin Scott Thomas), who is lying critically injured in a desert cave. But he is ... too late! She has already perished alone in the dark and cold. In *Camille*, Armand (Robert Taylor) finally understands that Marguerite has sent him away not because she doesn't love him but rather to save his social standing and future; he rushes to her bedside, but it is ... too late! Her tuberculosis, worsened by her broken heart, has progressed too far, and she dies in his arms. As Linda Williams has detailed, this aching oscillation between in-the-nick-of-time! and too-late! ratchets up the tension and emotional investment of the moviegoer and accounts, at least in part, for the response to melodramas. The "too-late" regret distinguishes melodrama from tragedy proper: Oedipus and Lear and (I would argue) Michael Corleone are fated to fall, no matter what, from the beginning of their stories. In melodrama, one believes that if the sought-for remedy had arrived just a day or moment earlier, the unhappy ending might have been avoided.

A third factor that increases melodramas' emotional pull—again stemming from its theatrical heritage—is the use of melodramatic acting and gesture. As we hear in *Tempest and Sunshine*, dialogue can be very hyperbolic. Only in a melodrama can someone utter the ending line of *Now, Voyager*, "Don't let's ask for the moon, we have the stars," or the foreshadowing lines of *Anna Karenina*, "You and I are doomed, doomed to unimaginable despair or to bliss, unimaginable bliss." Emotional scenes call for actors to pull out all the stops: think of James Dean's performance in *Rebel Without a Cause* or Meryl Streep's in *Out of Africa*.

In terms of gesture, the players perform as if in some dreamlike romantic fantasy. Lovers dance all night alone on the floor while European musicians play just for them. Strong men carry weakened damsels. Devoted women cradle their suffering men. People dissolve into tears and faint. In *Jezebel*, begging forgiveness from Pres (Henry Fonda) for her transgressions, Julie curtsies down to the floor, with her (now white) gown flowing about her. Asking his wife's forgiveness for years of infidelity, Wade Hunnicutt (Robert Mitchum) in *Home from the Hill* gets down on his knees. In *Imitation of Life*, Sarah Jane (Susan Kohner) throws herself on her mother's coffin. In *Titanic*, the lovers fly on the prow of the ship. In *The English Patient*, Count Almásy carries Katharine, who has been injured, up a hillside to a cave. The white parachute that he has wrapped her in drags behind them like a wedding train (or a shroud)

Nell (1994) Shot in the Fontana Lake district of North Carolina, *Nell* integrates the natural setting as a character in this story about an isolated, incommunicative, almost feral young woman who is discovered by society after her mother dies. Nell (Jodie Foster) knows nothing about the outside world, but she is at one with nature. She ventures outside her cabin mostly at night, and all these scenes of lake, sky, sunset, and moonlight are filled with a magical beauty, a beauty that mimics her innocence, imperiled by both scientists' cruel probing and legal intervention. The kindly local doctor (Liam Neeson) is determined to protect her from the world of modern sterile hospitals and courtrooms.

as she finally tells him she has always loved him. In a famous moment in *Now, Voyager,* Jerry (Paul Henreid) lights two cigarettes in his mouth, and then passes one to Charlotte.

Visually, the films employ a pattern of anti-realism and excess. Beautiful cinematography of nature in all its sublime beauty typifies those films shot on location. These are the films where sea, sky, sunset, and mountains speak for the characters.

In terms of art direction, often they gravitate toward glamour and upper-class settings. Even when the characters are supposedly only middle class, their lifestyles are preposterously comfortable, and when the characters are supposed to be wealthy, they live in mansions and model furs and baubles. Being a "fallen woman" often means striding around in gold lamé and jewels. Melodramas put on display all of the dream factory's craft in creating images of style, opulence, and luxury. One of the pleasures of the genre stems from how it fulfills our longings to see beautiful art direction displayed in stunning visual patterns.

But the mise-en-scène is more than glamorous; it participates in the story, becoming fraught with meaning. On those occasions when the story is set in modest or poor circumstances, the production design is still exaggerated (see Lucas's shack in *Peyton Place*); it still participates in speaking for the characters. Discussing the excess found in melodrama, many film scholars argue that whatever the characters can't say out loud is embodied in the settings around them.

In *The Age of Innocence*, characters are trapped by their high social status and their objets d'art become expressions of their psyches. Director Martin Scorsese demanded meticulous research about the customs of upper-class New Yorkers in the 1870s to make the melodrama more convincing. Every china piece, flower arrangement, and overstuffed footstool speaks of the social strictures that entangle Newland Archer (Daniel Day-Lewis) into upper-class respectability and make it impossible for him to break free and run away with his love, Ellen (Michelle Pfeiffer). As for Ellen, every picture in her room, every outfit that she wears, every hairdo she models is just a little bit distinct from those of her set: freer, more independent, and more sensual. When Archer visits Ellen's lodging, he becomes even more intoxicated with her. The film sets up a whole conversation through flowers: the delicate, pink roses Archer gives his virginal and very strictly proper fiancée, May, contrast with the yellow roses, redolent of warmth and life, that he sends to Ellen. Scorsese even flushes the screen with color washes, turning everything yellow so that the image embodies the characters' emotional states.

Melodramas have been, and continue to be, an enormously important part of Americans' emotional lives. One can see the deleterious side of this genre's influence: filling young girls' heads with romantic

***The Age of Innocence* (1993)** In taking on this adaptation of Edith Wharton's novel, Martin Scorsese, a moviemaker more famous for his gangster films than for melodramas, studied classic melodramas in depth. This shot shows the importance of mise-en-scène in the genre. Just as each word and event is pregnant with significance, each prop, costume, and color signifies a specific emotional state of the characters or moves the story forward. Here Newland (Daniel Day-Lewis) and May (Winona Ryder) are visiting an aviary. The white cages show how trapped Newland is by the expectations of his fiancée, her family, and his social set. Even the carefully placed greenery encases him in another snare.

longings that will never be fulfilled; brainwashing women into guilt about their mothering; holding up impossible and restricting ideals of proper manhood; circulating and recirculating racial stereotypes. Nevertheless, key melodramas, such as *Uncle Tom's Cabin*, in all its myriad adaptations, and Jonathan Demme's *Philadelphia* (1993), have had a progressive influence on American culture. Overall, in their insistence on the importance of feelings, and on the centrality of loving relationships, melodramas have provided oases of emotional plentitude. These refuges have sustained receptive audiences through modern industrialization into postmodern global capitalism.

Melodramas are not plausible, nor are they meant to be. Viewers do not believe in any film completely, and as the lights go down, signaling the start of a melodrama, we have already been cued by publicity to consciously turn up the dial on our suspension of disbelief. Spectators of melodramas are neither stupid nor naïve; they know the difference between the real and the ideal. What we find in melodramas, at their best, are stories that genuinely touch us through their unabashed courage in facing emotional currents generally kept hidden or unspoken. In a paradoxical way, melodramas do focus on the "one true thing": how we feel.

CLOSE-UP

Fumbling for Tissues While Watching *Million Dollar Baby*

A very good friend of mine named Angelica Huston called me and said there's something I want you to read. And if you don't cry when you read this don't call me back. And she gave me "Million $$$ Baby." And I read it that night and I swear I had tears streaming down my face. And my wife said, "What are you reading?" and I said, "Nothing. I just got something in my eye, I'm not reading anything."

–*Albert S. Ruddy, producer*[2]

Some people cry in movie theaters, others do not. Research has indicated that women are more likely to cry than men, but this may be

---

[2]"The Producers: Round 15," Disc 2. *Million Dollar Baby*, directed by Clint Eastwood (Burbank, CA: Warner Bros. Entertainment, 2004, 2005), DVD.

because it is more socially acceptable for women t⟨   ⟩tion than their stoic brethren. Some viewers are more apt to t⟨   ⟩ the happy endings of romantic comedies when the tragedy of a life of loneliness is narrowly averted and love wins out after all—just in time. The same emotion motivates the tears of joy at the end of many sports films, such as *The Natural* (1984), when Roy Hobbs (Robert Redford), wounded and humbled, narrowly snatches victory from the jaws of personal and team defeat, and hits a home run so herculean that it smashes the bulbs out of the stadium lighting, sending cascades of sparks streaming through the sky.

However, let us concentrate here on films that ⟨   ⟩ or at least, *me*) cry because they focus on separation, loss, ⟨   ⟩ any viewers first experience film's power to traumatize the⟨   ⟩en: *Bambi* (1942), *West Side Story* (1961), or *E.T.* (1982) might b⟨   ⟩ first exposure to the primal grief of separation from a loved on⟨ ⟩.

New melodramas, as noted before, often focus on illness. *Stepmom* (1998) and *One True Thing* (1998) share plots focusing on the terminal illness of the mother figure. In the first, Isabel (Julia Roberts), who has married Jackie's (Susan Sarandon) ex-husband, must deal with Jackie's impending death from cancer and her feelings of inadequacy to take over as the mother figure for her two stepchildren. Todd McCarthy wrote in *Variety*:

> Tears are jerked with strenuously sincere calculation in "Stepmom," which sees some very talented thesps working over the most mawkish conventions as if they were freshly minted. The combined efforts of five screenwriters ensured that not a single cliché of the modern feel-good tragic melodrama genre has gone unturned, resulting in a soggy heart-tugger that will be last on any guy's Chr⟨ ⟩mas want-see list but will attract, and connect with, more than e⟨ ⟩gh women to make it a solid hit.[3]

Stepmom is not a great film, but McCarthy's comments typify the misogynous attitude toward the genre. In *One True Thing*, another film of that year more praised by critics, Ellen (Renée Zellweger), a modern career woman living in New York, reluctantly gives in to her father's pressure to move back home when her mother, Kate (Meryl Streep), is

---

[3] Todd McCarthy, "Stepmom," *Variety*, December 9, 1998, 1.

found to have cancer. *One True Thing* is the starker text, making the viewer experience the mother's gradual decline and demise.

Rather than focus on either of those *maternal* melodramas, however, I want to concentrate on *Million Dollar Baby* (2004), a *paternal* melodrama hiding inside a sports story. *Million Dollar Baby* tells the story of Frankie Dunn (Clint Eastwood), an aging boxing manager who owns a run-down boxing club, where he employs a washed-up, elderly fighter, Scrap (Morgan Freeman), as a custodian. Maggie Fitzgerald (Hilary Swank) buys a membership in the club and asks Frankie to train her as a boxer, but he refuses, noting that being in her early thirties makes her too old, and, anyway, he doesn't believe in female boxers. Maggie's determination soon impresses Scrap, and Scrap maneuvers Frankie into taking her on. Maggie comes from a hardscrabble life and sees boxing as the only way to win a sense of respect and accomplishment: she trains so hard and fights with such aggression that she soon is boxing professionally and knocking opponents out in the first round. Maggie gains money (winning close to a million dollars in purses) and prestige, although her efforts to win the pride and affection of her greedy, trailer-trash family prove fruitless. Maggie, who misses her deceased father, and Frankie, who is painfully estranged from his only daughter, slowly build a father-daughter relationship.

At the climax of the sports subplot, Maggie fights a championship bout in Las Vegas against Billie "The Blue Bear," the reigning champion. After the bell has rung and the fighters are returning to their corners, Billie throws a late punch at Maggie, who has turned around; Frankie (in agonizing slow motion) reaches for the stool to pull it out of the way of Maggie's fall but he is...too late! Maggie falls onto the edge of the corner stool, breaking vertebrae in her neck. She is paralyzed below her face. Despite the best medical care, her condition is hopeless.

After months of unconcern, Maggie's family members visit the rehabilitation center and show themselves to be irredeemably selfish and venal: all they want is Maggie's money. Maggie's condition deteriorates; an infected bedsore leads to amputation of her leg. She begs Frankie to end her life as her father once put down his beloved dog when it was paralyzed. Frankie, a Catholic, refuses. But Maggie's will to die is so strong that she continually tries to kill herself by biting into her tongue and causing blood loss, leading the doctors to sedate her. Scrap convinces Frankie that Maggie should be allowed to die now, while she still recalls her triumphs. Late at night, Frankie sneaks into the hospital, finally tells

Million Dollar Baby (2004) When Frankie agrees to train Maggie he makes her promise not to cry. She never breaks down, not through all her travails, until her last moments. But these are tears of joy and relief, because Frankie has just kissed her, called her his darling, and agreed to end her life. Through a phenomenon that psychologists term "social contagion," her tears draw more tears from the viewer.

Maggie that his Gaelic stage name for her, "Mo Cuishle," means "my darling, my blood," and kisses her cheek for the first time. While tears of joy run down her cheek, Frankie ends her life. He leaves Los Angeles, never to return, believing himself to be damned for eternity, but facing that fate out of love for Maggie. Scrap writes to Frankie's estranged daughter to tell her what kind of man her father really was.

So for its first two-thirds, *Million Dollar Baby* presents the story of the underdog about to beat all the odds and become a champion, and then in the last third it becomes an agonizing story about disability, assisted suicide, and death. But the parts are not as disconnected as a synopsis might indicate. Henry Bumstead, the experienced scenic designer, makes the Hit Pit gym speak for the characters in its aged seediness and hopelessness. And darkness pervades the whole film. We never see a bright or sunny exterior. The film often looks as if it were shot in black and white. Tom Stern, the director of photography, works with large pools of dark and sharp shadows bifurcating the actors' faces, avoiding fill or back light. The strikingly dark poster for the movie captures the film's bleak visual and emotional landscape.

Moreover, we must take account of the music, which is credited to Eastwood. Instead of triumphal music like that used in *Rocky* (1976), the main melody is played by a solo piano, a simple tune of descending thirds that sounds like a lullaby, until it is picked up by lush strings, with cellos in the lead. Later, a solo acoustic guitar plays the second, very similar theme. Both the piano and the guitar are miked very closely—you can hear the guitarist's fingernails strike the strings. The music creates a sense of intimacy, loneliness, and simplicity.

Like all melodramas, *Million Dollar Baby* must have a villain. Actually, it features several. First in line comes Billie, the fighter who injures Maggie. Dialogue informs viewers that Billie frequently breaks all the rules of fighting and deliberately tries to hurt her opponents: the blow that decks Maggie is clearly a despicable act, thrown illegally. To make sure we hate Billie, Scrap's narration tells us that she is a former prostitute from Berlin, and the music and shadows that accompany her as she comes down to the ring portray her as ominous. In a long article on Eastwood's career, film scholar Tania Modleski has pointed out patterns suggestive of racial stereotyping. This seems evident here as Billie and her trainer are dark-skinned and foreign-looking versus the whiter-than-white, "Irish" complexions of Maggie and Frankie, another factor that might unconsciously set some audience members against these antagonists.

The members of Maggie's family count as additional villains. The Fitzgeralds' welfare fraud, criminality, laziness, and hedonistic gluttony contrast with Maggie's work ethic, self-denial, and ambition. Melodrama's preoccupation with *class* emerges prominently in *Million Dollar Baby. They* are content with their deep-fat fryers, Oreos, and Disneyland T-shirts; *Maggie* wants to be somebody, to make her mark on the world; *Frankie* is learning Gaelic and reads Yeats. The Fitzgeralds' cold-hearted, grasping selfishness and the hypocrisy they demonstrate when they come to visit Maggie in the hospital contrast with Frankie's months of quiet devotion and care. Though we fear that Maggie, who has always sought her family's approval, will sign over her assets to her mother in a pathetic bid for love, incapacitated though she may be, she wins another round against evil. Nineteenth-century melodramas would have promoted the sanctity of family. However, F. X. Toole's original story and Paul Haggis's screenplay take a more contemporary approach: now one creates one's "family" with non-blood relations through bonds of affection and respect. Throughout the genre's history, while *maternal* melodramas do not necessarily vilify the father (plot twists explain away his absence or ignorance of the state of affairs), *paternal* melodramas often go out of their way to justify the father's taking a leading role in the care of the child, often through making the mother more concerned about herself than her child's welfare, as happens here.

As in many parental melodramas, sex plays no part in *Million Dollar Baby*. Maggie and Frankie's relationship has a flirtatious (Freudian) side to it: he tells her that if she wins the fight in England, he'll propose to her; later, when she says he reminds her of her father, Frankie says that her father must have been a very handsome, intelligent man. But Eastwood as director never shows Frankie as trainer massaging her or touching her body. He touches her only after she's been injured, sponge bathing her as a father would a child. In many melodramas, sex with the "wrong" person (the evil seducer who tricked you into a sham marriage, your gardener, your stepfather, or someone who is already married) serves as an indication of a breaking or testing of social mores. However, *Million Dollar Baby* doesn't need to use sexual relations for this purpose. Maggie, Frankie, and Scrap are already all washed-up outcasts because of their outsider status and because they are involved in a disreputable sport that highlights brutality, and one that is even more disreputable for a woman. Moreover, all three are too old for a sport based on youth and vitality, leading Modleski to remark that the film "tacitly mourns the loss—as much Eastwood's as his characters—of masculine potency, and herein lies much of the film's poignancy."[4]

In *Million Dollar Baby*, as in *Peyton Place*, the viewer knows more than most of the characters. With Scrap as our all-wise narrator, we have insights into the events that the other characters do not share. We know—as presumably Maggie does not—that Frankie writes to his estranged daughter every week, that her letters come back to him marked "Return to Sender," and that he is a persistent but questioning churchgoer. We know—as presumably Frankie does not—that Scrap sets up a meeting between Maggie and another trainer who might bring her along faster, but that Maggie turns him down flat, her loyalty to Frankie absolute. Rather improbably, Scrap is even hiding in the dark shadows of the rehabilitation center when Frankie kills Maggie, a witness to the story's denouement.

The bond between Frankie and Maggie leads us into other major themes of melodrama. Clearly, the film focuses on the centrality of

---

[4] Tania Modleski, "*Million Dollar Baby*: A Split Decision," *Cineaste* 30, no. 3 (2005): 11.

Million Dollar Baby (2004) The film's darkness and sharply edged pools of light stand out in this shot from when Frankie first commits to training Maggie. This lighting pattern pervades the film. Maggie is always training alone in the darkness of the gym. Similar dark sequences with sharp shards of white light occur when Scrap talks to Frankie about Maggie's right to die, and when Scrap hides in the corridor of the nursing home at the end.

self-sacrifice. Frankie does not want to lose Maggie or be a party to euthanasia. His priest tells him that if he does this, he will be irretrievably lost. Frankie does so anyway: sacrificing himself for her. Toole concludes his short story with this sentence after Frankie checks that Maggie has no pulse: "With his shoes in his hand but without his soul, he moved silently down the rear stairs and was gone, his eyes as dry as a burning leaf."[5]

The yearning for a place of innocence figures several times in the film. Toward the end, Frankie reads aloud to Maggie Yeats's "Lake Isle of Innisfree," and they discuss moving to a cabin, but this fantasy only highlights that obviously Maggie is medically too needy for such a life. Another salient moment recalling innocence occurs earlier on, when Maggie sees a young girl and her dog in a pickup truck at a gas station; the camera lingers on the exchange of glances between the two. Maggie tells Frankie about her father and the dog he loved enough to end its suffering. Soon after this scene, they stop at a diner that Maggie associates with her father. It serves homemade lemon pie, Frankie's favorite

---

[5] F. X. Toole, "Million $$$ Baby" in *Rope Burns: Stories from the Corner* (New York: Harper-Collins, 2000), 101.

dessert. Eastwood softens the end of the story from Toole's original: the last shot of the film shows the outside of this diner, implying that Frankie has returned to the place of innocence where he and Maggie once shared a simple pleasure.

Scrap, who does not appear in this Toole story but makes an appearance (along with Danger and Shawrelle) in another tale in his collection, "Frozen Water," serves as the voice of morality in the film. That he is played by the much-beloved actor Morgan Freeman adds credibility to his arguments, as do his actions early in the film, such as believing in Maggie and defending Danger. It is Scrap who teaches the moral lesson and provides forgiveness. He tells Frankie,

> I found you a fighter. And you made her the best fighter she could be...People die everyday, Frankie, mopping floors, washing dishes. You know what their last thought is? "I never got my shot." Because of you, Maggie got her shot. If she dies today, you know what her last thought will be? "I think I did alright." I know I could rest with that.

Some religious viewers object to Scrap's value system and claim that the film promotes assisted suicide. Rush Limbaugh has called it a "million dollar euthanasia movie." The Catholic Church condemns the film as morally offensive. Advocates for the disabled decry the film's inference that a disabled life is not worth living: obviously Maggie was clinically depressed; what she needed was psychological intervention. But I find it as hard to imagine this fictional character talking to a therapist about her dysfunctional childhood as to envision her going to college and studying algebra in a wheelchair moved by blowing into a straw. The whole story up to this point has painted her as a woman who has never swerved from her chosen goals, whether to become a boxer, or to get Frankie to train her, or (at the end) to be granted the graceful exit her father gave his dog. By making a film that portrays assisted suicide in a positive light, despite his conservative bent, Eastwood has intervened in a major contemporary problem and come down on what some would describe as the liberal side.

At what point did I start crying the first time I watched the film? I think it was during the conversation between Scrap and Maggie in the hospital soon after her injury, when, instead of blaming Billie, Maggie faults herself for dropping her guard and not following Frankie's mantra about always protecting herself, and shows that her primary worry is about Frankie's pain. She asks Scrap to apologize to Frankie for her, and he angrily rejects her self-abnegation. As the philosopher Noël Carroll notes, we admire the victims of melodrama not just as victims but for their fortitude. For me, it was all downhill from here; I was fortunate that my friend had a packet of tissues in her purse, because I had not come prepared. I am obviously not the only one who lost it while watching the last third of *Million Dollar Baby*. Al Ruddy describes a preview screening that Eastwood arranged for tough-as-nails studio executives:

> The whole—I'm talking about the Warner Brothers executives [*gestures wiping his face, choking*]—wiping their eyes. Everyone's crying. Even without the score, without any effects tracks, Foley, nothing. The power.... Everyone got up at the end—they had tears in their eyes.[6]

Movies make us cry for several interrelated reasons. First, we empathize with the characters' plights and admire their uncomplaining stoicism: Maggie's, of course, but Frankie's too. Maggie hasn't just lost her career and her dreams she worked at so indefatigably: she's a full quadriplegic, and bedsores are rotting away the flesh she worked so hard to make invincible. Frankie, so lonely and isolated, abandoned by other contenders he has taught, has finally gained the daughter figure he has pined for over a lifetime, but her suffering and her indomitable will force him to kill her. The irreconcilability of their needs creates additional pathos: as is the case with *Stella Dallas*, two equally valid emotional mandates (Stella's willingness to sacrifice herself for her daughter's happiness and her daughter's heartsickness at her mother's missing her wedding) clash implacably. The characters and the viewer struggle, but once the punch is thrown and the stool grabbed too late, pain follows.

In life, pain is not gratuitous but inevitable. Keith Oatley, a psychologist, postulates that in fiction we experience pain from a safe place, where we know that we, and our loved ones, are not in peril. However, because of the aesthetic heightening of the fictional text, so ratcheted up by the music, the lighting, the performances, we are even more inclined to weep than in the midst of distracting ordinary life. He argues, however, that audiences feel genuine sadness: our emotions are not counterfeit. The

---

[6] "The Producers: Round 15," Disc 2. *Million Dollar Baby*, directed by Clint Eastwood (Burbank, CA: Warner Bros. Entertainment, 2004, 2005), DVD.

tears you may shed at *Million Dollar Baby* are as real as your tears when your cat dies. Your brain and body do not make a distinction.

On another level, however, the fictional setting does make a crucial difference. Psychologist Melanie Green and her co-researchers theorize, "To the extent that people take risks they live life fully. Stories enable recipients to identify with and mingle with risk takers—to live life even more fully." They continue, "Even if the story protagonists are doomed, the audience member is safe." They believe that "the most enduring stories echo mythology plotlines involving descent into danger coupled with eventual survival. The consequent enjoyment stems at least in part from experiencing intimations of invulnerability, of immortality."[7]

Maggie has died, Frankie is lost, but when the movie is over we are as we were, whole and hearty, if rather shaken. We have seen a film that moves us, that makes us feel powerful emotions, and have come out the other side from this descent into danger. Through *Million Dollar Baby* we have experienced/witnessed crippling, death, euthanizing a loved one, losing one's soul, and the awe-inspiring nobility of acting for others. And yet, when the lights come on and we hurriedly try to wipe our runny noses and wet faces while meeting no one's eyes (for we've been taught that tears are a sign of childishness, weakness, loss of control, and *femininity*), we feel, along with sadness, a slight exhilaration: like a mythic hero, we have descended into the world of the dead and come back wiser, but unscathed. Our cat was *not* run over. The emotions were real, but the consequences just pretend. With *One True Thing*, we experience our mother's death, only to realize at the credits, with great relief, that she is still alive. Like Scrooge in "A Christmas Carol" who has "what if" visitations, we've gone through a "what if" nightmare.

To deeply experience true emotions, undulled or distracted by the contradictions and noisy muddle of everyday life, is one of the main pleasures of movie going. When you finish *Million Dollar Baby*—as is the case with other great melodramas—you feel as if your world and your heart have been enlarged.

Sarah Kozloff

[7] Melanie C. Green, Timothy C. Brock, and Geoff F. Kaufman, "Understanding Media Enjoyment: The Role of Transportation into Narrative Worlds," *Communication Theory* 14, no. 4 (November 2004): 316.

QUESTIONS FOR DISCUSSION

1. Why is crying at a movie more embarrassing than laughing, screaming, or shuddering?
2. Describe the ways in which a thriller or action film that seems far away from melodrama-as-a-genre is actually deeply dependent on the melodramatic mode.
3. How will the general cultural move away from Freudian explanations of human psychology affect the genre? Have characters become more well-rounded in new melodramas, such as *Titanic*?
4. Is the increased focus on male characters in new melodrama a positive development in terms of equality of the sexes?
5. American cinema is not the only one to be influenced by the melodramatic mode: for instance, both Latin American *telenovelas* and Indian Bollywood films are highly melodramatic. Why is melodrama international in its appeal?

FOR FURTHER READING

Basinger, Jeanine. *A Woman's View: How Hollywood Spoke to Women 1930–1960*. New York: Knopf, 1993.

Brooks, Peter. *The Melodramatic Imagination: Balzac, Henry James, Melodrama, and the Mode of Excess*. New Haven, CT: Yale University Press, 1976.

Carroll, Noël. "Film, Emotion, and Genre." In *Passionate Views: Film, Cognition, and Emotion*, edited by Carl Plantinga and Greg M. Smith, 21–47. Baltimore: Johns Hopkins University Press, 1999.

Gledhill, Christine, ed. *Home Is Where the Heart Is*. London: British Film Institute, 1987.

Jacobs, Lea. *The Wages of Sin: Censorship and the Fallen Woman Film, 1928–1942*. Madison: University of Wisconsin Press, 1991.

Kehr, David. "The New Male Melodrama." *American Film* 8, no. 6 (1983): 42–47.

Klinger, Barbara. *Melodrama and Meaning: History, Culture, and the Films of Douglas Sirk*. Bloomington: Indiana University Press, 1994.

Landy, Marcia, ed. *Imitations of Life: A Reader on Film & Television Melodrama*. Detroit: Wayne State University Press, 1991.

Lutz, Tom. "Men's Tears and the Roles of Melodrama." In *Boys Don't Cry?: Rethinking Narratives of Masculinity and Emotion in the U.S.*, edited by Milette Shamir and Jennifer Travis, 185–203. New York: Columbia University Press, 2002.

Mercer, John, and Martin Shingler. *Melodrama: Genre, Style, and Sensibility.* New York: Wallflower Press, 2004.

Modleski, Tania. "Clint Eastwood and Male Weepies." *American Literary History* 22, no. 1 (Spring 2010): 136–58.

Singer, Ben. *Melodrama and Modernity: Early Sensational Cinema and its Contexts.* New York: Columbia University Press, 2001.

Williams, Linda. "Melodrama Revised." In *Refiguring American Film Genres: History and Theory,* edited by Nick Browne, 42–88. Berkeley: University of California Press, 1998.

———. *Playing the Race Card: Melodramas of Black and White from Uncle Tom to O. J. Simpson.* Princeton, NJ: Princeton University Press, 2002.

Bringing Up Baby (1938)

Romantic Comedy

LET'S START WITH SHAKESPEARE. Although some scholars reach back to the comic plays of Aristophanes and other Greek writers, Shakespeare's comedies—especially *The Taming of the Shrew, A Midsummer Night's Dream, Much Ado About Nothing, As You Like It*, and *Twelfth Night*—offer more well-known and relevant predecessors: witness the contemporary romantic comedies that directly remake Shakespearian works, such as *Much Ado About Nothing* (1993 and 2012), *10 Things I Hate About You* (1999), *She's the Man* (2006), and the blatant reference to *As You Like It* in *Never Been Kissed* (1999).

In Shakespeare's plays young people meet and fall in love, but numerous, often funny, complications ensue: humorous misunderstandings, mistaken identities, infatuations with the wrong people, and parental/official disapproval. Other impediments inevitably arise, as in *Taming* and *Much Ado*, from the lovers' pride and character defects. Subplots involving associates of the central couple supply supplementary entanglements that further confound the characters—and sometimes the audience as well. Finally, the plays conclude with characters discarding their disguises, recognizing each other, and discovering their own wishes and needs. All this fast-paced confusion serves to demolish the young people's fears, resistance to change, or initial arrogance; it makes them better people, more appropriate partners for each other, and ultimately capable of true love. When the Shakespearian couple unites, their union serves as a birth of a new, better society, the triumph of spring over winter.

If the groundlings of the Globe Theatre could sit in our local AMC multiplex, they would wonder if anything had changed in four hundred

Shakespeare in Love (1998) This inventive mixture of biography, fantasy, and Shakespeare's plays, which won an Oscar for Best Film, ends with Viola (Gwyneth Paltrow) and Will (Joseph Fiennes) being torn apart. Instead of focusing on the pain of the lost romance, however, the viewer rejoices as Viola courageously strikes out for the New World and takes delight in Will's bright future as the world's most famous playwright. The separation ending is one modern variation filmmakers offer within the romantic comedy genre. Even with this "go their separate ways" conclusion, however, such films can still be classified as comedies because they end on a life-affirmative note, stressing change and renewal.

years. In its essence, the romantic comedy genre has remained extraordinarily constant over the centuries. Although contemporary filmmakers struggle to differentiate their works in myriad ways, their efforts normally amount to surface variation over a consistent "marriage plot": 1) meet, 2) separate, 3) unite; or, in the "remarriage" variation, 1) be married, 2) separate, 3) remarry. The most radical film alterations divide the couple at the conclusion. *Roman Holiday* (1953), *Annie Hall* (1977), *My Best Friend's Wedding* (1997), and *Shakespeare in Love* (1998) all adopt "go their separate ways" endings. Despite the viewer's regret that the love affair has broken off, these films still manage to finish on an affirmative note, rejoicing in the individuals' growth and new prospects. If these movies concluded sadly, we would not classify them as romantic comedies.

This constancy of narrative structure does not prevent romantic comedies from responding to historical and social changes. Tempted though we may be to ascribe romantic comedy to some universal, evolutionary, biological urge to mate, we know that many seemingly static institutions and categories—marriage, love, sexuality, gender roles—have changed radically over the centuries. For instance, marriage had been primarily a business arrangement, an alliance between families, until the concept that one should marry for love gradually took hold in Western culture during the eighteenth century. The idea that husband and wife should not only find each other sexually attractive but also be each other's best friends and closest companions—forging what scholars call a "companionate marriage"—is a very recent model. In the twentieth century, many cultural factors, such as increased mobility, the decline of extended family households, and employment by corporations rather than ownership of individual enterprises, conspired to make marriage of preeminent importance. Cultural scholar David Shumway sees marriage today as the last refuge of a nurturing human connection in a colder, more impersonal world, meaning that it carries a burden for our ongoing personal happiness that it didn't use to shoulder.

As we know, the most essential relations between men and women have also changed radically in the last century, particularly as women have won more rights and independence. For centuries, no one would have thought of women as equal partners in a relationship: women were property to be sold, and their role in the unit was to honor and obey rather than to question or act independently. Concurrently, mores related to sexuality—whether in or out of wedlock, whether confined to one's own race or ethnicity or interracial, whether heterosexual or homosexual—have shifted enormously. Romantic comedies cannot help but reflect the changing relations between the genders and the ever-evolving sexual customs in the shifting iterations of their established plot lines.

Romantic comedy remains one genre where the film industry, the casual moviegoer, and film scholars all agree regarding classification; that is, producers overtly market certain films as "romantic comedies" and we accept that label as an accurate description. Nevertheless, just as with other genres, classification questions arise. Because 90 percent of Hollywood movies include romance as the main plot or as a secondary subplot, hybrids abound. Most musicals, such as those with Fred Astaire and Ginger Rogers and those by Rodgers and Hammerstein, revolve around the creation of a romantic couple. Thrillers often involve a central couple in an exciting series of events that are entangled with the progress of a love story. Alfred Hitchcock's British films, such as *The 39 Steps* (1935) and *The Lady Vanishes* (1938), typify this mixture, but the mélange persists in more contemporary examples as well, such as *Mr. and Mrs. Smith* (2005). The endings of *Speed* (1994) and *The Bourne Identity* (2002), showing the central couples in loving clinches, could be final shots of romantic comedies. Sports stories also frequently cross with romantic comedy to create a hybrid subgenre, exemplified by *Bull*

Runaway Bride (1999) Showcasing megastars Julia Roberts and Richard Gere, *Runaway Bride* was a box-office hit in its own right, but the viewing experience is much richer if one sees its deliberate parallels to *It Happened One Night* (1934), in which Ellie (Claudette Colbert) runs away at the last moment from wedding the wrong man and ultimately into the arms of Peter (Clark Gable). The differences between 1934 and 1999 are wryly highlighted by the means the heroine uses to make her escape: Maggie's hitching a ride on a passing FedEx truck makes a witty comment about the speed-crazy, commercial texture of our lives at the turn of the century. Romantic comedies frequently contain allusions to earlier works and figuratively wink at their audiences with intertextual references.

Durham (1988), *Tin Cup* (1996), and *Leatherheads* (2008), all interweaving the development of the romance around a suspenseful athletic contest (so as to attract both male and female viewers?).

How is it that, although resolutely formulaic, romantic comedies succeed in pleasing audiences year after year? Why don't we get bored watching the same old story endlessly? Partly, we can never have too much reassurance that winter (the toils and troubles of life) will eventually cede to spring (a promise of emotional plentitude and renewal); we can never get our fill of joy. When a romantic comedy succeeds in capturing the elation of love requited, it creates a warm bath that splashes through the screen to drench the viewer. In addition, to borrow a phrase from film critic Robert Warshow's discussion of Westerns, romantic comedy is an "art form for connoisseurs, where the spectator derives his pleasure from the appreciation of minor variations within the working out of a pre-established order."[1] From the poster and the credits we surmise—we

---

[1] Robert Warshow, "Movie Chronicle: The Westerner," in *Film Theory and Criticism*, 6th ed., ed. Leo Braudy and Marshall Cohen (New York: Oxford University Press, 2004), 713.

hope—that the Major Male Star and the Major Female Star will end up together, but we delight in seeing exactly how cleverly the events unfold *this* time. Moreover, romantic comedies refer to one another constantly in ways that forge bonds between films and congratulate viewers who are in the know. Such self-referentiality promotes connoisseurship.

Finally, the major pleasure of romantic comedy comes from its stars, and directors utilize every cinematic technique to highlight their attractiveness and sexual appeal—lingering close-ups, flattering lighting, careful costuming, etc. Individual responsiveness to stars comes into play here. If, like some of my students, you find Carole Lombard or Julia Roberts annoying, you will avoid their films. If, like me, you can't bear to spend time with Woody Allen, you'll be tempted to throw his films out of the canon. But when viewers fall a little bit in love with the stars, the genre seduces us. Many film lovers can think of few greater treats than spending two hours with Cary Grant, Barbara Stanwyck, Hugh Grant, Emma Thompson, Meg Ryan, Matthew McConaughey, Julia Stiles, or Heath Ledger.

History

Histories of romantic comedy generally start in the sound era because the verbal banter between the protagonists defines the genre. However, to do so overlooks silent-era antecedents.

Romantic comedy requires a facility with transmitting complicated narrative information, so it was not one of the first genres to appear in early cinema. However, by 1908—with one-reelers running approximately fifteen minutes—filmmakers possessed the narrative tools to undertake more intricate storylines. Indeed, bold production companies tackled the classics of world literature in an attempt to earn prestige for their fledgling medium. Biograph, Vitagraph, Kalem, and other early production companies adapted *The Taming of the Shrew* in 1908, *As You Like It* in 1908 and 1912, *A Midsummer Night's Dream* in 1909, *Twelfth Night* in 1910, and *Much Ado About Nothing* in 1913.

By 1913, romantic comedy was an established genre. Evidence exists in two films Alice Guy directed that year, *Matrimony's Speed Limit* and *A House Divided*. In the first, a young woman tricks her financially strapped fiancé into marrying her by sending him a fake telegram from an aunt, saying that he will inherit a fortune if he marries by noon. In the second, a newly married couple suspects one another of infidelity; on their law-yer's advice they live together but communicate only by note, which cleverly turns the screen's silence into an aesthetic device. Of course, as in most romantic comedies, they reconcile at the end.

A House Divided is an early example of the remarriage plot. The remar-riage plot is important to the genre because, as in *Mr. and Mrs. Smith*, it extends the excitement and adventure of courtship into wedded life. Spurred by the "new morality" of the Jazz Age—the acceptability of divorce and the changing position of women in American society—Cecil B. DeMille was making remarriage comedies as early as 1919. In *Don't Change Your Husband* (1919) and *Why Change Your Wife?* (1920)—just as in *The Awful Truth* (1937)—couples separate, learn to change and appreciate one another, and get back together.

The famous comic films of the 1920s mostly showcased the slapstick talents of male comedians such as Charlie Chaplin, Buster Keaton, and Harold Lloyd. Their movies, so-called "comedian comedies," empha-sized the individual performers' special skills, rather than a romance plot. However, we also know that major female stars in the 1920s, such as Constance Talmadge, Dorothy Gish, and Marion Davies, specialized in romantic comedies, although many of these films are unavailable for general viewing today. Luckily, we do have access to two classics, one starring Mary Pickford and the other Clara Bow. Pickford's *My Best Girl* and Bow's *"It"* (both 1927) display their leading ladies' charms in winning tales of disguise and misunderstandings. Intriguingly, both movies feature department store settings, and conclude with a shopgirl's marrying the owner of the store.

When sound came in during the late 1920s, Hollywood changed dramatically. The studios needed writers who could craft dialogue, so they imported a coterie of East Coast newspapermen; perhaps not sur-prisingly, to this day a remarkable number of romantic comedies casts one of the principals as a journalist of some sort. The studios also hired playwrights who brought with them the Noël Coward style of sophisti-cated comedies then current on Broadway.

Film historians enshrine 1934 in the history of the genre as a banner year, particularly because Frank Capra's *It Happened One Night* swept the Academy Awards. *It Happened One Night* was a signal event not only for its story of a runaway heiress, Ellie Andrews (Claudette Colbert), who meets a washed-up newspaper reporter, Peter Warne (Clark Gable), but also because it—along with other films of that year, such as *The Thin Man*

"It" (1927) Clara Bow here prefigures the screwball heroine. She unabashedly chases Cyrus Waltham Jr. (Antonio Moreno), the son of the owner of the department store in which she sells lingerie. Upon first laying eyes on her boss, she quips: "Sweet Santa Claus, give me *him*." She's also a tough cookie, fighting off the social workers who try to remove her best friend's out-of-wedlock child, claiming that the baby is hers, which complicates her love affair with Cyrus. Note, too, her short hair bob: a sign of female rebellion and independence in the twenties. *"It"* exemplifies the role major female stars played in the romantic comedies of the 1920s.

and *Twentieth Century*—sparked a particular style of romantic comedy, a style we call screwball.

Screwball comedy reigned from 1934 into the early 1940s, creating works of enduring enchantment. The screwball variant of romantic comedy is particularly unrealistic, fast-paced, and unsentimental. Several factors contributed to its distinctive style, most significantly, censorship. Starting in 1934, censors strictly enforced the Production Code that regulated onscreen morality, banning the blatant sexuality of Ernst Lubitsch's *Trouble in Paradise* (1932) and early Mae West films. Thus, directors had to find indirect ways to siphon off (or, in Freudian terms, "displace") sexual energy, such as into dazzling dialogue, slapstick action, and wildly improbable events. In *Easy Living* (1937), the plot starts with a fur coat falling out of the sky and landing on Mary (Jean Arthur). In *My Man Godfrey* (1936), Irene (Carole Lombard) leaves a horse in the library. In *Bringing Up Baby* (1938), Susan (Katharine Hepburn) lets a leopard loose in the Connecticut countryside.

Screwball also took its energy from the building wave of reforms in the status of American women, who won the right to vote in 1920. As many scholars have noted, screwball comedies get their special flavor from the prominence given to their female stars. This era is characterized by the "fast-talking dames," all imbued with high spirits that critics saw as "madcap," stars such as Colbert, Hepburn, Lombard, Irene Dunne, Barbara Stanwyck, and Rosalind Russell.

Among major directors who specialized in screwball comedies, How-

The Awful Truth (1937) Some critics consider *The Awful Truth* the epitome of the screwball era. Jerry (Cary Grant) and Lucy Warriner (Irene Dunne) each suspect the other of infidelity. They quarrel and file for divorce. One hitch in their separation, however, concerns custody of Mr. Smith (Skippy, who also played Asta in the Thin Man movies), the dog they both adore. Jerry gets dog-visitation rights, which leads to his sabotaging Lucy's engagement to a dull-witted Oklahoman, Dan Gleeson (Ralph Bellamy). Lucy pays him back by visiting the home of Jerry's stuffy new future in-laws disguised as his alcoholic sister and behaving outrageously. The couple reconcile in a cabin in the country just before their divorce becomes final.

ard Hawks popularized fast, overlapping dialogue and combative relationships between the sexes, directing a trio of masterpieces in quick succession: *Bringing Up Baby*, *His Girl Friday* (1940), and *Ball of Fire* (1941). George Cukor worked closely with Hepburn, making *Holiday* (1938) and *The Philadelphia Story* (1940). Preston Sturges, a screenwriter-director with a wild imagination, a flair for dialogue, and a disdain for convention, directed and/or wrote such screwballs as *The Good Fairy* (1935), *Easy Living*, *Remember the Night* (1940), *The Lady Eve* (1941), and *The Palm Beach Story* (1942).

Although Sturges continued to work in this genre into the 1940s, World War II and its immediate aftermath were not particularly hospitable to screwball's froth. The late 1940s and 1950s saw several different strains of romantic comedy. Cukor's films with Hepburn and Spencer Tracy, *Adam's Rib* (1949) and *Pat and Mike* (1952), and his three works featuring Judy Holliday, a brilliant actress who played a daffy blonde— *Born Yesterday* (1950), *The Marrying Kind* (1952), and *It Should Happen to You* (1954)—recast romantic comedy into more conventional and less freewheeling stories than those of the screwball era. Audrey Hepburn, charmingly fey but not as challenging as the screwball heroines, starred in a series of films highlighting romance over comedy: *Roman Holiday*, *Sabrina* (1954), *Love in the Afternoon* (1957), *Breakfast at Tiffany's* (1961), and *How to Steal a Million* (1966).

As the fifties progressed, the tight strictures of the Production Code loosened, leading to more sexual content. This shift is demonstrated in Billy Wilder's Marilyn Monroe films, *The Seven Year Itch* (1955) and *Some Like It Hot* (1959). Though no one is bedded onscreen, these more suggestive romantic comedies would not have been allowed in earlier decades dominated by strong censorship. Late in the 1950s and into the 1960s, Doris Day's films mixed prudishness and verbal licentiousness in odd proportions—lots of smarmy innuendo and leering but no actual sex—in a series of so-called "sex comedies," the most famous of which is *Pillow Talk* (1959).

During the early 1960s, romantic comedy plots often featured children who needed a second parent, so the union of the main couple also stabilized a traditional family. *The Courtship of Eddie's Father*, *My Six Loves* (both 1963), and *Father Goose* (1964)—like the megahit *The Sound of Music* (1965)—use romance to provide the missing parent for a brood. However, Hollywood's traditional take on marriage at this time was behind the changing social zeitgeist, which saw the launching of the modern feminist movement with the publication of Betty Friedan's *The Feminine Mystique* in 1963. Through the stir following Friedan's critique

Roman Holiday (1953) Audrey Hepburn's first starring role was in *Roman Holiday*. She plays a princess who runs away from the palace for a day, encountering Joe (Gregory Peck), a newspaper reporter. He recognizes her and plans to write a scoop about her but changes his mind when they fall in love. In this scene they are standing in front of a Roman sculpture, *The Mouth of Truth*, which—legend has it—bites off the hands of liars. They are lucky the sculpture has lost its magic, because they are both lying to one another. *Roman Holiday* is much more romantic than the movies of the screwball era.

of women's place in society, and political events such as the founding in 1966 of the National Organization for Women (NOW), the country had to acknowledge how unhappy—even enraged—women were made by domestic and economic arrangements previously taken for granted, such as the condescending cult of housewifery, women's exclusion from many professions, and unequal pay.

By 1968, the motion picture trade association replaced the restrictive Production Code with a much more flexible ratings system that assigns movies letter designations (G, PG, R, etc.). The sexual revolution (partly spurred by the invention of oral contraceptives in 1960) had changed attitudes involving sex in daily life and on the screen: intimacy no longer functioned as the prize at the end of courtship but instead as one of the stations on the road to commitment. For the next few years, the film industry seemed as confused about male-female relationships as Ben Braddock in *The Graduate* (1967). Most of the Young Turk directors who were part of the New Hollywood of the 1970s—Spielberg, Coppola, Scorsese, Altman, Lucas, Friedkin, and others—avoided romance like the plague.

Frank Krutnik writes, "In the post-1960's world, heterosexual engagement is posed as a perilous voyage into unmapped territories beyond the frontiers of the old cartographies, where lovers must steer between the wrecked vessels of romantic discourse and the abysmal prospect of emotional limbo."[2] In 1972, Peter Bogdanovich consciously tried to revive screwball with *What's Up, Doc?*, an homage to *Bringing Up Baby* that fell flat with both critics and moviegoers. As the 1970s lurched forward, the key filmmaker focusing on relationships was Woody Allen, who created a new style of romantic comedy scholars label the "nervous romance." In the nervous romance all the psychological and emotional stresses of relationships are laid bare and the conclusion for the couple remains uncertain. *Play It Again, Sam* (1972), *Annie Hall*, and *Manhattan* (1979) reveal deep suspicions about whether love, romance, and marriage are possible in an era so different from earlier times. Hal Ashby's *Shampoo* (1975), another nervous romance, centers on a hair stylist (Warren Beatty) who has sex with all of his rapacious clients but can't figure out where his heart lies. By the late 1970s, the wars between the sexes

---

[2] Frank Krutnik, "Love Lies: Romantic Fabrication in Contemporary Romantic Comedy," in *Terms of Endearment: Hollywood Romantic Comedy of the 1980s and 1990s*, ed. Peter William Evans and Celestino Deleyto (Edinburgh: Edinburgh University Press, 1998), 18.

appeared so dire that the scholar Brian Henderson, punning on the title of a forgettable 1977 film—and, thankfully, mistakenly—predicted the end of the genre in his 1978 article "Romantic Comedy Today: *Semi-Tough* or Impossible?"

During the conservative Ronald Reagan era of the 1980s, studios regrouped and produced movies that proved the endurance and profitability of the genre. *Tootsie* (1982) finds a way to incorporate watered-down feminism into its plot, by turning a man into a woman (at least for a while). Meanwhile, *Splash* (1984), *Moonstruck* (1987), and *Bull Durham* offer unusual premises, witty scripts, and attractive stars. The end of the decade, though, saw the genre move onto another plane of critical and popular approval: in 1989 Nora Ephron co-wrote and Rob Reiner directed *When Harry Met Sally...*, a tremendously popular success, topped a year later by Gary Marshall's *Pretty Woman* (1990). These ushered in the contemporary era of the films called the "new romance," or the "neotraditional" romantic comedy, a cycle that (arguably) continues to this day.

The "Big Three" female stars dominated the 1990s: Meg Ryan, Julia Roberts, and Sandra Bullock. Ryan is the smallest of stature and the

***When Harry Met Sally...* (1989)** Meg Ryan, one of the leading stars who made new romances so popular with audiences, here plays Sally, who chats with Harry (Billy Crystal) in a restaurant, catching up on life events since they last met. She is talking about her realization that she wants a family, and that the freedom she and her ex-boyfriend shared was never as fulfilling as they thought it would be. New romances often reaffirm traditional values such as having children, monogamy, and marriage. Ryan's fresh prettiness, comic timing, and touch of poignancy fit perfectly into the genre's latest incarnation.

most kittenish; in Peter Williams Evans's words, "To look at Meg Ryan is to contemplate a world free of demons and terror."[3] Roberts, tall and coltish, with an unusual beauty, is more "unladylike," and spontaneously emotional, exemplified by her dazzlingly wide smile and seemingly spur-of-the-moment laughter. Bullock shows the least vanity, often slightly mocking herself and the stories she appears in, and emerges as the most bristly and independent. Hugh Grant, who emerged as the major male star of new romance in a series of British films beginning with *Four Weddings and a Funeral* (1994), leavens his too-handsome face with stuttering, bumbling, insecure (winning) mannerisms.

In the first decade of the 2000s, romantic comedies multiplied like rabbits. By one account, production companies have released more than three hundred of them in the last fifteen years. Jennifer Aniston, Drew Barrymore, Cameron Diaz, Anne Hathaway, Katherine Heigl, Jennifer Lopez, Reese Witherspoon, and Renée Zellweger each appear in several (though none of them has broken through to the superstardom of the Big Three). George Clooney, Will Smith, Harrison Ford, Kevin Costner, Richard Gere, and Hugh Jackman appear as male leads, but because they are also cast in a variety of other genres, audiences don't associate them exclusively with romantic comedy. The only contemporary male stars who unabashedly specialize in this genre are Matthew McConaughey and Ashton Kutcher. As he has aged, McConaughey has sought out grittier roles.

Romantic comedies became plentiful in recent decades partly because they are (comparatively) cheap to produce and return healthy profits to Hollywood. No need for large budgets to support the special effects or dazzling visual spectacles demanded in science fiction and action adventure movies. Another reason these films remain reliably profitable is because they are directed primarily at female viewers. Women—and men—not eager to spend two hours with explosions, violence, or horror respond to the character focus of romantic comedy. *My Big Fat Greek Wedding* (2002), about a young Greek woman who falls in love with a WASP man and must deal with her family's ethnic culture shock, became the top-grossing romantic comedy of all time. Written by and starring Nia Vardalos, it is an indie film that cost a mere $5

---

[3] Peter William Evans, "Meg Ryan, Megastar," in *Terms of Endearment: Hollywood Romantic Comedy of the 1980s and 1990s*, ed. Peter William Evans and Celestino Deleyto (Edinburgh: Edinburgh University Press, 1998), 180.

***Desperately Seeking Susan* (1985)** Written, directed, and produced by women, *Desperately Seeking Susan* is a landmark romantic comedy. The focus here is partly on the romance between Roberta (Rosanna Arquette) and Dez (Aidan Quinn), but the emphasis is really on the parallels and contrasts between Roberta and Susan (Madonna), who switch roles: Roberta leaving her stultifying marriage and the trap of being a suburban housewife to become more liberated, and Susan taming her unruliness. The before and after photos of each woman (drawn from different scenes, and never shown in split screen as here pictured) show how they both change.

million to produce and has grossed over $240 million domestically. Even when Paramount, a major studio, produced *What Women Want* (2000), with expensive stars Mel Gibson and Helen Hunt, the film cost only $70 million, while returning a domestic gross of $180 million. Many romantic comedies double their gross in international distribution, and the genre does very well in ancillary markets such as DVD rental and sales, because they do not depend upon spectacle, and thus fit the smaller screen.

Whether due to their own inclinations, or because they've been shut out of other more expensive, "male" genres, female filmmakers have found a home in romantic comedy. Susan Seidelman, for example, a pathbreaking director in the mid-1980s, created *Desperately Seeking Susan* (1985) and *Making Mr. Right* (1987). In more recent years, Nora Ephron became a lauded screenwriter and director: her hits include *When Harry Met Sally…*, *Sleepless in Seattle* (1993), *You've Got Mail* (1998), and *Bewitched* (2005). Nancy Meyers directed *What Women Want*, *Something's Gotta Give* (2003), *The Holiday* (2006), and *It's Complicated* (2009). Anne Fletcher directed *27 Dresses* (2008) and *The Proposal* (2009). Lisa Cholodenko wrote and directed *The Kids are All Right* (2010). Mira Nair, an Indian director based in New York, brought her international perspective to *Mississippi Masala* (1991), about the love affair between an Indian woman and an African-American man, and *Monsoon Wedding* (2001). Dig down in the credits, and you will often find women producers and screenwriters as integral participants in romantic comedies.

Although one can find romantic comedies starring Sidney Poitier as early as *Paris Blues* (1961), *For Love of Ivy* (1968), and *Guess Who's Coming to Dinner* (1967), films focusing on African-American romance have become particularly notable in recent years. *Coming to America* (1988) and *Hitch* (2005) were wildly profitable thanks to the star power of Eddie Murphy and Will Smith, respectively. Smaller-budget productions such as *Brown Sugar* (2002), *Deliver Us from Eva* (2003), and *Perfect Holiday* (2007) recast romantic comedy conventions for the African-American community and provide expanded opportunities for a new generation of black filmmakers, such as Ricky Famuyiwa, Gary Hardwick, and Lance Rivera.

Similarly, romantic comedy has long included gay characters and themes, though mainstream offerings tend not to challenge traditional prejudices directly; instead they often make the gay character the lead's "best friend," so as not to depict homosexual romance. Still, *Victor/Victoria* (1982) flirted with transvestitism, while *The Wedding Banquet* (1993), which was nominated for an Academy Award in the category of Best Foreign Language Film, involves a gay man whose parents are pressuring him to marry and have children. *In and Out* (1997) and *The Object of My Affection* (1998), the former about a popular high-school teacher (Kevin Kline) who discovers he is gay and the latter about a woman (Jennifer Aniston) who falls in love with a gay man (Paul Rudd), played in major cinema chains all over the country. However, bolder independent films, such as *The Incredibly True Adventure of Two Girls in Love* (1995), *Kissing Jessica Stein* (2001), and *All Over the Guy* (2001), have been ghettoized into smaller exhibition venues. With the recent rise of the gay-marriage movement, homosexual romance will undoubtedly move into more mainstream romantic comedies.

Although the Production Code now belongs to the dustbin of Hollywood history, many studio releases continue to demonstrate a level of self-censorship. Though the typical romantic comedies of the last two decades are substantially more open about sexual desire and activity than they were during the screwball era—in *The Wedding Date* (2005), for example, the heroine (Debra Messing) ravishes the male escort (Dermot Mulroney) she has hired to accompany her to her sister's wedding festivities—they nevertheless strive to earn a PG rating and remain suitable (sort of) for young teens. Characters discuss sex obliquely; lovemaking scenes fade out; if people are nude, the camera frames them strategically. Filmmakers design their movies this way to keep them acceptable to parents, mature viewers who dislike vulgarity, and open-exhibition venues such as airplanes. Yet this self-censorship also has the benefit of encouraging clever indirection and substitution.

Film scholar Leger Grindon argues that the affirmative, traditional quality of new romance has been replaced since 1997 by a trend toward what he labels the "grotesque and ambivalent." We see the "grotesque" influence in those R-rated films that get comic mileage out of frankness about sexual and bodily matters. These include those "gross-out" comedies, such as *There's Something About Mary* (1998), *Knocked Up* (2007), *Forgetting Sarah Marshall* (2008), and *Bridesmaids* (2011), which foreground crude speech, explicit sex, bodily functions, and full nudity. By knocking love down from its glossy, magical place, they flout authority. These films are designed to have more appeal for young men than more genteel romantic comedies, and indeed, by bringing in a larger demographic, they have performed particularly well at the box office.

Grindon's "ambivalence" manifests in films that, like the nervous romance, question whether romance is possible in today's society. Especially in "art films" such as *Punch-Drunk Love* (2002), *Before Sunrise* (1995), *After the Sunset* (2004), and *Eternal Sunshine of the Spotless Mind* (2004), characters are hesitant to accept or believe in love. This ambivalence characterizes another new strand of romantic comedies as well, those that present multiple story lines and offer a panoply of couplings, such as *Love Actually* (2003) and *He's Just Not That into You* (2009). Spreading romance around among numerous couples allows a filmmaker to present a variety of scenarios (straight/gay; monogamous/unfaithful; committed/breaking up), illustrating a variety of approaches to courtship and love and providing both comparisons and contrasts. Multiple-couple films offer more options regarding romance than the traditional single-couple happy ending, and reflect the changing nature of relationships in the second decade of the twenty-first century.

Despite Grindon's able description of short-term cycles, I believe that the "reaffirmation of romance" typical of new romance still thrives.

One has only to look at the popularity of *Silver Linings Playbook* (2012)—where love conquers serious mental illness—to witness American films' will to love.

Typology, Themes, and Theories

Along with the basic plot structure of meet/separate/reunite (or, in the remarriage variation, be married/divorce/remarry), romantic comedies frequently manifest a characteristic narrative structure that the scholar Rick Altman terms "dual focus." In a dual-focus film, scenes centering on one lover alternate with parallel scenes centered on the other. For example, in *Pillow Talk*, we see scenes of Brad Allen (Rock Hudson) in his apartment, and then of Jan Morrow (Doris Day) in hers. In *Sleepless in Seattle*, scenes with Annie Reid (Meg Ryan) in New York alternate with those showing Sam Baldwin (Tom Hanks) in Seattle.

This choice of alternating focus has important thematic implications. As we gain more knowledge about each character, we understand that each is missing what the other can provide. Typically, one pole of the couple is responsible, cautious, and high achieving (read: sexually inexperienced and/or uptight), while the other is unconventional, free-spirited, and irresponsible (read: sexually experienced and liberated). The union of David Huxley (Cary Grant) and Susan Vance (Katharine Hepburn) in *Bringing Up Baby*, or of Elizabeth Masterson (Reese Witherspoon) and David Abbot (Mark Ruffalo) in *Just Like Heaven* (2005), creates a happy mean that makes the participants more blessed and more fulfilled as a couple than they were as singles.

Classic dual focus highlights additional differences besides sexual experience. In the screwball era, the lovers often come from different social classes and/or have diverse approaches to careers. Sandro (Francis Lederer) in *The Gay Deception* (1935) is a prince, while Mirabel Miller (Frances Dee) is a secretary. Johnny Case (Cary Grant) in *Holiday* is a self-made man, while Linda Seton (Katharine Hepburn) is an heiress. The dichotomy in social class continues down through the decades to *Working Girl* (1988), *Pretty Woman*, and *Maid in Manhattan* (2002). Along with social class, the dichotomy between the lovers often involves high achievement and careerism versus less ambition and a more relaxed attitude toward life. In earlier movies, such as *Ball of Fire*, *Sabrina*, and *The Apartment* (1960), the male characters are losing out on life because

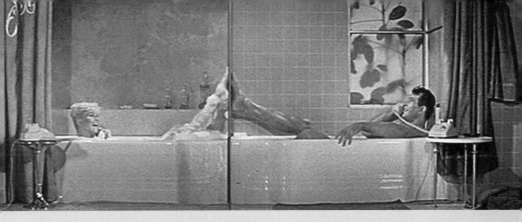

***Pillow Talk* (1959)** The famous split-screen shot in *Pillow Talk* captures the dynamics of the dual-focus narrative usually achieved via alternating parallel scenes. She is a prissy, career-obsessed interior designer; he is a lackadaisical songwriter whose real interest is in bedding women. They share a party-line telephone, which leads to their mutual hatred. By this scene, however, Brad (Rock Hudson) has disguised himself as Rex Stetson, an ultra-gentlemanly Texan visiting New York who is wooing Jan (Doris Day). His feigned sexual reticence brings out her sexual desire. When they go away to a cabin in the country, however, Jan discovers Rex's true identity. Such a dual structure, common in many romantic comedies, allows the viewer to learn more about each character, discover what each is missing in his/her life, and understand how the other person can provide the missing balance.

they can't pry their noses out of work long enough to smell the roses. Although movies continue to chastise men for single-minded ambition, in recent offerings the career-obsessed boot fits the female characters' smaller feet. Elizabeth in *Just Like Heaven* is unadventurous in terms of personal relationships because she can't detach from her profession as a doctor. Melanie (Michelle Pfeiffer) in *One Fine Day* (1996), Melanie (Reese Witherspoon) in *Sweet Home Alabama* (2002), and Kate (Catherine Zeta-Jones) in *No Reservations* (2007) elevate their work above openness to life and romance. Many films of the 1980s onward set about teaching women not to let their career ambitions close them off to love. Others, such as *Knocked Up*, criticize the slackers' immaturity and the striver's obsessiveness.

While many romantic comedies employ this dual focus, others utilize single focus; they privilege one side of the couple and sometimes even allow that character to narrate via voice-over. Recent examples include *Legally Blonde* (2001), *Bridget Jones's Diary* (2001), and *About a Boy* (2002). In these movies, we learn very little about the needs or feelings of the other member of the romantic couple. *About a Boy* doesn't even introduce the leading lady until midway through the film. Ironically, *About a Boy* nevertheless does contain a dual-focus tension, not between the lovers, but between Will (Hugh Grant), who is irresponsible, self-centered, and cool, and the young boy, Marcus (Nicholas Hoult), who is loyal, selfless, and hopelessly nerdy. "Bromances," such as *The Odd Couple* (1968) and *I Love You, Man* (2009), replicate dual-focus structure between male characters of contrasting personalities.

As in Shakespeare, modern romantic comedy plots frequently hinge on role-playing and deception. The tagline for *How to Lose a Guy in 10 Days* (2003) reads: "One of them is lying. So is the other," which pretty fairly sums up the dynamics in nearly all of these films. Whether on purpose or by accident, characters fall into playing a part: in *The Lady Eve*, Jean (Barbara Stanwyck), a cardsharp, pretends to be British nobility to get revenge on Charles Pike (Henry Fonda). In *Splash*, the mermaid (Daryl Hannah) pretends to be human to win Allen (Tom Hanks). In *While You Were Sleeping* (1995), Lucy (Sandra Bullock) has a crush on Peter (Peter Gallagher), a man to whom she has never spoken. When he is hospitalized in a coma, she deceives his family by pretending that

Love & Basketball (2000) Like many romantic comedies from the 1980s onward, *Love & Basketball* initially questions the heroine's intense desire for an ambitious career—in this case, she wants to play pro basketball—and shows the price that she pays for her obsession. Such films often suggest that women who strive for success close themselves off from the possibility of romance. *Love and Basketball*, however, validates the dream Monica (Sanaa Lathan) has of becoming a professional athlete. Here, at the film's conclusion, she challenges her about-to-be-married-to-someone-else true love, Quincy (Omar Epps), to a desperate, nighttime contest of one-on-one, the stakes being the future of their relationship. The film ends refreshingly with Monica on the professional court, as Quincy sits in the stands, cheers her on, and tends to their child.

she's his fiancée. The family loves her, and all is going well while Peter lies unconscious, but the course of true love never runs smoothly in romantic comedies: tangles ensue when Lucy falls in love with Peter's brother, Jack (Bill Pullman) and must reveal her lies to the family. In *The Shop Around the Corner* (1940) and its second remake, *You've Got Mail*, the man discovers that the anonymous pen pal he's fallen in love with is the woman in his life he can't stand; he strings her along until the combative antagonism fades to reveal the attraction underneath. In *Roxanne* (1987), *IQ* (1994), and *The Truth About Cats & Dogs* (1996), would-be lovers resort to the central trope of the 1897 play *Cyrano de Bergerac*, employing proxies to help them woo the objects of their affections, which, predictably, leads to mayhem. As Puck says in *A Midsummer's Night Dream*, "Lord, what fools these mortals be!"

Deception serves as a double-edged sword in the romantic comedy genre. On the one hand, when *x* misleads *y* in order to write a newspaper story about *y*, the deception is self-serving and immoral; the romance cannot come to fruition without a process of discovery, humiliation, and forgiveness. Although we anticipate that everything will work out, romantic comedies always contain the possibility that the deception will not be resolved in time, or that the hurt partner will not be able to forgive the deceiver. Romantic comedies gain their poignant quality as they extend the scenes of anger and irreconcilability and keep the audience wondering whether the relationship will ultimately thrive. As film scholars Kathleen Rowe and Tamar McDonald point out, melodrama and heartbreak lurk like sharks underneath romantic comedy. As viewers we hold our breath, hoping—praying—for a last-minute reconciliation, which is sometimes strung out in a chase scene, and sometimes—as in *Never Been Kissed*—in a five-minute countdown in the center of a baseball field, which serves no purpose other than to prove that Josie (Drew Barrymore) is so ashamed of her behavior than she will undergo this achingly painful public contrition and humiliation.

Yet playacting and deception also have the potential to liberate people from their mundane daily ruts. In *Never Been Kissed*, Josie's love interest, Sam (Michael Vartan), says, apropos of *As You Like It*: "See, the point Shakespeare's trying to make is that when we're in disguise, we feel freer, we do things we wouldn't do in ordinary life." And the movie proves his point by having Josie come out of her nerdy-loser shell when she impersonates a high-school student to write about high-school life for her newspaper. For many characters, only by breaking away from their everyday identity can they move forward: through pretending to be someone else, they are free to find themselves and someone to love as well.

Deception takes the form of cross-dressing with surprising frequency in this genre. In *Sylvia Scarlett* (1935), *Some Like It Hot, Victor/Victoria, All of Me* (1984), *Tootsie, Shakespeare in Love, Good Advice* (2001), and *She's the Man*, characters all learn more about their inner feelings and prepare themselves for love through such disguises. These films put into question many of our social assumptions about what it means to be a man or a woman and to what degree gender roles are merely social convention. In fact, some go further: they posit that by assuming the gender of the opposite sex, even if only by altering superficial details of one's appearance, one can become a more rounded human being, and more fully understand the inner life of the person whose love one craves. This knowledge can take the form of little instances—such as how demeaning it is to be called "Babe" in *Tootsie*—to far larger lessons, such as the problems posed by the cultural roles each gender must conform to in order to find a place within society. Ultimately, men understanding women and women understanding men teach each the problems the other gender faces and prepare them for maturity and love.

Twentieth-century romantic comedies promote a therapeutic ethos; that is, they believe that people can grow and repair their character defects when the pain, humiliation, and thrill of love make them reexamine traits they stubbornly hold on to. Characters can move on from grieving for past lovers (*Sleepless in Seattle*), medicate their obsessive-compulsive disorder [*As Good as It Gets* (1997)], overcome their fear of flying [*French Kiss* (1995)], repent for their judgmentalism [*The Philadelphia Story, Pride and Prejudice* (2005)], and generally grow up (too many to list). They take a journey—often literally—from their past problems to a brighter future.

According to Hollywood's rules, learning to be more sexually attractive is part of the therapeutic thematics. Starting with DeMille's silent films, romantic comedies stress the importance not only of inner maturity but also of outer display. As we all know, romantic comedies specialize in makeovers: Gracie (Sandra Bullock) in *Miss Congeniality* (2000) and Albert (Kevin James) in *Hitch* submit themselves to painful treatments to enhance their sex appeal. Even those films that don't officially "make over" a star predictably build tension toward "dress up" scenes: a climactic prom, party, wedding, or other occasion where the characters put on fancy clothes, and the camera ostentatiously pauses, or pans up their bodies, in admiration of their newly revealed sexual appeal. (Such narratives also form the basis of a slew of contemporary reality-based TV programs, from *What Not to Wear* to *The Ultimate Makeover*.) Viewers applaud these makeovers as positive signs of the characters' gaining self-confidence and accepting their sexual desires. Moreover, viewers derive vicarious satisfaction from seeing Cinderella rise from the ashes to become a beautiful princess, as in *Maid in Manhattan*, when the hotel housemaid goes to a benefit at the Metropolitan Museum. We believe that with the right clothing and expert help we too could morph from our ugly duckling quotidian frumpiness into swanlike gracefulness. However, students of this genre should not ignore how exterior makeovers can indoctrinate us into overvaluing the products of our consumer-oriented society and coerce us into strict normative standards of beauty.

The lesson of nearly all romantic comedies is that the way to win love is to go shopping on the ultra-expensive Rodeo Drive in Los Angeles and get your eyebrows shaped by an expert makeup artist. Women, in particular, are not lovable until they are as conventionally pretty as Hollywood can make them. You are not charming until you appear in designer duds. Actually, *How to Steal a Million* is one long commercial for Givenchy fashions, which, indeed, Audrey Hepburn, as slim and graceful as any model, displays fetchingly. Consumerism reaches its acme of absurdity in *Sex and the City* (2008) when Big (Chris Noth) proves his love for Carrie (Sarah Jessica Parker) by building her the ultimate walk-in closet. Not surprisingly, this is the site where they have sex and ultimately reconcile.

Some academics suggest that the upper-class settings of romantic comedy are not important in themselves but merely free up the characters from bills and responsibilities so that they can concentrate on eros. I disagree. The romantic comedy is the American genre most consistently and profoundly culpable for displaying and advertising the luxuries of American consumerism. Although the 1930s screwball comedies show a conscience about the Depression and criticize the rich, curiously, all the couples seem to end up quite financially comfortable. Another possible exception to the consumerist ethos might be those films featuring a repeated plot motif in which protagonists progressively lose all their possessions until they rediscover themselves in a more elemental situation, as occurs in *It Happened One Night* and *Romancing the Stone* (1984).

The Devil Wears Prada (2006) When Andrea (Anne Hathaway) starts working at *Runway* magazine, she is indifferent to high fashion. Gradually, she falls under its spell and makes herself over into the kind of fashionista she originally despised, adhering to the demanding code of beauty espoused and disseminated by her ruthless boss, Miranda Priestly (Meryl Streep). The most clever sequence features an Andy-on-her-way-to-work montage that match cuts her into a series of haute couture outfits as she walks down the street, enters the subway, comes out, goes into her building and office. Each change of clothing is for our viewing pleasure, shows the passage of time, and demonstrates her acceptance of a new set of values. Such makeovers indoctrinate viewers into overvaluing the expensive goods of our consumer-oriented economy and pressure audiences (particularly women) into blindly slaving to achieve a shallow ideal of beauty.

However, this plot motif doesn't actually lambaste consumerism; it just offers an exciting "adventure vacation," with the protagonists eventually returning to their normal lifestyle. Other films that appear to criticize consumerism actually demonstrate bad faith: *The Devil Wears Prada* (2006) supposedly advocates renouncing high fashion for a simpler and more moral life, but its camera fetishizes the ensembles that the characters wear and lingers over the fantasy of a Parisian excursion.

Obviously, this emphasis on beauty, fashion, and consumer goods stems from filmmakers' assumptions that these topics will interest their female audiences (and from product placement deals with companies). But it also arises from a deeper level: *the thematic connections between consumption and courtship.* Marriage in Western culture was once primarily a financial pact: a deal, involving families negotiating the dowries and settlements to their best advantage. Today, without matchmakers or extended families' help, individuals have to *market themselves* and portray their advantages in the most appealing light; hence, the emphasis on display, and the preeminent importance of instantly, physically, telegraphing one's beauty (read: healthiness and suitability to propagate), class, and social standing (read: resources to protect future offspring.) As relationships and sexual connections have become more casual, individuals "shop around" for mates just as they shop for consumer goods, surfing choices on the Internet, where a host of dating sites assumes the matchmaking role. Individuals "try on" different mates to see if they fit and ultimately "purchase" the one that suits them best. As the tagline for *27 Dresses*'s puts it: "She's about to find the perfect fit."

Thus, courtship is like consumerism; however, consumerism is also like courtship. Admit it: most of us get deep emotional satisfaction from our prized possessions. We yearn for a certain object, we hunt for it, we commit to it, and we triumphantly possess it. If the luster wears off, we either dust off the object and renew its appeal or dump it and search for a new one. The new car or the perfect pair of shoes is not just a utilitarian purchase, but one that gives us a pleasure that is partly sexual in nature. The plot of *Ninotchka* (1939) hinges on the title character's desire for a fashionable hat: the hat is a fetish object that stands in for her need for frivolity, love, and sex. All the displays of diamonds, fashion, yachts, and resort hotels in romantic comedies enhance the sexual charge of these films. We feast our eyes not only on the handsome stars but on the handsome goods and luxurious surroundings.

The critical literature on romantic comedy is fascinated by the issue of what the genre tells us about gender relations in American society. Some scholars (Kathleen Rowe in *The Unruly Woman* makes the most eloquent case) see it as potentially liberating, as subversive. Rowe highlights female characters she sees as "unruly," breaking the bonds of conventional behavior through open displays of intelligence, assertiveness, independence, and blatant sexual desire. We can trace the unruly woman throughout the sweep of the genre: from Ellie diving off the yacht in *It Happened One Night* to Theodora (Irene Dunne) going wild in a film literally and amusingly titled *Theodora Goes Wild* (1936), to Hildy (Rosalind Russell) physically tackling a policeman in *His Girl Friday*, to Sugar (Marilyn Monroe) wielding her sex appeal like a flamethrower in *Some Like It Hot*, to Annie (Susan Sarandon) schooling baseball players in *Bull Durham* (1988), to Audrey (Melanie Griffith) kidnapping Charles (Jeff Daniels) in *Something Wild* (1986), to Elle (Reese Witherspoon) upending all male expectations in *Legally Blonde*, to Eva (Gabrielle Union) cowing her brothers-in-law in *Deliver Us from Eva*. Unruly women mock male pretensions and arrogance. They turn the tables on male superiority.

They dare anything and everything. They own their own sexuality and pursue their own desires.

On the other hand, many scholars criticize the genre as merely offering feints toward equality between the sexes, the better to conquer women's desire for independence and teach them a lesson about their proper role in society. Diane Carson opens our eyes to a scary pattern: how many times in these movies men strike or otherwise physically abuse the women and how often the women are literally silenced: see, for example, the ending of *The Proposal*, filmed in 2009. Emphasizing the endings of movies in which the man inevitably conquers the unruly woman and she subsides into the role of predictable bride or lover, this school of thought sees romantic comedies as compulsively repeating the taming of the shrew. The more unruly the woman, the more credit redounds to the man (like Shakespeare's Petruchio) who ropes her in, teaches her a lesson, makes her submit, and ties her down with the silken cords of her own love.

Certainly, *Overboard* (1987) belongs in the Pantheon of Most Sexist Films of All Time. Starring Goldie Hawn as Joanna, a spoiled, rich woman who gets her comeuppance from a carpenter, Dean (Kurt Russell), it ends with her learning to love being the domestic slave to his four children. I also propose a special award for *The Thrill of It All!* (1963), in which a husband (James Garner) plots to make his wife (Doris Day) give up her high-paying career starring in soap commercials and find fulfillment in just being a pregnant wife. You may have other nominations. However, we can't ignore that some films—for example, *Bringing Up Baby*, *About a Boy*, *Forgetting Sarah Marshall*—put more emphasis on taming the unsocialized male animal, making *him* fit for love. The genre is so commodious that within its bounds one finds a wide spectrum of models of relationships between the sexes.

Nevertheless, we need to recognize that one end of the spectrum is indeed chopped off: romantic comedies by definition do not advocate the independent, single path, or a lifestyle of serial sexual adventure. They advocate love and commitment—and, for nearly all of their history, heterosexual love. If one believes that coupledom per se is an outmoded institution oppressive to men and women, or one feels rejected by these films' constant stress on heterosexuality, then the whole genre becomes propaganda for a conservative viewpoint, a way of socializing moviegoers into traditional gender roles and cultural conventions.

Iconography

The distinctive aesthetics of romantic comedy come from its dialogue, not its images. The best romantic comedies spring from the wittiest scripts delivered by the most skillful actors. Romantic-comedy dialogue sabotages the language of love; it uses insults as part of the mating ritual. Here is a meeting of two future lovers: in *10 Things I Hate about You*, Patrick (Heath Ledger) approaches Kat (Julia Stiles) on the soccer field, trying to chat her up:

> *Patrick:* Hey there, girlie. How you doin'?
> *Kat:* Sweating like a pig, actually, and yourself?
> *Patrick:* Now there's a way to get a guy's attention, huh?
> *Kat:* My mission in life. But, obviously I struck your fancy so you see it worked. The world makes sense again.

Progressing further through courtship rituals, in *Moonstruck*, we get this unusual declaration of love by Nicolas Cage to Cher:

> *Ronnie:* I love you.
> *Loretta:* [*slaps him twice*] Snap out of it!

This style of combative relationship lasts even through divorce. In *His Girl Friday*, Hildy says to her ex-husband (Cary Grant): "Walter, you're wonderful, in a loathsome sort of way."

Romantic comedies don't merely sabotage the language of love, they use their dialogue to deflate all serious subjects. In *Two Weeks Notice* (2002), George (Hugh Grant) is a real-estate developer talking with the very liberal parents of his girlfriend, Lucy (Sandra Bullock); he purposely misunderstands questions and the conversation veers off like a drunken sailor:

> *George:* This whole project is worth about fifty million in profits.
> *Ruth:* No offense, but I think it's *immoral* for one person to acquire that much wealth. How do you sleep at night?
> *George:* Well, I have a machine that simulates the sound of the ocean.
> *Larry:* Do those really work?
> *George:* Oh, yes, quite well actually.

Other sequences have the rhythm of stand-up comedy, building up to a punch line. In *When Harry Met Sally...*, Sally is describing to Harry what caused an earlier romance to falter:

Sally: Well, if you must know, it was because he was very jealous, and I had these days-of-the-week underpants.
Harry: Ehhhh. I'm sorry. I need the judges' ruling on this. Days-of-the-week underpants?
Sally: Yes. They had the days of the week on them, and I thought they were sort of funny. And then one day Sheldon says to me, "You never wear Sunday." It was all suspicious. Where was Sunday? Where had I left Sunday? And I told him, and he didn't believe me.
Harry: What?
Sally: They don't make Sunday.
Harry: Why not?
Sally: Because of God.

Alongside the funny dialogue, romantic comedies use slapstick action—particularly pratfalls. In *The Lady Eve*, Jean/Eve gets Charles Pike so confused he goes *splat!* three times in one scene. In *French Kiss*, Kate (Meg Ryan) is trying to spy on her ex-fiancé when she tumbles into the dessert cart. *Just Married* (2003) crashes and smashes its central couple around with such frenzy one wonders they aren't in body casts. Such physical comedy adds humor—and humbles the characters.

By far the most common locale for romantic comedies is New York City. Nearly all the screwballs take place there. In recent decades other yuppie cities, such as Seattle, San Francisco, Boston, or London, sometimes substitute for New York, but Manhattan is still the ur-location, the home of many of the screenwriters, the center of money, fashion, and culture. The couples at the heart of these dramas are sophisticates, not hicks. They have swanky jobs as journalists, book editors, advertising executives, and the like. They live a glamorous high life. Their Manhattan is a stage set for romance—a glorious confection of sidewalk cafes, Lincoln Center, nightclubs, rooftops, galas at the Met, riverside promenades, and boats on the Hudson.

Yet often, to discover their true feelings, characters must leave the surroundings where they are most comfortable and travel to what the literary scholar Northrop Frye calls "the green world." The green world is a more pastoral setting where the characters can discover themselves.

Maid in Manhattan (2002) This poster embraces the iconography of New York City. The film includes nearly every convention of romantic comedy, such as mistaken identity, a make-over scene, a heroine who speaks her mind, a dog who brings the couple together, and a holiday ending. Note the print at the bottom: "This Christmas…love checks in," indicating a Christmas season release. What is unusual about the film, however, is that the romance between Marisa (Jennifer Lopez) and Christopher (Ralph Fiennes) is interracial. In fact, *Maid* mixes together both race and class: Marisa is a hotel maid, working her way up from housekeeping to management. In several scenes, she criticizes Chris's silver-spoon perspective and shows pride in her social station. One might notice, that for all its political progressiveness, this poster lightens Lopez's complexion in the background graphic.

The forest of Arden in Shakespeare's *As You Like It*, and the woods outside Athens inhabited by the fairy rulers Oberon and Titania in *A Midsummer Night's Dream* provide prototypes. A modern equivalent to this Elizabethan "green world" appears in *Bringing Up Baby*, when Susan and David journey to her aunt's place in Connecticut, and in *27 Dresses*, when the lovers drive up to rural Rhinebeck. In *The Palm Beach Story*, Geraldine (Claudette Colbert) and Tom Jeffers (Joel McCrea) travel separately to Florida; in *Forgetting Sarah Marshall*, Peter (Jason Segel) and Sarah (Kristen Bell) end up in Hawaii, the latter to be with her new lover and the former to forget her. Sometimes, instead of literally leaving the city, the couple find the green world close at hand, such as in Central Park or on a landscaped rooftop.

Like the green world, dogs play a pivotal role in romantic comedies because they straddle the realms of the wild and the domesticated. *Must Love Dogs* is the commandment not only in the personal ad in that 2005 movie but also for romantic comedy aficionados. Skippy, the famous wire-haired terrier who plays Asta in the first two of the Thin Man movies, and shows up again in *The Awful Truth* and *Bringing Up Baby*, has sired litters of descendants. Dogs are partially about love—the dog's affection for Melvin (Jack Nicholson) in *As Good As It Gets* proves that at heart he is lovable even when his behavior is at its worst. Yet dogs blend cuteness with unpredictability—they run, they bite, they bark; they pull their owners in unexpected directions; they steal intercostal clavicles. In short, as well as fleshing out the best and sometimes the worst in the genre's cast of characters, they bring the green world indoors.

Even more than barking, music proves to be the food of love in romantic comedy. Particularly in the new romances after 1989, this genre leans toward popular song, the more familiar the better. Songs such as "All of Me," "Down With Love," "One Fine Day," "Sweet Home Alabama," "Peggy Sue Got Married," "Something to Talk About," "Pretty Woman," and "Love Potion #9" provide the titles of movies in which they are heard. Old standards from the American songbook, "It Had to Be You," "Stardust," "Fly Me to the Moon," and "You Were Meant for Me," live again on the genre's sound tracks. Filmmakers cleverly harness our nostalgic affection for these romantic classics to engender similar feelings for the story at hand. Music also forges interfilm connections. For instance, both *How to Lose a Guy in 10 Days* and *Kate and Leopold* (2001) include "Moon River," the theme song from *Breakfast at Tiffany's*. The romantic-comedy connoisseur feels a flush of pride at recognizing the reference.

Northrop Frye notes that comedies signal the appearance of a new society by some kind of party or festive ritual. The most common festivals in romantic comedy are holidays and weddings. Christmas songs, Christmas trees, Christmas dinners, Christmas gifts stack higher and higher with each new romantic comedy produced. Hundreds of romantic comedies take place at the time of the winter solstice and the turning of the earth toward sunlight. Those few that don't take place at Christmas choose New Year's Eve, Valentine's Day, Thanksgiving, or, occasionally, Midsummer's Eve. These nodal points of the year are recognized and ritualized times when society as a whole celebrates emotional connection and renewal. While studios tend to release action blockbusters in summer, for students out of school, they traditionally hold romances for the winter season.

As for weddings, who can keep track of the number of weddings seen on the screen in romantic comedies? Weddings, weddings, weddings—planned, cancelled, fled, and interrupted. Wedding, weddings, weddings—quiet elopements, vulgar Vegas chapels, full-regalia extravaganzas in churches and on seashores and mountaintops. On the one hand, I hate these wedding scenes because they buy into the

***Sense and Sensibility* (1995)** *Sense and Sensibility*'s dual focus is on the two sisters' disparate approaches to romance: Elinor (Emma Thompson) and Marianne (Kate Winslet) each find that something of the others' temperament is essential to true happiness. This ending shot occurs after the sisters' double wedding, where Colonel Brandon (Alan Rickman) throws coins up into the air, a gesture demonstrating generosity and community. The music soars as the coins glitter and tumble down like rain, spreading the magic of a world set right. This ending, like so many concluding scenes, seeks to include the audience in the new society created by love.

consumer madness of the U.S. wedding industry and promote the lie that the best way to declare your love and start your future is to bankrupt your family on fleeting, extravagant, and ostentatious trappings (which on television leads brides to act like maniacs). But if we look at these ceremonies as anthropological rites, weddings are the ultimate festive rituals, celebrating family, connection, and hope, and they belong in this genre.

Some ancient Greek comedies ended with the actors inviting their audiences to an imaginary banquet. Frye notes that this is only fitting, because romantic comedies are communal; they ask the audiences to join in an imaginary wholeness and the satisfaction of misunderstandings resolved. While their music soars, romantic comedies typically conclude with some kind of onscreen frolic that captures the joyfulness and hopefulness of the world set right, creating a mild buzz of euphoria that temporarily sustains us, as the lights come on, and we leave the theater to face the cold wind and traffic.

(Still) Believing in Love in (500) Days of Summer

Summer: There's no such thing as love. It's fantasy.
Tom: Well, I think you're wrong.

(500) DAYS OF SUMMER (2009) walks on a knife-edge between ambivalence and reaffirmation of romance. According to one of the screenwriters, 75 percent of the story derives from two failed relationships he suffered through. The tale revolves around Tom Hansen (Joseph Gordon-Levitt), who works at the improbably named New Hampshire Greeting Cards Company (improbable because the business is located in downtown Los Angeles). Tom becomes infatuated with the new secretary, Summer Finn (Zooey Deschanel), who has a relationship with him but ultimately breaks it off and leaves the company. Although Summer tells Tom from the beginning that she isn't looking for commitment, Tom continues to believe that he can win her over; thus, when she dumps him he grieves deeply. They meet again by accident on the way to the wedding of a former coworker, and this enchanting encounter rekindles Tom's hopes, but a week later he sees that Summer is wearing another man's engagement ring. After going through a bottomless depression, Tom quits his job and decides to return to his original training/interest as an architect.

When the director, Marc Webb, says on the commentary track that this film is a "coming-of-age story masquerading as a romantic comedy," he reveals that he doesn't know what we know: *all* romantic comedies stress lovers' journeys toward maturity. Tom must reevaluate the relationship and grow up, realizing, first, that Summer was always honest with him, second, that he had overidealized the relationship, and finally, that he is responsible for his own life and happiness.

In the last scene Tom meets another young woman, someone who has noticed *him* before (when he was oblivious to her). Unlike Summer, whose career interests the film never mentions, this young woman is also seeking employment as an architect. Instead of Summer's quirky, childlike, hipster garb, this woman wears a tailored pants suit. In her five minutes on screen, she makes a delightful impression. Tom makes a date with her for coffee. Her name is Autumn.

***(500) Days of Summer* (2009)** Tom's (Joseph Gordon-Levitt) infatuation with Summer (Zooey Deschanel) infects the cinematography. This sequence occurs on the train to a coworker's wedding, where the two run into one another. The warm orange color, the soft focus, the hand-held camera, and the background music, "Sweet Disposition," indicate how seeing her again sweeps Tom off his feet. The mise-en-scène mimics the romantic glow that catapults him back into infatuation.

Although divorce has been a plot point of romantic comedy since the silent era, romantic comedies of the last two decades often focus on the impact of parental separation on their grown-up children, and the ways in which the scars of those breakups have affected their offspring's openness to romance. *Reality Bites* (1994) features Winona Ryder and Ethan Hawke in an exploration of recent college grads lost in a world of un- and underemployment, afraid of AIDS, but mostly traumatized by their parents' divorces and stuck in terms of moving forward in life and love. In several studies the popular psychologist Judith Wallerstein has found that the prevalence of divorce is reshaping American society in many ways; she theorizes that children who grow up with no model of a successful relationship may either over-idealize love or become commitment-phobic. *(500) Days of Summer*'s opening narration highlights exactly these themes:

> This is a story of boy meets girl. The boy, Tom Hansen of Margate, New Jersey, grew up believing that he'd never truly be happy until the day he met The One. This belief stemmed from early exposure to sad British pop music and a total misreading of the movie *The Graduate*. The girl, Summer Finn of Shinnecock, Michigan, did not share this belief. Since the disintegration of her parents' marriage she'd only love two things. The first was her long, dark hair. The second was

how easily she could cut it off and feel nothing. Tom meets Summer on January 8th. He knows almost immediately she's who he's been searching for. This is a story of boy meets girl, but you should know up front, this is not a love story.

(500) continues to stress the changing nature of American family structures at the start of the story proper. Day 1 begins in Tom Hansen's office, where his friend McKenzie is proposing a new occasion for greeting cards:

> Maybe playing it safe is the wrong approach. The nuclear family is dead, and we need a new holiday that recognizes that. May 21st— [*he turns over an easel to show a prototype card*] *Other* Mother's Day.

Ultimately, however, *(500)* is a completely uncynical film. It believes fervently in old-fashioned romance. Rather than accepting a new model of loose relationships comprising tangential connections of friends, lovers, and associates—the "island chains" embraced by *About a Boy*—this movie is saying: "If you love someone and this person doesn't love you back, you are wrong to give up hope or believe your life is ruined. Your crush just was not The One. Love still exists out there." To impart this romantic, hopeful statement in a cynical time, *(500)* walks a fine line between innovation and convention.

(500) Days of Summer departs from the typical romantic comedy because it is resolutely single-focused, and moreover it focuses on the *man's*—not the woman's—search for love. Although the narrator tells us a few things about Summer, and the opening credits present a split-screen montage of their dual childhoods, the present-day story never includes a scene of her alone without Tom, and we always see her through his smitten eyes. Many romantic comedies feature a character whom Tamar McDonald calls "the unsuitable partner," such as Bruce (Ralph Bellamy) in *His Girl Friday* and Walter (Bill Pullman) in *Sleepless in Seattle*, yet these suitors' characterizations and the ways in which they are lit and framed clue the viewers into their unsuitability from the moment we meet them. In *(500)*, however, we see Summer only through Tom's eyes, through the eyes of his infatuation. She is mysterious and fetching, with a husky Jean Arthur voice. Moreover, unlike typical romantic comedies, we don't meet the suitable partner until the very end. Summer is not "The One" for Tom, but the unreliable camera leads us astray.

Along with its key switch away from dual focus, *(500)* throws onto the screen every technique for archly noting its own self-awareness. Romantic comedies always wink at the audience and often include cute transitional devices such as dividing *Love and Basketball* into the quarters of a basketball game or including airplane trajectory maps in *Sleepless in Seattle*. But *(500)* goes to extremes. In addition to the narrator with an overly sonorous voice who comes in from time to time, and who is not wholly trustworthy, the film uses intertitles noting which day the scene takes place and reshuffles chronology so that the presentation leaps back and forth in time. It switches to black-and-white footage for key moments, such as a montage of the Tom and Summer growing up, and when Tom imagines himself in European art films. The filmmakers mix in animation, both to stress the passing of the seasons on the intertitles and to mark Tom's feeling of self-erasure when his heart breaks. The screen splits in half several times, most effectively to contrast Tom's fantasy of what will happen when he goes to Summer's rooftop party versus the reality of what actually takes place. In one sequence, characters talk directly to the camera as if they were being interviewed for a documentary about love. After Tom and Summer sleep together for the first time, the movie temporarily morphs into a musical, with all the passersby in the street turning into backup performers for Tom as he dances and sings to a popular song while fountains surge in time to the music and a cartoon bluebird perches on his shoulder. Although some critics and viewers find the film too cute, I agree with *Sight and Sound* that these distortions from realism make the film an "almost indecently charming indie-whimsical romantic comedy."[4]

Along with being self-conscious about its own status as a movie, *(500)* is completely self-aware about the ways in which previous romantic comedies and other cultural products have colored our ideas about love. We see Tom at about age fourteen watching *The Graduate*; he thinks the ending is happy, that Ben (Dustin Hoffman) and Elaine (Katharine Ross) have managed to escape their parents and their problems and run off toward a blissful future. Nothing shows the unbridgeable gap between Summer and Tom so well as her (more accurate) understanding that the film's ending is bleak and Tom's inability to see why it leaves her crying inconsolably.

Although *(500)* provides no evidence that Tom ever understands *The*

---

[4] Kate Stables, "(500) Days of Summer," *Sight and Sound* 19 (2009): 64.

(500) Days of Summer (2009) During the scene in the park at the end of film, Summer tells Tom that he was right to believe in love, "but it just wasn't *me* that you were right about." Note how the camerawork is now more "objective"; the gray day, still camera, and the sharper focus let viewers know that this is truly happening, and that Tom is seeing clearly now. Tom's pain is real, but he is no longer willfully blinded by his infatuation.

Graduate, eventually he realizes how he has been taken in by pop culture. On Day 442 in a scene at the greeting-card company, Tom explicitly spells it out for the viewer.

> This is lies. We are liars.... It's these cards, *and the movies and the pop songs* [my emphasis], they're to blame for all the lies and the heartache, everything. And we're responsible. *I'm* responsible. I think we do a bad thing here. People should be able to say how they feel, how they really feel, not, ya know, some words that some strangers put in their mouths. Words like "love," that don't mean anything. Sorry, I'm sorry, I um, I quit. There's enough bullshit in the world without my help.

Such a caustic indictment is inconceivable in *Sabrina* or *While You Were Sleeping*. Even Woody Allen—who knows full well how movies influence our perceptions—would never attack his beloved *Casablanca* (1942) in such a manner.

(500) also differs from many other romantic comedies in its relatively modest budget and casting. While the R-rated *Forgetting Sarah Marshall*, another movie that focuses on a young man who loved and lost, cost $30 million to make, was produced by Judd Apatow, and was distributed by Universal, the PG-13–rated *(500)* was an independent

production made for $7.5 million and distributed by Fox Searchlight. More like *High Fidelity* (2000), *Juno* (2007), and *Easy A* (2010), *(500)* did not open at multiplexes around the nation, but instead premiered at the Sundance Film Festival and was catapulted to fame from there. The stars, too, were comparative unknowns at the time the film was made. Throughout the history of the genre, from Clara Bow and Clark Gable to Jennifer Aniston and Hugh Jackman, romantic comedies have traditionally featured the most glamorous, sexiest, biggest stars around. Gordon-Levitt, by contrast, was then familiar to fans of the television series *3rd Rock from the Sun* (1996–2001), while Deschanel was known for her career as a singer and supporting player on TV and in movies. Neither actor projects the assurance, glow, or narcissism of a major star: both are relatively believable as ordinarily attractive young adults, floundering as they try to establish their lives' trajectories. Some viewers didn't like *(500)* because they don't respond to Deschanel, and/or they find Summer too selfish and unpleasant. I believe we are supposed to be distanced from Summer.

In other respects, *(500)* follows the conventions of traditional romantic comedy. Summer is another manifestation of the unruly woman. She is madcap in rather trivial ways, such as her insistence on shouting "penis" in the middle of a public park and threatening to do so at Millie's wedding, and in making the first move by kissing Tom in the copy room. Summer is also, like many unruly women of the genre, quite blunt in expressing her opinions, open about her sexual desire, and more than a little selfish: although she tells Tom she just wants to be friends, she dances with him at the wedding because she wants to, oblivious of or uncaring about how this leads him on. (Her transgressions, however, don't really compare to the completely freewheeling, out-of-control kookiness of Susan in *Bringing Up Baby* or Clementine in *Eternal Sunshine of the Spotless Mind*). What is unusual is her disavowal of the traditional female goal of seeking love and marriage. She asks Tom and McKenzie: "You don't believe that a woman could enjoy being free and independent?...I just don't feel comfortable being anyone's girlfriend. I don't actually feel comfortable being anyone's anything, you know?" She continues, "I like being on my own. Relationships are messy, and people's feelings get hurt. Who needs it? We're young, we live in one of the most beautiful cities in the world, might as well have fun while we can and save the serious stuff for later." In a role reversal, Summer takes the stereotypical position of many commitment-phobic men, such as Brad Allen in *Pillow Talk* and Connor Mead (Matthew McConaughey) in *Ghosts of Girlfriends Past* (2009).

Yet Summer, like all the romantic comedy heroines who break convention, is ultimately tamed. As the filmmakers remark in their commentary, Summer is a closet romantic. She does fall in love, and does want marriage and commitment—just not with Tom. At the film's end, wearing more expensive clothes and jewelry, acknowledging that Tom was right all along to believe in love, she has become someone else's (more docile?) wife.

Although *(500)* includes no dogs, no Christmas or New Year's holidays, and no disguises, it follows romantic comedy iconography in other respects. Here, the city, the antithesis of the boring Shinnecock, is not Manhattan, but Los Angeles. The filmmakers carefully shoot around the tackiness of contemporary strip malls and billboards to focus on the most historic buildings and neighborhoods of L.A., to make it appear like a hip venue where one can walk along sidewalks and dip into record stores and coffee shops. Only one scene takes place in a car, and no one ever hits traffic or looks for parking.

The green world emerges in two key locations in *(500)*. The first is the small hillside park that is Tom's favorite spot in Los Angeles. Tom takes Summer to this patch of green when he first starts talking about architecture; she looks for him there when she wants to explain herself; and Autumn says that she has previously noticed Tom there. The green world also appears as San Pedro, the location of Millie's wedding, a beautiful outdoor venue for the ceremony and reception that leads to Tom's reinfatuation.

On first hearing, the music track of *(500)* seems transgressive. Instead of Jimmy Durante croaking "As Time Goes By," as in *Sleepless in Seattle*, Ella Fitzgerald crooning "I Love Paris," as in *French Kiss*, or the classic Frankie Valli song, "Can't Take My Eyes Off You," as in *10 Things I Hate about You*, *(500)* turns to lesser-known, quirky, indie bands from Canada, the U.K., and Australia, singing songs less inflected by the audience's previous associations and nostalgia. The Smiths, an indie band famous in England in the 1980s, who bring Tom and Summer together, are not household names but a mark of exclusive hipness. Although the sound track includes some familiar pieces, such as Simon and Garfunkel's "Bookends," Hall and Oates's "She Makes My Dreams," and Patrick

Swayze's "She's Like the Wind," these serve more as grace notes or ironic commentary than as theme songs. Yet *(500)* does use music to create romance and tug at our heartstrings. The closest thing to a theme song is "Sweet Disposition" by Temper Trap, a very up-tempo piece, with electric guitars reverberating as the group sings, in a high register, lines such as "We won't stop to surrender" and "Won't stop till it's over." The song voices Tom's refusal to give up on Summer. The film's trailer features "Sweet Disposition."

As befits an indie film, Summer does not wear Prada or go shopping on Rodeo Drive. But that doesn't mean that *(500)* avoids consumerism. It carefully includes a "dress up" scene: the camera lingers over both Summer and Tom in their going-to-a-wedding finery, just as it lingers over Loretta and Ronnie at Lincoln Center in *Moonstruck*. *(500)* also venerates IKEA, the mother lode of all furnishing for young couples, and foregrounds the pleasures of records and movies.

To me, *(500)* qualifies as a "new" romance rather than an "ambivalent" or "nervous" one questioning whether love is real or possible, because its director designed the film to be sincere and hopeful. The commentary track includes a fascinating argument between the screenwriters and director over the film's two final scenes. The screenwriters believe Tom might possibly be imagining his last interaction with Summer, the crucial scene in the park when he lets go of his bitterness. The director, however, says this scene is real, and *that is how he shot it*; unlike other whimsical moments in the movie, no cinematic techniques mark this scene as fantasy.

Also, the screenwriters say they are not sure that Tom's relationship with Autumn will work out. But Webb is very careful to give viewers every indication that it will. First he shoots the top of the elevator gears, the wheels of the universe moving. Then the narrator comes in again.

> Most days of the year are unremarkable. They begin and they end with no lasting memories made in between. Most days have no impact on the course of a life. May 23rd was a Wednesday.... If Tom had learned anything, it was that you can't ascribe great cosmic significance to a simple earthly event. Coincidence, that's all anything ever is. Nothing more than coincidence.... Tom had finally learned there are no miracles. There's no such thing as fate. Nothing is meant

to be. He knew; he was sure of it now. Tom was—[Tom stops walking toward his interview and goes back to Autumn—in the waiting area] he was pretty sure.

Here, as at the beginning when the narrator warned us "this is not a love story," we must weigh his words carefully against other evidence. After Tom makes his date with Autumn, he looks at the camera. The intertitle starts over on Day 1, but *this time with rays of sunshine streaking from the sun in the sky.* Most important, as the credits start to roll, the ending song, "She's Got You High," speaks directly to the viewer. It tells us that romance is alive, and admits that we all want a happy ending. *(500)* gives us the happy ending: Tom, now mature, can stand on his own two feet, and Autumn is The One. Ultimately, *(500)* IS a love story.

Sarah Kozloff

QUESTIONS FOR DISCUSSION

1. Which romantic comedy stars do you respond to, and why?
2. Which romantic comedies would you nominate for the Pantheon of Most Sexist Films?
3. Aside from the festive ritual explanation given above, why would romantic comedies often include Christmas scenes?
4. Another way to categorize romantic comedy is by age group: teen, young adult, and mature. How do the conventions discussed here change by demographic subset?
5. Imagine a romantic comedy that truly resisted the consumerist bent of the genre. What would it be like?

FOR FURTHER READING

Abbott, Stacey and Deborah Jermyn, eds. *Falling in Love Again: Romantic Comedy in Contemporary Cinema.* London: I. B. Tauris, 2009.

Carson, Diane. "To Be Seen but Not Heard: *The Awful Truth.*" In *Multiple Voices in Feminist Film Criticism*, edited by Diane Carson, Linda Dittmar, and Janice R. Welsch, 213–25. Minneapolis: University of Minnesota Press, 1994.

DiBattista, Maria. *Fast-Talking Dames.* New Haven, CT: Yale University Press, 2001.

Evans, Peter William and Celestino Deleyto, eds. *Terms of Endearment: Hollywood Romantic Comedy of the 1980s and 1990s*. Edinburgh: Edinburgh University Press, 1998.

Frye, Northrop. *The Anatomy of Criticism*. Princeton, NJ: Princeton University Press, 1957.

Gehring, Wes D. *Romantic vs. Screwball Comedy: Charting the Difference*. Lanham, MD: Scarecrow Press, 2002.

Grindon, Leger. *The Hollywood Romantic Comedy: Conventions, History and Controversies*. Malden, MA: Wiley-Blackwell, 2011.

Harvey, James. *Romantic Comedy in Hollywood from Lubitsch to Sturges*. New York: Knopf, 1987.

Henderson, Brian. "Romantic Comedy Today: *Semi-Tough* or Impossible?" *Film Quarterly* 31, no. 4 (1978): 11–23.

Karnick, Kristine Brunovska, and Henry Jenkins, eds. *Classical Hollywood Comedy*. New York: Routledge, 1994.

Kendall, Elizabeth. *The Runaway Bride: Hollywood Romantic Comedy of the 1930s*. New York: Knopf, 1990.

Kozloff, Sarah. "About a *Clueless* Boy and Girl: Romantic Comedy Today." *Cinephile* 8, no. 1 (Spring 2012): 4–13.

———. "Word Play: Dialogue in Screwball Comedies." Chap. 5 in *Overhearing Film Dialogue*. Berkeley: University of California Press, 2000.

McDonald, Tamar Jeffers. *Romantic Comedy: Boy Meets Girl Meets Genre*. London: Wallflower Press, 2007.

Moddelmog, Debra A. "Can Romantic Comedy Be Gay?: Hollywood Romance, Citizenship, and the Same-Sex Marriage Panic." *Journal of Popular Film and Television* 36, no. 4 (2009): 162–73.

Neale, Steve. "The *Big* Romance or *Something Wild*?: Romantic Comedy Today." *Screen* 33, no. 3 (Autumn 1992): 284–99.

Rowe, Kathleen. *The Unruly Woman: Gender and the Genres of Laughter*. Austin: University of Texas Press, 1995.

Harry Potter and the Deathly Hallows: Part 2 (2011)

The Fantasy Film

"CLAP YOUR HANDS IF YOU believe in fairies!" Or if you believe in fantasy. Peter Pan's famous command to the young at heart to save Tinker Bell would seem to tell us that the fantasy genre provides a whimsical way to pretend that the impossible and the fantastic are real. However, this conventional, slightly condescending definition contains only a partial truth. Some fantasy films *are* pure escapism containing technologically induced special effects intended solely to amaze children, or the child in the adult. But more evolved fantasy films stretch the ordinary understanding of reality for a higher, more serious purpose: to encourage an expanded sense of the possibilities that are necessary if we are to avoid a clichéd and limited, ultimately hopeless attitude toward our lives.

The Wizard of Oz (1939), based on *The Wonderful Wizard of Oz*, a children's book by L. Frank Baum, allows its heroine, Dorothy, and the audience to leave the hardscrabble Kansas of the period for the wonderland of Oz in order to move, in spirit, beyond the tyranny of the small-minded Almira Gulch, the richest, most vindictive woman in town. Other films of approximately the same period bent the limits of the real to show us the oppressive capitalist system (*Lost Horizon*, 1937); often overlooked everyday heroism (*It's a Wonderful Life*, 1946), and frequently mocked alternative masculinities (*Harvey*, 1950) from unusual and enlightening perspectives. And when the hero of a Hollywood film climbs down off the screen in *The Purple Rose of Cairo* (1985), our sense of the pathos of escapism in a harsh world is suddenly complicated by a cluster of insights into the heartwrenching fragility of hope and the consolations of fantasy. Even the child-oriented Harry Potter series (2001–2011) pushes back the boundaries of ordinary life through fantasy to give us a chance to see the repressiveness of modern Western culture through the eyes of a magical boy. The fantasy genre has continued to be escapist in part, but as it has developed, it has also continued to engage with social criticism and philosophical speculation. These two forms of fantasy emphasize a positive outlook on life and offer us opportunities to avoid getting stuck in a rut, emotionally, intellectually, and spiritually.

Because fantasy knows no geographical limits, there are no typical settings for fantasy films. Where Westerns are almost invariably set in barely populated small towns and the open plains, deserts, and mountains of the "old West," fantasy films might be located in a jungle, an urban department store, a mythical kingdom, rural Kansas, or a New Jersey movie theater. Because fantasy is part of every artist's vocabulary, important stars and directors sometimes make live-action fantasy films, but until recently none has been primarily associated with them. A recent exception is Tim Burton, who, beginning with *Beetlejuice* (1988), has become a celebrated director of fantasy films. Earlier, technicians Willis O'Brien and Ray Harryhausen, about whom more below, became famous for innovations that made fantasy easier to visualize, and The Walt Disney Studios is particularly significant to the development of animated film, which is inevitably a part of the fantasy genre. However, the bulk of fantasy films have emerged from a variety of studios and have been brought to life by a wide range of actors and directors. What is the history of this almost boundless genre? How can it be defined? What is its iconography?

History

The fantasy film did not start in Hollywood, but in France, with a former magician, Georges Méliès, when the movies were a new form of entertainment. As early as 1896, Méliès pioneered the use of special effects in short films like *The Devil's Castle* and *The Vanishing Lady* (both 1897), and in 1902 he made the famous animated fantasy film called *Le Voyage dans la lune*, a.k.a. *Voyage to the Moon*, which is sometimes referred to as the first science-fiction film. However, it is so whimsical and so innocent of the technological realism associated with science fiction that it can, perhaps with more accuracy, be identified as one of the first fantasy films. Méliès made 551 films that pushed forward the European development of the genre. In the United States, there was no such early champion, and fantasy films were relatively rare before the 1930s. We have little information about American silent fantasy films. However, we do have the full prints of the four whimsical screen adaptations of Baum's *The Wonderful Wizard of Oz*—much changed from the original—made between 1910 and 1933: *The Wonderful Wizard of Oz* (1910), *His Majesty, the Scarecrow of Oz* (1914), *The Wizard of Oz* (1925), and *The Wizard of Oz* (1933). The 1933 version, which is animated, depicts the scenes in Kansas in black and white and Oz in color, and in the world-famous 1939 adaptation of this story, director Victor Fleming followed suit.

Among the most inventive of the pretalkie fantasy films of the 1920s were short animations of Max and Dave Fleischer, especially Dave's Koko the Clown character. The Fleischers made at least twenty-one Koko cartoons between 1925 and 1927, combining live and cartoon action. The Fleischers used live-action footage of an animation artist drawing Koko as a still image, after which Koko would "come to life." Koko was so central to Dave Fleischer's career that he and his brothers, Max and Lou, named their company "Out of the Inkwell Films." Highly unusual in the 1920s, Fleischer's Koko remains unique even today; fantasy films rarely show us the construction of their illusions. Fleischer's other inspired animated creation is Betty Boop, a cheerful cartoon flapper with a high, nasal voice who endures today as a favorite cult fantasy heroine.

Because of their romanticized costumes, their dreamlike settings, and their highly improbable events, certain kinds of American adventure/romance films made in this early period are also included by some critics in the category of fantasy films. Matinee idol Rudolph Valentino's films are set in fantasy versions of India and the Middle East—for example, *The Sheik* (1921) and *The Young Rajah* (1922). Similarly, the swashbuckling films of action-adventure star Douglas Fairbanks are often referred to as fantasies, for example *The Thief of Bagdad* (1924) and *Don Q, Son of Zorro* (1925). In the same category of fantasy films are the silent Tarzan movies, which take place in an Africa of the imagination. In 1918, Elmo Lincoln starred in a pair of Tarzan adventures, *Tarzan of the Apes* (1918) and *The Romance of Tarzan* (1918), which recount onscreen the popular stories by Edgar Rice Burroughs set in a pristine corner of African jungle ruled by a white man who was raised by apes after surviving a plane crash in the jungle that killed his parents.

The advent of synchronized-sound film in 1927 opened up new opportunities for fantasy films. Early synchronized-sound fantasy films continued to transport the audience to visually daydream-like adventures, but now the fantasy world was also a domain of fantasy sound. The six Tarzan films of the 1930s and 1940s made by MGM show Tarzan wrestling wild animals and performing great athletic feats, including swimming, since this Tarzan was played by Olympic swimming champion Johnny Weissmuller. They also enriched the fantasy with the sounds of his environment. The Tarzan soundtracks resound with the music of the indigenous black Africans who live near Tarzan's special preserve, known in the Weissmuller films as The Escarpment, with the sounds of the animals who are Tarzan's friends and enemies, and with conversations between Tarzan and Jane Parker (Maureen O'Sullivan), the beautiful English woman brought to Africa by her father. But, most important, sound permitted Tarzan a characteristic cry. In the first of the Weissmuller Tarzan films, *Tarzan the Ape Man* (1932), the audience hears Tarzan's cry before it sees him. Tarzan's cry—once heard, never forgotten—became an important signal to the audience that either he himself or the friendly herds of animals under his command were on the way. All subsequent Tarzan movies define the jungle hero partly by that cry.

In another jungle fantasy from early sound pictures, *King Kong* (1933), Kong, a twenty-foot gorilla, is also heard by the audience crashing through the jungle underbrush of Skull Island before he is seen. Sounds made by Kong and by the other prehistoric animals on the island are a big part of this wild tale of Karl Denham (Robert Armstrong) and his group of filmmakers, who find Kong in a mysterious uncharted location where they plan to shoot an adventure film. Even more crucial was a technique, new at the time, developed by Willis O'Brien, called stop-motion animation, which brought Kong to life, and thereby revolutionized the fantasy film.

More sinister and conjuring more fear than the usual fantasy film, *King Kong* is sometimes classified as a horror film. The only rationale for including it in the fantasy category is that, unlike most horror films, it also includes a touching love story, the affection of the great ape for Ann Darrow (Fay Wray), a petite blonde actress Denham brings with him to star in his doomed film. Through the miracle of stop-motion animation, at the end of the story, Kong escapes from Denham's show and turns New York City upside down, finally scaling the Empire State Building, as he tries to find a place to be alone with Darrow. After Kong ascends the façade of the world-famous New York landmark, he is shot down by a fleet of airplanes, one of O'Brien's most notable contributions to the history of fantasy film, and Ann is reunited with Jack, her true (human) love.

The increased production of fantasy films during the 1930s was not only a function of improved sound and animation techniques; it was also the result of Hollywood's attempt to capitalize on national suffering during the Great Depression. Although money was scarce, movie attendance was high, as films helped Americans forget their hunger and fears for a few hours. Fantasy films were especially distracting, and once synchronized sound made it possible for movies to tell stories using music in a more central way, the fantasy genre began to include the fantasy musical, which wrapped the audience in glittering imaginary spectacles permeated by captivating melodies. One of the most charming fantasy musicals of the Great Depression was *Babes in Toyland*, a.k.a. *March of the Wooden Soldiers* (1934). It was a vehicle for the well-known comedy team of (Stan) Laurel and (Oliver) Hardy, who play Ollie Dee and Stannie Dum, two lovable nitwits who work in a toymaker's shop in a fairy-tale village and lodge in the big shoe in which Widow Peep (Florence Roberts) lives with her many children.

This movie, though on the surface a frothy musical comedy, has an interesting contemporary subtext that links characters from Mother Goose rhymes and well-known children's fairy tales with the financial problems of the American public. The village is a happy place, where the Three Pigs, Little Miss Muffett, Old King Cole, and many other fantasy characters sing and dance happily until a money problem rears its ugly head. Widow Peep falls on hard times and can keep her shoe house only if she gives her beautiful daughter Bo-Peep (Charlotte Henry) to the rich villain Silas Barnaby (Henry Kleinbach), who owns the mortgage on the Peep shoe. When Widow Peep tells him she hasn't got enough money for the mortgage payment, Barnaby threatens to turn the Peep family out into the street unless Bo-Peep becomes his bride. Bumbling Stannie and Ollie come to the rescue by arranging a daffy fake wedding in which they substitute Stannie under a heavy bridal veil for Bo-Peep. Barnaby is so enraged when the veil is lifted that he organizes an invasion of the blissful storybook village by a pack of monstrous "boogeymen."

But no villain can win when Ollie and Stannie are around to turn the world upside down. A mistake they have made at the toymaker's workshop with Santa Claus's order saves the day. Instead of building six hundred toy soldiers that are each one foot high, they have made one

Babes in Toyland, a.k.a. **March of the Wooden Soldiers (1934)** This heroic pairing of the soldier and the sweet, innocent little girl, projects a fantasy image of the stereotypical American hero whom old Hollywood typically brought in to save the day. There is even a trumpet call that precedes the march of the soldiers into the fairy-tale village reminiscent of the arrival of the cavalry in classical Western films. The soldier's woodenness can be seen as an inadvertent satire on the typical too-good-to-be-true heroes of mass market melodramas of the time. And the little girl, with her blond curls, recalls the Mary Pickford type of movie heroine from the days of silent movies.

hundred toy soldiers that are each six feet high. The toymaker's fury about this mix-up turns to glee, when, in a rip-roaring, funny climax, to a rousing version of Victor Herbert's "March of the Toys," Stannie's and Ollie's enormous mechanical militia routs the bogeymen—and Barnaby. Surely most of the audience was hoping that a battalion of wooden soldiers would save them from the Depression-era poverty they were forced to endure.

Snow White and the Seven Dwarfs (1937), the first full-length animated film, created by The Walt Disney Studios, did its part to comfort Depression weary Americans by enveloping the audience in a full-color, moving, talking, and singing picture book. By the time *Snow White* was released, the worst of the Depression was over, but the climb back was often grueling for many Americans and the trauma of abject poverty for people who had thought of themselves as middle class would last a lifetime. *Snow White* was not just for children. There was a large adult audience for the magical tale of the gorgeous princess with raven hair, red lips, and snowy skin and the adorable seven dwarfs who save her from her evil stepmother. Disney's animators embroidered the traditional fairy tale with events from the daily lives of the dwarfs and the lives of a wild-life community of birds, deer, rabbits, and other small animals who love and serve Snow White with as much devotion as Tarzan's elephants and chimps serve him. What's more, the songs Disney added to his fantasy define the longings and hopes of the Depression generation slowly returning to employment: primarily "Heigh Ho"; but also "I'm Wishing"; "Someday My Prince Will Come"; "Whistle While You Work"; and "With a Smile and a Song."

Walt Disney Studios has continued to make successful full-length, fantasy animated films that reflect the changing social conditions in America through timeless fairy tales. Among the most the most important of these are *Pinocchio* (1940), *Bambi* (1942), *Cinderella* (1950), *Peter Pan* (1953), *The Little Mermaid* (1989), and *Beauty and the Beast* (1991). The Disney Studios cartoon shorts starring Mickey Mouse, Donald Duck, and Pluto, which preceded *Snow White* by a decade and depicted fantasy versions of ordinary American domestic life lived by anthropomorphic animals, also continue to make up an important part of the American fantasy genre.

Likewise, *The Wizard of Oz* (1939), the tale of Dorothy (Judy Garland), a Kansas farm girl, and her adventures in Oz, contains not only a beautiful fantasyland, but also imaginative components that spoke eloquently to America just as it was lifting itself out of financial turmoil and facing a new challenge, the international storm brewing in Germany that would become World War II. The longing to escape to a better, anxiety-free place expressed by the song "Over the Rainbow," which Dorothy sings when daily life gets her down, could easily stand as the theme song for the entire fantasy film genre, and also as a coherent emotional articulation of the feelings of the average American of the period. Dorothy's wish to return home once she does reach the wonderful land of Oz might equally stand for the desire of the country to return to normality after its economic debacle. Moreover, hidden under this fantasy were a few other serious concerns. Dorothy and her friends the Scarecrow (Ray Bolger), the Tin Woodman (Jack Haley), and the Cowardly Lion (Bert Lahr) encounter angry talking trees, flying monkeys, and the Wicked Witch of the West (Margaret Hamilton), but they also learn the lesson that to be the best they can be they cannot rely on people like the Wizard of Oz (Frank Morgan) who make bogus claims to be "all-powerful," but rather that they must look to the power in themselves for transformation and growth. Their journey speaks to us in a fanciful way of familiar human dilemmas: rigidity (the tin man), lack of confidence (the lion), confusion (the scarecrow), and the problem of identity during the maturation process (Dorothy). Made at a time when dictators—Hitler, Mussolini, and Stalin—were rising in Germany, Italy, and Russia, the film is also eerily prescient, in its gentle way, about the danger of people putting their destinies in the hands of those who aspire to be all-powerful.

For the most part, the social meanings of *The Wizard of Oz* were inadvertent, and emerge only through acts of interpretation, but a slightly earlier film, *Lost Horizon* (1937), based on a novel by James Hilton, shows that sound also enabled a new kind of intentionally socially relevant fantasy film. *Lost Horizon* tells the story of five Americans and Britons who crash in the mountains of Tibet and discover a secret utopia called Shangri-La where no one is poor, all suffering is addressed by the community, and life is so healthy as a result that people live for hundreds of years. Slowly, all of the stranded passengers are detoxified by life in Shangri-La, where real brotherly love and cooperation are the order of the day instead of the cut-throat competition and greed that reign in the America and England they have left. Articulating the ideals of President Franklin D. Roosevelt's New Deal, which wrote into law an American government that took responsibility for the welfare of its people instead of espousing the sink-or-swim creed of the previous administration of Herbert Hoover, *Lost Horizon* pushed the envelope of the fantasy genre.

With its story of the noble Englishman Robert Conway (Ronald Colman), who finds love and peace in Shangri-La, *Lost Horizon* also introduces an interesting ambiguity to the fantasy film. Oz is unquestionably a dream, as are Toyland, Tarzan's Escarpment, and Snow White's castle. However, *Lost Horizon* suggests that Shangri-La might be real, a state of mind that can change life for the better if we learn to see the world in a different light. Although the fantasy genre in the 1940s continued to produce films that foreground fairy-tale elements and magic—for example, *I Married a Witch* (1942)—more fantasy films selling generosity of spirit and social responsibility followed in the wake of *Lost Horizon*.

Another example of this new type of fantasy film is *It's a Wonderful Life*, which celebrates the social responsibility of its hero, George Bailey (James Stewart), through the fantasy device of multiple time/space continuums. The film begins with an angel's-eye view of George and the ordinary daily life of Bedford Falls, the all-American small town where it is set, fusing the perspectives of angels and mortals to create multiple planes of existence. The angels watching George see him as a self-sacrificing idealist, and much as they may approve they also note that his philosophy is not working out too well. It's Christmas, and it looks like all of George's hard work to help his community is about to be destroyed by a combination of bad luck and a greedy businessman and slumlord named Henry F. Potter (Lionel Barrymore). In despair, George decides to commit suicide, feeling he is of no use to anyone. But he is stopped by Clarence (Henry Travers), a bumbling angel who will finally be given his wings if he can carry out a divinely inspired mission to give George something to live for.

Clarence, who makes up in heart what he lacks in brains, demonstrates to George the importance of his idealism when he gives him a glimpse of what life would have been like in his hometown if he had never been born. George's trip around Pottersville (what Bedford Falls becomes in the town's alternate reality as a result of there being no opposition to Mr. Potter) reveals to him that his very willingness to raise his voice on behalf of the little guy keeps his town from becoming the bitter, cold, miserable place it would be without him. Similar moralizing takes place in *Miracle on 34th Street* (1947), in which, also at Christmastime, a department-store Santa (Edmund Gwenn) insists that he is the real Kris Kringle. The pragmatic adults believe he is insane, but faith prevails, and by the end of the film, the holiday has returned to its true meaning of love, rather than the commercialized business bonanza it was at the beginning of the story. Is he or isn't he the real Santa? The film, which is full of contradictory clues about the old man's identity,

Miracle on 34th Street (1947)
In this frame from the first scene of the film, Kris Kringle (Edmund Gwenn) has just finished sternly lecturing a storeowner about an error in his Christmas display of Santa and his reindeer. Kringle is so convincing when he insists that the storekeeper has put the reindeer in the wrong order that the man and the audience can't help but wonder whether the old man is Santa Claus, as he claims, or a crazy old coot.

leaves us to ponder that question. Similarly, in Harvey, Elwood P. Dowd (James Stewart), a middle-aged man whose invisible friend is a six-foot rabbit named Harvey, shows his friends and family that what they think is mental disease is really a higher form of truth.

The decades that followed—the 1950s, 1960s, and 1970s—saw a temporary abandonment of this kind of idealistic fantasy and a proliferation of fantasy films based on the thrills of technological innovations that could produce increasingly spectacular special effects. The man most famous for creating the visual innovations of this time was Ray Harryhausen, who never made movies of the quality, fame, or importance of *The Wizard of Oz*, *Lost Horizon*, and *It's a Wonderful Life*, but who, by further developing Willis O'Brien's stop-motion animation techniques, made fantasy film extremely profitable.

Inspired by O'Brien's work in *King Kong*, Harryhausen modified the techniques used in that film to create his own movie of an exploited giant ape in love with a pretty young woman, *Mighty Joe Young* (1949). Unlike the special effects of the all-puppet stop-animation films made later by Tim Burton, Mighty Joe, like Kong, was an animated figure intended to interact seamlessly with live actors. Harryhausen went on to produce numerous highly successful fantasy films, like *The Beast from 20,000 Fathoms* (1953), *The Seventh Voyage of Sinbad* (1958), and, as late as 1981, *The Clash of the Titans*. But by 1973 his stop-motion animation was superseded in the fantasy genre by computer-generated imagery (CGI). In that year, CGI was first used in *Westworld*, a science fiction thriller, and has been increasingly used since then in all film genres. CGI, now a standard part of the commercial fantasy film, has been used by directors and set designers to create the atmosphere of blockbuster fantasy hits like the Lord of the Rings trilogy (2001–2003) and the Harry Potter films, two immensely popular series made possible by international collaborations between the United Kingdom and the United States.

Both Harryhausen's movies and the movies created through the magic of CGI tend to be of a piece with the preferred fantasies of the time, which were built on escapist formulas that flatter audience delusions of omnipotence, generating fantasies about getting a free pass from ordinary human limits. These films, inhabited by people and objects with unusual characteristics, include *Mary Poppins* (1964), a children's film about a flying nanny, and *Chitty Chitty Bang Bang* (1968), a family entertainment about a flying car. *The Lovebug* (1968), featuring Herbie, a talking car, was the first of a series of Herbie films. Other fantasy films of the period contain characters who could change shape. In *The Incredible Mr. Limpet* (1964), a man is granted his wish to be a fish. And in *Freaky Friday* (1976 and 2003), a mother and daughter find themselves in each other's bodies. During this period, the fantasy genre often "brought the comics to life." The Superman movies, starring Christopher Reeve (1978–1987), for example, allowed audiences to identify with the power of its superhero. There have since been recurring rashes of superhero films, including numerous Batman movies [*Batman* (1989), *Batman Returns* (1992), *Batman Forever* (1995), *Batman Begins* (2005), *The Dark Knight* (2008), and *The Dark Knight Rises* (2012)], four Spider-Man films [*Spider-Man* (2002), *Spider-Man 2* (2004), *Spider-Man 3* (2007), and *The Amazing Spider-Man* (2012)], and, for women, the Lara Croft films [*Lara Croft Tomb Raider* (2001) and *Lara Croft Tomb Raider: The Cradle of Life* (2003)]. However, there is some merging of socially responsible fantasy films and the escapism of technological fantasy in the Lord of the Rings trilogy and the eight-film Harry Potter series, which are interesting examples of CGI-enhanced superhero films with a difference. While offering the public heroes who are unrealistically empowered by magic, they also seriously consider the problems posed by our desire to escape human limits. The young hero Frodo (Elijah Wood) in the Lord of the Rings stories is spectacularly successful in dealing with the adult world of power politics, making sure that the ring of the title never falls into the wrong hands, but he is fatally wounded in the process. Recent Batman movies, especially the controversial *The Dark Knight Rises*, which engendered extreme audience violence when it was first shown, also use fantasy to evoke problematic social conditions.

Alongside these CGI festivals, a much more serious and sophisticated form of fantasy film grew up in the 1980s. These films root their fantasies firmly within ordinary settings and resist the temptation to seduce audiences with impossibly potent, generally victorious protagonists. One of the most affecting of this breed of fantasy films is *The Purple Rose of Cairo* (1985), set in New Jersey during the Great Depression, in which Woody Allen examines the siren call of fantasy escapism by juxtaposing it against the harsh realities of American working-class life. In the story, Cecilia (Mia Farrow), a mousy waitress bullied by both her mean-spirited employer and her selfish, faithless husband, Monk (Danny Aiello), is fired and goes to the movies to console herself with a romantic adventure film called *The Purple Rose of Cairo*. After Cecilia watches it for the fifth time, Tom Baxter (Jeff Daniels), the handsome

The Purple Rose of Cairo (1985) Cecilia (Mia Farrow) witnesses a debate between an actor, Gil Shepherd, and Tom Baxter, the character he plays in the film-within-the-film *The Purple Rose of Cairo* (Jeff Daniels), as Shepherd aims to control his runaway creation. Woody Allen captures here not only the conflict between the greed and ambition of the Hollywood industry and the idealistic characters with which it enchants the American public but also a foreshadowing of the consequences of Hollywood's brand of deception. Poor Cecilia's romantic fantasy is the mental equivalent of a sugar rush. At first, her spirits are raised by the imaginary hero Tom Baxter, but when he is taken from her, Allen raises the question of the value of the fragile happiness we get from fantasy.

hero of the movie, walks off the screen and into Cecilia's real life. They begin a romance that prompts Cecilia to think of leaving Monk, but their plans are thwarted by Gil Shepherd (Jeff Daniels), the actor who plays Tom. The studio heads are not happy that a film character has escaped their control and have threatened Gil with the loss of his career if he doesn't get Baxter back into the movie where he belongs. To protect his bottom line, Gil stoops to manipulation and lies to Cecilia, offering her himself as a better alternative to her miserable life than Baxter can ever be. He convinces her that real people must not lose themselves in fantasy, with the result that both Tom and Cecilia are destroyed by reality. Once Tom goes back onto the screen, the studio heads burn all the prints of *The Purple Rose of Cairo* and Gil goes back to Los Angeles, breaking his promises to Cecilia and abandoning her to her loved-starved, oppressive life.

In this film, Allen plays with the distinctions between fantasy and reality to arrive at a wistful portrait of the human condition. He suggests that in some ways fantasy may be more real than daily life in an America ruled more by a lust for money than a love of life and creativity. Gil Shepherd's creation of Tom Baxter, which should be a source of pleasure and pride to him, becomes a threat to his economic well-being and the economic interests of the movie studio, which fears that a virtual army of Tom Baxters will leave the screen in movie theaters all over the country and create chaos in the entertainment industry. This turn of events reveals an ironic split within Gil, who lives a life ruled by money, while his fantasy alter ego, Baxter, is more life affirming than the actor. With an intensity and intellectual focus never before seen in the fantasy genre, Allen turns the gaze of the genre on itself and demonstrates that if it is well made, fantasy, far from luring us away from life, can actually make us appreciate it more. In a final irony, Allen asks which is most fantastic, a character filled with love or the faith that real, greedy people put in green paper?

The boundary between fantasy and reality has steadily become a central issue in other popular and important fantasy films of the last twenty years, among the most provocative of which are *Edward Scissorhands* (1990), *Donnie Darko* (2001), and *The Curious Case of Benjamin Button* (2008). These films, although they are genre films, have an auteurist edge: the personal visions of their directors, as in *Purple Rose*, propel their stories. Tim Burton's views about the place of fantasy in American life are embedded in *Edward Scissorhands*, a story about a man fabricated by an inventor. The adventure begins when Peg (Dianne Wiest), an Avon Lady, finds Edward Scissorhands (Johnny Depp) alone in the now dead inventor's deserted mansion on a hill above her suburban community and brings him home. Gentle and loving, Edward was never finished by his creator, who died before he could make Edward's hands, and so he must live with what were supposed to be temporary hands made out of scissors. Like Tom Baxter, Edward is not real, but, like Tom Baxter, Edward is more loving than any of the characters of woman born.

At first, Edward charms the locals with his difference. Uneducated in the ways of normal life and possessed of his special "hands," he creates wonderful fantasy topiary for the neighborhood gardens, grooms pets innovatively, and designs one-of-a-kind hairstyles for the women in the community. But his scissor hands are also clumsy and dangerous, as he attempts to negotiate simple daily chores like sleeping and eating, and his naïveté makes him a patsy for bullies and a victim of both a sexually predatory woman and a religious fanatic who sees his difference as demonic. Eventually, Edward must run for his life from the community. With the help of Peg's daughter Kim (Winona Ryder), Edward makes the community believe he is dead and returns to his former isolation. Burton challenges his audience to think about whether America is capable of including the life-affirming and wondrous aspects of the imagination in our ordinary lives, considering the tyranny of the conformism that we call normal.

Similarly, Richard Kelly's *Donnie Darko* (2001) pits the power of the imagination against the repressive realities of materialist America. This film is the story of an imaginative suburban California boy, Donnie Darko (Jake Gyllenhaal), considered mentally ill by his family and his community. However, from the perspective of the film, Donnie has more options than ordinary people do and is more generous than "normal" people. The story focuses on the way his imagination grants him something rare in the selfish, materialistic world in which he lives, the willingness to sacrifice himself for the people he loves. At the beginning of the film, Donnie is on antidepressants, or is supposed to be, and regularly sees a therapist, whose goal is to socialize him. What his doctor and his family do not know is that Donnie is not taking his medicine and that he regularly has meetings with a six-foot rabbit who guides him toward acts of civil disobedience. Early in the film a crucial incident takes place. While Donnie is out talking to his giant rabbit, a piece of an airplane falls from the sky and lands on his empty room; in effect, his fantasy life saves him. Toward the end of the film, Donnie, the only character in the film who isn't consumed by looking out for number one, realizes that if he doesn't reverse the outcome of the airplane incident, his mother, sister, and girlfriend will die. With the help of Roberta Sparrow (Patience Cleveland), a strange recluse who was once a brilliant physicist, he turns time back to the moment when the plane part fell, and sacrifices himself to save his loved ones. Even more than in *The Purple Rose of Cairo*, this fantasy uses humane values to counter the "greed is good" philosophy of a money-mad America.

Donnie Darko borrows from many of the important fantasy films that preceded it: the double time continuum of *It's a Wonderful Life* and the giant rabbit of *Harvey*; the appreciation for the real granted by fantasy that drove *The Purple Rose of Cairo*, and the resurrection of Lois Lane by Superman when he turns back time in *Superman* (1978). Kelly reconfigures all these elements to add specific social commentary about the influences of vapid and ignorant cultural forces on the young people of Southern California, showing a school in which books are censored and the curriculum is influenced by a huckster, secretly involved in child pornography, who pedals half-witted self-help theories for the sole purpose of getting rich. Kelly also makes specific political references to the 1988 election campaign, during which George H. W. Bush ran against Michael Dukakis for president of the United States, and to the Republican sympathies of Donnie's parents.

David Fincher's *The Curious Case of Benjamin Button* (2008) transforms a witty short story of the same name (1921) by F. Scott Fitzgerald into a fantasy ode to the triumph of the human spirit. *Benjamin Button* is the story of a man who is born old but who grows younger as his life unfolds. When he is born, his mother dies and his father is so disgusted by his baby's strangely aged body that he abandons him on the steps of an old-age home, where he is taken in, loved, and cared for by Queenie (Taraji P. Henson), a black woman who works there. In the film, Button (Brad Pitt) has many adventures, including a passionate love affair with Daisy (Cate Blanchett), a beautiful, normal woman, who ages as Button gradually turns into a baby and dies in her arms. Set in New Orleans, the story of Button starts when he is born, as a clock that runs backward is set in motion in the main railroad station of the city by a clockmaker who wants to turn time back to a simpler age before the battlefield horrors of

The Curious Case of Benjamin Button (2008) In this frame, Benjamin (Brad Pitt) is seven years old but has the physical appearance of an old man weakened by ill health. Benjamin, abandoned by his father, has been brought by Queenie (Taraji P. Henson), a black woman who loves and cares for him, to a meeting of a southern black evangelical church, where she asks for a blessing that will give her and her husband a child, and another that will cure Benjamin so that he can walk. The congregation's embrace of Benjamin is a representative sample of director David Fincher's assertion that difference is only respected and nurtured on the margins of American society.

World War I. Fincher's film ends as the flood waters of Hurricane Katrina are pouring into the city and Daisy is dying. Whereas most literature and most films, including Fitzgerald's classic novel *The Great Gatsby*, tell us that you can't turn back the clock, in showing us time as a slippery river that runs many ways at once, *Benjamin Button*, calling on the power of fantasy, helps us see the human capacity for love in a new way.

Another glimpse into a seemingly impossible world, but one that also reflects our humanity, can be seen in the magical world of wizards. The Harry Potter series divides the turf of England between "muggles," human beings with narrow opinions about what is possible, and wizards, human beings who embrace a tradition in which time, space, and physical objects are all subject to an infinite number of permutations and combinations. Pictures and staircases are full of motion, not finite and stable. An abundance of magical meals and treats and the love and loyalty of animals and creatures such as elves are the natural right of wizards, while muggles are enclosed within much narrower, less exciting parameters. The conflict Harry Potter (Daniel Radcliffe) has with arch-villain Voldemort (Ralph Fiennes) takes him in and out of suburban England and London, as well as through the education system of Hogwarts as a representative of openness, and freedom of mind and spirit, while Voldemort represents solipsism, selfishness, and tyranny. The magical battles between Harry and his allies and Voldemort and his conspirators are complicated by the fact that a piece of Voldemort is in Harry. The fantasy paradox of Harry's adventures is that Harry's death at Voldemort's hands is the only way to kill Voldemort and save Harry's life. Harry is both dead and alive at the end of the saga. A real triumph over evil is only possible through going beyond the powers and skills of ordinary life. The Potter films strike a chord even with adults, who often find that pushing the envelope is the only way to deal with our moments of greatest human ordeal.

More recently, in *Midnight in Paris* (2011), Woody Allen distinguishes between the potency of genuine fantasy and the destructive influence of a different kind of fantasy, one that detaches us from a vibrant engagement in life. Allen opens the film with an extraordinarily long montage of the city that ravishes us with its beauty. Unlike *Purple Rose*, which is photographed with a gritty reality, *Midnight* is rich in saturated colors that depict Paris as a magical place that glows gold and white, even at night. As the story begins, we can see that the protagonist, Gil (Owen Wilson), is less sensitive to the glory around him than he should be because he lets it do little more than feed his illusions that Paris in the 1920s was infinitely superior to today's reality. Inez (Rachel McAdam), Gil's small-minded, though sexy, fiancée, recognizes the unfortunate hold this "golden age" fantasy has over Gil. But if Inez, who resembles her rich, shallow parents, can spot Gil's false illusion, she is not the solution to his problems, because of her own materialist fantasies. Viewing Paris as a big store, she too is completely blind to the real magic of Paris as it is today. It is only after Gil travels back in time that he comes to grips with the uncertainty of the present that has made him long for the past. The vehicle for time travel is a yellow 1920s Peugeot that stops for Gil at midnight; thus, this unscientific mode of leaving the present is not science fiction but pure fantasy, compounded by Gil's encounters with the great artists of the early twentieth century: Ernest Hemingway, F. Scott Fitzgerald, Gertrude Stein, and many others. Even delusional fantasy can be a potent form of travel. Gil's magical time travel broadens his perspective; he comes to understand that, in the words of William Faulkner, "the past isn't dead; it isn't even past." But at the same time, Gil learns not to idealize it. His education about the limits of the reductive fantasy of a golden age teaches him that people in all times look backward for perfection. Through productive fantasy, Gil is released from his narrow focus in the present, which has caused him to become engaged to the selfish Inez and to dream foolishly of living in a different time. He is rejuvenated and able to face in a mature way not only his anxieties about the present but also the promise it presents to him.

If we consider Allen's time-travel fantasy, Fincher's Benjamin Button fantasy, and the Harry Potter series, we find that the American entertainment industry is getting better and better at generating full-strength fantasy to tease our minds with multiple perspectives on a universe that seems, at least while we are watching the films, renewed and thrillingly alive with potential.

Typologies, Themes, and Theories

The fantasy film has taken many shapes in its long history, but one constant characteristic is that it has a "What if?" rather than a "This is" quality. Fantasy characters and stories are products of asking what would happen if someone knew more than ordinary human beings can know; or were stronger, smarter, or more creative. They ask what would happen if someone lived among beings who defy the laws of science; or animals and plants that fly, talk, or intentionally enter into human affairs as allies or enemies.

However, a film is not a part of the fantasy genre just because it contains a dream or a few frames of animation. Some films include fantasy sequences but are not fantasy films. In the musical comedy *Anchors Aweigh* (1945), for the first time, a live-action actor, Gene Kelly, dances on screen with a cartoon figure, a mouse called Jerry, from the Tom and Jerry cartoons. (Kelly was supposed to dance with Mickey Mouse, but Walt Disney refused MGM permission to use its character.) In the suspense thriller *Vertigo* (1958), Alfred Hitchcock famously includes a highly original dream sequence for the hero, Scottie Ferguson (James Stewart). In *American Beauty* (1999), a dark comic satire, the hero, Lester Burnham (Kevin Spacey) has a recurring daydream in which a young girl with whom he is erotically obsessed appears to him in a vision in which she is submerged in rose petals. None of these films is a fantasy film. They merely include fantasy sequences.

To qualify as part of the fantasy genre, a film may have some scenes that take place in ordinary reality, but it must contain a "What if?"question in its central premise. In *It's a Wonderful Life*, for example, at least half the film takes place within a realist framework, but the basic question in the film is a fantasy premise: "What if a man could see how the world would be if he had never been born?"

The "What if?" premise is also crucial to the horror film and the science fiction film. But fantasy films differ in several significant ways from the horror and science fiction genres. First, in horror films, the dominant emotion is fear, while in fantasy it is wonder. Fear, anxiety, and suspense are often part of the fantasy drama, but they don't overwhelm the spectator as the horror film does. Fantasy films differ from science fiction films primarily in their settings. Like fantasy films, science-fiction films often take place in locations no one has ever seen in real life. But the differences between science fiction locations and real places are founded on technology, or something like it, and the differences between fantasy locations and real places are founded on magic, or something like it—for example, the time-travel car in *Midnight in Paris* alludes to no principles from physics, unlike the spaceship in the television series *Battlestar Galactica*, for example.

Magic or forces equally inexplicable are behind fantasy films set in strangely changed ordinary locations and those that remove the

***It's a Wonderful Life* (1946)** Here, George Bailey (James Stewart) meets Clarence (Henry Travers), his guardian angel, who George thinks is an old man he has saved from committing suicide by drowning. Frank Capra chose to give Clarence and their meeting none of the conventional dramatic signs of divine intervention. Rather, both angel and encounter have the appearance of humble reality.

audience to whimsical places like Oz. The inexplicable forces are some-times explicitly associated with traditional magical creatures like witches, as in the Harry Potter films, which straddle both categories of fantasy films by featuring both a special place, the Hogwarts School of Witchcraft, and an unusual picture of the ordinary streets of England, in which ghosts and wizards might emerge at any time. But more often the events at the core of fantasy films are simply unfathomable. To fol-low the story of *The Purple Rose of Cairo*, when Tom Baxter walks off the screen, it is necessary to accept the strange event without explanation. Similarly, the ability of Herbie the car to talk and drive himself and the ability of Mary Poppins to levitate must be accepted at face value, as in dreams. By contrast, in the movies in the Star Trek series, every event is accompanied by a detailed, if fictionalized, technological explanation.

The strange occurrences that invade reality in fantasy films often challenge our faith in the stability of personal identity, a characteristic that is also typical of the horror genre. But in horror movies like *The Invasion of the Body Snatchers* (1956 and 1978), in which pod creatures rob people of their identities, there is a terror of losing oneself, while fantasy transformations suggests the wonderful consequences of expanding one's point of view. There have been numerous fantasy films in which characters are improved when identities fly between bodies, including *Goodbye Charlie* (1964), *Freaky Friday* (1976 and 2003), *All of Me* (1984), *Big* (1988), and *Switch* (1991). In both *Goodbye Charlie* and *Switch*, womanizing men who die return to life as women to experience men behaving badly from a different perspective. In *Freaky Friday*, the identities of a warring mother and daughter are switched, and they discover what it is like to walk in the other's shoes. In *All of Me*, the soul of a dying millionairess winds up in her male lawyer's body, opening up his perspective on gender. In *Big*, a little boy who wakes up in an adult body gets a preview of what it is like to be a man. Expansion of perspective is also an aspect of fantasy films in which the protagonist's personal identity is itself unusual, as in *It's a Wonderful Life, Donnie Darko*, and *The Curious Case of Benjamin Button*. They teach people the value of difference. Another example is *Being John Malkovich* (1999), in which an unsuccessful puppeteer discovers how to enter the mind of the actor John Malkovich. At first, he and his friends are interested only in how they can make money with this discovery. But ultimately, the importance of the merging with the actor creates new possibilities for them.

However, some critics, notably Joshua David Bellin in *Framing Monsters: Fantasy Film and Social Alienation*, have seen darker implications in films in the fantasy genre, arguing that they are inevitably predicated on subtextual attacks against minorities and marginalized groups. For many, this will sound like an outrageous idea, but a closer look at fantasy films, especially in the early sound period, suggests that it is exaggerated rather than completely baseless. For example, there is arguably subtextual anti-Semitism and racism that taints the sugary fantasy *Babes in Toyland*. Although neither Jews nor African Americans are explicitly present in Toyland, they are represented by the villain, Silas Barnaby, in stereotypical anti-Semitic makeup, and the monster bogeymen, costumed to replicate then-common racist images of African Americans. At the same time, the toy soldiers that rescue the village evoke the stereotypically heroic white Christian middle-class men of Hollywood films of the period.

However, if this is so, it is dangerous to assume definitive subtextual social messages on the basis of incomplete evidence. For example, some critics read the Tarzan films of the 1930s and the 1933 *King Kong* as categorically reactionary because of their treatment of their black African characters. However, while it is true that both the MGM Tarzan films and *King Kong* deal in racist stereotypes of black tribal peoples, we must also consider other subtexts. Side by side with the racism is a highly critical, progressive condemnation of the greedy exploitation of nature by Americans and Europeans. For example, there is more than just a "cute factor" to the many scenes of affectionate mother animals and their offspring and depictions of animal–human interaction in the Tarzan films. It is these scenes that validate Tarzan's rage at the white men who come to the jungle to sell and otherwise commodify the animals, ignoring their existence as feeling, intelligent beings who are part of living communities.

A similar mixture of racial narrow-mindedness and criticism of capitalist greed exists in *King Kong*. In this film, Africans are depicted as inferior in many ways to the white characters, and there is sexism in the way Ann Darrow is characterized as an object of passion rather than an active person in her own right. A typical damsel in distress, she spends the film screaming and crawling in terror, waiting for a man to rescue her. At the same time, there is a subtextual suggestion that Denham and company have no business pillaging Skull Island as they do. Animator Willis O'Brien subtly criticizes Denham's use of Kong as nothing more than a commodity by turning the huge ape into a character for whom we have so much sympathy that we may shed tears when he is killed at the end of the film. Clearly, this was not the intention of the filmmakers, but when Denham, the entrepreneur who brought Kong from Skull Island to New York, says that it wasn't the airplanes but rather beauty that killed the beast, some viewers may be thinking that it was neither planes nor beauty but greed that was responsible. If Denham had not taken Kong out of his natural habitat, the ape would not have created chaos in New York and wouldn't have had to die.

By the time that Peter Jackson remade *King Kong* in 2005, it was clear that progressive ideas had become dominant in the fantasy genre. Jackson told his version of the story of Kong by raising the subtexts of the original Kong film into the text of the film. Jackson both satirizes the racism and sexism of the original film and brings its themes of greed and exploitation to the surface. Moreover, Jackson does away with the implicit sexism of the 1933 version. Jackson's Ann Darrow (Naomi Watts) is not a pure victim. Although she does her share of screaming, she brings to bear enormous resources when she is Kong's prisoner. Her femininity becomes a civilizing force; she is not merely a sexual object and possession. Unlike the original Darrow, who is rendered oblivious by her nonstop hysteria, the updated Darrow gains insight into and sympathy for Kong. Jackson's remake touchingly and explicitly favors the difference that Darrow and Kong both represent from the greed of Denham (Jack Black) and the commercialism and militarism of American culture that produce the Denhams of the world.

The notion that fantasy films are *always* prejudiced against marginal people is also rendered suspect by the way *The Wizard of Oz, Miracle on 34th Street*, and *It's a Wonderful Life* advocate for the underdog and heap contempt on people who hold mainstream views about business: in these films, lives lived for the purpose of making money are also shown in an unflattering light. The villains of *Oz* and *Wonderful Life* are the richest people in town: Almira Gulch (Margaret Hamilton) in *Oz*, who is so lacking in humanity that she threatens the life of Dorothy's cherished dog, Toto, and Henry Potter in *Wonderful Life*, who drives the hero, a loving soul, to think of suicide. Similarly, the villain of *Miracle* is the Macy's psychologist, Granville Sawyer (Porter Hall), who has been so absorbed into the commercial culture that he attempts to get Santa Claus placed in a mental institution. Interestingly, in that film, R. H. Macy, the millionaire who owns the store, is not the villain, but only because he understands that it is to his economic advantage not to persecute Santa Claus!

Lost Horizon goes further than simply positioning the wealthy characters as villains. This is a film that defines paradise as a place where everything is shared, and people receive what they need, not just what they can afford, as under the capitalist system. Although its leader is a former priest who founded the utopia to make Christian values a political reality, Shangri-La is in many ways built on the ideals of communism and socialism, with its disdain for the profit motive, its emphasis on collective living, and its representation of a harmonious society built on the collective ownership of essential business enterprises. All the travelers from the outside world who get stranded in Shangri-La are defined by the kinds of character flaws that Karl Marx attributed to the bourgeoisie under capitalism. They get caught up in status and power struggles; they never think of doing anything for anyone but themselves; they are motivated only by money; they have problems with love relationships; and they suffer physical disorders from the nervousness associated with "getting ahead."

Nevertheless, this film also teaches us how inadvisable it is to read fantasy films simplistically. Its idealism is complicated by a good deal of

Lost Horizon (1937) This frame typifies the lush romanticism by means of which the social ideals of Shangri-La are represented. As Sondra (Jane Wyatt) explains the nature of society in Shangri-La to Robert Conway (Ronald Colman), the two are surrounded by the images of springtime and first love.

implicit racism. The explanations given by the founder of Shangri-La of his motivations are quite racist by today's standards, such as his opinion that the culture of Europe, which he has imported into his secret Tibetan hideaway, is the essence of genuine civilization. His prejudices are evident in the structure of Shangri-La where, primarily, Europeans rule and Tibetans do the manual work, Europeans teach and Tibetans learn—European culture. In the eyes of the film, Shangri-La is a cure for what ails European people.

On the whole, though, the destructive conformity of the majority is and has long been a major preoccupation of fantasy films. In *Harvey*, Elwood P. Dowd, the hero, is atypical of ideal American manhood, and yet it is he and not the mainstream Americans who is depicted with sympathy and admiration. Soft-spoken and dreamy, he displays none of the force and urge to dominate that "real" American men are expected to possess. "Real men" especially are not supposed to be best friends with an invisible six-foot rabbit named Harvey. Yet by the end of the film, *Harvey* has made the audience doubt the virtues of "real men" and the sane world, as it prompts us to see that what makes life truly worth living are the qualities of love and imagination that Dowd possesses in abundance. This too is a kind of political statement, about gender politics specifically. As with the fantasy films discussed above, however, there are competing and somewhat contradictory messages. Another part of the gender politics of this film is that it is particularly cruel in

***Harvey* (1950)** Elwood P. Dowd (James Stewart) politely waits for the invisible Harvey to precede him through the wrought-iron gate of his home. This image captures the essential details of the Dowd's situation as a middle-class man living with all the comforts of his social position, as well as the sense, sharply conveyed by the fence around his house, that he is imprisoned by his perquisites. Stewart's embodiment of Dowd's sunny refusal to permit himself to be constrained is also summoned up in this moment, as he blithely departs the premises with his fantasy friend.

its mockery of older women, who are portrayed as hopelessly foolish and unattractive; in fact, it is women who stand for the unimaginative normality of middle-class society, who look down on Elwood. Nevertheless, the film assures us that the world has been somewhat humanized by Elwood's presence.

For the most part, later fantasy films are less sexist. Certainly this is true of *The Purple Rose of Cairo, Edward Scissorhands, Donnie Darko,* and *The Curious Case of Benjamin Button.* The urban societies of *Purple Rose* and *Benjamin Button* are shown to lack tolerance for differences in both women and men in ways that cast light on a variety of social problems. In *Purple Rose,* Cecilia lives in a bleak sexist reality and finds release only at the movies. In *Benjamin Button,* issues of class and race arise when the central character's father, a rich white man, abandons him as a baby because he is different, and the task of the boy's up bringing is left to the poor black community, which tolerates Button's difference and loves him because they know only too well about being on the margins of society.

The suburban worlds of *Edward Scissorhands* and *Donnie Darko* are criticized for their materialism and conformity and for leaving little or no room for the differences that define the films' heroes or for the twists and turns of the human spirit. As in the urban films, there is little or nothing admirable about the suburban values of the majority. In *Scissorhands*, the identical pastel boxes in which the suburbanites live with their almost identical pastel cars are contrasted with the imaginative castle-like house on the hill above them where the inventor who created Edward lived. The people in the boxlike houses are the very personification of bored and miserable conformity; in contrast, Edward is loving, creative difference personified. The mainstream world is too narrow and too emotionally damaged to accept him, and ultimately chases him out of its domain. Darko's Southern California community is less oppressive and much more individuated than the *Scissorhands* world, but it constantly mistakes the aberrant for the truly marvelous and the truly marvelous for the aberrant. Darko's talents are mistaken for insanity

***Edward Scissorhands* (1990)** As Edward (Johnny Depp) looks into the mirror in a teenage girl's bedroom we see the sharp contrast between him and the suburban community to which he has been transported by a well-meaning Avon Lady. Suburbia is, in director Tim Burton's vision, essentially a feminized place, full of consumerism, icons of false beauty, and the tyranny of conformity with social norms. Edward, on the other hand, is associated with the masculine texture of leather and metal and an intractable and lonely originality. The pallor of Edward's face suggests that his difference is set apart from the sunny "normality" of his hostess's life.

while the perverse pedophilia of the local self-help guru is mistaken for creative intelligence.

Still, though neither Edward nor Darko finds his bliss, each leaves behind a legacy of beauty and love.

Iconography

Surprisingly, the magical creatures and situations prevalent in fantasy films are not as easily categorized as the iconic images we find in some other genres, like the cattle drive in the Western and the guns, cars, and molls in the gangster film. In many ways, the iconic figures of fantasy films perform the same function as poetry, giving us concrete images for feelings that are hard to express prosaically. Although there are some prototypical plots and figures in the genre, the iconography of fantasy film tends toward the particularity of a movie, a character, a plot, a situation, a song, as a permanent part of the American imagination that enduringly becomes part of private conversation and public commentary.

So, while many characters, songs, and images from *The Wizard of Oz* are burned into the imagination of the United States, and perhaps the world, the fantasy genre is not populated by numerous generic Tin Woodmen or Scarecrows, or little girls carried off to magical lands by tornadoes. Rather, the images of Dorothy as played by Judy Garland, with her auburn braids, her blue checked pinafore, her ruby slippers, and her little black Scottie, Toto, as well as the famous images of the metallic Tin Man, the seemingly boneless Scarecrow, and the Cowardly Lion may be evoked in full or in part in all kinds of movies, television shows, and even in political cartoons, to refer to particular kinds of problems and feelings.

Brian Sibley, a British blogger who has spent decades building his website into a clearinghouse that facilitates conversation about fantasy, and lists publications about fantasy film, has opined that fantasy is the most primal category of fiction, the closest to the earliest imaginative stirrings of human culture. The images of Dorothy and her friends appear to validate his idea. Singing "If happy little bluebirds fly beyond the rainbow / Why, oh why, can't I?" Dorothy is the icon of the longing for something more than ordinary reality. Constantly asking how she can return to Kansas, she is also the icon of the desire for a place in

***The Wizard of Oz* (1939)** This grouping is perhaps the most famous iconic fantasy film image in the world. Part of its universality is its suggestion of a comprehensive connection among the human, the animal, the vegetable, and the mineral, as the story pursues the struggle to find an appropriate place and identity. The image of Dorothy (Judy Garland) and friends (from left, Jack Haley, Ray Bolger, and Bert Lahr) also forms a continuity with the Hollywood practices of using the young girl as an icon of the most innocent, vulnerable, and lovable aspect of humanity.

ordinary reality. Her ruby slippers are icons of the desire to be anywhere but where one is. This image is used in David Lynch's *Wild at Heart* (1990), in which, when the heroine feels utterly powerless and vulnerable to attack by a potential rapist, she clicks her red high heels three times, as Dorothy did. Images and scenes in *Oz* are also icons of the unsuspected power we all have over our lives and destinies, since, as Glinda the Good Witch (Billie Burke) points out, Dorothy had the ability all the time to go home. The four friends on the yellow brick road are icons of human longing for understanding, compassion, courage, belonging.

The iconicity of the Disney creations is another kind of story. In many ways the Disney Studios has made its films iconic through marketing, which brings the Disney figures to life. In the various Disney theme parks, children can hug a walking, breathing figure who looks like Cinderella or Mickey Mouse. Disney also infiltrates American life through easily attainable objects. Everyone can wear a pair of Mickey Mouse ears, or a shirt with the pictures of almost all of the characters from the films, or purchase statuettes of the characters, furniture, and framed reproductions of scenes or figures from the movies. Still, it is a fact that the emotions these fantasy figures elicit are strong enough to make many fans want to live with them and around them in their daily lives, even though it may be hard to pin down with precision what the actual attraction of the Disney figures is. It's clear why little girls are fond of the cartoon heroines who populate Disney's cartoons—they are pretty and get their wishes granted. The longevity of Disney's iconic songs is also easy to understand. "When You Wish Upon a Star," from *Pinocchio*, can be placed alongside "Over the Rainbow" as the essence of the desire at the heart of the fantasy genre. Similarly, "Someday My Prince Will Come," from *Snow White*, and "So This Is Love," from *Cinderella*, have understandably expressed generations of romantic dreams. But why do Americans identify with a gentle, squeaky male mouse when the ideal American man is rugged, virile, and aggressive? Does the fantasy give overstressed Americans an opportunity to affirm other kinds of masculinities? And why do so many of the most popular and iconic Disney films evoke the pathos of the loss of the mother? One of the most famous scenes in film history is in *Bambi*, in which the young hero of the film, a deer named Bambi, loses his mother when a hunter kills her. Her self-sacrificial cry, "Run, Bambi!" after which she takes the bullet so that her son can escape, haunts the American imagination, even in the case of many people who are in favor of gun ownership and hunting.

The jungle fantasy images of King Kong and Tarzan are also complexly iconic, particularly the image of Kong at the end of the film, on top of the Empire State Building as he fights off the airplanes that are attacking him, and the scene in *Tarzan, the Ape Man* in which Jane teaches Tarzan how to speak English. These scenes evoke diametrically opposite but fundamental human reactions. In the case of Kong, there is the double threat from and to our instinctive nature. Kong is a fearsome figure, but his passionate energy is also menaced by civilization and its technologies. The language lesson in Tarzan evokes our wonder at the moment when we rise from the inexpressiveness of the primal to receive the gifts of civilization, but it is also the beginning of Tarzan's exit from the simple paradise of the jungle. These moments are indelibly burned into our culture. Kong on the Empire State Building has been on countless T-shirts and posters, in numerous ads, and in the windows of the *Mad* magazine offices in the Empire State Building, where there was a huge picture of Kong, as if he were climbing outside the office. The line "Me Tarzan, you Jane," supposedly from the famous scene in which Jane Parker gives Tarzan language lessons, has been used over the decades in jokes, as a way of representing male domination of women. It is a misquotation, since in the scene, Jane is in charge, and Tarzan is struggling to learn from her, by connecting the word Tarzan with himself and Jane with her. Tarzan's exact line is: "Tarzan [*punching himself*]; Jane [*punching her*]; Tarzan [*punching himself*]; Jane [*punching her*]." This continues until Jane gets tired of being punched. But misquotation or not, the common evocation of this moment testifies to its cultural resonance.

Among the few prototypical fantasy film devices that exist, we may count the plot of *It's a Wonderful Life*, which provides an iconic structure that both expresses our fears that we are too small and unimportant to matter in this world and reassures us that we do matter. The fantasy of George Bailey's trek in a parallel universe has often been imitated, particularly on television, as a tried-and-true way for a character to explore his or her fears and insecurities. To name but a few, one episode of *Moonlighting*, the comedy series of the 1980s starring Bruce Willis and Cybill Shepherd, featured this plot, as did fantasy sequences on the daily soap

King Kong (1933) Kong atop the Empire State Building, fighting off attack planes, is a potent fantasy image of the embattled animal instincts in human beings amid the technical marvels of modern life. Kong's complex fusion of the most derogatory stereotypical representation of African Americans and a sweetness coupled with fierceness stands as an enduring enigma. Just what does Kong reflect of American values during the 1930s?

***Tarzan, the Ape Man* (1932)** Considered little more than commercial entertainment for the uneducated when it was made, this film, as we see in this image, is visually sophisticated. The shadows of leaves and branches and the chiaroscuro of the dappled sunlight on Tarzan (Johnny Weissmuller) and Jane (Maureen O'Sullivan) create a visual vocabulary for the wild charm of Tarzan and his jungle environment for this highly civilized English rose. The scene itself constructs, by means of the fantasy genre, a gender dynamic that is inventive and arguably groundbreaking, suggesting a tender collaboration between female and male strengths and sensibilities.

operas *General Hospital, Santa Barbara,* and *One Life to Live.* The *Wonderful Life* plot device has also been featured in episodes of weekly shows like *Smallville, Saturday Night Live, Chapelle's Show, South Park, Buffy the Vampire Slayer,* and *The Sopranos.*

However, the most often reproduced fantasy plot device is that of the protagonist with multiple identities. As with many other characteristics of the fantasy film, this too is shared with the horror film and the science fiction film. But while the multiple-identity story in those genres tends to split the personality of a distinguished person to reveal an appalling, hidden, abnormal physical and/or psychological disorder—as in *Dr. Jekyll and Mr. Hyde* (1931 and 1941)—in the fantasy film it chronicles an identity split that enhances life in one or more wonderful ways, as in the examples of Superman, Batman, Spider Man, Wonder Woman, and other assorted superheroes. The "real" Bruce Wayne is a frivolous playboy, but as Batman he is a serious asset to society. Clark Kent is a shy, bumbling reporter, but as Superman he is an assertive achiever. Peter Parker is Clark Kent–like in his ordinary life as a news photographer, but as Spider-Man he is intrepid and successful. Wonder Woman is Diana Prince in her daily life—seemingly only an ordinary woman—but unbeknownst to most people she was born a princess in a tribe of Amazons and has secret superpowers of perception and intuition and a magical plane that she can call on when necessary.

The iconic category of fantasy double-identity hero, like many fantasy creations, is subject to multiple interpretations. In addition to expressing the secret wishes of many ordinary people to be amazing in ways that other people don't suspect, these characters may also be understood as expressing an uncanny sense about the body as an unreliable aspect of human life that can be both vulnerable and a source of protection. Or we can interpret the double identity as a way of discussing sexual ambiguity. Multiple-identity fantasy heroes traditionally elicit great interest from the opposite sex but neither marry nor commit themselves to a lover. Although the official explanation for their solitude is that it is a form of protection for anyone they might love, it may also be a form of protection *from* anyone who might love them. For this reason, these films are sometimes given queer readings, which interpret the secrecy of the lives of these heroes as a metaphor for the gay closet. As a result, some more recent fantasy superhero films have attempted to short-circuit the possibility of queer readings. Some recent Batman films have eliminated Robin, often read as a proof of Batman's homosexuality, and the second and third films of the Spider-Man series give their hero (Tobey Maguire) an explicitly heterosexual relationship with Mary Jane Watson (Kirsten Dunst), despite the ambiguity of their relationship in the comics.

Perhaps it is possible to say that the fantasy genre as a whole reveals a cultural double identity in the American filmgoer. Americans are reputed to be tough-minded pragmatists, moved more frequently by the economics of their own situation than by idealistic beliefs that involve the larger picture of society. Americans have also been criticized as conformists who are uncomfortable with what strays beyond the norm. Yet in fantasy films, another side of America is revealed: a whimsical preference for wonder, a faith in miracles, an optimism that life is always filled with unexpected promise, and a delight in difference.

The Purple Rose of Cairo

Both *The Wizard of Oz* and *The Purple Rose of Cairo* employ fantasy to create an original and unforeseen perspective on the human condition. But *The Wizard of Oz* draws a pretty clear line between fantasy and reality, as was typical of early Hollywood fantasy films. Dorothy lives in Kansas; the Cowardly Lion, the Tin Man, and the Scarecrow are not in Kansas. They are in Oz, which is "only a dream." One of the most fascinating aspects of late twentieth- and early twenty-first-century fantasy films is the way they employ plots and visual and sound images to blur that line. In later fantasy films like the Harry Potter movies, there is no such thing as "only a dream." The magical world Harry can see exists in places between buildings that ordinary people think is the whole of reality: railroad tracks invisible to muggle (ordinary) eyes that are squeezed between commercial British Railway tracks. In *Harry Potter and the Deathly Hallows, Part 2* (2011), Harry, in the middle of a fight with archfiend Voldemort, finds himself in a misty realm that looks a little like the King's Cross railway station, conversing with the now dead Dumbledore. When he asks Dumbledore if they are really talking or if their meeting is in his head, Dumbledore replies, "Of course it's in your head." He then adds with a sly grin, "But that doesn't mean it isn't real." Similarly, in *The Purple Rose of Cairo*, Woody Allen changes the terms of the relationship between the real and the imaginary by merging elements of films with elements of everyday life.

The Purple Rose of Cairo begins by invoking the kind of absolute distinction between fantasy and life that it will muddy. Fantasy is represented by the song played over the main title, Fred Astaire's recording of "Cheek to Cheek," a lilting romantic tribute to the magic of love, from *Top Hat* (1935). The key sentence in the lyric speaks of bliss, "Heaven, I'm in heaven, and my heart beats so that I can hardly speak; and I seem to find the happiness I seek, when we're out together dancing cheek to cheek." When the film cuts to the bedazzled face of Cecilia, its heroine, looking at the poster, the soundtrack of Astaire's song is interrupted by a clunking noise that breaks her reverie. A metal letter from the theatre marquee falls to the ground in back of her—a warning that the nuts and bolts of everyday life stand in opposition to our desires for happiness, or heaven. For a while, subsequent scenes continue this dichotomy. Cecilia talks about, thinks about, and repeatedly goes to see a film called *The Purple Rose of Cairo*, which is full of rich, bored, romantic people who represent a fantasy about the good life that couldn't be more distant from the endless pressure, abuse, privation, and drudgery that oppress her at her job in a diner and in her marriage.

But very soon the fantasy epitomized in *Purple Rose* not only penetrates Cecilia's ordinary life; the two show themselves to be powerfully interconnected. After she is fired, Cecilia goes to see *Purple Rose* for the fifth time as a form of self-medication against misery, and a character named Tom Baxter, of the obviously privileged "Chicago Baxters," fascinated by Cecilia, walks off the screen, stopping the movie in its tracks and stunning the movie's other characters, the audience, and the theater's manager. The separation between art and life, fantasy and reality is compromised. But what exactly is Allen showing us about what draws Tom to Cecilia and Cecilia to Tom? An economist might conclude that Allen is engaging us in a Marxist interpretation of Hollywood film as

The Purple Rose of Cairo (1985) Gil Shepherd (Jeff Daniels) takes time out from the rat race with a moment of free desire and pleasure with Cecilia (Mia Farrow) and a woman who owns a music store (Loretta Tupper). We see the part of the actor that went into the creation of Tom Baxter.

the opiate of the masses who never think about changing their situation because they are being fed daydreams to pacify them by rich Hollywood moguls who profit from their misery. But this film could have easily been made about a very rich but equally miserable woman; Allen is going for a commentary not about the difference between rich and poor, but between a real world ruled by necessity and money, and a fantasy world ruled by desire and love, and the ties that bind these polarities to each other.

Tom is a handsome, gentle, playful fantasy figure, attentive to the very real Cecilia, and the movie shows us clearly that he can be the ideal lover because he is uninterested in "chasing a buck." In his freedom from any economic motive, Tom is also the stuff the dreams of the rich are made of. Unlike the actual rich, Tom is not subject to any kind of limit or necessity, nor are the people he associates with in the film. Real rich people certainly have more and better material possessions than the rest of us, but there are all kinds of demands on them that they must bow to if they are to keep their wealth. But the people in *Purple Rose*, the film-within-the-film, are fantasy versions of the rich. They *can* go anywhere and do anything they want to do whenever they want to, and they never have to worry about anyone judging their behavior. When Allen shows the main title of *Purple Rose*, he emphasizes their fantasy existence as people without limits. The names of the actors and crew are printed in elegant calligraphic letters on the kind of card that is used for formal invitations, a main-title design often used in classic Hollywood comedies and romances, but here the image also invokes life as one long invitation to these devil-may-care, fancy-free people to enjoy the world at will. The relationship between Tom and Cecilia is built on the dichotomy between the circumstances that have created Tom, who is a creature of love and desire, and Celia, who is a daughter of the world of necessity and money.

This freedom to indulge desire is foregrounded as the primary element of the magic of the movies in the opening line of *Purple Rose*, spoken by a playwright who feels bored and wants to get out of town for fun. He apparently hasn't any deadlines to meet, press agents to listen to, or writer's block to struggle with. His life is about packing a suitcase and corralling some friends to go to some exotic place of his dreams. His friends, hanging around his penthouse, similarly unpressured by commitments, are ready to drop everything and go with him. These are people whose reservations fall into place without any hitches and who don't have to worry about getting on each other's nerves. If they do, they just say something witty. Similarly, when they meet explorer Tom Baxter in a tomb in Egypt, he drops his archeological work, almost in midsentence, when they invite him to go off to a nightclub in New York with them. When they get there, a glamorous songstress sings about going with the flow of life. Their nonchalance and the ease of their days enchants Cecilia, for whom everything is a struggle—as it is for all real people, whatever their income.

That the allure of Hollywood movies is their picture of lives unconstrained by necessity becomes even clearer when Tom is roaming around the real world. He has a pocketful of cash, but it's all make-believe money, a wonderful way of depicting the contrast between the fantasy life of money in *Purple Rose* and its role as an iron necessity in Cecilia's life. Moreover, when Tom runs into a prostitute by chance and follows her back to her brothel, Allen portrays the fantasy life of sex in Hollywood films. The girls in the brothel know better than anyone that in the real world sex is generally a matter of power relations. They understand sex as a consumer service traded for money or security, and are willing to tailor their services to fit the customer's preferences. Tom's point of view, which he offers the ladies of the night, is completely free of economics or power. He fuses sex with ideal love and reverence for the miracle of life created by sex. The prostitutes, worldly wise as they are, are so enthralled by the picture of love that he paints for them that they want to give him a sex party for free, but he gently and sweetly refuses in the name of his love for Cecilia. She's the only one he wants. "Are there any other guys like you out there?" asks one of the women.

We get the answer to that question when Gil Shepherd, the actor who plays Tom, arrives in New Jersey. Gil's entire life is pressure, from the public, from his agent, and, most of all, from the men who control the industry and have made it clear that he is finished if he doesn't get Tom back onto the screen. So the answer is "yes" and "no." Gil is Tom, but Tom is his free, life-loving side. From the point of view of reality, Tom must be sacrificed if the actor is to lead a successful life. We see how dear that freedom is to Gil when he and Cecilia have a mini jam session in a music store with the song "I Love My Baby," Cecilia playing the ukelele, Gil singing, and the old woman who owns the store playing the piano. But he can't afford it in the real world. It has to be relegated to the world of fantasy and shut out of his daily life, as we see in the extraordinary scenes in which Gil confronts Tom.

***The Purple Rose of Cairo* (1985)** Director Woody Allen imports images from old black-and-white films of merrymakers moving seamlessly as if the limitations of time and space didn't exist from one site of pleasure to another. In Cecilia's life, this quotation from the vocabulary of Hollywood cinema takes on a particular poignance in its contrast to her daily life that is so burdened by limits imposed by the economics of the Great Depression.

Their first meeting, early in the film, establishes the dialogue between fantasy, which Allen partially identifies with creativity, and the money that rules reality. It takes place in an abandoned amusement park, a perfect location for the meeting between character and actor. Gil and Tom begin by bickering about whether Tom has an autonomous reality or is the possession of the actor who created him. Surrounded by wooden horses and images of clowns, Tom represents desire and Gil the rules created by society. Can the sweet Tom become real if he loves Cecilia enough and tries hard enough? Or will Gil be able to conquer that kind of desire by calling on the power of society—comically, Gil threatens Tom with the might of the FBI, the courts, and the actors' union—to put Tom in the place that culture says he belongs: on the screen? Ultimately, the ambitious side of Gil triumphs over the yearning in him for bliss. The triumph of necessity means the reestablishment of the iron law of reality over Cecilia.

This is a fantasy about the simultaneous fragility of both the real and the fantastic. The real is threatened by the power of bliss after Tom's exit from the screen. But the fantastic is threatened by the power of the real. In fact, everything hinges on the choice of Cecilia, a woman who has never before had power in her life. She is happy for one of the few times in her life, when, in a clever turn of the plot, the fictional character Tom Baxter takes her into the movie of *The Purple Rose*, and she experiences the limitless bliss of his "existence" firsthand. But, just as E.T., the character in Steven Spielberg's science fiction film of the same name, must go home, Allen presents Cecilia's decision to choose reality as inevitable. The evaporation of bliss, then, is also inevitable. Cecilia cannot choose Tom, and once he goes back into the movie, Gil abandons Cecilia to save his career. But Gil too has made a sacrifice. He was happy with Cecilia, as he is not happy in Hollywood. His betrayal of her appears to fill him with regret, as we see in a wordless close-up of him on the plane back to Los Angeles. Because this scene is wordless, we don't know if he was really as happy with Cecilia as it seemed when they sang together in the music store, or if he simply feels sorrow at manipulating an innocent person. Maybe there's a bit of both. Whatever the case, in this wistful image of the fleeing Gil, Allen insists that he is not a villain but a man yielding to reality, just as Cecilia did when she chose him over Tom.

Through links between the fantastic and the real, *The Purple Rose of Cairo* releases the audience from the seemingly iron grip of economic necessity. We experience, briefly, as does Cecilia, a sweetness of spirit infiltrating the daily grind. Allen, one of the creators of the recent, sophisticated trend in fantasy film to acknowledge the complex relationship between fantasy and reality, forces us, in the last frames of *Purple Rose*, to ponder the nuances of the power of fantasy to produce inner freedom and a larger vision of possibilities. In the end, Allen seems to be saying that fantasy and reality are not two separate things but part of the same system of the real. Gil and Cecilia are caught in a culture that creates misery, but the fantasy figure Tom permits us to ask larger questions about why we suffer. The last image in this film is of Cecilia watching *Top Hat*, the blissful Fred Astair–Ginger Rogers musical, in which a character can sing, "Heaven, I'm in heaven..." and retain his paradise. We are left with a bittersweet conundrum. Is it a positive or a negative thing that we can dream of bliss? Cecilia's temporary respite from her depressing life with Monk changes nothing about her daily suffering. And yet without some experience of inner freedom through the imagination, could she, and by extension we, find the strength to cope with drudgery and emotional disappointment? It is up to the audience to answer this question, but Allen makes a strong case that fantasy is inextricably a part of the world as it is, in which, as he says in his later film *Crimes and Misdemeanors* (1989), human happiness does not seem to have been figured into the equation.

Martha P. Nochimson

QUESTIONS FOR DISCUSSION

1. In looking at the full range of American fantasy films, would you say that the fantasy genre is antagonistic to or supportive of difference, minorities, and marginalized people?
2. What is the difference between good magic and bad magic in the Harry Potter series? How does this fantasy of muggles and wizards better enable us to think in large terms about our ordinary lives?
3. Part of *The Wizard of Oz* takes place in Kansas, and part takes place in the land of Oz. Why is it considered a fantasy film rather than a realistic film with a fantasy interlude?
4. Woody Allen's films *The Purple Rose of Cairo* and *Midnight in Paris* are both fantasy films and both reflect on the potentially oppressive effect of financial pressures on human beings. How are they different in exploring this subject? How are they similar?
5. People often speak of the Tarzan films as depicting a sexist relationship between Tarzan, the naturally dominant man, and Jane, the submissive woman. Looking carefully at *Tarzan, the Ape Man*, would you affirm this belief, or is it a misinterpretation? Is *Tarzan, the Ape Man* a sexist film, or does it have unexamined feminist aspects?

FOR FURTHER READING

Attebery, Brian. *The Fantasy Tradition in American Literature*. Bloomington: Indiana University Press, 1988.

Bellin, Joshua David. *Framing Monsters: Fantasy Film and Social Alienation*. Carbondale: Southern Illinois University Press, 2005.

Gabler, Neal. *Walt Disney: The Triumph of the American Imagination*. New York: Vintage Books, 2007.

Goldberg, Lee, Randy Lofficier, Jean-Marie Lofficier, and William Rabkin. *The Dreamweavers: Interviews with Fantasy Filmmakers of the 1980s*. Jefferson, NC: McFarland, 1995.

Harryhausen, Ray, and Tony Dalton. *Ray Harryhausen: An Animated Life*. Rev. ed. London: Aurum Press, 2009.

Harryhausen, Ray, and Ken Ralston. "Commentary": Disc 1. *King Kong*, special ed. DVD. Produced and directed by Merian C. Cooper and Ernest B. Schoedsack. Atlanta: Turner Entertainment, 2005.

Irwin, W. R. *The Game of the Impossible: A Rhetoric of Fantasy.* Champaign: University of Illinois Press, 1976.

Morton, Ray. *"King Kong": The History of a Movie Icon from Fay Wray to Peter Jackson.* New York: Applause Theatre and Cinema Books, 2005.

Nicholls, Peter. *Fantastic Cinema: An Illustrated Survey.* London: Ebury Press, 1984.

Nochimson, Martha P. "Johnny Weissmuller and Maureen O'Sullivan: Tarzan and Jane." Chap. 2 in *Screen Couple Chemistry: The Power of 2.* Austin: University of Texas Press, 2002.

Rickitt, Richard. *Special Effects: The History and Technique.* London: Virgin Books, 2000.

Rushdie, Salman. *The Wizard of Oz.* BFI Film Classics. London: British Film Institute, 2008.

Todorov, Tzvetan. *The Fantastic: A Structural Approach to a Literary Genre.* Ithaca, NY: Cornell University Press, 1993.

Worley, Alec. *Empires of the Imagination: A Critical Survey of Fantasy Cinema from George Méliès to "The Lord of the Rings."* Jefferson, NC: McFarland, 2005.

Young, Paul. *The Cinema Dreams its Rivals: Media Fantasy Films from Radio to the Internet.* Minneapolis: University of Minnesota Press, 2006.

West Side Story (1961)

The Musical

NO GENRE MORE CLEARLY REFLECTS what is often labeled the classical era of Hollywood (roughly 1930 to 1960) than the musical. The films of the so-called "dream factory," with their glitzy glamour, larger-than-life stars, and comforting promise that life's problems will all disappear for an entertaining ninety minutes, find no better exemplar than the lush, romantic, singing-and-dancing fantasies of the classic Hollywood musical. Almost every studio made musicals: the surprisingly gritty looks behind the scenes of show business characteristic of the Warner Bros. contributions to the genre; the dynamic bundle of energy that is the curly-topped Shirley Temple starring in 20th Century–Fox's Americana-laced movies; the talented teens falling in love and putting on the show (or the other way around) in MGM's Mickey Rooney and Judy Garland vehicles; the silver-throated Jeanette MacDonald and husky-toned Maurice Chevalier loving and singing their way through a mythical Europe at Paramount; and the most famous dancing duo in the history of the silver screen, Fred Astaire and Ginger Rogers, making black and white truly colorful in globe-trotting terpsichorean fantasies that never left the studios of RKO.

While most of the major Hollywood genres (especially those that straddled the classical and postclassical eras) rarely find their entries collecting the coveted gold statuette come Oscar season, musicals have received the Best Picture prize no fewer than eleven times since the academy began giving out its self-congratulatory awards in 1929. The Oscars handed to musicals during the turbulent 1960s provide a general gauge of both the respect the genre commands and the way the Hollywood studios—in a perhaps desperate attempt to hold on to its fading mainstream audience—turn to the musical to deliver family pleasers. The musical dominated the otherwise contentious decade as no other genre ever ruled any era, winning four of the ten Best Picture prizes. In years that a musical did not win the big honor, one was nominated for Best Picture on three separate occasions; in two of the years that a musical did win, another musical was also nominated. In all, of the fifty films up for Oscars in the Best Picture category during the 1960s, nine, which is to say almost 20 percent, were musicals.[1] Even during the auteurist-dominated 1970s, musicals managed a handful of nominations despite undergoing the kind of shift that seemed, for a while at least, to toll the genre's death knell. But, unlike a vampire, a good genre never dies—no matter how many stakes are driven into its heart. The musical showed surprising life and vitality, morphing into clearly postclassical models and then remorphing into the kind of film even the old studio heads could embrace, as yet another century of cinema began.

History

The musical was the premiere beneficiary of the Hollywood sound revolution. Even an intuitive definition of the genre incorporates sound as a necessary precondition for its emergence. Yet if the musical required the coming of sound, so, too, the coming of sound required the musical. While Warner's *The Jazz Singer* (1927) was neither the first sound film (short films with competing sound technologies preceded it) nor the first sound feature film (it was a silent film with a few sound sequences), its sound was music and the music was box-office gold. Al Jolson, at that time the biggest star on Broadway, was cast as a singer in this otherwise standard, even old-fashioned intergenerational saga of Old World values versus New World aspirations. Then, when virtually every other major studio got into the manufacturing of sound films, they produced the

---

[1] The Oscar-winning musicals are *The Broadway Melody* (1929), *The Great Ziegfeld* (1936), *Going My Way* (1944), *An American in Paris* (1951), *Gigi* (1958), *West Side Story* (1961), *My Fair Lady* (1964), *The Sound of Music* (1965), *Oliver!* (1968), and *Chicago* (2002). The films nominated for Best Picture in the 1960s, aside from the aforementioned winners, are *The Music Man* (1962), *Mary Poppins* (1964), *Doctor Dolittle* (1967), *Funny Girl* (1968), and *Hello, Dolly!* (1969).

"All Talking, All Singing, All Dancing!" variety. Given the unfortunate timing of sound's being introduced just ahead of the stock market crash of 1929, when finance capital was at a premium, the excitement of music and dance became the glittering inducement for studios and audiences to fork over ever-scarcer resources for a technology that substantially added to the already enormously successful and influential medium of the silent cinema. And excitement there was! The studios produced so many musicals in 1929–1930 that they glutted the market—so much so that industry wags declared the genre dead. While around 125 musicals were made in these two years, only about twenty appeared during the next two years. But as the Great Depression worsened in 1932–1933, the seemingly counterintuitive strategy of virtually ignoring it to highlight scenic opulence and international insouciance was widely adopted.

This was not the case at Warner Bros., however, where, in 1933, the musical confronted the Depression head on, albeit sifted through the surrealistic imagination of dance director Busby Berkeley. With a penchant for the swooping camera, scads of scantily clad chorines, and wildly surrealist imagery, Berkeley's style and panache redeemed the musical, while the studio ensured that the stories were, if not quite ripped from the headlines, at least recognizable to audiences confronted by massive unemployment, lengthy bread lines, and an uncertain future. *42nd Street*, which set the standard for the backstage musical for years to come, involves a Broadway musical whose director has been made destitute by the stock market crash; in *Gold Diggers of 1933*, which inaugurated a series that included three more films by 1938, the producer of a stage show featuring four struggling actresses who share an apartment is forced by creditors to shut down rehearsals because he can't pay his bills; and *Footlight Parade* features James Cagney, in a role that reminded audiences he could do more than play a vicious gangster, as a failed director of Broadway musicals struggling against unscrupulous competition to remake his career. Together, the Warner films breathed new and lasting life into the genre.

As if these were not enough, 1933 saw RKO, the newest of the major studios and on uncertain economic footing, pair Fred Astaire—a veteran of the vaudeville and Broadway stages, but a newcomer to the movies—with Ginger Rogers—who had already appeared in *Gold Diggers of 1933* and *42nd Street*. Their one musical number and supporting roles in *Flying Down to Rio* created enough of a stir for the studio to pair them again, this time as the leads, in *The Gay Divorcee* (1934). The nine

***Footlight Parade* (1933)** Though more famous as the avatar of screen gangsters and tough guys in Hollywood's classical period, James Cagney started his show business career as a dancer. Equally adept at comedy and drama, able to sing and dance as well as shoot and fight, Cagney had the uncanny ability to capture his era—be it the Depression-ridden 1930s, as in *Footlight Parade*, or the war-torn 1940s, as in *Yankee Doodle Dandy*. The "Shanghai Lil" number featured here was typical of the kind of Orientalism that once pervaded Hollywood (note the "yellowface" impersonation of a Chinese woman by the stalwart Ruby Keeler), but Cagney's energetic, if eccentric, dancing is its real highlight.

Astaire-Rogers films of the 1930s, most memorably *Top Hat* (1935) and *Swing Time* (1936), are luminous visions of Art Deco brightness, sparkling repartee, inimitable song stylings, and, of course, dance numbers of unmatched creativity and dexterity. Moreover, the music they sang and to which they danced was created by some of the most influential and successful composers of pop tunes America has ever produced; Cole Porter, Jerome Kern and Dorothy Fields, George and Ira Gershwin, and, of course, Irving Berlin gave the Astaire-Rogers films prestige and sophistication. This initially strange coupling of a not conventionally handsome man with a perhaps too brassy lady thus became part of American movie history, their onscreen magic most succinctly described in the oft-quoted phrase (attributed to Katharine Hepburn): "He gives her class. She gives him sex." Whatever the reasons for their appeal, when Astaire and Rogers sang and danced, America was dazzled.

As the 1930s progressed, musicals became an industry staple. Over at 20th Century–Fox, the studio's fortunes were hoisted onto the tiny shoulders of Shirley Temple. Ultimately, she proved to be one of the most durable stars in the history of the American cinema, becoming not only a musical sensation but the object of every stage mother's dreams of stardom for her little girl. Though her individual films are largely forgotten, they did make a major contribution to American popular culture by featuring, in four of them, dancing star Bill "Bojangles" Robinson. Subject as he was, like all of Hollywood's African-American stars, to marginalization and racial stereotyping, the preservation of his innovative and influential dances remains one of the major legacies not only of Shirley Temple's star vehicles, but of the musical film itself.

Top Hat (1935) With a score by Irving Berlin, *Top Hat* is one of Astaire and Rogers's most sparkling and successful films. The Art Deco sets designed by Van Nest Polglase define their films as much as the musical scores—though perhaps nothing remains in memory so much as the dance duets of this most famous musical pairing. Rogers's flowing gowns (designed by Bernard Newman) accentuated her lines as she floated along to Astaire's gentle guidance. The rehearsals that went into making their dances seem so effortless and spontaneous were, however, notoriously grueling.

In this context, it should be recalled that Hollywood made a handful of musicals featuring major black stars, thus segregating African-American performers from major roles in mainstream films but also giving significant talents a chance to escape the horrific, stereotypical roles to which they were otherwise confined. Early in the sound era, MGM assigned King Vidor to direct *Hallelujah!* (1929), one of the finest of these vehicles. Over at Fox that same year, black stars Stepin Fetchit and Clarence Muse appeared in *Hearts in Dixie*. The 1930s saw the production of *The Green Pastures* (1936) at Warner Bros., while in 1943 MGM quickly followed up *Cabin in the Sky* with *Stormy Weather*. These films, while low-budget by A-feature standards, nevertheless received the full Hollywood treatment. This is in contrast to other movies with all-black casts, many directed by white filmmakers, which were made primarily for the black audiences, though some did have limited crossover appeal. Lena Horne's film debut, for instance, *The Duke Is Tops* (1938), was produced at Million Dollar Productions, which specialized in all-black films. To capitalize on Horne's beauty and growing fame following the success of *Stormy Weather*, it was rereleased five years later to general audiences under the title *The Bronze Venus*. On the even lower end of the budgetary scale one can find the films of singing star Herb Jeffries (a.k.a. Herbert Jeffrey), who rose to movie fame with *Harlem on the Prairie* (1937) and followed that up with the trilogy *Two-Gun Man from Harlem* (1938), *The Bronze Buckaroo*, and *Harlem Rides the Range* (both 1939). Jeffries's role as a singing cowboy owed its origins to the films of "the Singing Cowboy" Gene Autry—examples of musical Westerns that had great success as short subjects or B features. Such black-cast musicals form part of a tradition, it may be argued, that extends through films like *Carmen Jones* (1954) to *The Wiz* (1978), which features Lena Horne, and into more contemporary times with a film like *Idlewild* (2006).

The decade closed with one of the most beloved of all film musicals and of all films in general: *The Wizard of Oz* (1939). Its innovative use of color—the deliberately drab black and white of Kansas juxtaposed with the saturated Technicolor phantasm that is Oz, memorable musical numbers ranging from the plaintive "Over the Rainbow" to the jaunty "Follow the Yellow Brick Road"; and witty dialogue, together with the emergence of a superstar in Judy Garland, make the film a veritable paradigm of the musical and of Hollywood in the 1930s. Just as Dorothy eventually learns that there is indeed "no place like home," MGM also discovered there was no place like its home for the musical.

206

While World War II reduced demand for some film genres (the romantic comedy, for instance) and created a new one (the World War II Combat Film), the musical rolled merrily along. The patriotic fervor with which Hollywood imbued all its films, including the musical, after the Japanese attacked Pearl Harbor on December 7, 1941, found a high-water mark in James Cagney's performance as George M. Cohan in *Yankee Doodle Dandy* (1942). Although Cagney might be best remembered today for his tough-guy roles in gangster films, it was for this role, which had him gleefully dancing down the White House stairs, that he won his only Academy Award. With this and other morale-boosters made during the war, the studios put the Hollywood musical on a path that would lead to a second golden age (1944–1958), and the creation of what are, along with the films of Fred Astaire and Ginger Rogers, the best-loved, most artfully made musicals in the history of world cinema.

The casting of Judy Garland in *Meet Me in St. Louis* (1944) paired her with the man she would marry the following year—director Vincente Minnelli. Perhaps no less important, it gave Minnelli his first opportunity to direct a major star in a full-length film with all of the vast resources MGM could command. Minnelli had previously directed the all-black *Cabin in the Sky* (1943), but *Meet Me in St. Louis* was certainly his breakthrough.

It was on *Cabin in the Sky* that Minnelli first worked with MGM's major producer of musicals, Arthur Freed, as part of what is called the Freed Unit. They made nine films together, creating a string of commercial, critical, and artistic successes that remain a tribute to the Hollywood system and to the American cinema itself. Such films as *The Pirate* (1948), *An American in Paris* (1951), *The Band Wagon* (1953), and *Gigi* (1958) gave stars like Judy Garland, Gene Kelly, Fred Astaire, and Leslie Caron roles that allowed them to attain cinematic immortality. Freed also mentored the directing team of Stanley Donen and Gene Kelly, which led, once again, to timeless films that continue to enchant modern audiences: *On the Town* (1949), *It's Always Fair Weather* (1955), and, of course, the incomparable *Singin' in the Rain* (1952).

Yet a dark cloud hovered on the horizon, coming, ironically, from the success of the Broadway musical. A crucial connection had always existed between the film musical and its Broadway counterpart. Broadway plays were often the source of movie musicals even in the 1930s. Though the best musicals were typically either new creations for the

***On the Town* (1949)** The directing team of Stanley Donen and Gene Kelly brought many innovations to the Hollywood musical, not the least of which was location shooting for their first teaming, and Donen's directorial debut, *On the Town* (starring, from left, Frank Sinatra, Jules Munshin, and Kelly). Previously the genre had been not simply confined to the admittedly lavish and spacious soundstages of the studio lots, but given over more to fantasy than to reality. Shot on location in New York, this cinematic tribute to the city that never sleeps works to transform the potentially gritty and alienating urban landscape into a fairy-tale land of wonder and romance.

screen or adaptations that rendered the original almost unrecognizable, one of the highlights of the 1930s musicals was James Whale's stylish and powerful adaptation of the already-beloved Jerome Kern–Oscar Hammerstein II extravaganza *Show Boat* (1936). Memorable for its Expressionistic cinematography, the charming performance by Irene Dunne, and its subtle but unmistakable indictment of racism, it also showcases the powerful voice and commanding presence of Paul Robeson in an unforgettable vocal and cinematic rendition of "Ol' Man River." Its montage of black laborers toting barges and lifting bales as the mighty Mississippi rolls on demonstrates what film can do that the theater cannot. Unfortunately, the 1951 MGM version, produced by Freed in Technicolor, reveals in overproduced microcosm the slow creative decline of the genre.

Along with the stunning achievements of so many original scripts in the 1950s came the continued adaptation of Broadway shows. Stage shows that themselves revolutionized the form—*Oklahoma!*, *Carousel*, *South Pacific*, *Flower Drum Song*—were adapted into big-budget but typically stultifying films that contributed little to the genre except to purge the musical written expressly for the screen from the Hollywood landscape. By the time *West Side Story* swept the Academy Awards in 1961, the original film musical was virtually dead; the genre kept itself artificially alive mostly by big-budget film adaptations of beloved shows. Attempts to keep some form of the original film musical viable were American International's series of beach movies starring former Disney Mousekeeter Annette Funicello and teen idol Frankie Avalon. This small handful of films, made from 1963 to 1965, utilize a mild form of rock and roll that, along with their pleasant young casts, capitalized on the growing youth market. Similarly, a number of Elvis Presley vehicles set in exotic locales—Hawaii, Acapulco, Las Vegas—proved reasonably popular with young audiences until the 1960s came to its fiery close amid ever-increasing social unrest. And, of course, *Mary Poppins* (1964) was a (mostly) live-action example of the Disney musical magic.

Occasionally throughout the last three decades of the twentieth century, the musical showed legs, often quite literally, as when John Travolta carried two very different sorts of musicals to stunning box-office grosses. Released within six months of each other, *Saturday Night Fever* (1977) and *Grease* (1978) reveal both a new direction for the form and some life in the classic variety. *Grease*, a witty adaptation of the pleasantly retro Broadway show, has emerged as one of the most successful films ever made—even in unadjusted dollars it ranks in the all-time top one hundred U.S. domestic box-office successes; in adjusted dollars, it's in the top twenty-five. *Saturday Night Fever*, with its R rating, didn't pull in quite the revenues of *Grease*, but Travolta's tribute to disco dancing still gyrated into one of the biggest hits of the 1970s. More to the point, it offered a new opportunity for the musical to speak to a more cynical generation, demonstrating the significance of dance to the formation of community and friendship and celebrating an alternative vision of life's possibilities. Successful films from *Flashdance* (1983) and *Footloose* (1984) all the way to *Save the Last Dance* (2001) and *Step Up* (2006) owe

All That Jazz (1979) Bob Fosse was an innovative choreographer and sometime dancer on stage and screen. As a director, he infused adaptations of risqué Broadway shows like *Sweet Charity* (1969) and *Cabaret* (1972) with a creative terpsichore not previously seen in films. With *All that Jazz*, he turned his choreographic focus to autobiography to tell the tale of a driven Broadway director who injects more than a little sex, as well as alcohol, cigarette, and drug abuse, into the staid musical and, far from putting on the show and getting the girl at the end, meets only his death. It was more sad than ironic, then, that Fosse himself died at the young age of sixty.

their structure to *Saturday Night Fever*—films that kept the musical alive until the Walt Disney Studios revived it yet again.

As the adapted musical was demythologized by critically acclaimed films like Robert Altman's *Nashville* (1975) and Bob Fosse's *All That Jazz* (1979)—both films netted Oscar nominations for Best Picture—the original screen musical found new life in a somewhat surprising form: the animated film. The unprecedented string of commercial hits with sparkling musical scores that the Disney Studios inaugurated with *The Little Mermaid* (1989) and followed with *Beauty and the Beast* (1991), *Aladdin* (1992), and *The Lion King* (1994) were in the tradition of the studio's classic animated musicals, such as *Snow White* (1937), to be sure. Yet their popularity, which spawned many direct-to-video sequels and successful Broadway shows, indicated that the preteen crowd hardly found the musical moribund. Disney then launched a series of projects designed for both television and the big screen, led by the popular *High School Musical* (2006), its televisual sequel, *High School Musical 2* (2007), and its theatrical follow-up, *High School Musical 3: Senior Year* (2008). And surely no tweener alive, or her parents, doesn't know the name Hannah Montana, the eponymous lead character (played by Miley Cyrus) of a TV series broadcast from 2006 to 2011 and a movie released in theaters in 2009. The retro sensibilities of the High School Musical series certainly resonate with those who fondly recall the classical-era musical. Yet unlike those seemingly innocent song-and-dance extravaganzas of yesteryear that had near-universal appeal, the Disney-brand programming is geared almost exclusively to children and young adults. This sort of audience segmentation was inimical to Hollywood's attempt to create a unified cultural landscape through pan-demographic and pan-geographic productions.

Similarly, the big-budget adaptations of cutting-edge Broadway shows that achieved a good deal of box-office and critical success in the early 2000s were tilted toward Hollywood's more typical demographic of twenty- and thirtysomethings. The tough and cynical *Chicago* (2002); the peek behind the scenes of the music industry provided by *Dreamgirls* (2006); the poignant social commentary on view in *Hairspray* (2007); and the strictly nostalgic appeal of *Mamma Mia!* (2008) are fairly far away from any golden age. And some Broadway shows that had record-breaking runs or cultlike appeal found few cinematic takers. The lush romanticism of *The Phantom of the Opera* (2004) did not translate to the silver screen—ironic, considering the number of successful versions in its prior nonmusical form. The innovative and socially engaged *Rent* (2005) was also a box-office failure. And the disappointing reception of *Sweeney Todd* (2007)—despite its being the first full-scale adaptation of a Stephen Sondheim show—indicates the uncertain status of the genre, dependent as it is on particular films rather than overall generic vitality. As the generation weaned on Disney's shining musicals comes of age the original film musical, with its multigenerational appeal, may reappear.

Typologies, Themes, and Theories

For classical Hollywood, any film containing three or more songs performed within its narrative was classified as a musical. Time and scholarly revisions have, however, been less than sanguine about this simple definition. Few, for instance, still consider the Paramount classics starring the Marx Brothers, e.g., *Animal Crackers* (1930) and *Duck Soup* (1933), musicals. By the same token, despite Bing Crosby's musical talents, his numerous pairings with Bob Hope in their Road escapades generally fall under the broader category of comedy. Many instances of generic hybridity might, in some sense, be classified as musicals. Martin Scorsese's intense drama *New York, New York* (1977) also stands as his tribute to the musical. Francis Ford Coppola, another auteur, also tried to (re)mythologize the form via a combination of artifice and realism. Yet, like Scorsese's film, Coppola's *One from the Heart* (1982) was a failure both commercially and in the context of his brilliant and influential career up to that point. A later attempt on his part to utilize the form for *The Cotton Club* (1984)—critically well received but commercially far less so—grafted the musical onto the gangster film.

Yet generic hybridity had always been part and parcel of the musical. As Rick Altman notes, many other film genres influenced the Hollywood musical from the start: romantic comedy, the Western, melodrama.[2] The Western, for example, has been quite hospitable to music, and Hollywood produced both musical Westerns, e.g., *Destry Rides Again* (1939) and Western musicals, e.g., *Annie Get Your Gun* (1950) with great success along with some generic confusion. A number of musicals were remakes of romantic comedies: *The Philadelphia Story* (1940) was transformed into *High Society* (1956); *Ball of Fire* (1941) found musical expression in *A Song Is Born* (1948); *The Strawberry Blonde* (1941) became *One Sunday Afternoon* (1948). Perhaps the clearest example of these mixed genres has been the long-lived propensity of the musical to combine itself with the biopic, a process that began as early as 1936 with *The Great Ziegfeld* and has continued all the way into the twenty-first century with films like *Ray* (2004) and *Walk the Line* (2005).

The presence of musical numbers within a film may not guarantee a conventional generic fit, yet the lack of any musical numbers surely disqualifies a film from fitting the form. The question then becomes the *function* of the musical numbers within the diegesis (narrative story line). For a film to qualify as a musical, the music itself must be integral to the plot, whether or not the musical performance is for an audience in the film or integrated into the story in some other way. In other words, the music must advance the plot in some fashion or be reflective of a character's desires, goals, and state of mind or inner being. Of course, a musical will typically have more than one performed number,

---

[2] Rick Altman. *The American Film Musical* (Bloomington and Indianapolis: Indiana University Press, 1987), 129.

and these inevitably belong to different types, depending on the plot and the subgenre (see below) to which the film may belong.

The variety of musical types, or subgenres, makes defining the form difficult beyond the presence of musical numbers that advance the plot or are central to its functioning. To that end, Rick Altman identifies three subgenres that incorporate the majority of the classical-era musicals. Although elements of these three subgenres may be found in post-classical musicals, many more recent films may not so easily fit. Yet for the classical musicals that have stood the test of time, these subgenres work remarkably well. It should be noted, however, that Altman's categorizations follow on the heels of an older grouping worth considering first because it introduces complex problems of categorization and canon formation: how scholars decide precisely—and sometimes quite imprecisely—which films are put into what genres.

Before Altman categorized the musical film, it was subdivided along the following lines: the revue; the operetta; the backstage story; the star vehicle; the musical biography; the integrated musical. The revue basically links a series of individual musical numbers or acts by only the most minimal of plots. In the earliest days of sound in the cinema, many films were presented without benefit of plot at all; they simply followed the theatrical practice, common at the time, of showing a series of individual musical acts. The revue format lasted little beyond the formative years of the genre, reaching an artistic apogee in *Ziegfeld Follies* (1946), far less a biopic of the legendary impresario Florenz Ziegfeld than the creative restaging of songs made famous by or in the style of the once-popular Broadway revue that bears his name.

The operetta, a European mode, derived (as its name indicates) from opera, boasting a coherent, if usually quite light, story set in mythical or quasi-mythical European or exotic locales. One significant feature distinguishes this from opera: it contains a good bit of dialogue and is thus one of the precursors to the "book show" that came to define the Broadway musical. Operetta depends on trained singing voices, especially light sopranos and tenors. It enjoyed a vogue on the American stage in the 1910s and '20s and then flourished in the early sound film era. Paramount was especially notable for its operettas, including *The Desert Song* (1929), *The Vagabond King* (1930), *The Smiling Lieutenant* (1931), and *Love Me Tonight* (1932). The movies of Jeanette MacDonald and Nelson Eddy, for instance, *Naughty Marietta* (1935), *Maytime* (1937), and *Bitter Sweet* (1940), and a number with Kathryn Grayson, such as *The Toast of New Orleans* (1950) and *The Vagabond King* (1956), represent the two major cycles of operetta after the Paramount films of the early 1930s.

The backstage story focuses on the efforts to mount a show of some sort, typically a big-budget musical or an amateur show, or some other kind of production (e.g., *Singin' in the Rain* and the fabrication of sound musical movies). The most famous examples of these remain the Broadway Melody films, the Gold Digger entries, and, especially, the Depression-era dramas from Warner Bros. choreographed by Busby Berkeley (e.g., *42nd Street*). Popular throughout the classical era, this format survives into contemporary times with films that concentrate on music students who must work to put together a performance piece as a kind of audition to move on to greater professional training or a career, like *Fame* (1980) or dance-oriented films like *Step Up* (2006).

Love Me Tonight **(1932)** The operettas produced at Paramount in the early 1930s not only helped solidify the musical genre but brought to provincial America a genuine cosmopolitanism. Directed by sophisticated European émigrés, including Ernst Lubitsch and Rouben Mamoulian (*Love Me Tonight*), the films also introduced Americans to the Gallic charms of Maurice Chevalier (here with Jeanette MacDonald), who combined typical French insouciance with a great deal of charm. Mature sexual banter, sparkling tunes, and a creative handling of the musical numbers—especially in terms of integrating real sounds—brought a new level of sophistication to the Hollywood cinema.

42nd Street (1933) *42nd Street,* the archetypal "backstage musical," seems like a bundle of clichés until one realizes that this is where the clichés originated: the driven producer who desperately needs a hit; the snooty leading lady; the callow, but likable male lead; and, most of all, the chorine, who must go from unknown to star when the leading lady, literally rather than figuratively, breaks a leg. Their boy-and-girl-next-door looks and talent made stars of both Dick Powell and Ruby Keeler.

The star vehicle was particularly popular during Hollywood's classical period, when the studios had actors under contract for whom they would create films that fit their particular talents and personae. Plots were constructed to take advantage of the stars' special abilities, focusing the musical numbers on what they did best. Thus, for Eleanor Powell, MGM created vehicles that enabled her to show off her ability as a tap dancer, such as *Born to Dance* (1936), *Rosalie* (1937), and *Lady Be Good* (1941). The Astaire-Rogers films gave Fred an opportunity to do a specialty number and to create situations where he and Ginger could dance together in romantic duets. The most obvious examples of this sort of film may be found at 20th Century–Fox, which signed Olympic figure-skating sensation Sonja Henie to a multifilm contract in 1936 and crafted a series of films, beginning with *One in a Million,* in which she plays, unsurprisingly, a figure skater, and at MGM, which featured Esther Williams in a series of "aqua musicals" in the 1940s and '50s to take advantage of the former teenage swimming champ's aquatic abilities (not to mention her athletic figure and good looks), including *Bathing Beauty* (1944), *Neptune's Daughter* (1949), and *Dangerous When Wet* (1953).

The musical biography—perhaps the most long-lived of the subgenres—was a biopic revolving around the life and work of a musical entertainer. Though singing stars remain the most popular subjects for film—from the sultry songstresses portrayed in *The Helen Morgan Story* (1957), *Lady Sings the Blues* (1972, with famed pop star Diana Ross as

Billie Holiday), and *Sweet Dreams* (1985, the story of Patsy Cline), to the popular male entertainers in many musical modes who are the subjects of *The Jolson Story* (1946), *The Buddy Holly Story* (1978), and *Ray* (about Ray Charles)—other creators and performers have also seen the light of celluloid. Composers, for instance, have proved popular subjects, perhaps because their works provide numerous opportunities to stage musical numbers in a variety of styles. Jerome Kern's life was given the biopic treatment in the lavish tribute *Till the Clouds Roll By* (1946); songwriting duo Rodgers and Hart got the Hollywood treatment in *Words and Music* (1948); Cole Porter was the subject of two biopics, first in *Night and Day* (1946) and later in *De-Lovely* (2004); even Mozart found himself on screen in the Oscar-winning *Amadeus* (1984).

The integrated musical represents the Platonic ideal of the form—that mode to which all previous forms aspired. This epitome was achieved almost simultaneously on stage, with *Oklahoma!*, which premiered on Broadway in 1943, and on screen with *Meet Me in St. Louis*. This subgenre marries all of the elements in the work—story, dialogue, music, lyrics,

***Ray* (2004)** Musical biographies were popular during Hollywood's golden age and were instrumental in keeping the musical alive after the genre's tailspin in the 1960s. One of the many dramatic stories based on the lives of rock, country, and rhythm and blues musicians is *Ray*, in which Jamie Foxx uncannily channels the persona of famed blind singer-songwriter Ray Charles to Oscar-winning acclaim. Though he doesn't do the singing (Charles's own recordings are used), Foxx captures Charles's unique performance style.

dance, set design—to further the plot, an integration to tell a coherent, often dramatically moving story. With *Meet Me in St. Louis* setting the trend, the Freed Unit's subsequent films all adhere to this model, as do many of the other films made at MGM in the 1950s, such as *Kiss Me Kate* (made in 3-D in 1953) and *Seven Brides for Seven Brothers* (1954), produced by Jack Cummings.

The weaknesses of categorization according to these six subgenres are many. For Altman, the revue is not a musical at all: it lacks narrative. Some sort of story and characters are required to fulfill the basic entertainment and ideological functions that make the musical a particular mode of popular discourse. By that same idea, concert documentaries are not musicals but a subgenre of documentary. Defining a particular film as an operetta requires a technical explanation of the kind of music it employs, whereas defining a film as a backstage story requires a structural explanation of the kind of plot it employs. At some level, almost every musical is a star vehicle meant to highlight the particular abilities of its leading man or lady. A star vehicle can also fit into another subgenre: is *Yankee Doodle Dandy* a star vehicle for James Cagney or the story of George M. Cohan? If the biopic and star vehicle overlap, at what point does the star vehicle give way to the integrated musical? Surely *Meet Me in St. Louis* is a showcase for Judy Garland's sublime singing voice, *The Pirate* for Gene Kelly's acrobatic dancing, and *The Band Wagon* for Fred Astaire's unearthly gracefulness. In short, defining subgenre by recourse to these properties is untenable.

Instead of such categories, Altman designates three major subgenres, each fundamentally definable by a variety of shared characteristics of setting, structure, form, and function. These not only provide definitions using the same criteria, they also subsume the earlier categories. In addition, they provide a fit for many, if not all, of the postclassical varieties, though the de-emphasis on musical variety within many modern musicals demonstrates either a true morphing of the genre or the need to eliminate such films from the canon of musicals. Thus the older categories yield to more elegant and accurate categories: the fairy-tale musical, the show musical, and the folk musical. The fairy-tale musical includes the category of operetta but also many of the integrated musicals; the show musical includes the backstage musical, the musical biography, and certain of the star vehicles; the folk musical handles the majority of the integrated musicals, as well as some of the star vehicles. While the iconography of each subgenre will be dealt with in the next

Meet Me in St. Louis (1944) The first film generally acknowledged to represent a complete integration of music with plot, *Meet Me in St. Louis* is also a good example of the folk musical. Yet there is more here than seems immediately apparent: Though made in 1944, when World War II still raged in both Europe and the Pacific, the film may be seen as starting the process of reintegrating men into the joys of small-town, family life. While the men all seem drawn to distant parts away from the bosom of the family—represented by the numerically superior number of women—the film works to demonstrate the pleasures of hearth and home. Thus, couched in the nostalgia of turn-of-the-century Middle America, it belies its seemingly simple story.

section, Altman's subgenres also contain the structural features that allow us to understand not just the form but also the function of the musical.

Were the musical to consist merely of a group of subgenres without any overarching generic characteristics, then each subgenre would, in fact, be a discrete genre. But such is not the case. The musical, overall, is a genre devoted to creating the couple. It fashions this couple out of paired opposites, using music and dance to visualize and thematize the romantic coupling and the overcoming of opposition of personalities. In addition, the musical functions to comment on the place and value of entertainment in our daily social and personal lives and to overcome other sorts of oppositions in the culture at large. In essence, then, the musical utilizes singing and dancing to smooth over cultural tensions and assuage societal concerns.

First of all, the musical often relies on a dual-focus narrative that does not depend on chronology to present its protagonists but rather progresses both simultaneously and alternatively. That is to say, the narrative draws parallels between the male and female characters until such time as they merge in marriage. Altman uses the example of *New Moon* (1940) to demonstrate cutting between the characters of Jeanette MacDonald and Nelson Eddy before they meet each other. Similarly, *The Pirate* alternates between scenes of Judy Garland and Gene Kelly, both getting their own sequences, but this swinging back and forth between characters establishes the dual focus, the shared spotlight. Another example is *The Music Man* (1962), which offers scenes of Robert Preston's Harold Hill and Shirley Jones's Marian the Librarian separately before they meet on the screen. Naturally, these alternations foreshadow the eventual encounters and, this being a musical, the ultimate joining of the couples.

Yet the dual-focus alternation also brings with it opposition—the parallels are drawn to contrast the two personalities and often the different social situations of the main characters. Thus, in *New Moon* Mac-Donald is free, wealthy, rich, and cultured; Eddy is poor, imprisoned to start with, tenacious, and has no time for niceties. In *The Pirate*, Kelly is free, wild, open, and energetic; Garland is repressed, confined, and controlled. These same respective characteristics are associated with Harold and Marian in *The Music Man*. The male as wild, free, energetic, a wanderer, and the woman as controlled, contained, repressed, a home-body, are typical (but not universal) gendered associations in the musical. Most significant, the couple represent contrasting characters and values. It is the work of the musical to marry (literally) these contrasting characteristics, overcoming structural oppositions that are otherwise incompatible. The musical overcomes these oppositions by allowing each of the characters to assume qualities of the other: in *The Pirate*, Kelly settles down with Garland and gives up his roving eye and wandering ways; Garland is allowed to express more of her inner desires and is freed up in the process.

For Altman, the dual-focus narrative split between male and female overlays other, or secondary, dualities. One such duality is between work and entertainment and its subsidiary, seriousness versus fun. Typically, the musical equates the man with the entertainment/fun side of the equation, the woman with the work/serious side. (This may be seen as a variation of the gendered nature of sexual difference in the Western, where the man is the free, wandering spirit, the woman the embodiment of domesticity and stability.) Even when the roles are reversed, for example in *The Sound of Music*, in which Maria (Julie Andrews) brings fun into the stuffy home of Christopher Plummer's Von Trapp family, the dichotomy holds: one side is associated with work, seriousness, and business, the other with play, fun, and entertainment. By overcoming these secondary dichotomies through the marriage of the couple, the musical reconciles a competing discourse in American culture, that between work and play, or high art versus entertainment, as in *The Band Wagon* and *Funny Face* (1957); it does so through a kind of marriage that might, revealingly, be called "show business." This dichotomy between work and play, art and entertainment, and its overcoming by the union of a couple who represent the competing sides of the equation, might be one reason that, while other cultures have something like musicals, no other nation has produced what might be called a large body of "work" devoted to the pleasures of "play," which is to say that "American musical" is, precisely, the best term for the genre.

Second of all, there is the issue of the musical's ideology. Critics point to its supposed retrograde nature as a genre devoted to heterosexual coupling and the sanctification of bourgeois institutions like marriage and capitalism, but also to what the genre offers that life itself does not or cannot provide. In other words, what pleasure is derived, beyond the spectacle of entertainment itself (a not inconsiderable joy, to be sure), from a form that prizes falling in love while putting on a show; meeting your true love in some mythical kingdom; or just finding that special someone in Anytown, USA? Richard Dyer, without denying the very real contradictions of capitalism and the frequent repression of issues of race, class, and sexuality, was the first commentator to note the "utopian" sensibility of the genre. The musical responds to needs created by the culture and offers up visions of abundance, energy, intensity, spontaneity, and community as opposed to society's scarcity, exhaustion, dreariness, manipulation, and fragmentation. Musicals accomplish this either through settings that deny the reality outside of the theater or, perhaps even more interesting, transform reality into a vision of utopia. In this sense, we can better understand a film like *Saturday Night Fever*, in which both the plot and the film work to transform Tony's dreary, fragmented life into something else, something he can get glimpses of on Saturday nights at the disco and which, through John Travolta's energetic performance, especially his dancing, the audience can similarly understand and experience. Yet far from being unique in this respect, *Saturday Night Fever* typifies a genre whose work, whose business, it is to provide glimpses of something else, something out there, perhaps somewhere over the rainbow or maybe right next door.

Iconography

Musicals are not easily definable by a specific setting within history or geography, like the typical Western. A musical may take place in any historical period—*A Funny Thing Happened on the Way to the Forum* (1966), for instance, takes place in the Roman Empire and *New Moon* in the eighteenth century; numerous musicals are located in the nineteenth century or in the early part of the twentieth. Similarly, musicals may be situated in the United States, Europe, Latin America, or some never-never land. Characters in musicals may be show people—professional entertainers or would-be stars or even amateurs content with their status. Yet frequently they are not and instead encompass a wide variety of characters from sailors and soldiers to psychiatrists. While the Western is characterized by icons like six-guns, horses, saloons, and frontier forts; the gangster film by machine guns, flashy cars, snazzy clothes, and bars and nightclubs; horror by monsters, haunted houses, sharp knives, dark woods, and creaking sounds; science fiction by space ships, alien planets, supercomputers, and cyber beings, the musical seems to lack such consistent iconography. Aside from the use of music itself in the form of song and dance, the musical's settings vary from small towns to Broadway; from log cabins to luxury apartments; from the ghetto to the Land of Oz. In other words, the semantic features of the genre fail to guarantee a definition or fit. Recourse to the various subgenres as defined by Altman, however, does allow for the isolation of semantic features particular to those types.

The fairy-tale musical is set in a kind of never-never land, even if it is vaguely situated in a recognizable locale. Of course, a film like *The Wizard of Oz* makes explicit this never-never-land "geografancy," as does Disney's animated and live-action versions of *Peter Pan* (1953, 1960). Other musicals use fictional locales that clearly owe much to the never-never-land ideal in that the locale is entirely divorced from any sense of the mundane world. A fine example of this is Minnelli's *Yolanda and the Thief* (1945), set in a fictitious Latin American country, but shot entirely in a studio with suggestive sets, and in saturated Technicolor. So, too, the Caribbean locale of *The Pirate* is more far more fantasy than documentary. *Brigadoon* (1954), again directed by Minnelli, adapts the Lerner and Loewe stage fantasy set in the Scottish Highlands. This aspect of the fairy-tale musical, one derived from the stage operetta and reinvented in cinema, goes all the way back to Lubitsch's *The Love Parade* (1929), with its location in the mythical kingdom of Sylvania. (In a bit of intertextual play, Paramount would again use the name of Sylvania as the comic foil to the equally mythical kingdom of Freedonia in the Marx Brothers' comedy-with-music *Duck Soup*.) Though typical of operetta, this tendency remains apparent as late as the 1960s, in the adaptation of *Camelot* (1967).

A variation of the fictionalized mythical locale transforms an exotic or unfamiliar locale into a fairy-tale universe. This is also typical of operetta, but no less so for more strictly Broadway-style plays and films. The desert sheikdoms of the Middle East, for instance, have been used in films as varied as *The Desert Song* (remade in 1943 and 1953), *Kismet* (1955), and *Harum Scarum* (1965). Further east, the exotic Orient, as it was once called, is the setting for *The King and I* (1956). Filmmakers often gave actual South American locations the fairy-tale treatment, as in *Flying Down to Rio, In Caliente* (1935), *Down Argentine Way* (1940), and *Fun in Acapulco* (1963). Although far more common in the show musical subgenre, New York City also proves amenable to the fairy-tale treat-ment in *Swing Time, Bells Are Ringing* (1960), *Sweet Charity* (1969), and even, despite the apparent grittiness, *Rent*. But the Hollywood conver-sion from real to fairy tale was most apparent in the numerous films that have romanticized Paris. *Love Me Tonight* musicalizes the city in its opening number, and countless films follow the lead, including *Roberta* (1935), *Gold Diggers in Paris* (1938), *April in Paris* (1952), *Daddy Long Legs* (1955), *Funny Face* (1957), *Gigi*, and, of course, *An American in Paris*. The Parisian fairy-tale romance extends all the way to *Moulin Rouge!* (2001). Woody Allen managed to combine the fairy-tale qualities of both New York and Paris (with a stopover in Venice) in his tribute to the musical, *Everyone Says I Love You* (1996).

To go along with the overall fairy-tale quality of the setting—never-never land or transformation of the real world—this subgenre situates its characters in a variety of fanciful spaces, be they kingdoms with their castles or their modern-day equivalents. Luxury liners provide mobile variations of these surroundings as well. The settings also mandate the kinds of characters to be found in them: counts and countesses, dukes and duchesses, the fabulously wealthy, or the magical inhabitants

***Moulin Rouge!* (2001)** The fantasy elements of the musical find their clearest expression in the fairy-tale subgenre. This is perhaps best expressed in the transformation of real locales into romantic wonderlands. Such is the case with the multinational *Moulin Rouge!* With an Australian director and a cast drawn from Australia, the United Kingdom, and the United States, and with influences ranging from Broadway to Bollywood, Baz Lurhmann's stylish film is at once delightfully retro and studiously postmodern. Although the action occurs in fin-de-siècle Paris in the Montmartre nightclub made famous in the paintings by Henri de Toulouse-Lautrec, the anachronisms abound—most notably in the use of many well-known pop songs of a decidedly modern sensibility (including songs by Elton John and Madonna). Stunning sets and lush staging, along with the operatic emotions of the characters, capture the essence of the classical musical. (Pictured above is Ewan McGregor, with Nicole Kidman.)

of these mythical realms—talking scarecrows, singing mermaids, and genies who grant wishes. As noted above, polar opposites often counterbalance the royals, and this subgenre is populated equally by commoners. Often, therefore, we find entertainers, or artists of a sort, working stiffs trying to make an honest dollar or con men trying to make a dishonest fortune, orphans mentored by mysterious millionaires, or millionaires posing as commoners.

Characters in the folk-musical subgenre inhabit worlds far different from those in the fairy-tale variety. Mostly everyday people—even when the protagonists seem somewhat exotic, like the mobsters in *Guys and Dolls* (1955), the gang members in *West Side Story*, the carneys of *Carousel* (1956), the baseball players of *Take Me Out to the Ball Game* (1949), and the gold prospectors in *Paint Your Wagon* (1969)—these figures possess a rootedness, a sense of belonging to a place audiences can recognize as at least possibly real. The most typical ordinary people in this subgenre are denizens of small-town America. Nothing extraordinary or fanciful defines the characters in *Meet Me in St. Louis*, who are members of a typical multigenerational household. Yet in setting the films among ordinary people in Middle America, this subgenre foregrounds an important icon that further helps define it: the family. As Altman notes, no other musical subgenre features families so prevalently. Parents or parental figures, youthful lovers, adolescents on the cusp of adulthood, and little children abound in this form. Conventional spaces, then, are found in small towns where families naturally congregate: the home, for instance, is a major locale (perhaps no film outside of a melodrama has been rooted so specifically in the home as *Meet Me in St. Louis*). Other icons of small towns or coherent neighborhoods predominate in the settings, like the park, saloon, malt shop, or street.

While the spaces characters occupy and the sorts of characters who inhabit them differ vastly from the folk to the fairy-tale musical, a similarity still exists in the transformation of the setting into a quasi-mythical realm. Initially, at least, rural Oklahoma seems immensely different from a desert kingdom, Catfish Row, the black section of Charleston, South Carolina in *Porgy and Bess* (1959) from lily-white Sylvania, and the backwoods in *Seven Brides for Seven Brothers* from the gardens of Paris, yet a sense of escapism links each to the other. Though certainly not every folk musical is set in the past or attempts overt escapism (*West Side Story* and *Flower Drum Song*, for instance, are clear exceptions), many of these films invoke nostalgia as their dominant emotional tendency. Setting the films in the past, for example, allows for the elimination of racial issues—not because such issues didn't exist but because they were little discussed. Paradoxically, the all-black musicals similarly avoid racial issues by focusing exclusively on an all-black setting, as if these characters lived in a mythical land (unlike the America of their time) where white people either didn't exist or had no negative impact on black life. In that sense, an element of the folk subgenre takes on certain of the fairy-tale qualities, at least in terms of overall setting and certain thematic aspects. But in the kinds of characters and the types of musical numbers they perform, the folk musical is distinguishable from its fairy-tale cousin because its setting is distinctly recognizable—and recognizably American, at that.

The settings of the show musical, however, tend to be more grounded in everyday realities, despite some overlap between subgenres. Just as the fairy-tale and the folk varieties clearly display certain similarities in their settings, so, too, the show variety can overlap with the folk-variety films that focus on show business of one sort or another, such as *Show Boat*, *Summer Stock* (1950), and *Annie Get Your Gun*. Still, one can typically define the show musical by a narrative drive that overtly features the trials and tribulations of putting on a production. The final result need not necessarily be a Broadway performance, though that destination typifies the subgenre. The final outcome can be movie musicals, as in *Singin' in the Rain*, or USO shows during wartime, as in *Stage Door Canteen* (1943), or the revue-like *Stormy Weather*, with its focus on various venues within the narrative. But the majority of films within this subgenre specifically devote themselves to making it on the Great White Way, Broadway. This quest for popular success means, of course, New York City and its environs, but it also encompasses the apartments of the well-to-do and the less so, the dressing rooms of the cast, and the stage itself, in rehearsal and in performance.

The show-business setting of this subgenre brings with it a rather limited cast of characters, specifically, show people. They may be fit into clear types—even more familiar archetypes than the characters in the fairy-tale and folk variety. These include the driven director—a figure of respect (the Warner Bros. films of the early 1930s) or a figure of gentle satire (*The Band Wagon*); the temperamental star who will either not make it into the final production or who must learn humility despite his/her superior talent; the pleasant juvenile male lead; and the unknown chorus girl upon whose untested and slender shoulders the success of the show may ultimately rest. This subgenre also features a recognizable set of hangers-on, from the well-to-do who fancy themselves patrons of the arts to the low-level tough guys (typically rendered harmless in the classical era) who romance the equally tough chorus girls who, unlike the lucky one plucked from obscurity, are destined never to make it big.

Yet, the seemingly discrete nature of the subgenres should not disguise the commonalities across the genre. One such commonality, of course, is the importance of music. Beyond this obvious and tautological assertion lies a more important proposition, however: that the musical consists of both a number of songs and a variety of song types. Song types usually mean such things as: solo, duet, dance duet (a derivation of the ballet pas de deux), chorus or ensemble number, and specialty numbers. Solos themselves might be broken down into such categories as declarative numbers, with which a character asserts his or her personality in a forceful way; love solos, which express joy at the newly born romance; and plaintive songs of longing or regret. Duets might be comically argumentative or mutual declarations of love; specialty numbers might be the province of the protagonist, the couple, or a supporting character. Though not every classical musical might contain all of these types of numbers, enough make the inclusion of such numbers iconographic of the form itself, part of both its semantics (the very types themselves) and its syntax (where they fall in the unreeling of the plot). One reason that the contemporary film musical revolving around, say, would-be dancers, street entertainers, or young people who perform in a marching band may not seem quite the same kind of musical as is generally understood by the term may be due to this lack of variety in the music.

Take a film like *Oklahoma!* The variety of musical numbers indicates just how many types of integrated songs can create setting, mood, character, conflict, and a sense of community, among other necessities. Though admittedly more typical of the Broadway stage than the original film musical (some structural needs of a live show, such as ensemble numbers and secondary-couple songs, which give primary couples chances to rest from the rigors of being constantly on stage, obviously are not necessary in film), *Oklahoma!* demonstrates how musical numbers can vary in their type and function. Curly's (Gordon MacRae) opening solo, "Oh, What a Beautiful Mornin'," provides not only the musical's setting but also something of Curly's personality—self-contained but optimistic, fancy free but romantic. The more comic number "I Cain't Say No" tells a great deal about the comically sexy Ado Annie (Gloria Grahame), who will form one half of the secondary couple. "Kansas City," an ensemble number, not only gives the stars a chance to rest but provides a sense of spectacle by incorporating a large number of singers and dancers while simultaneously lending the piece its air of nostalgia. (*Oklahoma!* is a folk musical set in 1906, the year before Oklahoma was granted statehood.) The show's second number, "The Surrey with the Fringe on Top," sung by Curly to Laurey (Shirley Jones), functions as a courting song, a playful attempt by Curly to convince Laurey to go to a dance with him. It also furnishes some of the turn-of-the-century flavor necessary to create nostalgia for the bygone era. As Curly's early solo offers information about his character, so Laurey's later solo, "Many a New Day," reveals much about her: mainly her feelings for Curly in the obvious attempt to deny them. The title song itself is a paean to the territory (and to rural life) that is about to become a state.

Besides providing the state with its official song (and a slogan— OKLAHOMA IS OK—for a previous version of its license plate), *Oklahoma!* was a novel show in every respect. Certainly its most influential innovation

***Oklahoma!* (1955)** The dream ballet, pioneered on stage by Agnes de Mille and on film by Gene Kelly, became a staple of the film musical to narrate the emotional conflicts and feelings of the characters through the expressive means of dance. The ballet, even more than the Broadway stage, was the province of urban sophisticates and had very much a European taint to it, but the pioneering choreography of de Mille and Kelly Americanized the form to some extent, and in general made ballet accessible to audiences far and wide.

was the "dream ballet" performed by Laurey. This lengthy dance, built on the ballet style pioneered by George Balanchine and Martha Graham and choreographed by Agnes de Mille (her first foray on Broadway), narrativized dance in the musical as never before, fully integrating aspects of the character and themes. De Mille went on to create other dream ballets and innovative choreography for Broadway productions of *Carousel* (1945), *Brigadoon* (1947), and *Paint Your Wagon* (1951). The dream ballet, in particular, found a welcome home in the film musical and was particularly popular in the 1940s in films like *Yolanda and the Thief* and *The Pirate*.

The dream ballet and other lengthy dance sequences in balletic mode also owe something to the "Slaughter on Tenth Avenue" number danced by Gene Kelly and Vera-Ellen in *Words and Music* (1948). Originally choreographed by George Balanchine for the Rodgers and Hart stage musical *On Your Toes* (1936), Kelly adapted it to film. Specifically, he took advantage of his muscular dancing style and sense of choreography for the camera to make the number completely self-contained. Under the impetus of de Mille's choreography for the Broadway stage and sequences like "Slaughter on Tenth Avenue," the dream ballet and other fantasy-like modern-dance sequences became part and parcel of the classical musical. The most memorable of these include the very lengthy sequence in which Minnelli and Kelly transform the banks of the river Seine into a dream world for the romantic "An American in Paris Ballet"; Kelly's reimagining his shore leave in "A Day in New York" in *On the Town*; Astaire and Cyd Charisse's channeling of Mickey Spillane in the "Girl Hunt Ballet" in *The Band Wagon*; Leslie Caron's fantasizing about her guardian angel in the "Daydream Sequence" in *Daddy Long Legs*; and the "Broadway Melody Ballet" in *Singin' in the Rain*. Of course, the prevalence of these types of numbers in the films of Astaire and Kelly as stars and choreographers contributed a great deal in creating the iconic patterns of the musical.

Another crucial icon of the genre is the specialty number, also exemplified in the films of Astaire and Kelly. Though many films built around the particular talents of a particular star would find ways to integrate musical numbers to highlight this, these sequences became icons in the films of Astaire and Kelly. Such numbers were not simply dancing or singing solos, but rather dance numbers designed to take advantage of choreographic ingenuity along with the star's particular, unique style. The sets, props, and staging were all integral parts of the dance. In the Astaire canon such numbers include "Top Hat, White Tie and Tails" from *Top Hat*; "Bojangles of Harlem" from *Swing Time*; "Sunday Jumps" and "You're All the World to Me" (this is the famous number where the camera revolves along with the room itself) from *Royal Wedding* (1951); and "Shine on Your Shoes" from *The Band Wagon*. These are just some of the musical items that bear Astaire's immortal stamp.

For Kelly, who is not identified as part of a romantic duo as are Astaire and Rogers,[3] almost all of his most famous screen moments are specialty numbers: dancing with a mop, a couple of different brooms, on furniture, with anything other than a dame, in *Thousands Cheer* (1943); to his own mirror image for the "Alter Ego" number in *Cover Girl* (1944); with Jerry the Mouse (of the cartoon duo Tom and Jerry) in *Anchors Aweigh* (1945); on roller skates for the number "I Like Myself" in *It's Always Fair Weather* (1955); acrobatically tapping and leaping with the Nicholas Brothers to Cole Porter's "Be a Clown" in *The Pirate*; and, of

---

[3] Altman, *The American Film Musical*, 55.

***Swing Time* (1936)** "Bojangles of Harlem" represents one of Fred Astaire's most complex specialty numbers, with its use of multiple silhouetted images of the dancer, first mirroring his movements and later conflicting with them. Yet certainly most notable is that Astaire performs in blackface. One of the most controversial of all American musical modes, blackface entertainment has been unalterably tainted by the tinge of racism. Though cinematic blackface performances in the studio era were hardly deliberately racist, they do reveal the continuity of this problematic performance style. Moreover, in this instance, by allegedly paying tribute to Bill "Bojangles" Robinson, "Bojangles of Harlem" reveals the racism that underlies blackface by the very absence of the figure being feted—indeed, it points to the very absence of black actors in most musicals, a form which drew so heavily from black expressive culture.

course, with an umbrella and a rain shower in what might be the single most famous number in the annals of the musical, the title track from *Singin' in the Rain*. These typify the Kelly specialty sequence.

Specialty numbers are not always the province of the stars. Though most of the ensemble cast of *On the Town* are allowed to shine in their own moments (i.e., their own specialty is given a chance to come to the fore), Ann Miller's "Prehistoric Man" is something of a showstopper. The same is true of Donald O'Connor's unforgettable acrobatics in "Make 'em Laugh" in *Singin' in the Rain*. In the musical revue, one could argue that every performance is a specialty number. Still, with the appearance of recognizable musical stars or significant costars, one crucial icon that helps define the musical is the specialty number.

Yet if one type of number best represents the musical, with its dual-focus narrative leading to the creation of the romantic couple, it is the duet—especially the pas de deux. Singing and dancing well together overtly confirms the rightness of the couple's being together. Over and over, across the decades of the form, the seemingly spontaneous ability of the musical couple to sing or dance in perfect harmony or coordination is indicative of the essential rightness of the union. Tony (Astaire) and Gaby (Charisse) think they are from two different worlds in *The Band Wagon*: tap versus ballet, popular versus high art, Broadway versus

Singin' in the Rain **(1952)** In what is justifiably the single most famous musical number in all of film history, Gene Kelly's performance of the title number from *Singin' in the Rain* captures the very essence of the musical. Don Lockwood's joy at falling in love leads to a moment of sheer exuberance. Instead of seeing the rain as an inconvenience, it becomes an opportunity to cavort in childlike glee, seen when the intricate and athletic choreography gives way to the act of stomping through rain puddles. This anarchic spirit animating the body to express its ecstatic feelings comes to a halt, symbolically enough, when Lockwood comes upon a policeman, the sign of authority. Appropriately for a film about the coming of sound to the movies, the song itself was introduced in *The Hollywood Revue of 1929*, the second feature-length musical released by MGM.

legitimate theater. Yet when they step out into Central Park to the strains of "Dancing in the Dark" and begin to move together—magic. This was always the in-joke, so to speak, of the plots of the Astaire-Rogers films. Fred would pursue Ginger; she'd resist; but the magic they made together on the dance floor would always translate to the enchantment of romance. The song-and-dance duet became de rigueur in their films and in some ways came to define the form itself. "Night and Day" in *The Gay Divorcee*, "Let's Face the Music and Dance" in *Follow the Fleet* (1936), "Never Gonna Dance" in *Swing Time*, and, most famously, "Cheek to Cheek" in *Top Hat* are far more important to the creation of the couple than are the mechanics of the plot.

Kelly's films were not immune to the magic of the pas de deux, either. He is paired with Vera-Ellen in a charming number, "When You Walk Down Mainstreet with Me," in *On the Town*; Tommy (Kelly) and Fiona (Charisse) make beautiful music together to the strains of "The Heather on the Hill" in *Brigadoon*. Of course, Kelly is not alone in discovering that dancing with a partner is sometimes more satisfying than dancing alone. Tony Manero learns that lesson when he connects with Stephanie in *Saturday Night Fever*. Young women learn this same lesson in *Save the Last Dance* and *Step Up*. Thus, for over seventy years of Hollywood movie musicals, the lesson remains the same: making beautiful music together means that you belong together, that the show will go on forever in a world of entertainment.

CLOSE-UP

Saturday Night Fever

Perhaps no film has ever been so intimately associated with its sound track as *Saturday Night Fever*. For some audience members the music makes the film; for others, the film is an artistic success aside from the music. For any discerning viewer, it is clear the film needs its music as much as its music benefits from John Travolta's star turn. An immediate blockbuster success, with a sequel following some six years later, the film continues to have a life in popular culture. Yet one thing *Saturday Night Fever* seems not to be for most critics, and perhaps most audiences, is a musical.

Saturday Night Fever is an adaptation of a supposedly nonfiction magazine story about Brooklyn working-class youth who essentially live for Saturday nights and their time at the local disco. Though the story was eventually revealed to be wholly made up (British author Nik Cohn based his article, "Tribal Rites of the New Saturday Night," on the British mod movement of a decade earlier—a predominantly working-class youth movement which at least provided the origin of *Saturday Night Fever*'s working-class focus), the film attains a rare level of authenticity through its location shooting, incisive script, and excellent performances from a cast of relatively unknown young actors—only Travolta among the leads had any particular résumé or fame at the time. The strong, wholly realistic dialogue, the lack of any attempt to glamorize the locales, and the often foolish behavior of the protagonists suggest a rare level of insight concerning marginalized and alienated young people. Perhaps the dismissal of the music by so many critics then (and now) has something to do with the film's milieu. Yet it is this very dismissal that prevents critics and certain audience segments from seeing the film for what it is, in its essence: a musical.

Given that all of the musical numbers within the film's narrative either are performed at the disco or depict rehearsal at the studio in preparation for the dance contest, the film resembles the classic backstage musical [though the disco contest, far from representing a triumphant climax, is rather anticlimactic, save that it contributes to Tony's (Travolta) increasing sense that he is outgrowing his Bay Ridge roots]. Its use of New York locales recalls *On the Town* and *West Side Story*, and reproduces the latter's insistence on ethnic specificity and refusal to turn New York into the kind of utopia that critic Richard Dyer characterizes as an essential part of the genre. Indeed, not only does *Saturday Night Fever* not glamorize its locales or underplay ethnicity, it revels in the ordinariness, even seediness, of much of the Brooklyn landscape and the truly dark side of family and interethnic conflict. The harsh language; intense, if only occasional, violence; frequent sordid sexuality, and ambiguous ending also seem far from any notion of classical Hollywood's feel-good musicals. And yet, despite these features, the film's structure and, ultimately, its sense of the redeeming power of music as a form of imagination fit the film into a generic mold that is worth exploring.

If the musical numbers are either performed in the disco or rehearsed in anticipation of the disco contest, these numbers nevertheless function as music does in the integrated classic musical: as revelatory of the essential fit between a man and a woman, as the raucous expression of spirit and energy, and as an aid to the spontaneous formation of community. In addition, there is another kind of "performance" style in the film, that between the image track and the sound track. Rarely, if ever, has the relationship between the score and what is on screen been so intimately connected. Far from merely used as underscoring to guide our emotions, the music functions as an integral part of the narrative: what happens on the musical track is just as important as what we see on the image track. This element is seen most clearly right at the start when Tony walks down the street to the tune of "Stayin' Alive." His walk, a confident strut, is cut precisely to the Bee Gee's beat. This sets the tone, then, for the importance of the relationship between music and image, gives us insight into Tony's character, and possesses its own infectiousness, as if we were experiencing time not on the grimy streets of Brooklyn but in the more sensual world of the disco. In a sense, this is the very theme of the film—the disjunction between the workaday world of Tony's low-level job (he is carrying a paint can)—and the triumphant spirit to be found in the dance club, 2001 Odyssey.

The lyrics, too, express many of the themes—appropriate for an opening number. Just as Tony Hunter (Fred Astaire) in *The Band Wagon* expresses both his sense of isolation and his determination in that film's

"Well, you can tell by the way I use my walk…" Tony, carrying a paint can, struts his stuff.

opening number, "By Myself," so "Stayin' Alive" tells us of Tony's pluck and the alienation he feels.

> Well, you can tell by the way I use my walk,
> I'm a woman's man, no time to talk.
> Music loud and women warm,
> I've been kicked around since I was born.
> And now it's all right. It's okay.
> And you may look the other way.
> . . .
> Well now, I get low and I get high,
> And if I can't get either, I really try.
> Got the wings of heaven on my shoes;
> I'm a dancin' man and I just can't lose.

His sexual confidence and the importance of dance to his self-image are in conflict with the indifference of the city and, as the following scene reveals, the indifference, even hostility, of his family. Only at the disco does Tony come alive.

The spontaneous formation of community around music and performance, a key component of the classic musical, is seen in the first sequence at the disco. Tony takes to the dance floor and grabs two girls around the waist and begins to dance with them; and soon, to the strains of the Bee Gees' "Night Fever," he leads an ensemble in the Electric Slide. The number is an important component of the narrative in that it shows Tony's leadership at the club, his dancing skills, and the way Annette (Donna Pescow) pushes through the group to dance next to him. This formation of community around dance has a real-life component in the film—the close-knit community of Italian-American youngsters who resent outsiders, be they Puerto Ricans or Manhattanites slumming in Brooklyn.

As in any classic musical, the leading man gets his specialty number. For Travolta this is his solo number performed, appropriately enough, to the strains of the Bee Gees' "You Should Be Dancing." Tony simply abandons his dance partner and takes over the floor. Since Travolta is an excellent dancer, the film allows him a number of fairly lengthy takes that show off his ability. However, the film also feels it necessary to cut occasionally to onlookers admiring Tony's skills. This kind of built-in audience is also typical of musicals set in clubs or in performance spaces to motivate the musical number. But more typically the musical number

Tony leads the spontaneous dance line as they perform a variation of the Hustle and the Electric Slide.

takes over and the audience is abandoned, so to speak. Less so here, for the film insists that Tony's dance is performed in the midst of his admiring community; that it is not a Busby Berkeley sort of impossible fantasy but an outgrowth of Tony's energy and enthusiasm, his way of working off the week's pressures and disappointments.

Another key component of the classic musical is the creation of the couple. The couple's suitability is almost always signaled by their fit in duets, with at least two musical numbers together—the first some sort of spontaneous dance that reveals their natural connection, and the second a performance number that solidifies their relationship and leads to some dramatic highlight. Here, again, the film fits the bill. Though Annette pursues Tony, and has a natural dancing talent, Tony is attracted to the more worldly and aloof Stephanie (Karen Lynn Gorney). He first sees her in 2001 Odyssey as the DJ puts on a Latin number. Tony is angry at this, not believing the music to be danceable. However, he spots Stephanie doing a salsa with an older man and is immediately impressed by and attracted to her. When he says, "She can dance; she has the wrong partner, of course," we know who he has in mind as the right one. And indeed, at their first rehearsal together to prepare for the dance contest, their duet reveals their natural compatibility. Like Fred and Ginger dancing cheek to cheek and arm in arm, Tony and Stephanie trip the light fantastic with spontaneous grace. They dance to the

Tony's solo number at the dance club has also become one of the film's iconic moments.

strains of "More Than a Woman," perhaps revealing that Stephanie will, indeed, be more than a woman to Tony and become more of a mentor than a lover. Although they will kiss and attempt a date, their fit together is almost wholly on the dance floor. Whereas in the classic musical, dancing was something of a substitute or stand-in for sex and certainly revealed the natural suitability of the couple, in this postclassical musical, Tony and Stephanie have almost nothing but dancing. Until Tony can grow out of using dance as an escape, can learn to treat women as more than either sex objects or, for that matter, dance partners, he is not a suitable partner for Stephanie. He realizes this and goes to her at the end, a different man.

In fact, it might be argued that although they dance well together, their second duet is not a transcendent moment in the film. The musical number—the disco contest—danced again to the strains of "More Than a Woman" (except this time it is the Bee Gees' version and not Tavares's, as in the rehearsal) wins them the contest. But Tony, at least, recognizes that the Puerto Rican couple danced much better than he and Stephanie and he is angry that his friends—even Stephanie—cannot admit as much. This moment is primarily used to demonstrate that Tony has come to recognize the provincialism of his life, not to mention the racism that infuses his community. But symbolically we may say that the quality of the duet reflects on Tony as someone who still has growing and learning to do, as good a dancer as he is. Thus, the musical numbers function much as they do in the classic musical: as revelatory of character, as aid in the spontaneous formation of community, as revealing the special talent and ability of the leading man, and in demonstrating the potential suitability of the couple. Though the music is, then, highly significant to the film's plot and characters, the film's climax is most distinctly—except as we will see in an ironic way—not a musical number.

The final straw of Tony's disillusionment with his life takes place during the film's second scene on the Verrazano-Narrows Bridge. Bridges are an important motif in the film. The Verrazano Bridge, which connects the New York City boroughs of Brooklyn and Staten Island, is a liminal space for Tony and his friends. When they get drunk or high, the group drives in Bobby's (Barry Miller) car to the bridge to let off steam. They never actually cross the bridge. Instead, they stop in the middle and Joey (Joseph Cali) and Double J (Paul Pape) perform dangerous stunts on the scaffolding and walkways. The first time they go to the bridge, we notice that Bobby does not engage in any such stunts, preferring to remain in the car with Annette. Later in the film, Tony will borrow Bobby's car to drive Stephanie to Manhattan, crossing the Brooklyn Bridge to the instrumental strains of "How Deep Is Your Love"—filmed in such a way as to seem like a climactic moment as a helicopter shot follows them across the famous bridge's majestic span, moving ever upward until the car is almost too small to be seen, as if it were triumphantly leaving Brooklyn behind. Of course, the movement from Brooklyn to Manhattan represents Stephanie's step up to a larger world—a world in which she interacts with the likes of Laurence Olivier, whom Tony knows not by name but because the famous actor once did TV commercials for Polaroid. Stephanie's attempts to better herself are contrasted with Tony's

The creation of the couple in their duet rehearsal—though more work needs to be done both as dancers and as a couple.

utter lack of horizons; his only feelings of accomplishment stem from the small raise he gets at work, for which his unemployed father belittles him; his dancing; and his fascination with the Verrazano Bridge—which Stephanie cogently points out he never crosses but only reads about.

Yet the film's climax does indeed take place on that very bridge. Bobby, who worships Tony with the same kind of idolization and homosexual attraction reminiscent of that of Sal Mineo's Plato toward James Dean's Jim in the youth classic *Rebel Without a Cause* (1955)—to which *Saturday Night Fever* bears more than a passing resemblance in other ways, as well—is upset that Tony didn't call him one night as promised. Bobby has gotten a girl pregnant and is contemplating marrying her after finding out from Tony's brother, a priest, that the pope will not give a dispensation for an abortion. Exactly what Bobby wants to talk to Tony about we do not know, but certainly his feeling of hurt and betrayal at Tony's not calling him is more traditionally associated with a woman's reaction when a man who has promised to call does not. (Bobby has frequently been visually linked with Annette throughout the film, thus feminizing him and making him, like Annette, a would-be lover whom Tony rejects.) In obvious despair, Bobby begins to perform stunts on the bridge's cables as if he were some mad circus performer. His friends try to talk him down, but all he can do is call out to Tony to admire his fearlessness. Tony's attempts to get Bobby down off the cables and walkway reminds us of nothing so much as a failed duet—Tony reaches for Bobby as Fred

A kind of failed duet, Tony reaching for Bobby, but their hands never meet.

A sense of ethnic identification and solidarity with the underdog are evoked in Tony's poster of *Rocky*.

to Ginger, but to no avail. Bobby's plunge off the bridge to his death is interpreted by Tony as suicide, certainly an astute observation. Of course, we may interpret this suicide as Bobby's feeling trapped and hopeless at the prospect of marrying perhaps the only girl he ever slept with, but a deeper reading would be Bobby's inchoate recognition that heterosexual marriage itself is the fate he dreads—that he could never face his real feelings for Tony, given the rampant homophobia that also character- izes Bobby's friends, as seen when two gay men walk past the group and Joey and Double J tease and harass them. For Tony, though, Bobby's death represents everything about his community that he has come to resent—whether it's a knee-jerk Roman Catholicism that forces marriage onto teenagers who get pregnant, a son who joins the priesthood as the greatest good of all but a tragedy when that same son decides to turn in his collar, or deep-seated racism and homophobia. Tony finally makes the move out of Bay Ridge—perhaps ironically not by crossing any bridge but by taking the subway under the river, arriving the next morning into the light of Manhattan and perhaps a new day for him.

Saturday Night Fever is very much a film of its time. Though casual audiences understand this in terms of the posters hanging on the wall in Tony's room, including one of Sylvester Stallone in *Rocky* (released the year before *Saturday Night Fever*), one of Al Pacino in *Serpico* (1973), to whom Tony is compared by a girl at the disco, and one of Farrah Fawcett, or the film's disco dancing and leisure suits, more discerning eyes will note its deep connections to the 1970s cinematic zeitgeist, its clear con- nections to the Hollywood renaissance. Though director John Badham is not usually thought of as one of the "movie brats," his deconstruction and reconstruction of the classic musical puts him squarely in the camp of those directors, like Francis Ford Coppola, Brian De Palma, and, especially Martin Scorsese, who put classic genres through a ringer and came up with potent new forms and formulas. Indeed, *Saturday Night Fever* recalls *On the Town* or *West Side Story* less than it does Scorsese's more personal cinema, such as *Who's That Knocking at My Door* (1967) and *Mean Streets* (1973). (Coincidentally, Scorsese evinced interest in the musical the same year as *Saturday Night Fever* with *New York, New York*.) The injection of strong elements of social class, its refusal to exoticize or romanticize its ethnic dimensions, and its ability to resist glamorizing its locales, turned *Saturday Night Fever* into a rare Hollywood film of great depth and seriousness. At the same time, it managed to continue to participate in a genre that pays tribute to the values of Hollywood entertainment through the transcendent use of music and dance.

David Desser

QUESTIONS FOR DISCUSSION

1. It is well known that musical stars like Cyd Charisse routinely had their singing voices dubbed. Both Natalie Wood and Rita Moreno were dubbed in *West Side Story*, as was Audrey Hepburn in *My Fair Lady*. Ironically, Debbie Reynolds had her singing voice dubbed over in one number in *Singin' in the Rain*. Though not uncommon, then, does this fact detract from the reality of the musical, one value of which is the ability of the characters to sing and dance as expressions of higher emotions and sheer professionalism?

2. Though the entire Hollywood cinema, past and present, is a collaborative art, the auteur theory arose to separate out a group of authors who managed, despite studio, stars, genre, and screenwriters, to put their individual stamp on their films. The musical is perhaps more heavily dependent on a variety of collaborative talent, including the composers and lyricists and the choreographers and stars. Directors like Vincente Minnelli, Gene Kelly, and Stanley Donen are certainly credited with innovative filmmaking and personal contributions. Yet other directors of significant musicals, like Mark Sandrich and Charles Walters, are given far less stature. How applicable is the auteur theory, then, to the musical, given the extensive input and even centrality of other creators involved?

3. Walt Disney's animated classics like *Snow White and the Seven Dwarfs*, *Dumbo*, *Cinderella*, and on through the modern blockbusters like *The Little Mermaid*, *Beauty and the Beast*, *Aladdin*, etc., all feature original music and rely on it strongly for plot and character development. Yet these films are rarely thought of as musicals. According to the discussion of the genre in this chapter, in what ways are these films musicals?

4. Given the crucial significance of music to the characters and the number of musical performances within the films, in what ways can we say that films like *Drumline* (2002), *You Got Served* (2004), and *Stomp the Yard* (2007) are musicals? If they are musicals, into what subgenre might they fit? And if they are not musicals, why not? And what about films like *Bring It On* (2000) and its numerous direct-to-video sequels in which cheerleading—a form of dance, after all—is central to the plot? Are these musicals?

5. The decline of the classic musical in the late 1950s corresponds to the end of the classical era of Hollywood. Though the musical remains a somewhat vibrant force in the postclassical era, was there an intimate connection between the studio system and the musical, or were other factors involved in the musical's decline?

FOR FURTHER READING

Altman, Rick, ed. *Genre, the Musical: A Reader*. BFI Readers in Film Studies. London: Routledge, 1981.

———. *The American Film Musical*. Bloomington and Indianapolis: Indiana University Press, 1987.

Cohan, Steven. *Hollywood Musicals: The Film Reader*. New York: Routledge, 2002.

Dyer, Richard. "Entertainment and Utopia." *Movie* 24 (Spring 1977): 2–13, reprinted in Altman, ed. 175–89.

Feuer, Jane. *The Hollywood Musical*. 2nd Ed. Bloomington and Indianapolis: Indiana University Press, 1993.

Knight, Arthur. *Disintegrating the Musical: Black Performance and American Musical Film*. Durham and London: Duke University Press, 2002.

Mast, Gerald. *Can't Help Singin': The American Musical on Stage and Screen*. Woodstock, NY: Overlook Press, 1987.

Parkinson, David. *The Rough Guide to Film Musicals*. Rough Guide Reference. London: Rough Guides, 2007.

Rubin, Martin. *Showstoppers: Busby Berkeley and the Tradition of Spectacle*. New York: Columbia University Press, 1993.

The Outlaw Josey Wales (1976)

The Western

TWO GUNFIGHTERS CONVERGE on the main street of town as prairie dust billows around them. Instead of blazing away with their guns, they silently face one another. The duel is decided in this moment of silence, and when they draw, the ritual is complete. Few scenes in the movies are as famous as the gunfight in a Western, or as deeply ingrained in the culture of America. Indeed, no genre connects as broadly or deeply with the nation's history and mythology or with ideas and images held about America throughout the world. Words like "cowboy," "gunfighter," and "stagecoach" swiftly evoke a stock of story situations and images. Clint Eastwood, one of the genre's key filmmakers, has stated that jazz and the Western are the great, original American art forms.

As a genre, an idea, and a cultural category, the Western predates cinema. The first public exhibition of motion pictures took place in 1895, but by then Westerns were already thriving in literature, painting, photography, and theater. James Fenimore Cooper largely invented the genre in his epic set of five novels The Leatherstocking Tales (1827–1841). Comprising *The Deerslayer, The Pathfinder, The Last of the Mohicans, The Pioneers,* and *The Prairie,* the novels tell of the exploits of the frontiersman Natty Bumppo and his attempts to escape encroaching civilization. The most famous of the novels, *The Last of the Mohicans,* has been filmed numerous times (1911, 1920, 1932, 1936, and 1992).

As Cooper was writing his novels, painters like George Catlin were traveling throughout the West, sketching and painting the Indian communities they found along the way. Catlin painted the Comanche, the Sioux, the Fox, and the Saulk with an ethnographer's eye for detail, costume, and ritual. The action paintings of Frederic Remington in the 1880s look like scenes from Hollywood movies. Remington's dynamic compositions depict outlaws riding into town, Indians chasing a stagecoach, and Indian gunfire pinning down the cavalry.

Like painters, photographers visualized and documented the West and the vanishing Indian communities. Photographic portraits of Geronimo, Red Cloud, Quanah Parker, and Chato show these warriors in later life; the camera also caught such other figures of legend as Tom Horn, Wyatt Earp, Pat Garrett, Billy the Kid, and Buffalo Bill.

One of the chief popularizers of Western mythology, and his role within it, was William Cody, better known as Buffalo Bill. During his career on the frontier, he had been a scout for General George Custer and received the Medal of Honor for his work with the Third Cavalry; later he appeared in a play in 1872 called *The Scouts of the Prairie*, in which he portrayed himself alongside another Western legend, Wild Bill Hickok. Buffalo Bill's Wild West show began in 1883 as a touring theater company featuring the likes of Sitting Bull and Annie Oakley, and dramatizations of Custer's Last Stand and the Pony Express. Cody and his show toured the United States and Europe, making him an international celebrity and his show one of the defining narratives of the West.

History

When cinema arrived, then, it inherited a massively popular cultural category—the Western—that already existed in the visual arts, literature, and the theater. But the movies did more than any of these other art forms to spread and popularize the genre and to make it singularly identified throughout the world with the life and culture of America. Remington's action paintings are cinematic, but they are static images. The movies invigorated the Western by bringing the dramatic stories of wagon trains, gunfighters, the Indian wars, and cattle drives to life in exciting imagery that *moved*.

Until the 1970s, Westerns were a thriving genre. From 1908 to 1913, the director D. W. Griffith worked at Biograph Studios, and of his 571 Biograph films, nearly seventy were Westerns. The most famous of these, *The Battle at Elderbush Gulch* (1913), shot on location in California, depicts warfare between white settlers and Native Americans. As early as 1910, 21 percent of all American films were Westerns, and over succeeding

The Great Train Robbery (1903) Westerns were plentiful before the invention of cinema, and they immediately became one of the new medium's most important and popular genres. At first, they were filmed on the East Coast. *The Great Train Robbery*, for example, was made in New Jersey. It tells a familiar genre story of robbers attacking a train and being pursued and gunned down by a posse. With its use of multiple storylines and parallel editing, this film marked a key advance in early cinema's narrative capabilities.

decades that number remained relatively steady, fluctuating between a low of 13 percent in 1933 and a high of 34 percent in 1950.[1] The greatest number per year were produced in the mid-1920s. In 1925, for example, Hollywood made 227 Westerns; the following year, it made 199. By the 1960s, the overall number of features began to decline, although Westerns were plentiful on television in that era. Forty-six Western series were broadcast in 1960, for example.

Several reasons exist for the immediate bond between early cinema and Westerns. One is that filmmakers could shoot outdoors, and the Los Angeles area, then still primitive, featured abundant unspoiled landscapes. But another reason is that for early filmmakers, the frontier was still a reality. Hollywood at the time was a remote location, a primitive town, and vestiges of the frontier remained. Cattle ranches operated near the movie colony, which employed many ranch hands. Director Raoul Walsh, stuntman Yakima Canutt, and actors Ben Johnson, Tom

[1] Figures cited here and elsewhere from *The BFI Companion to the Western*, ed. Edward Buscombe (Boston: Da Capo Press, 1988), 426–28.

Mix, and Slim Pickens were all cowboys before they got into the movies. Wyatt Earp lived in Hollywood in the 1920s and worked as a film consultant, and he became friendly with Tom Mix and the director John Ford. Bill Tilghman, who had been marshal of Dodge City, directed himself in *The Bank Robbery* (1908), which is about his pursuit of the outlaw Al Jennings, who played himself. The Comanche chief Quanah Parker has a cameo in the movie, which was shot near Cache, Oklahoma. Thomas Edison's *Cripple Creek Bar Room* (1899) depicts contemporaneous times following the 1891 Colorado gold strike at Cripple Creek.

Westerns were very real, then, for the early filmmakers working in this genre. Before 1907, though, most Westerns were filmed on the East Coast. The most famous and significant of these, *The Great Train Robbery* (1903), was, like *Cripple Creek Bar Room*, shot in New Jersey. But by 1907, the Selig and Essanay film companies were shooting out West, and in 1910 the Bison company settled in Santa Ynez Canyon and became a significant producer of early Westerns. That same year, Bronco Billy Anderson, who had appeared in a small role in *The Great Train Robbery*, emerged as the first Western star. Dressed as a cowboy but sometimes playing a genial outlaw, Anderson had a ten-year run of popularity in pictures like *Bronco Billy's Redemption* (1910) and *Shootin' Mad* (1918).

Two other major silent screen stars offered highly influential variations on the cowboy. William S. Hart—*Hell's Hinges* (1916) and *Tumbleweeds* (1925)—incarnated the silent, taciturn loner, slow to anger but capably violent once roused. Hart's persona influenced the demeanor of such later Western stars as Gary Cooper, Randolph Scott, James Stewart, and Clint Eastwood. In contrast to Hart's moral seriousness, Tom Mix packaged the Western cowboy as a figure of flamboyant entertainment. His films, such as *Riders of the Purple Sage* (1925), *Tony Runs Wild* (1926), and *King Cowboy* (1928), bristled with stunts, chases, and fistfights; his horse had a name (Tony); and his heroic, gallant characters lacked the moral darkness that Hart embodied.

The Western often assumes an epic form because of its vast landscapes and great historical themes, and large-scale Westerns soon appeared in the silent and early sound eras. Shot on location in Utah and Nevada, James Cruze's *The Covered Wagon* (1923) dramatized the migration of settlers via the overland trails in the 1840s, and the movie was a huge popular hit. John Ford's *The Iron Horse* (1924) portrayed the building of the first transcontinental railroad. Raoul Walsh's *The Big Trail* (1930) depicted waves of Conestoga wagons sweeping across the overland trails. Walsh shot the movie in 70 mm widescreen and filled the huge frame with impressive action and epic landscapes. The film featured John Wayne in his first major role, as the scout leading a wagon train, but its box-office failure sent Wayne back to B movies for the rest of the decade. He did not have another lead role until John Ford's *Stagecoach* (1939).

The B studios, which were sometimes referred to as Poverty Row and included Republic, Monogram, Producers Releasing Corporation, and other independents, were major producers of Westerns. From 1941 to 1945, the B studios produced 645 features, of which half were Westerns. By contrast, in these years Westerns represented 13 percent of all films produced by Hollywood's major studios (Paramount, Warner Bros., MGM, Columbia, 20th Century–Fox, RKO, Universal). The Bs produced

The Toll Gate **(1920)** William S. Hart was one of the genre's first and biggest stars. Hart had been a professional stage actor but was drawn to film because of his love for the West and his interest in offering realistic portraits of the frontier. He established the iconic Western hero—taciturn, solitary, slow to anger but deadly when roused—that later stars, like Gary Cooper and Henry Fonda, perpetuated. In *The Toll Gate*, Hart plays an outlaw trying to escape his lawless past. Like that of Western stars Clint Eastwood and Charles Bronson, his face looks carved in stone.

most of the Westerns—62 percent—made throughout the industry in these years. These movies were shot quickly on low budgets and emphasized action. Many were series Westerns, with popular stars, such as Roy Rogers and John Wayne, who appealed to a juvenile audience. In terms of sheer numbers, the B Westerns represented the base of the genre in this period, but its critical reputation rests almost exclusively with the A pictures made by Hollywood's major studios.

Nearly all of Hollywood's major directors worked in the genre; the notable exception is Alfred Hitchcock. Sometimes the visit was occasional but resulted in noteworthy films, as with George Stevens: *Shane* (1953), Henry King: *The Gunfighter* (1950), Fred Zinnemann: *High Noon* (1952), and William Wyler: *The Big Country* (1958). Not typically identified with the Western, these directors made significant contributions to it by adding an uncommon degree of psychological depth to the characters and sometimes by taking it in unusual political directions. Zinnemann's *High Noon*, for example, is an allegory about the fragility of democracy and how appeals to patriotism can be a cover for political repression. Working more regularly in the genre were William Wellman: *The Ox-Bow Incident* (1943), *Yellow Sky* (1948), *Track of the Cat* (1954); Raoul Walsh: *The Big Trail* (1930), *They Died with Their Boots On* (1941), *The Tall Men* (1955); and Delmer Daves: *Broken Arrow* (1950), *3:10 to Yuma* (1957), *Cowboy* (1958).

Unquestionably, the genre's most important directors during the classical Hollywood studio era of the 1930s, '40s, and '50s were Howard Hawks and John Ford. Hawks's *Red River* (1948) is one of the genre's great classics, an epic about the first cattle drive over the Chisholm Trail. It features a brilliant performance by John Wayne as a cruel trail boss, one that redefined his career and established his chops as a serious actor. Hawks continued working with Wayne in *Rio Bravo* (1959), *El Dorado* (1966), and *Rio Lobo* (1970). These collaborations helped to define Wayne's star persona, one of the most important in the genre.

But it was Ford who established the most enduring partnership with Wayne and who is arguably the genre's finest filmmaker. Ford made more great Westerns than anybody else, films that are not simply genre classics but rank among American cinema's greatest films, period. These include *Stagecoach*, *My Darling Clementine* (1946), *Fort Apache* (1948), *The Searchers* (1956), and *The Man Who Shot Liberty Valance* (1962). Ford's use of Monument Valley, on the Arizona-Utah border, made it the most iconic of the Western's landscapes, and his films look more deeply into

***Stagecoach* (1939)** Universally regarded as one of the industry's top filmmakers, John Ford would unpretentiously introduce himself by saying, "I'm John Ford. I make Westerns." He made more great Westerns than anybody else and launched John Wayne's career as a major star in *Stagecoach.* Wayne had spent the decade in low-budget B movies when Ford gave him the lead role as the Ringo Kid. Here he makes his dramatic entrance in the film and into legend.

the relation between history and myth than anyone else's. In his early work, such as *The Iron Horse* and *Three Bad Men* (1926), Ford presents the ideals of Manifest Destiny and other Western myths in an optimistic and uncritical fashion. As he aged and his work deepened, he began to question these ideals, and in pictures like *Fort Apache, The Searchers,* and *The Man Who Shot Liberty Valance,* he shows that a nation's mythology often distorts, denies, or suppresses complicated and unpleasant historical truths.

As the studio system began to ebb in the 1950s, two important filmmakers emerged and fashioned a series of idiosyncratic films around the personae of stars James Stewart and Randolph Scott. Anthony Mann, who had specialized in crime films during the 1940s, created a series of rough, rugged, and often extremely brutal films starring Stewart in much darker roles than he previously had played. *Winchester 73* (1950), *Bend of the River* (1952), *The Naked Spur* (1953), *The Far Country* (1954), and *The Man from Laramie* (1955) feature a poetically harsh use of landscape and Stewart alternating between obsession, revenge, and brutalization. In contrast with the flamboyance of Mann's films, those directed by Budd Boetticher and starring Randolph Scott are more spare, terse, and minimalist. In *Seven Men from Now* (1956), *The Tall T* (1957), *Decision at Sundown* (1957), *Buchanan Rides Alone* (1958), *Ride Lonesome* (1959), and *Comanche Station* (1960), small, spare films that were tightly crafted morality plays, Boetticher pitted Scott's elegant loner against a series of often charming villains. The Mann-Stewart and Boetticher-Scott films are regarded today as among the genre's most important works.

In the later 1960s and into the 1970s, the Western's base of popularity began to erode as the nation's culture underwent wrenching transformations associated with the civil rights movement, the Vietnam War, and the women's movement. The cumulative effects of these transformations led to a breaking apart of the genre's classical structure, in which the values associated with civilization—the conquest of the frontier, the displacement of Native Americans, and traditional gender role division—were no longer taken for granted. One result was a new complexity and self-consciousness in the genre, often a new cynicism in the handling of its character types and stories. *Little Big Man* (1970), for example, shows Custer as deranged, the cavalry as bloodthirsty and brutal, and Native Americans as virtuous and heroic rather than as the stock villains typified in many past Westerns. The shadow of Vietnam hangs heavily over *Ulzana's Raid* (1972), a cavalry-versus-Indians story about the military misadventure of fighting without understanding an adversary. *McCabe and Mrs. Miller* (1971), a seemingly traditional genre story about the founding of a town, depicts civilization as corrupted by money and as politically controlled by big business. At the end the hero dies alone in the snow, forgotten and abandoned by the town he helped create.

The Good, the Bad and the Ugly (1966) Clint Eastwood became a star in three "spaghetti Westerns" that he made in Italy with director Sergio Leone. The films became international box-office successes. Leone brought a new level of cynicism and violence to the genre and a brilliant cinematic style. Extraordinary examples of widescreen filmmaking, Leone's movies exerted a powerful influence over subsequent Westerns.

The genre's transformation and its new moral cynicism and skepticism were fueled in the mid-1960s by the spectacular box-office success of Sergio Leone's trilogy *A Fistful of Dollars* (1964), *A Few Dollars More* (1965), and *The Good, the Bad and the Ugly* (1966). Leone established a new iconic character, played by Clint Eastwood: a cold-blooded bounty hunter who doesn't play by a gentlemen's rules and may be apt to draw first, a stone killer who never hesitates. Made in Italy and released in the United States by United Artists in 1967, Leone's films were more vicious, violent, and cynical than Hollywood's Westerns of the period, and they opened the door for even more brutal depictions of the West. Accordingly, the most important director of Westerns after John Ford took the violence of Leone's films and married it to the cultural transformations of American society. In his depictions of a dirtier, bloodier, more psychopathic West, Sam Peckinpah was the natural successor to Ford. His greatest film, *The Wild Bunch* (1969), was a bloodbath about Western outlaws caught up in the Mexican revolution in 1913. *The Wild Bunch* connected the Western clearly to the Vietnam War, and the film's grandeur, scale, and scope made it into one of the genre's climatic expressions of artistry. Peckinpah followed it with two more original and idiosyncratic Westerns, *The Ballad of Cable Hogue* (1970) and *Pat Garrett and Billy the Kid* (1973).

The other major director to emerge in this period—and to date the last of the genre's major filmmakers—was Clint Eastwood. Like John Wayne, Eastwood acted in a large number of Westerns. He reinterpreted the character type of the laconic, violent loner, first incarnated by William S. Hart, in pictures such as *Hang 'Em High* (1968), *Two Mules for Sister Sarah* (1970), and *Joe Kidd* (1972). But unlike Wayne, Eastwood proved to be a formidable director as well, and his films *High Plains Drifter* (1973), *The Outlaw Josey Wales* (1976), *Pale Rider* (1985), and *Unforgiven* (1992) are impressive accomplishments, with *The Outlaw Josey Wales* and *Unforgiven* among the genre's classics.

Since the 1980s, the production of Westerns has become infrequent. Distinguished Westerns have appeared—*Dances with Wolves* (1990), *Open Range* (2003), *The Assassination of Jesse James* (2007), *Appaloosa* (2008), *True Grit* (2010)—but the rarity with which a new Western appears makes each one a singular and heralded occasion, irrespective of its merits. Westerns will continue to be made, but the popular audience has moved on to other genres—horror, fantasy, and science fiction chief among them—and it may be that Westerns hold more appeal for filmmakers today than for audiences. Nevertheless, the Western is American film's most iconic genre and certainly one of its most important.

Typologies, Themes, and Theories

Westerns have a basis in history but are not themselves historical; they aim for myth and poetry, for a cultural reimagining of the events and conflicts that surrounded the expansion of settlements into the plains, prairies, and mountains of the middle and far West. The genre has drawn from this history in very selective ways, emphasizing such events as migration via the overland trails between 1840 and 1860, the period of the mountain men and fur trappers and traders in the 1840s, and, from the 1850s onward, the construction of the railroads, the great cattle drives to cities served by rail lines, the slaughter of buffalo that the railroads facilitated, and the wars against powerful Indian tribes in the northern and southern plains and the more dispersed and low-level conflicts with the Navaho and Apache. The selective way that Westerns draw from history is evident in their construction of Native American characters. Indian communities were extremely diverse and were distributed throughout the continent; they included the anglicized Five Civilized Tribes living in the southeastern United States and the fishing villages of the Chinook on the Pacific coast in the far northwest. But Westerns have focused nearly exclusively on the warriors of the Great Plains, nomads on horseback, groups that included the Sioux, found in the Dakotas; the Apache, Comanche, and Kiowa, found in Arizona, New Mexico, and Texas; the Cheyenne, found in Wyoming; and the Blackfoot and Crow, found in Montana, Idaho, and Wyoming.

Because Westerns draw their stories from historical events, while exercising considerable poetic license, this genre is more bounded in time and space than other American film genres. It is important, therefore, to ask, "When is a Western?" and "Where is a Western?" Is *The Last of the Mohicans* a Western? It features conflicts among frontier characters—settlers and Mohican and Huron Indians—that are characteristic of many Westerns. But the time frame is the 1750s, during the French and Indian War (1756–1763), which is considerably earlier than the period in which most Westerns occur. Though the Cooper novel is one of the chief literary influences on the genre, it is difficult to classify *The Last of the Mohicans* as a true Western. The story takes place in upstate New York, in the Appalachian region that was the frontier at that time. But the frontier line was continually shifting west. By 1820, for example, the Mississippi River marked the frontier.

Considered in terms of space or locale, then, Westerns typically take place west of the Mississippi. Territories bordering the eastern side of the river that achieved statehood (Illinois, 1818; Tennessee, 1796; Mississippi, 1817; Louisiana, 1812) did so in periods that few Westerns have depicted, and so their territories tend to be excluded from the genre. The 1820s–1840s was the era of the fur trappers and traders and mountain men, which many Westerns have depicted: *How the West Was Won* (1962), *Jeremiah Johnson* (1972), *The Mountain Men* (1980). This era marks the inception of the genre's time frame, but many Westerns occur after the Civil War ended, in 1865, which is when migration to the interior of the country increased, the cattle drives occurred, the gunfighters and outlaws appeared, and the Indian wars accelerated. A convenient way, then, of marking the temporal boundaries of the genre is to place the Civil War at its far side, allowing for the era of the fur traders to influence key films, and to place the other marker closer to modernity at World War I. *The Wild Bunch* takes place just on the eve of that war, and other key Westerns focusing on the Mexican revolution of 1910–1920 include *The Professionals* (1966), *Vera Cruz* (1954), *Duck, You Sucker* (1972), *Bandido* (1956), and *Villa Rides* (1968). World War I ushered in a scale of slaughter and mechanized death that is at home in the war genre but foreign to the Western. Therefore, with the birth of modernity that it represents, the war marks the end point of the Western's imaginary world. Thus, movies set in the West in the modern era, such as *The Last Picture Show* (1971), *Junior Bonner* and *The Honkers* (both 1972), and others, are not truly Westerns. They overlap on the edge of the genre but fall outside its time frame. *Lonely Are the Brave* (1962), for example, depicts a cowboy on the run from police who pursue him in jeeps and helicopters. He could escape but cannot bring himself to leave his horse behind, and this leads to his downfall. The film depicts a Western character in a mechanized world, hemmed in and harassed by the paraphernalia of modernity; it is a film self-conscious in its relation to Westerns but is not itself a Western. Helicopters don't fit into this most rule-governed of all film genres.

The Wild Bunch (1969) Many Westerns take place in Mexico, often during the revolution of 1910–1920. In Peckinpah's film, a gang of train robbers flees across the border and becomes entangled with the civil war raging there. Such films propose that as the United States became more settled, the frontier shifted south to Mexico. Other examples of this trend include *The Magnificent Seven* (1960) and *Vera Cruz* (1954). In variations on the theme, American gunmen seeking the frontier travel to Bolivia—*Butch Cassidy and the Sundance Kid* (1969)—and Australia—*Quigley Down Under* (1990). In the climax of *The Wild Bunch*, Peckinpah's outlaws fight with hand grenades and a machine gun, emblems of a modern, post-frontier era.

In *The Six-Gun Mystique*, film scholar John Cawelti writes that Westerns by definition take place on or near a frontier, and he describes the frontier as the meeting point between the forces of savagery and civilization, with the former threatening the latter. For Cawelti, there are three basic character types in Westerns—savages, including outlaws, Indians, rustlers, and gunmen; townspeople, who are personified as bankers, schoolteachers, and farmers; and the hero, a violent character who has elements of savagery within but who often becomes aligned with a town or settlement or other civilized characters. The genre's richness and complexity are evident in the diversity of ways that it may portray these character types. An optimistic and idealized view of civilization often is embodied in a town or settlement, with families, churches, and schools representing a desirable vision of social life, as in *My Darling Clementine*. The town may represent the future, and the lawless violence embodied by savage characters typically threatens its safety or even its existence. But Westerns also may offer a critical and pessimistic portrait of town life. In *The Gunfighter, The Searchers, Hombre* (1967), *The Wild Bunch*, and others, towns and settlements contain bigotry and powerful forces of social and political corruption. In *The Gunfighter*, for example, the outlaw Jimmy Ringo (Gregory Peck) visits the town of Cayenne aiming to reunite with his wife and son, who live there. His presence in town incites hatred, bigotry, and even violence among the townspeople. This leads the marshal, himself a former outlaw, to remark, "The problem isn't him demoralizing the town; it's the town demoralizing him." At the end of *Stagecoach*, as the outlaw (John Wayne) and the saloon girl (Claire Trevor) ride out of town, the doctor observes ruefully, "They're saved from the blessings of civilization." As these examples suggest, Westerns are often ambivalent in their view of domestication and the settled life, and this ambivalence is rooted in the genre's core political outlook and its view of modernity. I will return to these points in a moment.

Indians have personified the savage characters in many Westerns, such as *Stagecoach*, *Northwest Passage* (1940), and *Red River*, being depicted as purely violent and malevolent characters. In *The Iron Horse*, they periodically ride onscreen to shoot at the workers building the transcontinental railroad; beyond this plot function, they have no role in the film. But while many Westerns have stereotyped Indians, it is incorrect to stereotype Westerns as uniformly unreflective, hostile, or unsympathetic toward Native Americans. Indeed, many Westerns have depicted Native Americans with considerable sympathy and aligned the genre's elements of savagery with the white civilization that sought to conquer or exterminate them. While John Ford stereotyped Indians in such pictures as *The Iron Horse* and *Rio Grande* (1950), he offered heroic and politically sympathetic portraits in *Fort Apache* and *Cheyenne Autumn* (1964) and scathing depictions of white racism in *The Searchers* and *Two Rode Together* (1961). These varied portraits in Ford's work mirror the diversity of outlook at large in the genre. Portraits of Native American heroism and honorable resistance to white expansion increased significantly in the 1950s in such films as *Broken Arrow*, *Devil's Doorway* (1950), and *Apache* (1954). More recent instances include *Little Big Man* and *Dances with Wolves*.

Other Westerns have personified the savage characters as outlaws and cattle rustlers. The key point delineating savage characters is that they threaten the spread of settlements and practice forms of violence that the genre regards as unacceptable. These include hanging, whipping, knifing, scalping, and back-shooting. Violence in Westerns is governed by fixed rules that stipulate who may use it, under what conditions, and in what forms. In his essay "Movie Chronicle: The Western," Robert Warshow noted this attribute of Westerns when he wrote that they provide a serious orientation to the problem of violence and

***Dances with Wolves* (1990)** The Western has a long and complex relationship with Native Americans. Many films present Indians simply as stock villains, as obstacles to progress and development. But a significant number of Westerns take a more enlightened view and present their Native American characters with empathy and admiration. *Dances with Wolves* creates a countermyth to Manifest Destiny, the idea that the winning of the West was a noble undertaking, by showing the Lakota Sioux as a civilization being wiped out by the spread of settlements and the ferocious violence of the U.S. Army. Graham Greene (pictured here) plays Kicking Bird, who sees the gravity of the threat to his people.

a means for reflecting on it. Among all American film genres, Westerns are governed most by rules when it comes to violence. The best-known, most famous, and most iconic scene in a Western is the draw, that is, the showdown between hero and villain, a gunfight in which the hero coolly waits until the villain pulls his gun first. The gunfight is a ritual occurrence in Westerns; it proceeds according to rules that stipulate how it should occur and under what conditions. In this respect, the gunfight separates the hero from the chaotic and sprawling violence perpetrated by outlaws and other savage characters. They resort to violence quickly and without hesitation. The hero, by contrast, is reluctant to kill, is slow to provoke, and is temperate in his response when the time does come. The most elegant and beautiful depiction of a classical gunfight in these terms occurs in *Shane* (1953) when the hero (Alan Ladd) faces down Wilson, a skilled and deadly gunfighter, in the town saloon. Shane waits until Wilson draws, and Wilson is fast, but Shane is faster and puts him down with a single shot. As Warshow has noted, the aesthetic of the draw imposes a clean discipline upon the messy work of killing by insisting that it be done at a distance and according to agreed-upon rules, and that it come in its own proper time and place. The proper place may include the town's main street or its saloon or the mountains or prairie of the wilderness. It does not include schools, churches, stores, and other places of daily business. When outlaws massacre a wedding party in *Tombstone* (1993), the action establishes their credentials as savages.

All rules can be bent and broken in meaningful ways, and many Westerns revise the genre by taking familiar scenes in new directions. In the climax of *Lawman* (1971), the federal marshal, Jared Maddox (Burt Lancaster), takes aim and deliberately shoots a man in the back as he runs away from the gunfight. The action is meant to complicate our moral assessment of Maddox, the film's hero. In *Tom Horn* (1980), a cattle rustler ambushes the hero, Horn (Steve McQueen), as he comes out of a store on the town's main street. Horn drops the man with a single shot; then, seeing that he is wounded, Horn coldly finishes him off with a bullet to the head. In *Unforgiven*, the film's hero is outlaw William Munny (Clint Eastwood), a cold killer of women and children. In the film's climax, he uses a shotgun to kill an unarmed man. The extremely graphic bloodshed in *The Wild Bunch* announces to the viewer that this is not a traditional, classical view of the West with clean, distanced gunfights where people follow the rules of the draw. At the end of the film, the wild bunch fights with a machine gun and hand grenades, inflicting a level of violence on their enemies that is more characteristic of war films than of Westerns. And throughout, the hero, Pike Bishop (William Holden), never takes his six-gun out of its holster.

Whether the genre's depictions of violence are clean or "dirty,"

***My Darling Clementine* (1946)** Henry Fonda is Wyatt Earp, pausing here on his way to a showdown with the Clanton gang. Ford's low angle composition helps elevate Earp to a mythic level. The Western hero is solitary and determined, at home in a world of violence and reluctant but ready to engage in the ritual of the gunfight.

rule-bound or chaotic, one of its core themes is the conflict between violence and social life, between unregulated aggression and lawful order. Westerns offer symbolic dramas about the resolution of this core conflict. In many films, the hero uses his skills at violence to protect the town and defeat the savages. Having done so, however, he may find it difficult to lay down his guns and live peacefully. Like the savage characters, the hero is a wilderness figure, at home with violence, which often renders him unable to adapt to settled life. Many Westerns, *Shane* and *The Searchers* among them, begin with the hero's emerging from the wilderness and making entry into a town or settlement and end with his returning again to the wilderness because his own savagery renders him unfit for civilized life. Such Westerns solve the dilemma inherent in the relation of violence and social order by postulating a moment when a progressive kind of violence—that of the hero against the savages on behalf of the town—is necessary for social progress. But having transacted that progressive violence, the hero must be banished from the social order that he has helped protect.

There is thus a melancholy tone to many Westerns; the genre identifies

The Searchers (1956) The Western hero tends to be a wilderness character, traveling through the mountains, plains, and deserts of the far West. As many Westerns begin, the hero leaves the wilderness to enter a town or settlement, where he is drawn into conflict between settlers and savages. In the opening moments of *The Searchers*, Ethan Edwards (John Wayne) emerges from the desert to join his brother's family at their cabin. The setting and action help give Ethan a mysterious, mythic, and majestic stature.

The Professionals (1966) The "end of the West" is a theme in many films, where modernity spells the downfall of the Western hero. The genre uses automobiles, telephones, and other signs of a modernizing world to convey the idea that the wilderness is declining and the frontier vanishing. In *The Professionals*, the heroes looking for some old-time excitement cross the border into Mexico. Here, the film's hero, Fardan (Lee Marvin, left), travels by car to meet with a railroad baron who has promised him employment.

with that which is lost—the hero and the wilderness life of which he is part. This tends to complicate the genre's portraits of modernity. In the Western, a modern world is always just emerging or is on the cusp of doing so. A telephone in *The Shootist* (1976), automobiles in *Ride the High Country* (1962), *The Professionals*, and *The Wild Bunch*, the National Guard supplanting a town marshal in *Tom Horn*—the paraphernalia and institutions of modernity signal that Westerns are set in a transitional era when a frontier way of life was swept away by the encroachments of advanced technologies, more densely concentrated populations, great urban centers, and vast economic and political power. Many Westerns celebrate empire building, *The Iron Horse*, *Red River*, and *How the West Was Won* in particular. But the genre's view of the transition to modernity is remarkably unified. The genre's political vision tends to be a populist one. Populism was a late-nineteenth-century movement among western farmers and small businessmen that aimed at forestalling the growth of centralized business, banking, and political interests. Populism was aligned with an ideal of "the people," and Westerns share the antipathy of populism for big business, big bankers, and national politicians. Railroad barons are frequent villains in Westerns, as in *The Professionals* and *The Wild Bunch*, because they represent a concentration of wealth and power that the genre views as a source of corruption.

Westerns are about a world that no longer exists, and the melancholy associated with a vanished world is an essential component of the genre and of the culture's larger understanding of the historical experience on which these films are based. By the 1880s the West was vanishing quickly, and Frederic Remington felt driven to paint it before it was gone forever. His paintings, and others by George Catlin, as well as Edward Curtis's photography of the wilderness and of Indian tribes, were forms of documentation as well as nostalgic remembrances. Remington wrote, "I knew the railroad was coming. I saw men already swarming into the land. I knew the derby hat, the smoking chimneys, the cord-binder, and the thirty-day note were upon us in restless surge. I knew the wild riders and vacant land were about to vanish forever."[2]

Portraying a vanishing way of life, Westerns look backward, even when they offer a positive vision of a settled and civilized life as the way of the future. The genre's heart is almost never with this future but with the wilderness and with the loner hero who inhabits it. Thus, despite the many Westerns in which marriage, families, child rearing, schools, and settlements are portrayed in positive terms, the genre, in fact, is in flight from domesticity. In *Shane*, the gunfighter-hero rides away from the family that he loves. In *The Searchers*, Ethan (John Wayne) is an exile from home and hearth. In *The Gunfighter* and *Tom Horn*, the heroes find themselves rejected by the women they love because of their violence. Domesticity sometimes becomes a mark of weakness in Westerns. Male townspeople, for example, lack virility and often shrink from challenge. Marriage can sometimes make a man dead meat in a Western. In *Red River*, Dan Latimer is a gentle soul, is married, and stutters, all qualities that mark him in the film as weak, and when he goes on the cattle drive and the herd stampedes, Dan is trampled to death. Of the three Earp brothers in *My Darling Clementine*, James is the youngest and is engaged to be married; he also cooks the meals for his older brothers on the trail. All of these qualities mark him as feminine and domesticated. In the opening moments of the film, he is gunned down by the Clanton gang of rustlers.

The hero's skills at violence and his bond with the wilderness mean that he is far less susceptible to domestication, though sometimes it happens. In *Saddle the Wind* (1958), Robert Taylor plays a reformed outlaw

---

[2] Edward Buscombe, "Painting the Legend: Frederic Remington and the Western," *Cinema Journal* 23, no. 4 (Summer 1984), p. 158.

peacefully operating a large ranch. In *Angel and the Badman* (1947), John Wayne plays an outlaw whose lawless ways are tested by his love for a Quaker woman. In many Westerns, the hero is a lawman who is living a settled life in a town, but almost invariably outlaws or other savages threaten his family or the town. In response, he picks up his guns again. In *The Last Hard Men* (1976), for example, Charlton Heston is a retired sheriff living with his daughter when an old enemy from the past brings violence back into his life. A Western narrative almost always builds toward the necessity for a climactic and violent confrontation between the hero and the savages, no matter what the hero's values may be when he first appears in the film. *High Noon* (1952) provides a paradigmatic example. Gary Cooper is Will Kane, a town marshal who has just retired and gotten married to a Quaker woman, Amy (Grace Kelly), when the

High Noon (1952) Westerns offer a rigid set of roles for women. These include school-teacher, dance-hall entertainer, wife, and mother. Violence tends to be the prerogative of men in Westerns, and women represent values in opposition to violence. In *High Noon*, Amy (Grace Kelly) is a pacifist and here tries to persuade her husband, Will (Gary Cooper), to leave town rather than face outlaw Frank Miller. Eventually she goes against her principles and picks up a gun to defend Will. But she breaks the genre's rules and ethics of engagement by shooting one of the villains in the back.

film begins. Their plans for a peaceful future are jeopardized by an old enemy, Frank Miller, who returns to town with his gang to kill Kane. Amy tells Will that she will leave him if he picks up his gun again, that they should leave immediately and run. Westerns acknowledge the value of law and order and social peace, but Kane voices the genre's core outlook when he straps on his gun belt and says to Amy, "It seems to me I've got to stay." But Amy doesn't see it that way, even after being chastised by Kane's former lover, Helen Ramirez (Katy Jurado), who asks Amy what kind of woman she is. If Kane were my man, she says, I'd be at his side with a gun. In the end, Amy comes around, picking up a six-gun and shooting one of Miller's men when he is about to ambush Kane. But it is a hard choice for her to make, and in making it she acknowledges that the law of the West is frontier law, resting at its base on violent force. In *The Man Who Shot Liberty Valance*, John Wayne as the frontier character tells Ransom Stoddard (James Stewart), a lawyer from the East who believes in written law, that in the West a man settles his own conflicts. He brandishes his pistol at Stoddard to show how it is done.

The genre's ambivalence toward domestication and the settled life, and its belief in the necessity for violence, inform another of its structural characteristics, namely, the rigid and traditional gender roles that prevail. Westerns are a male-oriented genre that provides very limited roles for women. Women tend to be schoolteachers, mothers, wives, or dance-hall entertainers. The latter category is an interesting one because it is sly and tricky about what it designates. During the classical Hollywood era, prostitution was a taboo topic for filmmakers; they were constrained from explicitly portraying it onscreen. In many Westerns of this period, dance-hall entertainer is a cleaned-up and sanitized category connoting prostitution. It wasn't until the 1960s and afterward, in such films as *Ride the High Country* (1962), *The Cheyenne Social Club* (1970), and *The Cowboys* (1972), that Westerns became more candid about frontier prostitution.

With female characters so rigidly typed in the genre, there is little room for them to participate in the core action of the narratives. Violence is a male domain in Westerns and the genre's protagonists, its heroes and savages, who transact violence and enact the bloody transition between the frontier and modernity, are almost always men. One is tempted to say "are always men" except that a very few Westerns have experimented with placing women in the genre's traditionally male roles. *Johnny Guitar* (1954) features an armed showdown between characters played by Joan Crawford and Mercedes McCambridge. In *Bad Girls* (1994), a gang of four women is on the run from the law. In *The Quick and the Dead* (1995), Sharon Stone plays a gunfighter, a cool killer who beats numerous men to the draw. Whatever the merits of such films, they are deviant examples of the genre, and a viewer watching them knows that they are standing the genre on its head by reversing the normative distribution of gender roles. But the rigidity of its gender patterning does not mean the Western is without fine performances by women playing well-written characters. Jean Arthur subtly portrays a restless, discontented mother in *Shane*, one tempted to leave her family for the rootless Shane. Gail Russell convincingly makes the Quaker life a real temptation for John Wayne in *Angel and the Badman*. Cathy Downs personifies all that is refined and elegant about the East in *My Darling Clementine*. These are vibrant, wonderful performances, essential components in the classic status each of these films has achieved. It is just that when one thinks of Westerns, one doesn't tend to think of their female characters. This is especially surprising when one considers the wide variety of roles that woman played on the frontier. These included army scouts, outlaws, cattle drivers, gold prospectors, and Indian fighters. Perhaps the Western's rigid patterning of gender roles is one reason that Westerns have fallen out of favor with contemporary audiences. The women's movement gathered force in the late 1960s and began influencing filmmaking in the mid-1970s, and it transformed the culture's understanding of men and women, how they should be permitted to behave and interact, and what they are capable of doing. Westerns did not keep pace with these changes. The Western has remained a hardened, rule-bound genre; it has not accommodated in any profound, enduring, or extensive way the culture's changed understanding of male–female relations.

The genre's great stars are men. Gary Cooper, Clint Eastwood, John Wayne, Henry Fonda, Burt Lancaster, James Stewart, Kevin Costner, Robert Duvall, Randolph Scott, William S. Hart, Charlton Heston, Gregory Peck—they convincingly embody the laconic loner who typifies the Western hero. Robert Warshow brilliantly observed that the Western hero differs greatly from Hollywood's movie gangsters. The gangster is always in motion and talks fast and furiously; the gangster is ambitious and pursues wealth and power. The Westerner, by contrast, is a figure of stillness and repose, few words, and fewer possessions.

Cooper, Eastwood, Wayne, and these other stars project a quiet authority onscreen; their movements are loose and relaxed; their temperaments are calm and collected. All are essential elements in the persona of the Westerner. Most important, they know how to handle a horse and how to look good in the saddle and standing with a six-gun strapped to their thigh. They are convincingly at ease amid the paraphernalia of a frontier world. One of the problems afflicting the genre today is a relative lack of new stars that can inhabit the Old West convincingly. Male stars today are associated more often with action and cop genres and with science fiction and fantasy. Riding a horse, leaping from the saddle, throwing a rope, walking through a herd of cattle—Westerns require a repertoire of physical skills from their performers, which cannot easily be faked. Henry Fonda and Ben Johnson do some incredibly fast and tough riding on horseback over broken, rocky terrain in *My Darling Clementine* and *She Wore a Yellow Ribbon* (1949). It's not a trick; the actors are doing the riding. They are successful as Westerners because they physically inhabit their roles according to what the genre demands. Moreover, the vocal inflections of the genre's great stars are perfectly suited to the oddly stilted and anachronistic pitch of Western dialogue. Henry Fonda can murmur "I'd admire to, Ma'am"; Eastwood can utter "I ain't like that no more"; John Wayne can caution "Whoa, take 'er easy there, Pilgrim"; Robert Duvall can declare "I aim to kill Baxter and those that done this"; Gary Cooper can insist "I've got to, that's the whole thing"—these lines ring with the authenticity of Western frontier life when delivered by such iconic performers, whose currency in the genre is unquestioned.

Iconography

The enduring imagery of the Western is established by landscape, by costuming, and by recurrent patterns of action in the genre. In terms of landscape, the genre is defined by its setting, which is typically centered on the Great Plains and the arid deserts and mountains of the far West. The parched, rocky terrain of New Mexico and Arizona, for example, forms the backdrop for many Westerns about the Apache wars, such as *Stagecoach* and *Ulzana's Raid*. The mountains of Grand Teton National Park in Wyoming mark the frontier and furnish a majestic backdrop to the action in *Shane*. Occasionally, a deviant landscape appears, one unusual for the genre. *McCabe and Mrs. Miller* is set in Washington State, with heavy forests and perpetual rainfall. But lushness is rarely found in the genre's landscapes. Typically, Westerns stress the harsh and unforgiving nature of the frontier, and mountains and desert provide powerful visual embodiments of terrain where violence is a way of life. When John Wayne emerges from the Texas desert at the beginning of *The Searchers* (actually filmed in Utah), the barrenness of the land becomes a statement about his character. The opening of *Duel at Diablo* (1966) magnificently captures the stark deserts of Utah, as an army scout and Apache warriors hunt one another amid rocky outcroppings jutting above the desert floor. A helicopter shot enlarges perspective to show the vastness of the open, unsettled, and inhospitable land.

The most famous and iconic of all Western landscapes is Monument Valley, a vast, flat desert with red mesas and huge sandstone buttes rising hundreds of feet in the air. John Ford prominently featured the location in many of his Westerns (*Stagecoach, Fort Apache, The Searchers*), and Italian director Sergio Leone filmed a few shots there for *Once Upon a Time in the West* (1968), which was otherwise shot in Europe. Leone showed the valley in its most famous and panoramic view, with the East and West Mitten Buttes and Merrick Butte prominently displayed. In using the location, Leone was paying homage to Ford and to the genre's most famous setting. Ford loved the location because of the dramatic vistas

***Once Upon a Time in the West* (1969)** The striking sandstone monoliths of Monument Valley made it the genre's most iconic and recognizable landscape. John Ford used it frequently in his films, and when Italian director Sergio Leone wanted to self-consciously reference Ford and the Western in a movie otherwise shot in Europe, he traveled to Monument Valley to capture its famous beauty.

offered by the rocky outcroppings, and the poetic contrast afforded by the huge, vertical buttes and the vast, flat valley floor. Ford had a painter's eye and was sensitive to the epic contrast that these differences could create, especially when small human figures were placed in the frame. Monument Valley gave his films an epic scale.

The ways in which landscape is deployed in imagery and action lends the Western many of its distinctive features. Images of riders on the horizon line were one of John Ford's favorite compositions, which he often utilized when filming in Monument Valley. The precariousness of settlements along the frontier is visualized by showing the ways that the wilderness encroaches upon schools and homes and other postings of domestic order. The dust from Monument Valley blows right into the town of Tombstone in *My Darling Clementine*, and the desert overtakes an abandoned town in *Yellow Sky* (1948). The desert is just outside the doorways of Texas settlers in *The Searchers*. A gun, a noose, and a legal tome keep lawlessness at bay west of the Pecos in *The Westerner* (1940), because the wilderness sprawls everywhere, with nary a settlement in sight. The town in *Shane* is a few wooden buildings perched in the valley below Grand Teton and looking like a strong wind from the mountain would sweep it away.

Like landscape, costuming provides the Western with distinctive imagery. A hat, chaps, a vest, a kerchief, rope, boots, and a six-gun give the Westerner his distinctive and unmistakable markings. There is tremendous variation in costuming throughout the genre, with fashion trends suddenly appearing. The villains in *The Man Who Shot Liberty Valance* wear dusters—long, ankle-length coats—but it wasn't until Sergio Leone's films in the mid-1960s that dusters became a common item of Western costuming. The Westerner is also a man with a horse, and images of a solitary, taciturn figure on horseback in the wilderness are iconic elements of the genre. Horses, as John Cawelti noted, provide cowboy, gunfighter, Indian, and outlaw with a principal tie to the wilderness and an emblem of personal freedom: the ability to come and go as one chooses. But horses also provide almost all essential transportation in Westerns, whether by mount, stage, or buggy. The only common exception to this is travel by rail. As a result, Westerns tend naturally toward a slower, more measured pace than action genres set in the present day. Shots showing cowboys driving a herd of cattle or a rancher traveling by buggy can't be hurried. This is possibly another reason that the genre has fallen into disfavor with contemporary audiences.

Red River (1948) The genre's classic imagery derives from the action afforded by its recurring stories and settings. Wagon trains, cavalry charges, stagecoach robberies, and cattle drives furnish familiar imagery in countless Westerns. *Red River* portrays the first cattle drive over the Chisholm Trail, and a river crossing is always part of the journey. The imagery is indelibly Western.

Similarly, the technologies of violence in Westerns help make the genre relatively anachronistic for today's audiences. The amount of carnage that six-guns, Winchester rifles, and bows and arrows can inflict is quite limited compared to the automatic weaponry that proliferates in action, cop, and war films. The body count in those genres tends to be much higher. Nineteenth-century technologies of violence showcased by the Western help give the genre its restraint and rules of engagement, modest compared to today's more popular action genres.

Recurrent patterns of action derived from story formulas help to give the Western its defining imagery. Westerns about cattle drives—*Red River, The Cowboys, Open Range*—provide opportunities for filming men on horseback with a moving herd contending with blizzard, rainfall, river crossings, and attack by outlaws or Indians. "Town taming" Westerns—*My Darling Clementine, Warlock* (1959), *Tombstone*—provide opportunities for staging classical gunfights on the main street, probably the genre's most indelible story element. "End of the West" stories—*Will Penny* (1968), *The Wild Bunch, Monte Walsh* (1970), *Tom Horn*—provide opportunities for portraying a wilderness hero hemmed in by the modern era and defeated by it. "Wagon train" Westerns typically include a sequence in which Indians attack the convoy, and in such films as *Red River* they ride in circles around the cluster of wagons, shooting at the settlers, in another of the genre's most famous and emblematic images. Many Westerns feature travel by stagecoach, and such scenes carry the high probability of an attack by outlaws or Indians, in which case the stagecoach will be driven at breakneck speed through canyon and desert as the attackers pursue. Cattle drives, gunfights, stagecoach robberies—these and other recurrent story situations have generated the genre's stock of famous images, ones that have defined the Western in enduring terms.

The Western is more than a film genre. It is a cultural category based in historical experience and the myths born of that experience. Although it has been delineated by painting, photography, literature, and theater, cinema has been the most important medium disseminating the genre as a popular entertainment worldwide. Westerns are not only movies, but the movies have had more to do with the genre's persistence over time and its popular appeal than any other medium. Westerns are one of American cinema's fundamental genres, the one that talks most extensively about the idea of America and about the contradictions of race, violence, individualism, and law and order, tensions that run deep inside American culture and society. Without Westerns, there'd be no movie cowboy. And without the cowboy, there'd be no America as we know it, for better or for worse.

My Darling Clementine

Of all the directors who worked in the Western genre, John Ford had the most poetic and profound sensibility for its historical and cultural meanings and their potential for cinematic expression. Ford had a painter's eye for composition, for the arrangement of space onscreen in dramatic and thematically significant ways. While many filmmakers have this ability, Ford's gift for composition was especially fine, and his sense for making visual poetry out of the genre's thematic material was instinctive.

Ford's early Westerns, made during the silent era, demonstrate his pictorial talents and his affinity for the genre. A massive land rush—scores of would-be homesteaders in wagons and on horseback galloping to stake their claim on acres of free land—provides the climax in *Three Bad Men*, and Ford choreographs the action in epic style. Throughout the scene, his camera consistently finds visual grandeur in the arrangement of figure and landscape, as it does in *The Iron Horse*, an epic about the building of the transcontinental railroad.

Landscapes are crucial to the Western because they embody cultural ideas about the wilderness, and Ford was inventive in his treatment of landscape. He used red filters on the camera, for example, in *Fort Apache* to darken skies and make cloud formations pop in a dramatic way. A red filter blocks blue light, and when black-and-white film shot in this manner is developed and processed, blues become black, accentuating a contrast effect when clouds are present, and adding considerable drama and tension. Ford also placed his horizon line either low in the frame

Fort Apache (1948) Ford used red filters on the camera to block blue light from registering on black-and-white film. As a result, blues look black, darkening skies in this dramatic fashion. Ford's pictorial compositions enhance the epic scale of this film's final act, which depicts a foolhardy colonel who leads his cavalry into a Custer-like ambush by Apache warriors.

or high up, rather than in the middle. He felt very strongly that effective Western landscape compositions must adhere to this principle. It enhances the scale of the shots.

Ford loved working outdoors in the West, but his feeling for landscape is balanced by his deep respect for and attraction to the rituals and social bonds of settled, domestic life, as found in homes, families, and such institutions as schools and churches. Ford's sensibility equipped him superbly well for making Westerns because he understood and was drawn to the genre's fundamental tensions between wilderness and civilization, between the wandering and the settled life.

My Darling Clementine illustrates how the genre can function as a template for a director's cinematic style and vision and also as a focus of social currents of meaning and value. *Clementine* was the first film Ford made after World War II. During the war he was a commander in the U.S. Naval Reserve and headed the Office of Strategic Services' combat photographic unit, making documentaries about the fighting. Ford witnessed the D-day landings on Omaha Beach and filmed the carnage there. He also filmed the Battle of Midway, during which he was wounded by shrapnel. The Navy praised his bravery during the war, and when he resumed making feature films, he turned immediately to the Western as the genre in which he felt most at home.

While *Clementine* reflects Ford's war experiences, at its most immediate level it is a version of the oft-filmed saga of Wyatt Earp and the gunfight at the O.K. Corral in the town of Tombstone. Ford changed the town's location from its true site in southern Arizona to Monument Valley, 460 miles due north. This change accentuated his ability to visualize the wilderness–civilization conflict. In the film, the desert and rocks of Monument Valley surround the town, making a statement about the precariousness of the life in relation to the harshness of the wilderness.

At the same time, Ford makes the film a story about Wyatt's (Henry Fonda) change from wilderness character to one who is increasingly involved with and sympathetic to town life. We first meet Wyatt in the expanse of Monument Valley as he and his brothers are driving a small herd of cattle to market. Unshaven, a cowboy in duds, Wyatt feels at home in the desert; the settled nature of town life is not for him.

When his brother James is murdered by the Clantons, who also rustle the Earp cattle, Wyatt's savage skills—the ease with violence that marks him as a wilderness character—emerge as he swears vengeance on those

My Darling Clementine **(1946)** One of the genre's core narratives deals with the transformation of a wilderness into a life-sustaining community. Ford visualizes that change by showing a transformation in both the film's main character, Wyatt Earp (Henry Fonda), and in the town of Tombstone. Wyatt first appears as a nomadic wilderness figure and then is softened by the town, a process Ford shows symbolically in a scene in which Wyatt gets a haircut and a shave, his grooming framed by the barber's mirror.

***My Darling Clementine* (1946)** Tombstone's aspirations to become a mature community with enduring institutions get a mythic treatment by Ford in the scene where Wyatt escorts Clementine (Cathy Downs) to Sunday church services. The wilderness looms nearby in the towering monoliths of Monument Valley. The unfinished scaffolding for the church points to the town's transitional status, while the flags emblemize a desire for connection to the nation.

responsible. Ford visualizes Wyatt's potential for killing when he sees the Clantons in Tombstone—his face is grim, the low-angle framing accentuates his strength and authority, and the low-key lighting makes the atmosphere tense and ominous. Wyatt tells Old Man Clanton (Walter Brennan) that he's agreed to be town marshal because it will enable him to find James's murderer. Tombstone is shown at this point in the film as—symbolically—a place of darkness and chaotic violence.

But as the film progresses, Tombstone becomes more sunlit, more settled, and more civilized, and Wyatt changes with it. A barber cuts Wyatt's hair and applies a cologne that other characters describe as the scent of a desert flower, a description that Ford intends as an analogy to the town's transformation from desert to garden, from wilderness to civilization. The barber holds out a mirror so Wyatt can survey his new look, and Ford shows Wyatt's face framed in the mirror, a composition that speaks about the way this violent wilderness character has been encircled by civilization.

Wyatt steps outside and checks his appearance as reflected in a shop window, the glass also reflecting the desert and rocky outcroppings of Monument Valley, a visual reminder of the town's transitional state, evolving from a lawlessness associated with the wilderness to a more domesticated life that enforceable law makes possible.

Wyatt has gotten barbered on Sunday morning, and scads of people are riding into town for a church meeting. Ford provides a masterly composition that visualizes the lingering difference between Wyatt and the townspeople. Wyatt stands erect, in place, facing into the desert while wagonloads of churchgoers move past him in the other direction. The contrast of movement and character orientation in the shot prefigures Wyatt's eventual decision to leave the town once he has settled with Clanton and gotten justice for James. Although Wyatt is drawn to the rituals of town life, he remains a wanderer, like most Western heroes, and at film's end will ride away from the town, back into the wilderness.

As Wyatt watches the gathering churchgoers, Ford creates one of the greatest sequences in all of American cinema, the scene where Wyatt escorts Clementine Carter (Cathy Downs) to church. Clementine is a refined woman from the East, whose presence helps to soften Tombstone's rough edges, and an unspoken affection prevails between her and Wyatt. Clementine asks Wyatt to walk with her to church, and Ford invests this action with great solemnity and dignity. His respect for the rituals of social life enables him to show the action with affection and an integrity that is unique to him as a filmmaker. Ford presents it as a reverent moment in which Wyatt is inducted into the life of the community.

Ford's low camera angle juxtaposes the looming monoliths of Monument Valley with Wyatt and Clementine as they walk to the church. The church itself is unfinished, a wooden floor with the framing for a bell tower, and the desert surrounds the tiny structure, a poetic image pointing to the town's transitional status. A civilized Tombstone represents the future, but that future isn't here just yet, not while the Clantons and the wilderness still pose a threat. The church is a work in progress, as is the town itself, and the national flag that adorns the church's framing points toward the community's desire for social development and for unity with the nation itself. These aspirations will move Tombstone beyond the savage state in which Wyatt first finds it.

Dances are an enduring ritual in Ford's films; a dance represents the bonds among members of a community. These interested Ford far more than solitary individuals or lone heroes. Wyatt truly becomes a member of Tombstone when the church elder welcomes him to the dance and clears space for Wyatt and Clementine—"our new marshal and his lady fair"—to participate. Wyatt's ceremonial induction into the life of the church redefines his position in the town; no longer simply a gunman with a badge, he now holds an intimate place in the spiritual life of the community.

But he remains a wilderness figure and close friend with Doc Holliday (Victor Mature), the tubercular physician who has come west seeking his own death. Holliday represents the dark side of the frontier. Whereas the civilized rituals taking root in Tombstone embody the benefits of personal and social development, Holliday's embrace of violence represents the obliteration of the kind of higher self that these rituals nourish. Clementine has come west searching for Doc because they had once been a couple and she wants to try to save him, but he spurns her and chooses dissipation and self-destruction. "The man you once knew is dead," he tells her.

Tombstone moves beyond its frontier origins with the deaths of Holliday and the Clantons, characters who embody savagery in the film. As a figure midway between civilization and savagery, Wyatt is the intermediary who assists this transition, and Ford, ever sensitive to the genre's rules and rituals, gives Wyatt a mythic stature as he walks down the town's main street toward the O.K. Corral and the gunfight with the

Clantons. Ford films Wyatt from a low angle, accentuating his stature, and he's attentive to the beauty of Fonda's physical movements, especially the lean and graceful way he walks. Ford films Wyatt as a man alone, on a dusty street, with one six-gun in his hand and another on his thigh, headed for a confrontation he cannot and does not wish to avoid. It's one of the Western's great heroic images.

With Doc's and his brother Morgan's help, Wyatt vanquishes the Clantons and fulfills his promise to James. Earlier, Ford had given us a scene in which Wyatt visits James's grave and makes a heartfelt speech to his dead brother, telling him that he'll make the town safe for young people so that their lives will not be extinguished too soon by violence, as was James's. Throughout his career, Ford filmed many graveside oaths, scenes in which a character, haunted by a loss, visits a loved one's grave. Such scenes, as an ongoing motif in Ford's work, show his veneration

My Darling Clementine (1946) Ford served in the navy during World War II, and *Clementine* was the first film he made after the war. His experiences in that conflict influenced the film, especially in this scene where Wyatt visits the grave of his younger brother, James. Ford's films have many such scenes, where a grieving survivor visits a loved one's grave. Here, the sadness references the many lives lost in the war and demonstrates how the Western can use its period time frame to comment on the present.

for the past, for the social bonds that nourish one's identity, and also point to his melancholy over the wounds and privations that life inflicts.

In this case, the dates on the gravestone show that James was eighteen when he died. The violent and premature death of an eighteen-year-old young man has a special and particular resonance in a movie made in 1946. It carries the legacy of the war and the loss of a generation of young Americans, and Wyatt's grief over James is also meant by Ford as the emblem of a collective grief over all young Americans killed in the war.

Thus, at film's end, when Wyatt returns home with his one surviving brother to tell their father what has happened, he is weighed down in ways that embody the collectively sober conscience of Americans who survived a war that inflicted much personal and national damage. The ending is right for a Western. Wyatt enacts the ritual of the gunfight and, afterward, elects to leave town, saying goodbye to Clementine because he is at heart a wanderer, as are most Western heroes. But he bears now a deeply personal loss and sadness, one that Americans in the period understood and one certainly that Ford felt with regard to what he had witnessed in the war. *My Darling Clementine* portrays the foundation of a town and a community, but, as the lyrics of its title song state, it is also about something now lost and gone forever.

Stephen Prince

QUESTIONS FOR DISCUSSWION

1. A filmmaker who is interested in exploring the history and mythology of America might choose to make a Western. Would this be an appropriate choice? Why?

2. This chapter has argued in favor of a strict conception of the genre, requiring that Westerns fit within clear boundaries as to time frame and setting. Offer a counterargument claiming that Westerns could take place in the modern era, before the Civil War, or even outside of the United States.

3. Imagine that you are a producer casting a Western. Which contemporary actors would you choose? What criteria would you use in fitting these performers to the genre?

4. Many Westerns from the late 1960s and early 1970s—*The Wild Bunch, Soldier Blue, Ulzana's Raid, Little Big Man*—have been interpreted as

commentaries on the Vietnam War. To what extent can a genre that is set in the past comment on a modern period?

5. Many genres feature violence as an important element of story and style. In what key ways does the Western portray violence?

FOR FURTHER READING

Buscombe, Edward, ed. *The BFI Companion to the Western*. Boston: Da Capo Press, 1988.

Cawelti, John. *The Six-Gun Mystique Sequel*. Madison, WI: Popular Press, 1999.

Cowie, Peter. *John Ford and the American West*. New York: Harry N. Abrams, 2004.

Eckstein, Arthur M., and Peter Lehman. *The Searchers: Essays and Reflections on John Ford's Classic Western*. Detroit: Wayne State University Press, 2004.

Frayling, Christopher. *Spaghetti Westerns: Cowboys and Europeans from Karl May to Sergio Leone*. London: I. B. Tauris, 2006.

Kitses, Jim. *Horizon's West: Directing the Western from John Ford to Clint Eastwood*. London: British Film Institute, 2008.

Lenihan, John H. *Showdown: Confronting Modern America in the Western Film*. Champaign: University of Illinois Press, 1980.

McGee, Patrick. *From "Shane" to "Kill Bill": Rethinking the Western*. Hoboken, NJ: Wiley-Blackwell, 2006.

Mitchell, Lee Clark. *Westerns: Making the Man in Fiction and Film*. Chicago: University of Chicago Press, 1998.

Seydor, Paul. *Peckinpah: The Western Films—A Reconsideration*. Champaign: University of Illinois Press, 1999.

Simmon, Scott. *The Invention of the Western Film: A Cultural History of the Genre's First Half-Century*. Cambridge: Cambridge University Press, 2003.

Slotkin, Richard. *Gunfighter Nation: The Myth of the Frontier in Twentieth-Century America*. Norman: University of Oklahoma Press, 1998.

Smith, Henry Nash. *The Virgin Land: The American West as Symbol and Myth*. Cambridge, MA: Harvard University Press, 2007.

Studlar, Gaylyn, and Matthew Bernstein. *John Ford Made Westerns: Filming the Legend in the Sound Era*. Bloomington: Indiana University Press, 2001.

Tompkins, Jane. *West of Everything: The Inner Life of Westerns*. New York: Oxford University Press, 1993.

Warshow, Robert. "Movie Chronicle: The Western." In *Film Theory and Criticism*, edited by Leo Braudy and Marshall Coen, 703–16. New York: Oxford University Press, 2004.

Wright, Will. *Sixguns and Society: A Structural Study of the Western*. Berkeley: University of California Press, 1977.

Saving Private Ryan (1998)

The Combat Movie

TO SCRUTINIZE FULLY what cinema scholars commonly classify as "war narratives" would entail a cultural stretch across the centuries from *The Aeneid* (29-19 BCE) to *World War Z* (2013)—and beyond. Its inventory would inevitably crisscross a range of other genres, particularly science fiction [e.g., *Star Wars* (1977)], fantasy [*The Lord of the Rings* (2001)], melodrama [*Mrs. Miniver* (1942)], comedy [*Shoulder Arms* (1918)], and even the musical [*This Is the Army*, (1943)]. Given the impossibility of adequately encompassing such an enormous diversity of subject matter and style, this chapter focuses on the American fictional combat movie: films about United States soldiers fighting in historical battles. War historian Gary Freitas argues that six basic themes or narratives dominate these combat movies: combat hell, unit conflict, war is crazy, combat duels, military command, and the big battle. At their best, combat movies that fall into these patterns fuse powerful, often disturbing, visual spectacles depicting the sweep of history with intense, personal narratives about the romance of danger, the heights of love, the depths of loss, and the cruel necessity to kill for one's country and way of life.

Concentrating on fictional American combat movies based on historical events, particularly the Civil War, World War II, Vietnam, and contemporary conflicts, this chapter eliminates some films associated with war but that do not focus on, and sometimes never even include, battle scenes, such as *The Birth of a Nation* (1915), *Gone with the Wind* (1939), *Casablanca* (1942), *The Best Years of Our Lives* (1946), *The Bridge on the River Kwai* (1957), *The Great Escape* (1963), *M*A*S*H* (1970), *Coming Home* (1978), *Born on the Fourth of July* (1989), *Independence Day* (1996), and *Inglourious Basterds* (2009), among many others. Most important, it overlooks the crucial significance of documentaries and newsreels despite their immense contributions to both wartime society and the dynamics of feature film production. In particular, both newsreels and documentaries have brought significantly higher levels of visual realism to fictional combat imagery by means of their sense of immediacy and aura of authenticity. Studio productions quickly incorporated many of their filming techniques, technical innovations, and documentary footage into their fictional narratives to provide viewers with a more direct and visceral sense of actual wartime experiences.

Why does the combat film compel viewers? Why do wars occupy such a central role in human culture? Sebastian Junger's book *War* (2010) provides some basic answers to these questions. He was embedded as a journalist for weeks at a time (June 2007–June 2008) with a platoon headquartered in a remote and precarious outpost in the Korengal Valley (Eastern Afghanistan), and his wartime truths have echoed across the decades in almost every combat movie. Characterizing fighting as an adrenaline rush, he exults that "twenty minutes of combat is more life than you could scrape together in a lifetime of doing something else" (144). In an environment where "lives are measured in inches and seconds and deaths avoided by complete accident" (197), "men form friendships that are not at all sexual but contain much of the devotion and intensity of a romance" (155); as a result, says Junger with a mixture of wonder, sadness, and admiration, young men "fall in love with combat" (234). In such a world, therefore, a Zen-like paradox arises when "who you are entirely depends on your willingness to *surrender* who you are" (276)—"heroism is a negation of the self" (211). As many writers and soldiers have said about those who risk their lives in wars, from Troy to Afghanistan, Junger too comes to realize that the bond between men "is the core experience of combat." "Courage," Junger concludes, "*was* love" (239).

History

Military men designate battle zones as "theaters" of war, yoking combat sites to dramatic productions, and every war America fights influences Hollywood's re-creation of past wars, as well as events beyond the screen. While combat movies remain situated within the social and historical context that nurtured them, an era's cultural memory of past events never remains static. Current attitudes, therefore, cannot help but color depictions of past events because no artist can fully escape the surrounding culture. So, for example, *Glory* refracts the Civil War through a lens crafted in 1989, examining racial problems from a twentieth-century rather than a nineteenth-century point of view. Realizing this neither disregards nor disparages the meticulous attempts at historical accuracy evident in this and many other combat movies. It simply recognizes the continual interface between fact and fiction: actual combat affects cinematic productions, and those reflections of reality, in turn, influence tangible wartime actions.

THE CIVIL WAR

During both the silent and sound eras, moviemakers have found the clash on American soil between North and South fertile ground for dramatic situations. According to Gary Gallagher, a Civil War scholar, Hollywood has offered four major interpretive traditions regarding Civil War movies: 1) the Ex-Confederate Lost Cause tradition, which ignores the slavery issue and paints the southern fighters as gallant but doomed; 2) the Union Cause tradition, which focuses on maintaining the United States as one country against seditious secessionists; 3) the Emancipation tradition, which envisions the Civil War as a struggle to eliminate slavery; and 4) the Reconciliation Cause tradition, which attempts to reunite the nation under one government. The earliest silent Civil War movies address these themes, and all, to some degree or another, demonstrate bigoted attitudes during this period, most notably in the sympathetic portrayal of the Ku Klux Klan and racist depictions of blacks in D. W. Griffith's *The Birth of a Nation* (1915).

Buster Keaton, a genius of the silent era, made a Civil War movie, *The General* (1926), that featured many fundamental themes found in subsequent and more ostensibly serious combat films, but he approached them comically. Made some eight years after World War I ended, with Americans keenly aware of the inhumane savagery of trench warfare, *The General* was far less cavalier about combat than many of its prewar predecessors. When Confederate Army recruiters will not allow Johnnie (Keaton) to enlist because they deem him too valuable as a train engineer, he is emotionally crushed and his girlfriend refuses to see him again "until he is in uniform," an outward validation of his masculinity that prevails in combat movies from the silent era to current times.

The General (1926) After World War I, Americans fully understood the disastrous impact of the conflict on both the winners and losers, particularly the appalling savagery of trench warfare that doomed a generation of young soldiers. Buster Keaton's *The General* displayed a comic tone, but it was far less casual about combat than many of its prewar predecessors. The film also demonstrates an early conflation of combat and masculinity, a pervasive theme throughout the combat genre.

While earlier Civil War movies often focus on costumes and romance, more modern productions assume a murkier, often more skeptical, tone and present more brutal depictions of battles. *Gettysburg* (1993), a re-creation of the famous battle that turned the tide against the South, shows points of views from both armies, as well as personal stories, about, for example, old friends fighting on different sides. Its gory high-point occurs with Major General George E. Pickett's (Stephen Lang) ill-fated infantry charge against Union troops dug in on Cemetery Ridge. *Gods and Generals* (2003), a prequel to *Gettysburg*, incorporates many of the actors from the earlier movie, with detailed concentration on battles prior to Gettysburg, including Fredericksburg and Chancellorsville. Yet with the flamboyant Stonewall Jackson at its center, the film relegates the crucial issue of slavery to the margins of the action.

Unlike *Gods and Generals*, *Glory* positions the brutal facts of racism clearly at its center, interweaving the stories of various characters with epic battle scenes. The film offers viewers a fictionalized version of the Fifty-fourth Massachusetts Infantry Regiment, the first fighting force composed entirely of African-American volunteers. The letters home from its idealistic white commander, twenty-six-year-old Colonel Robert Gould Shaw (Matthew Broderick), form the basis of the movie's narrative, delivered in first-person voice-overs at points in the movie. The film's other characters represent various segments of black society at the time of the war, particularly Thomas Searles (Andre Braugher), a scholarly black man who finds army life difficult; Trip (Denzel Washington), a bitter and volatile escaped slave; Jupiter Sharts (Jihmi Kennedy), a free black man; and John Rawlins (Morgan Freeman), a grave digger who serves as a father figure to the younger men. Although hindered by racism and corruption within the Union Army, the Fifty-fourth distinguished itself and ultimately led a perilous charge on South Carolina's heavily defended Fort Wagner in July 1863. Combat becomes the proverbial melting pot that forges "the other" into indisputable Americans, but outsiders must adopt the discipline of the white military culture to partake in this rite of passage. The radical transformation of Trip from disruptive wildness to heroic soldier dramatically demonstrates this conversion from defiant outsider to dedicated patriot.

Glory (1989) *Glory* foregrounds the brutal facts of racism with its fictionalized version of the Fifty-fourth Massachusetts Infantry Regiment, the first fighting force composed entirely of African-American volunteers during the Civil War. Embedded in *Glory* lies the ideological precept that continues in current combat movies as well: for traditional outsiders, such as blacks and by extension other immigrant groups, serving in the military remains a passageway to genuine social acceptance; the willingness to die for America validates marginalized outsiders as legitimate and socially acceptable citizens.

WORLD WAR I

Because most of the best fictional combat films about World War I were made after the battles ended, they lack the fervent patriotism that characterizes films made during actual fighting, such as in World War II. Rather than immediacy, these films offer remembrance, often colored with bitterness and regret, usually lit up by courageous feats of personal bravery on the ground or in the air. By the mid-1920s, first-hand accounts of the horrors of World War I—a total of 9.7 million military personnel dead, along with 6.8 million civilians—were widely circulating free from any government censorship. Often in the form of memoirs, novels, paintings, war memorials, and other art forms, these accounts inspired substantial antiwar sentiments that found their greatest film expression in *All Quiet on the Western Front* (1930) and *Sergeant York* (1941). *Sergeant York* was one of the first of many "conversion movies":

Sergeant York (1941) *Sergeant York* epitomizes the "conversion movie" evident throughout the combat genre, in which the protagonist foregoes his personal ideals for the good of the group and the country. The movie follows the conflict of conscience behind the heroic exploits of Alvin C. York, a sharpshooter who single-handedly killed twenty-three German soldiers, captured 132, and became the most decorated American soldier of World War I. Despite his proficient marksmanship, York (Gary Cooper) initially refuses to kill because of his religious convictions. Here, torn between his religious faith and duty to his country, he contemplates his ethical dilemma; ultimately, he decides to fight not for glory but to save American lives.

the protagonist ultimately gives up his personal ideals for the good of the group—and the country. Despite the strong isolationist movement following World War I, at the time the movie was made, America was edging toward entering World War II, and the changes in York's morality reflect those attitudes. Indeed, the real Alvin York barnstormed across the country telling the public why America needed to join the Allies in fighting Hitler. As soon as America entered World War II, most film-makers abandoned World War I as a topic, and only a few films about the Great War (as World War I was originally known) have been made since that time, including *War Horse* (2011).

WORLD WAR II

Although the U.S. film industry lost some of its major markets in Europe and Asia during World War II, an average of sixty million Americans still went to movie theaters each week from 1942 to 1946. As the war continued, new technological advances in lighting, sound, color, cinematography, and, particularly, special effects allowed moviemakers to document actual battles and, in turn, to re-create them more realistically in fictional films than during any previous era. Gripping combat footage—whether real or staged—allowed home-front audiences to experience the distant sights and jarring sounds of armies at war. Manufacturing countless reels of stridently ideological footage, the prolific dream factories assembled influential fictional and documentary productions to inspire the troops abroad and to educate the folks waiting for them at home. It also permanently altered the status of the Hollywood cinema and, by extension, the role that mass media has played in American culture. In 1946, the year after World War II ended, domestic attendance at the movies reached a high of ninety million per week, or 60 percent of the U.S. population.

If World War II had not actually occurred, Hollywood would probably have invented it. With one in every ten citizens in uniform, the war supplied American filmmakers with a prepackaged series of exciting plots, exotic settings, and courageous men of action engaged in deadly battles on the land, on the sea, and in the air (each with its own set of subgenre conventions). The subject matter and the visual opportunities the war offered were perfectly suited for the movies. Men and women from every corner of the United States and every level of society were ripped from the complacency of their daily lives and cast in a historic confrontation to determine the fate of the world. The pictures of men from across the United States slogging their way through overgrown jungles on remote Pacific islands and dodging bullets in the war-torn cities of Europe mesmerized moviegoers. Early World War II combat movies depict American soldiers engaged in heroic, almost mythic, crusades against the malevolent powers of darkness and oppression beyond the imaginations of Tolkien and Rowling.

Wartime combat movies pit decent citizens against evil aggressors whose regimes threaten to destroy America. U.S. servicemen onscreen demonstrate their moral authority and earn their ultimate victory by fighting bravely, honorably, and fairly; they kill only when necessary and treat their prisoners with respect. As film scholar Kathryn Kane notes, the honorable American soldier is depicted as a reluctant but decent and ethical warrior who personifies his country's morally superior values. Ironically, however, the decent and courageous American soldiers who fight to protect individual liberties must abandon those freedoms in wartime. In most World War II combat movies, the common soldier never questions such contradictions, articulates overarching political motives, or pronounces lofty patriotic sentiments; such nationalistic language is left to generals and politicians, who often prove far less admirable than the ordinary bands of brothers who risk their lives to protect their loved ones, homes, and buddies.

In updating her influential work *The World War II Combat Film: Anatomy of a Genre* (2003), Jeanine Basinger outlines several evolutionary waves of World War II combat movies, noting that such generalizations always contain individual exceptions. Her organizing structure provides a useful model to categorize these movies by focusing attention on representative works in each wave.

THE FIRST WAVE. Released between the Japanese attack on Pearl Harbor, on December 7, 1941, and December 31, 1943, the first-wave films define the basic conventions of the World War II combat movie and often use wartime events for basic plotlines. *Air Force* (1943) is a representative film from this period, released at the height of World War II and loosely based on true incidents, which falsifies some important historical facts—most noticeably by positing that Japanese Americans knew about the clandestine attack on Pearl Harbor and were involved in sabotaging military efforts there. By spreading this misleading information, as did other

***Air Force* (1943)** This film becomes a morale-renewal project that takes revenge for Japanese attacks on American bases that shook American society's self-confidence. Every bomb they release and every ship they blow up erases some of the shame suffered at Pearl Harbor. Winocki's (John Garfield) transformation from disgruntled outsider to valued part of the crew epitomizes a recurrent theme in World War II combat movies: Americans must put aside their petty differences to become a unified force. He sets into motion one of the most repeated narrative arcs in the combat genre: the conversion of the malcontent into a man who recognizes his patriotic duty, ultimately accepts his military responsibilities, and, finally, becomes an important part of the fighting unit.

films during this time, *Air Force* helped stoke xenophobic fears about Japanese citizens living along the Pacific coast and played a role in conditioning the public to accept the internment of some 110,000 Japanese Americans into so-called war relocation camps.

The crew of a B-17 bomber, christened *Mary Ann*, contains an ethnic (although all-white) jumble from various sections of the country. After the men witness the devastation resulting from Japan's sneak attack, they help destroy another enemy fleet in an extended combat sequence that expertly blends newsreel footage and staged sequences. *Air Force* clearly demonstrates the country's intense desire to gain revenge for Pearl Harbor, strives to restore faith in our military, and reaffirms American masculine pride. The ending foretells American victory, as the crew takes off to bomb Tokyo accompanied by the stirring music of "Off We Go Into the Wild Blue Yonder" and inspiring words from President Roosevelt.

THE SECOND WAVE. Aware of their predecessors' work, the directors of the second-wave movies, released between January 1, 1944, and January 31, 1946, solidify the established generic formats and conventions. Characteristically, these films use technical devices pioneered in newsreel and documentary footage. Like its predecessor *Air Force*, the second-wave film *They Were Expendable* (1945) somberly depicts the initial Japanese victories in the Pacific; Imperial forces relentlessly advance from their savage attack on Pearl Harbor to conquer the Philippines, despite the courageous efforts of American soldiers memorialized in such films as *Bataan, So Proudly We Hail, Salute to the Marines, Corregidor* (all 1943), and *Back to Bataan* (1945). Although released after the war, the episodic *They Were Expendable* depicts one of our country's most humiliating surrenders but simultaneously pays homage to the American fighting man's bravery, professionalism, and sense of duty in the face of overwhelming odds that doomed many to imprisonment or death. That the film ends with a sense of gloomy defeat, despite the fact that America had already won the war, argues for a rather somber view of combat, one that stresses the need for American military vigilance and recognizes that the last battle is never the final one.

THE THIRD WAVE. After a period of respite (1946–1949), when, Basinger notes, combat movies virtually disappear, retrospective films emerge again from November 1, 1949, to December 31, 1959. These include a series of movies whose narratives incorporate the generic conventions established in the previous two cycles, although still integrating historical events into the plotlines. This combination often results in films attentive to military details but lacking the gory brutality of earlier World War II combat movies. Produced in the midst of the Korean War and contemporary Communist threats, third-wave films introduce variations by probing the combatants' psychological states of mind, including one of the most famous, profitable, and representative third-wave movie, *Sands of Iwo Jima* (1949). Set in 1943, *Sands of Iwo Jima* stars John Wayne in a signature role as John M. Stryker, a tough, embittered, and alcoholic marine sergeant assigned to mold a rifle squad of raw recruits into a fighting unit. Because of his abusive training methods, constant bullying, and harsh punishments, the squad views Stryker as a cruel martinet, not knowing that his anger springs from his wife's having left him and refusing him access to his son. Eventually, the men come to admire Stryker, and the unit fights bravely in the perilous invasions of

Tarawa and Iwo Jima. *Sands of Iwo Jima* demonstrates a distinct evolution in the combat movie, incorporating a smattering of cynicism absent in earlier movies, such as one soldier's definition of war as "trading real estate for men."

THE FOURTH WAVE. This series, characterized by epic recreations of historical events, often with international casts, runs from January 1, 1960, to December 31, 1970. These films usually employed veterans who actually fought in the battles, were made on the actual locations of these clashes, and paid meticulous attention to even the most minuscule of historical details. Made some two decades after the end of World War II, fourth-wave movies often view historical events with an overlay of nostalgia and romanticism. *The Longest Day* (1962), a representative example of fourth-wave films, concentrates on historical accuracy rather than individual stories. Featuring an all-star cast of forty-two British, American, and French actors, the movie chronicles the important events that occurred during twenty-four hours of the D-Day landing at Normandy (France) on June 6, 1944. Its multiple perspectives present the miscalculations and heroism of Allied and German soldiers, running the gamut from the highest commanders making tactical decisions down to the grunts risking their lives to carry them out. Made with the help of thirty-seven military advisers and actual D-Day veterans, *The Longest Day* remains one of the most authentic combat movies of all time.

THE FIFTH WAVE. The mounting antiwar culture spawned by America's escalating military presence in Vietnam and by a rebellious generation's challenges to the entrenched authority of establishment institutions greatly influenced the themes and attitudes of the fifth-wave combat films, made between January 1, 1965, and December 31, 1975, and overlapping the fourth wave. The resulting productions invert, subvert, parody, and even ridicule many of the sacred genre conventions inherited from previous eras, stretching the margins of the genre almost to the breaking point. These macho fantasy movies feature a cynical attitude toward combat and an increasing level of violence. They function as dark, sometimes satiric, counterpoints to the previous waves of more patriotic fare by recasting established conventions, demythologizing them, and destabilizing traditional generic assumptions.

The Dirty Dozen (1967) typifies this group and makes few claims to authenticity, since transforming twelve convicted criminal men into a crack fighting unit lacks any realism. However, many of the character-istics of previous combat movies remain evident: an all-star cast, the multiethnic and multicultural platoon (although the armed forces were still segregated in 1944), and the strict attention to external details. Yet the film sabotages these conventions. Most obviously, this rebellious platoon contains no square-jawed, red-blooded American patriots sali-vating for an opportunity to smash the Huns but rather, as the film's psychiatrist notes, a "twisted bunch of antisocial nuts with a bushel of psychopathic deformities" that includes murder, religious fanaticism, rape, racism, and sexual deviancy. Ironically, however, the film initially determined to reverse hallowed combat movie customs ultimately reaf-firms the most revered convention of all: to survive, a diverse group of men must abandon their individuality and function as a team. That most of this surly, violent, defiant collection of misfits ends up sacrific-ing their lives for their country demonstrates how this powerful and pervasive theme resonates throughout the genre, even in its most sub-versive examples.

THE SIXTH WAVE. This category moves beyond the Basinger model. Stretching from the late 1970s to the present, it showcases a mixed bag of epics, nostalgic recreations, and ideological reconsiderations from a spectrum of viewpoints. Among the most fascinating yins and yangs within the combat movie genre are Clint Eastwood's re-creations of the battle for Iwo Jima in two overlapping films, *Flags of Our Fathers* (2006) from the American point of view and *Letters from Iwo Jima* (2006) from the perspective of the outnumbered Japanese. Although both films con-tain gruesome combat sequences detailing the ferocious battle for this strategic air base, each foregrounds elements of the genre rarely empha-sized in previous movies. By revealing the dismal personal stories lurk-ing behind Joe Rosenthal's famous photo of the U.S. flag being raised on Iwo Jima, *Flags of Our Fathers* focuses on how combat affects soldiers psychologically as well as physically and, more centrally, on the symbi-otic relationship between those engaged in war and those who report it: each group feeds off the other and continually seeks to manipulate its counterpart to control wartime narratives. While many films rehabili-tate the Germans by incorporating sympathetic portraits of some Nazi combatants, few films provide a similar regeneration for Japanese fight-ers. In *Letters from Iwo Jima*, viewers observe a spectrum of soldiers from the highest general, Kuribayashi (Ken Watanabe), to the lowest private,

Saigo (Kazunari Ninomiya). The film salutes their bravery in valiantly defending their homeland against overwhelming odds, including committing suicide rather than surrendering.

Saving Private Ryan, the most influential contemporary World War II combat movie, renders the story of eight soldiers sent to remove the last surviving Ryan brother from combat. Many of the film's dilemmas radiate outward from one essential question: is it ethical to dispatch these soldiers, all with loved ones of their own back home, to salvage one man and return him to safety? Under what conditions (if any) is it appropriate to sacrifice the many for the one? According to the conventions of the combat film, the sacrifice-of-the-individual-for-the-group mentality

Flags of Our Fathers (2006) Two overlapping films re-create the battle for Iwo Jima: *Flags of Our Fathers* from the American point of view and *Letters from Iwo Jima* (2006) from the perspective of the outnumbered Japanese. The cynical realism of war as "showbiz" drives the movie by showing the weary public manipulated into buying war bonds and by revealing how legends become truths through the power of the media. *Letters from Iwo Jima* counters the pervasively negative depictions of Japanese soldiers by individualizing them and saluting their bravery in valiantly defending their homeland. It renders a perspective of Pacific-theater action rarely seen in combat movies: American fighting men depicted as the enemy. In this upside-down, parallel universe of movie combat, we are not quite sure whom to root for and whom to fear.

is mandatory. By contrast, in *Saving Private Ryan* most of the members of the platoon are sacrificed to save the one. As the film unfolds, other conventions are also inverted: heroic men behave immorally, good men are sacrificed needlessly, cowardly men survive, and honorable men die because they act ethically. Although plagued by doubts, fears, and insecurities, this platoon ultimately lives up to the combat genre's conventions by dying as a unit to serve a larger cause.

THE KOREAN WAR

Wedged between the epic Second World War and the catastrophic Vietnam War, the Korean War (June 25, 1950–July 27, 1953) remains aptly called "the forgotten war" or "the unknown war." Many of the movies about Korea recycle familiar World War II themes and plot structures, including protagonists who fought in that earlier war and ethnically mixed platoons, although fanatic communists replace evil Nazis, newer weapons of war emerge, more minorities materialize, and racism becomes a more frequent topic. Released in February 1951, a few months after fighting began, *The Steel Helmet* stands as the first American film about the Korean War, and its central figure, Sergeant Zack (Gene Evans), personifies a new and more disparaging image of the American soldier. *The Steel Helmet* finishes not with the traditional "The End" but rather with the sadly prophetic words of warning: "The Story Has No Ending."

THE VIETNAM WAR

Like an unwelcome guest, the legacy of the Vietnam War remains a living presence in American life and cinema. No filmmaker can ignore Vietnam's enduring power as a media-saturated war reconstructed mainly through visual representations: photographic images, TV programs, and war movies. Lasting from November 1955 to April 1975, the war saw American troops join South Vietnam forces to wage a campaign of conventional fighting, while the Vietcong mainly employed hit-and-run guerrilla tactics that ultimately defeated its technologically superior enemies. By the end of the war, America's vast military complex, a symbol of the country's strength and power, was a staggering Goliath struck down in a faraway land by Punji sticks and men in black pajamas. Widely recognized as a total military and diplomatic collapse, the Vietnam

The Steel Helmet (1951) Leftover clichés from World War II proved inadequate to represent the fighting in Korea, and a new vocabulary of images had not yet been inscribed into the genre. *The Steel Helmet*, the first American film about the Korean War, depicts an American soldier more concerned with himself and his survival than with his buddies. Sergeant Zack (Gene Evans), a pugnacious World War II veteran and cantankerous racist, presented moviegoers with a far different image of the American soldier. Zack ultimately loses his temper and shoots an unarmed North Korean POW needed for interrogation. Recovered from his raging, he famously tells him, "If you die, I'll kill you." Equally unconventional are the conversations among the men, most crucially when the North Korean hostage attempts to sow seeds of bitter racial discord among the exhausted soldiers. His efforts fail, demonstrating that American principles of democracy, even if not fully realized, remain superior to communist propagandistic rhetoric.

"quagmire" demonstrated that the United States could not enforce its will unilaterally across the globe and that some wars are simply not winnable in the conventional, World War II manner.

Other than the Civil War, no U.S. military action has ever divided American citizens as dramatically and pervasively as the Vietnam War. This protracted, bitter, and disruptive conflict shattered fundamental American beliefs and lacerated the public psyche. During the Vietnam era, unlike periods of other foreign wars, drugs from pot to heroin became a pervasive part of military life that soldiers transported stateside as well. The combat films reflect this turmoil. These Vietnam combat movies challenge, destabilize, and ultimately sabotage all the previous generic conventions. Given the widespread perceptual shift from World War II's reluctant American troops heroically triumphing in a "good" war to Vietnam's crazed baby killers participating in an "evil" imperialist incursion—and losing—representative Vietnam combat movies encapsulate the madness, anger, and antiwar zeitgeist of this tumultuous era. *The Boys in Company C, Go Tell the Spartans, The Deer Hunter* (all 1978), *Apocalypse Now* (1979), *84 Charlie MoPic* (1984), *Platoon* (1986), *Full Metal Jacket, Hamburger Hill* (both 1987), and *Casualties of War* (1989) foreground the irrationality, meaninglessness, confusion, cruelty, futility, waste, and other inherent tragedies of combat.

A sprawling epic that ignited a firestorm of complaints about its portrayal of traumatized veterans and stereotypical Asians, *The Deer Hunter* divides its narrative into three sections dynamically woven together to illustrate the war's insidious impact on working-class Americans, both

***The Deer Hunter* (1978)** Many combat films about Vietnam, like *The Deer Hunter*, conflate a rash and reckless war with the men fighting it, personifying volatile soldiers as deranged incarnations of the brutality surrounding them; irreparably damaged by both physical and psychological traumas, these unstable hollow men usually cannot adjust to civilian life. Most famously, sadistic Vietcong guards force their prisoners to play Russian roulette against each other (which had no basis in fact) as they bet on the outcome, a powerful metaphor for the omnipresent element of chance that either saves or dooms soldiers during combat. The film, which began with a joyous wedding, ends with a somber funeral, a poignant communal sacrament concluded at breakfast with the assembled friends singing "God Bless America," a touching if ambiguous moment infused with lost innocence and unresolved dilemmas.

those fighting in Southeast Asia and those remaining at home. The first part presents an intertwined character study of four Russian Americans and their community: Michael (Robert DeNiro), Steven (John Savage), Stan (John Cazale), and Nick (Christopher Walken). The second segment abruptly shifts to a firefight in Vietnam, shot with a jumpy handheld camera for realism. Most famously, vicious guards force the prisoners to play Russian roulette against each other (which has no basis in fact), a powerful metaphor for the omnipresent element of chance that either saves or dooms a combat soldier. *The Deer Hunter*'s final portion follows three lives drastically altered by the war: an alienated and subdued Michael travels back to a chaotic Vietnam in a futile attempt to salvage the deranged Nick; a despondent and severely crippled Steven remains confined to a wheelchair and estranged from his family; and a heroin-addicted and shell-shocked Nick wanders around Saigon, participates in a Russian roulette club to earn money, and ultimately shoots himself.

The Vietnam films made closest to wartime culminate in the episodic and surrealistic *Apocalypse Now*, loosely based on Joseph Conrad's *Heart of Darkness*. His commanding officer assigns Colonel Benjamin Willard (Martin Sheen) to assassinate the charismatic and highly decorated Green Beret Colonel Walter Kurtz (Marlon Brando), a brilliant officer turned renegade warlord. A hallucinatory energy fuels *Apocalypse Now*, endowing it with a psychedelic mélange of exhilarating and terrifying scenes. In a justly famous scene, flamboyant Lieutenant Colonel Bill Kilgore (Robert Duvall) orders a phalanx of Ninth Air Calvary helicopters, accompanied by Wagner's "Ride of the Valkyries," to drop bombs and napalm on a peaceful village, a horrifying and yet savagely magnificent visual sequence that ends with Kilgore's oft-quoted line "I love the smell of napalm in the morning." Willard butchers Kurtz in a ritualistic scene cross cut with the sacrificial slaughter of a water buffalo, the colonel's last words, "the horror, the horror," taken from Conrad's book, echoing on the sound track. The dazzling imagery in *Apocalypse Now* compels us to watch the Vietnam War as if it were a ravishing vision of hell on LSD, while simultaneously forcing a confrontation with the murky aspects of America's soul.

The Deer Hunter and *Apocalypse Now* represent the most significant early films about the Vietnam War. Almost a decade later, during the more conservative Ronald Reagan era, three equally provocative films, *Platoon* (1986), *Full Metal Jacket* (1987), and *Casualties of War* (1989), confront combat's inherent contradictions differently from their cinematic

Apocalypse Now (1979) *Apocalypse Now* is a rambling voyage deep into a psychedelic mélange of exhilarating and terrifying scenes. Loosely based on Joseph Conrad's *Heart of Darkness*, Colonel Benjamin Willard's (Martin Sheen) hunt to find and assassinate the charismatic Green Beret Colonel Walter Kurtz (Marlon Brando), a highly decorated officer turned renegade warlord, functions as the excuse for a rambling voyage deep into America's murky psyche, stripping away the thin veneer of civilization that conceals savagery. Willard butchers Kurtz in a ritualistic scene cross cut with the sacrificial slaughter of a water buffalo, the colonel's last words, "the horror, the horror," echoing on the sound track. *Apocalypse Now* captures the paradoxical nature of combat—horrible and hypnotic, violent and visceral. Its dazzling imagery compels us to watch the Vietnam combat footage as if it were a ravishing vision of hell on LSD, while simultaneously forcing a confrontation with the darker aspects of America's soul.

ancestors. Although they follow the common practice of showing war from "the grunt's" point of view, these movies undermine one of the combat genre's most cherished conventions: the melting-pot corps of very different types of men who ultimately band together to form a cohesive unit, fight and defeat a common enemy, and thus personify the superiority of American democracy. The protagonist's final lines in *Platoon* epitomize the intense social and ideological clashes within fighting units that proved divisive and sometimes even lethal: "We did not fight the enemy. We fought ourselves and the enemy was in us." All three films strive for a visual patina of battle verisimilitude even as disruptive cultural issues ignored in previous combat movies claim the foreground, including race, class, educational level, economic status, and substance abuse. Vietnam veterans were stigmatized by these pervasive film images of psychotic soldiers fighting an insane war, the former conflating with the latter to generate the most negative portraits of the American military in cinema history.

CONTEMPORARY COMBAT FILMS

Contemporary combat movies fall into three historical categories: 1) The Gulf War [*Courage under Fire* (1996), *Three Kings* (1999), and *Jarhead* (2005)]; 2) Somalia [*Black Hawk Down* (2001)]; and 3) the Iraq War [*The Hurt Locker* (2008)]. As of this writing, the war in Afghanistan has generated no American fictional combat movies. While there is a paucity of theatrical movies about these controversial wars, TV movies and documentaries covering them have filled the void, including a few that have had widespread theatrical releases, particularly *Gunner Palace* (2004) and *Restrepo* (2010). Audiences seem disinclined to pay for pretend combat stories about ongoing wars when compelling images appear nightly on their TV screens, cycled as they happen and then recycled as history: combat as entertainment, entertainment as combat. The bombing of Baghdad, for example, was the second-most-watched television event in history, although its antiseptic presentation onscreen provided little fodder for heroic combat movies.

Concurrent with this lack of interest in combat movies, however, increasingly realistic video games (called "military shooters") such as the Call of Duty series continue to rack up extraordinary sales. America's Army, a free download series of video games developed by the U.S. Army to stimulate declining recruitment numbers, has also been very successful: an MIT study concluded that the game had more impact on recruits than all other forms of advertising combined. So why are these combat video games so popular? The so-called "first-person shooter" games thrust individual players into virtual battlefields often based on actual warfare locations and incorporating soldiers sporting historically accurate weapons and uniforms. Yet no matter how enhanced the graphics and realistic the audio, video games offer excitement without consequences. As a result, gamers can vent their aggressions in a socially sanctioned manner, as virtual combat provides a sense of immersive participation and direct agency impossible to achieve sitting passively in the movie theater. Some critics, however, allege that virtual bloodletting numbs players to carnage and may even encourage violence beyond the screen. Others claim that the merging of combat video games with the news media's presentation of fighting has produced an American population that increasingly conceptualizes combat as a video game rather than a lethal enterprise.

Courage Under Fire (1996), the first big-budget Hollywood film to confront the Gulf War, merges intense air and ground battles with a murder mystery. It also remains one of the few combat movies featuring a woman in command of men, U.S. Army Captain Karen Walden (Meg Ryan). Like the Vietnam films, *Courage Under Fire* illustrates how the military establishment manipulates the media and lies to protect its reputation. Its multiple flashbacks dramatically convey the slippery nature of truth under combat conditions, as well as how the precious bond between soldiers can foster deceit and treachery in the name of brotherhood.

Although its gritty and realistic style combined with graphically violent scenes marks its lineage as a post-Vietnam combat movie, the cynical humor of *Three Kings* (1999) makes it feel more akin to *M*A*S*H* than to *Courage Under Fire*. As U.S. troops engage in mop-up operations at the end of the Gulf War in March 1991, a group of soldiers discovers a map locating a bunker where Saddam Hussein has stashed a fortune in stolen gold bullion. Major Archie Gates (George Clooney), a disgruntled Special Forces officer relegated to escorting reporters around the war zones, joins forces with three reservists to pilfer the gold. Suddenly, however, a quirky caper flick turns into a daring rescue movie when the four men must choose between riches and saving a desperate group of civilians. As with its tone, the technical and visual elements of *Three Kings* designate its unique status among combat movies, demonstrating that new types of wars demand inventive imagery. While many scenes are shot in deep focus, with the actions in the foreground, midground, and background of the frame simultaneously in focus and commenting on each other, other segments feature a roving camera, wide-angle shots, oblique angles, disturbing close-ups, and distorting jump cuts. Jarring whip pans whisk the viewer from one scene to the next, while various sections mimic the zooming and panning style of CNN reporting. One of the most remarkable shots in the movie graphically illustrates the effects of a bullet entering the body.

Like *Three Kings*, *Jarhead* (a slang term for Marines because of their haircuts) also upends generic conventions by becoming a combat movie that contains no fighting. As the war ends, sniper Anthony Swafford (Jake Gyllenhaal) has never fired his weapon. Based on real events in Somalia, *Black Hawk Down* focuses on the courage of Americans despite

***Three Kings* (1999)** During the Gulf War, Americans avidly watched their TV screens as planes pinpointed their targets and dropped their payloads, the live images bearing an eerie resemblance to computer games and triggering an apt nickname: "The Video War." A realistic style combined with graphically violent scenes mark *Three Kings* as a darkly cynical post-Vietnam combat movie. The technical and visual elements of *Three Kings* designate its unique status among combat movies. Many scenes are shot in deep focus, while diverse segments feature a roving camera, wide-angle shots, oblique angles, disturbing close-ups, and distorting jump cuts. Jarring whip pans whisk the viewer from one scene to the next, mimicking the zooming and panning style of CNN reporting. The film's color palette replicates the hue and tint of wartime newspaper photographs. One of the most remarkable shots in the movie illustrates the effects of a bullet entering the body, the abdominal cavity filling up with bile.

the humiliating failure of a mission during the Battle of Mogadishu, in October 1993, showing valiant soldiers fighting bravely against overwhelming odds. *The Hurt Locker* (where a soldier lands after an explosion) takes place during the postinvasion period in Iraq and follows three members of the army's Explosive Ordnance Division as they detonate or deactivate improvised explosive devices. The film explores the psyches of men who participate in this hazardous mission.

Typologies, Themes, and Theories
CULTURAL MEMORY AND HISTORICAL EVENTS

Those who have never actually participated in combat can know about it only from the words and pictures of others and, thus, share what Alison Landsberg calls "prosthetic memories": widely circulated, technologically generated memories that become as important a part of a person's sense of identity as actual lived experiences. Because stories and images that simulate past experiences and manufacture memories express more about the cultures within which they are produced than the ones they ostensibly describe, prosthetic memories become manifestations of current points of view and ideological agendas that never remain static. Their contours shift and slide, their meanings remaining adaptable to negotiations between competing societal demands. The ingredients in combat films, therefore, are akin to records at an oldies radio station: some are played repeatedly, some are resurrected and then ignored, and some languish in the dustbin of obscurity. By blending historical facts and dramatic narratives, combat films also become implicit commentaries on previous combat movies. In *Jarhead*, for example, the marines awaiting battle cheer the famous Kilgore scene while watching *Apocalypse Now*, and other films about modern warfare, such as *Full Metal Jacket*, overtly mock the staged heroics of John Wayne. The wartime histories propagated in motion pictures—be they totally replicated visuals of incidents crafted after they occurred, edited constructions of images captured during the actual situations, or some intermingling of the two—make movies into communal photo albums commemorating shared national experiences. As such, combat films form a repository of communal memories and continue to play a central role in the negotiation and codification of historical events in American culture.

HISTORICAL ACCURACY

Derived from historical events, combat movies are continually subjected to the slings and arrows of outraged historians and actual participants in the battles themselves. For instance, Ken Burns, who made the documentary *The Civil War* (1990), attacked *Glory*'s lack of historical precision and likened its characters to the stereotypical figures in World War II movies. Film scholar Robert Eberwein questioned why the only historical figure incorporated into *Glory* is the white officer Shaw, when information about the blacks who served in the regiment was readily available. Other commentators noted that the film implies the unit was made up of former slaves when, in fact, it was predominately composed of free black men from Massachusetts and Pennsylvania. Sometimes a combat movie gets criticized for what it omits, such as when critics condemned *Saving Private Ryan* for including only American soldiers and ignoring the role of foreign troops in the D-Day invasion. Critics often object to conventional subplots in the genre, most often romances, arguing that their alternation with battle sequences robs combat films of their legitimacy and turns them into semimelodramas.

During times of war, combat films literally become part of the military arsenal; they can bolster the home front, solicit funding, solidify public opinion, taunt the enemy, and inspire soldiers. After World War II, General George Marshall commented that "the war had seen the development of two new weapons: the airplane and the motion picture." As film historian Thomas Doherty points out, World War II feature films that entertained as they informed played an active and significant role in American life, bringing new prestige to filmmaking, recognized importance to the industry, and a role for it in national politics. So the question arises: do combat movies have a moral responsibility to present historical events as accurately as possible? No work of art can capture every aspect of a historical event, and combat films, like all movies, are inherently subjective: directors choose a specific point of view from among a multiplicity of possible perspectives and offer interpretations of events. Because moviemakers consciously strive to entertain as well as to enlighten, their use of outward accuracy—the incorporation of correct uniforms and precise firearms—usually overlays obviously fictional events meant to engage the audience. The realism of costuming and props, therefore, can lull the audience into accepting unreal plots as genuine history. That said, when directors of combat films wrap them in the cloak of historical authenticity, they do incur a responsibility to present images and narratives as precisely as possible, realizing that films reach a large audience and are often taken as factual.

MASCULINITY

For most of the late nineteenth and entire twentieth centuries, the Western's individualistic cowboy-hero dominated formulations of masculinity in American society, an idealized creation shaped and circulated by literary writing, cinema productions, and TV programming. Now, with the addition of video games and the Internet to these traditional media outlets, the Western's preeminent role has been usurped by the combat movie: the frontier has been converted into the front line, the savage Indians transformed into enemy soldiers, and the rugged cowboy replaced by the battle-hardened veteran. Issues of masculinity have always been an inherent part of the combat movie. *Sands of Iwo Jima* paints a far from totally positive portrait of an enduring symbol of masculinity, the iconic Sergeant Stryker, and contains a running battle about what constitutes manhood. Stryker's self-destructive pathology, brooding misery, and psychological weaknesses alternate with his combat strengths. In one famous scene, Stryker courageously destroys the enemy machine gunners butchering his marines. Does he do so out of concern for his men or as the desperate act of a man with little to live

***Sands of Iwo Jima* (1949)** The symbiotic connection between combat films and military institutions can strongly influence and overtly intervene in productions. To boost their sagging public image at the end of World War II, Marine Corps leaders approached John Wayne to make a movie about the battle of Iwo Jima, where 6,318 Marines died. The popularity of *Sands of Iwo Jima* helped keep the Marines Corps alive, functioning as a powerful recruiting tool far beyond its sheer entertainment value. *Sands of Iwo Jima* offers a complex portrait of its seriously flawed hero, Sergeant Stryker (Wayne). Despite the character's overt flaws, Wayne's portrayal of Stryker came to embody the guts and spirit of the American soldier during World War II, an emblematic image and one of the most indelible representations of the military man in combat.

for? Despite his overt character flaws, Stryker came to embody the guts and spirit of the American soldier, an emblematic image and one of the most indelible representations of the World War II fighting man. In a more modern conception of masculinity, Captain Miller's (Tom Hanks) sobbing breakdown and shaking hands in *Saving Private Ryan* present a far more nuanced image of masculinity than previously seen in combat films.

Interwoven seamlessly with the hypermasculinity that defines most combat films is a strand of homoeroticism rarely so evident in other genres. Sometimes this thread is displayed as a spectacle/fetish with the near-naked male body, as when the camera lingers over Sylvester Stallone's bulging torso in the Rambo movies (1982–2008). Because squad members depend on each other to survive, intense relationships between soldiers under perilous conditions dominate the genre and make combat movies the ultimate "buddy" films. The constant threat of death relentlessly hovering over soldiers endows these tough men with an intrinsic vulnerability that, in turn, gives them license to cast away some of the social prohibitions that govern their civilian lives; this reckless freedom often results in actions—sometimes marvelous and other times appalling—they would never consider engaging in stateside. The combat film remains one of the few genres in which men can express deep emotional affection for each other while simultaneously displaying extreme physical courage. Even when romances between men and women bloom in the midst of the death and desolation of combat movies, the bonding relationships between men transcend the common connections of daily life and define the genre, while the presence of women mainly affirms the soldiers as heterosexual.

NATIONALISM

From its earliest days, Hollywood filmmakers have assembled clusters of communal facts and fantasies into genre films that have fulfilled a shifting assortment of national needs and desires. The combat genre reshuffles a series of potent mythologies containing valiant heroes, dangerous quests, malevolent villains, recognizable iconographies, repeated narrative patterns, and recurring conventions to design compelling allegories to define themselves and identify America's salient values. The ubiquitous ethnically diverse platoons that populate combat movies become microcosms of American life and values, the pristine ideals of nationhood erected upon a foundation of racial and religious equality. The American flag flutters into the majority of combat movies, a stirring symbol of American pride and patriotism—as well as of its bloody history. Military superiority or the assumption of it also plays a significant role in the formation of American identity, and ongoing media representations of "the sting of battle" become significant building blocks in the shaping of our communal sense of national selfhood.

A war does not end when the shooting stops; instead, the cessation of fighting signals the beginning of intense debates about its meaning and place in American culture. Combat movies navigate through the muddy fields of wartime sagas, offering competing representations of historical events that negotiate and reaffirm America's distinctive principles. Combat films made during a conflict usually express the fears of a country and those produced subsequently serve as interpretations, or reconfigurations, of what happened during those fearful struggles. Film scholar Marita Sturken observes that American productions inevitably blur the boundaries between images and histories, conflating facts and fantasies to configure a shared mélange of wartime experiences and fabrications. Thus, reenactments of events in combat movies play a significant role in conceptualizing the meaning of American national identity and the recurring questions of what it means to be an American. We can be certain an event occurred, but its meaning and significance shift with the tides of history. "History," says a character in Julian Barnes's novel *The Sense of an Ending* (2011), "is that certainty produced at the point where the imperfections of memory meet the inadequacies of documentation" (18).

REPRESENTATIONS OF WOMEN IN THE MILITARY

The vast majority of combat movies present clichéd female characters or express overt sexism in dialogue or imagery. Predominately masculine, the world of combat movies inevitably relegates women to emblematic roles as mothers, wives, girlfriends, daughters, and sexual necessities. In the pre-Vietnam movies about World War II, women personify what the soldiers risk their lives to defend: love, family, and home. While this attitude lingers in a few post-Vietnam films, the allusions to women change as the genre evolves. In *Full Metal Jacket*, much of the language during boot camp training equates weak recruits with crude references to their femininity (or homosexuality), while *Casualties of War* incorporates the brutalization of women as an ongoing consequence of combat. Many films show soldiers incessantly worrying about their stateside women being unfaithful and their fears of losing them.

A few movies defy this fundamental assumption that men fight and women wait, struggling to break free of the stereotypes that dominate this genre. *Courage Under Fire* confronts shifting aspects of military combat never tackled by Stryker or Ryan: gender equality and hostility, mental health status, and the accidental killing of one's comrades. The painful necessity for Karen Walden to leave her daughter behind as she marches off to war demonstrates the complications of a cultural transition that challenges the traditional roles of men in combat movies and women at home. Because Walden is dead as the film begins, men relate her story from their perspective, a narrative strategy that renders her unable to provide her unique version of events—or even to give her a voice. Yet her authoritative role inherently rebels against the machismo tradition prevalent in previous combat movies.

REPRESENTATIONS OF MINORITIES IN BATTLE

Minority characters in combat movies—usually part of multiethnic platoons—exemplify the advantages of democracy over other forms of government. As the later films emerge, the ironic juxtaposition of men fighting for a country in which they are second-class citizens discriminated against by the people they seek to defend forms a recognizable subtheme. Yet the very fact that such characters are willing to sacrifice their lives for their nation, despite facing relentless prejudice stateside, demonstrates the enduring vitality of the American Dream. Combat films epitomize the ideological precept that fighting for one's country remains the primary passageway to genuine citizenship for traditional outsiders; the willingness to die in combat validates marginalized immigrant groups as legitimate Americans. The vast majority of war movies identify combat as the primary crucible, the proverbial melting pot that forges "the other" into indisputable Americans. To do so, however, the outsider must first become disciplined by adopting the traditional hallmarks of white military culture. In combat film conventions, martyrdom in battle becomes the price of public acceptance.

WARTIME ATROCITIES

Early combat movies depict American soldiers as morally superior to their despotic enemies. As actual World War II battles faded into cultural mythology, some combat movies muddied this supremacy, creating a picture of U.S. servicemen as similar to their enemies. Vietnam pictures often envision American soldiers as morally inferior to their counterparts, indiscriminately killing civilians and raping women. They also reveal some unsavory realities of combat, particularly that the best soldiers are often the least civilized of men: the harsh necessities of war provide justification for their belligerent, sometimes sadistic, actions. Combat zones leave little room for the niceties of prolonged contemplation or grand gestures of nobility. In *The Dirty Dozen*, the platoon drops grenades and pours gasoline through air vents into a locked room filled with unarmed German officers and civilians (including women) and then sets them ablaze without a second thought. Such an action conducted by the enemy would be considered a war crime, but given the audience's emotional investment in these nasty antiheroes, the resulting incineration elicits cheers rather than horror. These movies often acknowledge two seemingly contradictory facets of human nature that struggle for the soul of future combat movies: when necessary, ordinary men can rise above their petty concerns to achieve extraordinary heroism and, under battlefield conditions, cruel atrocities inevitably occur even among those fighting with God on their side.

COMBAT MOVIES AND GOVERNMENT/ MILITARY INFLUENCE

The symbiotic connection between combat films and governmental offices can strongly influence and overtly intervene in productions. *Hearts of the World* (1918) provides an early illustration of this link. D. W. Griffith was the only director authorized to go to the front lines of the battlefield during World War I. Why was such access granted? The British War Office Cinematography Committee appealed to Griffith to make a feature that would help sway Americans to enter the war. In exchange, he would have free rein to shoot on actual battlefields and present genuine war scenes. Thus, *Hearts of the World* is essentially a commissioned piece of propaganda made to generate sympathy for the Allied cause and one of the first movies to entwine itself with a governmental agency. More recent examples exist as well, such as the post–September 11 meeting between forty Hollywood executives and officials of the Bush administration about how to help fight terrorism and a November 8 meeting they had with Karl Rove, a senior White House adviser, for a more focused discussion about how Hollywood might help the war effort. In response to the 9/11 attacks, some movies that might have proved controversial, such as *Collateral Damage*, *Buffalo Soldiers*, and *The Quiet American*, were shelved for a time, and others that might stir patriotism, like *Black Hawk Down* and *We Were Soldiers*, were moved to the front of the distribution line. Examples like these dramatically illustrate how combat films can be overtly constructed for purposes far beyond their sheer entertainment value.

Every combat movie functions as either a recruiting poster or a dire warning against joining the military. All the branches of the armed forces realize the power of films to sway or repel potential volunteers. If combat movies such as *Platoon* and *Courage Under Fire* contain far too negative portrayals of fighting men, requests for assistance by filmmakers are routinely denied. If the military approves the trajectory of the narrative—which basically means foregrounding battlefield heroism and honor—and the positive presentation of its fighting men and women, it usually contributes substantially to the filming, often loaning bases, equipment, uniforms, weapons, stock footage, and even men to fill various production needs, as was the case with *Pearl Harbor* (2001). This quid pro quo saves film companies large amounts of money. In addition, the armed services routinely supply experienced advisers to contribute recommendations during shooting, but these combat experts can also act as censors. Their threat of withdrawing military support provides leverage to reinforce their suggestions and guarantee serious consideration. All of this "official" attention to military verisimilitude finds its way into the prerelease hype for the movie and provides fodder for the inevitable "special features" section of the DVDs.

THE AMERICAN SOLDIER

Throughout American history, societal attitudes toward U.S. soldiers expressed in combat movies have functioned as a barometer of general opinions toward various wars. Although films exist about major historical figures, most American combat movies feature common men carried forth by the currents of history. The following generalizations form the broad outlines of how combat films present fighting men, recognizing that exceptions exist in all eras. Those who fought the ground battles in World War I are depicted as heroic but essentially betrayed soldiers who bravely volunteered for an epic struggle but found themselves trapped in mud-soaked trenches and commanded by incompetent, even venal, officers. At the opposite end of the spectrum, World War I pilots engage in a romantic environment populated by gentlemen following strict codes of honor, dressed in flamboyant outfits, and performing daring feats among the clouds. American films rendered World War II combatants as courageous men fighting nobly in the so-called Good War. The ethnically varied platoons composed of everyday grunts become symbolic of an idealized American society where social and racial differences disappear in a cooperative effort to defeat a fanatical enemy. While post-Vietnam movies about World War II tarnish this bright image, these men never fully lose their shine, despite their rough edges.

Combat imagery was never quite the same after World War II. As befits a forgotten war, both moviemakers and the American public essentially ignored the soldiers who fought in Korea. Leftover clichés from World War II proved inadequate to represent them, and a new vocabulary of cynical images had not yet been fully inscribed into the genre. Vietnam combat films conflate a reckless war with the men fighting it, personifying volatile soldiers as deranged incarnations of the brutality surrounding them; irreparably damaged by both physical injuries and psychological traumas, these unstable hollow men cannot adjust to civilian life. Later films transport World War II images of America's courageous fighting man into Vietnam by showing him rescuing POWs stranded in the jungle, thereby separating the vilified war from the soldiers engaged in combat. Contemporary filmmakers seem uncertain how to represent soldiers in America's ongoing wars, but they separate the men from the conflict. Soldiers often behave bravely and honorably despite being engaged in what many consider an unnecessary, futile, and imperialistic chain of conflicts around the globe.

TECHNOLOGY

Because the vast majority of Americans come into contact with war only through the camera's lens, combat films are intimately connected with developments in technology both on and off the screen. Continual advances in recording technology allow moviemakers to capture indelible images as they happen and to construct more realistic fictional films using the same equipment employed by reporters and documentary filmmakers. In the Gulf War, for example, TV sequences of the heavy Baghdad bombing and "smart" surgical strikes positioned viewers as spectators/partakers inside missile sensor systems as they sped downward, coining the phrases "technowar" and "MIMENET" (the military-industrial-media-entertainment-network) war. The constant stream of immediate combat images available on television and the Internet not only transmitted wartime events as they occurred, unhampered by the necessity to process film, but demanded that fictional movies replicate this level of realism to maintain any sense of authenticity. On-screen, some combat films showcase individual acts of courageous men fighting gigantic machines of war, individual soldiers attempting to demolish marauding tanks, dodging strafing aircraft, and knocking out machine gun bunkers. Yet American soldiers usually maintain technological superiority, although (as in the Vietnam movies) this increasingly sophisticated equipment does not always guarantee success and often generates overconfidence.

Iconography

The fundamental visual ingredients of the combat genre are apparent at first glance. Attention to historically accurate military uniforms and decals, side arms, rifles, and larger weapons of war (from machine guns and tanks to aircraft and ships) is paramount for authenticity. Of course, budget considerations and military access affect the availability and correctness of these items, but particular visual images seem yoked to specific wars. Thus, no matter the limitations of budget and access, all combat movies use their available resources to make their iconography conform to audience expectations about what that particular war looked like at the time.

Two diametrically opposed visual settings characterize World War I combat movies: trench warfare enacted on ravaged landscapes and aerial battles waged across endless skies. The frigid, soggy, muddy trenches contain drenched and shivering soldiers dressed in drab uniforms and huddling together wherever they can find shelter from the nasty weather. Between these enemy channels lies a hazardous terrain filled with hidden land mines, barbed wire, deserted foxholes, remains of bombed buildings, broken tree trunks, and enemy snipers. On this killing ground, soldiers relentlessly charge back and forth, never seeming to gain ground, watching their comrades die, and ultimately retreating to their own furrows. Not surprisingly, then, a second visual image appearing in many World War I combat movies is a landscape covered with crosses.

Among the clouds, however, the scene is far different. High above the trenches, brave men in spotless uniforms, accessorized by flowing silk scarves and goggles, struggle for supremacy in picturesque biplanes. Their aircraft catch fire and plunge downward, the absence of parachutes assuring certain death. Unlike soldiers being shot and dying in the ground war, the gallant pilot's body smashing into the earth is never seen in close-up. A gentlemen's code of honor governs these thrilling skirmishes filled with graceful dips and glides, riveting acrobatics, and exciting dogfights. These gods of the air duel fearlessly but courteously, their battles characterized by a chivalric kinship between enemies who respect their adversary's proficiency and nerve. Such intrepid exploits captured the imagination of a generation.

World War II has been the subject of a massive array of movies over the decades. The European, Pacific, and African theaters all offer very different locations, from bombed out ruins, to sweltering jungles, to scorched deserts. Jeanine Basinger's comprehensive study of the combat genre breaks it into three sections—war on the ground, on the sea, and in the air. Each contains a set of mechanized images that define its basic nature, including land weapons (tanks to machine guns), warships (submarines to carriers), and aircraft (bombers to fighter planes). The varying uniforms of soldiers, sailors, and pilots also delineate rival clusters of servicemen. Robert Eberwein lists a number of basic male and female characters, narrative cycles, and common elements, including, among others: writing letters, receiving mail from home, listening to the radio, spontaneous play to relieve tension and boredom, singing, burials at sea, leaves from combat, and reflections on the nature of the enemy. All of this is accomplished with cigarettes dangling from the lips of men on even the slightest break from the rigors of war.

Many updated but roughly similar images appear in the Vietnam combat movies, but one is especially emblematic: the helicopter. The instantly recognizable sound of whirling rotor blades as a copter whips

Wings (1927) *Wings* is the paradigmatic silent World War I aerial warfare film, a romanticized and spectacular production depicting honorable men jousting with skill and daring. Its dazzling flying sequences highlight the stark differences between muddy ground battles and idealistic air fighting. The flamboyant flyboys resemble knights of old, obeying rules of chivalry and honor, accessorizing their fashionable uniforms with colorful silk scarves, engaging in spectacular dogfights, and dying in a blaze of glory. *Wings* also spotlights the homoerotic strand that runs throughout the combat films. Deep emotions between men intensified by their wartime experiences are not overly sexual but rather cherished examples of manly bonding under extreme circumstances, a convention that runs throughout this genre.

up a blast of wind and majestically rises is inexorably linked with this conflict. Whether firing down upon hapless civilians mingled with fleeing Vietcong guerrillas, evacuating wounded men from the field of action, or lifting terrified refugees from the rooftop of the U.S. embassy in Saigon, the enduring sights and sounds of helicopters define Vietnam combat movies. They are the symbol of America's technological dominance, but also of the military's failures. The other immediately identifiable Vietnam combat image is of soldiers lighting up joints as frequently as they smoke cigarettes. This conspicuous shift from alcohol to drugs for decompression and relaxation delineates crucial distinctions

***Apocalypse Now* (1979)** The instantly recognizable sounds of whirling rotor blades and the sight of a helicopter lifting into the air become emblematic of the Vietnam War. The sights and sounds of helicopters became the permanent image of America's technological dominance, but also an ironic symbol of the military's failures as well: sailors pushing Huey and Chinook helicopters into the South China Sea during the evacuation of Saigon put a decisive exclamation point on America's tragic misadventure. Using helicopters as its metaphor, *Apocalypse Now* demonstrates how the military risks brave men's lives for trivial reasons. In a justly famous scene, flamboyant Lieutenant Colonel Bill Kilgore (Robert Duvall) orders a phalanx of Ninth Air Calvary helicopters accompanied by Wagner's "Ride of the Valkyries" to bomb a village so that a professional surfer can demonstrate his skills. The sequence ends with Kilgore's oft-quoted line as he walks shirtless among the exploding armaments, "I love the smell of napalm in the morning."

between previous veterans and a new generation of soldiers, who are less professional, reliable, and disciplined.

Another mechanical innovation dominates current combat movies: night-vision devices. These tools, which once provided only distorted images, have progressed to become a prominent part of America's weapons arsenal, particularly in Iraq and Afghanistan. Filtered through the ghostly green images (the human eye can differentiate shades of green more readily than any other color), these instruments allow soldiers to perform covert missions in the dark, such as capturing Osama bin Laden in *Zero Dark Thirty*. On a visual level, they necessarily shift the viewer into total alignment with the character on the screen; we see only what he/ she sees. Such a direct connection often compels audiences to adopt a sympathetic attitude toward that character, since we perceive the world through a particular set of eyes and share, quite literally, his/her vision.

The Landing on Omaha Beach in *Saving Private Ryan*

Saving Private Ryan's depiction of American troops landing on Omaha Beach on D-Day (June 6, 1944) remains one of the most powerful and influential re-creations of combat ever put on film. This lacerating twenty-five minutes, with its harrowing mélange of indelible images and sounds, invokes an awful beauty that compels the viewer. To borrow phrases from Tim O'Brien's Vietnam novel *The Things They Carried*, the Omaha Beach landing "fills the eye" with the horrible "moral indifference" of combat.

To understand the techniques that produce such a visceral punch, it seems useful to break the Omaha Beach sequence into five segments: 1) time spent on the boats and in the water; 2) time spent on the initial landing; 3) time spent moving up the beach; 4) time spent trapped by enemy fire; and 5) time spent overrunning the German machine gun pillbox. Before this sequence, however, the film begins with sounds rather than pictures, a lone trumpet and snare drum and the American flag fluttering in the wind. The camera opens by tracking behind a man, his family following him, walking down a tree-lined path as the trumpet, now harmonized by other solemn brass, and flag sounds continue. The man (Harrison Young) moves through a field of grave markers, obviously searching for a particular name. Eventually, he falls to his knees in front of one marker and begins to sob, the camera slowly panning in to an extreme close-up of his eyes accompanied by the ever-louder noise of crashing waves. This transition from present to past events creates an illusionary point of view, a sly sleight-of-hand trick that ultimately confounds the audience's narrative expectations. Because the first individual most viewers immediately recognize is Tom Hanks, they naturally surmise that he and the man back among the graves are same person at different points in his life. Retrospectively, one realizes that Ryan was not present on the beach that day in June 1944, so what initially seems like a first-person remembrance becomes a conjectured third-person account, pieced together long after most of the events actually transpired.

ON THE BOATS AND IN THE WATER

The first visual images shown are rows of metal hedgehogs, barriers along the shoreline, with waves lapping and curling against them. "June 6, 1944" establishes the date, followed by "Dog Green Sector / Omaha Beach" to set the place and provide a documentary feel to the sequence. Next, a quick series of long shots shows a squadron of Higgins boats straining toward the drop-off point. Men vomit over the sides of the boat. The camera cuts to a man's hands shaking as he twists open his canteen and raises it to his lips. The bars on his helmet are the only bright spot in a darkly foreboding frame. This, as we come to know, is Captain Miller (Tom Hanks). An unsteady, handheld camera moves back to reveal the men who surround him; Sergeant Horvath (Tom Sizemore) plops a wad of tobacco into his mouth. More vomiting. "Clear the ramp! Thirty seconds! God be with you!" screams the boat's captain, followed by a volley of orders issued alternately by Miller and Horvath: "Move fast and clear those murder holes. . . . Keep the sand out of your weapons. Keep those actions clear. I'll see you on the beach." A series of close-ups of men waiting anxiously to disembark from the boat catches the fear lurking in their eyes and creeping around the corners of their mouths; some pray and one kisses his crucifix. But other than Miller and Horvath, we have no inkling of who will be part of the continuing narrative and who will be left sprawled on the beach. The sound of a whistle slices through the air, a wheel spins quickly, the front of the boat slaps down, and bullets clank against the metal hull and mow down the first row of soldiers. The horror has begun.

For the first time in the sequence, the viewer experiences a shift from the point of view of the disembarking American soldiers to that of their enemies firing down on them. Shot now with a jerky horizontal pan from behind the backs of the Germans, and glimpsed between spewing machine guns being fed belts of ammunition, the running Americans seem small and helpless on a darkling plain. Maintaining this point of view for just a few furious seconds, the image cuts back to men desperately seeking a relatively safe patch on the beach, then shifts back to the Higgins boats with more men tumbling over their sides and into the sea, the camera slipping underwater with them. The blue sea and the bubbles of breath that surround the wriggling bodies momentarily muffle the sound of combat, like a wet blanket wrapped tightly around

Saving Private Ryan (1998) *Saving Private Ryan*'s depiction of American troops landing on Omaha Beach on D-Day (June 6, 1944), where some twenty-five hundred soldiers lost their lives, remains one of the most powerful—and influential—re-creations of combat ever put on film. With its harrowing mélange of indelible images and sounds, of technical brilliance and grisly replication, this lacerating twenty-five minutes has become the model against which all subsequent combat scenes will be judged. The sequence calls out for post–World War II generations to acknowledge the debt they owe to the men and women who fought to defend America. But the film is not an unambiguous celebration of American bravery. The search for Ryan has no military target and no direct bearing on the outcome on the war. Rather, it offers viewers an insistent inquiry into what constitutes moral behavior within a wartime landscape dominated by violence, brutality, and death.

their bodies. Rifles and helmets slide into the darkness beneath their dangling feet. As they struggle to untangle themselves from the heavy gear dragging them downward, some of the men drown; bullets slice through the water, first missing and then finding their targets, mixing red into the blue water.

Following some men swimming upward, the camera breaks above the waves, the sounds of battle resuming its loud and disjointed cacophony, then bobs beneath the surface again, then into the air, then below again, and finally stays above the depths for a few moments. We catch glimpses of men helping their comrades ashore, of others clinging to the hedgehogs or lying dead in their metal arms; we hear bullets clinking against the steel. A man Miller drags toward shore is shot and sinks beneath the water. Slowly, the Americans inch forward, their feet eventually finding dry land. Quick cut back to the enemy pillbox to remind us of who holds the high ground and who remains vulnerable. A few bullets whiz past Miller, who sinks to his knees in the shallow water, blood swirling around his legs. For an instant, we fear that the film will dare to kill off its most recognizable actor. This uncertainty remains because Miller is outside the frame while the camera catches a man stepping on a land mine, flying into the air, and having his left leg ripped from his body. Behind him, Miller, slowly crawling toward land, finally clings to a hedgehog for a momentary respite.

THE INITIAL LANDING

At this point, the scene abruptly shifts from a third-person perspective and drags us into Miller's subjective point of view. The concussions from exploding munitions render him temporarily unable to hear properly. Sounding as if he were standing under a waterfall, a steady roar dominates his hearing and ours. Other sounds don't totally disappear, but they seem distant—less pronounced and not entirely discernable. His numb gaze takes in the scene. He watches frightened soldiers huddling beneath the hedgehogs. A soldier gathers up his right arm from the ground and runs off with it. Miller gingerly picks up his helmet, now filled with red seawater, and replaces it on his head, the rivulets of blood crisscrossing his face and giving him a weird, kabuki-like appearance. A soldier hollers into his face, but Miller cannot hear him. Finally, the whining explosion of a bomb restores his hearing: "What the hell do we do now, sir?" shouts the enlisted man. Turning to Horvath, he commands, "Move your men off the beach." "What's the rallying point?" inquires one of the men. "Anywhere but here!" answers Miller.

MOVING UP THE BEACH

Ripping us away from Miller's first-person perspective, the camera returns to the third-person, plunging us back into the chaotic confusion of the men working their way up the beach. But Miller remains the focal point around which the action dips and dives. The camera tracks along parallel to Miller's progress as the pushes his way past dead and mangled bodies. In one of the film's most gruesome moments, a soldier lies dying on the sand, his guts literally spilling out from his body as he cries out plaintively, "Mama. Mama." The relentless assault on our senses continues. Miller stumbles on a platoon of medics clustered behind a hedgehog and, as he speaks with their leader, a man right in front of them gets shot repeatedly. They never miss a beat in their conversation or even take notice of the dead man's riddled body. At one point in his progression, Miller drags a wounded soldier toward safety when a bomb explodes and severs the man's body in half. Miller finds himself lugging his upper torso, now sheared off from its legs. Eventually, Miller sprints forward, joined by a makeshift group of those who survived the brutal assault. They fling themselves down on a sandbar beneath the German gun emplacement, survivors more by chance than by skill.

TRAPPED BY ENEMY FIRE

Miller orders the radio operator to relay to headquarters that "Dog One is not open," that the objective has not been achieved. He rolls to his right and asks a soldier who preceded him, "Who's in command here?" "You are, sir," comes the reply. Some other survivors arrive, slamming themselves down on the sand. The camera cuts back to a close-up of Wade (Giovanni Ribisi), a T/4 medic, struggling to stem the bleeding of a fatally wounded soldier. The overlapping noise never relents during this sequence: the sounds of bullets and explosions blending with the voices of screaming men. Stripping rifles and ammunition from dead and dying soldiers, the improvised group readies for an assault on the German stronghold. One man sustains a bullet that ricochets harmlessly off his helmet. "Lucky bastard," says his comrade as the man hastily removes the steel pot to check his head for wounds. The next bullet splats squarely in the forehead and kills him. Luck is a temporary commodity on Omaha Beach. While Wade tends to the wounded, the rest of the men ready themselves to attack the German pillbox, crawling their way behind a stone structure.

OVERRUNNING THE MACHINE GUN PILLBOX

Demonstrating his ingenuity, Miller uses chewing gum to paste a mirror onto a knife blade, slides it around the corner, and gets a bead on the German position. Inch by inch they move closer to the deadly pillbox but remain pinned down by the German fire. Miller calls for Private

Saving Private Ryan **(1998)** In the Omaha Beach sequence, *Saving Private Ryan*'s Captain Miller (Tom Hanks) epitomizes the idealized American soldier, the prototype of the common man called upon to perform uncommon deeds. For Miller, concrete images of ordinary daily life function as snapshots that drive him to get home. But, as befits a post-Vietnam soldier, he is no hypermasculinized John Wayne inspired by patriotic platitudes. Miller's shaking hand, the initial image presented to viewers and one stilled only by death, betrays his internal fears and frailties. The captain's sobbing breakdown reveals how excruciating it is for him to make the necessary decisions that doom men and presents a far more nuanced image of masculinity than what was screened in previous decades of combat movies. *Saving Private Ryan* transforms individual patriotism from a collection of abstract concepts and jingoistic expressions into a shifting constellation of concrete objects and particular people, a sepia-tinted portrait of hearth and home and a nation of brave men forced into desperate situations and personified by Captain Miller during the D-Day landing.

Jackson (Barry Pepper), the southern sharpshooter we recognize as the man who kissed his crucifix on the Higgins. The camera offers a close-up of Jackson's squinting eye as he mouths a prayer and squeezes off a round that kills a German soldier. The frame is suddenly filled with praying men, common soldiers and chaplains giving fallen warriors the last rites. Again, the camera closes in, this time on Jackson's lips as he asks God to steady his aim. The prayer is answered, as more Germans flop forward. Now the Americans move quickly upward toward the pill-box, as Horvath screams out, "We're in business!"

Next appears a long shot of the beach, the first one that furnishes any real sense of geographical perspective and would commonly serve as the opening establishing shot. Having denied viewers this conventional shot and plunging right into the lethal chaos alongside the advancing soldiers, the camera finally looks back to the oncoming waves of Americans landing on the beach. But this is only a temporary reprieve. The camera immediately swings around and rejoins the small platoon in its ongoing assault. Higher and higher the men climb, killing the fleeing Germans who are abandoning their posts. Once they reach the pillbox, the Americans shoot more Nazis as they emerge into the daylight. Finally, a flamethrower ignites the entire structure, and the remaining Germans pour from its bowels. The angry GIs shoot several Germans attempting to surrender. Having seen so many of their friends just maimed and killed on the beach, they mow down the Germans like frightened cattle. Mercy is not an option on this bloody day. Dog One is open at last, but at a terrible cost.

After some interplay, the camera again zeroes in on Miller's shaking hands as he lifts the canteen to his lips and takes a long, slow drink. For the moment, they can all rest. "That's quite a view," says Horvath to Miller. "Yes, it is," comes the bone-weary reply, as the camera moves from a close-up of Miller's face and eyes (reminiscent of the similar shot of the old man in the cemetery) back to the blood-soaked waves slapping rhythmically against the beach and the lifeless bodies carelessly strewn along the shoreline. Finally, a long traveling crane shot comes to rest on the backpack of one dead soldier lying facedown, spread-eagled on the wet sand. His name, stamped on it in black letters: Ryan.S.

One can never be never sure if a genre movie creates a cultural moment or if it just rides atop the waves of the social zeitgeist. With the most broadly resonant genre films, it remains almost impossible to separate the dancer from the dance as cultural attitudes ripple far beyond movie theaters. Whatever the case, *Saving Private Ryan* certainly helped inspire a vast and renewed national interest in World War II. For example, tourism shot sharply upward at the Omaha Beach memorial in France, seen in the opening and closing segments of the film, with tour guides having to tell disappointed visitors that no grave exists for Captain John Miller. As *It's a Wonderful Life* (1946) has become the traditional film shown at Christmastime, so *Saving Private Ryan* has emerged as the movie to accompany Veterans Day. Yet the film clearly demonstrates how current events shape past memories within genre formulas and conventions. *Saving Private Ryan* amalgamates some of the most hallowed tropes from the World War II combat movies, such as the multiethnic platoon and the courage of American fighting troops against overwhelming odds, with a brooding sense of Vietnam War realism, as evidenced in the Omaha Beach sequence and the continual questioning of the mission to save Ryan. By conflating Ryan's deliverance with the generic convention of fighting to protect the homeland, the movie transforms individual patriotism from a collection of abstract concepts and jingoistic expressions into a shifting constellation of concrete objects and particular people; the sepia-tinted portrait of hearth and home encapsulated within Ryan's idealized Iowa farmhouse, for example, is an image that could fit comfortably within any World War II movie.

Yet while invoking and paying homage to some very traditional combat movie traditions, *Saving Private Ryan*'s central narrative structure simultaneously runs counter to a well-established and recurring motif of conventional genre film history. Hollywood genre films have been hugely instrumental in helping to encapsulate and disseminate revered American ideals of masculinity, traditionally glorifying the rugged individualist as a venerated figure worthy of emulation. Mainstream genre movies habitually center on a lone figure's willingness to face danger, and even to risk death, to insure the survival and reinforce the values of the larger group: the single gunman battling outlaws or Indians to defend the settlers or townsfolk, the space explorer sacrificing him/herself to save the rest of the crew, the private eye facing mortal danger to restore order to the community. These types of selfless acts remain the surest method for characters to demonstrate bravery, gain redemption, and garner audience identification. In the combat film, the sacrifice-of-the-individual-for-the-group mentality is mandatory: communal objectives must inevitably replace private divisions and goals or else the group and its values will not survive.

Saving Private Ryan fits this conventional combat film pattern in its first and last sections as the platoon participates in the landing at Omaha Beach and the defending of the bridge at Remelle, but the film's whole middle section, as the men search for Ryan, has no military target and consequently no direct bearing on the outcome of the war. This is not a case of brave men risking their lives to liberate Bataan, Midway, or Guadalcanal. Men engaged in those deadly missions rarely consider the broader implications of their actions; they just try to survive as best they can. But the members of *Saving Private Ryan*'s doomed platoon have the luxury to question the wisdom of their superiors, challenge the logic of their mission, and contemplate their fate as they hike across the French countryside. Each situation they encounter generates a new series of ethical questions, a deeper and more insistent inquiry into what constitutes moral behavior within a wartime environment dominated by violence, brutality, and death. In an instance of dark irony, Captain Miller's most moral decision—to free an unarmed German prisoner—ends up costing his life, as that soldier kills him during the battle at Remelle. By the end of the movie, five of these eight American soldiers will be dead—and for what?

Captain Miller embodies the combat film genre's archetypal citizen soldier, the conventional ideal of the common man called upon to perform uncommon deeds. But Miller is no hypermasculinized John Wayne storming the sands of Iwo Jima to replicate another World War II combat movie hero. Neither is he a steroid-fueled, vengeful Rambo seeking redemption from the Vietnam-era debacles. Instead, Miller finds the strength and ability to lead his men in spite of his psychological demons and frailties. The fallible, brave, and cerebral Captain Miller may be the only realistic model of the American soldier possible in the post-Vietnam era. Thus, while *Saving Private Ryan* uses the generic conventions of combat movies to call upon post–World War II generations to acknowledge the debt they owe to the men and women who fought to defend the United States during the 1940s, the film is simultaneously an ambiguous celebration of American bravery during a time of acute national crisis. In this sense, *Saving Private Ryan* utilizes the generic traditions derived from World War II combat films to pay homage to military sacrifices made during the 1940s but filters these cinematic conventions through the American perceptions and values prevalent in the 1990s.

Lester Friedman

QUESTIONS FOR DISCUSSION

1. Select one World War II combat movie and one Vietnam War movie. Compare and contrast how each does the following: depicts battle scenes, portrays enemies, and presents relationships between men within fighting units.

2. Discuss the connections between masculinity as depicted in combat movies and in Westerns. What are the similarities and differences between what defines manhood in each genre?
3. While the combat genre is primarily about men, women do fill various roles. Looking at examples from different wars, how does the image of women evolve? What roles do women traditionally play in early combat films as differentiated from later movies?
4. Technology, both inside and outside the frame, plays an important role in the combat genre. Discuss how earlier combat films, particularly their battle scenes, are filmed in relation to more modern movies. Which techniques seem more evident and which ones disappear over time? How do the films that strive for realism achieve authenticity?
5. The American soldier in combat movies is a social and dramatic construction. Compare and contrast representative figures from different wars to trace the evolution of this image over the decades.

FOR FURTHER READING

Ambrose, Stephen. "Blockbuster History." In *World War II, Film and History*, edited by John Whiteclay Chambers II and David Culbert, 97–106. New York: Oxford University Press, 1996.

Barker, Martin. *A "Toxic Genre": The Iraq War Films*. London: Pluto Press, 2011.

Basinger, Jeanine. *The World War II Combat Film: Anatomy of a Genre*. Middletown, CT: Wesleyan University Press, 2003.

Boggs, Carl, and Tom Pollard. *The Hollywood War Machine: U.S. Militarism and Popular Culture*. Boulder, CO: Paradigm Publishers, 2007.

Chapman, James. *War and Film*. Trowbridge, England: Reaktion Books, 2008.

Clarke, James. *War Films*. London: Virgin Books, 2006.

Doherty, Thomas. *Projections of War: Hollywood, American Culture and World War II*. New York: Columbia University Press, 1999.

Eberwein, Robert. *Armed Forces: Masculinity and Sexuality in the American War Film*. New Brunswick, NJ: Rutgers University Press, 2007.

———. *The Hollywood War Film*. Oxford: Wiley-Blackwell, 2010.

———, ed. "Introduction." In *The War Film*, 1–19. New Brunswick, NJ: Rutgers University Press, 2006.

Freitas, Gary. *War Movies*. Brandon, OR: Robert Reed Publishers, 2004.

Friedman, Lester. *Citizen Spielberg*. Urbana: University of Illinois Press, 2006.

Gallagher, Gary W. "Causes Won, Lost, and Forgotten: Hollywood and the Civil War since Glory." Washington, D.C.: American Historical Association website. www.historians.org/perspectives/issues/2008/0805/0805fil2.cfm.

Junger, Sebastian. *War*. New York: Hachette Book Group, 2010.

Kane, Kathryn "The World War II Combat Film." In *Handbook of American Film Genres*, edited by Wes D. Gehring, 85–104. New York: Greenwood Press, 1988.

————. *Visions of War: Hollywood Combat Films of World War II*. Ann Arbor, MI: UMI Research Press, 1982.

Keser, Robert. *"What Price Glory?"* Melbourne, Australia: Senses of Cinema website, August 17, 2007 (Issue 44). www.sensesofcinema.com/2007/cteq/what-price-glory/.

Kinnard, Roy. *The Blue and the Gray on the Silver Screen: More than Eighty Years of Civil War Movies*. Toronto: Carol Publishing Group, 1996.

Landsberg, Alison. "Prosthetic Memory: The Ethics and Politics of Memory in an Age of Mass Culture." In *Memory and Popular Film*, edited by Paul Grainge, 144–61. Manchester, UK: Manchester University Press, 2003.

————. *Prosthetic Memory: The Transformation of American Remembrance in the Age of Mass Culture*. New York: Columbia University Press, 2004.

O'Brien, Tim. *The Things They Carried*. New York: Houghton Mifflin, 1990.

Robertson, Linda. *The Dream of Civilized Warfare: World War I Flying Aces and the American Imagination*. Minneapolis: University of Minnesota Press, 2005.

Slocum, David J., ed. *Hollywood and War, The Film Reader*, 1–21. New York: Routledge, 2006.

Strupples, Peter. "Visual Culture, Synthetic Memory and the Construction of National Identity." *Third Text* 17, no. 2 (2003), 127–40.

Sturken, Marita. *Tangled Memories: The Vietnam War, the AIDS Epidemic, and the Politics of Remembering*. Berkeley: University of California Press, 1997.

Westwell. Guy. *War Cinema: Hollywood on the Front Line*. London: Wallflower Press, 2006.

Star Trek: The Motion Picture (1979)

Science Fiction

"SPACE: THE FINAL FRONTIER..." Surely there isn't anyone invested in the pop-culture landscape who doesn't know these words. Similarly, it is hard to imagine many who can't place the phrase "A long time ago, in a galaxy far, far away." But those only generally familiar with the spoken and written introductions to television's *Star Trek* (1966–1969) and the big screen's *Star Wars* might not quite realize their respective sources' unprecedented and astonishing impact on American culture. Between them, they have been the basis of eighteen feature films—Star Trek (twelve) and Star Wars (six)—have generated five live-action and two animated television series with a total of over 750 hours of programming time, and have earned almost $6 billion in worldwide box-office grosses. Hundreds of spin-off books have been published detailing new adventures of the familiar characters and introducing new ones, and a number of comic-book series have similarly extended the two universes into New Media.

Yet just three decades before the launch of the Star Trek franchise, even the most imaginative science-fiction writer could not have pictured such a scenario. In its written format, science fiction was then the province mainly of boys and boyish dreamers, the genre having reached new heights of popularity in the late 1920s and 1930s in monthly magazines with garish names and gaudy covers, like *Astounding Stories* and *Thrilling Wonder Stories*. On the screen, it was the lowest of the low, the worst of the Bs. *Star Trek*, of course, was hardly alone in changing the status and stature of screen science fiction. A handful of works in the 1950s, on the page and on the screen, brought critical respect to the genre before

Gene Roddenberry's space opera—not that *Star Trek* was an immediate critical darling or ratings blockbuster. Other works in the 1960s and early 1970s helped cinematic sci-fi move up the intellectual food chain, but it was *Star Wars* that finally put an end to the genre's second-class status. *Star Trek* and *Star Wars* demonstrated that imaginative works told with humor and panache could not only achieve great popularity and more than a modicum of critical respect but, more important, could inspire others with the same sense of wonder that led their creators to reach for the heavens and beyond.

History

The early history of cinematic science fiction lies outside the United States. Though the science is more in the technology of the cinema itself than in the plots of his films, French magician turned cinematic illusionist Georges Méliès is credited with creating the first cinematic sci-fi. His flights of fancy include *A Trip to the Moon* (1902), *The Impossible Voyage* (1904), and *20,000 Leagues Under the Sea* (1907). Inspired by works of his fellow Frenchman Jules Verne, the films rely on Méliès's imaginative sets and groundbreaking special effects.

While fantasy in the cinema took off under Méliès's influence, sci-fi did not. Occasional Hollywood releases—like the 1916 version of *20,000 Leagues Under the Sea*, notable for its pioneering use of underwater cinematography, and an adaptation of Sir Arthur Conan Doyle's *The Lost World* (1925), distinguished for its A-list cast and the special effects of Willis O'Brien—were rarities. Germany produced the most outstanding sci-fi films of the 1920s, though here, too, they were far outnumbered by horror and fantasy films. Yet two works by Fritz Lang set a tone and style that were taken up by both science fiction and science in the decades to come. The first of these, *Metropolis* (1927), combines Expressionistic styling and horror-film motifs for its futuristic tale of a city divided between the upper and lower classes, the haves and the have-nots, the intellect and labor. With its soaring skyscrapers, flying cars, and a sexy cyborg, this film continues to exert a powerful influence on the genre. The same is true of *Woman in the Moon* (1929). The science of this story marked an advance measurable in light-years from what was then typical of the genre. So convincing was its portrayal of rocket science and space travel that Germany's Nazi government withdrew the film from circulation to protect its own military experiments with rocketry. Later, the film's dramatic countdown to launch was adopted by NASA. Yet for all their special-effects innovations and their genuine attempt to incorporate science into science fiction, Lang's films did not lead to the immediate creation of a generic canon.

The Soviet Union, best known in the 1920s for its montage-based propaganda films and the futuristic art of Constructivism, turned its attention to sci-fi for a single, albeit quite spectacular, foray. *Aelita*, a.k.a. *Aelita: Queen of Mars* (1924), boasts art direction, set design, and costumes at once modernist and deliberately kitschy. Its framing narrative—a dream about a trip to Mars—makes its Martian locale stand in for pre-revolutionary Russia, but in that respect the film sets a standard for the use of science fiction to allegorize contemporary concerns—something the genre later did in the United States with great regularity beginning in the 1950s. Many historians believe that *Aelita* influenced both the Flash Gordon and the Buck Rogers serials of the 1930s.

Back in the United States, *Just Imagine* (1930) is a lavishly produced, *Metropolis*-inspired musical (courtesy of the famed songwriting team of Buddy DeSylva, Lew Brown, and Ray Henderson) that flopped commercially and entered the annals of legend for its sheer oddity. Yet so many of the motifs it employs—a troubled utopia, soaring urban landscapes, rocket ships to Mars, managed population control, loss of individuality and freedom of choice—were already familiar sci-fi tropes and prescient of the cinematic genre to come.

Of a more significant nature, films like *Frankenstein* (1931), *Island of Lost Souls* (1932), and *The Invisible Man* (1933) were part of the developing horror genre revolving around mad scientists, yet they also contained—or at least foreshadowed—important motifs, such as cloning or issues of what it means to be human, that postwar sci-fi took up in interesting ways.

A handful of serials, produced in the 1930s and '40s at the minor-major studio Universal or in the so-called B-hive studios like Mascot and Republic, furnished cinematic sci-fi with its first generic regularity. (At the end of the studio era, around 1970, many of these serials—twelve to fifteen episodes of twenty minutes each—found their way to Saturday-morning or -afternoon television, where their running times and serialization suited a medium in search of content suitable for younger viewers.) *The Phantom Empire* (1935), starring popular radio star Gene Autry (the Singing Cowboy), was an early trendsetter, combining elements of the Western and the musical. Set in a high-tech underground city, its set design and costumes owe a lot to *Aelita*; it also contains a veritable hodge-podge of gadgets, gizmos, and gauges that never try for any scientific verisimilitude yet are vastly entertaining in their innocence.

Subsequent serials took on a similar goofiness, a sheer joy in their adolescent imaginings of evil empires underground or out in space, icy blond villainesses, virginal heroines, and steadfast all-American heroes. Buster Crabbe played Buck Rogers in 1939 and Flash Gordon in three serials, made in 1936, 1938, and 1940. Crabbe embodied virile American masculinity: an Olympic swimming champ, he possessed good looks and an athletic build that contrasted starkly with the misshapen aliens he came into contact with in his sci-fi serials. Not surprisingly, given the prevailing cultural attitudes of the time, racism taints many images of the villains: *Flash Gordon*'s Ming the Merciless (Charles Middleton) is clearly "Oriental" and, in costuming and make-up, quite similar to the evil Fu Manchu.

The two most significant sci-fi texts of the 1930s do not belong to the world of cinema, yet both look forward to the way in which sci-fi later had, on the one hand, commercial viability and, on the other, critical respect.

When *Action Comics* #1 appeared in April 1938, it introduced our most enduring comic-book superhero, who, before winging his way onto the silver screen, made stops on the radio, in animated shorts, and on television. But Superman, in whatever medium, cannot be ignored as an underpinning of the sci-fi genre. *Superman* comic books inspired a rash of new superhero characters that would be grouped into something of a separate genre by the early 2000s, but the influence of superheroes on sci-fi remains considerable (and vice versa), and Superman is their fountainhead.

Radio was the pathway for H. G. Wells to enter popular mythology, also in 1938 and appropriately enough on Halloween, when an adaptation of *The War of the Worlds*, written and produced by and featuring Orson Welles, was broadcast as an episode of the weekly series *The Mercury Theatre on the Air*. The live performance on the nationwide CBS radio network convinced a large segment of the listening public that Martians were invading Earth. Welles's radio play demonstrates an uncanny ability to mimic the structure of radio news. It was convincing enough to start a panic—in the Northeast many people loaded up their cars and fled; miscarriages and premature births supposedly occurred in some numbers; churches were packed by prayerful people. When the public realized that they had been fooled, outrage followed. This sci-fi-themed broadcast brought Welles to Hollywood (where he did not work in science fiction) a couple of years later and is certainly what he is most remembered for in his pre-Hollywood career. It remains the stuff of legend.

World War II dampened the already minimal enthusiasm for science fiction in the cinema, although superheroes and costumed crusaders continued to flourish in comic books. Republic Studios produced the last of the kitschy serials at the end of the decade, *King of the Rocket Men* (1949). Its twelve episodes essentially mark the end of the movie sci-fi serials, after which their naïveté, B budgets, and casts all migrated to television. One could hardly imagine then that the very next year, the start of a new decade, would inaugurate a true golden age of science fiction on the screen.

A number of factors generated the sci-fi boom of the 1950s, most notably the atomic bomb and the Cold War. Less frequently cited but no less potent was the rise of the teenage audience. Although small at this time in terms of numbers, the teenage demographic was the most reliable filmgoing audience. Teens were drawn to the drive-in theater, an exhibition space that provided them with a place to socialize and to take advantage of the privacy of the automobile. In 1950 there were about 150 drive-in theaters, but by 1957 that number had ballooned to nearly four thousand. A new kind of inexpensive film form, produced by a new generation of exploitation-minded showmen working with more imagination than budget, found a welcome home at the drive-in.

The cinematic sci-fi in the 1950s demonstrated its true generic status both by the number of films produced—nearly two hundred—and by their range of budgets and of subject matter. Stretching from classy A features with respectable casts to swarms of Bs starring unknowns and made on a shoestring, the stories concerned men who became monstrously large or frighteningly small; benevolent beings from outer space with Earth's best interest at heart, or alien invaders bent on conquering and killing; visions of rampant conformity or staunch individualism; sophisticated robots possessing the milk of human kindness, or mindless, mutant, marauding bugs grown to gargantuan proportions. These found both critical respect and dismissive derision. But audiences, especially those pesky teens, couldn't get enough of them.

Most of the '50s sci-fi films seemed little more than feature-length versions of the cheesy serials that characterized '30s sci-fi. In the early years of the decade, films such as *The Flying Saucer*, *Rocketship X-M* (both 1950), *Flight to Mars*, *Lost Planet Airmen*, and *The Man from Planet X* (all 1951) did little to increase respect for the burgeoning sci-fi genre. With even more obviously exploitation fare like *Prehistoric Women* (1950), *Captive Women* (1952), *Cat-Women of the Moon*, and *Mesa of Lost Women* (both 1953), any chance of mainstream appeal and impact seemed a long shot. Yet a handful of films set a new tone for the genre.

The first of these serious attempts to make the genre more intellectually and scientifically germane to contemporary concerns was *Destination Moon* (1950). Based on a novel by Robert A. Heinlein, one of the deans of literary science fiction, and produced by George Pal, one of the true visionaries of the cinema, the film made every attempt to be true to the science behind rocketry and space travel. Though fueled by Cold War paranoia, the film manages to imbue space travel with a scientific, not just patriotic, urgency. An Academy Award for Best Effects is testimony to the film's careful production design, and its use of color lends it a big-budget air of spectacle lacking in its B-feature counterparts. Its no-star cast was a bit more typical of the genre. Unfairly lumped together with less thoughtful screen sci-fi, *Destination Moon* deserves a greater appreciation for being a true "first" in many respects.

Although *Destination Moon* is somewhat forgotten, *The Day the Earth Stood Still* (1951) has morphed into a classic. Few who see the film can resist the temptation to amuse their friends and family with the command "Klaatu barada nikto!" But the movie offers pleasures other than catchy lines. It was the first film to seriously consider it likely that alien races with greater technology and morality at their command exist out there. Most movie sci-fi sees aliens as fearsome creatures out for our destruction, but this film finds them a bit friendlier, with just enough threat to back up their beneficence. The film's use of a giant, indestructible, quasi-sentient robot called Gort encouraged audiences to take robotics seriously, and Gort itself became the first in a series of screen machines that extends all the way to R2-D2, C-3PO, and beyond. Most important, the film questioned the moral, not just scientific, basis for atomic weapons and warfare—this at a time when Cold War tensions and the arms race were ramping up. Despite its black-and-white cinematography and modest special effects, *The Day the Earth Stood Still* remains far more effective and memorable than the effects-driven remake released in 2008.

The Day the Earth Stood Still (1951) "Klaatu barada nikto!" The flying saucer and the robot have proved to be among the most definitive and most durable of cinematic science-fiction iconography. In *The Day the Earth Stood Still*, the mysterious saucer unloads an alien life form along with a gigantic robot whose very size and silence are meant to be both mysterious and menacing. At a time when the arms race was an unqualified and unquestioned patriotic necessity, this plea for nuclear sensibility and worldwide cooperation was indeed brave. Such liberal sentiments, however, became increasingly rare as the decade wore on.

The Thing from Another World, a.k.a. *The Thing* (1951), another modestly budgeted film, took advantage of its minimal sets to create an atmosphere of claustrophobia and dread. Featuring an isolated locale (above the Arctic Circle), a predominantly male group of scientists, and the need for courage (because they are menaced by a powerful creature from outer space), the movie has much in common with the mainstream cinema of Howard Hawks, who is often credited with inspiring the movie and, perhaps, directing much of it. With obvious elements of the horror film, *The Thing* still keeps its focus on the "science" and speculates about alternate life forms. It also questions reason and communication as the preferred means of dealing with the unknown. This film was remade in 1982. With John Carpenter, director of *Halloween* (1978), at the helm, it is no surprise that the horror elements predominate.

The War of the Worlds (1953), yet another 1950s classic that was eventually remade, was one of many alien-invasion narratives released that same year. Some of them were quite stylish and effective in their own right, such as *Invaders from Mars* and *Phantom from Space*; others were far more routine, like *Killers from Space*. But, based on the same H. G. Wells novel that Orson Welles adapted to terrify radio audiences a decade and a half earlier, *The War of the Worlds* had an immediate impact few other such narratives could claim. Its big budget garnered it an Oscar for Best Effects, which went along, more unusually for early sci-fi, with an Oscar nomination for Best Editing. Rich color cinematography, frightening Martian robots, and a deeply human, religiously tinged morality make the film both a genre classic and one that transcends genre.

Classics of a different sort—more campy than the others—appeared in 1954, both part of the hybridized science fiction–horror cycle and separate from it. These are the "creature features," which, rather than focus on monsters from outer space, depict familiar but malformed animals whose origins rest right here on Earth, their mutations the unintended consequence of atomic radiation. *Them!* boasts a decent cast (James Whitmore, Edmund Gwenn, James Arness), passable special effects, and a simple but frightening premise: nuclear irradiation has turned ordinary ants into giant, almost indestructible predators. Likewise utilizing what are derogatorily called BEMs (bug-eyed monsters), *Tarantula* and *It Came from Beneath the Sea* (both 1955), *The Deadly Mantis* (1957), and *Attack of the Giant Leeches* (1959) would follow, but *Them!* retains its status as the foundation of atomic-radiation paranoia manifested in the creature features.

Other sci-fi classics of this period have clear linkages to the horror genre, most notably *Invasion of the Body Snatchers* (1956), which is marked by a paranoid ambience evoking loss of control and rampant, mindless conformity, and the micro-budgeted *The Incredible Shrinking Man* (1957), which postulates, after a number of B movie–style set pieces, that the infinitely small scale of atoms and molecules is as exciting and mysterious as the infinitely large scale of solar systems and galaxies.

One colorful exception to the general run of B movies in this era is *Forbidden Planet* (1956), as much an intelligently imagined foray into psychosexual dynamics as an interplanetary space adventure. A deft combination of Freudian psychoanalysis and Shakespearean drama by way of *The Tempest*, the film has provided screen sci-fi with its most memorable robot since Gort. More lovable and cuddly than Gort, Robby the Robot, named for its engineer/designer Robert Kinoshita, was conceived to be a feature attraction of the film, an android Ariel to the film's Miranda, here in the shapely form of Anne Francis as Altaira, daughter of Prospero/Professor Morbius (Walter Pidgeon). The Caliban of the piece is the alien Krell technology that gives rise to the famous "monsters from the Id"—bringing Freud to a galaxy far, far away. Reviews at the time certainly singled out Robby but gave high marks to the entire production, making it one of the best reviewed of golden age science-fiction films.

At the other end of the critical scale stands *Plan 9 from Outer Space*. Made in 1959, it brought the first golden age of screen sci-fi to a screeching halt. Often considered the worst movie ever made, *Plan 9* is sometimes thought for that reason to be good. That a director so monumentally untalented as Ed Wood (subject of a likable 1994 biopic by Tim Burton, the sci-fi/fantasy/horror maven and kindred—though far more talented—spirit) would be drawn to the genre reveals its "B"-grade status despite the occasional, happy exception.

The creature features and other types of B movies dominating the genre kept sci-fi in the twilight zone of critical respect during the next decade. Only a couple of films of the early to mid-1960s can be counted in any serious history of the genre: *The Time Machine* (1960), based on an H. G. Wells novel and which has good special effects and a quasi-grim view of the future, and *Fantastic Voyage* (1966), which also features innovative special effects in its trip through the inner space of the human body; but no films shook up or added appreciably to the genre. However, exactly thirty years after Superman and Orson Welles brought attention and controversy to science fiction, two movies appeared that had immediate success at the box office, garnered great critical respect, and influenced screen sci-fi for a generation to follow, ushering in a second golden age of science fiction in the cinema.

Planet of the Apes, released in February 1968, was an immediate hit. A more than respectable cast, including Charlton Heston, Roddy McDowell, Kim Hunter, and James Whitmore; an intriguing premise; and a shock ending netted the film the kind of cultural cachet little seen in the genre's history. Oscar nominations for Best Costume Design and Best Musical Score, along with an Honorary Award for makeup, attest to its mainstream appeal. An allegorical call for more humane treatment of animals or, more richly, a displaced examination of America's ongoing efforts to deal with race and racism, the film artfully blends intelligence and excitement. Few members of the audience failed to leave the theater without exclaiming the famous line: "Take your stinking paws off me, you damn dirty ape!" The film's generally literate script, coauthored by Rod Serling, the famed TV writer and creator of *The Twilight Zone,* proved another reason for the film's success. *Planet of the Apes* gave rise to four

***Planet of the Apes* (1968)** The look of absolute shock and horror displayed by Taylor (Charlton Heston) when he sees that his fellow human astronaut (Jeff Burton) has been subjected to a full lobotomy in the name of "science" functions as an effective metaphor for animal cruelty and brutal racist practices of the Euro-American past. Released in the era of fierce civil rights struggles, *Planet of the Apes* could not and would not hide its symbolic concerns. By speaking so directly to the current climate, the sci-fi cinema managed to achieve a modicum of critical respect while, with groundbreaking makeup and other special effects, increasingly finding large and appreciative audiences.

sequels from 1970 to 1973 that followed the law of diminishing returns typical of sequels—less critical respect and fewer ticket sales. Still, they did well enough to inspire a couple of TV shows and to live on in the hearts of sci-fi fans even to the point of being revived in theaters on occasion in a marathon showing of all five features. Not unexpectedly, the series was revived, in 2001.

If *Planet of the Apes* impresses with its makeup, solid acting, and shock ending, *2001: A Space Odyssey*, released just two months later, takes sci-fi into another realm entirely. Directed by Stanley Kubrick and written by Kubrick and famed science-fiction author Arthur C. Clarke, *2001: A Space Odyssey* is an almost completely visual experience with minimal dialogue (the first words are not spoken until some twenty-five minutes into the film) and even more minimal characterization. A deeply philosophical, if ambiguous, meditation on man's technological progress and human evolution itself, the film seems wide open to interpretation. Kubrick and Clarke speculate on alien intervention in man's shift from ape to proto-human through the discovery of tools. Indeed, one of the cinema's most famous associative edits arises when the bone used as a weapon is flung into the air by our apelike ancestor and, in graceful slow motion, gives way to a spaceship floating in orbit to the strains of a Johann Strauss waltz ("The Blue Danube"). Is this same monolith that inspired the use of tools also going to be responsible for humankind's next evolutionary step? It seems so, as the protagonist Dave Bowman (Keir Dullea) hurtles through a wrinkle in space, rapidly ages, and is transformed into the famous image of the star-baby.

While the film's ultimate meaning remains open to speculation, its many contributions to the science-fiction genre are beyond dispute. Primary among these is the endowment of a computer with the longing for self-preservation. HAL 9000 (a name derived from shifting the letters of IBM and based on early work with artificial intelligence and computer interactivity at the University of Illinois at Urbana-Champaign) becomes the most memorable character in the film as he schemes, plots, and finally seems pitiful in his near-human desires. The film also launched a new generation of special effects and, arguably, set the genre on course for special effects being an integral part of any big-budget effort. Douglas Trumbull emerged as the first of the new generation of screen effects wizards employing new forms of sophisticated animation. For *2001*, he created the slit-scan technique, memorably employed in the "star-gate" sequence of the film to simulate a new kind of space. Slit-scan photography, though eventually replaced by computer-generated imagery (CGI), became the preferred—even definitive—mode to represent faster-than-light space travel and nonlinear spaces. Trumbull's name and contribution to future sci-fi films, like *Silent Running* (1972, which he also directed), *Close Encounters of the Third Kind* (1977), and *Star Trek: The Motion Picture* (1979), became important components to their advertising and reception. *2001*'s special effects and simulation of space travel also came from another source in the form of consultant Frederick I. Ordway III, a rocket scientist who had worked on the X-1 and X-15 experimental aircrafts and was eventually employed at NASA. *2001: A Space Odyssey* was an even bigger hit than *Planet of the Apes* and garnered what were the first, and still among the very few, major Oscar nominations for a science-fiction film, including Best Director and Best Original Screenplay.

The first sci-fi film to get a Best Picture nomination came almost a decade later. Thanks to films like *THX 1138* and *The Andromeda Strain* (both 1971), *Soylent Green* (1973), and *Logan's Run* and *The Man Who Fell to Earth* (both 1976), sci-fi was gaining respectability, but a new level of esteem was reached in 1977, when *Close Encounters of the Third Kind* and

Star Wars made eyes pop out and mouths hang open, with box-office numbers not only never seen in science fiction but little seen in the history of film. In any other year, *Close Encounters* would have been the run-away box-office champ, but *Star Wars* made it a distant second. *Star Wars* stills ranks third on the list of highest-grossing films ever released in the United States, and second in adjusted dollars. Its ten Oscar nominations, including the Best Picture nod, only added to its incalculable impact and influence. Interestingly, the film is as much fantasy as sci-fi, and its borrowings from other genres, including the Western, the combat film, and the old sci-fi serials, make it truly an eclectic film, with something for everyone. Its five sequels hardly diminish its luster, with George Lucas's coherent vision and increasing budgets giving the series a unique place in the annals of popular culture.

After 1977, the genre never lost its audience appeal, and occasionally garnered mainstream critical respect as well. *Alien, The Black Hole*, and *Star Trek: The Motion Picture* all hit the movie screens in 1979—a potent year for science fiction. The first film launched a new generation of science fiction–horror, while the second, a Disney effort, attempted to trade on *Star Wars* iconography with a bit of harder science, and the third brought the cult TV series to the big screen and was followed by a large number of sequels. The special effects of all three films are notable, though *Alien*'s are certainly the most memorable, especially H. R. Giger's design for the nearly indestructible creature. A figure out of a nightmare, lizard-like yet erect, with an ever-morphing body, the alien itself evolved in the three sequels, becoming one of the most truly frightening beings the cinema has ever seen.

With the genre well established and the Star Wars sequels leading the way, the 1980s marked one of the most important decades yet for screen science fiction. In 1982, for instance, the Disney Studios introduced the first generation of video game-influenced movies with the computer-effects driven *Tron*. Though its plot leaves something to be desired, it is the most purely visual film after *2001* and, more important, brings computer animation to the foreground, demonstrating media "synergy"—a film inspired by video games itself then gave rise to video games in the sort of cycle that has characterized industry practices ever since.

If *Tron* has it supporters today, they are greatly exceeded in number by those of *Blade Runner*, released that same year. Though not a huge box-office hit at the time, *Blade Runner* has been reevaluated as one of the most intelligent sci-fi films ever made. Certainly its special effects, in the form of the most complex production design since *Metropolis*, do not fail to impress; its film-noir stylings, sense of claustrophobia, and classic femme fatale lend the film an extra dimension of cinematic layering. A thoughtful, if violent, meditation on what it means to be human, *Blade Runner* exemplifies a film that equals or surpasses its respected source, in this case Philip K. Dick's novel *Do Androids Dream of Electric Sheep?* (1968), as a major contribution to science fiction.

Yet even the combined box office of *Tron*, *Blade Runner*, and other sci-fi films of the year, such as the remake of *The Thing* and *Star Trek II: The Wrath of Khan*, couldn't equal the take of *E.T. the Extra-Terrestrial*. The biggest box-office hit since *Star Wars*, and fifth all time, Spielberg's film, like his earlier *Close Encounters*, takes an optimistic view of space aliens. *E.T.*'s success sheds light on *Blade Runner*'s relative failure: unashamedly optimistic where *Blade Runner* is darkly ambiguous, its clean and bright suburban setting and lily-white characters similarly contrast to *Blade Runner*'s urban grit and ethnic hodgepodge. Although "E.T., phone home" is not quite the catch phrase it once was, it certainly had its cultural moment.

***E.T.: The Extra-Terrestrial* (1982)** This iconic moment from Steven Spielberg's blockbuster captures the sense of childlike wonder and awe that makes sci-fi a genre capable of capturing the hearts and minds of the adolescent in all of us. Spielberg's optimism that the universe holds many mysteries of a magical nature make his films *Close Encounters of the Third Kind* (1977) and *E.T.* tributes to the innocent belief that not everything unknown is out to hurt us; that this world and others offer up hope if only we retain our own innocence and commitment to our true nature. The use of children as the primary protagonists and grown-ups as the villains of the piece speaks to Spielberg's insistence that children and the childlike are the best hope for universal peace and harmony.

Video-game imagery and a plot to match are the hallmarks of *The Last Starfighter*, a succesful youth-oriented film of 1984. A bit more adult oriented is John Sayles's examination of race relations and racism in *The Brother from Another Planet* (1984), which boasts virtually no special effects. *The Terminator* (1984), in contrast, ups the ante of effects-driven, kinetic excitement. Arnold Schwarzenegger's famous line—"I'll be back"— in the villainous title role certainly proved prophetic as the film gave rise to three sequels (1991, 2003, 2009), with Schwarzenegger appearing in the first two. Schwarzenegger also found himself launching another sci-fi franchise when he starred in *Predator* (1987), a deft combination of high-explosive action-thriller and sci-fi allegory. A direct sequel followed in 1990 and a spinoff series, AVP: Alien vs. Predator (2004, 2007), came next, though Schwarzenegger does not appear in any of these. Another film that combined high-octane violence with an interesting sci-fi premise is *RoboCop* (1987). A dystopic vision of the future, a violence quotient that originally netted the film an X rating (until certain cuts were made), and a wicked sense of humor combined with a sensitive examination of the intersection between the human and the cyborg to make the film a blockbuster hit and critical darling. Sequels followed in 1990 and 1993.

The creature feature made a big-budget comeback courtesy of the Jurassic Park series (1993, 1997, 2001), whose box-office success was truly of T-rex proportions and whose computer-driven special effects seamlessly integrates with the live-action characters. The special effects of *Independence Day* (1996), including a realistically shocking destruction of the White House, were similarly up-to-the-minute, even if its ideology is rather retro, much like the BEMs that attack Earth. It seems as if every big-budget sci-fi blockbuster was finding a way to introduce new effects into their creation of alternate worlds, something especially true of *The Matrix* (1999), which became another of those sci-fi films that seems a touchstone for its moment. Though the remainder of the trilogy introduced only more ambiguity into the film's complex mixture of computer paranoia, martial-arts mayhem, and religiomystical musings, the first film provoked a good deal of intelligent conversation. It also gave the world what came to be known as the Matrix effect—a digitally enhanced simulation of slow- and stop-motion photography pioneered by the French videomaker Michel Gondry and originally called bullet time. Seen in music videos and a famous television ad for Gap jeans, it is used in *The Matrix* to simulate the path of a bullet in superslow motion and in other effects to indicate a digital or cyber reality.

The Matrix (1999) "Bullet time" is the term given to superslow-motion, variable-speed effects. It has been utilized in animation, music videos, TV commercials, and video games, but was popularized in *The Matrix* (with Keanu Reeves) and expanded on in the subsequent films of the trilogy. It can be achieved in numerous ways—animation, video effects, multicamera photography, and through CGI. Its usage in numerous media is a clue to the way in which this effect is itself one of the primary attractions that link films to numerous other entertainment formats. The transmedia usage of this effect is indicative of the links that audiences perceive and expect in an era when discrete media are becoming a thing of the past. Thus, its use in the forward-looking genre of sci-fi is significant.

Sci-fi films often embody a very conservative ideology. The vast majority of them not only feature white males as the dominant characters, but they also personify a vision of unproblematic heterosexual masculinity in their pursuit of the twin goals of defeating the aliens and rescuing the damsel in distress. Perhaps this conservatism can be accounted for by the genre's very origins at a moment when masculinity was in some crisis from the freedoms experienced by women during World War II, when whiteness was in danger of losing some of its privileges due to racial integration and the civil rights movement, and when associations between communism and homosexuality, not to mention the blacklist, made any variation from the norm suspect and seemingly subversive. Sci-fi films in general are virtual bastions of white-male heterosexuality, which remains largely true to this day. One can count on the fingers of one hand the number of black or multicultural characters in mainstream sci-fi. Harry Belafonte stars in *The World, the Flesh and the Devil* (1959), a postapocalyptic melodrama that deals explicitly—and uniquely in golden-age sci-fi—with issues of race and racism, and which Belafonte's own company produced. Nichelle Nichols and George Takei relieved some of the overall whiteness on TV's original *Star Trek*. A black astronaut appears in *Planet of the Apes*, though this film allegorizes its real racial concerns. The use of black star James Earl Jones as the voice of *Star Wars* archvillain Darth Vader caused a good deal of controversy, as his was the only black presence in this film; to make up for this, one suspects, Lucas introduced Billy Dee Williams as Lando Calrissian at the end of *The Empire Strikes Back* (1980) and gave the world a black Jedi in the form of Samuel L. Jackson's Mace Windu in *Star Wars: Episode III—Revenge of the Sith* (2005). Emerging superstar Will Smith had a refreshing role as a hotshot fighter pilot in the blockbuster *Independence Day* and as a driven scientist in the big-budget, effects-driven remake of *I Am Legend* (2007), while Laurence Fishburne and Idris Elba broke the mold to star as ships' captains in the big-budget *Event Horizon* (1997) and the very high-profile *Prometheus* (2012), respectively.

***The Brother from Another Planet* (1984)** Writer-director John Sayles cut his mainstream cinematic teeth by scripting low-budget genre films, including the charming sci-fi adventure *Battle Beyond the Stars* (Jimmy T. Murakami, 1980). Though the budget is certainly no larger than those of his exploitation efforts, Sayles's *The Brother from Another Planet* (with Joe Morton) has more than drive-in audiences in mind with this deceptively powerful film. With few sci-fi trappings, the film nevertheless must be considered an important entry into the genre, with its deeply humanistic look at the formation of community, racial solidarity, and legacies of slavery and civil rights struggles. The picture of Bruce Lee in the background reveals the strong connection between the martial arts superstar and the black community.

Yet too often issues of race are allegorized to the detriment of black actors. One interesting film along these lines that tries to have it both ways is *Enemy Mine* (1985). African-American actor Louis Gossett Jr. costars, yet he is cast as an alien, unrecognizable under convincing makeup. The film is quite obviously an allegory about the qualities that link us rather than the differences that separate us. Only as late as the Matrix trilogy do numerous black characters occupy significant positions in the narrative, along with women. The same is true of Asian characters occupying a primary position in the narrative (and offscreen in the notable martial-arts sequences). This reminds us that our examination of race in American cinema should also extend to representations of Latinos and Asians. Here as well, Hollywood sci-fi remains monochromatic and unicultural.

It is certainly true that women have fared a bit better since the golden age ideal of BBBs (big-breasted babes) being the prize for defeating the BEMs. Yet the very notoriety given to Sigourney Weaver's portrayal of Ripley in the first Alien film and the hard-bodied Linda Hamilton in 1991's *Terminator 2: Judgment Day* (she was a more standard damsel-in-distress in the first film of the series) indicates just how rare it continues to be for the woman to take on the action role in screen sci-fi.

This world of white males extends to the forces behind the camera. No black director has yet been responsible for a big-budget sci-fi film. [If one allows the comic-book blockbusters into the fold, then Tim Story qualifies as the lone exception, with *Fantastic Four* (2005).] A singular exception to the all-male helmers of sci-fi is Kathryn Bigelow, whose *Strange Days* (1995) certainly qualifies as a major studio production. Here, Angela Bassett does double duty in breaking the white-male hegemony of screen sci-fi as the action hero of the piece, with her costar Ralph Fiennes, taking the more traditionally passive female role. Bassett appeared in two more sci-fi films, *Contact* (1997) and *Supernova* (2000). That one can briefly outline the appearance of black characters in sci-fi in basically one paragraph is a disappointment that should give us pause about our present situation and our imagination of the future. Hollywood may espouse liberal ideas allegorically in its science-fiction films, but the history of the genre demonstrates that the industry rarely actualizes such sentiments. That no black directors and only one woman have forayed behind the camera means that though space may be the final frontier, much remains to do back here on Earth.

Typologies, Themes, and Theories

One basic tenet of genre theory holds that film formulas are products of the sociocultural context in which they arise and that they respond to specific cultural needs, issues, and anxieties. Cinematic science fiction proves especially interesting from this angle. To begin with, the genre manifested itself simultaneously in the post–World War II era in different places. Although some Hollywood film genres have counterparts in the international cinema, most tend to be associated with specifics of American history and culture. Science fiction, however, was almost immediately transnational. By the middle of the 1950s, American screen sci-fi was joined by British and Japanese efforts; over the years since, France has joined the sci-fi parade in significant ways. Equally important, while specific cycles in individual genres owe much to the impact of a current cultural moment, science fiction has always been intimately tied to timely concerns. Arguably, then, sci-fi films offer some of the best sites to catch a glimpse of any era's zeitgeist. Nineteen-fifties nuclear paranoia, for instance, arises not just in the general milieu of postwar fears of atomic warfare in light of the Cold War and the arms race, but also very definitely in the production of the creature features which, as shown above, began in 1954. Revealingly, this cycle appears after the nuclear tests in the Pacific Ocean at the Bikini Atoll in 1953. The destructive power of the new generation of nuclear weapons and the accidental irradiation of a Japanese fishing trawler brought home just how much force such weapons could unleash and how easily they could have unintended consequences. If this was the hidden origin behind *Them!*, it was the overt inspiration for the Japanese mega-hit *Gojira* (*Godzilla*, 1954; released in dubbed and modified form in the United States in 1956 as *Godzilla: King of the Monsters*).

The blockbuster sci-fi hits of 1968, *Planet of the Apes* and *2001: A Space Odyssey* arose out of different aspects of 1960s politics and culture, the former arising from the civil rights movement, and the latter especially latching on to a younger audience with its psychedelic imagery and sense of an LSD trip. Later, sci-fi would tackle emerging issues of ecology, environmentalism, and overpopulation (*Soylent Green, Logan's Run, Blade Runner*), while the increasing reliance on computers, along with advances in robotics, gave rise to films that cast a wary eye on such developments, including *Demon Seed* (1977), *WarGames* (1983), and the Terminator series. The emergence of cyberspace, the outcome of computer networking that has had the greatest impact on global culture of any technological development since television, has similarly given rise to paranoia and grave concerns, as seen most memorably in the Matrix trilogy. Sci-fi cinema has dealt with these and other significant issues, all tied to a moment of cultural and technological shifting that altered the topography of our daily lives.

Like all genres, science fiction is hardly a closed system with clearly defined borders and boundaries. It intersects, for instance, with horror. As the historical survey above reveals, many sci-fi films can just as easily fit into the horror genre. While scholars might debate the categorization of individual films, one broad, useful manner of differentiation would be to follow the influential analyses of noted sci-fi theoretician Vivian Sobchack, who distinguishes between the "monsters" of horror and the "creatures" of science fiction. For her, the horror monster proves interesting, significant, or otherwise emotionally appealing, whereas

***Aliens* (1986)** Critics justifiably accused *Alien* (1979) of a less-than-necessary bit of exploitation in the climactic scene that features lithesome star Sigourney Weaver wearing a skimpy undershirt and bikini briefs. It seemed unlikely that the heroic final girl of the film would have to face the fearsome monster dressed as if appearing in an R-rated sexploitation potboiler. As if to compensate, at the end of *Aliens*, she armors up to go mano a mano with the mobile monster seen clearly in all its horrid glory throughout the film. The transformation from the nubile femme to the fearsome mom (taking on the maternal in her protection of Newt) desexes Ripley but makes her a whole lot tougher.

the sci-fi creature usually has little personality or pathos attached to it. Moreover, the monster found in the horror genre is typically a singular figure, whereas in science fiction, the danger might very well come in large groups. Think of the original version of *The Thing* or the Alien films compared with Frankenstein's monster or the Wolf Man. We feel only fear and revulsion for the hideous and motiveless creatures in the sci-fi films but share some sympathy for the doomed monsters in the horror movies. According to this formulation, then, the former films are more science fiction, the latter classic horror.

Though few would mistake a science-fiction film for a Western, that most venerable of genres has affected more recent science fiction almost as greatly as horror, especially in terms of character types and the idea of the frontier. Not for nothing did *Star Trek*'s creator, Gene Roddenberry, whose early days in television found him writing episodic Westerns, claim that his new show was "*Wagon Train* in space." *Outland* (1981) is an acknowledged adaptation of *High Noon* (1952); *Westworld* (1973) relies on the classic image of the gunfighter to stage its robots-versus-humans

Star Wars (1977) The iconography of the Western seems ingrained in film viewers of every generation, even those who had little direct experience of the classical Hollywood genre—such as many who have made *Star Wars* a cult favorite of unprecedented proportions to this day. The scene at the Mos Eisely Cantina deliberately, obviously, and humorously recalls many a Western saloon sequence, from the gruff bartender who claims "We don't serve his kind" (in reference to C-3PO), to the thugs who confront Luke and Obi-Wan to Han Solo's (Harrison Ford) drawdown, of a sort, with bounty hunter Greedo. The presence of beings of all sizes and stripes similarly recalls the melting-pot atmosphere of life on the Western frontier. The creative mix of the familiar and the fantastic make the film a viewing experience with something for everyone.

saga; *Star Wars* and its sequels and prequels not only draw upon familiar Western iconography, such as the saloon, but frequently and quite specifically reference *The Searchers* (1956), the ur-text of postclassical Hollywood. Sci-fi films of a certain type were at one time called, perhaps derogatorily, space operas in the way that Westerns were called horse operas and the melodramas soap operas.

So, too, the sci-fi genre borrows a good deal from the combat film. *Aliens* is virtually a World War II combat film right down to the ethnically mixed platoon (adding women to the mix, to be sure). *Independence Day* has all the iconography of the sort of World War II aerial combat sequences that similarly make *Star Wars* so exciting. And *Starship Troopers* (1997) utilizes the "why we fight" ideology of the combat films in its vision of recruitment and the struggle against quite literal BEMs. This is only natural. The combat-film structure arose to reflect not only the realities of modern warfare but the ideology of cooperation necessary to win a war; in science fiction, this ideology of cooperation facilitates the fomenting of national ideals and values. By the same token, modern space flight is never within the purview of the lone individual. To an extent, then, screen sci-fi carries forward many of the icons and ideals of the Western and the combat film, and for similar ideological purposes.

If the science-fiction genre had merely grown out of horror or Western movies, or were indistinguishable from the comic-book blockbuster or simply an effects-laden variation of action films, it would hardly merit or sustain generic analysis on its own. Yet a simple feature distinguishes the form: a setting in the near or more distant future or an exploration of an unforeseen extension of current conditions. This is to say that science fiction may be defined as—to use a term popular with literary critics—"speculative fiction." Science-fiction narratives extrapolate present conditions or technologies and postulate their evolution in the future, or make dramatic but plausible postulations about the present. In a certain way, the genre continually poses the question "What if?" under a range of different circumstances For example, a whole category of sci-fi cinema asks, What if intergalactic space travel were possible? Allowing that to be the case, a host of other uncertainties are raised: What sorts of alien life would space explorers encounter? What kind of natural but unknown phenomena might arise? What effects would such travel have on the physical and psychological well-being of astronauts? The proposition that humanity might invent faster-than-light travel also suggests that alien civilizations might possess similar technology, confronting us with the classic 1950s scenario of the flying saucer and creatures from Mars. Then the questions become, If aliens arrived on Earth, would they be hostile or benevolent? Would their technology pose a threat to us? Would they be like Hal or Robby or Gort? What sort of form would they take and how might we know them? The list of speculations is almost endless.

Though the space opera emerged as the most prominent of science fiction's story types in the golden age, more serious films of recent decades have chosen to focus on Earth-bound issues. The most significant of these has been the response to the growth and development of computers, experiments in robotics, progress in artificial intelligence, and the plethora of connections that make up the Internet and the World Wide Web. Virtual reality, once the very definition of science fiction, has become more possible through advances both in video gaming—whose links with cinema, especially the science-fiction cinema, increasingly occupy both the imagination of business and the business of academics—and cyberspace. The questions here have expressed societal fears and anxieties: What if our computers turn on us? What if artificial intelligence becomes synonymous with and indistinguishable from natural intelligence? What if there comes a time when we cannot distinguish virtual reality from any other sense of reality? Is that time already here?

Related to questions of artificial intelligence and issues of an essentialized notion of humanity is the vexing moral problem of human cloning and genetic engineering. The science-fiction genre has long depicted the ethical issues our society struggles with, including choosing the gender of a baby, testing for genetic diseases, trying to engineer certain types of so-called desirable qualities, and cloning a human being. Sci-fi movies have confronted these complicated problems, usually with dramatically unforeseen results.

Other issues have also come to the fore, including linked concerns about environmentalism, population control, global warming, and possible shortages of crucial natural resources. These films, in particular, portray themselves as extrapolations into the future, asking fundamental questions such as, what if we continue on our reckless path of environmental destruction?

Because of these essential questions, the science-fiction genre deliberately provokes speculation from both its makers and its audience. To do so, it must create plausible worlds, technologies, and situations.

***Star Trek* (2009)** In the New Hollywood of the twenty-first century, the concept of the "reboot" has been added to older industry practices of the prequel, the sequel, and the remake. The venerable *Star Trek* got the prequel/reboot treatment in the form of a very successful summer blockbuster in 2009 (with Chris Pine, Zoe Saldana, and Zachary Quinto). It takes the familiar characters of the long-running franchise and imagines them in their younger incarnations yet finds a way to transform certain elements of the characters, thus making them both similar and different. Walking a tightrope between appealing to the large cult fandom of the franchise and rebooting it for a new generation is a feat the film performed with admirable dexterity. The reboot will itself generate sequels based on these new characters and the newly created reality of the Star Trek universe.

Science-fiction films, therefore, rely heavily on special effects. Yet the effects that some fans demand and expect function only as subsidiary elements to create coherent, alternate characters and universes. Here appears another crucial characteristic of science fiction: its penchant for sequels, series, and multipart story arcs. The sci-fi genre is not unique in producing sequels. Although rare in the classic Hollywood studio era, sequels, prequels, and remakes emerged as standard business practices in the postclassical Hollywood, but the sheer number of sci-fi films that generate sequels or initially appear as part of a series make it a defining characteristic of the genre. Only the horror genre has been defined by as many sequels and series, and for similar reasons. Star Wars (six films) Planet of the Apes (five), Alien (four), the Terminator (four); trilogies like the Matrix, RoboCop, and Jurassic Park; and an odd hybrid like Alien vs. Predator (two films, following two Predator movies as well), among others, speak to a situation in which business success may only partially account for this prevalence. Like horror, sci-fi appeals to the primary moviegoing audience of the last few decades, the kind of adolescent audience that wants to see these texts extended through other media like comic books, novels, and video games beyond the life of just one film. As such, sci-fi films often remain open-ended, allowing not only for sequels but for the formation of cult audiences that latch on to them, learn all there is about them on and off the screen, and incorporate them into their own daily lives. Fan fiction is just one manifestation of this phenomenon. Another, more prevalent occurrence has been "cosplay" (costume roleplay), which first appeared in Japan as a response by anime fandom but which has developed into a regular feature at the increasingly popular world of comic-cons. These events began as comic-book conventions but have morphed to encompass sci-fi, horror, anime, and fantasy. So (in)famous have Star Trek fans and their conventions become, for instance, that there was even a popular documentary made on the subject: *Trekkies* (1997). Adolescent audiences find in the fully realized, provocative worlds of speculative fiction the ability—perhaps even the need—to insert themselves into these universes and to wish never to see them come to an end.

Iconography

At first glance, the science-fiction genre seems to lack the kind of recognizable setting that characterizes a number of other genres, like the frontier of the Western, the urban jungle of the gangster movie, and the haunted houses of the horror film. After all, science fiction can be set literally anywhere: twenty thousand leagues under the sea, the center of the Earth, the moon, Mars, and beyond, in galaxies far, far away. Yet there is one distinctive setting that identifies the form: the future. This future may look vastly different from film to film, but a setting in times to come—near or distant, on Earth or beyond—certainly marks a movie as science fiction. Of course, many of the genre's films take place in the present, so the future setting is not necessary to the form; yet a film set in the future must in some ways always be considered as science fiction, though it may fall into different genre categories as well.

Concomitant with a setting in the future, the technologies that the future may contain—whether of space travel, computing, robotics, cyberorganisms, genetic engineering, military hardware and weaponry, or even household consumer goods—also characterize the science-fiction genre. The very need to create coherent worlds requires a rich panoply of devices and designs that provide audiences with a concrete sense of a possible future—or at least a visually compelling one. Along with this comes a production design that bespeaks a sense of architecture of future possibilities. Soaring skyscrapers; flying cars; walkways hundreds of stories high; rounded, sleek, metallic surfaces—combinations of modernist architecture and postmodern, usually Asian, cities—make science fiction a screen genre of surfaces and graphic design. Of all the genres, therefore, science fiction contains the most possibilities for exuberant imaginations to delight us with spectacular visual delights and stun audiences with dazzling special effects.

The future setting or a setting in a present time that exaggerates a specific feature of technology makes the sci-fi genre recognizable by certain specific semantic elements. The most prevalent icons filmmakers employ to create these plausible or sometimes implausibly spectacular visions include, first of all, the spaceship. As Vivian Sobchack points out, the spaceship has no consistent image or stable symbolic role in science fiction, unlike, say, the railroad in the Western, which is inevitably an agent of change. The film that began the first golden age of science fiction, *Destination Moon*, uses its rocket ship to propel characters and audience on an exciting, wholesome adventure, thereby functioning as a force for good. *When Worlds Collide* (1951) sees the ship as a means of salvation; the U.S.S. *Enterprise*, in all its various incarnations in the Star Trek adventures, provides all the comforts of home and more, while sleekly hurtling through space on its continuing mission to explore strange new worlds. But the spaceship itself can take on what Sobchack calls a "demonic" character. The *Discovery* of *2001* becomes a deathtrap for most of its astronauts when Hal, the heart of the ship's operation, goes a little haywire; in *Silent Running*, one of the astronauts kills his fellow travelers and is left alone for the rest of his days with only robots as his companions, the ship a flying coffin-to-be. The *Nostromo* of *Alien*, a hulking, lumbering deteriorating freighter, provides far too many hiding places for the eponymous creature; the ship which gives *Event Horizon* its title may be the repository of some inexplicable horror. Yet, as Sobchack also notes, the spaceship may be neutral, merely the vehicle to get its cast from one place to another—the adventure will occur when they get there and not on the way.

The spaceship is also linked to another crucial icon of science fiction: the alien. Indeed, the look of the ship itself is often thematized. Earth ships of the 1950s are powerful, phallic rockets, while alien ships are often sleek saucers, womblike and thus feminized, in keeping with the hypermasculinized ideology of Cold War films. Although the association of flying saucers with evil aliens has not been confined to 1950s science fiction, the sight of the giant saucers hovering over some of Earth's most notable landmarks in *Independence Day* leaves room for doubt about their intentions only to some (misguided) characters. Similar threats are equally evident in Steven Spielberg's *War of the Worlds* (2005). Though flying saucers are not universally the product of evil aliens, their manifestations always seem at least ambiguous and typically are not resolved in Earth's favor.

The alien beings themselves may be benevolent or malevolent, and the Earthlings must determine where they lie along the spectrum. Like spaceships, aliens come in a number of shapes and sizes; sometimes all but indistinguishable from humanity, [e.g., *The Day the Earth Stood Still, Invaders from Mars, I Married a Monster from Outer Space* (1958), *Starman* (1984), *They Live* (1988)]; sometimes looking far different but nevertheless essentially peaceable (*Close Encounters, E.T.*); and sometimes, well, they are just as mean as they are ugly. Yet the presence of the alien on Earth or met in outer space remains a defining icon of science fiction. That is one reason, for instance, *Alien* fits securely in this chapter; were it more of a horror film, it might be called *Monster*.

Aliens help science fiction ask one of its fundamental questions: what does it mean to be "human," which is to say, what attributes, values, qualities, and characteristics do we ascribe to beings that makes them (or us) worthy of preservation, dignity, and respect? Another way that science fiction has dealt with this is through the linked imagery of robots, androids, and cyborgs. Though the machinelike qualities of Gort or Robby do little to make us imagine them as particularly human, the more they act in our image the more uncomfortable we may feel in so easily dismissing them as mere machines. George Lucas, very much aware of this function of robots, designed his R2-D2 as an even more cuddly version of Robby and endowed C-3PO with all-too-human characteristics of a more negative, if amusing variation.

Robots can also be used to segment off the nonhuman from the human, no matter how lifelike they may appear. For example, *Westworld* plays with the image of the gunfighter as a cold-blooded killer by making the antagonist a no-blooded killer, a robot with no conscience but, rather, an implacable sense of programmed mission. So, too, the robot-killer of *The Terminator*. Once the relatively inexpressive form of Arnold

***Forbidden Planet* (1956)** Beauty and the beast? Certainly Anne Francis qualifies as the former, but is Robby the Robot the latter? Indeed not. In what may be the first instance of a truly domesticated, virtually feminized, robot in sci-fi, the "character" of Robby acts as a way to tame fears of technology while the film continues a trend in which technology—run amok for one reason or another—is indeed seen as something frightful. Yet the artificial intelligence of Robby is in some ways preferable to the cold intelligence of the otherwise all-too-human Dr. Morbius (Walter Pidgeon), whose inner demons produce the "monsters from the Id" that the alien technology makes manifest.

Schwarzenegger is stripped away, the even more completely machinelike steel assassin is revealed. The robots or androids in these films make for particularly effective killers precisely because they have no feelings; there is no way to reason with them or sway them from their deadly missions. It is precisely when robots or androids or, for that matter, computers begin to develop feelings, a sense of empathy that comes from a sense of self, that the line between human and other becomes blurred and dangerously thin.

One strategy science-fiction films use is to have these robots—these artificially created beings—animated by actual actors and not by machines or computer-generated effects. The very implacability of the gunfighter in *Westworld* and of the Terminator becomes all the more frightening because these characters are played by flesh-and-blood actors, such as Yul Brynner and Arnold Schwarzenegger, who bring along recognizable and defined personae.

A.I. Artificial Intelligence (2001) explores not only the issue of the "humanity" of robots (even using actors to play them) but also points

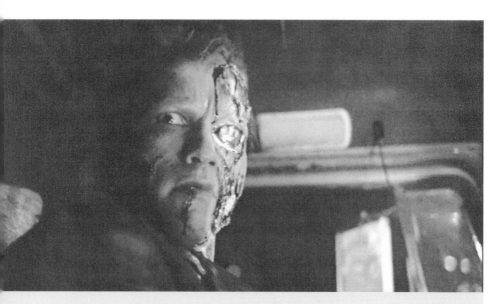

***The Terminator* (1984)** Austrian-born bodybuilder Arnold Schwarzenegger was an interesting choice to play the humanoid, soulless cyborg. Having appeared in only a handful of roles, most prominently the action-fantasy Conan duology (1982, 1984), he had yet to achieve the superstardom that allowed him to play his roles straight and yet with a sense of irony and self-reflectivity. Here his limited emotional range, overbuilt body, and odd sense of alienness blend to create an image of a being not quite one of us. The humor his character displays combines with a talent for violence and mayhem both eerie and entertaining. That he would shift from villain to hero in the later installments of the franchise mostly reflects his increasing stardom and popularity, beginning primarily with the success of this film.

out the cavalier way such creations might be disposed of and the fear they may engender in people. David (Haley Joel Osment) is a little boy-like robot bought to replace a lost child. When the child returns, David is summarily dismissed and must fend for himself. The outside world that he encounters in his quest for love and to be, Pinocchio-like, a "real boy," is a nightmare of cruelty, callousness, and discrimination against the A.I. beings (called mechas). The sight of humans cheering as mechas are destroyed in an aptly named Flesh Fair intentionally makes us uncomfortable, recalling such atrocities as the Holocaust and the lynchings of blacks.

A more subtle evocation of the human–nonhuman conundrum lies at the heart of *Blade Runner*. Its futuristic production design—the soaring pyramidal skyscraper that dominates the near-future Los Angeles skyline—and lived-in look are the attractive window dressing for a richly philosophical meditation on the nature of personhood and being. With references to Milton's *Paradise Lost*, the poetry of William Blake, and, most of all, Mary Shelley's *Frankenstein*, the film examines man's relationship to a creator, the creator's responsibility to his creation, and the definition of humanity amid advances in robotics, cybernetics, and artificial intelligence. What distinguishes the androids, here called replicants, from previous cinematic incarnations of artificially produced beings is that they are in every way human—in some ways, as the Tyrell Corporation that manufactures them has it, "more human than human." Certainly they are stronger, faster, and smarter and the women are quite beautiful. What makes them feared in the narrative of the film, and illegal residents of Earth, is that they have been "conceived" in commercial venues to have specific roles—and a set number of days before they expire. The allegory to slavery is unmistakable, recalling similar arguments in the eighteenth and nineteenth centuries over the humanity of black people and the breeding they underwent to fulfill certain functions on the plantation. *Blade Runner* was a tour-de-force in every respect, and its growing critical reputation is due predominately to the rich manner in which it examines definitions of the human.

Yet another variant of the robot/android/replicant is the cyborg. Cyborgs represent the literal merging of man and machine and reflect many advances in medical science along with the increasing utilization of computers as part of everyday life. The cyborg (cybernetic organism) has proved amenable to the action variant of science fiction, with such films as *Cyborg* (1989), the Nemesis series (1992 and following), *Cyborg Cop* (1993), *American Cyborg* (1994), and others. The most fascinating of these films is doubtless *RoboCop*, for the complicated issue of just how much humanity remains when scientists add robotic equipment to a human shell. This concept of a "shell" is implicated in one of the most respected of all Japanese anime, *Ghost in the Shell* (1995), a similarly themed tale of cyborg identity. For the soulless corporation that transforms Officer Alex Murphy (Peter Weller) into the RoboCop, the idea that some shred of himself—a self—would remain is unthinkable, for the corporate men are themselves already dehumanized by the overly mediated, hyperviolent society of the near future. Amid all the killing, however, some sense of Murphy's human personality remains.

As cloning and genetic engineering have become both increasingly common and controversial, they have found their way into the science-fiction genre. Though introduced into science-fiction literature via Aldous Huxley's wide-ranging novel *Brave New World* (1932), genetic engineering never appeared onscreen until social reality made it a lively topic. One important film in this mode is *Gattaca* (1997). Here, those not genetically manipulated in utero are subject to high levels of discrimination, a nice reversal of more typical science-fiction motifs that products of genetic tampering or mutations are to be feared. In a world where such engineering is the norm, those who are more "normal" find themselves very much on the outside. Alternately, medical experimentation—seen in hybrid sci-fi–horror films such as *Frankenstein* (1931, 1994) and *Island of Lost Souls* (1932), remade as *The Island of Dr. Moreau* (1977, 1996), for instance—finds its way into sci-fi actioners that have some depth beneath the mayhem, including *Universal Soldier* (1992). The ethics of cloning, a variation of genetic engineering, have also come in for some

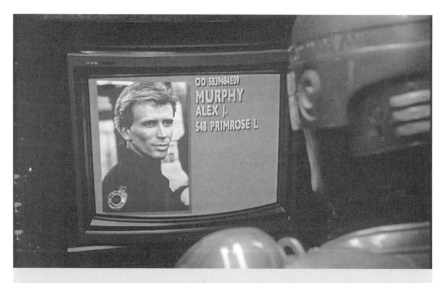

RoboCop (1987) The intersection of the human and the machine, flesh and circuitry, is at the heart of this witty, violent, dystopic view of corporate America in the near and all-too-possible future. *RoboCop* (with Peter Weller) offers up a perhaps surprisingly whole worldview of mindless media entertainment, urban decay, corporate greed, and governmental ineffectiveness. Yet behind all of this there is a deeply humanistic message that postulates the persistence of humanity not just in the transformation from man into cyborg (a common motif of the sci-fi cinema, especially seen in Japanese anime), but amid the dystopian world that is all too plausibly imagined.

IV-2 LOGIC TERMINAL IV-3 LOGIC TERMINAL MEMORY TERMINAL

***2001: A Space Odyssey* (1968)** "I'm afraid, Dave." It is surely a deliberate irony on the part of author Arthur C. Clarke and famed director Stanley Kubrick that the most plaintive and pathetic moment in *2001: A Space Odyssey* comes courtesy of the ship's computer. As astronaut Dave Bowman (Keir Dullea) begins tearing out Hal's memory chips, the increasingly desperate and emotional pleas that he utters makes the audience uncomfortable with the sense that this is a living being, in contradistinction to the emotionless people who have populated the film following the highly charged Dawn of Man prologue. The film pioneered many elements of science fiction, not the least of which is the issue of sentience and "humanity."

examination in the years since the process itself became a scientific possibility. *The Island* (2005) deals with the question of identity. One basis of humanity is thought to be the unique characteristics of an individual. Cloning considers the issue from the point of view of an individual who is by definition not an individual at all. Arnold Schwarzenegger got into the act with a story about clones programmed for nefarious purposes with *The 6th Day* (2000)—a nice allusion to the biblical story of Genesis in which God created man.

Genetic engineering, human cloning, man-machine hybrids, robots, and artificial intelligence are all linked issues. Another connected topic, and a well-utilized icon of the sci-fi genre, is the computer. Advances in computing started in the 1950s but took a while to find a home on sci-fi screens. But once they did, inaugurated by *2001*'s Hal, they emerged as a potent visual image. Like the robot or the android, the computer can take on malevolent characteristics, especially when it attempts to achieve a kind of "life" of its own. *Colossus: The Forbin Project* (1970) envisions what is now called a supercomputer. When two such computers are connected, the resulting mayhem threatens the entire world. This idea of a computer—invented by humankind to protect itself—turning on its creators lies at the heart of the Terminator series, in which the supercomputer network, Skynet, determines that the world would be better off without people in it. *Demon Seed* imagines a computer possessed not only of artificial intelligence but intense sexual desires, giving new meaning to the concept of plugging in and rebooting.

Connected computers, as in *Colossus*, are an imagination of the now very real world of the Internet and the resulting creation of cyberspace. We live daily in a science-fiction world that routinely blurs the line between virtual reality and actual reality. Obviously, the Matrix trilogy explores the fears about supercomputers and virtual reality in blockbuster fashion, but many films have taken cyberspace and virtual reality out of the computer and into real life, at least onscreen. Most of these films use the syntax of the thriller and thus create a kind of hybrid genre. The visualization of these films relies strongly on CGI, appropriately enough, thereby creating a nice dialectic between computer-as-menace and computer-as-pleasure. *The Lawnmower Man* (1992) is an innovative look at computer–human interaction in the new virtual reality mode, injecting a human into cyberspace. The opposite idea, that of a being that exists only in virtual reality entering into the real world, was the intriguing subject of the big-budget *Virtuosity* (1995). *Dark City* (1998) envisions our very existence as a type of virtual reality, a computer game in which we wander around in a simulated environment we mistake as real.

Finally, a common image pattern worth noting in the sci-fi genre is dystopia. This also takes many forms. The postapocalyptic action-adventure common to the modern B film, in which nuclear war or ecological disaster obliterates the bulk of humanity, and life for the survivors is both tenuous and brutal, is exemplified by the cult favorite *A Boy and His Dog* (1974) and the Australian *Mad Max II: The Road Warrior* (1981) and its many and numerous knock-offs [e.g., *Omega Doom* (1996), *Steel Dawn* (1987)]. Before *Star Wars*, George Lucas created a nifty little dystopic world with his modestly budgeted *THX 1138*. Urban decay, youthful alienation, and governmental cynicism create an unpleasant but very stylish world in *A Clockwork Orange* (1971). And the old hippie adage "Don't trust anyone over thirty" gets an interesting treatment in *Logan's Run*. Perhaps a dystopian vision is simply more dramatic than the utopia that technological advances always promise at world's fairs and international expositions. Certainly, with home computers as ubiquitous as television and the Internet more popular than the multiplex, people trust their technology far more than the movies do.

Blade Runner

In the annals of serious screen sci-fi, few other films have commanded the attention of Ridley Scott's *Blade Runner* (1982). Though something of a box-office disappointment at the time of its release, it has subsequently come to achieve the kind of status reserved for the likes of *Metropolis*—to which it bears more than a passing resemblance—and *2001: A Space Odyssey*. This is owed to a combination of stunning production design (modeled on Osaka, Japan, and Hong Kong), a convincingly grim imagined near-future (one at great variance with Philip K. Dick's source novel, *Do Androids Dream of Electric Sheep?*), and a rich meditation on questions of identity and definitions of humanity. In this bleak future society, a blade runner is a specialized cop who hunts renegade replicants who have fled to Earth, where their presence is banned. Unless they choose to reveal their superior strength and speed, or are subjected to a sophisticated personality test, called the Voight-Kampff, replicants can blend easily with humans, from whom they are otherwise indistinguishable. The test measures autonomic responses to emotions like compassion and empathy, things which distinguish man from animal, human from machine. Yet, as the film reveals, not all humans are necessarily compassionate and not all replicants lack empathy. It is precisely at the borders between the human and the cyborg, the person and the personality, that *Blade Runner* locates its brave new world.

The film utilizes a dual-focus narrative structure, tracing Rick Deckard (Harrison Ford) as he hunts down the escaped replicants, Leon (Brion James), Zhora (Joanna Cassidy), Pris (Daryl Hannah), and their leader, Roy Batty (Rutger Hauer), as they attempt to locate their "maker"—Eldon Tyrell (Joe Turkel), the head of the Tyrell Corporation, which manufactures replicants—to override their built-in "fail-safe"—a four-year lifespan—or otherwise hold him to account. In his search,

Deckard grows more and more conflicted about his assignment, espe-cially after he discovers a fifth replicant—Tyrell's assistant, Rachael (Sean Young)—who is almost indistinguishable from humanity even in taking the Voight-Kampff test, and as he himself discovers more of his own humanity. And in their search for Tyrell, the replicants, too, discover more of their own (supposed lack of) humanity and grow ever more sym-pathetic to viewers, who come to understand their condition as slaves, bred for specific tasks (sex for the women, manual labor for the men) and desirous of nothing more than acceptance and normalcy. Their four-year life spans give them a taste for life, for experience, a body of knowl-edge, a sense of belonging, and they want more; yet in acknowledging that they want more, they also reveal what is at the heart of humanity: the ability to learn, grow, love, and experience loss. The surprising turn of events, in which a blade runner falls in love with a replicant, and a replicant saves the life of a blade runner, is a meeting in the middle, in which a human who has become too much like a machine interacts with machines who have become all too human.

One question that has fascinated critics and commentators is that of Deckard's humanity. Is he a replicant? Ridley Scott has claimed to believe that Deckard is indeed a replicant. For Scott, the definitive answer comes subtly through the use of the origami figures that fellow blade runner Gaff (Edward James Olmos) leaves at scenes where he has been hunting replicants. Deckard dreams of unicorns and when Gaff places an origami unicorn outside Deckard's apartment, Scott believes that Deckard definitively realizes that the image has been implanted in his mind, just as Rachael's "memories" of her girlhood are merely manu-factured images. Yet the unicorn left at Deckard's apartment could just as easily indicate Gaff's recognition that Rachael, with whom Deckard is now in love, is a replicant. Deckard realizes that Gaff knows both that Rachael is a replicant and that Deckard is in love with her. The unicorn could simply be a sign that Gaff (who has been rather mysterious and unfeeling himself, suggesting that all of the blade runners may be rep-licants) has spared Rachael's life. He even says to Deckard immediately before that, "It's a pity she won't live. But then again, who does?" Yet even without the unicorn dream (which is not in the original U.S. the-atrical release), there is much evidence that Deckard is, or at least may be, a replicant. When, after hours of testing Rachael, Deckard finally concludes that she is a replicant, Tyrell informs him that even Rachael

***Blade Runner* (1982)** Gaff's (Edward James Olmos) origami unicorn was originally supposed to signify that Deckard was a replicant. But an earlier scene to which this is specifically referred was cut out of the original theatrical release.

does not know this. Deckard asks, "How can it not know what it is?" The same may be said of Deckard.

Deckard shares with the replicants a fascination with photographs. He finds a stack of photos in Leon's hotel room when he investigates Leon's shooting of Holden, the first blade runner we meet. Rachael similarly relies on photographs to provide her with a sense of memory. Deckard has framed pictures throughout his apartment and a stack of mostly black-and-white photos. He takes them out and looks through them after returning to his apartment after his first confrontation with the replicants. Deckard's lack of emotionality, said to characterize replicants (which is, ironically, far from the truth of things), certainly defines his character. In the original theatrical version, his voice-over tells us that his ex-wife called him a "cold fish," while Rachael wonders if he ever administered the Voight-Kampff test to himself. And if it is possible that the blade runners are themselves replicants, it is noteworthy that, seen in long shot, Holden (played by Morgan Paull, who stood in for Harrison Ford in screen tests during the casting phase), closely resembles Deckard, as if blade runners came in a set of different basic models, as we learn is the case with replicants. In fact, in Dick's source novel, Zhora and Pris, two of the renegade replicants, are actually identical in appearance, to emphasize the assembly-line origin of the androids.

***Blade Runner* (1982)** In shadow, Morgan Paull resembles Harrison Ford, another indication that Deckard is a replicant.

Other clues that Deckard may be a replicant are found in lines of dialogue that can be taken in more than one way. For instance, when chasing Deckard through the Bradbury Building at the film's climax, Roy calls to him, "Show me what you're made of." That is, show me what you've got, of course, but also, show me whether your skin, muscle, bones, etc., are natural or manufactured. Similarly, after Roy's death Gaff calls to Deckard, "You've done a man's job, sir." This could simply mean that he's done a very difficult job or that he has, literally, done the job of a man, not a replicant.

Finally, we may note that the Nexus-group replicants are stronger, faster, and, in Roy's case, smarter than humans, yet Deckard survives— he recovers from Zhora's vicious chop to his windpipe (she is a combat replicant, not just a beautiful exotic dancer); Leon tosses him all over the street and into cars; Pris gets him in a powerful leg lock and seems to twist his head around at an impossible angle; and Roy breaks two of his fingers, which doesn't prevent Deckard from hanging on by the fingers of just one hand, as he dangles from a rooftop. Deckard may simply be an earlier model of replicant but otherwise possessed of superior sight, shooting ability, and strength in his own right. Ultimately, however, whether Deckard is a replicant—earlier model or not—is less important than the fact that his essential humanity is uncovered and redeemed by these replicants, especially his love for Rachael and his final confrontation with Roy Batty.

The film first uses the two renegade replicant women, Zhora and Pris, to demonstrate not only their sense of self-preservation but the pathos of their outlaw status through their deaths. Zhora's death is handled in a particularly dramatic and poignant way, considering that she is the first of the replicants to be killed. After striking Deckard in the throat and nearly strangling him to death, Zhora runs out of the nightclub with Deckard in hot pursuit. The film then spends the next three and a half minutes watching as Deckard searches for her amid the crowds and noise of the bustling city. When he finally spots her, she runs again; he shoots twice and misses. In her desperation to flee from the blade runner, Zhora crashes through the glass of a department store window as the film switches to slow motion. The camera angle also switches, from behind Zhora as she runs, to in front of her. This slow-motion continues throughout the rest of the sequence, as Deckard's next shot finds its target and we see agony cross her face, and then as she falls to the floor. Vangelis's mournful music rises on the sound track as an underscore to her death throes. Zhora crashes through more glass, this time into a diorama of a winter scene; as she dies, artificial snow falling around her, Deckard walks forward and sees her lifeless body, eyes open, but unseeing. The sequence establishes Deckard's efficiency as a blade runner along with his regret at killing Zhora, while insisting on the humanity of Zhora and the pathos of her death.

Blade Runner (1982) The killing of Zhora prompts Deckard to consider not just the humanity of the replicants but also his own.

Deckard's killing of Pris is also somewhat drawn out by the film, as he initially searches for her amid the dolls, both mobile and still, that populate J. F. Sebastian's apartment. When he approaches what he thinks might be either her or a heavily made-up life-size doll, he learns the hard way that she is very real. She gets him in a powerful leg lock, nearly twisting his head off. She lets him loose to make a gymnastic run at him, but he manages to get off a shot that strikes her in the torso. Pris, with a childlike fury, throws a temper tantrum at the prospect of dying, kicking her legs and smashing her hands on the ground. Deckard shoots again, hitting her in the side, which drives her to the floor. Slow motion is only used for an instant, to capture Pris's final death throes. In fact, Roy's death, much more quiet than that of either Zhora or Pris, is also filmed in slow motion—his head slumps forward and he releases a white dove that he had grabbed a bit earlier. The dove takes off in slow motion toward a whitening sky. The women's deaths have released Deckard's pent-up feelings of pathos. Early on he had been cynical about replicants, having said to Rachael, "Replicants are like any other machine; they're either a benefit or a hazard. If they're a benefit, it's not my problem." But now he feels remorse. With Roy's death, Deckard becomes fully human.

Interestingly, following the killing of each of the woman replicants, Deckard is confronted by one of the men—Leon—after he kills Zhora

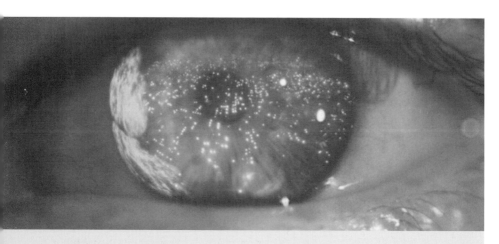

Blade Runner (1982) Eyes—windows to the soul, index of humanity—are a recurring motif in the film.

and the other—Roy—after he kills Pris. We can see that both men are deeply affected by the deaths of their female counterparts and both men torment Deckard in preparation for killing him. And both say essentially the same thing to him as they demonstrate their superior physical capabilities: Leon says, "Painful to live in fear, isn't it?" while Roy remarks, "Quite an experience to live in fear, isn't it?" Further, as Leon is about to kill Deckard, he says, "Time to die." At that point he is shot through the forehead by Rachael, who thus saves Deckard's life. Later, when Roy also says "time to die," he does not mean it for Deckard but for himself, just after he rescues Deckard. In saving Deckard, Roy has opened up Deckard's eyes to what life really means.

And this brings up one of the film's most notable motifs—one is tempted to say "visual motifs," since the film in fact relies strongly on the recurring image of eyes. The first such instance occurs right at the start when a large, disembodied eye reflects the fiery furnaces belching flames high atop the polluted city. (Fire and burning are other prominent motifs.) Next is the Voight-Kampff test, which registers small reactions in the pupils of the eyes, involuntary responses to stress or emotional triggers. Further highlighting of eyes comes as Leon and Roy search for answers to questions about longevity, inception dates, and possible changes to their makeup. They first confront Chew, whose part in the replicants' design is the genetic engineering of eyes. As Chew is confronted by the two replicants, he stammers, "Eyes; I just do eyes." Roy smiles and says, "Chew, if only you could see what I've seen with your eyes!" Later, Leon is about to kill Deckard by poking his fingers through his eyes. Later still, Roy simultaneously crushes Tyrell's skull and pokes his thumbs deep into his eye sockets, a fact much clearer in the so-called Final Cut than in either the theatrical version or the intermediate "director's cut." The blood running down his empty eye sockets is a horrifying sight, but it is in keeping with the film's insistence on eyes. Finally, when Roy has finished chasing Deckard across the rooftops, he laments, "I've seen things you people wouldn't believe.... All those moments will be lost in time, like tears in the rain." Instead of having blood running out of their eyes, both Roy and Deckard appear to be crying as the rain falls on their faces.

It is in the final scene where the film makes clearest the thin line separating human and replicant, man and machine. One could say that Deckard and Roy have been linked throughout the entire film. Of course, as in any action film there must be the inevitable showdown between protagonist and antagonist. In this case, the film uses a dual-focus structure, alternating scenes of Deckard in his pursuit of the replicants with scenes of the replicants as they pursue answers to their questions. But in the climactic showdown, the links between the two of them are made explicit. Both Deckard and Roy have severe pain in their right hand—Deckard because Roy has broken two of his fingers and Roy, who is losing sensation in his limbs as his expiration time draws near, has put a spike through his right hand to keep sensation alive. The film cuts between the two men, each wounded, each soaked by the rain, until finally, as Roy dies, instead of cutting back and forth, the film dissolves from Deckard's face to Roy's, momentarily superimposing them.

Of course, the replicant equally responsible for Deckard's reclaimed or discovered humanity is Rachael. His falling in love with her is the surest sign of his emotional regeneration. The film handles Rachael's characterization quite interestingly through costume and lighting. Rachael wears very old-fashioned clothes, more characteristic of the 1940s than 2019. In hairstyle and costume she resembles Joan Crawford in Michael Curtiz's 1945 noir classic, *Mildred Pierce*, set in L.A. That *Blade Runner* evokes *Mildred Pierce* is interesting, but Scott's film more generally evokes film noir through its use of low-key lighting, especially in the scenes with Rachael, even using the famous "blinds" effect—hard shadows of dark and light as if filtered through Venetian blinds. In keeping with

***Blade Runner* (1982)** The dissolve from Batty to Deckard visually links the two.

***Blade Runner* (1982)** The evocation of film noir—in lighting, costume, and in the possibility that Rachael is a femme fatale.

the motif of eyes, however, despite the low-key lighting and other noir effects, Rachael's eyes are always visible (most likely through the use of an eye light). The evocation of film noir lends Rachael an air of the classic femme fatale, which works to keep her true nature and motives ambiguous. Film noir and its close generic cousin, the hard-boiled-detective story, are further highlighted in the original theatrical release by the use of voice-over supplied by Harrison Ford for Rick Deckard. The voice-over tries for a cynical, world-weary tone, characteristic of those noirs derived from the works of Dashiell Hammett, James M. Cain, and, especially, Raymond Chandler. Though this voice-over was eliminated as early as the director's cut, enough noir recollections remain to give *Blade Runner* a curiously retro feel despite its postmodern gloss. The world of noir is a world of paranoia, cynicism, and alienation, a far cry from the science fiction of contemporary films like *Star Wars, Close Encounters,* and *E.T.* Yet whatever the box-office at the time, *Blade Runner* has emerged as one of the most influential of all sci-fi films, standing as a rich and compelling look at the genre's most poignant questions: what does it mean to be human, and who gets to decide?

David Desser

QUESTIONS FOR DISCUSSION

1. Special effects are of particular importance in science fiction and they were crucial in the silent era—in Italy, France, Germany, and the United States. Yet the genre has barely a presence in pre–World War II cinema. What do you imagine kept the genre from thriving in the United States or in other nations with active film industries?

2. Why do you think the science-fiction genre developed in the United States, Britain, and Japan in the 1950s, but other nations with active industries either latched on to the genre later (e.g., France) or not at all (e.g., Italy)?

3. There is a long association between genres and stars. Think Fred Astaire and Gene Kelly in the musical; John Wayne in the Western; Cary Grant in romantic comedy. Although Charlton Heston appeared in a handful of important sci-fi films and Arnold Schwarzenegger starred in more than half a dozen sci-fi smash hits, we don't necessarily associate these stars with science fiction or, for that matter, do we consider any particular stars iconic to the genre. Numerous sci-fi films boast no stars at all—think of the original *Star Wars*. Why does sci-fi have this feature?

4. The question of "humanity" has become an important theme in sci-fi films since the 1980s. Can this be related to other issues prevalent in modern science fiction, such as cloning, genetic engineering, and human–animal relations?

5. Which sci-fi films of the new century will likely become the sort of cult favorites that appeared in the last quarter of the twentieth century? Why?

FOR FURTHER READING

Anderson, Craig W. *Science Fiction Films of the Seventies*. Jefferson, NC: McFarland, 1985.

Brosnan, John. *Future Tense: The Cinema of Science Fiction*. New York: St. Martin's, 1978.

Cornea, Christine. *Science Fiction Cinema: Between Fantasy and Reality*. New Brunswick: NJ: Rutgers University Press, 2007.

Kuhn, Annette, ed. *Alien Zone: Cultural Theory and Contemporary Science Fiction*. London: Verso, 1990.

———. *Alien Zone II: The Spaces of Science Fiction*. London: Verso, 1999.

Slusser, George, and Eric Rabkin, eds. *Shadows of the Magic Lamp: Fantasy and Science Fiction in Film*. Carbondale: Southern Illinois University Press, 1985.

Sobchack, Vivian. *Screening Space: The American Science Fiction Film*, 2nd edition. New York: Ungar, 1993.

Telotte, J. P. *Replications: A Robotic History of the Science Fiction Film*. Urbana: University of Illinois Press, 1995.

———. *Science Fiction Film*. New York: Cambridge University Press, 2001.

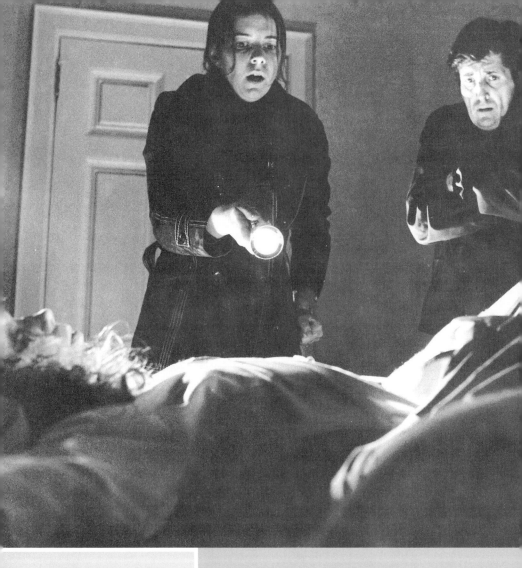

The Exorcist (1973)

The Horror Film

THE MONSTERS, GHOULS, AND PSYCHOPATHS found in horror films are among cinema's most popular and iconic characters. Few moviegoers don't know of Dracula or Frankenstein's monster, of *Psycho*'s Norman Bates or *The Silence of the Lambs*' Hannibal Lecter. Fan sites in cyberspace celebrate Freddy Krueger and Jason, the killers who stalk through the Nightmare on Elm Street and Friday the 13th series. Fan magazines such as *Fangoria* and the now-defunct *Famous Monsters of Filmland* profile the makeup and special-effects wizardry that create memorable werewolves and flesh-eating zombies. A paradox—viewers are attracted in these movies to characters and creatures they would run from in real life—lies at the heart of horror's appeal. These movies address some of our deepest anxieties about life and the nature of being human, and in doing so, never go out of fashion.

History

While all cultures have stories about ghosts, demons, evil spells, and the undead, the narrative basis for horror in the cinema originates with the gothic novels of nineteenth-century Europe, which emphasize old dark houses, tombs, crypts, family curses, ghosts, vampires, and themes of madness and the sinister double or doppelgänger. Cinema readily made use of these atmospheric devices and quickly released many adaptations of such novels as *Frankenstein* (1818), *The Vampyre* (1819), *The Hunchback of Notre Dame* (1831), *The Strange Case of Dr. Jekyll and Mr. Hyde* (1886),

The Picture of Dorian Gray (1891), *Dracula* (1897), *The Turn of the Screw* (1898), and *The Phantom of the Opera* (1910).

The first horror (and vampire) movie is probably Georges Méliès's *The Haunted Castle* (1896), although Méliès was more interested in presenting special-effects trickery than in arousing fear and terror. The first film adaptation of Mary Shelley's *Frankenstein* is an Edison two-reeler from 1910; a feature-length film, titled *Life without Soul*, followed in 1915. Two U.S. versions and a German version of *Dr. Jekyll and Mr. Hyde* appeared in 1920, along with, from Italy, another version of *Frankenstein*. Elaborate and expensive Hollywood studio productions of *The Hunchback of Notre Dame* (1923) and *The Phantom of the Opera* (1925) pointed to the popularity of horror in early cinema and to the enduring appeal of the gothic novels. Another key horror character showcased in cinema's first decades is the Werewolf, the subject of two American releases (1913, 1925) and one from France (1923). Edgar Allan Poe's gruesome stories furnished cinema with key narrative templates and were adapted continuously across many decades. Poe's "The Tell-Tale Heart" first appeared as D. W. Griffith's *The Avenging Conscience* (1914) and his "Masque of the Red Death" as the German *The Plague in Florence* (1919). Hulking monsters and synthetically created beings flourished in *The Golem* (1915) and its sequels (1917 and 1920), all from Germany, and *Alraune* (German and Hungarian versions in 1918, others from Germany in 1928, 1930, and 1952).

Horror and the art film often coincided in cinema's earliest decades. Top-rank international filmmakers regularly trafficked in horror. The great Swedish filmmaker Victor Sjöström made *The Phantom Carriage* (1921), focusing on the netherworld of spirits and the damned, and a decade later the extraordinary Danish filmmaker Carl Dreyer made a dreamy, horror-art film in *Vampyr* (1932). Universal's big-budget *The Hunchback of Notre Dame* and *The Phantom of the Opera* showed how prestigious horror could be as a silent-film genre. Both feature Lon Chaney, the genre's first great star, in the title role. The son of deaf parents, Chaney found fame playing grotesque characters, such as the Hunchback, the Phantom, a pointy-toothed (but fake) vampire in *London After Midnight* (1927), and Alonzo the Armless in *The Unknown* (1927). He subjected himself to painful, torturous makeup procedures to create his memorable characters. To create the Hunchback, he wore an extremely heavy hump and harness and a dental device that prevented him from closing his mouth, and he blackened his eye sockets and used wire to

The Phantom of the Opera (1925) Horror films were plentiful during the silent era, though it is doubtful that the format was yet a genre. Lon Chaney became a major star by specializing in grotesque and gruesome makeup designs. He underwent torturous procedures to transform his face and body, and the unmasking scene in *Phantom* (with Mary Philbin) is one of horror cinema's classic moments. Chaney used wire, nose plugs, and greasepaint to create a skeletal, death's-head face.

pull up his nose for the death's-head face of the Phantom. These elaborate procedures became part of the studio publicity for the films, and so famous was Chaney for his makeup metamorphoses that he was called the Man of a Thousand Faces. A Hollywood joke went, "Don't step on it! It might be Lon Chaney."

The grotesque found its most enduring home during the silent era in Germany. The Expressionist art movement appeared first in German theater and painting and then flourished in cinema during the 1920s. Its antirealist, antinaturalist style, emphasizing dark, chiaroscuro (or pinpoint) lighting, sharply angled set designs, and character types such as monsters and madmen, furnished natural ingredients for horror films. Numerous classics of silent horror date from this period of German Expressionism. *The Cabinet of Dr. Caligari* (1920) shows the world from the perspective of a lunatic confined in an asylum. Accordingly, the sets lurch at odd angles and lighting effects (painted on the sets!) present violent slashes of illumination and shadow. The story features a mad doctor and a somnambulist he directs to terrorize remote villages and small towns by abducting and killing their inhabitants.

***Nosferatu* (1922)** In the silent era, art films regularly included an emphasis on horror. The renowned German filmmaker F. W. Murnau applied his brilliant visual style to this version of the Dracula story. Max Schreck as the vampire looms menacingly in the doorway of his castle. Note the fusion of performer and architectural design—the elongated body of the vampire inside the arched doorway. This blend of performance and architecture was a characteristic feature of Expressionism.

F. W. Murnau created the definitive early version of Dracula in *Nosferatu* (1922), another visionary work melding the horror genre with art-film aesthetics that is visually more expressive and cinematic than Universal's *Dracula* (1931), which stars Bela Lugosi and is based on a stage play (and stiffly shows these origins). Murnau went on in *Faust* (1926) to depict Satan as a huge, bat-winged creature spreading pestilence and death.

Horror films, then, were widespread throughout silent cinema, though it is generally thought that these productions did not constitute a genre. While certain stories—*The Hound of the Baskervilles* and *Dr. Jekyll and Mr. Hyde*, for example—were adapted repeatedly into silent-era films, horror remained more a subject or a style than a genre. There had not yet been established a gallery of recognizable character types, situations, and locales that were repeated often enough as to be considered enduring formulas and conventions.

It was the huge outpouring of films from Universal Studios (one of the Hollywood industry's smaller studios) during the early sound era that solidified horror as a genre. Universal provided horror with its first real golden age by defining its first set of classic movie monsters and their definitive visual renditions. Nineteen thirty-one saw the release of both *Dracula* and *Frankenstein*, with performances, by Bela Lugosi as the vampire count and Boris Karloff as the monster, that remain the standards. Karloff returned the following year as *The Mummy*, creating another classic monster. Sequels began with *Bride of Frankenstein* (1935) and *Dracula's Daughter* (1936) and continued with *Son of Frankenstein* (1939), *The Mummy's Hand* (1940), *The Ghost of Frankenstein* (1942), *Frankenstein Meets the Wolf Man* (1943), *Son of Dracula* (1943), *House of Frankenstein* (1944), *The Mummy's Ghost* (1944), *The Mummy's Curse* (1944), and *House of Dracula* (1945).

Most of these sequels are pale imitations of the original films, but their repetition of stories and characters enabled a horror genre to emerge. Another classic monster reappeared in this interval in *The Wolf Man* (1941), although it was not Universal's first try at a werewolf movie. *Werewolf of London* (1935) had failed to provide a memorable or definitive portrait of lycanthropy. The approach worked in 1941 because Lon Chaney Jr. portrays Larry Talbot, the Wolf Man, as an anguished victim,

Frankenstein (1931) Horror became a film genre in the early sound era as Universal Studios gave the classic monsters their definitive portraits and then reissued them in sequels over the next decade. Among the many film versions of Mary Shelley's *Frankenstein*, this one offers the most enduring image of the monster, achieved in Boris Karloff's performance and in the makeup design perfected by James Whale, director, and Jack Pierce, who ran the studio's makeup department and designed many of the classic monsters.

giving the character a haunted dimension that Karloff had also captured in Frankenstein's monster. Hans Salter's music score is so fine that Universal continued using it in subsequent monster movies. But most important are the makeup designs of Jack Pierce, who more than anyone at Universal was responsible for defining the look of these classic monsters. Pierce also created the makeup effects for *Dracula, Frankenstein, The Mummy*, and all of their sequels.

But horror production at Universal was more widespread than the movies about classic monsters. Other outstanding pictures include *Murders in the Rue Morgue* (1932), *The Black Cat* (1934), and *The Raven* (1935), all of which achieve such heights of gruesome sadism that the industry was hit with a public backlash calling for censorship and a halt in horror production. A woman, for example, is tortured to death in *Rue Morgue*, and a man is skinned alive in *The Black Cat*. Viewers today might have difficulty realizing how troubling these films were at the time of their release because the limits of violence in the genre have broadened considerably. But these movies were regarded in their day as unacceptably horrifying and violent.

They were popular, however, and the success of Universal's horror pictures led other studios to begin producing their own. Classics from the period include Paramount's *Dr. Jekyll and Mr. Hyde* (1931, still the best version of this story) and *Island of Lost Souls* (1932), MGM's *Freaks* (1932), *Mark of the Vampire*, and *Mad Love* (both 1935), RKO's *The Most Dangerous Game* (1932) and *King Kong* (1933), and Warner Bros.' *Doctor X* (1932) and *Mystery of the Wax Museum* (1933).

The 1930s represented Universal's high period of creativity. By the 1940s, the classic monsters had appeared onscreen so often they stopped being scary, and the end of the line came when they met the popular comedy duo Abbott and Costello. *Abbott and Costello Meet Frankenstein* (1948) teams the comedians with Dracula (again played by Lugosi), the Wolf Man (Chaney Jr.), Frankenstein's monster (now played by Glenn Strange), and even the Invisible Man (Vincent Price). The success of this film led to numerous sequels: *Abbott and Costello Meet the Invisible Man* (1951), *Abbott and Costello Meet Dr. Jekyll and Mr. Hyde* (1953), and *Abbott and Costello Meet the Mummy* (1955). The success of this series points to an important relationship between horror and comedy that I will discuss later in this chapter.

Beset by so many lackluster sequels during the 1940s, horror was mostly in a retrograde phase. But at RKO Pictures, producer Val Lewton

Cat People (1942) Val Lewton's horror series at RKO emphasizes shadows, ambiguity, and the unknown instead of the literal monsters who populate Universal's horror movies. Although Lewton did not direct the films, his control as producer ensured that they maintain a unity of style, emphasizing a poetic, evocative tone and horrors that are vivid but unseen. In *Cat People*, Irena Dubrovna (Simone Simon) fears she is marked by a family curse under which females metamorphose into predatory jungle cats. In this scene, her rival in love (Jane Randolph, with Kent Smith) is stalked by a black panther that may, in fact, be Irena. The use of shadows and offscreen space is wholly characteristic of the Lewton style.

launched an outstanding series of nine films that rank among the decade's best work in the genre: *Cat People* (1942), *I Walked with a Zombie* (1943), *The Leopard Man* (1943), *The Seventh Victim* (1943), *The Ghost Ship* (1943), *Curse of the Cat People* (1944), *The Body Snatcher* (1945), *Isle of the Dead* (1945), and *Bedlam* (1946).

Whereas the Universal films have literal monsters—vampires, werewolves, mummies—Lewton's pictures do not. They emphasize sources of horror and terror as might be found in the real world—satanic cults, voodoo, serial murderers, insanity, sadism, and pestilence—and stylistically foreground suggestion, atmosphere, and the ambiguities of perception. Instead of viewing monsters through the camera, Lewton views dark, shadowy places where something bad might be lurking. Horror is felt but often not seen. His low-budget films are poetic masterpieces that arouse a sense of dread in the viewer's mind rather than putting something literal onscreen. They are not about monsters but about the psychological sources of fear.

The horror genre declined in the 1950s in favor of science-fiction movies about monsters engendered by radiation and nuclear fallout. England's Hammer Films, however, launched an influential series of remakes focusing on the classic monsters. *The Curse of Frankenstein* (1957), *Dracula* (1958), *The Mummy* (1959), and *The Curse of the Werewolf* (1961) are more graphically sexual and violent than the Universal pictures. In this way, these remakes pointed toward the future of horror as a genre that would often transgress boundaries of good taste, beginning with the ultraviolent, low-budget productions of Herschell Gordon Lewis. The first of these, *Blood Feast* (1963), portrays a victim being scalped and her brain extracted, and a killer ripping the tongue from another woman's mouth. Color cinematography shows the copious amounts of blood in hypersaturated detail, and Lewis's actors hold real entrails and organs up before the camera.

While Lewis's films are the first in the genre to dwell on body mutilation, it is Alfred Hitchcock's *Psycho* (1960) that definitively marks the onset of the genre's modern period. Hitchcock's film about a serial murderer shows the coldness of tone and the savage treatment of characters and of viewers that are now hallmarks of modern horror. Hitchcock said that his only objective in *Psycho* was to make audiences scream, and he brutally kills off the female lead before the halfway mark, dispatching her with a flurry of knife blows in a bathroom shower that has become the single most influential scene in modern horror. It is a

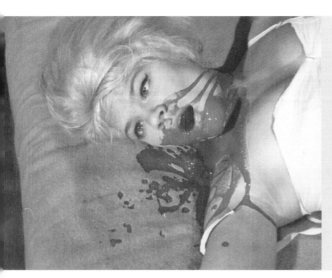

Blood Feast (1963) Horror as splatter—its presentation in terms of graphic violence— originates with the low-budget films of Herschell Gordon Lewis. In the first of these, *Blood Feast* (with Astrid Olson), a deranged Egyptian caterer butchers young women and uses their body parts to reanimate an ancient goddess. A heart, tongue, and other entrails are displayed on camera. The film plays better than its plot summary sounds, largely because Lewis is gleeful and good-natured in his celebration of bad taste.

***Psycho* (1960)** This is the film that marks the onset of the genre's modern period. Hitchcock takes horror away from the tombs, crypts, castles, and foreign locales that had been so common in the genre and relocates it in the banal surroundings of ordinary life. The "monster" is the charming, boyish Norman Bates (Anthony Perkins), a serial killer who preys on victims at the motel that he manages. Hitchcock portrays Norman's madness and refuses to explain it away. In the film's chilling final shot, a triple exposure shows Norman's grinning face superimposed on the leering skull of his murdered mother, with both atop the image of a car containing one of Norman's victims being dredged up from the swamp. The chain lifting the car seems to go straight into Norman's heart.

calculated assault on the viewer's sense of safety and security. If someone can be killed without warning by a psychopath in the privacy of a bathroom, Hitchcock is saying, if the world is that irrational, then no place is safe. Because Hitchcock raised the bar, horror films made after *Psycho* went to greater lengths to assault the audience and undermine its sense of safety.

Hitchcock was a major filmmaker visiting the horror genre, rather than one who regularly worked there, and after *Psycho* the genre's films diverged along two channels of production. On the one hand, big-budget, prestigious horror films made by name directors aimed solidly at the box office and at critical respectability. These include Roman Polanski's *Rosemary's Baby* (1968), William Friedkin's *The Exorcist* (1973), Richard Donner's *The Omen* (1976), and Stanley Kubrick's *The Shining* (1980). At the same time, scrappy, low-budget movies achieve much greater impact by ferociously assaulting audience sensibilities with extreme violence

***The Exorcist* (1973)** Extremely gruesome makeup and physical effects helped to catapult this film to blockbuster success. Like many horror films of the period, it focuses on anxieties and emotional turbulence within the family. Regan's (Linda Blair) satanic possession shatters her home life and relationship with her mother. The film's graphic violence, profanity, and gross-out effects (which include projectile vomit) are calculated shocks aimed at the audience.

and with a disregard for critical favor. George Romero's flesh-eating (but organ meat–preferring) zombies in *Night of the Living Dead* (1968) revived the long-dormant zombie theme in horror. Tobe Hooper's *The Texas Chainsaw Massacre* (1974) depicts a family of cannibals preying on a group of young teens and brilliantly evokes psychologically punishing tension and fear. Another cannibal holocaust occurrs in Wes Craven's *The Hills Have Eyes* (1977), and a traveling band of serial killers kidnap, rape, and kill two young women in Craven's *The Last House on the Left* (1972). The crude filmmaking technique on display in these movies works to their advantage by enhancing a sense of realism. They are less glossy and far more amateurish than the big-budget studio productions, and their violence and grim, almost nihilistic outlook has exerted a huge influence on the genre.

Violence-based horror entered the mainstream when John Carpenter's *Halloween* (1978) became a huge box-office hit. Made on a low budget as a film buff's homage to *Psycho*, it spawned the era of "slasher movies" dominated by stalk-and-kill scenarios in which teenagers fall victim to hulking, merciless killers. Film series based on *Friday the 13th* (1980, with more than ten sequels) and *A Nightmare on Elm Street* (1984, with nearly ten sequels and a television series) influenced numerous stalk-and-slash imitators, such as *Terror Train* (1980), *Prom Night* (1980), and *My Bloody Valentine* (1981). The unending violence in the films sparked a critical backlash akin to the 1930s response to Universal's classic monsters. Critics charged that the films are exercises in unrestrained sadism and promoted a puritanical view in which sexuality was violently punished.

Eventually, the proliferation and repetition of the slasher formula made it ripe for parody, which Wes Craven supplies in *Scream* (1996) and Keenen Ivory Wayans follows up on in *Scary Movie* (2000), both of which poke self-conscious fun at the formulas. The teen victims in these movies have grown up watching slasher films and know all the rules and conventions, though this doesn't prevent the killers from working their mischief. The innovative and assaultive techniques of *Night of the Living Dead*, *Halloween*, *The Last House on the Left*, and *The Texas Chainsaw Massacre* had reached a dead end in the uninspired knock-offs that *Scream* and *Scary Movie* lampoon. But even as this wave of exploitation filmmaking crested and then broke, visionary work continued to occur in the genre. A rejection of lurid violence and a return to the psychological style of Val Lewton typify *The Blair Witch Project* (1999), *The Sixth Sense* (1999), and *The Others* (2001), which generate tension and fear from things that remain hidden, ambiguous, suggested, and not revealed before the glare of the camera. Audiences responded enthusiastically to this older style, and each of these films was a significant critical and box-office success.

But like Freddy Krueger and Jason, ultraviolent horror has kept coming back, recently in the so-called "torture porn" films—*Saw* (2004, with six sequels thus far) and *Hostel* (2005, with two sequels)—and in a sustained effort to reboot the classics of the 1970s. This effort stemmed from the film industry's recognition that these movies had been followed by too many increasingly bad sequels and that the originals retain a primal power that might be evoked again in remakes that bring a fresh approach. Thus far, the reboots include *The Texas Chainsaw Massacre* (2003), *Night of the Living Dead 3D* (2006), *Halloween* (2007), *The Last House on the Left* (2009), *Friday the 13th* (2009), *My Bloody Valentine* (2009), and *A Nightmare on Elm Street* (2010). Audiences have been receptive to these remakes, most of which performed well commercially.

Measured by the number of productions and the dedication of its fan base, horror remains among the most robust of American film genres, yet it also remains a genre in which few major filmmakers work for long.

A Steven Spielberg might visit by directing *Jaws* (1975) or producing *Poltergeist* (1982), a Kubrick might drop in to make a single picture, but most of the genre's key filmmakers do not graduate to A-list pictures. The relative inability of horror filmmakers to develop careers outside the genre points to a ghettoization of horror that other genres do not experience. And yet, because of the unending anxieties we have about our world, horror remains a vital part of contemporary popular culture and one that, conceivably, will never diminish.

Themes, Typologies, and Theories

Horror tends to be a permeable genre, its boundaries more porous and flexible than those of the gangster film, the war film, or the Western. It bonds readily with other genres; many horror films are hybrids, combining one or more genres. A very large number of horror films, for example, are comedies. *The Ghost Breaker* (1922) and *The Cat and the Canary* (1927) are early examples of horror-comedy hybrids. More recent examples include *Young Frankenstein* (1974), *Love at First Bite* (1979), *Motel Hell* (1980), *The Evil Dead* (1981), *An American Werewolf in London* (1981), *The Howling* (1981), *Gremlins* (1984), *Fright Night* (1985), *Arachnophobia* (1990), *Tremors* (1990), and *Shaun of the Dead* (2004).

Laughter has always been part of the audience response to horror movies. Like comedies, horror films aim to produce a physical reaction in their viewers. Typically, this reaction is one of anxiety, fear, or revulsion, but frequently it includes laughter. After a good jolt or shock, viewers often laugh to release tension; alternatively, laughter may be symptomatic of mounting tension. It may also signal disbelief if viewers refuse to go along with the shock effect a movie intends to deliver. William Paul's book *Laughing Screaming* explores the connection in horror between these responses, which are not as far apart as they might seem initially.

Horror has also bonded quite extensively with science fiction. Movies such as *Alien* (1979) and *The Thing* (1951, 1982) can be classified in either genre. The setting of *Alien* is futuristic, and both movies involve visitors from outer space. But at heart they are monsters-on-the-loose stories, with the monster threatening a small, isolated group of people. *Predator* (1987) is another example of a sci-fi monster movie, and by this logic one could include the huge run of sci-fi pictures from the 1950s

***Predator* (1987)** Horror is a protean genre, that is, it bonds readily with elements from other genres. *Predator* (with Arnold Schwarzenegger), for example, is a monster-on-the-loose story, which is one of horror's classic narrative types. But the story blends horror with elements of science fiction and the war film. While battling guerrilla soldiers in a Central American jungle, a unit of American commandos is attacked by an alien being that has traveled to Earth from another world. The film emphasizes terror and shock, but the sci-fi premise and the combat action make the film a generic hybrid.

that featured giant beasts unleashed by radiation [*The Beast from 20,000 Fathoms* (1953), *Them!* (1954), *Godzilla* (1954)].

Even musicals may bond with the horror genre. *The Little Shop of Horrors* (1986) is a musical comedy about a man-eating plant. *Sweeney Todd* (2007) portrays cannibalism, *Rockula* (1990) is a vampire musical, and *The Rocky Horror Picture Show* (1975) offers singing, cross-dressing monster makers. Even Westerns might be horror films. *Curse of the Undead* (1959) portrays a vampire stalking the Old West who is killed in a gunfight by a straight-shooting preacher. The titles of *Billy the Kid vs. Dracula* (1965) and *Jesse James Meets Frankenstein's Daughter* (1966) tell all.

The genre, then, is protean, capable (like a vampire) of assuming different forms and shapes. Across this variation, however, horror has been responsive to major social and political events and issues. Indeed, commentators on the genre often view it as a kind of social safety valve, operating to release collective tensions by projecting these onto a monster whose configuration resonates with the anxieties that are prevalent in a given period. As an art movement and a style, Expressionism flourished in Germany in response to the slaughter of World War I, and horror films in the 1920s and 1930s implicitly addressed the war's carnage. The stitched-together body of Frankenstein's monster and the mutilated faces and limbs of the monsters in other films, such as *Island of Lost Souls*, evoke the landscape of postwar Europe in which large numbers of disfigured veterans were a common sight. Many of the cinematographers, composers, screenwriters, and production designers who worked on these films were émigrés from Europe.

A decade later, human beings were again smashed and blown apart, this time by World War II. While Hollywood newsreels did not show this carnage, the horror film did picture it in the physical mutilations appearing in Universal's huge run of Frankenstein sequels. Moreover, the Wolf Man, that era's great addition to the gallery of horror icons, was responsive to the Nazi fascination with wolf imagery and werewolf arcana. Curt Siodmak, screenwriter of *The Wolf Man*, left Germany when the Nazis took power, and he intended *The Wolf Man* to be an allegory of this period, with the pentagram that identifies a werewolf's victim being reminiscent of the Jewish Star of David, which the Nazis used to identify Jews and persecute them.

The turn toward graphic violence in the modern horror film was partly instigated by the Vietnam War. Effects artist Tom Savini helped pioneer the use of foam latex and prosthetics to simulate dismembered limbs and skin that could be gouged and torn off on camera. Savini had been a combat cameraman in Vietnam, and he transposed what he had seen on the battlefield into the fantasy scenes in horror movies.

In addition to the traumas induced by war, horror films are responsive to collective fears about sexuality. *The Thing* (1982), *The Fly* (1986), and *Bram Stoker's Dracula* (1992), are parables about AIDS, for example. Monster movies have offered coded depictions of homosexuality and reflected shifts in society's views on that subject. Horror films about demonic children, such as *The Exorcist* and *The Omen*, point toward sociological conflicts involving gender roles and the family unit that intensified during the 1970s as the women's movement began to gain momentum. Recently, the so-called torture porn movies—*Saw, Hostel*, and their sequels—are widely regarded as responses to the prisoner abuse carried out at Abu Ghraib prison in Iraq and the detention camp at Bagram Air Base in Afghanistan. The zombie movies *28 Days Later* (2002) and *Homecoming* (2005) include explicit references to the Iraq War.

Scholars and critics tend to agree that horror films can offer a symbolic transformation of social anxieties and issues, but what of the genre's underlying structural features, those that transcend the formulations of particular eras? Across the genre's tremendous variation, what are its underlying and unifying characteristics? Film scholar Robin Wood has proposed the most elegant and productive formulation of the genre's structural unity. According to Wood, a horror film is defined by a situation in which normality is threatened by a monster. This is a simple and powerful formulation. Note that the terms "normality" and "monster" may be given various definitions; indeed, the genre's richness lies in the multitude of ways that films have responded to these concepts. Hollywood's horror films of the 1930s, for example, often defined normality in terms of the heterosexual couple, married or engaged, who are endangered by monsters and mad scientists. At the end of these films, the couple prevails, the monster is destroyed, and normality is safeguarded from further threat. Of course, this could be a relatively rigid formula, and numerous films work interesting variations on it. Larry Talbot in *The Wolf Man* is a haunting character because he is a tragic victim. He becomes a werewolf through no fault of his own, and the curse destroys him. As the film begins, Larry personifies normality. As he is destroyed, normality is destroyed.

Normality in this period is often depicted in rather pale terms, and the monsters and madmen are often more interesting characters than the hero and heroine. In *Island of Lost Souls*, Edward Parker (Richard Arlen), the hero, is stranded on a remote island and is attracted to the mysterious Lota (Kathleen Burke), a beautiful woman who turns out to have been created from a panther by the mad Dr. Moreau (Charles Laughton). When he finds out who and what Lota is, our hero is naturally horrified, although this is a conventional and therefore somewhat uninteresting reaction. In contrast, it is the tragic Lota and the insanely transgressive Moreau who linger as the film's vivid characters.

Many horror films personify normality in terms of the family and then go on to question the integrity of the institution or to show its destruction. In *Parents* (1989), the suburban married couple turn out to be cannibals. *The Hills Have Eyes* and *The Texas Chainsaw Massacre* present grotesque versions of the family in clans of cannibal killers, negative inversions of bourgeois family values. *The Exorcist* shows the breakdown of domestic order when an adolescent girl suffers a satanic possession. The psychotic serial killer in *The Stepfather* (1987) desires to have the perfect family. He marries a succession of single mothers and kills them along with their children when they inevitably fail to measure up to his impossible ideals of true family life. And children in numerous horror films are monstrous offspring, whose debauched existence offers a critique of family values. Damien, the son of Satan in *The Omen*, succeeds in killing his parents when he is still a child. The adolescent Regan in *The Exorcist* spews profanity, urinates in public, masturbates with a crucifix, and kills several people. Even a child's doll can be lethal and malevolent, such as the Chucky character in *Child's Play* (1988) and its sequels.

Horror films tend to identify "normality" in terms of heterosexuality, monogamy, marriage, family, and children, but the genre's films construe these in divergent ways. They may be accepted uncritically as givens, but they may also be subverted, criticized, or attacked. Monsters too are treated in flexible and divergent ways. They may be vampires, werewolves, giant beasts, or other types of nonhuman beings, but they may also be simply and disturbingly human. Henry in *Henry: Portrait of a Serial Killer* (1986) and Hannibal Lecter in *The Silence of the Lambs* have no special

***The Silence of the Lambs* (1991)** One of the most unnerving lessons of modern horror is that ordinary people may be the source of unspeakable horror. Monsters need not be vampires or supernatural beings; they can be all around us, indistinguishable from a next-door neighbor. Hannibal Lecter (Anthony Hopkins) is cultivated, intelligent, charming, polite, funny, and sophisticated. He also takes great pleasure killing and eating other people. The bleakness at the heart of modern horror films lies in their suggestion that this kind of monster cannot be recognized or defended against.

powers. They are merely remorseless killers who enjoy being predators, and the portrait of horror offered by their films invites viewers to contemplate the oneness of monstrosity and human being. At the end of *Henry*, Henry kills the one person in the film with whom he has formed a fragile emotional connection. He remorselessly chops her up and leaves her body in a suitcase by the roadside, then moves on to a new town and another set of victims. The ending is bleak and desolate and leaves no positive, affirmative values intact. (In this respect, it is more uncompromising than *The Silence of the Lambs*, in which the institutional authority of the FBI offers a heroic set of values to counter Lecter's depraved example.)

Modern horror films, like *Henry: Portrait of a Serial Killer*, are more aggressive in their assault on the sensibilities of the audience than was horror in earlier decades (until that point where Hitchcock brutally dispatched the heroine of *Psycho* in the shower). In the silent era and during the early sound period, viewers knew that the monster would be definitively destroyed at film's end. Dracula would be staked, Frankenstein's monster burned or dropped into a sulphur pit, the Wolf Man clubbed with a silver knobbed cane or shot with a silver bullet. But in contemporary horror films monsters are not so easily destroyed. *The Silence of the Lambs* ends with Hannibal Lecter on the loose. John Carpenter's *Halloween* spins a shrewd morality tale about evil coming to a bucolic small town. But the town turns out to be devoid of sustaining values or relationships; it is a ghost town with no one on the streets, and this void spawns and attracts the evil personified in the character of serial killer Michael Myers. He cannot be killed or stopped. After being stabbed, choked, and shot numerous times, he continues to rise and seek victims, a true bogeyman. Carpenter ends the film with the sound of Michael's breathing filling the town, an audio overlay accompanying shots of key locations in the story. This evil now infests the town; it cannot be eradicated. In its closing moments, *Halloween* establishes the paradigm for modern horror—the monsters are everywhere, and they cannot be destroyed. In *The Devil's Rejects* (2005), a sadistic killer taunts his victims before their death. They pray and cry out to God for help; the psychopath listens to their entreaties, amused, and then kills them anyway. This bleak vision of ultimate annihilation is very typical of the modern horror film and offers a striking contrast to the more comforting formulas that operated in earlier decades.

Wood's formula mentions a monster, but must all horror films have a monster? Vampires or werewolves are clearly monsters, but is Hannibal

Don't Look Now (1974) Many horror films evoke the uncanny, a sense of strangeness and dread, an overwhelming feeling that all is not right and that something terrible is about to occur. John Baxter (Donald Sutherland) is in Italy helping restore the artwork in a church when he begins to have strange visions, unaware that they are premonitions of his own impending, violent death. When he realizes their meaning, it is too late.

Lecter a monster? When we describe him as such, we actually are speaking metaphorically to say that his behavior is like that of a monster's. This is very different from claiming that he is a vampire or can turn into a wolf. What about a film like *The Sixth Sense*, about a decent man, Malcolm Crowe (Bruce Willis), who is dead but does not know it? He tries to communicate with his wife, but she seems not to know that he is in the room. Only at the end of the film does he understand the reason for her perplexing behavior, namely, that he has crossed over from life to a twilight realm in which his consciousness lingers on after death. Or *Don't Look Now* (1973), in which another decent man, John Baxter (Donald Sutherland), has recurring visions of his own violent death but does not realize what they are until it is too late to avoid his fate? These are films of the uncanny, not of monstrosity. "Uncanny" is a term that designates things and experiences that are mysterious, strange, and disorienting in ways that provoke dread, a sense that something terrible is about to happen. *The Others* is an upside-down ghost story in which a widow, Grace Stewart (Nicole Kidman), lives in a country house with her two children. Bizarre, unexplained things happen that suggest the house is haunted, and Grace experiences a terrible dread that something bad will occur and struggles to protect her children. It turns out that Grace and her children are the ghosts, and the noises they've been hearing are from the flesh-and-blood occupants of the house. The story is upside-down because the spirits don't know what they are and confuse their realm with that of the living.

The Sixth Sense, Don't Look Now, and The Others are films about the uncanny that work by providing psychological suspense rather than dwelling on graphic violence. Does the fact that these movies lack monsters mean that they are not horror films? A comprehensive and flexible definition of the genre ought to include them, and therefore we should expand Wood's notion to incorporate categories of the uncanny and supernatural and of psychopathy, alongside monsters, as essential ingredients, provided in each case that a film's aim is to evoke in the viewer sensations of anxiety, fear, and/or revulsion. The genre employs monsters, the supernatural, and madness as mechanisms for the evocation of these states of mind. Monsters, then, are important in the genre, but many horror films do not have them.

What do these horror formats—monstrosity, the uncanny and supernatural, psychopathy—have in common? Their evocation of anxiety, fear, and revulsion is based on violating the logic by which reality is organized according to cultural and social systems of meaning. Horror films specialize in portraying such violations. Cultures and societies impose meaning upon existence, in part, by creating sets of basic distinctions: male and female, living and dead, edible and inedible, human and animal, self and other. These distinctions are extremely important for members of a social group, and all societies maintain laws and taboos that enforce the logic of the distinctions. Brother and sister may not marry. Human flesh is not to be eaten. Animal flesh is to be cooked before being eaten. The supernatural experiences, the monsters, and the madmen (and women) in horror movies provoke fear and revulsion because they fail to conform to these categorical distinctions. Vampires are neither living nor dead but are undead. Werewolves transgress the social and biological separation between human and animal. Ghosts and other supernatural manifestations suggest that life reaches other conclusions beyond death or religious resurrection. Graphic imagery of dismemberment and other grievous wounds challenges belief in the integrity of the body as the repository of personhood and mind. If the body can be so easily and disgustingly destroyed, then so too can the self.

By challenging the logic of these cultural systems of meaning, horror films provoke the experience that we call "horror," resulting from the introduction of disorder and a perverse counterlogic into our perceptions of an ordered universe. Cultural anthropologist Margaret Mead suggested that human beings were deeply uncertain about what separated them from the animal world and feared that people couldn't be expected to remain reliably human, that is, to behave always as human beings. Thus, she said, cultures guarded their sense of humanity with rituals and taboos that were designed to shore up a collective sense of self by enforcing a conceptual order on the world.

Horror films speak to this fundamental uncertainty about the nature of being human. They respond to the existential question—what is required to remain human?—by presenting the issue in its negative form, that is, by showing the loss of humanness. The genre's story situations show grave threats to human identity. People become undead. They change into predatory animals, become cannibals, pass beyond life into a haunted realm where they know no peace, have their bodies mangled and mutilated in horrific ways, become impregnated by demons or other life forms, or lose all that they cherish in unspeakable ways. The ritual nature of these films, the repetitive visiting and revisiting of these traumas by an audience and upon an audience, suggests that these are core anxieties felt at the root of human existence. Thus the genre keeps returning to the same primal question—what is required to remain human?—by showing how easily humanity may be lost. In horror movies, the zombies, psychopaths, or ghosts are always on the verge of overtaking the embattled characters whom they threaten. Apocalypse at the individual or collective level is always threatened in a horror film. And audiences never tire of being reminded that their world and their sense of self is a fragile thing and easily imperiled. The genre thus remains a lively one, continuously speaking to the changing landscapes of our present nightmares.

Iconography

More than any other genre, horror films involve threats that lurk just out of sight. Accordingly, offscreen space is tremendously important, and the horror genre employs shot compositions that convey to viewers the sense that something bad or evil or sinister is present just beyond the

The Others (2001) The unseen and the unknown furnish powerful sources of horror because they invite viewers to supply the imagery that is missing on-screen. By exploiting offscreen space, a filmmaker can infuse the scene with dread and a sense of foreboding. A viewer knows that something awful lurks just beyond the frame, where the camera is not looking. In this film, Nicole Kidman plays a woman plagued with fears that her house is haunted. Ghostly noises infest the space of this deserted room, surrounding Kidman with unseen menace.

borders of the frame. Offscreen space enforces a distinction between the seen and the unseen, and horror film compositions play on this distinction to create anxiety and dread. Characters in the scene may or may not suspect the danger, but viewers are made to feel it. Monsters lurk there. Moreover, horror-movie characters often show really bad judgment, continually going down into dark basements or up into shadowy attics, rummaging in crypts or burial chambers, or rushing into a dark forest or moor despite clear signs that vampires, savage animals, zombies, or serial killers are on the loose. Shadows, darkness, unseen but palpable threats—these acquire visual force by aggressive and clever uses of offscreen space. When a horror-movie character, for example, rushes down creaky stairs into that dark basement from which mysterious noises have been coming, the shots will often tightly frame the character. This restricts the viewer's ability to see the surroundings, accentuating the sense of offscreen danger.

While the compositional use of offscreen space is prevalent throughout the genre, horror films are not as tied to a specific type of setting as are war films, Westerns, gangster movies, and film noir. This enables genre iconography to range widely and to be a function of recurring story situations. Thus, the many "mad scientist" movies—*Murders in the Rue Morgue, The Fly, Saw,* and the many versions of the Frankenstein story—emphasize laboratories and other types of lair where the crazed genius dwells and plots mischief. The set designed by art director Charles D. Hall for the 1931 version of *Frankenstein* became the most influential such space, replete with oversize machinery, spinning dials, blinking lamps, and arcing electrical current. Buffalo Bill's basement hideaway in *The Silence of the Lambs,* where he imprisons and torments his captives, and Jigsaw's similar dungeon in *Saw* are stylistic descendants of Hall's *Frankenstein* set. These sinister, isolated rooms create a special space in the films' narratives where horror dwells, split off from the banal world of ordinary reality.

Cemeteries, crypts, and burial grounds flourish in horror films because they contain the lurking dead who frequently return to harass the living. *Night of the Living Dead* opens in a cemetery where the undead burst forth from their graves. Dracula and other vampires haunt cemeteries and sleep in their coffins. *Frankenstein* (1931) opens in a graveyard as a funeral concludes and Dr. Frankenstein (Colin Clive) waits with his assistant to plunder the freshly buried corpse. An Indian burial ground in *Poltergeist,* atop which sits a suburban housing development, spews spirits to haunt and afflict the hapless family that is its principal target. The terrors of premature burial dominate *Isle of the Dead* and *The Vanishing* (1988 and 1993). In the latter film, a clever serial killer specializes in drugging and then burying his victims alive. Graves are a threshold place, marking a boundary between the living and the dead, and horror films emphasize them as tokens for creating terror, for upsetting viewers' metaphysical sense of the world. The shocker at the end of *Carrie* (1976) is the image of a hand suddenly springing forth from beneath the earth of a freshly dug grave.

Probably the most famous and indelible setting for a horror film is an old dark house, often of vast proportions, that holds signs of evil or portents of dread, frequently involving something terrible that has happened in the past. The prevalence of forbidding, sinister houses in horror films derives from the genre's gothic roots. Such buildings appeared throughout gothic fiction and can be found in such novels as *The Castle of Otranto* (1764), *The House of the Seven Gables* (1851), and *The Turn of the Screw.* In *Psycho,* Alfred Hitchcock pointed to this tradition by setting the Bates Motel, where the film's serial killer preys on his victims, next to a gothic house perched on a hill.

In cinema, old dark houses furnish splendid locations for stories about ghosts and the supernatural. If they are large and cavernous and have many rooms and wings, they afford numerous opportunities for ghosts to lurk and plot their mischief. In *The Changeling* (1980), for example, a grieving music professor (George C. Scott), whose wife and child have been killed in a car accident, moves to New England, where he rents a huge abandoned residence. He hears strange noises and, following them to their source, discovers a boarded-up doorway that leads to an old decrepit bedroom in an upstairs wing of the house he didn't know existed. It's a child's bedroom, and it proves to be the source of the ghostly emanations that torment him and prevent the house from being at rest. Many decades ago, a child was murdered in this room,

***The Changeling* (1980)** Old dark houses are a frequent image in horror movies because, being vast and ancient, they harbor secrets, crimes, and spirits. Stories about haunted houses are among the genre's most traditional and effective types. Fleeing tragedy, John Russell (George C. Scott) rents an abandoned historical house and comes to realize that something else lives there. In this scene, the spirit has just bumped him with an unmistakable message.

and his spirit is reaching out through the house to make contact with the professor.

The site of a haunting need not be a residence. It can include hotels [*The Shining, 1408* (2007)], apartment buildings (*Rosemary's Baby*), and orphanages [*The Orphanage* (2007)], provided that the structure is remote or vast and baroque and contains plenty of hiding places for ghosts or other lurking presences. *The Shining* is about the power that an old, massive hotel, the Overlook, exerts on the unbalanced mind of its caretaker, Jack Torrance (Jack Nicholson). Progressively unhinged by the sinister energies of the Overlook, Torrance becomes a menace to his wife and child, eventually devolving into lunacy and delirium. The large range of films with action focusing on a haunted or otherwise sinister structure includes *The Old Dark House* (1932), *The Uninvited* (1944, 1993), *The House on Haunted Hill* (1959, 1999), *The Haunting* (1963, 1999), *Legend of Hell House* (1973), *The Lady in White* (1988), *Stir of Echoes* (1999), *Poltergeist*, and *The Others*.

Old dark houses are not the only legacy of the gothic tradition to be found in the genre. A predilection for foreign or exotic locations is prevalent in horror. Many of the classic Universal films were set overseas—*Dracula* in Transylvania, *Frankenstein* in Bavaria, *The Mummy* in Egypt, *The Wolf Man* in Wales. In *The Black Cat* (1934), a couple honeymooning in Austria seek shelter from a storm in a mansion built by an insane architect and devil worshipper (Boris Karloff) atop the site of a World War I–era massacre. The back alleys of Paris furnish the setting for *Murders in the Rue Morgue*, where a deranged scientist, Dr. Mirakle (Bela Lugosi), prowls for victims to use in painful and illegal laboratory experiments. At times, the foreign locales are wholly imaginary. *Frankenstein Meets the Wolf Man* takes place in the fanciful European domain of Visaria.

It wasn't only the Universal productions that located horror in distant and exotic locales. Val Lewton's *Isle of the Dead* takes place on a remote island during the Second Balkan War (1913) between Greece and Turkey. Full of plague, the island has been quarantined. Unable to leave, its inhabitants succumb to madness and superstition. The island of St. Sebastian in the West Indies is the site of a voodoo curse in *I Walked with a Zombie*. Mysterious, uncharted islands regularly harbor monsters or diabolical experiments aimed at turning animals into humans or madmen who hunt humans for sport, as in *King Kong*, *Island of Lost Souls*, and *The Most Dangerous Game*.

Throughout this period, the most iconic of the genre's stars conveyed a sense of the foreign in their names and vocal inflections—Boris Karloff, Bela Lugosi, Peter Lorre. Perhaps it was due to a provincialism in American culture that horror seemed synonymous with foreign lands, and such a convention may have created a distancing effect for viewers that offered comfort. Horror was always "over there" rather than close to home. If one wants to avoid vampires, don't travel to Transylvania—it's that easy. If you don't go, they won't get at you. At the same time, however, the foreign settings might also convey for viewers an estrangement and disorientation that accentuated experiences of anxiety and dread. Foreignness in the horror film held these contrary effects. On the one hand, it suggested that monsters wouldn't turn up in one's own house or hometown. On the other, the setting worked to heighten the traveler's indelible sense of vulnerability. This latter effect perhaps explains why the use of distant locales as a setting for horror has continued in today's films. *Hostel* presents a group of mostly American tourists traveling through Slovakia, where they fall prey to a ring of torturers. The city of Bratislava seems quaint and harmless, and the local hostel where they stay seems innocuous. But appearances are deceiving, and the tourists are captured, imprisoned, and subjected to lengthy, painful deaths. In the sequel (2007), the victims are women unfortunate enough to visit the same place that houses a torture industry catering to wealthy international bidders. These desire nothing so much as the privilege of torturing a victim to death. Both films augment the terror by focusing on travelers in an unfamiliar culture who lack the support of family and friends when they get into trouble. *The Ruins* (2008) depicts two vacationing American couples who run afoul of man-eating plants when they visit Mayan ruins in a remote Mexican location. *Turistas* (2006) places American tourists traveling in Brazil in harm's way when they encounter a sinister doctor who wants to harvest their internal organs. *Anaconda* (1997) showcases the predatory powers of a giant snake attacking small boats of travelers in the Amazon. In each case, the foreign locale functions in the manner of an old dark house. It holds lurking horrors that the characters are slow to recognize and that shatter their comfortable sense of reality.

One of Hitchcock's great achievements in *Psycho* is his shifting of the terrain of horror from the foreign and distant to the familiar and banal. Thus, while the tradition of foreign horror has continued, horror has also accommodated, since *Psycho*, the near-at-hand. Hitchcock's brilliant strategy involved placing the irrational inside the everyday by taking a bathroom and presenting it as a killing ground. The motel bathroom where Marion Crane (Janet Leigh) meets her end is far removed from the genre's old dark houses where one expects bad things to occur. The entire point of the Hitchcock scene is that Marion is relaxed, alone, enjoying a private moment, secure in her sense of safety. The killing violates all of that, along with the audience's sense of belief in these things. It is, therefore, a double violation, of the character and of the audience. And Hitchcock goes further still by refusing to provide an explanation for the madness of Norman Bates (Tony Perkins), the killer. In the last sequence, a psychiatrist (Simon Oakland) summarizes Norman's history and suggests that Norman went insane after killing his mother, that Norman coped with his guilt by splitting his personality to accommodate the mother as a part of his own mind. The explanation is there for those who want it, but Hitchcock ends the film with a close-up of Norman's grinning face superimposed on the skull of his dead mother. In doing so, Hitchcock suggests that madness resists explanation, that irrationality is its essence, and that it can be observed but not accounted for. This is truly a terrifying philosophy, and it led in the modern horror film to all of the monsters and psychopaths who are indestructible and unstoppable, and indistinguishable from ordinary people.

Post-*Psycho*, horror can be found anywhere and everywhere: a roadside motel (*The Devil's Rejects*); the church frequented by a handsome bachelor (*The Stepfather*); a drive-in movie theater where an all-American boy turned multiple murderer sets up his rifle and begins to shoot the patrons [*Targets* (1968)]—even the yard where a beloved family pet has turned killer [*Cujo* (1983)]. Numerous safe zones prevailed in earlier decades of horror, provided one remembered not to travel by the full moon or to visit Castle Dracula. There are no safe zones in today's horror films. A suburban kitchen and an ordinary family breakfast can turn to sudden horror, as in *The Believers* (1987); the home where a kindly woman takes the victim of a traffic accident can become a prison presided over by a lunatic, as in *Misery* (1990).

Imagery redolent of sexuality figures strongly in horror films because sex is one of the primal forces in life, and throughout history it has aroused cultural anxieties and phobias. One of the supreme, recurring images in horror is of a woman being abducted by a monster, and scholars of the genre tend to view the monster in such situations as the projection of a culturally repressed or otherwise distorted sexuality. Countless horror movies threaten females with kidnapping and ravishment by monsters and climax with imagery of them being carried off to fates that include death but often threaten to be worse than that. *The Cabinet of Dr. Caligari* climaxes with Cesare, the serial killer, carrying the heroine across the rooftops with angry villagers in pursuit. A rampaging gorilla in *Murders in the Rue Morgue* does likewise, and *King Kong* takes this premise to mythic heights as the ape scales the Empire State Building carrying a shrieking Fay Wray (1933) or Naomi Watts (2005). Genetically spliced with a housefly and now turning into a giant, mutated version of one in *The Fly*, Seth Brundle (Jeff Goldblum) bursts into his girlfriend's apartment and bears her off. The climax of *Jeepers Creepers* (2001) features the demonic monster bursting into a police station and carrying off the heroine (Gina Phillips) to cannibalize her.

These narrative situations in which a helpless, screaming woman is abducted by the monster did not survive the 1970s women's movement with their logic intact. Instead, during the 1980s the slasher film introduced an alternative narrative development but one still centered on anxiety about sexuality. Slasher movies depict hulking killers eliminating in cleverly gruesome ways clusters of nubile and sexually active teenagers. As Carol Clover has pointed out, one of the conventions of such films is the "final girl," the lone survivor of the massacre who proves to be the most resourceful woman in the bunch. She often escapes from the killer or turns the tables and finishes him off (at least until the next sequel). More generally, the final girl can be seen as a quasi-feminist inflection of the retrograde gender politics of earlier horror movies in which the monster's most abject threat is always understood to be directed at the film's heroine. In *Alien* and *Aliens* (1986), the triumphant last woman attains the proportions of an Amazonian warrior as she combats the monster with brainpower as well as brawn. *The Descent* (2005) works a variation on the final-girl formula. A group of women spelunkers is set upon in the bowels of an uncharted series of caves by monsters that dwell there, and the most resourceful, Sarah (Shauna Macdonald), manages to escape and return to safety aboveground—or so she thinks. In the film's final seconds, the escape is revealed to be a hallucination. She is still belowground, encircled by the ravening creatures that are about to close in.

The anxieties about sexuality that are rampant in horror films are linked to a more general set of social fears and taboos that center on the

The Descent (2005) Sarah (Shauna Macdonald) is the sole survivor among a group of friends that has been attacked by monsters dwelling below ground in uncharted caves. She is the most humane and resourceful member of the group, and according to horror-movie conventions she ought to live through the experience as the final girl. But the film's bleak closing moments reveal that she has hallucinated her escape, that she is still in the caves, and that the creatures are closing in on her. As released to theaters in North America, however, these last moments were cut to produce a more upbeat ending, and a sequel was released in 2009 in which Sarah is still alive. Although horror is the most transgressive of all film genres, it still faces marketing pressure to moderate its impact.

body, particularly its effluvia—blood, semen, pus—and the spectacle of the body in torment, broken, with its internal matter spilling out. Contemporary horror films emphasize these areas of focus, in part, because the special-effects advances that latex and prosthetics achieved in the 1980s and that the digital revolution took to a new level a decade later have enabled filmmakers to simulate body violence in convincing ways. Of course, censorship had posed an ongoing problem for the Hollywood studios and particularly for earlier horror films. Many states and cities operated censor boards that demanded cuts before giving a film clearance to be exhibited in local theaters. Because of their often gruesome content, horror movies, more than any other genre, drew the attention of the censors. But, by the end of the sixties, censorship was over; the U.S. courts had found the censor boards to be unconstitutional. The fall of censorship freed horror movies from the restrictions faced by filmmakers working under the old studio system.

As a result, since then, the genre portrayed virtually every conceivable physical trauma, has pictured bodies coming apart and being sundered in hundreds of ways, and has concentrated attention on the primal forces of sexuality, birth, and death. The visualization of birth trauma, for example, is a central focus in *Alien* and its sequels, as the baby monsters gestate in their human hosts and then violently burst forth from their chests. Sexual trauma is central to *Rosemary's Baby*, as Rosemary (Mia Farrow) is impregnated by the devil, and it is arguably one of the primal fears that animate the zombie movies, in which a single bite from a slavering zombie is sufficient to turn the victim into one. The cancerous decay induced by physical disease is a prime focus in *The Fly*, and physical collapse and erosion after death are abundantly illustrated in zombie movies.

There is no end of horror in the world. The terrorist attacks of September 11, 2001, displayed it on a collective, international scale, and in this most porous of genres, the various documentaries about 9/11—or about the Holocaust—share many affinities with horror films and arguably could even be characterized as a part of the genre, with the important qualification that they are not fictional. For at its core, horror portrays the cruelties and brutalities that arise from living as a finite being in the world and from being subject to the predatory impulses of fellow beings. This focus makes it coextensive with the world today and most certainly with the world as it always was. As long as passengers on an airplane glance nervously at fellow passengers to see if they are lighting a bomb fuse in their shoe, or people fear the onset of a new viral plague, act of bioterrorism, or cancer diagnosis, the horror genre will speak to its audiences in urgent, alarmist, and perhaps even in cathartic tones. Monsters are undying. *The Wolfman* is born again in a 2010 remake starring Benicio Del Toro. As long as there is cinema, the dark genre and its secrets will claim our attention.

CLOSE-UP

Visual Space in the Horror Film

The design of compositional space onscreen is strongly coded in the horror genre. Filmmakers use shot composition to evoke the viewer's sense of fear and revulsion. Strategies for framing a scene's action often emphasize methods for eliciting feelings of suspense, anxiety, and dread in viewers. While composition is not the only means of attaining such an end in the genre, the way that a scene's action is framed is especially important in horror because it offers filmmakers very effective ways of scaring viewers.

Composition is a filmmaker's way of designing visual space, the area visible onscreen bordered by the edges of the frame. In horror films, visual space often contains something that is threatening—a monster, a ghost, a killer—whose exact whereabouts may be unknown to characters in a scene but who is presumed to be nearby. Visual space in the genre, therefore, furnishes a zone of danger and threat that clever filmmakers find ways to exploit.

John Carpenter's *Halloween* portrays a deranged killer named Michael Myers, who returns to his hometown on Halloween and proceeds to stalk a group of teenagers and kill them one by one. The story focuses mainly on Laurie Strode (Jamie Lee Curtis), and Michael remains a lurking presence for much of the film, except for moments where he appears suddenly to threaten Laurie or one of her friends.

Carpenter's camera is in continuous motion, circling and following the characters in ways that replicate the type of stalking behavior that Michael engages in. As such, the moving camera elicits a subtle unease in viewers. In the film's first scene, Carpenter has identified the moving camera with the killer's point of view. In an extended subjective shot,

Halloween (1978) The killer, Michael Myers, stalks Laurie (Jamie Lee Curtis) and her friends, drawing ever closer to them. In many scenes, his presence is known to viewers but not to the other characters. Here, as Laurie walks away from the camera, Michael lurches into view in the foreground of the shot. Carpenter holds the composition, creating an increasing tension the longer Michael hovers in the frame unseen by Laurie.

the camera assumes Michael's perspective as he stalks and then murders his sister. Although there are no more point-of-view shots beyond this scene from the killer's perspective, camera movement and composition in subsequent scenes suggest Michael's presence. During many scenes, for example, where Laurie or her friends walk around outside, the prowling camera and wide-screen framing create a pronounced sense of threat. Viewers feel that Michael may appear at any moment inside the frame.

In an early scene showing Laurie and a young boy walking to school, Laurie stops at the old, abandoned Myers house to drop off a key that her father, a Realtor, needs to show it to prospective buyers. As Laurie walks up the sidewalk to the front porch, the shot composition places the camera inside the house, looking out at Laurie through the curtained front-door window. It is an anticipatory framing, because Carpenter then cuts back outside to show another view of Laurie approaching the house. Then the interior framing is repeated, this time with the shadowy presence of Michael next to the window, watching Laurie.

The scene's action then shifts back outside as Laurie says good-bye to the boy and walks away from the camera, down the sidewalk, into the background of the frame. Carpenter holds the shot, however, and after a pause, Michael looms into the edge of the wide-screen frame, his back to the camera and in the immediate foreground. Only the edge of his shoulder and neck are visible; he stands and watches Laurie walk away, and Carpenter holds the shot for a very long time, as the viewer watches Laurie being stalked unawares. The shot does not have much depth of field (Michael, in the foreground, is in soft focus), and Carpenter's decision not to edit or cut away but to hold the frame creates a remarkable amount of tension as the viewer is made to understand the level of threat and danger that is drawing closer to Laurie.

In other scenes Michael looms suddenly into the frame, rising up from the rear seat of a car to strangle one of Laurie's friends or materializing swiftly from the shadows of a kitchen hallway to stab another girl's boyfriend. When Laurie goes into a neighbor's house where her friends have been partying and finds them murdered, a lighting change in the shot slowly reveals that Michael is standing directly behind her.

In the film's climax, Michael attacks Laurie, and she fights him off in a series of confrontations that Carpenter stages in terms of the invasion of space. Laurie runs out of the neighbor's house and back home. Michael follows her. She locks the doors and windows, but he gets inside.

Halloween (1978) Michael Myers sits up behind Laurie, who believes that she has finally killed him. It is a moment calculated to make the audience scream, as viewers try to alert Laurie to her danger. Viewers see what is happening behind her, but Laurie cannot. The screen space in the shot is partially seen, accessible to the audience but not the character, and this difference creates an excruciating suspense.

They fight in the living room, and she stabs him in the neck with a knitting needle, seeming to kill him. He falls behind the sofa, but then, after a pause, lurches back into the frame to menace her anew.

Laurie runs upstairs and hides in a closet. Michael invades this space too, breaking through the flimsy closet door, and seems to die once again when Laurie, cowering on the closet floor, stabs him repeatedly. Laurie crawls out of the closet and sobs in terror. The shot frames her in the foreground with Michael's body visible but out of focus in the background. Carpenter holds on this composition. As Laurie slowly calms down and starts to feel some relief at the thought that she has prevailed, Michael slowly sits up behind her and then gets to his feet. Audiences watching the film are screaming at this point to alert Laurie because the suspense is unbearable. Michael keeps coming on, invading areas of space that had seemed safe.

Michael *is* the bogeyman, a legendary figure of malice that cannot be stopped or killed. Carpenter has choreographed wide-screen space throughout the film in ways that identify it with zones of threat and danger, and in the film's closing moments he expands this design to suggest that Michael is everywhere, that no safe places remain anywhere. The psychiatrist (Donald Pleasance) who has been pursuing Michael and who comes to Laurie's rescue by shooting him discovers that Michael hasn't stayed dead, that his body is not where it fell. The film ends with several shots that reprise locations seen earlier—the downstairs living room where Laurie and Michael fought, the exterior of several houses where Michael stalked and killed his prey—and these shots are accompanied by amplified audio of Michael's husky breathing. The audiovisual design suggests that Michael's malevolence is now coextensive with all spaces in the town, that the evil he represents, which came home to roost, is now everywhere and that it cannot be stopped. Zones of danger are everywhere. All spaces are lethal.

As Carpenter's camerawork in *Halloween* exemplifies, the choreography of visual space in the horror film establishes a sense of threat and menace by playing on a viewer's awareness of offscreen space. The viewer is made to understand that something uncanny, supernatural, psychopathic, or threatening is out there, nearby, and, while unseen at the moment, is likely to burst into view in ways that will bring horrific consequences to the characters in the story.

In this respect, visual space in horror movies points beyond itself. It conveys more than it shows. It suggests that horror may be found just beyond the borders of the frame, where neither camera nor characters are looking. Visual space is laden with the anxieties that the unseen generates and, in this respect, has a quality of pointing beyond itself, designating thresholds between what is seen and what is felt but unseen. This expressive principle is linked to a common method of staging action that relies on suggestion and indirection. Suggesting that a dreadful action is occurring is often more effective at eliciting horror than showing it directly and at length.

Saw, for example, has the reputation of being an explicit, bloody, and torture-centered horror movie. It was so profitable and popular that it has spawned numerous sequels, and its storyline—about two men chained in a basement warehouse and subjected by a diabolical killer to harsh mental and physical abuse—earned the film the designation "torture porn." The film's title offers the lurid promise of grotesque physical mutilation. It refers to climactic action in which one of the men, Lawrence (Cary Elwes), saws off his foot to escape from the shackles that imprison him.

And the killer doesn't disappoint. His other victims are burned alive or are forced to crawl through razor wire until they bleed to death or, in the case of Amanda (Shawnee Smith), are strapped into an explosive face mask wired to a timer and told that the key to unlock the mask can be found in the stomach of the semicomatose man who is her cellmate.

***Saw* (2004)** The scene depicting the torture of Amanda (Shawnee Smith) is ferociously grim and includes some explicit violence. Most of this, however, occurs offscreen, and the scene plays mainly on her face, capturing her emotional responses to the hellish situation in which she finds herself. This visual design gives the scene a psychological focus that makes it more disturbing than if it had concentrated mainly on graphic violence.

If she uses a knife to gut him and remove the key, she stands a chance of freeing herself.

While these story situations are extremely gruesome, the film's visual approach is oblique and relatively suggestive. The deaths of the burn and razor-wire victims are shown quickly, in flashback, and are distorted by being presented in a few seconds of very fast action footage, in which the events are sped up to an almost cartoon-like degree. Amanda's ordeal occupies more screen time, but when she goes to work with the knife to retrieve the key, the low-angle camera framing shows her but not the comatose cellmate as she stabs and slashes. A quick shot of intestines in her hands is the only moment of explicit, onscreen violence.

The scene is excruciating not because of its physical violence but because of her extreme distress and suffering. Fear, anxiety, and dread can be contagious emotions, and when a character displays them in the intense way that Amanda does, viewers experience similar emotions. The scene's design, then, emphasizes the character's psychological anguish, and visual space is choreographed to minimize explicit physical violence while emphasizing Amanda's extreme duress.

Similarly, Lawrence's amputation of his own foot is filmed with the camera aimed mainly at his face. A quick shot shows the saw cutting into his skin, but the action concentrates on Lawrence's expressions of pain and on the horrified gaze of his cellmate as he watches the self-mutilation. Audio detailing the sounds of the cutting is far more graphic than anything the images are showing.

Saw is a grim and carefully made film that evokes conditions of extreme horror by relying on a suggestive and oblique presentation of violence while emphasizing the characters' psychological and emotional distress in ways that make these contagious for viewers.

In this regard, *Saw* is like *The Texas Chainsaw Massacre*—both films create an intensively violent and grotesque atmosphere while showing very little actual onscreen violence. The poetics of horror often reside in such indirection. Suggestion and atmosphere count for much in this genre, and producer Val Lewton was the master of oblique, indirect horror.

In Lewton's films, horror is felt more often than it is seen. In *Cat People*, when a panther stalks a woman who has sought refuge in a swimming pool, the onscreen images show the flickering light and shadow from the pool's surface reflecting onto walls. The audio track, carrying a panther's growls, establishes that something is in the room with the swimmer, but only for a brief moment do the flickering shadows assume the vague outline of a jungle cat. In *Isle of the Dead*, a woman who has been buried alive awakens inside her coffin and shrieks in terror. The camera moves slowly toward the coffin, showing only the outside, as the character's horrific situation is conveyed through audio information. The viewer hears her scratching at the wood with her fingernails and then the shriek of panic and terror.

Saw (2004) The climax comes when Lawrence (Cary Elwes) takes the saw and hacks off his foot to get free of his shackles. It is violent action that has been promised by the film's title, and viewers have been anticipating it. As in the scene with Amanda, the visual design plays mainly on Lawrence's face, capturing his agony rather than on the lurid details of self-mutilation. What viewers picture in their own minds, as a result, is arguably more horrible than what a filmmaker might show directly.

***Isle of the Dead* (1945)** A simple close-up of a coffin shows the viewer little that is horrifying, if taken in strictly visual terms. But the narrative situation—a woman has been buried alive—and the audio information—her fingernails clawing at the wood inside the casket, the steady drip of water inside the mausoleum, her scream—supply the details that make the image horrifying. Suggesting rather than showing—this strategy has provided an effective route to horror throughout the genre's history.

Lewton understood that suggestion and indirection can produce powerful results and that the design of visual space in the genre is inherently linked to these elements. Indeed, most filmmakers who work effectively in the genre have learned to choreograph visual space to establish zones of danger and threat whose unknowable or unpredictable nature serves to unsettle the viewer.

Stephen Prince

QUESTIONS FOR DISCUSSION

1. Anxiety, fear, dread, and revulsion are negative emotions. Ordinarily they are unpleasant to experience. Why then do audiences seem to enjoy experiencing them in the context of a horror film?

2. The monsters in the classic Universal films—Dracula, Frankenstein's monster, the Mummy, the Wolf Man—seem hardly frightening to modern audiences, and yet in their day they were considered disturbing,

unacceptably gruesome, and dangerous for impressionable viewers. How might one account for this change?

3. Horror films often furnish a symbolic way of expressing collective traumas and social fears. Is this kind of expression more likely to occur in this genre than in others? Why or why not?

4. Since *Psycho*, horror films have become more graphically violent. How essential is graphic violence for the experience of horror? Might it interfere with or get in the way of other essential components in producing the sensation of horror?

5. What are the ingredients essential to a well-made horror film?

FOR FURTHER READING

Benshoff, Harry M. *Monsters in the Closet: Homosexuality and the Horror Film.* Manchester, UK: Manchester University Press, 1997.

Carroll, Noël. *The Philosophy of Horror: Or, Paradoxes of the Heart.* New York: Routledge, 1990.

Clover, Carol. *Men, Women and Chainsaws: Gender in the Modern Horror Film.* Princeton, NJ: Princeton University Press, 1993.

Freeland, Cynthia. *The Naked and the Undead.* Boulder, CO: Westview Press, 2001.

Grant, Barry Keith, ed. *The Dread of Difference: Gender and the Horror Film.* Austin: University of Texas Press, 1996.

Hardy, Phil, ed. *Horror.* New York: Overlook Press, 1995.

Palmer, Randy. *Herschell Gordon Lewis, Godfather of Gore: The Films.* Jefferson, NC: McFarland, 2006.

Paul, William. *Laughing Screaming: Modern Hollywood Horror and Comedy.* New York: Columbia University Press, 1995.

Phillips, Kendall R. *Projected Fears: Horror Films and American Culture.* Praeger, 2008.

Pinedo, Isabel Cristina. *Recreational Terror: Women and the Pleasures of Horror Film Viewing.* Albany: State University of New York Press, 1997.

Prince, Stephen, ed. *The Horror Film.* New Brunswick, NJ: Rutgers University Press, 2004.

Skal, David J. *The Monster Show: A Cultural History of Horror.* New York: W. W. Norton, 1993.

Tudor, Andrew. *Monsters and Mad Scientists: A Cultural History of the Horror Movie.* Hoboken, NJ: Wiley-Blackwell, 1989.

Wood, Robin. "The American Nightmare: Horror in the '70s." In *Hollywood: From Vietnam to Reagan . . . and Beyond*, edited by Robin Wood, 63–84. New York: Columbia University Press, revised and expanded 2003.

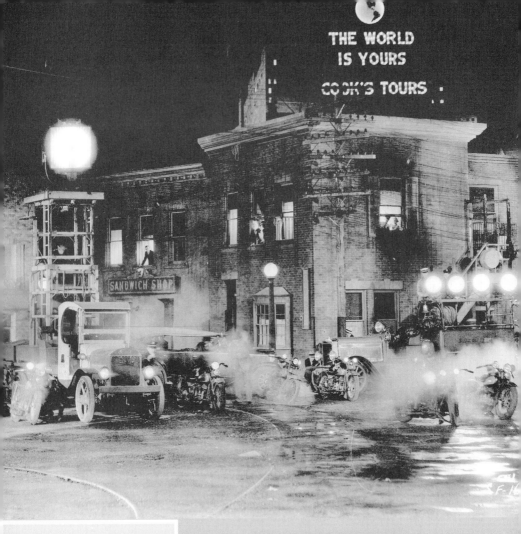

Scarface (1932)

The Gangster Movie

THE GANGSTER MOVIE, with its stories told from the point of view of characters on the wrong side of the law, is among the most controversial of the film genres. Since the 1930s, the decade many think of as its heyday, it has come under periodic attack for inciting public immorality, glorifying violence and sexism, and casting ethnic aspersions. It is also one of the most commercially profitable genres, commanding large audiences and impressive box-office receipts, which may be why it is the genre that will not die, despite sustained attempts to kill it, first by the Production Code Administration (PCA), the official watchdog of the industry from 1930 to 1967, and more recently by privately funded ethnic-defense organizations. The gangster movie's resilience is counted as a blessing by enthusiastic filmgoers, as it was by Robert Warshow, the first critic to analyze it as a serious and important part of American culture. Warshow saw in gangster films the only Hollywood genre that speaks the truth about an American society steadfastly in denial about its problems. His claims are given credibility by the indelible impressions made by many of the larger-than-life actors who have worked in gangster films over the years: James Cagney, Edward G. Robinson, Humphrey Bogart, Paul Muni, Al Pacino, Robert De Niro, Joe Pesce, Gabriel Byrne, Albert Finney, and, in *The Sopranos*, the film genre's televisual brother, James Gandolfini. The mobsters created by these acting powerhouses do seem to reveal a side of America that is usually hidden from view.

The charge that gangster movies are principally a guilty pleasure that indulges desires forbidden by normal social rules is undermined by the genre's longevity. If gangster films provided nothing more than illicit thrills, they would have played out long ago. Thrills get old quickly, and many other genres are much more accomplished at reproducing unrestrained taboo spectacles. A close examination reveals that more important than the gun battles and the lurid sex and glitz in gangster movies are the interesting home truths they tell about American cultural values, especially the cherished American Dream, that shining faith that America is a land of opportunity, open to all, where wealth and happiness are possible for anyone willing to try hard enough to achieve these goals. The gangster film scrutinizes some dark realities behind these generalizations.

History

The gangster film began as a narration of temporary lapses in a social landscape still paying lip service to time-tested morals and ethics. In the beginning of the twentieth century, before synchronized sound in movies, the genre told its stories against the background of an ongoing nativist movement, which identified the floods of immigrants from Europe to American shores as the cause of what they saw as an ethical decline in the United States. Nativists suggested that the newcomers challenged the stability of society, especially in the big cities. However, from the start, the gangster film contested nativist assumptions, depicting a universal modern malaise among immigrants and "real Americans" alike. And the gangster film still implies that, with respect to modern ethical confusion, there is not much difference between Americans born in the United States, whose ancestors were immigrants, and recently arrived Americans.

The film generally identified as the oldest gangster film is a silent short titled *The Musketeers of Pig Alley* (1912). Seventeen minutes in length, it is a comic anecdote framed within the context of nativist prejudice against immigrants.

Two of the main characters are the Little Lady (Lillian Gish) and her husband the Musician (Walter Miller), obviously temporarily in the immigrant section of the city in which the film is set. With their chiseled, pale Nordic features, and good manner, wearing clothes that are inexpensive but in good taste they represent what nativists of the day would have called "real" Americans, those born here. The Little Lady, dressed as a typical silent film ingénue, and the Musician, dressed in what would have been identified during that period as "artistic" clothing, contrast sharply with the third main character, the Snapper Kid (Elmer Booth), who represents what nativists saw as the threat to real Americans. An immigrant gangster, Snapper is an early version of the film gangster, with his sharp clothes and his wiseguy manner. When the Musician is forced to leave the Little Lady on her own in order to find work and money to support them, Snapper almost immediately makes a play for the virtuous wife, fulfilling the worst fears of the nativists. However, she is more than a match for Snapper, and he respects her from then on. We clearly see the esteem in which Snapper holds her when, after the Musician returns and Snapper makes it necessary for him to leave his wife alone again by stealing the money the Musician has earned, Snapper comes to her rescue. While the Little Lady is alone, her friend takes her to the Gangster's Ball to cheer her up, and one of Snapper's rivals slips a drug into her drink, intending to take advantage of her. Snapper saves her, ruffling nativist expectations, and does not use the opportunity to take advantage of her himself. Later, although the Musician, who has now retrieved the stolen money from Snapper, knows that Snapper stole it in the first place, he somewhat bemusedly acquiesces when the Lady gives Snapper an alibi when the police try to arrest him, in payment for the good turn he did her. The immigrant gangster turns out not to be as bad as is generally imagined, and the real Americans, the Musician and the Little Lady, turn out not to be as good as is generally supposed.

To modern eyes, *Musketeers* may not seem like a gangster film. It contains none of the iconography that was later inextricably associated with the genre. The criminals don't even seem like "gangsters." Although Snapper has a few scenes in which he and his rival fight each other, there is little to identify the two as part of different factions. It all looks like some disorganized street crime.

Ten years later, gangster films were no longer laughing at the compromised state of morals and ethics in America. The light-hearted tone of *Musketeers* bears little or no relation to what was to come. Nevertheless, this little movie does take a few tentative steps in the direction of depicting a gangster protagonist, as opposed to a gangster villain, and it is of further interest because it was directed by one of the fathers of the American film industry, D. W. Griffith, and featured Lillian Gish, the person who is often credited with creating the art of film acting.

Much closer to later gangster films are two other silent-era ancestors of the genre: *Regeneration* (1915), a feature-length film of seventy-five minutes, and *Underworld* (1927), an eighty-minute feature. *Regeneration*, based on an autobiography popular in the early twentieth century, *My Mamie Rose: The Story of My Regeneration* (1902), written by a newspaperman named Owen Kildare, tells the story of a gangster redeemed by the love of an altruistic society girl. Long on moralizing, it makes an attempt to directly address the problems of an era when immigration was high and integrating the masses of newcomers into America was a national issue. In *Regeneration*, a socialite, Marie "Mamie Rose" Deering (Anna Q. Nilssen) shows herself to be different from the other members of high society when she decides to live and work in the immigrant area of the city as a social worker. When Owen Conway, a gangster, (Rockliffe Fellowes) falls in love with her, his desire for salvation defines the immigrant as a potentially good person if given a chance.

But as the gangster story evolves, the protagonists become more violent and less interested in reformation. *Underworld*, also the story of the redemption of a mob leader, this one named Bull Weed (George Bancroft), was a harbinger of the new developments that were only a few years away. Bull stands as a transitional figure between the more benign mobster that preceded him and the more violent mobster to come. A tough, street-hardened gang boss, he spends most of the film bullying everyone around him. Only at the last moment is he transformed by a sudden realization that true love exists, when he is struck by the way it has enabled his moll, Feathers (Evelyn Brent), to redeem an alcoholic, upper-class lawyer nicknamed Rolls Royce (Clive Owen). But Bull's recognition that there is something better than the predatory life of a gangster comes too late to save him. His insight motivates him to let the police take him off to jail as the film and the era of the chivalrous movie gangster came to an end.

Enter the volcanic gangsters who populated the genre during the early days of the studio system. Taking on a specific look and identity in the 1930s, gangster films became the territory of desperate but charismatic men who inhabited the mean streets that could be constructed at a moment's notice by studio in-house set builders and designers and filled by studio contract players, writers, and directors. The classics of this period were made by the Warner Bros. studio, which, within a matter of days, could throw together a convincing imitation of poverty-stricken immigrant streets, a suitable script, and an electrifying cast of immigrant mob characters. The Production Code, presented to the Hollywood community in drafts between 1930 and 1934, attempted to keep the gritty 1930s gangster film within acceptable bounds by prescribing limits on its depiction of sex and violence and by requiring the punishment of its criminal protagonists. However, audience enthusiasm for mob stories encouraged Warner Bros. and other studios of the 1930s to persist in making them. These gangster films drew massive amounts of customers to the theaters for reasons beyond a taste for violence. Gangster films were, in many ways, like looking into a mirror for many people caught in the financial upheavals of the Great Depression, not only immigrants and their children but also native-born Americans.

The Great Depression, which began in 1929 and ended with America's entrance into World War II in 1941, was a worldwide collapse of the financial infrastructures of the industrialized countries of the West, which had seen a decade of out-of-control financial expansion that depended on short-term profits and allowed for no oversight by regulating bodies that could bring stability through long-term planning and enforcement of limits on business practices. Gangster films were not about the industrialists responsible for the crash of the stock market in the United States, but rather about the atmosphere of greed they had created that affected the immigrants searching for a way to survive in their new land. Gangster films suggested that some new immigrants learned bad habits from that atmosphere of greed.

The business to which the gangsters turned to make their short-lived but spectacular fortunes was the manufacture and sale of illegal liquor, much in demand because of Prohibition, the other historical event that had a profound impact on the genre. In 1919, the National Prohibition Act, also known as the Volstead Act, was passed by Congress over the veto of President Woodrow Wilson, and effectively made it impossible to legally produce, bottle, sell, or serve alcohol in public establishments. Intended to deal with alcoholism in the United States, it had quite a different effect. The Volstead Act is widely given credit for the upsurge in gangster presence in America; through the illegal liquor trade, gangsters amassed fabulous fortunes. Because the criminal manufacture of liquor was completely unregulated, the product was substandard, sometimes poisonous and even lethal. But gangs could not be compelled by law to sell untainted liquor, so Prohibition insured only that most people who consumed alcohol were at risk.

Prohibition was ended in 1933, soon after Franklin D. Roosevelt became president, but by then the damage had been done: gangster networks had gained a foothold in America. The gangster films of the 1930s reflected the rise of gangster empires during Prohibition. And a spectacular rise it was, often accompanied by a spectacular fall, which Hollywood was forced by the PCA to end their stories with, so that, as the PCA insisted, the public would not take the dynamic criminal protagonists as role models. However, PCA zeal failed to fool most filmgoers, who knew that many historical gangsters became even more powerful after Prohibition by using the fortunes they made when liquor was illegal to finance other illegal dealings, in gambling, prostitution, and, eventually, drugs.

The studio-system stars of the 1930s most closely associated with the movie gangster's meteoric rise and fall were Edward G. Robinson, James Cagney, Paul Muni, Humphrey Bogart, and George Raft, all of whom were under contract to Warner Bros. Robinson was the star of the first major gangster film of the period, *Little Caesar* (1931), based on a popular novel by W. R. Burnett, which ends with the once powerful mobster lying in the gutter asking, "Is this the end of Rico?" The other two most influential gangster films of the decade, *The Public Enemy* (1931), starring Cagney as Tommy Powers, and *Scarface* (1932), with Muni as Tony Camonte, also have spectacular closing scenes. Powers's final appearance is as a corpse. He is delivered to his mother's home swaddled in bandages like a mummy, and falls through the doorway in one of the most horrifying images to come out of the period. Camonte perishes in a hail of bullets in a shootout with the police.

Little Caesar (1931) Caesar Enrico Bandello (Edward G. Robinson) lies in the gutter, felled by police bullets at the end of this early gangster classic. "Is this the end of Rico?" he asks, not of the police, but of a higher power. Another instance of Hollywood's ability to work on many levels, *Little Caesar* gives its protagonist his due punishment but at the same time raises him to heroic status, as a frail soul confronting the meaning of life and the mystery of death. Robinson's expression of pure suffering conflicts in an interesting way with the goals of the PCA.

***Scarface* (1932)** This film bore the brunt of the antagonism of the PCA to gangster films. In the bitterly personal war between the PCA and director Howard Hawks that delayed the release of the film for years, a truce was finally reached when Hawks agreed to a number of conditions. Primary among them was the unmasking of the protagonist, Tony Camonte (Paul Muni), as a coward when stripped of his gun. After a career of macho bravado, Camonte is reduced to unmanly sniveling when the police have him cornered and are poised to come in for the kill. The shadow in the composition, which seems to be facing the other way, suggests his discarded, larger-than-life alter ego.

All three of these films feature immigrant gangster protagonists fired up with a passion to be someone and get ahead in the United States. The gangster hero of *Scarface* was clearly based on the historical immigrant gangster Al Capone; the other two had careers that might remind the audience of Capone's meteoric and brutal rise but do not tap into any of the famous details of his biography, like the scar on his face. But at the same time, the obstacles faced by these protagonists might resemble those faced by members of the movie audience in their attempts at upward mobility in Depression-era America.

The one gangster film about a female boss made by Warner Bros. is *Blondie Johnson* (Ray Enright, 1933). The film stars Joan Blondell, a very popular star of Warner Bros. musical comedies. *Blondie Johnson* breaks the mold of the Warner gangster movie, not only by giving the mob leadership role to a woman but also by changing its typical depiction of the

***The Public Enemy* (1931)** This frame features the uncanny, gruesome, upright corpse of the protagonist, Tommy Powers (James Cagney), just before it falls headlong through the door of the Powers home, a warning to all who might be tempted to a life of crime. This lurid image exemplifies how clever Hollywood could be in dealing with the pressures from civic groups and the PCA to use the gangster genre to teach a moral lesson. It is both politically correct for its day and sensational enough to provide commercially profitable thrills and chills for the audience.

mob boss as a struggling immigrant. By contrast, Blondie and her family are native-born Americans who are victims of the Great Depression and, because there were no unions at the time, the victims of the owners of American industry. In addition, Blondie rules her gang not through violence but with her brains and her ability to manipulate people by using drama. She is not destroyed at the end of the film; rather she's "learned her lesson" and looks forward to marriage and "going legit" after serving her jail sentence. As might be expected, Blondie received an equivocal reception from the PCA and the public, both of which did not take happily to the thought of a powerful woman. She was the first and last of her sex to occupy such a prominent role in a Warner gangster movie.

In 1935, the PCA amended its code to forbid the production of gangster films outright, but as with so many of its other rules, this one was not enforced to the letter. Cagney did experiment with playing law enforcers—in *G-Men* (1935), he's an FBI agent—but he made two of his most famous gangster films after the PCA tried to pull the kill switch on the genre: *Angels with Dirty Faces* (1938) and *The Roaring Twenties* (1939). Robinson, who publicly expressed his displeasure at being typecast as a gangster, made a number of comedies during the second half of the 1930s spoofing his roles as a mob thug, but he also made some of his best gangster movies at that time, including a classic study of the gangster and public attitudes toward crime, *The Amazing Dr. Clitterhouse* (1938).

The war years, 1941–1945, were not good for the genre. During this time, America preferred its crime films in the form of detective stories and an emerging genre eventually called film noir by French critics. The postwar years were not a good period for gangster films, either. But there were some mob films produced in the late 1940s and in the 1950s and 1960s that are interesting for historical reasons. They reflect the Cold War suspicion of immigrants and things "foreign" that gripped the United States after World War II, and also the gradual relaxing of restrictions on the movies as the PCA lost power. The gangster films of this period were also influenced by the Kefauver Commission, led by Senator Estes Kefauver in 1950 and 1951, which woke America up to new postwar trends among American gangsters, who had begun to adopt some of the tactics of corporate America.

A powerful, still available, but now largely forgotten film of this period that portrays the turn of American gangsters toward a corporate model is *The Gangster* (1947). It dramatizes the fatal discovery by an old-school gangster that his power has been taken away by a new, empowered corporate mob. By 1967, in *The St. Valentine's Day Massacre*, the first Technicolor gangster film, we find Al Capone's mob business being conducted in well-lit board rooms rather than in the old dark corners that were the mob settings on the Warner studio lots. That is, this film reflects a 1960s picture of the underworld, despite the fact that its story takes place in the 1920s.

The St. Valentine's Day Massacre demonstrates Cold War paranoia about immigrants and foreigners. This film portrays gangsters as repulsive psychopaths, unlike the old Warner films, which certainly highlight their characters' megalomania but also allow for their warmth, pathos, desperation, and, above all, charisma. Other examples of Cold

War gangster films that depict their central characters as almost entirely detestable are *Al Capone* (1959), in which Rod Steiger plays Capone as a charmless homicidal maniac; and *The Rise and Fall of Legs Diamond* (1960), whose protagonist seems to have ice in his veins. Such movies made money but have been relegated to the dusty warehouses of film history. The only Cold War gangster film to achieve real distinction and lasting fame, *White Heat* (1949), is leavened by the artistry of Cagney, who has written of how he forced some comedy into the film to humanize his character.

White Heat is the last of Cagney's great gangster roles and the last great gangster film to be directed by Raoul Walsh, who also directed one of the first American gangster films, *Regeneration* (see pp. 409–10). Both the narrative of *White Heat* and the story of how it came to be are full of the tensions of a paranoid postwar America riddled with the shocks of men returning from war and with fears fanned to frenzied extremes by Senator Joseph McCarthy, who preached imminent invasion by European Communists, allegations for which he never produced any credible evidence. In keeping with the tenor of postwar America, *White Heat* was planned as an FBI story that would focus on the transfer of power from an experienced agent to his young protégé, reassuring American citizens that the forces of law and order had postwar America under control. But because he was too big a star to be given a secondary role, when Cagney was cast as Cody Jarrett, a gangster the two agents sought to capture, the film was rewritten as his story, a study of unstable gangster psychology. It became a gangster film.

In the version of *White Heat* that reached the screen, the center of attention is the way Jarrett, a cold, psychotic murderer, evades pursuit by agents of the U.S. Treasury Department. Jarrett's characterization is complicated by his darkly comic dependence on his mother, a bond so powerful that he is unable to survive her death. Jarrett dies in the final scene speaking in a disoriented way to his dead mother, as though she can hear him, but there is a subtle difference between his death and the predictably violent deaths of previous Hollywood gangsters, who, as mandated by the PCA, die in humiliating circumstances: Jarrett remains a larger-than-life figure, the master of his own demise. A throng of government agents watches in helpless amazement as the gangster goes out in a literal blaze of glory when he sets fire to the gasworks. Moreover, Cagney's psychological portrait of a man outside the law is the ancestor of the kind of psychologically imagined gangster protagonists who started to rule the screen when the genre began its second golden age, in 1972.

Gangster films got a powerful second wind because of the confluence of several historical changes in America in the 1970s. This decade saw the collapse of the studio system, the emergence of many independent productions, and the demise of the PCA. Much that had been taboo in old Hollywood was now possible, and this new freedom was especially productive for gangster movies, which no longer had to be cautious about their use of sex and violence. Auteurs began to interest themselves in making films with personal perspectives on the American gangster instead of formulaic mob sagas. Add to this the civil rights movement and women's liberation protests in the 1960s, which stimulated various ethnic-pride movements, and the conditions for the production of *The Godfather*, a turning point for the genre, were in place.

The PCA had cautioned the studios to be as tactful as possible about ethnicity in gangster films, for fear that the ethnic identification of gangsters would adversely affect ticket sales. Francis Ford Coppola's *The Godfather* (1972) took just the opposite tack. Basing his film on the best-selling book of the same name by Mario Puzo, Coppola tells the story of Italian immigrants struggling to become Americans and finding the path of least resistance through the gangster world. When Michael (Al Pacino), the youngest son of Don Vito Corleone (Marlon Brando) decides to join the mob, he disappoints his father, who had hoped that Michael would become a leader within the legal framework of America. Coppola, with this issue, explicitly posed some hard questions about the United States.

Instead of motivating Michael by the economic need of the Warner Bros. gangsters or the psychosis of the Cold War gangsters, Coppola motivated his gangster through the psychology of family. Instead of terminating his film with the once obligatory death of the mob boss, Coppola shows Michael achieving upward mobility, a trajectory more in keeping with real life. Coppola pursues the implications of Michael's success to their logical conclusion in *The Godfather Part II* (1974), in which Michael acquires more wealth and power than his father ever had, but the price of his spectacular financial success is the loss of the kind of emotional depth that made his father a force for some good in the immigrant community. Michael's almost complete dehumanization requires us to think about the materialism of the United States and what success in America is really about. In 1990, when Francis Ford Coppola was contractually

***The Godfather* (1972)** This frame is from a crucial scene in which, although he never says the words, it is clear that Vito Corleone (Marlon Brando) hoped that Michael (Al Pacino) would become a "real American" highly placed in a legitimate profession. Vito had endured nativist scorn and would naturally yearn for his son's legitimacy. The question that haunts this film, the primary question posed by the fin-de-siècle gangster movie, is why the next generation remains in the mob.

forced to film *The Godfather: Part III*, a film which he himself has spoken about very critically in interviews, he undermined the hard-edged portrait of the Corleones in the first two films of the trilogy by sentimentalizing his gangster protagonist. In Part III, Michael takes an unmotivated turn toward being a sympathetic, loving father and a regretful ex-husband, as if the soul destroying life he had been leading had only had temporary effects. It is of interest that it is only *The Godfather* and *The Godfather: Part II* that have influenced the further development of the genre.

The frightening cultural implications of gangsters who succeed in America without being punished by the law were taken up by a series of brilliant, independent directors who came after Coppola. Interestingly, their films do not register an anxiety that the gangster has "gotten away" with anything. Rather, the post-*Godfather* films increasingly made the genre a way of confronting the spiritual void created by rampant American materialism. One of the most piercing contributions to the American gangster genre during this period is not a purely American film, but a globalized production. *Once Upon a Time in America* (1984), like many Hollywood productions from the 1980s to today, was the result of numerous international influences. It began with an American novel; was adapted for the screen by an Italian director, Sergio Leone; was filmed in the United States, Rome, France, and Canada; and was brought to life by American actors and writers, and an international crew. The novel Leone adapted to create *Once Upon a Time in America* is *The Hoods* (1952), about gangster life during Prohibition. Never a well-known book, *The Hoods* is a strangely ambiguous work. Its author is supposedly Harry Grey, but that might have been a pseudonym for a man named David Aronson, who claimed to have spent his early life in the Jewish mob, and it may have been based on actual events. Leone's film, however, much changed from the original, is unambiguously fictional.

The Hoods takes a hard-boiled approach to the gangster story, but Leone's film does not. The fairy-tale allusion in the film's title matches the phantasmic nature of the gangster America depicted by Leone. In a film saturated with opium and liquor, Leone creates a group of characters who journey through a surreal world of crime, violence, the psychology of male friendships, and an America moved more by fear than by love. As the nonlinear story unfolds back and forth in time, it uses dizzying flashbacks and flash-forwards to show how the friendship of four men who begin as the poverty-stricken children of immigrants is bargained away in a series of ruthless schemes to find success in America. One of the gangsters, Max Bercovicz (James Woods), to become completely integrated into straight America kills two of his friends and betrays Noodles Aaronson (Robert De Niro), the gangster pal he loves the most. But, like Michael Corleone, Max grows increasingly empty as his growing success leads him to more corrupt deeds, until life is worth nothing to him anymore, and he seeks his own death. Even though the law doesn't punish Max, in *Once Upon a Time in America*, and in other gangster films of this period, there is a subtle and sophisticated "crime doesn't pay" theme at work.

Similarly, Martin Scorsese has assured himself an immortal place in American cinema with *Goodfellas* (1990), a film containing rich, successful mobsters and extremely pessimistic undertones about the American promise to immigrants. *Goodfellas* begins with the amazing statement by the film's protagonist, Henry Hill (Ray Liotta), a real-life gangster whose biography Scorsese adapted for the screen, that as long as he can remember, he has always wanted to be a gangster. Using Hill's story

Goodfellas (1990) In this frame from the final scene of *Goodfellas*, Henry Hill (Ray Liotta) is in the federal witness-protection program. The expression on his face reveals his confusion about the unhappiness he experiences as a law-abiding citizen. Henry's sense that his life, no longer glamorous or luxurious, has reached a dead end is also expressed by the nondescript terry cloth robe he wears and the house he lives in, which is identical to all the other houses in the subdivision. Scorsese closes his film by challenging his audience to question the American materialism that allows gangsters to think of their immoral and destructive lives in glowing affirmatives.

about his lower-middle-class beginnings, Scorsese too distances the late-twentieth-century gangster film from the economic hardships that drove the Warner films and the mental disorders that drove the Cold War films. Hill and all the characters in *Goodfellas* are not motivated by necessity but by the mythos of glamour, power, and money, which they intend to get by any means necessary, a parody of the American Dream. The strength of Hill's delusions about what the good life means is revealed when he is forced into the government witness-protection program after it becomes clear to him that his former brothers in crime are about to kill him. As a rehabilitated citizen, however, Hill is never apologetic for the theft and murder of which he had been a part; he ends the film expressing only nostalgia and longing for the life of a gangster, which he remembers as a time when he ruled the city.

Scorsese uses all kinds of cinematic poetry to encourage us to wonder what has happened that would cause the immigrant dream of Hill's Irish-American family to lead Hill to aspire to a life of crime and to continue to long for it even after he and his family have suffered terribly from its excesses, amorality, and violence. In 2002, Scorsese made *Gangs of New York*, an even bolder depiction of the complex connections between immigration and gangster life, that, for the first time in the history of the American gangster genre, roots the gangster way of life in pre–Civil War New York, as it depicts the overwhelming environmental pressures on the newcomers to join gangs in order to survive.

Another exciting post-*Godfather* gangster film is *Miller's Crossing* (1990). In this film, the Coen brothers follow in the tradition of Coppola, Leone, and Scorsese, mining the gangster story to demonstrate the pervasive moral and ethical confusion of America. Set during Prohibition, *Miller's Crossing* features as its protagonist a loner named Tom Reagan (Gabriel Byrne), who has become the right-hand man of a mobster named Leo (Albert Finney), the boss of a criminal empire in an unnamed city. Reagan, whose isolation gives him a clarity about what's going on that the other mobsters don't have, wields a detached kind of control over events. But his very success as Leo's enforcer leaves him isolated and carrying the burden of guilt for what must be done to survive in a world gone totally mad. The Coens, like Leone, use surreal elements in this film to depict the psychology of materialistic America. Like all of late-twentieth-century gangster filmmakers, they also highlight the ethnicity of their characters, which in this case is the old New York immigrant mix of the Irish, Italians, and Eastern European Jews. In the tradition of post-*Godfather* gangster films, Reagan and Leo don't die for their illegal activities, but instead sustain emotional, spiritual, and/or mental wounds that inflict a living death.

The biggest recent events in the gangster genre concern ethnicity, race, and television. In 1992, Edward James Olmos directed *American Me*, a saga of a Hispanic gang, and in 2007's *American Gangster*, America, for the first time, produced an African-American gangster film, as opposed to a gangsta film, of which there have been a number since 1980. (We will shortly explore the differences between gangster and gangsta films.) And in the television series *The Sopranos* (1999–2007), David Chase pushed the spiritual, psychological, emotional, family, and ethnic aspects of the gangster film to new heights and depths. The current television series *Boardwalk Empire* (since 2010), possibly as a reflection of a contemporary deterioration in the financial situations of millions of Americans, marks an interesting return to the examination of immigrant gangsters forced by economic necessity into crime. As an inheritor of the film and television traditions of gangster stories, *Boardwalk Empire* stands at a new frontier in its examination of the links among immigration, money, the American belief in upward mobility, and crime. Unlike the 1930s

Warner Bros. classics, which look back on rise of Prohibition gangster culture immediately after the demise of Prohibition, this series takes advantage of a very long historical perspective of almost one hundred years, setting its sights on the rise of a politician-turned-gangster, Nucky Thompson (Steve Buscemi), in a very corrupt Atlantic City, at the beginning of Prohibition. Building on *The Sopranos'* piercing insights into the domestic lives of gangsters and the blurred line between ordinary American society and gangster attraction to violence and materialism, *Boardwalk Empire* adds a political dimension, continuing the gangster genre's focus on the fragility of the American Dream by way of the links it makes visible among family, crime, and national and local politics.

Typologies, Themes, and Theories

Delving into the history of the gangster film does not answer the question of what makes a gangster film, and, although there are some film genres that are harder to define, the gangster genre provokes some interesting questions as to its identity. One of the major difficulties of defining movie genres is caused by the amount of overlap among them, and overlaps between the gangster genre and other kinds of films abound. Is *Brother Orchid* (1940), a witty Edward G. Robinson vehicle that tells the story of a mob boss who discovers he's happier as a monk in a monastery than as a criminal in a penthouse, a gangster film or a comedy? Is any film containing a gangster character part of the gangster genre? Is any criminal a gangster? In *Double Indemnity* (1944), Walter Neff (Fred MacMurray), an insurance agent, helps a sexy client kill her husband for the insurance money, but most people are not likely to think of him as a gangster. Why? And then there is the problem of the outlaw film. In *Bonnie and Clyde* (1967) the eponymous couple, played by Faye Dunaway and Warren Beatty, barnstorms around Depression America robbing banks in the Midwest. They are certainly criminals, but are they gangsters? And how about Johnny Rocco in *Key Largo* (John Huston, 1948)? He's a gangster villain, and very important in the film, but does this make *Key Largo* a gangster film?

The answer is no, because one of the seminal defining characteristics of the gangster genre is that within this type of film, the gangster is the protagonist, not the villain. One of the crucial typological characteristics of the gangster film is that it tells its story from the point of view of a very unlikely hero, a criminal. If a film contains an important gangster character but he or she is seen from the perspective of the people who want to put him/her behind bars, then it might be a police drama, a detective story, a film noir, a thriller, or a crime melodrama, but it isn't a part of the gangster genre. So even though *Key Largo* contains one of the most famous gangsters in American cinema history, Johnny Rocco (Edward G. Robinson), it is a crime melodrama. We don't see Johnny in terms of his own passions and how and why he has embraced crime. Rather we see him as he is seen by the hero, Frank McCloud (Humphrey Bogart), who ultimately destroys Rocco as we cheer McCloud on.

While we don't approve of the gangster in his own genre and know he should be punished, we get so far inside the mobster protagonist that we can't see him from the point of view of the people who want to jail or kill him. Even the worst of the repugnant Cold War gangsters are sometimes seen by the audience in their own terms. This makes the gangster genre much more complex than any other form of crime genre except films about outlaws, which also feature protagonists who are criminals. So what's the difference between the gangster film and the outlaw film?

The big difference is that outlaw characters in films like *Bonnie and Clyde* are dropouts from society. Americans and insiders by birth, they *want to live outside* of ordinary culture. In contrast, gangster protagonists in films are born outsiders, almost always immigrants, who want to get to the top of the social order, to "be someone." Outlaws, by contrast, are individualists who can't stand authority, like Bonnie and Clyde, who are so incompatible with social order that they can have sex only when they are on the run. There are such great differences between Bonnie and Clyde and the main characters in gangster films that while they may all be called crime films, only films told from the point of view of criminals who band together to break into society can be called gangster films.

Similarly, we do an injustice to the gangsta film, a very powerful recent addition to the history of crime films, if we include it in the gangster genre. There are no racial motivations in the Hollywood gangster film, while the gangsta film is all about racial injustice. To confuse the gangsta film with the gangster film is to avoid important social issues. In gangsta films, crime is not a desperate attempt to belong to mainstream, nativist society, as it is in the standard Hollywood gangster movie, but rather an unfortunately violent response by justly angry black men to a white culture that has excluded them from competing for the American Dream. In *Belly* (1998), for example, Tommy "Buns" Bundy (DMX) and

Sincere (Nas), a pair of fierce Harlem gangstas, unlike Tony Camonte in *Scarface*, cannot break into mainstream society because of its racism. As a result of racism, in *Belly*, the point of view is with a posse of gangstas, who intend to operate as outsiders getting their own back on a hostile society. They are more like outlaws than gangsters. In fact, Sincere refers to himself and his pals as "outlaw niggers." But it is not an outlaw film either. Bonnie and Clyde get a rush from being outsiders. Buns and Sincere are not outsiders by choice; they have been forcefully excluded from mainstream American society and its dreams. At the same time, unlike the Warner Bros. gangsters, they neither can nor want to belong to society as is. Their hopes tend toward cultures different from ordinary white culture. Buns turns toward the Nation of Islam, an American religious movement into which he can fit without being a criminal. Sincere leaves the country and searches for his ethnic roots in Africa. The gangsta film, like the outlaw film, is a crime movie that needs to be considered in terms of a genre of its own, with its own themes and aesthetics.

That the desperation to belong to mainstream society is a continuing theme in the Hollywood gangster genre is illustrated by the two versions of *Scarface*, made fifty years apart. Even though the earlier film records the plight of Italian immigrants and the remake the plight of Hispanic immigrants, the goals of the two heroes are identical. In the 1932 version, Paul Muni stars as Tony Camonte, a man who frantically wants to be somebody in a society that treats newly arrived Italian immigrants like animals. While the film encourages the audience to be appalled by his violence, it shows us the protagonist's pathetic need to be respected by American society with such humor and such charm that we cannot help but feel for him. One of the many such scenes in the film depicts Camonte's attempt to make points with the blonde, American mistress of his mob boss, who laughs at his expensive bad taste, calling him effeminate, which he mistakes for a compliment. The PCA forced director Howard Hawks to give plenty of screen time to the police who condemn Camonte in rigid moralistic terms, but the reason this film continues to live is that Hawks brought to flaming life Camonte's struggle, wrong-headed though it may be, to make the American Dream his own, despite the barriers erected against immigrants. Fifty years later, Tony Montana (Al Pacino) in an updated Hispanic version of *Scarface* (1983) makes the same pilgrimage. Because in 1983 there was no PCA to rein him in, director Brian De Palma was freer to use violence than

Howard Hawks was, but Montana's longing for a place in the American community is as strong as Camonte's, and also takes the form of possession of the obligatory upper-middle-class mansion, cars, wardrobe, and, most important of all, a "real American" blonde.

In fact, it is a perverse obsession for middle-class respectability and affluence, coupled with a lack of understanding the importance of limits imposed by the laws and customs that define respectability, that drives the gangster genre. When television claimed its inheritance from Hollywood in *The Sopranos*, it too focused on the need for money as a passage into middle-class membership. However, after the Godfather films, and certainly in *The Sopranos*, love and family became even more central than possessions to the gangster's would-be bourgeois existence.

Gangster fables of powerful longings to be included in society reflect some historical truths about the motivation of real gangsters, but there is no gangster film, even among those that use the names of real gangsters, that accurately reflects the lives of real gangsters. Gangster films more resemble parables than newspaper accounts of real crime, and this is the way critics have typically read them. The gangster genre has been interpreted as a rare instance of American tragedy; a way for Americans to vent their guilt; a mode of speaking about the difficult history of immigration in America; and a parable of the fragility of modern American identity. The tragic view holds that the American concept of success involves so much aggression that those Americans who succeed are left feeling isolated from others and guilty of abuses committed in order to rise. As Robert Warshow wrote in the final paragraph of his famous essay "The Gangster as Tragic Hero," the gangster film reflects the double bind in which American men found themselves: "that failure is a kind of death and success is evil and dangerous, is—ultimately—impossible."[1] Critiques that connect gangster movies with immigration often opine that they allow us to consider the dark side of immigrant life in America. In doing so, they complete the media picture of America as a land of golden opportunity, a rosy view of America's significance for the oppressed of the world that is expressed in Emma Lazarus's passionate poem on the base of the Statue of Liberty, which ends with Lady Liberty saying that she lifts her lamp beside the golden door of America. Gangster films show immigrants receiving a much less gracious introduction

---

[1] Robert Warshow, *The Immediate Experience: Movies, Comics, Theatre and Other Aspects of Popular Culture* (Garden City, N.Y.: Doubleday, 1962), 133.

to American society. This is part of the critique of the "identity" school of criticism, which asserts that American gangster movies depict gangsters as immigrants so seriously disoriented by the loss of their birth culture and humiliated by the efforts of American authorities to intimidate them that they are pressured to fabricate "real American" identity through the acquisition of material possessions by any means necessary, including criminal means. This reading renders the gangster film a searing critique of American materialism. All these various readings of the genre suggest that although the gangster figure seems to show a kind of "otherness" to the good citizen, he is, at the same time, a way of speaking of the good citizen's hidden fears and anxieties: the shadow.

The theories behind these approaches contrast sharply with literalist ideas about the genre, which mistakenly see the gangster figure as a potentially destructive role model instead of as an ironic comment on life in the United States. According to serious critics, the early gangster films like *Little Caesar*, *The Public Enemy*, and *Scarface* all contain subtextual critiques of American society, and the post-*Godfather* gangster films' approach to social problems in the United States is quite overt. For example, Michael Corleone's story is essentially and explicitly about values, not money. He has the education to make himself materially comfortable, but he chooses to follow in the footsteps of his gangster father because he finds no values in American society that he can respect. When his all-American sweetheart Kay Adams (Diane Keaton)— her name alone connoting the America of the founding fathers—protests that his father is not, as Michael claims, like any other businessman because he kills people, Michael accuses her of being naïve. That she has no defense against his point of view suggests rot in the depths of the United States.

Similarly, the addiction of Henry Hill, a child of immigrants, to the excesses of the gangster life even though he, like Michael Corleone, is not forced into crime by poverty suggests serious corruption in America. In *Goodfellas*, Scorsese goes to great lengths to show that Hill's greed and lack of respect for law and hard work to gain success is very much a part of the America in which Hill lives, a greed from which Hill never recovers despite his supposed rehabilitation in the FBI witness-protection program. Indeed, the real-life Hill continued to get into trouble while he was in the program, so addicted was he to the highs of gangster violence and lawbreaking. The confusion of Hill's values is reflected and intensified in *The Sopranos*, which was inspired by *Goodfellas*, in the attachment of Tony Soprano and his associates to the high life and continual rushes of gang life which, as in Scorseses's chronicle, reflect an infantile America hooked on literal and figurative speed.

American Gangster, a twenty-first-century mob movie about black Americans that is not a gangsta film, features Frank Lucas (Denzel Washington), a protagonist closer to Tommy Powers and Tony Camonte than to gangstas Sincere and Buns, and may suggest a turn toward a more optimistic point of view in the genre, brief though it may be. Lucas intends to live the American Dream regardless of racial prejudice, even if that means being a criminal. *American Gangster* is based on a historically real black gangster, and the film doesn't kill him off in the traditions of the old Warner Bros. gangster sagas, or portray him as emotionally dead in the Coppola tradition, but rather is faithful to another possibility offered by real life. Lucas goes to jail and glimpses the possibility of a successful straight life after serving a long sentence, during which time the civil rights movement has changed the playing field. And *Road to Perdition* (2002), in telling the tale of a fictional gangster named Michael Sullivan (Tom Hanks), evokes the necessity for immigrants to take the gangster route if they wished to survive, but the film takes a turn into a Hollywood happy endings by buying the gangster genre back into the American Dream as it shows that Sullivan's son will become part of a virtuous America with good values. Both of these films are more optimistic than is typical of the gangster tradition in American movies. At the same time, the plot complications surrounding Chalky White (Michael Kenneth Williams), a black mobster in *Boardwalk Empire*, a more recent entry into the gangster genre, are not optimistic. They reflect strong American racism and economic trends that force Chalky into being a gangster, and they indicate that the more successful Chalky is in using crime to keep his family in material comfort, the more emotionally alienated he becomes from them.

Iconography

All genres are associated with signature visual and auditory images, but the gangster genre is especially rich in iconography. However, the images have changed significantly over the years. In the earliest gangster films, *The Musketeers of Pig Alley* and *Regeneration*, we find no distinctive iconography. But by the time of *Underworld*, the visual definition of the

Scarface **(1932)** This typical Warner Bros. gangster film street was recycled in the 1930s by the studio scenery department for all of its genre pictures. It is intentionally generic in character, indicating a low-end urban residential area that might be in any large city because the PCA determined that it would be bad for ticket sales to connect crime films with any particular city. This prohibition was not strictly adhered to even in the 1930s, and by the 1940s it was entirely gone.

gangster film had begun to take shape. *Underworld* features the seedy, claustrophobic, shadowy, urban settings emitting an aura of secrecy that became a staple of the Warner Bros. gangster films of the 1930s. Scenes that take place at night on empty pavements lined with small, dirty shops and dotted with ubiquitous lampposts became characteristic of the movie gangster milieu. In the post-*Godfather* era, gangster-film urban immigrant sets became more realistic and innovative, as in *Once Upon a Time in America* and *Gangs of New York*, which faithfully re-created from historically accurate documents the tenements of the early twentieth century and the slums of the mid-nineteenth century, respectively.

The appearance of the movie gangster also began to take shape in *Underworld*, which showed Bull Weed attired in suits, white shirts, and ties, clothing that differentiated him from the ordinary working man by its formality, but also differentiated him from upper-class Americans by a certain crudity of the material and its occasional garishness. Most important for the gangster image for the next decades was the fedora, also worn by Bull Weed, which became a staple of the mob wardrobe and was often worn indoors as well as out. The particular model of hat, with its formal appearance, that came to be associated with the gangster suggested the middle class to which he aspired at the same time that it projected a sinister doggedness and aggression.

Gangsters also have molls. In *Underworld*, the moll made her first appearance as Feathers McCoy, Bull Weed's woman, and she has since become an iconic feature of the genre. Feathers set the tone for her later sisters, as a good-looking, slightly hard, slim, unmotherly woman who wears too much makeup and dresses in fashionable, overly showy clothes. Above all, Feathers was the first in a long line of molls as modern girls, "real American" women who are the gangster version of a wife and who furnish proof of the gangster's place in society. Like Feathers, the conventional genre moll tended to be extremely verbal, brandishing a sharp, witty vocabulary that made her as lethal in her own way as the gangster. Feathers was a brunette, but the Warner Bros. molls who succeeded her tended to be blondes, another mythical credential of Americanness to wash the gangster clean of his immigrant roots.

When synchronized sound came to motion pictures, the gangster genre picked up another iconic marking: prominently displayed images of guns accompanied by their barking or rapid mechanical sounds when

***Once upon a Time in America* (1984)** The post–World War I locations in *Once Upon a Time in America* could not be more specific with respect to city and ethnic group. This is the famous Jewish section of the Lower East Side of New York City in the early twentieth century. Unlike the generally deserted Warner Bros. sets depicting American urban life in the 1920s, these mean streets are bustling with people, animals, and merchandise, an intense reminder of the immigrant environment of the gangster story.

Gangs of New York (2002) Scorsese's set of the infamous Five Points in 1861 New York, the site of the city's major crimes of the period, is unique in the history of American gangster films and gives a new face to the urban gangster scene. Constructed at Cinecittà, Rome's celebrated film facility, it roots the American immigrant gangster in the Civil War period and specifically in the Irish immigrant experience. Thematically, Scorsese sets his story in a period when guns constituted a modern addition to the gangster arsenal, unwelcome in the eyes of "old school" gangsters of the time. In this frame, the striking absence of automobiles, another part of the standard iconography of the genre, is equally provocative and unsettling to conventional expectations.

fired and cars with motors loudly growling and tires screeching as they careered around corners. For obvious reasons, guns and cars make less of an impression in silent gangster movies. *Little Caesar* set the pace for Warner Bros. sound gangster movies with a new look and a new sound. Its opening scene kicked off the decade when Caesar Enrico Bandello, or Rico as he comes to be known, pulls into a gas station at night in an automobile and, under cover of darkness, shots ring out. From there, Rico invades the big city, and firearms and cars are an integral part of the landscape. Rico's first big score is an attack on a pricey nightclub on New Year's Eve, depicted in an artful montage in which drawn guns punctuate the action though only one shot is fired. Guns are everywhere in this film, though gunfire is sparingly used, for example in a drive-by attack on Rico, until a somewhat restrained final shootout between Rico and the police that includes a speeding-police-car sequence. In *The Public Enemy*, the sound effects of gunfire proliferate in numerous major gun battles; and there is even more spectacular gun play in *Scarface*, despite all the complaints of the PCA. With the later weakening of PCA power, spectacles of violence grew in intensity. The last scene of *White Heat* trumps all of its predecessors by substituting for gunfire the explosion of a large gas-storage tank that resembles a nuclear detonation. And post-*Godfather* gangster films have become bloodier and more savage, as, for example, the 1983 remake of *Scarface*, in which the visualization of violence in American gangster films reaches its zenith.

However, in many respects, the biggest change in gangster films made after the 1970s is not increased violence but the way they define themselves in opposition to the major icons of the Warner Bros. years. Newer gangster films, like *The Godfather* and *Goodfellas*, moved their mob settings from the inner city to the outer boroughs, the suburbs, small American towns (as in the case of *Road to Perdition*); the wide-open spaces and neon-lit streets of Las Vegas; and even to Europe. Much of *Godfather I* and *II* takes place on a large suburban estate, and much of *Goodfellas* takes place in Queens

Miller's Crossing (1990) Gabriel Byrne, who plays Tom Reagan, and directors Joel and Ethan Coen collaborated to use Reagan's hat self-consciously as part of the iconography of the genre. Reagan explicitly uses the hat as a security blanket, as it implicitly functioned in the Warner Bros. classics. Reagan dreams about it, clings to it, and uses it as part of his complex courtship dance with the woman he desires. Unlike the Warner Bros. fedoras, which wear the gangster, this fedora is worn by Reagan, battered by his experiences and shaped by him, as though he has incorporated the symbol into his being. In the final scene of the film, Reagan performs a ritual with it, as though it gives him what meager shred of identity he has been able to retain in the perfidious and violent world of the mob.

***Scarface* (1932)** Poppy (Karen Morley) is the blonde American trophy Tony Camonte steals from the boss he defeats when he briefly becomes the king of the mob hill. In her boudoir, Poppy presents the clearest image of her function as a luxury object, as far as the men are concerned. Nevertheless, her highly intelligent, alert expression suggests an inner agency that the film never fully explores and only partially reveals in her cutting, incisive dialogue and self-possessed bearing.

and on Long Island. When David Chase set his series *The Sopranos* in New Jersey, he used as his main title montage a car leaving New York City.

Similarly, the appearance of the newer gangster protagonists stands somewhat in opposition to the iconic older gangster model. Michael Corleone takes on the iconic appearance when he decides to be a gangster, and the gangsters in *Miller's Crossing*, which is set in the 1920s, exaggerate the old images, particularly that of the fedora. However, Henry Hill and his associates dress in the loose-fitting shirts that define suburban casual as opposed to the gangster pseudo-formal of bygone days, as do the characters in *The Sopranos*. The gangsters in *Casino* (1995) go hatless in the Nevada desert, and the nineteenth-century gangsters in *Gangs of New York* wear clothes appropriate to that era.

The women in recent gangster films also clearly diverge from the iconic molls of old Hollywood. The new paradigm of the woman with whom the gangster protagonist is involved is a proper middle-class girl who marries her mobster lover and finds that she must deal with the consequences of her choice. Kay Adams in the Godfather trilogy is the prototype of this new female presence in the genre. More fully fleshed out than the moll, Kay has dramatic problems of her own and is not, as were the early molls, merely one of the gangster's possessions. Excommunicated from Michael's life and thus from the lives of her son and daughter when she has an abortion rather than bring a third child into a crime empire, Kay marks the entrance into the genre of a female awareness of the implications of enabling a mobster. Unfortunately, Coppolla's

***White Heat* (1949)** Verna Jarrett (Virginia Mayo) is the Cold War version of the traditional blond moll. Flashy and feisty, she is combative rather than witty, impulsive rather than intelligent. The degradation of the moll reaches its extreme in *The St. Valentine's Day Massacre* (1967), in which Myrtle (Jean Hale) is little more than a wild animal.

innovation is somewhat compromised in *The Godfather: Part III*, when Kay and Michael are allowed a rapprochement that erases the crucial moral and ethical questions that tear them apart in the first two films of the trilogy, as if those issues never existed.

In *Goodfellas*, Karen Hill (Lorraine Bracco), the wife of the protagonist, has not only her own point of view but also her own voice-over, the first female voice-over in the genre. Karen, a "nice Jewish girl," who is as excited by Hill's affluent, high-flying gangster lifestyle as he is, brings into the genre an explicit reference to the complicity of law-abiding America in the success of the mob and adds to Scorsese's picture of the confusion of values in materialistic America. The same can certainly be said for Carmela Soprano (Edie Falco) and Tony's psychiatrist, Jennifer Melfi (Lorraine Bracco), in *The Sopranos*, who are even more fully etched portraits of the seduction of the middle class by the nonstop highs and profligate wealth of the American mobster.

The old prototype of the moll remains only in the *Scarface* remake, in which Elvira Hancock (Michelle Pfeiffer) is featured as a 1980s version of the American, blonde, smart-talking moll who shores up the immigrant gangster's identity. By contrast, the many easy women that Tony Soprano beds are not molls in the old sense, but are either "goomars"—kept women who, unlike the moll, have little to no power—or quick assignations who appear only briefly in the story. And in *Miller's Crossing*, the brunette Jewish prostitute, Verna (Marcia Gay Harden), who is the object of desire of both mob boss Leo and his enforcer, Tom Reagan, while tough-talking and flashy in the old moll tradition, has an uncharacteristic independence. In *Once Upon a Time in America*, Deborah Gelly (Elizabeth McGovern), the principal woman in the film, is tragically bound by the ties of Jewish ethnicity and an immigrant childhood to Noodles and Max, but she too is very much her own person. On par with the male protagonists of the film, Deborah has actively struggled with the corroding influences of American materialism with as much vigor and just as little success as Noodles and Max. And like Noodles and Max, she has seemingly achieved the American dream of success, as a glamorous stage and film star.

Finally, there is the highly problematic issue of iconic ethnicity in the gangster genre. It is widely believed that the gangster genre constitutes an ethnic insult to Americans of Italian extraction. And certainly some of the most iconic screen gangsters are patently Italian Americans, many of them inspired by the historical figure of Al Capone: Caesar Enrico Bandello in *Little Caesar*; Tony Camonte in *Scarface*; Al Capone in *Al Capone*; the Corleone family in the Godfather trilogy. In the television

Scarface (1983) This apocalyptic scene of destruction, in which Tony Montana (Al Pacino) floats face down in the pool in the garish center hall of his mansion, is oddly a validation of PCA fears about the gangster genre at the same time that it obeys the PCA mandate to give the gangster protagonist a violent end, long after most of the films in this genre have opted for more interesting and thoughtful comments on the wages of sin. The violence in this scene is gratuitous, serving no purpose but to make the film more sensational. However, unlike Michael Corleone, also played by Pacino, whose emotional death-in-life because of his criminal activities interestingly comments on the terrible losses that go along with mob success, Montana has his life terminated in the clichéd shootout that ends almost all the Warner Bros. 1930s gangster movies.

series *The Sopranos*, which now enjoys primary iconic status among screen-gangster productions, the main characters are Italian-American. That said, however, the series implicates almost all ethnic groups in the United States in mob culture, painting Slavic Americans as perhaps the most savage of any of the groups it depicts.

Moreover, if Americans of Italian heritage dominate public conversation about gangster films, they do not dominate the genre, which depicts the full spectrum of immigrant mobsters, the key characteristic of almost 100 percent of screen gangsters being their immigrant status and not their particular nationality or religion. For example, James Cagney, perhaps the most enduringly celebrated of the actors associated with American gangster film, played iconic Irish American mobsters in three of the most important gangster films of the Warner Bros. era: *The Public Enemy*, *Angels with Dirty Faces*, and *The Roaring Twenties*. He also played the main character in the most defining of the Cold War gangster films, *White Heat*, Cody Jarrett, who might be Irish American, but who is evidently not Italian-American in any case. Irish American gangsters are the principal characters in *Miller's Crossing*, with Jewish-American and Italian American gangsters appearing in subordinate roles, as is the case in *Road to Perdition* and *The Departed* (2006). *Gangs of New York* focuses on Irish American gangsters, but its main point is the impossibility of finding any ethnic group in America that can take the high ground, including white Anglo-Saxon Protestants, since as a nation of immigrants, America was also a nation of gangs.

Goodfellas features a protagonist who has an Irish father and an Italian mother, and if he is a part of the Mafia, in which important privileges are granted only to full-blooded Italians, neither Henry Hill nor the Irish Jimmy Conway (Robert De Niro), the second-most important male character in the film, is that. Jewish American gangsters take center stage in *Once Upon a Time in America* and in *The Rise and Fall of Legs Diamond*, as well as in *Casino*. Al Capone's mob in *The St. Valentine's Day Massacre* is a rainbow coalition of Americans whose ancestors hail from all parts of Europe: Germany, Ireland, and the Slavic countries, as well as Italy. The remake of *Scarface* concerns Hispanic gangsters, as does *American Me* (1992), while *American Gangster* is a story of an African American gang kingpin, not an immigrant in the strictest sense of the word, but a person whose group continues to be treated as outsiders. The central figure in *The Gangster* (1947), Shubunka (Barry Sullivan), is a man of indeterminate Slavic origin, played by an Irish actor.

Thus, public discourse about the genre, and not the genre itself, is the problem. A discussion of American gangster films based on the evidence rather than a seriously skewed discourse will find the iconic screen gangster volcanic and charismatic, a troubled man of immigrant heritage who gives the audience insight into a confused and confusing America built on the fears as well as the work of immigrants, not an attack on any ethnic group.

Once Upon a Time in America

Part of the originality of the gangster genre is its ability to use cinema to replicate the confusion and alienation of its immigrant/outsider mob protagonists. Other crime films, like police and detective dramas and outlaw sagas, feature protagonists who have a secure lock on the difference between reality and illusion. But this is not the case with gangster protagonists, who, toward the end of their films, typically find that their definition of reality has become a blur. Never securely rooted in the culture, gangster protagonists are cut off in many ways from their environment, and the images onscreen make us experience their isolation and disorientation. Close reading reveals many extraordinary moments when the gangster genre sensitizes us to the traumatized gangster state of mind. In a famous scene in *Little Caesar*, director Raoul Walsh has the audience experience the fragility of the gangster's grip on reality when he gives us a point-of-view shot as Rico, intending to shoot his best friend because mob power politics seem to demand it, is overcome by confusion. The shot blurs Rico's (and the spectator's) view of Joe. We are in his head as he loses focus and cannot pull the trigger.

In the more recent *Goodfellas*, Martin Scorsese uses sophisticated visual and aural images that place us inside Henry Hill's grandiosity and at the same time create an ironic distance between us and Hill. When Hill shows his new girlfriend, Karen (Lorraine Bracco), that he doesn't have to wait in line to get into an exclusive night club, we accompany them through an alternative entrance by way of the chaotic kitchen, filled with people running around hectically, the refuse from food preparation, and the clutter of dozens of objects strewing their path. In this scene, the jubilant song on the sound track, "And Then He Kissed Me," allows us to experience along with Hill and his date their bedazzled euphoria about the kitchen as a magical pathway to ecstasy. Yet our awareness of the grimy kitchen gives us a consciousness that Hill *doesn't have* of the absurdity of his feeling privileged as a mobster and his disoriented detachment from actual reality. In television, Tony Soprano and Nucky Thompson, despite their affluence, live on the edge, at a point where ordinary life threatens to turn surreal, and they find themselves perplexed by dreams in which their subconscious minds challenge their conscious decisions. However, for gangster screen aesthetics, the prime example is *Once Upon a Time in America*, with its many brilliant ways of drawing us into the hallucinatory grandiosity and alienation of the mobster.

Following the lives of four Jewish men, the children of immigrants, during the Prohibition era in New York City, *Once Upon a Time in America* uses cinematic poetry to depict the double bind of protagonist Noodles Aaronson (Robert De Niro), who, if circumstances had permitted, would have been a bookish sort of a man, but who is forced to accommodate himself to the street politics of immigrant life that drives him into crime. Noodles highlights the intensely traumatic situation of the immigrant by fiercely trying to bring to the wide-open American experience the sense of limits and loyalty to friends and loved ones that are an innate part of the European culture from which he and his family have been torn. Every scene in which Noodles appears shows him attempting to balance American urban streetwise pragmatism with traditional values—and, as America overwhelms his efforts, reveals the impossibility of Noodles's position. His situation reaches its climactic moment in the enigmatic and disturbing scene in which he takes the love of his life, Deborah Gelly (Elizabeth McGovern), on a date that is supposed to realize their dreams, but which goes horribly wrong. Noodles's initial euphoria turns into an attack on the body of the woman he has always adored, a scene that calls out for interpretation within the framework of the disoriented and disconnected immigrant gangster figure, since it is a baffling moment; Noodles has never displayed violence toward any woman and Deborah is a woman he has long placed on a pedestal.

Fantasy rules Noodles's "night to remember" with Deborah, who has grown up in the same Jewish ghetto in New York as he. But while she has used the fantasy of the theater as her means to escape immigrant poverty and hopelessness, Noodles has fueled his escape with gangster

***Once Upon a Time in America* (1984)** The dreamlike evocation of Noodles (Robert De Niro) as he utilizes his gangster power to offer the best of everything to Deborah (Elizabeth McGovern), the love of his life.

fantasies. The film's visualization of this date evokes Noodles's detachment from reality and the excessive nature of his dreams of love, beauty, and happiness. Deborah, in her own way a self-created fantasy of success, colludes with him in his disorientation without understanding until it is too late the implications of the fantasies enveloping them for the evening. She presents herself in the image of a fairy princess, beautifully dressed in delicate, filmy white chiffon, sparkling beads, and white fur. Noodles, too, presents himself fantastically for this occasion that he believes will change his life. He is resplendent in immaculately tailored formal menswear, and he escorts her into a seaside restaurant that is officially closed for the season, but which his gangster money and power have given him the means to open specially for his evening with her.

The cinematography emphasizes the dreamlike quality of this date. Shot on location in a real seaside restaurant, obviously chosen by the filmmakers for its high, white ceiling; decorated with wedding-cake bas-relief sculptural carving; and its pure white symmetrical arches, the scene radiates an airy brilliance. The white glow is punctuated by the warm glow of highly polished wood floors; green plants; red and white carpets; and dozens of tables for two, dressed in pristine white linen, sparkling glassware and silver, and apricot-colored roses. Chandeliers and candles reflect even more brilliance on the setting.

Leone's camera glides smoothly in one take from an entrance gallery to the dining room, shooting what seems to be an endless row of white arches, tables, chairs, and waiting servers and musicians. Infinite abundance is the image achieved by the frame compositions, the sense of boundless, clean, elegant excess that has haunted the dreams of impoverished newcomers to the American paradise. Noodles has provided for this date so much more than is needed by any two people. But neither Noodles nor Deborah reacts with surprise to the superabundance of dozens of people assembled to serve them and to provide music while they dance; this is clearly the dreamscape of their hearts objectified. The song the orchestra plays is "Amapola," and it has a very special historical significance for Deborah and Noodles. When they were children, she would practice dancing to the tune, as Noodles spied on her through a hole in the wall made by removing a brick. She knew he was there and taunted him. The dance then was for his eyes only, but he was catching a forbidden glimpse of her. Now he is her partner as they move to the music together. But on this night, the walls have been removed and transgressive secrecy is a thing of the past—or so they want to believe.

The grandiosity of the moment is tempered, at first, by the tenderness of the fantasy. Deborah says the words that Noodles has longed for all his life, that he is only person she has ever cared about. He leads her to the floor on which they will be the only couple, to dance to the song she once danced to in the dusty back room of her father's restaurant. The camera moves to a high angle, nestled among the sconces, lights glowing through apricot-colored shades, and enfolds them in the context of their most delirious fantasies of plenty, beauty, and romance, as we see them surrounded by all the tables at which no one else is sitting. Slowly, the camera moves down into a tight shot of their heads cheek to cheek. But a warning note is sounded at this point. Amid all this glamour and riches, Deborah's expression is ambiguous. It exudes neither satisfaction nor ecstasy. Noodle's face is buried in her neck. What is the truth of these people captivated by old dreams?

A lap dissolve merges this image with the exterior of the restaurant, an architectural Arabian nights dream, complete with minaret and exotic, oriental stone-and-ironwork windows against an azure evening sky. When the camera pans down it finds Noodles and Deborah reclining on the beach on rugs and cushions. As Noodles speak to her, he narrates their lives up to this point as if the past were a straight line leading to this climactic moment of passion and fulfillment. But now the fairy tale cracks as Deborah tells Noodles she's going to Hollywood to try for a film career. What happens when the gangster's excessive fantasy unravels?

Noodles is initially unable to respond, as if all coherence has departed from his view of the world. He has been frozen in time, thinking, like F. Scott Fitzgerald's Gatsby—who also woos his lady by means of riches acquired through associations with mobsters—that time has stood still waiting for him to catch up to it and win the game that he, as an immigrant, seemed born to lose. Once the fantasy is shattered, Noodles is unable to speak. He cannot win Deborah by taking by force the riches that will make her his. So he takes *her* by force.

Noodles, who has always striven for limits and for loyalty to friends, is overtaken completely by the gangster violence that we have seen before in other contexts. As outsiders, Noodles and his mob buddies act out rage and humiliation at not belonging, which is exactly what Noodles does when he savagely rapes Deborah, who, for once in her life, has

Once Upon a Time in America **(1984)** The dance for which Noodles has been waiting his entire life. There is no one in the world but Noodles and Deborah, and he rules the world—or so it seems.

left herself open to someone, a thing she will never do again. Leone shoots this attack in images as gritty and horrifying as the dream date is ecstatic, and to be sure that the audience is under no illusions about the depth of Noodles's rage, Leone shows him raping Deborah a second time, ripping the pale, delicate fabric of her dress the way the pale, romantic fantasy has been torn.

The rape scene, which all too many critics who have not thought with sufficient precision about the gangster genre have read as an anomaly in *Once Upon a Time in America*, is in fact the emblem of all the immigrant gangster relationships in this film. The characters destroy what they love because of fantasies they have developed to survive the rigors of immigrant life. The rape is indeed analogous to what Max does to Noodles, his dearest friend. When Prohibition is over, Max, believing that his best option is to join the Mafia—or syndicate, as Max calls it—a plan he knows Noodles will never go along with, stages his own death, killing two of his friends, and leaving Noodles as a grieving survivor. While Max adopts a new identity that will lead to riches and power, Noodles flees New York, and the film jumps ahead thirty-five years, moving inexorably to a conclusion that carries gangster-film depiction of gangster disorientation to heights that have never been equaled by any other filmmaker working in the genre.

When we see Noodles next, he is an old man who has been lured back to New York. The gangster grandiosity that overtook him when he raped Deborah will now throw his world into a state of permanent disorientation. He has received a mysterious letter—sent to him by Max, as he eventually discovers. Max, who Noodles thought was dead, is alive—but not for long. When Noodles learns that Max sent the letter, he realizes that he has been brought back to kill him. As Max explains, someone is going to, and Noodles is the only one he can "accept it from." Max is now so far into the inner circle in America that he is a highly placed government official, but, in his soul, he is still a man on the outside. He has been caught in corruption and is sure that he will be assassinated by other government officials who believe that he will implicate them when he is forced to testify before an official hearing. The cinematic language through which the meeting between Noodles and Max, the first time they have seen each other in thirty-five years, is represented at the end of the film is, like the rape scene, rich with the aesthetics of the gangster's self-involved grandiosity and the instability of his life.

The prologue to their confrontation is Noodles's discovery of David

Bailey (Rusty Jacobs), the image of Max when he was a boy, leading Noodles to the shattering realization that Max, obviously David's father, could not have died thirty-five years earlier. Noodles also realizes that Max and "Secretary Bailey," the U.S. Secretary of Commerce whose implication in scandal is all over the news, are one and the same. But it is the audience alone who sees the return of Max into the film, as we peer through the red stained glass of a window in his home, before Noodles arrives there. As we watch, Max moves toward us in a sea of red (blood-stained?) light, as the stunningly beautiful nostalgia theme composed for *Once Upon a Time in America* by Ennio Morricone swells on the sound track. As he opens the window, we see Max in natural light. It is as though we have actually watched Max coming back to us by moving physically through time. Observing this image, we become one with Noodles, seeing the hated and beloved Max rising from the dead.

This image of connection is immediately followed by a scene that shatters all possibility of a human bond, mimicking the precise dynamics of the rape scene. Noodles arrives at Max's house and wanders around his luxuriously appointed study as Max places on the desk the gun he wants Noodles to kill him with, baiting him by reminding him of how horribly he has deceived him. Noodles refuses and leaves. It looks like Noodles has succeeded in grounding himself in reality instead of allowing Max to seduce him into the old life of gangster disconnection. And then Leone pulls the rug out from under both Noodles and the audience.

As Noodles stands outside of the Bailey mansion, he sees Max exit the gates of his estate and walk toward a garbage truck standing there—for what reason it is impossible to say. Suddenly the truck motor turns on and moves past Max, hiding him from Noodles's view for a few seconds. When the truck has receded into the darkness, Max is gone. What has happened to him? All that is visible is the grinding mechanism at the back of the garbage truck. Has Max committed suicide? But the only matter that is being mashed in the turning metal gears is vegetable refuse. Noodles is completely discombobulated. Nothing he sees makes sense.

Equally sudden is the appearance of two carloads of young people rushing past Noodles, as "God Bless America," recorded by Kate Smith in 1943, blares on the radios. Noodles is now outside the ordinary parameters of time and space. Abruptly, the image of Noodles outside of Max's estate is replaced by an image from Noodles's past. He is in the

***Once Upon a Time in America* (1984)** Deborah's point of view on Noodles's bliss. What is her dream?

opium den where we saw him the night Max supposedly died. We see Noodles puff on an opium pipe, and his anxious expression is replaced by the idiotic smile of drug-induced ecstasy.

The audience too has been forced from a secure relationship with time and space. We do not know where we are, whether we are in Noodles's confused and disoriented head, or whether, as some critics have suggested, the entire film is Noodles's opium dream after Max dies in 1933. The latter "just a dream" interpretation seems to be easier for some people, but ultimately it makes no sense. If the film is just a dream, then Noodles has successfully created in his subconscious in 1933 exactly what New York will look like in 1967. A better close reading is to see this as Leone's depiction of the alienation of the gangster, so much a part of the genre and so clearly indicated by the events of Noodles's life. Faced with the impossibility of his situation, Noodles withdraws from it. In this much larger, much more resonant reading, the importance of the gangster genre surfaces. The immigrant gangster comes to stand as a metaphor for modern man, beset by freedom, cut off from the old traditions that once seemed to organize the human landscape.

Pulled into Noodles's head, we find that his story is about us too. Looking closely at how Leone depicts his alienation, we find the fascination of the American gangster genre in its most beautiful and intense form. Fostering audience identification with a mobster who breaks the most fundamental rules of society but wants nothing more than to be a part of it is ultimately a moral enterprise, an examination of the dynamics of an American tendency to lose our grip on reality as we pursue our desires, particularly desires for success. Lacking a solid tradition to buttress us, like Noodles and the other vividly portrayed gangster protagonists, we are unable to know with secure certainty who we are under the powerful centrifugal pressures of American circumstances.

Martha P. Nochimson

QUESTIONS FOR DISCUSSION

1. What is the definition of a gangster film? How has that definition changed from *The Musketeers of Pig Alley*, its first appearance in 1912, to more recent gangster movies like *The Godfather*, *The Godfather Part II*, *Goodfellas*, and *Once Upon a Time in America*?
2. How has the role of women changed in the gangster genre?
3. Does the gangster film glorify violence, or does it make us think about the causes of violence? Does the answer to this question vary from film to film?
4. How does the gangster film deal with ethnicity and race?

FOR FURTHER READING

Doherty, Thomas. *Hollywood's Censor: Joseph I. Breen and the Production Code Administration.* New York: Columbia University Press, 2009.

Grieveson, Lee, Esther Sonnet, and Peter Stanfield, eds. *Mob Culture: Hidden Histories of the American Gangster Film.* New Brunswick, NJ: Rutgers University Press, 2005.

Leitch, Thomas. *Crime Films.* New York: Cambridge University Press, 2002.

Mason, Fran. *American Gangster Cinema: From* Little Caesar *to* Pulp Fiction. Basingstoke, Hampshire, UK: Palgrave Macmillan, 2003.

Munby, Jonathan. *Public Enemies, Public Heroes: Screening the Gangster from* Little Caesar *to* Touch of Evil. Chicago: University of Chicago Press, 1999.

Nochimson, Martha P. *Dying to Belong: Gangster Movies in Hollywood and Hong Kong.* Malden, MA, and Oxford, UK: Wiley-Blackwell, 2007.

Shadoian, Jack. *Dreams and Dead Ends: The American Gangster Film.* 2nd ed. New York: Oxford University Press, 2003.

Silver, Alain, and James Ursini, eds. *The Gangster Film Reader.* New York: Limelight Editions, 2007.

Warshow, Robert. "The Gangster as Tragic Hero." In *Immediate Experience: Movies, Comics, Theatre, and Other Aspects of Popular Culture,* edited by Robert Warshow, 97–103. Enlarged ed. Cambridge, MA: Harvard University Press, 2002.

To Kill a Mockingbird (1962)

The Social-Problem Film

HOW DO WE CLASSIFY MOVIES such as *Milk* (2008), *Hotel Rwanda* (2004), and *To Kill a Mockingbird* (1962)? "Message movies," "morality plays," "preachment yarns," "headliners," "semidocumentaries," "docudramas," and "propaganda": all of these terms have been used. The name "social problem" originally referred to a cycle of films made right after World War II that focus on anti-Semitism, racism, war trauma, and other social ills. Subsequently, film scholars applied the label to earlier and later films so that the contours of a genre emerged over time. This genre, however, does not offer instantly identifiable settings or characters, as is the case with Westerns and gangster films. Instead, it is distinguished by its subject matter: these films spotlight a contemporary issue larger than the personal problems of the protagonists. Such movies seek to prompt reflection, discussion, and, in many cases, action about a pressing concern of American social life.

An *exclusive* grouping of social-problem films would include only serious, realistic dramas set in contemporary times. An *inclusive* grouping would include comedies and satires, such as *Dr. Strangelove* (1964) and *Wag the Dog* (1997), that make their case by taking the problem into the land of the absurd. Another branch of social-problem film overlaps with the historical film by choosing a story set in the past, though the "past" is relatively recent in *Matewan* (1987) and the topic—unionization—is still relevant. Hollywood has produced many hybrid genres, such as social-problem Westerns, e.g., *Dances with Wolves* (1990), which is about the genocide of Native Americans; social-problem musicals, e.g., *West Side Story* (1961), which is about racial prejudice; social-problem thrillers, e.g.,

Gentleman's Agreement (1947) Part of the cycle of postwar social-problem films, *Gentleman's Agreement* won the Academy Award for Best Picture in 1947. It stars Gregory Peck as Phil Green, a journalist who pretends to be Jewish to "blow the lid off" anti-Semitism in America. Green's Jewish secretary (June Havoc) is shocked when she finds out that her boss has feigned his religion. Phil reproaches her: "Look at me hard. I'm the same man I was yesterday: that's true, isn't it? Why should you be so astonished, Miss Wales? You still can't believe that anybody would give up the glory of being a Christian for even eight weeks, can you? That's what's eating you, isn't it?…Same face, same eyes, same nose, same suit, same everything. Here, take my hand—feel it! Same flesh as yours, isn't it? No different today than it was yesterday, Miss Wales. The only thing that's different is the word Christian." This kind of explicit dialogue about a pressing American social problem is characteristic of social-problem movies.

Breach (2007), which is about treason; social-problem sci-fi, e.g., *The Day After Tomorrow* (2004), which is about global warming; and particularly, social-problem biopics, e.g., *Malcolm X* (1992) and *What's Love Got to Do with It* (1993), because biopics often focus on a person who was courageous enough to tackle an injustice.

But what constitutes a social problem and who gets to "frame" or define it? Is crime an outgrowth of poverty, calling for sympathy and more government services, or a consequence of weakness in law and order, calling for vigilante justice? Hollywood has produced plenty of films from both perspectives. Throughout its history, however, this genre treats themes from a primarily liberal standpoint: I can think of numerous courtroom plots where the big corporation is at fault, and no examples about the burden of frivolous lawsuits or greedy plaintiffs.

The table below highlights some common themes:

Sample Thematic Clusters of Social-Problem Films

Education of the Poor	Racism	Corporate Malfeasance	Oppression of Women	Corrupt Officials	Mining Conditions	Prison Brutality
Blackboard Jungle (1955)	Within Our Gates (1920)	It's a Wonderful Life (1946)	Her Defiance (1916)	The Life of Big Jim Sullivan (1914)	Black Fury (1935)	I Am a Fugitive from a Chain Gang (1932)
To Sir, with Love (1967)	In the Heat of the Night (1967)	The China Syndrome (1979)	Outrage (1950)	Mr. Smith Goes to Washington (1939)	How Green Was My Valley (1941)	The Defiant Ones (1958)
Stand and Deliver (1988)	Guess Who's Coming to Dinner (1967)	Silkwood (1983)	Diary of a Mad Housewife (1970)	Serpico (1973)	Salt of the Earth (1954)	Lonely Are the Brave (1962)
Dangerous Minds (1995)	El Norte (1983)	A Civil Action (1998)	The Accused (1988)	Prince of the City (1981)	The Molly Maguires (1970)	Cool Hand Luke (1967)
Freedom Writers (2007)	Do the Right Thing (1989)	The Insider (1999)	Dolores Claiborne (1995)	16 Blocks (2006)	Matewan (1987)	Brubaker (1980)
The Great Debaters (2007)	American History X (1998)	Blood Diamond (2006)	North Country (2005)	Frost/Nixon (2008)	Harlan County War (2000)	The Road to Guantánamo (2006)

History

Unlike many genres, which go in and out of fashion precipitously, the social-problem film has chugged along steadily. Filmmakers always want to make movies about contemporary issues, and many viewers hunger to see films that have a meaningful connection with their social conditions.

In fact, even during the early years of the silent era—a period often maligned as all ringlets and pranks—films were remarkably frank and political in their treatment of every social ill, from venereal disease and sex education to labor exploitation and poverty. This shouldn't be surprising; after all, movies were born in the Progressive Era (roughly 1890-1920), when activists loudly clamored for reform and when muck-rakers exposed the corruption or brutal working conditions fostered by many American companies and practices. Film scholar Steven Ross points out that because single-reel filming was relatively cheap and easy, from the very early years reformers and religious leaders, as well as labor unions, business, and political-interest groups, made films to try to sway public opinion toward their causes.

Margaret Sanger, the crusader for birth control, produced a film about the subject in 1917, titled, aptly enough, *Birth Control*. The suffrag-ist movement financed three melodramas—one of them with the provoc-ative title *Eighty Million Women Want—?* (1913). The National Child Labor Committee participated in the production of *Children Who Labor* (1912). Professional filmmakers also highlighted injustices. Edwin S. Porter, famous for *The Great Train Robbery* (1903), also made *The Kleptomaniac* (1905), which shows that a rich woman who shoplifts is acquitted, but a poor woman who steals a loaf of bread for her starving children is sent to jail. At the end, an allegorical figure of Justice holds scales—one side with a loaf of bread, the other with a bag of gold—and the gold wins out. Many of the shorts D. W. Griffith made for Biograph treat social issues: for example, *A Corner in Wheat* (1909) contrasts the decadent parties of the wealthy wheat speculator with hordes of people in a breadline.

Filmmaking became more expensive in the age of silent features, 1915-1927, and, therefore, interest groups had less access to the screen. Some historians believe that as the industry moved toward standardization—particularly with movie theaters opening up in wealthier parts of town and wooing a more middle-class audience—it promoted fantasy and comedy, while social comment vanished from the screen. Perhaps social-issue films attracted less attention during these years because their moralism was out of tune with the carefree hedonism and modern sophistication of the Roaring '20s, but they never disappeared. Griffith's *The Mother and the Law* (1919) lambastes hypo-critical titans of industry and capital punishment, while his *Broken Blos-soms* (1919) critiques racism and macho domination. The pathbreaking female director Lois Weber made movies in favor of birth control and against abortion, in favor of child labor laws, temperance, and livable wages for college professors, and against capital punishment. The pio-neering African American director Oscar Micheaux made *Within Our Gates* (1920), a film that features a horrible scene of whites lynching

***I Am a Fugitive from a Chain Gang* (1932)** The ending of this film is famous for it bleakness, and its refusal of a Hollywood "happy ending." The hero has escaped from a torturous prison, but he cannot rejoin normal life. At the end, he bids good-bye to his girlfriend, Helen, and disappears into the night. Helen: "Can't you tell me where you're going? Will you write? Do you need any money? [Jim shakes his head.] But you must, Jim! How do you live?" Jim: "I steal!" The ending is shocking in showing how paranoid, unbalanced, and criminal Jim has become due to the injustices he had suffered.

blacks, and *Body and Soul* (1925), which warns about hypocrisy in the Church. In the years corresponding to the Red Scare of the 1920s, filmmakers produced a whole slew of titles against communism.

Censorship became more organized in the 1920s when the Motion Picture Producers and Distributors Association hired Will Hays to bolster the industry's image after a series of scandals. However, the Catholic-oriented censors supported controversial material when they agreed with its moral uplift. Hays granted a special dispensation to *Human Wreckage* (1923), which is about drug peddling. The film, sponsored by the Los Angeles Anti-Narcotics League, stars Dorothy Davenport, whose husband, the movie idol Wallace Reid, had died in 1922 from complications of his addiction to morphine. Two years later, Davenport directed *The Red Kimona* (1925), which features a lower-class prostitute who is exploited by both her male lover and purient society matrons.

Hollywood converted to sound at the beginning of the Depression. Talkies led to many changes in the industry, one of which was the hiring of scores of East Coast writers, as well as the purchase of contemporary plays and novels. Since many of the writers and playwrights were deeply engaged in politics and social issues, this brought an infusion of committed left-leaning talent to Los Angeles. Besides, the times were dire: by the end of 1932, 28 percent of the population was trying to survive on no income whatsoever. The tenor of the times seeped into the movies, especially at Warner Bros., which made a policy of snatching its stories from current headlines. Movies of these years focused on women descending into prostitution to eat; homeless boys on the road; brutality in prisons, reform schools, and factories; and crooked lawyers.

As the 1930s progressed, other studios joined in; for example, Goldwyn produced the hard-hitting *Dead End* (1937), about young boys turned into hoodlums by their slum environment. Indeed, by the end of the decade, the press of developments, particularly the ominous situation in Europe on the verge of war, made typical Hollywood escapism seem hollow. Darryl Zanuck, the studio head most consistently committed to social commentary, stated:

> I kept on thinking that every single happening I was reading about in the newspapers and newsmagazines was the stuff of moving pictures. But they kept warning me to stay away from such things. "Give 'em cowboys, tits and gangsters," said Jack Cohn [Columbia]. "That's the way to keep 'em happy." Louie Mayer [MGM] put it more pompously. "Give them glamour," he said. Glamour! In 1939, when the world was going to pieces![1]

In 1939, the MPPDA changed its position from firmly advocating that movies are only for entertainment to officially welcoming their treatment of contemporary topics. With or without the MPPDA's permission, a rush of prestigious, high-budget social-problem films tumbled out. Frank Capra directed his most coherent political film, *Mr. Smith Goes to Washington* (1939). Even MGM got involved, though *Mrs. Miniver* (1942), a film supporting our British Allies during the Blitz, cast the ultra-beautiful Greer Garson as the "typical" British housewife. Zanuck, now at 20th Century–Fox, optioned John Steinbeck's *The Grapes of Wrath*

---

[1] Leonard Mosley, *Zanuck: The Rise and Fall of Hollywood's Last Tycoon* (New York: McGraw-Hill, 1985), 188.

The Grapes of Wrath (1940) Nunnally Johnson's screenplay originally ended with this shot of Tom Joad (Henry Fonda) walking off into the distance (a typically Fordian horizon shot), leaving his grieving mother (Jane Darwell) behind. However, the producer, Darryl Zanuck, added a final scene showing that Ma's courage and strength are unshaken. Zanuck's conclusion is more hopeful, while still striking a populist note. Endings of social-problem films are key sites of contention because they determine the film's overall message and approach to the issue under observation. This is where faith in the American Dream is either confirmed or questioned.

(1940). Although Zanuck insisted on changing the ending so the film concludes on a slightly more optimistic note than the book, John Ford's version shows a whole system of exploitation of dispossessed migrant workers, and even includes dialogue defending communism. Zanuck and Ford followed *The Grapes of Wrath* with *How Green Was My Valley* (1941), a story about a Welsh mining family coping with brutal workplace hazards, the desecration of their environment, and small-minded intolerance.

During the war, the Office of War Information censored films, demanding tales that painted the virtues and success of American democracy to keep up morale and present the country in a positive light to international audiences. Still, notable social problems were addressed: lynching in the *The Ox-Bow Incident* (1943), alcoholism in *The Lost Weekend* (1945), and crushing poverty in *A Tree Grows in Brooklyn* (1945). Immediately postwar, Hollywood filmmakers, sobered by their wartime experiences (including knowledge of the Holocaust, which forced everyone to recognize a level of crimes against humanity previously unimagined) and broadened by their exposure to documentary techniques, produced an impressive cycle of social-problem films. *The Best Years of Our Lives* (1946) swept the Academy Awards with its bleak portrait of returning veterans facing unemployment, disability, and alcoholism. *Gentleman's Agreement* (1947), a story about anti-Semitism, monopolized all the statues a year later. *Pinky*, *Home of the Brave*, and *Intruder in the Dust* (all 1949) tackled racism.

Although later, liberal critics judged these postwar films harshly for their evasions and compromises, in the late 1940s conservative forces found them threatening. Eric Johnston, Will Hays's successor at the MPPDA, proclaimed in 1947, "We'll have no more *Grapes of Wrath*, we'll have no more *Tobacco Roads*.... We'll have no more films that show the seamy side of American life."[2] In September 1947, fearing that communists and fellow travelers were inserting propaganda into Hollywood movies, the House Un-American Activities Committee (HUAC) issued its first subpoenas investigating the presence of the "red menace" in the film industry. The FBI investigated the creative teams behind ten films—including *It's a Wonderful Life* and *The Best Years of Our Lives*—for communist ties. One of the main consequences of the anti-communist probes and the blacklisting of liberal filmmakers that ensued (which lasted until 1959) was to take the wind out of the social-problem film's sails. Many of the professionals previously involved in those movies either were jailed, went into exile, or retreated to less controversial subject matter.

One historian has calculated that in 1947, 28 percent of the films released could be categorized as social-problem films; by 1954 that number had slipped to 9.2 percent. Nonetheless, social-problem films continued to be released throughout the 1950s. Ida Lupino directed a series of low-budget movies on issues such as rape and unwanted pregnancy. George Stevens adapted Theodore Dreiser's indictment of capitalism and social climbing, *An American Tragedy* (1951). Elia Kazan made *On the Waterfront* (1954), about mobsters on the docks of New York; Otto Preminger directed Frank Sinatra as a heroin addict in *The Man with the Golden Arm* (1955). Stanley Kramer produced and/or directed one message movie after another. As the civil rights movement gathered steam, Hollywood distributed more films that dealt with racial discrimination,

---

[2] Quoted in Thomas Schatz, *Boom and Bust: American Cinema in the 1940s.* History of American Cinema, vol. 6 (Berkeley: University of California Press, 1997), 382.

such as *No Way Out* (1950), *The Defiant Ones* (1958), and *A Raisin in the Sun* (1961).

Television enters the story here. During the 1950s, live television dramas on controversial subjects were written by left-wing writers working under pseudonyms. When the young writers and directors moved on to the big screen, or the older filmmakers migrated back, they brought with them these stories and attitudes. Sidney Lumet, whose television work was extremely political, made the transition to film with an adaptation of a television drama about racial prejudice in a jury room, *12 Angry Men* (1957), and he would go on to direct many films in this genre.

The early 1960s was a transitional time for Hollywood as the industry floundered financially and stylistically. The demise of the Production Code freed this genre to tackle grittier subjects more forthrightly. The Code had not only regulated sexual content and crime, it mandated respect for religious, legal, and national authority figures. Film historians often trace the birth of New American Cinema to 1967 with the release of *Bonnie and Clyde* and *The Graduate*. Cinema in the later '60s and throughout the '70s expressed the attitudes and discontent of a fresh generation of filmmakers and youthful audiences. And yet, however oppositional Arthur Penn, Robert Altman, Martin Scorsese, and Stanley Kubrick were to "The Establishment," they never attacked specific social problems, more often adopting positions of general cynicism, paranoia, or existential angst. For instance, Sydney Pollack's *They Shoot Horses, Don't They* (1969) ends with Robert (Michael Sarrazin) acceding to Gloria's (Jane Fonda) pleas by shooting her in the head, illustrating that American society is too far gone to reform—so one might as well die.

Less popular and less noticed than the big Hollywood directors, independent filmmakers increasingly made political films. A group of blacklisted filmmakers and nonprofessional actors actually produced *Salt of the Earth* (1954) at the height of the McCarthy period. A remarkable story about a strike at a zinc mine in New Mexico, it also treats male domination of women and anti-Hispanic prejudice. Conservative powers launched a national campaign to suppress the film—the story of the film's tribulations is fascinating, almost more exciting than the movie itself—and kept *Salt of the Earth* from being distributed.

In later decades, independent directors were often willing not only to engage with social issues but to experiment stylistically. *Nothing But a Man* (1964) , which copies the mode and feel of Italian Neorealism, is

Salt of the Earth (1954) This unusual film was made by a group of blacklisted film-makers in New Mexico. Based on a true story, it takes the side of Hispanic mine workers against Anglo town officials and mine owners and argues against exploitation, preju-dice, and male dominance. In this image, the wives of the miners take over the picket lines after courts have unjustly prohibited the men from demonstrating. The film was denounced on the floor of Congress, and conservative powers engaged in a conspiracy to suppress it by deporting Rosaura Revueltas, the main actress, to Mexico; whipping up violence against the production; blocking the negative from labs; and keeping prints from being projected in movie theaters. The campaign against the film shows how fright-ened some were that a movie would influence viewers.

Similar campaigns against other films (for instance, feminist protests against the 1980 psychosexual thriller *Dressed to Kill*) also testify that movies are widely credited with influencing social attitudes.

a quiet and devastating look at African-Americans coping with poverty and racism. The daring *Sweet Sweetback's Baadasssss Song* (1971), which also deals with racism, is confrontational in the style of French film-maker Jean-Luc Godard's counter-cinema. *Do the Right Thing* (1989) chal-lenges the viewer every step of the way to decide whether the right thing is Martin Luther King's nonviolent protest or Malcolm X's principle of aggressive confrontation. *El Norte* (1983) integrates magical realism with a gritty portrayal of the situation of illegal Guatemalan immigrants. John Sayles's films pioneered the multi-storyline structure, showing how all the inhabitants of a community are interwoven, in films such as *City of Hope* (1991) and *Sunshine State* (2002).

Another strand of social-problem films reappeared on television. The mega-success of two miniseries, *Roots* (1977) and *Holocaust* (1978), demonstrated how popular and influential serious subject matter could be. Ever since, television has carried a torch for this genre, sometimes in weekly series—e.g., *The West Wing*—but more often in made-for-TV movies. *The Day After* (1983) is a graphic and terrifying account of what happens when a nuclear strike hits Kansas; *The Burning Bed* (1984) is a still unparalleled account of spousal abuse; *An Early Frost* (1985) was one of the first discussions of AIDS. The cable stations Lifetime, Showtime, and especially HBO—in *Recount* (2008) and *Game Change* (2012)—have continued the tradition of made-for-TV social-problem films.

Back in the big-budget-feature world of the 1970s and '80s, scholars Ryan and Kellner highlight that liberal films often presented the conflict between a single, brave, and good person against corrupt institutions. Sometimes the protagonist wins out, validating American ideals of individual agency, but sometimes overwhelming forces prove too strong.

***Do the Right Thing* (1989)** This film addresses head-on the racial conflicts simmering on a hot day in Brooklyn. Spike Lee uses his camera in unconventional ways—canted angles, unusual lenses, tight close-ups—to ratchet up the viewer's involvement in the story. Here the camera is zooming in on a close-up of Stevie (Luis Ramos), who addresses the camera (and the viewer in her seat) directly with examples of the racist hate talk. This is part of a montage sequence during which people of different ethnic groups all virulently defame others. Lee makes us face the prevalence of racism and its ugliness.

Mainstream directors such as Martin Ritt, Oliver Stone, Sydney Pollack, Michael Apted, and Sidney Lumet kept the genre in the theaters with lauded films. A key film of that era was *Norma Rae* (1979), in which Sally Field plays a union activist so indomitable that she forces the textile mill to allow unionization. *Salvador* (1986) challenges the Reagan administration's actions in Latin America. *Absence of Malice* (1981) shows the devastation caused by ambitious reporters who pry into private lives. *Gorillas in the Mist* (1988) shows Dian Fossey's brave attempt to save animals in the wild. In *The Verdict* (1982), Paul Newman, as an alcoholic lawyer, wins a malpractice case for his client, but the film fits Ryan and Kellner's pattern of stressing personal redemption rather than a fundamental change of the system.

During the 1990s, social-issue documentaries crossed over to reach mainstream theater audiences. The most important figure in this trend is Michael Moore, whose *Roger and Me* (1989) uses humor and staged scenes to launch an indictment of the CEO of General Motors. Moore's influence has continued through *Bowling for Columbine* (2002), a documentary about gun control, and his denunciation of the Bush administration in *Fahrenheit 9/11* (2004). Other documentaries in this vein include *Super Size Me* (2004), *Enron: The Smartest Guys in the Room* (2005), *Inside Job* (2010), and *Waiting for "Superman"* (2010). Documentaries have brought political issues into mainstream theaters, attracted news coverage, and affected public commentary on a host of issues. Yet documentaries don't appeal to all viewers; some audiences are more drawn toward movies with big-name stars, the pleasure of a clear narrative, and high production values. According to Box Office Mojo, the fictional film *Mississippi Burning* (1988), which is in many ways a travesty of the true history of the civil rights movement, earned $35 million at the box office, while the documentary *The Untold Story of Emmett Louis Till* (2005) earned only $200,000.

One has only to peruse the Academy Awards of the 1990s and 2000s to see the prevalence of social-problem films, which seem to have been nominated for more of the major awards than any other genre. *Dances with Wolves* (1990), *Schindler's List* and *Philadelphia* (both 1993), *The Insider* (1999), *Erin Brockovich* and *Traffic* (both 2000), *The Pianist* (2002), *Crash* (2004), *Brokeback Mountain* and *Good Night and Good Luck* (both 2005), and *The Help* (2011) were acclaimed by tastemakers and earned respectable grosses.

A significant development in the history of the genre came in 2004 with the founding of a production company whose avowed mission is not money but social improvement—Participant Media, started by Jeff

Skoll, a billionaire philanthropist who was involved in the founding of eBay. Participant Media funds, cofunds, or distributes both fiction films and documentaries. Its roster in the last few years is impressive: *Good Night and Good Luck*, *North Country*, *American Gun*, *Syriana* (all 2005), *Fast Food Nation* (2006), *Darfur Now*, *Chicago 10*, *The Kite Runner* (all 2007), *Fair Game* (2010), *Contagion* (2011), *Lincoln* (2012), and the cultural blockbuster *An Inconvenient Truth* (2006). Aside from boosting awareness and fostering discussion, each film is linked to an Internet "campaign"—for example, *Murderball*'s (2005) site raises money for the Paralympics; *Syriana*'s suggests protesting the tactics of oil companies. The website for *An Inconvenient Truth* has specific suggestions for effecting change personally, locally, nationally, and globally. Participant Media seeks to change audiences from passive spectators into grassroots activists. Its mission statement, though, repeats the mantra of the genre, stressing first that its films will entertain, and then that they will motivate spectators into making a difference.

What's next for the genre? As YouTube and other New Media ventures allow nonprofessionals access (*Kony 2012*, a video about human-rights abuses committed by Joseph Kony, a murderous guerrilla leader in Uganda, went viral with more than eighty million viewers and changed international policy), the future may hold a return to the past: the ability of interest groups to use visual narratives to lobby for their cause. The technical revolution currently under way greatly expands the number and nature of the social problems that might be addressed and allows citizens to plead the case for reform in a wide variety of arenas.

Typologies, Themes, and Theories

Social-problem films blend two narrative modes: 1) realism, to prove that the story and problem are authentic, and 2) melodrama, to move the viewer to pity, outrage, and (perhaps) action. Many social-problem films are based in historical fact; of the roughly one hundred films mentioned in this chapter, about half involve a real person or event. (In most cases, the story first won renown in book form.) Where the tale is not the literal story of one historical person, as in the case of *The Grapes of Wrath* or *Traffic*, writers conduct broader research in order to make their presentation accurate.

Of course, when scholars scrutinize the *actual* story behind any of

***Philadelphia* (1993)** Andrew Beckett (Tom Hanks) dies of AIDS. At a memorial gathering in his honor at the end of the film, a TV plays a home video of Andrew as a child. The adorableness of the little boy—who could hate or fear this innocent child?—coupled with a very moving musical score, insists that the viewer feel this loss as a terrible tragedy. Thus, this social-problem film, like so many others, employs the techniques of melodrama to move the viewer toward pity for Andrew and outrage at his bigoted, homophobic antagonists.

these films they uncover how much is simplified, condensed, or prettified to make a Hollywood feature film. These changes work to bring out the melodramatic aspects of the story. Melodrama, a mode that seeks to highlight moral values in a confusing world, arouses pity for an innocent sufferer and outrage at the oppressors (see Chapter 2 on melodramas). Accordingly, social-problem films place enormous stress on the protagonist's suffering. The Nolan family's struggles in *A Tree Grows in Brooklyn* are heart-wrenching. In *The Insider*, Jeffrey Wigand (Russell Crowe) becomes paranoid and irrational and verges on suicide. Andrew Beckett (Tom Hanks) in *Philadelphia* suffers terribly from the ravages of AIDS and the hostility of homophobes.

In terms of characters, this genre often employs melodrama's tactic of dividing the world into absolute good and absolute evil. Filmmakers paint the antagonists in social-problem movies in the worst possible light. Winston (Craig T. Nelson) in *Silkwood* (1983) not only falsifies X-rays of nuclear rods, he letches after Karen (Meryl Streep) in a disgusting manner. The husband in *Dolores Claiborne* not only beats his wife but molests his daughter. Not only is Karen (Tilda Swinton) in *Michael Clayton* (2007) defending the company's abysmal pollution record, she's paying hit men to kill lawyers who oppose her. In *The Company Men* (2010), Salinger (Craig T. Nelson), who has just laid off thousands of employees, is building himself a luxurious new office. Sometimes the antagonists in these films appear so unremittingly evil that they might as well be wearing black capes and twirling long mustaches.

Both realism and melodrama contribute to a notable feature of social-problem films—the number of women protagonists. Historically, melodrama has had a penchant for women because their suffering can more easily evoke an audience's concern or pity. However, the twentieth century actually brims with women activists; the true stories behind *Birth Control, Norma Rae, Silkwood, Missing* (1982), *Gorillas in the Mist, Erin Brockovich, Dangerous Minds, Music of the Heart* (1999), *Boys Don't Cry* (1999), and *The Whistleblower* (2010) feature real women brave enough to challenge traditional powers and norms. Social scientists argue that in contemporary society women are particularly likely to play the role of whistle-blower because they don't feel as integrated into or as loyal to the "old-boy network."

The protagonists of social-problem films obsess over the injustice they strive against. They show tremendous perseverance in fighting against powerful odds and dangerous situations. In the late 1940s and the 1950s, in films such as *The Men* (1950), which is about a traumatized, disabled veteran, the love of a good woman "solves" the social problem. But over the history of the genre, romance is typically underplayed or frustrated. Frequently, the protagonists forsake the pleasures of love and family to pursue their causes. Girlfriends, boyfriends, wives, and

Karen Silkwood Silkwood was a union activist at the Kerr-McGee plant in Oklahoma, which manufactured nuclear equipment for power plants. She testified before the Atomic Energy Department about safety violations at Kerr-McGee. She was on her way to meet a reporter from the *New York Times* with a binder of information when she died in a one-car accident in 1974. Although the allegations of foul play were never substantiated, the case became a cause célèbre and fueled suspicions about the nuclear industry. Her story was the basis of *Silkwood*, a 1983 film starring Meryl Streep, Kurt Russell, and Cher, which was nominated for five Academy Awards.

This film, along with *Norma Rae* (1979), *Prince of the City* (1981), *What's Love Got to Do with It* (1993), *Milk* (2008), *42* (2013), and countless others, demonstrates the strong crossover between social-problem films and biopics, that is, films that trace a notable figure's biography. In social-problem biopics, however, the person is famous for fighting injustice or corruption, not for being a queen or explorer.

***In the Heat of the Night* (1967)** At the beginning of this film, the bigoted southern sheriff, Gillespie (Rod Steiger), is racist and hostile toward Virgil Tibbs (Sidney Poitier). By the end of the film, the sheriff has great respect for Poitier's character; Gillespie comes to admire Virgil's intelligence, expertise, and perseverance. Gillespie has been converted from a racist to a believer in equality. This film offers a good example of the "conversion story" plot type so common in the social-problem genre.

husbands leave the protagonist, who is giving his/her all to buck the system. Norma Rae's and Erin Brockovich's (Julia Roberts) homelives suffer. Romance never even enters as a subplot in *In the Heat of the Night* or *Michael Clayton*.

Three common plot formulas recur in social-problem films, sometimes in combination. The first is the *courtroom* case, where guilt and innocence will be publicly presented for the viewer to judge. The second is the *investigation*, when someone stumbles across an injustice or conspiracy, sleuths into its depth and seriousness, and tries to bring it to public notice. Finally, in the *conversion* story, a central character, who stands in for the viewer, is converted from his/her prejudices or lack of compassion to the side of the angels.

Thematically, social-problem films side with the poor, the downtrodden, and the humiliated against their victimizers. These films believe in justice and commitment; they celebrate individuals such as Paul Rusesabagina (Don Cheadle) in *Hotel Rwanda*, who risk their lives while others cower. Like muckraking novels, or investigative television programs on the order of *60 Minutes* and *20/20*, social-problem films believe in the power of the exposé: their subtext is, "If only the American people knew the true story of problem x"—x being chain gangs, or poor schools, or Matthew Shepard's brutal murder in Laramie, Wyoming—"then surely the public outcry will put an end to these outrages." What the genre never wants to acknowledge, however, breaks out into the open in Michael Mann's subtle film *The Insider*, when the whistle-blower is talking to the journalist:

> *Wigand:* You believe that because you get information out to people, something happens...
> *Bergman:* Yes.
> *Wigand:* Maybe that's just what you've been telling yourself all these years to justify having a good job. Having status. Maybe for the audience it's just voyeurism, something to do on a Sunday night, and maybe it won't change a fucking thing.

Wigand's misgivings about the utility of exposés are ultimately proved wrong in this story, but only due to Lowell Bergman's extraordinary dedication, and Bergman decides that he has to leave *60 Minutes* because of his misgivings about the show's integrity.

Two opposing doctrines about the role of film in American society have influenced all discussion of social-problem films. The first is the doctrine of "pure entertainment," according to which movies exist just for escape, just for fun. (This is what underlies your friend's veto of a serious drama in favor of a gross-out comedy or horror film.) The film industry, very aware of audience preferences, often promulgates this doctrine as official policy. Will Hays, then head of the Motion Picture Producers and Distributors Association, wrote in 1938:

> Entertainment is the commodity for which the public pays at the box-office. Propaganda disguised as entertainment would be neither honest salesmanship nor honest showmanship.... The movie theater can afford the soft impeachment that most pictures reflect no higher purpose than to entertain.... If entertainment and recreation are what 85,000,000 people weekly seek in American motion picture theaters, and they do, so much the better for the screen.[3]

Obviously, this doctrine avoids defining what individuals actually find *entertaining*. As mentioned above, many viewers find meaty films

---

[3] Quoted in Margaret Thorpe, *America at the Movies* (New Haven, CT: Yale University Press, 1939), 274.

more nourishing than fluff; in point of fact, they prefer films that engage with meaningful issues.

However, the "entertainment doctrine" is so dominant, so ingrained, that under questioning, the vast majority of directors, even those famous for their politically engaged films, will cagily respond that entertainment is their only or preeminent goal. Bruce Gilbert, the producer of *The China Syndrome*, a film designed to warn of the dangers of nuclear power plants, reveals why everyone involved in that movie's publicity deliberately spoke about it as "just a movie": "We believe that for the most part the public doesn't want to see films that they think are good for them.... We didn't want to keep anybody from seeing the film by positioning it in a way where they would believe that it was one of those films that would be good for them, like castor oil or medicine."[4]

The opposite point of view, which has been openly embraced by a few filmmakers and actively championed by many critics and scholars, is that the movies have a social responsibility. Commentators on the right and on the left sides of the political spectrum have promulgated this doctrine with equal force. Martin Quigley, one of the conservative, Catholic authors of the Production Code, stated firmly, "The function of art is to ennoble. Art is as much a servant and tool of civilization as science."[5] Joseph Losey, a director blacklisted for his communist associations, is quoted in *The Celluloid Weapon*, "Of course art has a social function. We are social beings and live in a society. If you don't want to recognize that then you have to live without the products of society, without any obligations to society and without any obligations on the part of society to you. Anyone who feels that strongly that art has no social function should go to the proverbial desert island."[6]

Trying to reconcile these two opposing doctrines has led to filmmakers adopting the strategy of making social commentary... *entertaining*. Darryl Zanuck, the studio head who played the greatest role in producing and promoting social-problem films from 1930 to 1960, addressed screenwriters at a conference in 1939: "We must play our part

[4] "Bruce Gilbert: Hollywood's Progressive Producer," in *The Cineaste Interviews: On the Art and Politics of the Cinema*, eds. Dan Georgakas and Lenny Rubenstein (Chicago: Lake View Press, 1983), 252–53.
[5] Martin Quigley, "Decency in Motion Pictures," in *The Movies in Our Midst*, ed. Gerald Mast (Chicago: University of Chicago Press, 1982), 340.
[6] Joseph Losey, "Speak, Think, Stand Up," *Film Culture* 50–51 (Fall and Winter 1970), 58.

in the solution of the problems that torture the world. We must begin to deal realistically in film with the causes of wars and panics, with social upheavals and depressions, with starvation and want and injustice and barbarism under whatever guise." He went on to admonish, "If you have something worthwhile to say, dress it in the glittering robes of entertainment." Unless the film is enjoyable, Zanuck was sure that "no propaganda film is worth a dime."[7]

Dressing the films in the "glittering robes of entertainment," however, has discredited the genre with film critics and theorists, leaving the social-problem film open to several interrelated charges of "bad faith" and futility. Most of the academics who deride this genre rely on tenets of Marxist film theory. One of the key assumptions, articulated in 1969 in the French journal *Cahiers du Cinéma*, is that films with explicit political content cannot be effective as critiques of society if they adopt conventional cinematic structure and style. According to *Cahiers* and its followers, unless you explode the conventions of Hollywood narrative (as Jean-Luc Godard does in his late films) by Brechtian techniques—such as openly avowing that the film is fictional or preventing viewers from identifying with the characters—you cannot make a movie that will truly be progressive. Moreover, Marxists and socialists have little truck with liberalism's philosophy of gradual amelioration of social injustices. In their eyes, no Hollywood film is brave enough to get to the heart of society's ills (the capitalist system). Instead, this genre offers fantasies whereby heroic individuals have the power to defeat straw villains as opposed to challenging America's fundamental economic base and inequities. Thus, for these critics, the social-problem film actually works to support the status quo by siphoning off social discontent and sending audiences out drained of revolutionary fervor.

The question of who has the right to speak for whom also dogs this genre. Can white, straight, upper-class men (who historically have dominated all Hollywood filmmaking) do justice to tales of oppression of the poor, the laboring class, minorities, immigrants, women, or gays? Have these men—wittingly or unwittingly—"stolen" these stories from those who should be telling them and inevitably weakened their critiques? Charges along these lines circled around *The Help*, which reveals the humiliating treatment of black domestic workers in the

---

[7] George F. Custen, *Twentieth Century's Fox: Darryl F. Zanuck and the Culture of Hollywood* (New York: Basic Books, 1997), 275.

Jim Crow South, but was written by a white woman and directed by a white man.

Related strong critiques of the genre circulate. Although critics from the first half of film history, such as Bosley Crowther of the *New York Times*, took it for granted that their task included judging a film's politics, many reviewers from the 1960s onward, including Andrew Sarris and Pauline Kael (who vehemently disagreed with each other about many issues), have a visceral distaste for social-problem films, resenting their preaching and pretension. To many critics, the genre has too many elements of Victorian "moral seriousness;" they see this genre as akin to the preachy elderly sisters who try to restrain the daring adventurousness of the high-spirited Huck Finn (who is more akin to Hollywood's traditional irreverence and speed). For them, the Academy Awards lavished on this genre provide ample evidence of Hollywood's hypocrisy (those overpaid, overpampered liberals in La-La Land have guilty consciences!) and smug self-congratulation (so eager to pat themselves on the back for tripe!).

Further accusations—more or less warranted, depending on the case—arise from conservatives that filmmakers choose sensitive or taboo subjects merely to exploit their sensationalism. *Moving Picture World*, a trade magazine in early Hollywood, charged that a cycle of films made in the 1910s about enforced prostitution ("white slavery") was "lewd and smutty entertainment cloaked in the guise of educational warnings.... You cannot fool your decent patrons by prattling about social uplift and terrible lessons."[8] The 1932 version of *Scarface* presents a bald example of filmmakers camouflaging a film as social critique just to get it released. Censors offered strong objections to the script, charging that the movie glorified violence and gangsters, which it does. The coproducer, Howard Hughes, wrote to director Howard Hawks: "Screw the Hays Office. Start the picture and make it as realistic, as exciting, as grisly as possible."[9] After the film was shot, they got around the threatened ban through some editing, by adding an introductory text claiming that the story was an outcry against the scourge of gangsterism, and by changing the title to *Scarface: Shame of a Nation*.

Critics routinely attack social-problem films not only for their bad

---

[8] Shelley Stamp commentary, *Traffic in Souls*, on *Perils of the New Land: Films of the Immigrant Experience (1910–1915)* DVD, Flicker Alley, 2008.

[9] Dawn B. Sova, *Forbidden Films: Censorship Histories of 125 Motion Pictures* (New York: Checkmark Books, 2001), 260–61.

faith but for their ineffectiveness. Most believe that social-problem films preach to the choir. A March 17, 2008, article in *Time* magazine cited the example of Mel Gibson's *The Passion of the Christ* (2004), a blockbuster hit. A poll queried audiences and found that only 0.1 percent of viewers became Christians after seeing the film, though nearly 18 percent were stirred to practice Christianity more devotedly. Thus, the journalist concludes, films don't change anyone's mind; at most, they help stir up the already committed.

Advocates of social-problem films counter these varied charges from numerous angles. In terms of Brechtian theory, Murray Smith has written a careful rebuttal, using *The Accused* (1988), which is about the true story of a public gang rape and starred Jodie Foster, as his example. He concludes that the advocates of alienation are not being fair to the complexity of Hollywood films or to the complicated ways audiences identify with and judge characters while viewing. We can ally ourselves with characters and be outraged by social injustices at the same time; feeling empathy does not stop us from seeing the need for change; we can—indeed, we always do—think and feel at the same time.

The melodramatic aspects of social-problem films have been fodder to those who charge the genre with hypocrisy, yet recent theoreticians have reevaluated and defended melodramatic tropes. The scholar Linda Williams argues that melodrama, with its search for a moral code and sympathy for the oppressed, underlies all of American film. Similarly, Elaine Roth argues that melodrama is uniquely capable of stressing the injustices done to those who are relatively powerless in American society, and that each melodrama puts the viewer in the position of a being a jury of sympathetic peers.

As for the issue of the filmmakers' sincerity, the deeper one goes into film history, the more one finds incontrovertible examples of filmmakers' *good* faith: King Vidor mortgaging his own home to make *Our Daily Bread* (1934); the makers of *Salt of the Earth* literally braving bullets and editing in a ladies' washroom to hide the print from its enemies; Sidney Lumet submitting *Daniel* (1983) to studios thirty-seven times before he could get it produced; Steven Spielberg setting up and funding his Survivors of the Shoah Foundation because he was so moved by *Schindler's List*; and Terry George putting up his own money to get *Hotel Rwanda* off the ground. Some actors, George Clooney or Susan Sarandon for example, have such strong reputations for activism that their casting serves as a sign of genuine commitment.

***Dead Man Walking* (1995)** Susan Sarandon, pictured here as Sister Helen Prejean, has been a committed activist for years. She has taken roles as a feminist desperado in *Thelma and Louise* (1991) and as an anti-apartheid activist in *A Dry White Season* (1989). She has narrated numerous liberal documentaries. Offscreen, she was part of a delegation to Nicaragua in 1984, worked for Ralph Nader's presidential campaign in 2000, donated her time to try to save death penalty prisoners, and participated in activities against the Iraq War and global warming. Social-problem films frequently feature actors—such as Sarandon, Henry Fonda, Sean Penn, and Gregory Peck—who have taken public stands on social issues.

Regarding the identity of the filmmakers, if you look beneath the famous directors' credits, you will often find evidence that the white, straight male sought out others with divergent life experiences—for example, Callie Khouri, not Ridley Scott, wrote *Thelma and Louise*, and Ron Nyswaner, a gay activist, was the screenwriter of *Philadelphia*. Moreover, film historians keep uncovering films made by women, African Americans, and homosexuals that never made it into the canon of famous movies. And in recent decades, especially in independent circles, members of underrepresented groups have increasingly succeeded in producing and directing social-problem films themselves—witness *Precious* (2009), with a black director, Lee Daniels, at the helm, and a black screenwriter, Geoffrey Fletcher, adapting the novel *Push*, which was written by a black woman, Sapphire, or the lauded films, *Fruitvale Station*, *Lee Daniels' The Butler*, and *12 Years a Slave*, all of which appeared in 2013.

In terms of effectiveness, reviews of social-problem films are often studded with such phrases as "surprisingly honest," "refreshingly hard-hitting," and "quite daring in its time period," which indicate that the writer personally felt the power of the social critique. This makes me wonder: has everyone occasionally felt this power? When I look back at my own viewing history, I recall that seeing *West Side Story*, *To Kill a Mockingbird*, and *In the Heat of the Night* as a child taught me something about racial prejudice; as a teen I was profoundly affected politically by Costa-Gavras's *Z* (1969), which is about government complicity in a political assassination in Greece. Certainly, a judge in New Jersey believed that a movie could affect viewers positively. When three teenagers vandalized a Jewish cemetery with painted swastikas in the spring of 1994, the judge ordered them to watch *Schindler's List* with him.

Social-problem films might be exonerated from the charge of ineffectiveness if they have psychological or educational impact on some portion of their audiences. Yet, in addition, they clearly can have an impact on American life. One scholar studied the 1959 reception of Stanley Kramer's *On the Beach*, which presents a story of worldwide contamination from nuclear fallout. Linus Pauling, a famous American scientist, commented at its premiere, "It may be that some years from now we can look back and say that *On the Beach* is the movie that saved the world." While G. Tom Poe does not quite conclude that the film saved the world,

On the Beach (1959) This original poster is in color: the atomic cloud in the background is an eyecatching and frightening shade of orange. Movies have an effect on culture at large through such ancillary avenues as magazine and newspaper ads, reviews, and word of mouth. Even people who didn't see the film itself might have caught the fear of nuclear holocaust through the surrounding buzz and publicity, or even through seeing such a chilling image as this.

gregory peck · ava gardner
fred astaire · anthony perkins

stanley kramer's production of **on the beach**

introducing donna anderson
screen play by john paxton · from the novel by nevil shute
produced and directed by stanley kramer. released thru [UA] united artists

he does deduce that it made large waves, not only for those who saw it but because of the press coverage, ad campaign, and secondary public discourse that the film sparked. Poe rightly focuses on the "ripple effect" of movies on the public sphere. Even people disinterested or politically opposed, who don't buy tickets, may get splashed by the widening circles of publicity and discussion about a movie and the topics it raises.

Actually, historians maintain that some films have had demonstrable (though not the sole) effect on changing attitudes or policies.

- *I Am a Fugitive from a Chain Gang* is credited with reforming prison practices.
- *The Snake Pit* (1948) led to reform in mental hospitals in twenty-six states.
- Thirty-seven percent of viewers polled in a survey credited *The China Syndrome* with engendering their opposition to nuclear power.
- The year after *Norma Rae* appeared, textile mill workers were unionized.
- *Philadelphia* has been seen as responsible for correcting American public misconceptions about AIDS.

Pursuing the subject of real-world consequences, *Time* magazine polled over one thousand voters. The poll revealed what seem to me amazing numbers, but the journalist, Rebecca Keegan, oddly presents them dismissively: "About 30 percent of respondents said a movie had changed their mind about an issue. Fewer than 20 percent said a movie had persuaded them to donate money to a charity or inspired them to volunteer for a cause. And only 10 percent said a movie had caused them to vote differently." Ten percent said a movie had caused them to vote differently! In the majority of elections, 10 percent is more than the margin of victory.

Iconography

Social-problem films are varied; they do not share imagery or costumes or props. Nonetheless, we can isolate a few common patterns.

Social-problem films often begin and end with text on the screen, the first telling us that the movie is based on a true story, the latter updating the audience about further real-life events connected to the story

Norma Rae **(1979)** A real Alabama textile mill served as the location for the filming of *Norma Rae*, the kind of scenery rarely pictured in other genres. Social-problem films focus on lower- and working-class settings, rather than on the glamorous or fantasy locations pictured in other genres. The machine noise in this mill is deafening.

we've just seen, and occasionally informing us of what actions to take to address this problem.

Realism extends into the visual style of the film. Scenes are shot on location, often in the places named in the story. The camera work often imitates that of documentaries in the use of hand-held sequences, black-and-white film, and the lack of studio lighting. We see spaces that "pure entertainment" movies tend to avoid, such as the working and living conditions of the lower class—mines, factories, tenements, prisons. Because these films interweave their stories with real events, they often include shots of newspaper headlines or cuts to television newscasts.

Some films of this genre include nonprofessional actors, "real people," as extras. Surprisingly often, notable public figures appear as themselves, blurring the lines between fiction and reality, and vouchsafing the movie's seriousness. Even more effective in blurring that line is when a movie, such as *Milk*, cuts from its re-creation of events to documentary footage.

In this genre, stars try not to look glamorous. One sign of a performer's seriousness about a role, and a film's earnestness about its subject, is the avoidance of makeup, jewelry, costumes, and other techniques that highlight his or her sex appeal.

The dialogue of social-problem films, however, often veers away from realism toward melodrama in its explicitness. In *Fail-Safe* (1964), in which a computer glitch and Cold War suspicions lead to American planes bombing Moscow and then the compensatory destruction of New York City, the president (Henry Fonda) articulates the movie's moral to his Soviet counterpart:

President: Two great cities may be destroyed. Millions of innocent people killed. What do we say to them, Mr. Chairman, "Accidents will happen?" I won't accept that.

Chairman: All I know is that as long as we have weapons—

President: All I know is that men are responsible. We're responsible for what happens to us. Today we had a taste of the future. Do we learn from it or do we go on the way we have? What do we do, Mr. Chairman? What do we say to the dead?

Chairman: I think if we are men we must say this will not happen again. But do you think it's possible, with all that stands between us?

President: We put it there, Mr. Chairman, and we're not helpless. What we put between us we can remove.

Melodrama also underlies the *coups de théâtre* scenes, those silent, climactic moments where the balance shifts: when the black convict escapee (Sidney Poitier) jumps off the train to stay with his white partner (Tony Curtis) in *The Defiant Ones*; when Norma Rae holds up her union sign on the table in the mill; when the images of his victims are superimposed on Matthew (Sean Penn) as he is executed in *Dead Man Walking*.

Social-problem films, like all other genre films, can be brilliant and stirring or schlocky and evasive about the injustice and its solution.

Traffic in Souls (1913) This was an early social-problem film about young women forced into prostitution. Authorities in the early teens were so convinced of the film's effectiveness that they showed it to incoming immigrants on Ellis Island. Twenty-first century viewers may be tempted to dismiss this film as outdated melodrama; in recent years historians have also critiqued the "white slavery scare" of the early 1910s as an overblown, Puritanical fear of women's sexuality. However, *Traffic in Souls* still has relevance in today's world because we know that vulnerable girls and boys are frequently sold or coerced into prostitution rings and virtually held prisoner, not only in other countries but in the United States as well. We should be careful before we dismiss a social-problem film as outdated and irrelevant to contemporary society.

Moreover, the passage of time can be particularly hard on them: the problem may seem trivial or the analysis shallow because of the privileges of hindsight. For instance, a contemporary reappraisal of *To Kill a Mockingbird* argues that for all its vaunted liberalism, the film is irredeemably tainted by class prejudice toward the "redneck" white characters. Nonetheless, we need to be careful before we cavalierly dismiss these movies. *Black Legion* (1937) presents a story about a working-class man (Humphrey Bogart) so angered by economic competition from foreign immigrants that he joins a hate group called the Black Legion, whose members dress up in hooded robes and terrorize their Polish, French, and Irish American neighbors. Film scholars have dismissed the film as cowardly in that it evades the real prejudices of the Ku Klux Klan and its lynching of blacks and Jews. But perhaps this was cleverly strategic—because a blatantly anti-Klan movie would not have been distributed in the South, whereas this allegory would be. And while we might regard the film's subject as outdated—anti-Polish prejudice seems absurd, belonging to some dusty, bygone era—we can see unfortunate parallels to the case of a gang of Long Island youths terrorizing, beating up, and killing Ecuadorian immigrants in 2008.

In judging a film's balance of realism and melodrama (and the sophistication of the film's sociopolitical analysis), one should look hard at the ending and how neatly it ties up the social problem. *The Pursuit of Happyness* (2006) suggests that if you just buck up under poverty and homelessness and study your textbooks through the night at a homeless shelter, you too can become a stockbroker. In the education subgenre, one committed teacher can defeat the evil school bureaucracies and can rescue students from entrenched social ills through love, understanding, and relevant assignments. Although surely the real-life teachers whose stories are being told would disagree, these happy-ending films could be used to argue that we don't need more money or reform of American schools: we just need such selfless teachers.

Films that duck the Hollywood "happy end" *feel* truer and more serious about social problems whether or not they are based on fact. The girl is beaten to death in the fictional *Broken Blossoms* (1919); *Black Legion* ends with the hero in jail for life and his wife devastated; *Fail-Safe* concludes with New York City obliterated by an atomic bomb; *Do the Right Thing* ends with Mookie refusing Sal's conciliatory offers. In each case the movie tells its audience what we know is truer than "true stories": that the last reel does not easily eradicate this social cancer, that it is intractable. Fighting against this injustice is going to take all our will and energy.

Social-problem films are about winning hearts and minds. When a social-problem film succeeds in sending its audience out of the theater thinking, "I want to be part of the solution," it has done its job.

Standing Up for Justice in *North Country*

In a cinematic culture that damages and demoralizes female characters with embarrassing regularity, making a film about sexual harassment seemed like a bold act. Nobody's made this film before.[10]

—*Niki Caro*

Like many social-problem films, *North Country* comes from a true story. The movie relies on a book, *Class Action: The Story of Lois Jenson and the Landmark Case That Changed Sexual Harassment Law,* by Clara Bingham and Laura Leedy Gansler (2002), which chronicles the case of *Jenson* v. *Eveleth Taconite Company.*

The film, directed by Niki Caro, a New Zealander, tells the story of Josey Aimes (Charlize Theron), who is loosely based on the real plaintiff, Lois Jenson. Because she is a single mother of two children, Josey, fleeing an abusive husband and disapproved of by her conservative parents, takes a job in the Pearson (Eveleth) Taconite mine despite warnings that the work environment is hostile toward women. Due to strong unions, the mines, the biggest employers in the Mesobi Iron Range, pay the highest wages in this desolate area of northern Minnesota. At Pearson, Josey finds that her male coworkers and foremen subject the women to constant "jokes," crudity, and even physical assault. After complaining through official channels and being labeled a troublemaker, she finally persuades a local lawyer, Bill White (Woody Harrelson), to represent her.

White realizes that Josey has no chance if she challenges the mine

---

[10] Pamela Paul, "Niki Caro: The Director of *North Country* Talks about Sexual Harrassment," *Slate* (October 20, 2005).

alone: the company's defense would be that she is unusually sensitive and humorless—in short, a malcontent. However, if the lawyer and his client can get several women working in the mine to agree to join a class-action suit, he can prove that the workplace violates the women's civil right to work in a safe environment. The judge declares that he will certify a class if White gets two other women to join with Josey. Unfortunately, the other women mine workers, even Josey's best friend, Glory (Frances McDormand), are very reluctant to get involved; all of them depend on these jobs for their livelihoods and all are terrified of retaliation, not only in the workplace but in the close-knit community.

The climax of the film occurs in a courtroom. (This film exemplifies the courtroom plot.) Pearson's lawyer subjects Josey to vicious cross-examination, criticizing her personal life and sexual morals. Josey is forced to admit a secret that she had kept for years: that her teenage son, Sammy (who is estranged from her and acting out because of the town's animus), was conceived when, at 16, she was raped by her high school teacher. The night after the revelation Sammy runs away from home, but returns and reconciles with his mother. The next day in court, her chief tormentor at Pearson, Bobby Sharp (Jeremy Renner), who had been her boyfriend in high school, initially claims that Josey's intercourse with the teacher was consensual. Under White's cross-examination, however, Bobby admits that he witnessed the teacher's assault and that he did not come to Josey's aid. White seizes upon the theme of moral courage and helping those who are being preyed on. In the film's climactic, didactic speech, he argues: "What are you supposed to do when the ones with all the power are hurting those with none? Well, for starters, you stand up. Stand up and tell the truth. You stand up for your friends. You stand up even when you're all alone. You stand up." At this moment, Glory, who has entered the courtroom late makes her presence known. She is so ill she cannot speak, but she bangs her hand to get attention. Her husband reads a statement: Glory is willing to join the class action. Glory looks challengingly at the other women miners in the room. In a wonderful, only-in-the-movies moment, one by one, with agonizing slowness (accompanied by a fast but lyrical melody played on a special Bolivian lute), the frightened women miners—and then several of the men who are disgusted by the treatment the women have received—silently, literally *stand up*, indicating that they too will join the suit.

When watching a film inspired by actual events, the viewer may justly be suspicious about the mixture of fact and fiction, about how much

North Country (2005) Josey's lawsuit hangs by a thread. By this point in the film, her friend Glory is so ill that she cannot speak, but she and her husband enter the courtroom at a climactic moment. Glory bangs her hand on a bench, until the judge stops the proceedings. Her husband reads aloud for her, "My name is Glory Dodge. And I'm not fuckin' dead yet. I stand with Josey." That Glory, in her extremis, is willing to do what is right, shames and challenges the others. After agonizing seconds, one by one the women miners defiantly, fearfully rise to support Josey, thus allowing the case to proceed as a class action.

is accurate and to what degree the "glittering robes of entertainment" that Zanuck recommended to filmmakers have been woven in to seduce us to the film's point of view.

The most important point to me about *North Country*'s veracity is that virtually every instance of harassment that it depicts—leaving semen on a woman miner's sweater, threatening rape, smearing feces on walls, groping the women's breasts while reaching for a cigarette, pranks with dildos, sending them into dangerous areas purposely to frighten them—was documented in the lawsuit. So too was the lack of facilities for women to relieve themselves and their pleas for Porta-Potties; the only incident not mentioned in the book that is dramatized onscreen is that of the male miners knocking over the grudgingly granted Porta-Potty with Sherry inside, though an anonymous commentator on IMBD reports this actually happened *three* times. In fact, the film leaves out of its dramatization hundreds of other incidents, including omnipresent pornographic pictures and graffiti, foul language, physical intrusion into the women's homes, and stalking by a deranged supervisor. The level of harassment portrayed in *North Country*, graphic as it may be, is less horrific than what really took place.

Other aspects of the film accurately reflect the historical record as well, for example, the fact that the mine hired women only because of federal pressure; that management didn't want them there and publicly said so; and that management and the union discounted every complaint brought to them. Eveleth *did* incite the union to believe that the women's lawsuit would lead to the closing of the mines and the loss of jobs; it *did* purposely pursue a "nuts and sluts" defense in the courtroom, claiming that women who were suing had to be either unbalanced or immoral; it *did* threaten women mine workers and pressure them to sign affidavits swearing they had never been harassed or upset by the misogynist acts they witnessed. In this case, the offenders in the conflict actually acted as badly as the villains of melodrama.

Elements of the film that some critics have complained about as being too melodramatic to be credible also turn out to be partially based on fact: Lois Jenson's son was conceived during a rape (though not by her teacher), and she never told him the truth about his father until it came out in court. The second plaintiff, Pat/Glory, a union representative, did suffer from and die of amyotrophic lateral sclerosis (Lou Gehrig's disease). Although before she started working at the mine Lois Jenson was not married to a man who beat her, during her years there she did endure a short and abusive marriage.

The film is accurate, too, in small details: Eveleth's main lawyer was female and she was merciless with the plaintiffs; the nightlife of these towns consists of country music bars; and ice hockey is the community's ruling passion.

The film was shot on location in the towns of northern Minnesota where the events happened. Many of the original plaintiffs were involved in the production, some as extras. Cinematographer Chris Menges's helicopter shots of bleak terrain and the snow-covered isolation capture the unforgiving nature of the surroundings. The interiors of the mine, shot at a copper mine in northern Minnesota, show us a scene from Dante's *Inferno*, an environment of noise, danger, dirt, and mammoth power machinery that would be an intimidating workplace for most white-collar Americans, male or female. The sound track alternates between instrumental music used in moments of high tension—particularly scenes that are shot without onscreen sound—and popular songs. Six of the songs are drawn from Bob Dylan's repertoire. Dylan was born in Hibbing, Minnesota, and the songs chosen capture his trademark yearning toward truth telling (in "Paths of Victory" written in 1964) and sadness ("Girl from the North Country," written in 1963, and "Tell Ol' Bill," written in 2005).

Charlize Theron, cast as Josey, is blonde, younger, and prettier than many of the other women who worked at the mines (as was the case with Jenson). Although Theron is not asked to remake herself as radically as she did for *Monster* (2003), in which she plays a lesbian prostitute who becomes a serial killer, in *North Country* she takes on the unglamorous costumes and appearance of a lower-class working woman, not a movie star. She wears work clothes, gets dirty, and goes without makeup.

In three areas, however, the film takes significant dramatic license: the time scheme of the events, the character of the lawyer, and the role of Josey's family.

Lois Jenson started working at the Eveleth mine in 1975. After putting up with nine years of abuse, she had an epiphany: "If she did not speak up, who would?" Her legal case started in 1984, when she first contacted the Minnesota Department of Human Rights, and the matter was referred to the state attorney general's office. The case plodded on until 1998, when it was settled out of court. *North Country* radically compresses these years, leaving out Jenson's vain attempts to get the state to help her, her arduous search for private representation, and the years of pretrial discovery and depositions. The film also elides the penalty phase of the trial after the class had been certified and the mine found guilty of sexual harassment. This was the most devastating part of the ordeal, during which the women had to bare all the details of their personal lives to prove that their emotional and physical ailments were caused by what happened at work and not by other events in their rough lives. The elderly, conservative, and, as it turned out, kleptomaniac judge appointed as "special master" to decide on penalties awarded minuscule damages to the women and publicly and gratuitously criticized them. The film also leaves out the plaintiffs' appeal of these penalties to the Eighth Circuit Court, which threw out the special master's decision on legal grounds, pointedly rebuked him, and sent the damages phase of the case back for retrial. Before the retrial, however, the mine owners settled with the female mine workers.

North Country thus focuses on only one short phase of this legal odyssey—the one that was most groundbreaking in terms of American jurisprudence—the certifying of the women employees of Pearson/Eveleth as a class, and thus the finding that each female employee did not have to prove her individual harm. The film begins in 1989 and ends

Inspired by a true story.

North Country (2005) Particularly at the film's beginning, the camera shoots from a helicopter. We see the desolation of the range of mountains that hold this precious ore, overhead shots of the ugly mines and the pits, and the loneliness of snow and forests. This shot captures the bleakness of the landscape and, like so many social-problem films, testifies to the story's authenticity.

in 1991, the year Judge Rosenbaum did indeed rule on such certification. We can date the action of the movie by the Anita Hill–Clarence Thomas Supreme Court hearing on TV, which took place in 1991, and which Lois Jenson and the other plaintiffs watched avidly. While a screenplay following the entire case would have been unwieldy, truncating a fourteen-year legal gauntlet (which in itself severely traumatized the plaintiffs) into a less arduous two-year period downplays the women's and their counsels' perseverance and fortitude, and the difficulties they faced in getting justice to prevail. The plaintiffs felt they were raped all over again by the legal system.

Screenwriter Michael Seitzman also made significant changes in the character of Bill White. The defense team in *Jenson* v. *Eveleth* was a Minneapolis firm, Sprenger and Associates, headed by Paul Sprenger, a nationally famous employment-discrimination lawyer. He was very experienced in this field; he worked with a team of other associates and experts; when he took the case on contingency he was sure that the mine would settle quickly; and he was happily married to another lawyer in his firm. The idea that a small-town local boy with a yen for pretty Josey Aimes could, by himself, win against the legal resources of the large corporation that owned Eveleth is pure Hollywood.

Finally, other than to point out that Jenson's father worked at Eveleth and did not approve of her taking a job there, *Class Action* says next to nothing about Lois Jenson's relationship with her parents. If the two alterations pointed out above soften the film's critique of American society and advance a conventional view of triumphant individual agency, the third, intriguingly, works to sharpen and broaden its look at gender dynamics. Hank Aimes (Richard Jenkins) is crucial to the film in that he literally represents "patriarchy," the power of the father. He has been ashamed of and judgmental toward his daughter since her out-of-wedlock pregnancy. His realization that she is brave and tough; his standing up for her in the union meeting; his kneeling before her in the kitchen the night Sammy runs away after he learns that she had been raped and never told anyone—together they make *North Country* "a conversion story" on the order of *In the Heat of the Night* and *Philadelphia*. Similarly, Josie's mother, Alice (Sissy Spacek), goes through a conversion—deciding to side with her daughter and leave her husband shows her journey toward political consciousness.

In fact, the screenwriter and director's choices throughout make the film a little less about the workplace and the courts as the main theaters of rights and responsibilities and more about domestic and familial equality and understanding. In this sense their choices lend the film's social message more universality: even those who haven't suffered at the workplace (or who find this degree of harassment extreme) can see traditional gender roles operating within and negatively affecting their own families.

Niki Caro skillfully draws our attention to the way these traditional gender roles pervade the characters' (and our) lives. Josey's daughter is playing with a Barbie doll in one of the first shots. The first scenes vividly show Josie being beaten by her husband and rejected by her father. Later we see a scene in church where young girls, dressed in white, are being confirmed—the stress on their virginal innocence displays the powerful forces, including religion, pressing down upon women. Meek Alice Aimes seems always to be on the move, doing a never-ending routine of women's chores, passing plates at a church supper, sewing, laundry, etc. Even when she temporarily walks out on her husband, she is so indoctrinated in her duties that she leaves him a sandwich for his dinner. The supportive, loving marriage of Kyle Dodge (Sean Bean), who is a gentle watchmaker, and Glory, the tough union official, is held up to Josey and the viewer as something special and enviable.

Film critics unanimously castigate the film for the melodrama that dominates its last third. The Bobby Sharp subplot, including his witnessing of the rape, failing to intervene, and crumbling on the stand under White's badgering, is not only fictitious and histrionic, it distracts us from the real crimes of the mine operators and the legal system, and makes the fictional teacher a personified figure of evil. Purists also hate the film's relatively upbeat ending, stressing the mother-son bond— seeing it as a cop-out, Hollywood happy ending. The actual plaintiffs suffered so much ostracism and emotional damage that most became physically and emotionally disabled, which no settlement money could repair. How much softening does a social-problem film need, how much draping with the glittering robes of entertainment, to entice audiences to the theater?

Even with its underdog-wins-out optimism, *North Country*, which cost $35 million to make, was not a financial success.

Participant Media did not develop a concrete action plan to go with the movie, vaguely hoping that it would raise consciousness. However, the company did reach out to the National Organization for Women, the Feminist Majority Foundation, and the Family Violence Prevention Fund, which together launched a campaign they called "Stand Up: A Campaign to End Sexual Harassment and Domestic Violence." NOW took the film to twenty college campuses; feminists used the film to urge involvement in a national "Coaching Boys into Men" program.

To counter the charge that the hostile climate portrayed in *North Country* is ancient history, Niki Caro points to the similarly vicious treatment of women in the U.S. military, which is well documented and ongoing, as portrayed in the documentary *The Invisible War* (2012). Presumably, most viewers seeing *North Country* would be more sensitized to inequalities in their work place. Moreover, by broadening the theme to include domestic relations, the film, rather than weakening its message, demonstrates better than most sociology lectures the way the personal and public are intertwined.

Class Action reports that two of the actual plaintiffs watched the 1980 comedy *9 to 5*, in which three secretaries get revenge on their chauvinistic boss, and found the movie hilarious. That movie, and the Anita Hill–Clarence Thomas hearing on TV, influenced their understanding of their predicament. Screening *North Country* powerfully affects viewers' understanding of the history of gender in the workplace in the United States and the ways in which that history still echoes today. Flawed though it may be, the film thus accomplishes the goal of a social-problem film.

Sarah Kozloff

QUESTIONS FOR DISCUSSION

1. What films have you seen that raised your awareness about a social problem or sensitized you in some way?
2. Why are the three plot formulas identified above—court case, investigation, and conversion—so useful for social-problem films? What films come to mind as examples of these plot formulas?
3. Filmmakers commonly take liberties with historical fact for dramatic ends. Is there a line that some filmmakers have crossed, losing credibility, and if so, what criteria do you use for setting that line?
4. Recent documentaries have borrowed a page from social-problem films and dressed their topics in "the glittering robes of entertainment." Discuss with examples.
5. Can you think of films that you have not seen personally but which nonetheless have affected cultural discussion? By what means have these films penetrated into general cultural consciousness?

FOR FURTHER READING

Biskind, Peter. *Seeing Is Believing: How Hollywood Taught Us to Stop Worrying and Love the Fifties.* New York: Henry Holt, 1983.

Bogle, Donald. *Toms, Coons, Mulattoes, Mammies, and Bucks: An Interpretive History of Blacks in American Films.* 4th ed. New York: Continuum, 2001.

Brownlow, Kevin. *Behind the Mask of Innocence: Sex, Violence, Prejudice, Crime: Films of Social Conscience in the Silent Era.* New York: Knopf, 1990.

Comolli, Jean-Louis, and Jean Narboni. "Cinema/Ideology/Criticism." In *Critical Visions in Film Theory: Classic and Contemporary Readings*, edited by Timothy Corrigan and Patricia White with Meta Mazaj, 478–86. Boston: Bedford/St. Martins, 2011.

Lorence, James J. *The Suppression of* Salt of the Earth: *How Hollywood, Big Labor, and Politicians Blacklisted a Movie in Cold War America.* Albuquerque: University of New Mexico Press, 1999.

Patton, Cindy. *Cinematic Identity: Anatomy of a Problem Film.* Minneapolis: University of Minnesota Press, 2007.

Roffman, Peter, and Jim Purdy. *The Hollywood Social Problem Film: Madness, Despair, and Politics from the Depression to the Fifties.* Bloomington: Indiana University Press, 1981.

Ross, Steven J. *Working-Class Hollywood: Silent Film and the Shaping of Class in America.* Princeton, NJ: Princeton University Press, 1998.

Russo, Vito. *The Celluloid Closet: Homosexuality in the Movies*, rev. ed. New York: Harper & Row, 1987.

Ryan, Michael, and Douglas Kellner. *Camera Politica: The Politics and Ideology of Contemporary Hollywood Film*. Bloomington: Indiana University Press, 1990.

Sayre, Nora. *Running Time: Films of the Cold War*. New York: Dial Press, 1982.

Sloan, Kay. *The Loud Silents: Origins of the Social Problem Film*. Urbana: University of Illinois Press, 1988.

Smith, Murray. "The Logic and Legacy of Brechtianism." In *Post-Theory: Reconstructing Film Studies*, edited by David Bordwell and Noël Carroll, 130–49. Madison: University of Wisconsin Press, 1996.

White, David Manning, and Richard Averson, *The Celluloid Weapon: Social Comment in the American Film*. Boston: Beacon Press, 1972.

Touch of Evil (1958)

Film Noir

WALTER NEFF (FRED MACMURRAY) slumps wearily in a chair, as the blood from the bullet wound in his shoulder leaks through his suit jacket. Dawn begins to light up Los Angeles outside the office windows. A match head flares under his thumbnail, and he draws deeply on a cigarette. Into a Dictaphone he confesses to a murder, saying, "I killed him for money—and a woman—and I didn't get the money and I didn't get the woman. Pretty, isn't it?"

In another year and on another long night, Jeff Bailey (Robert Mitchum) knows that an old lover and her boyfriend are setting him up to take the fall for a murder, but he can't figure out the play. Sitting in a taxi in the shadows, Bailey tells the driver, "I think I'm in a frame....I don't know. All I can see is the frame. I'm going in there now to look at the picture."

Like Bailey, Bradford Galt (Mark Stevens) is a victim. Framed twice for crimes he never committed, jailed, released, and now on the run from the police, Galt cries out, "I feel all dead inside. I'm backed up in a dark corner, and I don't know who's hitting me." More conspiracies, more set-ups, more fall guys—there seemed no end to them in Hollywood's bleak depiction of America in the years that followed World War II. It was a time of always-night; of hoods and cheap gunsels, dames, and gats; cops on the grift, jazz tunes, neon signs, and car rides on wet asphalt streets to the big nowhere. It was a time in the movies when Al Roberts (Tom Neal) knew, after his own brush with murder and a seductive, dangerous woman, that "fate or some mysterious force can put the finger on you or me for no good reason at all."

Neff, Bailey, Galt, and Roberts are the hapless protagonists in *Double Indemnity* (1944), *Out of the Past* (1947), *The Dark Corner* (1946), and *Detour* (1945), films whose pessimism and bleak vision typify the genre of film noir. "Noir" is a French word meaning "black." These, therefore, are black films, but the description must be understood in metaphoric terms. Blackness here designates a twilight world where the darkness is both visual and moral, a world where, in the words of Raymond Chandler, the streets are dark with more than night. Chandler's crime novels were major influences on film noir, and his phrase perfectly captures the pessimism and the anxiety that are such important elements in the films. The genre specializes in dark, foreboding films about crime, often set in urban locales. The titles of noir films are exceptionally poetic, and they evoke the special qualities of this genre and its twilight world—*The Big Sleep, Nobody Lives Forever* (both 1946); *Out of the Past*; *In a Lonely Place, Edge of Doom, Where the Sidewalk Ends* (all 1950); *Captive City, Sudden Fear* (both 1952); *The Big Heat* (1953); *The Big Combo* (1955); *Nightmare, While the City Sleeps* (both 1956); *Odds Against Tomorrow* (1959).

Noir in its purest form flourished in Hollywood movies during the 1940s and 1950s, but the genre's influence extends far beyond those decades. Pictures as diverse as *Blade Runner* (1982) and *Sin City* (2005) incorporate noir elements, and many contemporary filmmakers have been so influenced by the genre that they have made pictures, like *Body Heat* (1981) and *L.A. Confidential* (1997), modeled on the style of past noir films. In fact, a second period of noir, begun in the 1980s, is called "neo-noir," since its films most often are set in the modern rather than a retro period.

History

Noir differs from gangster movies, Westerns, science fiction, horror, war films, and other basic movie genres. These others emerged very early in film history, and some, like horror and the Western, existed before movies were invented. Noir, by contrast, doesn't appear until several decades after the invention of cinema. The glory years for film noir run from 1940 or 1941 (opinions differ) until 1959. This interval, the classical period for the genre, encompasses the years when it emerged and gained full aesthetic force in American cinema. The year of inception varies

***This Gun for Hire* (1942)** Alan Ladd and Veronica Lake were one of noir's earliest established screen couples, paired here and in *The Glass Key* (1942) and *The Blue Dahlia* (1946). Their cool, reserved demeanors blended together superbly well, and Ladd's character in *This Gun for Hire*—a stoical killer who loves only his cat—proved to be tremendously influential. Jean-Pierre Melville's classic *Le Samourai* (1967), for example, owes much to Ladd and to this film.

slightly because scholars differ in their identification of the "first" noir film. Some stipulate that the genre begins with *The Maltese Falcon* (1941), while others offer *Stranger on the Third Floor* (1940). But while disagreement exists over the exact point of inception, critics widely recognize the final film in the genre's classical phase to be Orson Welles's *Touch of Evil* (1958). They do so partly because of its grandiose and baroque visual and narrative design—a hugeness of style that is summative in a manner that designates appropriate conclusion for this phase of the genre— and also because the 1950s marked the end of Hollywood's black-and-white period. The great, classic noir films are in black and white. In the 1960s, color cinematography became the norm for feature filmmaking, and the genre has had a troubled and difficult relationship with this shift. Color complicates and diminishes a cinematographer's ability to render black as an absolute domain within the visible spectrum of light. In a very real sense, then, the onset of color cinematography brought an end to the classical phase of film noir.

Numerous influences commingled to bring to the fore films centered on dames, gats, fall guys, grifters, and hoods in snap-brim hats. One of the most important was the "hard-boiled" crime fiction that emerged in the 1920s and 1930s, penned by Dashiell Hammett, Raymond Chandler, James M. Cain, and Cornell Woolrich. They reinvented crime fiction by taking it away from the rarefied air of Edgar Allan Poe's stories, in the 1840s, and Sir Arthur Conan Doyle's work. Auguste Dupin and Sherlock Holmes solved cases by superior brainpower. The hard-boiled writers present hoods who act from venal motives and detectives, often halfway between the law and the underworld, who solve cases by taking a blackjack to the head or pulling a gat in a dark alley. (Hard-boiled crime fiction and the movies spawned by it have their own vocabulary. A gat is a gun, a gunsel is a hood, and lead poisoning is what they dispense.) In opposition to the rationalism of crime fiction in the hands of Poe and Doyle, the hard-boiled writers proffer physical action, moral ambiguity, and existential darkness.

The genre of noir formed as their work was adapted into movies. *The Maltese Falcon* and *The Glass Key* (1942) brought Hammett's novels to the screen. Chandler's work appeared as *Murder, My Sweet* (1944), *The Big Sleep*, and *The Brasher Doubloon* and *Lady in the Lake* (both 1947). Cain's work surfaced as *Mildred Pierce* (1945), *The Postman Always Rings Twice* (1946), and *Slightly Scarlet* (1956). Chandler worked in Hollywood as a screenwriter, and he adapted Cain's novel *Double Indemnity* and also scripted *The Blue Dahlia* (1946). Woolrich's novels appeared as *Phantom Lady* (1944), *Black Angel, The Chase, Deadline at Dawn* (all 1946), *Fear in the Night* (1947), *The Window* (1949), and others.

The figure of the private detective as created especially by Chandler and Hammett became one of the genre's essential character types. Hard-boiled crime fiction gave filmmakers in the period a template for exploring the themes and motifs so essential to noir. *Double Indemnity* and *The Postman Always Rings Twice*, for example, portray adulterous lovers fueled by a rampaging sexual desire that leads them to commit murder. Hard-boiled crime novels and the movies adapted from them are tough, unsentimental, hard-edged, violent, and cynical in their view of human behavior.

But it was not just literature that led to film noir. Equally important, painting and photography in the 1930s and 1940s provided a visual culture focusing on the city by night and on states of alienation and loneliness. Among painters, Edward Hopper depicted lonely city streets lit by spare lamps at some awful hour of the soul when sleep won't come.

Drug Store (1927) presents a bleak vision of urban desolation as the titular store stands illuminated on an empty street. *Nighthawks* (1942) shows the patrons at a café, isolated from one another, a dark street yawing behind them. Hopper's inspiration for the painting is thought to have been "The Killers," a short story by Ernest Hemingway that opens in such a café. The story and the painting it inspired led directly into the genre. In 1946, Robert Siodmak filmed the story, title intact, creating a classic noir film, and his lighting for the café sequence was clearly inspired by Hopper.

More important even than this cycle of painting focusing on urban alienation was the photography of Arthur H. Fellig, a.k.a. Weegee. An odd man who prowled the city with his camera, Weegee became the chronicler of nocturnal Manhattan. Monitoring a police radio in his apartment, Weegee raced to scenes of roadside carnage, mob hits, and drug and prostitution busts, photographing these in a candid, harsh, and unsentimental manner. Of seminal importance to the genre, his book of Manhattan photographs, *Naked City*, appeared in 1945, providing filmmakers with an extensive set of visual references and models for use in portraying crime in the streets and the look of the underclass, those beaten down by hard times, vice, or despair. One of the genre's subcurrents is a quasi-documentary style applied to depictions of city life and methods of crime detection, and Weegee's work influenced filmmakers here, too, inspiring one of the genre's key semidocumentary films, *The Naked City* (1948).

Two additional influences operated to help form the genre. One was the influx of European filmmakers fleeing the Nazis in the 1930s and 1940s. These included many producers, directors, cinematographers, and production designers who went on to work in film noir, among them Fritz Lang, Robert Siodmak, Otto Preminger, Billy Wilder, John Alton, and Rudolph Maté. Many had worked in German cinema in the silent era during the period of Expressionism, an exaggerated style that emphasizes shadowy lighting and moody, atmospheric set design. These motifs grafted naturally onto the emerging noir genre, with its predilection for staging scenes at night and making the urban environment into an expression of danger, fear, and anxiety.

A final technological and aesthetic influence on the genre enabled it to accomplish this visual design. Hollywood cinematography shifted from the soft, diffused lighting of 1930s films, where action was staged in a shallow plane of focus, to a hard-light and deep-focus staging in

Murder, My Sweet (1944) Nineteen forty-four was the magic year for film noir, with three critical and box-office successes that cemented the outlines of the genre. Dick Powell plays Raymond Chandler's hard-boiled private eye, Philip Marlowe, in an adaptation of Chandler's novel *Farewell, My Lovely* that established the private detective as an archetypal noir movie character. In this startling example of low-key cinematography, Marlowe sees the reflection of a giant thug (Mike Mazurki) looming in his office window. The monster stands behind him and is reflected on the glass by the city's lights shining from the rear. Low-key cinematography was the genre's most important means for achieving visual poetry.

the 1940s. Writing in 1941, at the very onset of film noir, cinematographer James Wong Howe [who went on to shoot the classic noirs *Body and Soul* (1947) and *Sweet Smell of Success* (1957)] traced the hard look of 1940s crime films to the influence of documentary photography in news magazines such as *Life* and *Look*, and he might have added the work of Weegee. The moody look of noir owes much to the highly controlled lighting designs that a shift to hard light made possible and, in particular, to the use of low-key cinematography.

From 1940 to 1959, Hollywood produced 270 noir films. Nothing initiates a cycle, trend, or genre of filmmaking faster than box-office success, and noir is a case in point. When a set of films appears that marks a new style or direction and scores well with critics and the public, the industry movies quickly to consolidate the pattern by making more like them. While several films early in the 1940s—*This Gun for Hire* (1942), *Shadow of a Doubt* (1943)—incorporate noir themes and imagery, the take-off year for the genre was 1944, when a group of films earned critical praise and box-office success and were perceived by commentators of the period as marking a new direction for crime films. The success of *Double Indemnity*, *Laura*, and *Murder, My Sweet* helped turn Hollywood crime films in the strongly psychological direction that noir epitomizes. *Double Indemnity* portrays an adulterous affair that leads to murder. *Laura* showcases a detective's amorous obsession with a murder victim. Seeing her portrait in a painting, he falls in love with her as he investigates her apparent death. *Murder, My Sweet* provides the first real showcase for the genre's hard-boiled private eye character type amid elaborate shadows created by flamboyantly low-key lighting designs. (*The Maltese Falcon* has a hard-case detective played by Humphrey Bogart but few distinctively noirish lighting designs.) These three films helped solidify the genre by refining its character types, narrative tropes, and visual design, while other noir pictures that year—*Phantom Lady*, *When Strangers Marry*—helped it flourish. Over the next decade, from 1945 to 1955, production of film noir accelerated. Whereas seven noir films were released in 1944, the number jumped in the next years to sixteen (1945), twenty-four (1946), and twenty-nine (1947). Thirty-one noir films were released in 1950, the genre's busiest year. By 1956, however, production began to decline, falling to nine films, and by 1959 only three noirs were in release. All of the major studios made noir films, with RKO producing the most—forty-two films from 1940 to 1959. Even the B-film studios— Eagle-Lion, Republic, Monogram, Producers Releasing Corporation— participated in the genre's boom, making eighteen noirs among them.

Prominent directors who worked frequently in the genre include Fritz Lang [*The Woman in the Window* (1944), *Scarlet Street* (1945), *The Big Heat*], Alfred Hitchcock [*Shadow of a Doubt*, *Notorious* (1946), *Strangers on a Train* (1951), *The Wrong Man* (1956)], and Orson Welles [*The Stranger* (1946), *The Lady from Shanghai* (1947), *Touch of Evil*]. But many of the genre's great films were made by second-tier directors who showed real flair at pushing noir's off-kilter moral and visual motifs to new extremes. These include Robert Aldrich [*The Big Knife*, *Kiss Me Deadly* (both 1955)], Jules Dassin [*Brute Force* (1947), *Night and the City* (1950), *The Naked City*],

Joseph H. Lewis [*Gun Crazy* (1950), *The Big Combo* (1955)], Anthony Mann [*T-Men*, *Railroaded* (both 1947), *Raw Deal* (1948)], and Robert Siodmak [*The Killers*, *Cry of the City* (1948), *Criss Cross* (1949)].

Just as these directors helped make noir a viable genre, many stars established close ties to it. Noir's distinctive flavor owes much to the insolence of Humphrey Bogart in *The Maltese Falcon*, *The Big Sleep*, *Dark Passage* (1947), and *Key Largo* (1948); to Alan Ladd's steely coldness in *This Gun for Hire* and *The Blue Dahlia*; and to Robert Mitchum's sleepy-eyed passivity in *Out of the Past* (1947) and *His Kind of Woman* (1951). Barbara Stanwyck personified noir's archetypal femme fatale—a siren with warm lips, a cold heart, and a hot gun—in *Double Indemnity*, *The Strange Love of Martha Ivers* (1946), and *The File on Thelma Jordan* (1950), but she had plenty of company in the likes of Yvonne De Carlo (*Criss Cross*), Jane Greer (*Out of the Past*), and Ava Gardner (*The Killers*). Other great ladies of noir include Gloria Grahame (*In a Lonely Place*), Lizabeth Scott [*Dead Reckoning* (1947)], and Veronica Lake (*This Gun for Hire*), each of them sultry, blonde, and quietly but fiercely loyal to fallen and tarnished men. And where would noir be without its assortment of gunsels and cheap hoods, personified by the likes of Richard Widmark [*Kiss of Death* (1947)], William Bendix (*The Glass Key*, *The Dark Corner*) and that ultimate loser and fall guy, Elisha Cook Jr. (*The Maltese Falcon*, *The Big Sleep*), born with a morgue-tag on his toe, destined to take the sap or eat the bullet in each and every film.

Noir took off in this period because of this gallery of superb film-makers and performers. Hollywood's great roster of talent, working under long-term contracts with studios, ensured that film noirs were peopled with a gallery of convincing low-lifes and hangers-on, thugs, dames, private eyes, and cops, played by actors who made these colorful characters live and spun each film into a convincing universe of blighted, desperate lives vividly rendered on screen. But as Hollywood's era of black-and-white cinematography drew to its close, and the studio system broke apart, so, too, did film noir; throughout the 1960s, the genre was mostly dormant, apart from rare films like *Cape Fear* (1962) and *The Naked Kiss* (1964) that harkened back to the former period. The early 1970s, however, saw filmmakers renew their interest in the genre's story conventions, character types, and visual motifs. Chandler's Philip Marlowe returned to the screen in Robert Altman's *The Long Goodbye* (1973), though the film was mainly a cynical satire of noir. It was Roman Polanski's *Chinatown* the following year that signaled that a great reawakening

***Chinatown* (1974)** Private detective J. J. Gittes (Jack Nicholson) stumbles onto a scheme to control Los Angeles's water supply, but the scale of corruption that he uncovers proves to be beyond his ability to challenge. *Chinatown* depicts classic elements of noir—a period setting in Los Angeles, a hard-boiled private eye, an apparent femme fatale, and low-key lighting. Roman Polanski's film signaled the return of noir as a major genre, and the period of neo-noir that it inaugurated accelerated during the 1980s.

of noir was in the offing. Influenced by the then-contemporary miasma of official corruption that was the administration of Richard Nixon and the Watergate scandal, *Chinatown* reimagines the genre's basic story of a private eye enmeshed in a world of conspiracy and corruption but does so using color cinematography. A brilliant script by Robert Towne, Polanski's direction informed by his tragic sense of an evil world, career-defining performances by Jack Nicholson as the detective and Faye Dunaway as the femme fatale who proves more victim than predator, and Richard Sylbert's remarkable production design envisioning Los Angeles in the 1930s make this a work comparable to *The Wild Bunch* (1969) and *2001: A Space Odyssey* (1968) among Westerns and science-fiction films: landmark works that transformed their genres.

    Chinatown brought color to film noir and inaugurated the era of neo-noir. The term designates a later, more contemporary period of production than that of the classical era, and today neo-noir flourishes, although it required several years to evolve. *Chinatown* elicited few comparable films in the 1970s. Only *Farewell, My Lovely* (1975), a remake of *Murder, My Sweet*, starring Robert Mitchum (one of the icons of the earlier noir era), playing a weary but still idealistic Philip Marlowe, showed a comparably keen interest in the tone, feel, and moves of 1940s noir. *Body Heat* (1981) is the important successor to *Chinatown*—it opened the gates to neo-noir production. Directed by Lawrence Kasdan, *Body Heat* is a contemporary reimagining of *Double Indemnity*, telling the familiar noir story of adulterous lovers driven by lust and greed to kill a spouse who stands in their way and then turning on one another with acts of betrayal. *Body Heat* brings noir into the present era with a story set in 1980s Florida rather than a period-era Los Angeles. It made noir contemporary. Color cinematography was an indicator of this new modernity in the genre, and numerous neo-noirs followed, some set in the earlier period, many not. Narratives that explicitly harken back to the classical era and are set in those years include *Mulholland Falls* (1995); *L.A. Confidential*; and *The Black Dahlia* and *Hollywoodland* (both 2006). But many others situate noir in the contemporary world, including *Taxi Driver* (1976); *D.O.A.* (1988); *The Grifters* and *After Dark, My Sweet* (both 1990); *Reservoir Dogs* and *Night and the City* (both 1992); *Red Rock West* (1993); *Blood and Wine* (1996); *Palmetto* (1998); and *Sin City*.

Typologies, Themes, and Theories

What makes film noir distinctive? How does the genre differ from other kinds of crime movies, such as gangster films? Many gangster movies are also classified as film noir—*White Heat* (1949), *The Asphalt Jungle* (1950)—but in general gangsters make poor characters for noir films: too extroverted, too full of energy and ambition, too active in setting goals for themselves, such as knocking over a bank, taking over a city's numbers racket, or bumping off the big shots who stand between them and their plans. The film noir protagonist, by contrast, tends to be a victim, set upon and manipulated by forces or people more powerful than he or she and who often shows a degree of passivity or resignation in accepting this fate. Gangster narratives look forward because the gangster wants things he doesn't presently have. Film noir narratives often look backward, focusing on something bad that happened in the past and that now threatens a character's life or chance for happiness.

"I did something wrong—once," Ole "Swede" Andresen (Burt Lancaster) says at the beginning of *The Killers*. Two hit men have arrived in a small town looking for Andresen. Suspicious that they mean him harm, Nick Adams (Phil Brown) races to warn Swede, but he quietly tells him

The Killers (1946) Swede Andresen (Burt Lancaster) meekly accepts his death in the opening of Robert Siodmak's film. Rather than flee from the assassins who have tracked him to his small apartment, he chooses to remain in bed, awaiting their bullets. "I can't do anything about it," he says, words that provide a classic expression of the genre's fatalism. This was a career-making performance for Lancaster, and he continued working in the genre for the rest of the decade. He teamed again with Siodmak on the classic *Criss Cross* (1949).

to go away. "There's nothing I can do about it," he tells Nick wearily. He waits for them to come and quietly receives the gunfire that they turn on him. Tired of running, Swede dies because he knows he can't elude his past forever. Jeff Bailey's plight in *Out of the Past* typifies the way that past actions haunt the present in noir. His chance for happiness now—he owns a gas station and is in love with a good woman—becomes imperiled when a hoodlum he once knew comes back into his life to ask for a favor. Bailey knows he's being set up to take the fall for some crime not yet committed, but he can't avoid the snare because at its center is the temptation offered by an old flame, Kathie Moffat (Jane Greer). So Bailey goes along to his doom.

The narrative structure of *Out of the Past* and *The Killers* is typical of noir—the movies present Bailey's and Swede's stories as extended flashbacks that tell the viewer how they got into such awful predicaments. Flashbacks, a common storytelling device in Hollywood films of the 1940s, are especially associated with film noir, along with voice-over narration. Bailey narrates the flashback in *Out of the Past*, as does Walter Neff in *Double Indemnity*, where that flashback explains how he came to have a bullet wound in his shoulder and how the murders that he's confessing to transpired. Because Swede dies at the beginning of *The Killers*, the film introduces a new character, an insurance agent investigating the death, who provides the mechanism for retrieving the past. The extended flashback in *Criss Cross* occurs at the film's beginning as Steve Thompson (Burt Lancaster), on the verge of robbing an armored car, explains how he came to this point of crisis. Frank Chambers (John Garfield), the narrator of *The Postman Always Rings Twice*, tells his story from death row as he awaits execution. *Sunset Boulevard* (1950) begins with a corpse floating in a swimming pool, and Joe Gillis (William Holden), in voice-over, promises to explain how the body got there. The macabre joke is that Joe is the dead man, and his tale reveals how he came to be murdered. *D.O.A.* (1950) is narrated by Frank Bigelow (Edmond O'Brien), a man dying from radiation poisoning, and in his last moments of life, he explains to homicide detectives why he was poisoned and how he tracked down the man who murdered him.

The flashbacks in noir account for one of the genre's strongest motifs: the idea of fate or predestined action. The noir protagonists—"hero" is the wrong term here because the protagonist tends to be a victim and because the stories offer little in the way of triumph—invariably make the wrong choice or have already made one in their past when the film begins. As he walks home in *Double Indemnity*, Walter knows he's doomed and that the murder plot he's hatching will fail. "Suddenly it came over me that everything would go wrong. It sounds crazy . . . but it's true, so

Double Indemnity (1944) With blood leaking from a shoulder wound, Walter Neff (Fred MacMurray) confesses to murder and betrayal. As the film begins, he relates the story of these crimes in an extended flashback, one of many that would distinguish film noir. Many of the genre's films are fixated on the past and its guilty secrets. Voice-over narration became such a familiar feature in the genre that only two years later a comedy, *My Favorite Brunette*, parodied the device of a hard-boiled tale told in flashback.

help me. I couldn't hear my own footsteps. It was the walk of a dead man." Steve, returning to his hometown in *Criss Cross* because he can't stay away from his old love, Anna Dundee (Yvonne De Carlo), says in voice-over, "I didn't come back on account of her.... I wasn't going to go looking for her. I didn't expect to run into her. I didn't particularly want to see her. I was sure of that if I was sure of anything. But then from the start, it all went one way. It was in the cards, or it was fate, or a jinx, or whatever you want to call it, but right from the start..." Lost in thought, he never finishes the line, but what is omitted is clear enough—that right from the start it all went wrong for Steve. The title of *The Postman Always Rings Twice* evokes the idea of fated action. The postman in this case is death, and you might cheat it once, but not a second time.

Here, then, is an important way in which noir characters differ from movie gangsters. The gangster, too, may fail, but his death tends to be a memorable one—even spectacular—in terms that provide a measure of his heroic stature. The protagonist in a film noir tends to be more introverted, more passive, more acted upon, and at most he or she hopes to avoid the snares that are closing in. Amnesia is a frequent affliction of noir characters. In *Street of Chance* (1942), *Deadline at Dawn*, *Somewhere in the Night* (both 1946), and others, the noir protagonist finds himself implicated in a murder or other crime but has no memory of it, and the story becomes a quest to find the truth. In many noir films the protagonist is a detective—*The Dark Corner*; *The Big Sleep*; *Murder, My Sweet*; *Chinatown*—but the cases typically prove complicated and labyrinthine, and the detective achieves only a limited measure of success, if success at all, in solving them. In *Murder, My Sweet*, Marlowe must find a client's missing lover. He does so but cannot prevent her death, and Gittes, the detective in *Chinatown*, fails miserably, causing the death of a woman he loves.

The protagonist in noir is generally male; often, therefore, these films feature a male victim who may be set up to take the fall for a crime committed by someone else, or who may be lured into committing a crime, or who is set upon in other ways by force of circumstance. Notable exceptions to this pattern exist. *Mildred Pierce* (1945) stars Joan Crawford as the title character, a woman who suffers great hardships and humiliations as she tries to make a good life for her daughter, Veda (Ann Blythe). Unfortunately for Mildred, Veda proves to be scheming, selfish, and hateful toward her mother, and she ultimately becomes a killer. This series of traumas virtually destroys Mildred as she discovers

Mildred Pierce **(1945)** Victims in noir are frequently men, but *Mildred Pierce* offers
a study of the title character, a devoted mother who suffers at the hands of her vicious
daughter, whose selfishness leads Mildred to financial ruin and to being ensnared in a
murder plot. Joan Crawford plays Mildred, and the flagged key light conveys noir's customary atmosphere of threat and anxiety.

a fundamental lesson of the noir universe—that one's life can come
undone utterly and through little or no fault of one's own. *Sorry, Wrong
Number* (1948) stars Barbara Stanwyck as Leona Stevenson, an invalid
confined to her bed who gradually discovers that her husband has made
arrangements for her murder. Much of the narrative develops from Leona's point of view and dramatizes her mounting alarm and fear. One of
noir's most extreme victims, she remains physically unable to avoid the
fate that looms for her.

The other character type central to noir is a counterpart to the
male victim: the femme fatale, the deadly but seductive woman who
manipulates her lover into committing a crime and may even lead him
to his death. *Double Indemnity* provides the archetypal femme fatale in
noir, Phyllis Dietrichson (Barbara Stanwyck), a serial killer who leaves
a long line of dead men and women in her wake as she struggles to rise
ever higher in wealth and social standing. Phyllis feels no sentiment or
soft emotions. She's all wickedness and calculation. As she says about

herself, "I'm rotten to the core." She is startled, therefore, when she hesitates to put a second bullet into Walter. Perhaps this hesitation means that she cares for him. Does she feel an improbable measure of affection for him? But her confusion is brief—Walter promptly puts a slug into her. There is little room in noir for softness or hesitation. Cora Smith (Lana Turner) tempts her lover into a murder plot in *The Postman Always Rings Twice*, and Anna lures Steve to his death in *Criss Cross*. Kathie Moffett kills Jeff in *Out of the Past* by crashing their car, and Robert Mitchum's character meets the same fate in *Angel Face* (1953) at the hands of Diane Tremayne (Jean Simmons), who had knocked off her parents earlier in the film.

The noir femme fatales rank among the deadliest villains ever put on the screen, but noir films also have their share of seductive women who are not lethal. Lauren Bacall makes a memorable partner for Humphrey Bogart in *The Big Sleep* and *Dark Passage*, as Lizabeth Scott does for Burt Lancaster in *Desert Fury* (1947) and *I Walk Alone* (1948), though she also plays a femme fatale in *Too Late for Tears* (1949). Gene Tierney, the haunting title character and apparent murder victim in *Laura*, turns out not to be dead. Though she is alluring and irresistible to homicide detective Mark McPherson (Dana Andrews), she is no danger to anyone. Quite the contrary—in the climax of the film, the killer makes a second try for her. But despite the range of women's roles in noir, the femme fatale remains the genre's best-known and most archetypal female character.

Because of this, and the associated presence of sexual manipulation and duplicity as key elements in countless noir films, many scholars suggest that the genre as a whole was a response to the sociological

***Criss Cross* (1949)** The noir femme fatale: Anna (Yvonne De Carlo) watches from the shadows as her lover, Steve Thompson (Burt Lancaster), is drawn into an armored car robbery that she has engineered. The strong key light has been flagged to illuminate only part of her face. The swift drop-off into shadow accentuates an aura of mystery and menace. The Angels Flight funicular railway is visible outside the window.

dislocations that ensued during World War II and its aftermath. Specifically, they cite these elements in noir as manifestations of upheavals in gender roles, as women entered the work force in numbers during the war years and then returned to the home to make room in the nation's factories for returning veterans. Correlation, though, does not prove causation. Although the femme fatale appeared in films during the years in which these gender-based labor conflicts were being negotiated, nothing in film noir establishes a direct connection between the femme fatale and the dislocations of World War II. Nevertheless, film noir tends to be interpreted quite often in sociological terms, as a body of films that held a mirror up to the neuroses and anxieties of postwar America. Why did so many pessimistic films appear in the years during and after the war? Why did the characters seem so alienated from the surfaces of American life? What were the sources of unease the films are alleged to be responding to?

In addition to the gender issues just mentioned, historians cite sources including the fears and traumas associated with the anticommunist campaign, the atomic bomb, which had closed the war in the Pacific with an unprecedented demonstration of deadly force, and the adjustment and reintegration of returning veterans. Many noirs, indeed, inflect their stories with these anxieties. *White Heat* and *Kiss Me Deadly* climax with apocalyptic explosions that reference the newly dawned atomic age. Other films depict their male victims as returning war veterans—*Spellbound* (1945), *The Blue Dahlia*, *The Chase* (1946), *The High Wall*, *Crossfire* (both 1947), *Kiss the Blood Off My Hands* (1948). The social hypotheses about noir thus find some grounding in the material of the films, but these hypotheses mainly involve relations of correlation. Therefore, while the connections may be alluring and provocative, they remain mostly speculative.

The central theoretical uncertainty about film noir is a rather different one than whether the films hold a dark mirror up to their era. It is a question about whether noir is, in fact, a genre or, alternatively, a style that can be applied to many otherwise diverse films. Scholars have not reached consensus on this issue. Genres such as the Western, the musical, the gangster film, the war film, and science fiction are clearly coded and patterned in terms of costume, setting, situation, and character types. Noir films are not as obviously coded in these terms. Noir also exhibits more diversity in subject matter and style; it ranges from heavily stylized and visually baroque productions, such as *Kiss Me Deadly* and *Touch of Evil*, to semidocumentary films, such as *The Naked City*. It includes movies about male victims, femme fatales, and private detectives; movies about gangsters; and police movies glorifying the methods that law enforcement officials use to apprehend criminals. *T-Men*, for example, is a hybrid film. It employs a Voice of God narrator, seemingly out of a documentary newsreel, to describe the enforcement mechanisms used by the Treasury Department in tracking felons, and much of the film lionizes the authority of this agency that, in the film's view, keeps America safe. But the movie also veers into recognizable noir territory with Joe MacDonald's marvelous cinematography emphasizing shadows, dark corridors, and isolated pools of light starkly illuminating night exteriors, along with the film's emphasis on the violence and brutality of the criminal netherworld. Noir films, it is said, also fail to show a unity of setting. *The Third Man* (1949) takes place in Vienna, *Cornered* (1945) in Switzerland and Buenos Aires, *Notorious* in Brazil, and *Touch of Evil* in Mexico. Noir also crosses genres, according to the manner in which some scholars construct it. *Pursued* (1947) and *Track of the Cat* (1954), for example, are Westerns often characterized as film noir, as is *Blade Runner*, a science fiction film.

Scholars who assert that noir is not a genre claim that it is merely a conceptual category, one that was created retrospectively by critics who, in later years, viewed these older Hollywood movies and perceived a common pattern of narrative and style in them. According to this view, the term "film noir" was invented after the fact to describe this recognized commonality. In this respect, the claim goes, noir differs from other genres. A Hollywood director making a Western, a musical, or a gangster movie was conscious of doing so because those genres existed in a self-evident way; film noir, it is said, did not.

In fact, however, the term "noir" was not retrospectively invented. Nor did commentators, filmmakers, or viewers in the period fail to see these movies as distinctive. When *Double Indemnity*, *Laura*, and *Murder, My Sweet* were released in 1944, a critic the following year described them as representative of a new trend of crime film, more psychological in focus, more hard-boiled, and more Freudian. In calling them Freudian, he was emphasizing their interest in neuroses and anxiety. In 1946, a French critic viewing the films was startled by their differences from past productions. He described them as "noir" and emphasized

The Big Combo (1955) John Alton was noir's most radical cinematographer. His blacks were deeper, his shadows more uncompromising, his depth of field more extended and expansive than anyone else's. Alton specialized in a kind of lighting minimalism when he worked in noir, pushing single- or two-source lighting to extremes of expression, as here. Three gangsters (Brian Donlevy, Lee Van Cleef, Earl Holliman) plan a murder in an apartment lit only by a table lamp. But the impression is deceptive. The effect light (the table lamp in the foreground) is supplemented with baby spotlights shining upward from the floor.

the importance of their use of flashback and voice-over narration, of femme fatale characters, and their social pessimism. *Panorama du Film Noir Américain* (1941–1953), the first book-length study of film noir, appeared in France during the genre's golden age.

Filmmakers, too, understood that noir represented a new pattern. John Alton, one of the genre's great cinematographers [*T-Men*, *Raw Deal*, *Railroaded, He Walked by Night* (1948), *I, the Jury* (1953), *The Big Combo*, among many others] wrote a book, *Painting with Light* (1949), that explained the art and techniques of professional cinematography. It was extremely unusual in this period for a cinematographer to make public the methods and secrets of the trade, and Alton devoted a full chapter to what he termed "Mystery Lighting," writing that audiences had grown tired of banal lighting designs and were demanding something more realistic and expressive. He called this new trend mystery lighting. Although he didn't use the term "noir," he clearly meant the style of lighting in vogue in this group of films, and he described many specific lighting scenarios of film noir. These included such things as "the effect of passing auto headlights on the ceiling of a dark interior," "fluctuating neon or other electric signs," "the hanging light on the ceiling of a cheap gambling joint," "searchlights of prisons," and "flashes of guns in absolute darkness."[1] Here, then, was one of the genre's leading cinematographers offering a primer on how one lights for film noir. Alton's chapter demonstrates that, though the term "noir" had not yet gained wide acceptance, this category of films and expressive designs was clearly established in the minds of filmmakers.

Like filmmakers, viewers were aware of noir even if they didn't call it by that name. As early as 1947, a full-fledged and wonderfully on-target parody of film noir appeared. Released by Paramount Pictures and titled *My Favorite Brunette*, it stars Bob Hope as Ronnie Jackson, a professional baby photographer who yearns to be a private eye, and not just any sort. He wants to be a hard-boiled private eye like he's seen in the movies. Across the hall from his office is one belonging to a private detective named Sam McCloud. Ronnie enters and sees McCloud sitting at his desk, back to the camera, talking on the phone. "Listen, baby, it'll take more than a couple of hopped-up gunsels to scare me off," McCloud growls into the phone. When he hangs up, Ronnie, who wants to be his partner, tells McCloud, "All my life I've wanted to be a hard-boiled detective like Humphrey Bogart, or Dick Powell, or even Alan Ladd." At this, McCloud turns, revealing that it *is* Alan Ladd in the role, an uncredited cameo appearance. Ladd was a noir icon in the period, appearing in *This Gun for Hire, The Blue Dahlia, The Glass Key*, and *Appointment with Danger* (1951). As McCloud, Ladd is dressed for noir—belted trench coat, fedora, smoking a cigarette, and packing a roscoe in a shoulder holster. The film pokes fun at other essential features of the genre, including flashbacks and voice-over narration (by Ronnie, from death row, telling the story of how he got there) and low-key cinematography. The existence of so thoroughgoing a parody suggests strongly that noir in the period was a distinctively recognized category of film.

Noir, then, is a genre, but the issues of classification that operate in all genre study are especially acute with noir. How one defines the category goes some way toward constituting the category. Is *Dirty Harry*

---

[1] John Alton, *Painting with Light* (Berkeley: University of California Press, 1995 reprint), 47–48.

(1971) a noir film? Some scholars classify it as noir, pointing to the film's attention to violence committed on both sides of the law. But its year of production falls between the end of noir's classical period and the onset of neo-noir. The film was released during a period in the 1960s and early 1970s when noir seemed defunct. The movie also lacks the striking low-key cinematography of classic noir; most of its scenes play in daylight. Furthermore, Harry (Clint Eastwood) is not an alienated character; he is angry with police bureaucracy, but his disaffection doesn't carry the existential qualities that afflict characters like Bradford Galt or Walter Neff. *Dirty Harry*, then, becomes a noir only if one focuses mostly on theme and not on the conjunction of theme and style.

But it is precisely this conjunction of theme and style that establishes noir as a genre rather than as a diffuse category. Noir can seem like a shapeless category if one employs a loose and permeable conception. Think, for a moment, in terms of Westerns; films set in the modern era, such as *Lonely Are the Brave* (1962) and *No Country for Old Men* (2007), could be construed as part of the genre, provided we employ a relaxed definition of Westerns. A strict definition, however, would exclude them precisely because they are set in the modern era. A strict definition of noir would exclude a picture like *Dirty Harry* because it lacks relevant features of noir, such as a cinematographic style emphasizing low-key lighting and an alienated central character. A restrictive definition of noir, then, can help us greatly in understanding the films as a genre and in undertaking the grouping and classifying operations necessary when studying genre. To count as noir, a film ought to have an urban setting; a central character who is alienated, victimized, or manipulated; a narrative structure emphasizing past transgressions or traumas; a focus on crime that is both psychological and physical; an extensive use of low-key lighting; an overall tone of threat, mystery, and fated action; and, finally, some combination of structural elements, including flashbacks, voice-over narration, and excessively dense and labyrinthine plotting. A noir film ought to have a preponderance of these features, even if one or more central items is lacking or deemphasized. *Out of the Past*, for example, features an often rural setting, but its other genre features are so emphatically noir that the movie unquestionably belongs in the genre. Adhering to a tight definition of noir, then, helps to address some of the thornier issues surrounding this category of filmmaking. Because the integration of style and theme is so important in constituting the genre, we turn now to a discussion of noir style.

Iconography

Many of noir's most famous images derive from the kinds of locations used in the films, from the visual possibilities afforded by clothing fashions of the 1940s and 1950s, and from the use of low-key cinematography. Because urban locales figure strongly, bars, nightclubs, cafés, neon signage, apartment buildings, and city landmarks help to create the genre's distinctive ambiance, as do Packards, Buicks, Studebakers, and other distinctive period automobiles. When fog, mist, or rain is added to these exterior locales and when story events are made to occur at night, then noir moves strongly toward the characteristic poetic and atmospheric effects for which it is famous.

Location shooting greatly enhances these attributes of urban locale and provides a major component of noir style. While the Hollywood norm at this time was to shoot most or all of a film on indoor studio sets, film noir often moved in a contrary direction, toward the use of real urban locales. *Kiss of Death* features extensive location work, with filming at the Chrysler Building, the Criminal Courts Building, the Hotel Marguery, and the Tombs detention center in Manhattan, as well as in Queens, the Bronx, New Jersey, and Sing Sing prison in Ossining, New York. Manhattan locations also figure prominently in *The Naked City*, including Roosevelt Hospital, the Williamsburg Bridge, and the city morgue. A common practice involved combining the use of studio sets with exterior work shot on real streets and with interior scenes shot inside actual buildings. One finds this pattern in *T-Men*, *The Big Combo*,

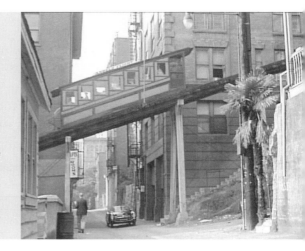

***Kiss Me Deadly* (1955)** Many noir films were set in actual urban locations rather than studios. This strategy added realism to the story and helped to make the city into a kind of character in the films. Extensive location work in *Kiss Me Deadly* includes scenes filmed on Los Angeles expressways and in the historic neighborhood of Bunker Hill, including this sequence that takes place along the Angels Flight funicular railway. One of Los Angeles's most distinctive landmarks, the original Angels Flight, built in 1901 and closed in 1969, used two cars operated by a cable-and-pulley system.

The Dark Corner, Double Indemnity, and *Kiss Me Deadly* (1955), among many other films. As a result, the urban settings in the stories acquire a powerful and tangible presence.

Los Angeles, in particular, figures in a great many noirs and becomes the archetypal noir city, established as such in Raymond Chandler's novels and then in Hollywood's numerous productions set there. Angels Flight, the distinctive funicular railway in Los Angeles, appears in *The Star* (1949), *Criss Cross*, *The Unfaithful* (1947), *Act of Violence* (1948), and *Kiss Me Deadly*. Bunker Hill, another distinguishing Los Angeles locale, appears extensively in *Criss Cross*, in exterior shots of the area's distinctive Victorian buildings, and in scenes shot inside area buildings and apartments. Another Bunker Hill location, the Third Street Stairs, paralleling Angels Flight, appears in *Criss Cross*, *Act of Violence*, and *Kiss Me Deadly*. L.A.'s gasworks, a huge storage facility for natural gas, shows up in numerous exterior scenes in noir, and several sequences in *711 Ocean Drive* (1950) take place there. Scenes filmed inside L.A.'s City Hall appear in *D.O.A.* (1950), *Crime Wave* (1954), *711 Ocean Drive*, *Tight Spot* (1955), *Tension*, and *Scene of the Crime* (both 1949). Other prominent Los Angeles locations appearing in noir include the Bradbury Building, MacArthur Park, and Malibu Beach.

The period's fashions in clothing play a significant role in noir iconography. Men and women tend to be well-dressed and accessorized.

***Out of the Past* (1947)** The distinctive look of noir in its classical period owes much to the clothing fashions of the 1940s. Here, Robert Mitchum is dressed for noir, in a belted trench coat, a fedora on his head, and a cigarette cupped in his hand. Lighting a cigarette in noir is a kind of ritual occurrence, providing opportunities for elaborate lighting effects. Mitchum holds a small arc light in his hand to simulate the match flare, which, in turn, acts as a small spotlight by virtue of the surrounding shadows. Costume and lighting design are formula elements in the genre that help to establish its tone of mystery, danger, and intrigue.

Snap-brim hats and fedoras provide many opportunities for dramatic effects by casting shadows to partially obscure the face, and trench coats offer good hiding places for handguns. Smoking was widespread in American society in this period, and the movies reflect this, but probably no genre stylized smoking as strikingly as noir. Lighting a cigarette becomes a major motif and ritual in such pictures as *Double Indemnity* and *Out of the Past*, staged with great dramatic effect as characters ignite a match using the thumbnail and lean into an elaborate lighting effect motivated by the flare. In his chapter on mystery lighting, John Alton emphasizes that lighting a cigarette in the dark of night provides great opportunities to create unusual and stylish effects by placing either a small arc light in the actor's hand or a larger lamp shining upward from the ground. In such cases the lighting creates an aura of intrigue and danger.

Indeed, more than any other ingredient, lighting establishes the characteristic noir iconography. Noir lighting is low-key, which means that the ratio of key light to other sources of illumination in the shot is high. (The key is the main light directed at an actor or scene.) As a result, low-key designs create extensive shadows, and the look of noir is defined by shadows and by small, selective areas of illumination within a dark visual palette. To create a low-key design, one must employ hard light because it is highly directional, that is, it is focused and brought to a point, selectively illuminating a small area while creating a fast falloff into shadow in surrounding areas. Soft light is diffused through a filter or bounced off a surface such as a wall, and it is much harder to control, tending to move in all directions at once. By contrast, hard light can be focused and flagged (flags are used to cut off a portion of light from a source), enabling sharp definition of precisely controlled areas of illumination.

In practice, low-key designs can be created using a single source of illumination or, alternatively, many lights. Alton's work in *The Big Combo* sometimes uses single-source illumination, while Joe MacDonald's cinematography in *The Dark Corner* employs intricate designs created by numerous lights. These include clothes lights to build up dark clothing, crosslights shining through the frame, toplights, kickers from high or low angles in the rear of the set, and fill lights and eye lights to emphasize the eyes of the performers. As this array of lamps suggests, it is inaccurate to assume that a shadowy, low-key scene necessarily features few lights. It might, but it often features very elaborate setups, with the

The Dark Corner (1946) The shadows in noir are deep, even in the daylight. Private detective Bradford Galt (Mark Stevens) stands in his Los Angeles office during daylight business hours, yet he is engulfed in shadows and darkness. At its most extreme, noir is a land of always-night, conveyed in low-key cinematography that often veers far from realism to embrace stylized expressions of mood and atmosphere.

underexposed areas calibrated to be read that way by the camera without necessarily appearing as such to the eyes of the actors or crew on set.

The industry-wide shift from soft to hard light in the 1940s helped film noir to emerge as a genre. Hard, directional light, high contrast, and fast falloff into shadow define the look of noir, and movies that do not feature low-key cinematography tend to move to the outer zones of the genre or outside of it entirely. Thus, a film such as *Dirty Harry* is not well qualified for inclusion in the genre. Low-key lighting did not originate with noir, nor was noir the only genre to employ it. It also may be found, for example, in horror films, such as Val Lewton's productions in this period for RKO studio [*Cat People* (1942), *The Leopard Man* (1943)]. As he was filming noirs in the 1940s, MacDonald also shot two Westerns, *My Darling Clementine* (1946) and *Yellow Sky* (1948), and in both he employed low-key-lighting designs. But this does not make these Westerns film noirs, because they lack the other elements of genre. While low-key designs, therefore, are not exclusive to noir, they found their most extensive and elaborate applications in noir movies, and therefore this aspect of iconography, more than any other, defines the look of noir and the meaning of the genre when combined with other key elements of character and narrative.

The importance of lighting design in the genre makes the period of neo-noir problematic. Low-key lighting can be utilized in color cinematography, as noirs like *Chinatown*, *L.A. Confidential*, and *Body Heat* demonstrate. But color tends to soften the high-contrast look produced by black and white. Color provides a great deal of information about objects and their separation from one another, information lacking in black-and-white film, which records only grayscale information. A filmmaker working in black and white has only shades of gray to discriminate and separate objects on screen. In grayscale, black can be employed as a more pure and extreme state than is typically the case in color cinematography, where illuminated areas of the frame will convey information about hue as well as luminance values. Thus, the neo-noirs tend not to showcase the kind of intensive and stark visual designs of classic noir. Their scenes may take place at night and be lit in a low-key fashion, but inevitably they convey a greater range of visual information than did noir in its earlier period. While neo-noir may feature shadows and darkness, these lack the aggressive thrust of noir in its classical period. Only *Sin City* among recent neo-noirs captures the starkness of classical low-key cinematography, and it does so because it employs a black-and-white look with isolated color effects. (To be precise, the

***Out of the Past* (1947)** Femme fatale Kathie Moffat (Jane Greer) pleads with Jeff Bailey (Robert Mitchum) to believe that she hasn't tried to set him up for a crime. But, of course, she has, and Jeff is too naïve for his own good. Note the striking visual effect achieved by side-lighting the actors, which places them in silhouette, while back and fill light separates and defines them relative to the rear wall of the set.

black-and-white look is itself an effect—the movie was shot in color, which was then drained from the image except for small areas that were allowed to retain their hue.)

Along with gangster movies, film noir remains American cinema's most enduring crime genre. Though it did not originate with the birth of cinema, its arrival in the 1940s gave audiences what amounted to a perfect genre, with image and narrative fused into an enduring pattern that furnishes a pervasive influence on contemporary film. Noir gave the movies much of what one thinks of in terms of style, not just darkly complected cinematography but a certain old-Hollywood glamour—Bogart in a trench coat; Veronica Lake's golden hair glowing in a halo of studio lighting; Lauren Bacall's and Lizabeth Scott's sultry, smoker's voices; Mitchum or MacMurray thumbing a match; Stanwyck or Lana Turner luring a weak man to his doom; and an indelible rich vocabulary—shiv, sawbuck, take the fall, newshawk, nailed, Mickey Finn, jack, jake, hooch, hop-head, gams, croak, copper, clip-joint—that, like the movies themselves, lingers today. Noir provides an essential template for today's filmmakers who want to make movies about crime, punks, fall guys, and floozies. Matty (Kathleen Turner), the great femme fatale in *Body Heat*, tells her lover, "You aren't too smart, are you? I like that in a man." Only noir gives filmmakers a home for hard-boiled patter like that.

The Imagery of Noir

The stories of crime and deception that are prevalent in film noir gave filmmakers many opportunities to create highly stylized images that evoke the genre's peculiar twilit world. While Hollywood movies in the 1940s and 1950s often follow a standard visual style, the noir genre enabled filmmakers to push the boundaries of Hollywood style in interesting and exciting ways.

Very often these departures from the standard visual template result in images that are exaggerated, unbalanced, garish, off-kilter, unstable, and startling in the aggressive ways that they evoke the landscape of noir.

At the beginning of *Kiss Me Deadly*, a crying, terror-struck woman (Cloris Leachman), clad only in a trench coat, runs along an isolated,

Kiss Me Deadly (1955) The off-kilter world of film noir is announced at the outset of *Kiss Me Deadly* with this peculiar credit sequence in which text scrolls backward down the screen. It turns the standard methods of beginning a film upside down and disorients the viewer by confounding expectations about how a narrative ought to get underway.

dark highway where private eye Mike Hammer (Ralph Meeker) almost runs her down in his sports car. He gives her a lift, and the film's opening credits scroll onscreen as they drive.

But this is no ordinary credit sequence. The titles scroll backward, from the bottom of the screen to the top, a very disorienting presentation. The camera is mounted on the rear of the car, directly behind Hammer and the mystery woman (who calls herself Christina), and as the car speeds forward, the camera sees only darkness, an impenetrable night, beyond the glare of the headlights. The night rushes to meet the characters.

As the credits scroll, the audio contains the amplified sounds of the woman sobbing and moaning and a song playing from the car's radio, Nat "King" Cole singing "I'd Rather Have the Blues Than What I've Got." The lyrics of the song describe a situation so terrible and alienating as to make the blues (a slang term for emotional depression) seem pleasant by comparison. The sequence is sustained—the backward-scrolling credits, the sounds of sobbing and the musical lament, the characters illuminated by the dashboard lights and surrounded by darkness—in a manner that emphasizes the essential noir qualities of alienation and threat.

The off-kilter qualities of the opening sequence extend throughout the film. When the credits end, gangsters ambush Hammer and force his car off the road. They kidnap and drug Hammer and torture

Kiss Me Deadly **(1955)** Mike Hammer (Ralph Meeker) and Christina (Cloris Leachman) drive along a lonely highway where the night is absolutely dark, bringing with it a sense of menace that engulfs and surrounds them. The world of noir is nocturnal and dangerous.

Christina until she dies. They put Hammer back into his car and send it over a cliff. This entire scene is framed so that the hoodlum in charge of the mayhem is glimpsed only by his feet and lower legs, providing a fragmentary view of the action consistent with compositional styles elsewhere in the movie.

When Hammer breaks into William Mist's house (Mist is an associate of the arch villain who tortures Christina), he walks through an art gallery downstairs. The camera travels with him, but shows only odd, partial views of the action—Hammer's lower legs crossing the tiled floor and low-angle traveling shots of the paintings that place them center frame, with the edge of Hammer's shoulder and center chest visible on the left of the screen.

No clear narrative reason exists for these peculiar compositions. But their perverse, oddly angled views are in keeping with the tone established by the film's opening imagery, which insists upon visual strategies for disorienting the viewer. Elsewhere in the film, extreme wide-angle perspectives exaggerate the graphic elements of staircases and work to thrust violent action directly out at the viewer.

In this regard, much of *Kiss Me Deadly* is designed to be visually transgressive, to work against the conventions of polished studio film-making. But these visual elements, so extreme in their design, are not just a formalistic exercise. They connect with the film's narrative project, which is to take film noir to a kind of ultimate point. The narrative is about both nothing and everything. Hammer wants to find out why Christina is killed and what the gangsters are searching for. His secretary describes this quest as a kind of great nothing, an abstraction. She calls it a search for "the great what's-it."

The what's-it turns out to be a box that contains an annihilating white light, emitted by a nuclear fission that burns and vaporizes whoever looks at it. The energy in the box is unidentified. The whiteness in the box designates a void—the abstraction of the great what's-it—but it also evokes the nuclear bomb, the ultimate everything that dominated and haunted postwar culture. As the film ends, the box "goes off," turning a beach house into ground zero.

Kiss Me Deadly **(1955)** The film's visual style frequently is decentered, unbalanced, harsh, and exaggerated. Wide-angle lenses make the visual perspective of many shots more extreme than normal. When Hammer visits a mysterious woman named Gabrielle (Gaby Rodgers), the staircase outside her apartment engulfs and diminishes his figure as he knocks at the door. The wide-angle perspective makes the stairs look unnaturally large and Hammer unnaturally small.

***Kiss Me Deadly* (1955)** Robert Aldrich's film connects the anxieties expressed in film noir to the nuclear age that began with the close of World War II, thereby suggesting that noir as a genre was motivated by, and responsive to, this new era in human history when collective annihilation became a real threat. Gabrielle (Gaby Rodgers) opens the box that contains the great what's-it and perishes in its burning white light.

The film thus connects the genre of noir with the bomb and suggests that noir's anxieties are indeed the anxieties of a new, nuclear age. In *Kiss Me Deadly*, the genre's off-kilter, destabilizing visual style furnishes tropes for the ultimate kind of destabilization that the bomb's entrance into human history represents.

While *Kiss Me Deadly* has one of the most extreme visual designs in the noir genre, its emphasis on garish images and flamboyant constructions of nocturnal landscapes are common throughout the genre. *The Killers,* for example, opens with a driving scene in which the titular assassins are silhouetted in a car whose headlights stab the darkness of a lonely, deserted highway.

A sign announces their arrival in Brentwood, New Jersey, and the next shot shows the diner and surrounding buildings in Brentwood, elaborately backlit, with sharp, slashing blades of light and heavy shadow. The two killers stride into this chiaroscuro landscape, menacing silhouettes casting long shadows, and head for the diner in search of Swede, the man they've come to kill. The darkened landscape and ornate shadows point to the violence represented by the killers and to the despair of their victim. Swede lies in bed in his darkened room and awaits their arrival, too full of sadness to run, no longer caring whether he lives. The noir tone is created by the lighting and by the aura of despair that clings to Swede. He reacts passively to his impending death. It is an abnormal reaction, one that establishes the narrative world in terms of disequilibrium and emotional disturbance.

Murder, My Sweet is one of many films based on Raymond Chandler's novels, and the opening scene plunges the viewer into a darkened room at a disconcerting and provocative angle. The camera looks down from a high, overhead view at a table and desk lamp. The lamp illuminates the table surface, and several figures are glimpsed seated around the table, but otherwise the room is dark. The camera slowly zooms forward (the zoom effect was produced on an optical printer rather than in-camera) until the blank table surface fills the screen, with the lightbulb reflected on its surface.

***Murder, My Sweet* (1944)** Private eye Philip Marlowe (Dick Powell, with Donald Douglas) has been blinded and wears a bandage around his head when he appears at the beginning of *Murder, My Sweet*. Facing a police interrogation, he narrates a flashback, explaining how he acquired his wounds. Imagery of the blind hero establishes a disquieting tone as the film begins, and Marlowe's loss of eyesight works metaphorically as a statement about the tangled, impenetrable conspiracies at the heart of noir.

The camera then abruptly pulls back and up, away from the table, to reveal three detectives questioning a man. The lighting is hard and low-key, and the detectives shift in and out of the shadows as they adjust their seating. The effect is that the table lamp casts the visible illumination, but the elaborate edge lighting on the characters creates a more pictorial effect than the desk lamp could actually accomplish. The pictorial effect, with its complex interplay and dynamic changes of light and shadow, is consistent with the genre's emphasis on elaborate and ornate depictions of darkness.

The detectives drill their suspect with questions that he deflects or refuses to answer. Another detective enters the room, and strikes a match, as the camera moves to reveal the suspect's face. Hitherto the character has been glimpsed from the back or obliquely. The flare of the match and the glare of the desk lamp show that the suspect—private eye Philip Marlowe (Dick Powell)—has his head and eyes covered in a large bandage. In this darkened room, Marlowe is blind, owing to some prior and as-yet-unspecified injury.

It's a startling moment, this abrupt revelation that the film's protagonist is crippled. Like many noirs, the events of *Murder, My Sweet* unfold in flashback, as Marlowe explains how he became involved in murder and acquired the bandage that prevents him from seeing his interrogators. The film's narrative is launched from a place of darkness and wounding.

Noir imagery derives from elaborate orchestrations of small pieces of hard light, creating complex, contrasting bands of illumination and darkness that ensnare characters in the stories. In this regard,

***The Big Combo* (1955)** Susan (Jean Wallace) uses light to entrap the film's villain, Mr. Brown (Richard Conte), shining the floodlight of an automobile on him when he tries to hide in the darkness of an airplane hangar. Working like a cinematographer, Susan lights the scene's action. She whips the light back and forth as he tries to evade it, and the scene becomes a self-conscious commentary on the role of lighting in the genre and of a cinematographer as a key collaborator in the creation of noir style.

cinematographers make major contributions to the noir style, and the genre can be regarded as being, in important respects, cinematographer-driven. The climax of *The Big Combo* resolves story issues in a sequence that showcases the work of cinematography.

Police Lieutenant Diamond (Cornel Wilde) has been relentlessly pursuing a mobster known as Mr. Brown (Richard Conte), and he finally corners Brown in an airplane hangar. Brown's henchmen are killed in a gun battle, and Brown, now alone, tries to flee. His girlfriend, Susan (Jean Wallace), helps Diamond by shining the floodlight of an automobile on Brown. The sequence becomes a symphony of light and lighting effects, as Brown tries to evade the floodlight and Susan sweeps it through the hangar, relocating Brown and catching him in its glare time and again. The beam of light punches through the darkness of the hangar and bounces off its tin walls. Diamond emerges from the darkness to capture Brown, who stands, helpless, in the glare of the light.

The sequence self-consciously points to the central role played by cinematography in noir style; the film's narrative issues are resolved using a cinematographer's tool—light itself and its choreography in service to drama. Susan effectively becomes a cinematographer, a surrogate for the film's real cinematographer, John Alton, using light to sculpt drama, to delineate character, to foreground story action. She lights the action in a manner that enables it to develop and conclude.

But this is noir, and light contains its own mysteries and sources of unease. After Brown is taken away, Diamond and Susan exit from the hangar in the film's concluding shot. They are framed at the entrance

***The Big Combo* (1955)** Cinematographer John Alton uses a backlit bank of fog to establish an iconic noir landscape, distinguished by the silhouetted figures of Susan (Jean Wallace) and Diamond (Cornel Wilde), the frame of the airplane hangar, and the nothingness that lies beyond. Susan and Diamond head toward the light, but the composition prevents the viewer from seeing where they are going. Their destination is poetically undefined; it lies on the murky landscape of noir.

of the hangar, surrounded by the interior darkness of the building, and they walk toward a brightly lit exterior that is undefined because it is shrouded in fog.

Alton wrote about the challenges of illuminating fog, which has a tendency to flatten contrast. He lit the scene in a higher key and with greater contrast than normal, shot it with a wide-angle lens to keep the fog in focus, dressed the actors in dark clothing so they would stand out as silhouettes, and illuminated the entire background with light to create a strong feeling of depth.

Diamond and Susan walk off into a void, the engulfing fog whose bright illumination holds both promise and mystery. The shot has become an archetypal statement on the meaning and style of noir, defining a landscape of mystery and threat, illuminated by light that conceals rather than reveals, hiding information instead of disclosing it. Light illuminates the noir world, showing things the characters might prefer not to see or know. The conclusion of *The Big Combo* provides one of the genre's most poetic statements about the paradoxical nature of light in noir, where illumination may be inadequate to reveal the truth or where what it does reveal might perhaps be better left in the shadows.

Stephen Prince

QUESTIONS FOR DISCUSSION

1. If a crime film has most of the ingredients of noir but does not use low-key lighting, can it still be considered a noir film? Why or why not?
2. Crime films have existed since the beginning of cinema. D. W. Griffith's *Musketeers of Pig Alley* (1912) is an early example of a movie about crime in the city. How did film noir, when it arrived, mark a new and different direction for crime films?
3. Film noir has been an enduringly popular genre. Why do audiences seem to enjoy visiting the dark side of life in these movies? What is the appeal of noir?
4. Enter the debate about whether noir is a genre or a generalized style. Build a case for each position. Which side in the debate seems stronger and more persuasive?
5. If you were a director making a noir film today, would you shoot it in black and white or in color? Why?

FOR FURTHER READING

Alton, John. *Painting With Light*. Berkeley: University of California Press, 1995.

Borde, Raymond, and Etienne Chaumeton, *A Panorama of American Film Noir, 1941–1953*, trans. Paul Hammond. San Francisco: City Lights Publishers, 2002.

Cameron, Ian, ed. *The Book of Film Noir*. New York: Continuum, 1992.

Hirsch, Foster. *The Dark Side of the Screen*. New York: A. S. Barnes, 1981.

Kaplan, E. Ann, ed. *Women in Film Noir*. London: BFI Publishing, 1980.

Naremore, James. *More Than Night: Film Noir in Its Contexts*. Berkeley: University of California Press, 1998.

Palmer, R. Barton. *Hollywood's Dark Cinema: The American Film Noir*. New York: Twayne, 1994.

Silver, Alain, and James Ursini. *Film Noir Reader*, 4 vols. New York: Limelight, 1996, 2004.

Silver, Alain, and Elizabeth Ward, eds. *Film Noir: An Encyclopedic Reference to the American Style*, revised edition. New York: Overlook Press, 1992.

Spicer, Andrew. *Film Noir*. Essex, UK: Pearson, 1992.

Vertigo (1958)

The Thriller

GAVIN ELSTER (TOM HELMORE) simply wants to protect the chic, sexy blonde he says is his wife, Madeleine (Kim Novak). That's why he hires a man he knew back in his college days, a reliable former police detective named Scottie Ferguson (James Stewart), to follow her. Now, why shouldn't Scottie believe his old acquaintance? Many reasons. Slowly, Scottie discovers that Elster has baited a trap with the beautiful "Madeleine" to take advantage of Scottie's weakness—his vertigo—and entangle him in a web of illusion. But by the time the detective understands that he has been used and abused, he is powerless to stop the chain of deadly events that Elster has set in motion. So it goes in Alfred Hitchcock's *Vertigo* (1958), arguably the greatest thriller of all time.

The thriller generates suspense and tension by setting its hero the task of negotiating a seemingly endless and confusing maze, and *Vertigo* is stunning in its evocation of how the thriller hero becomes ensnared in the coils of his inner life, trapped inside his own fears and erotic passions. Of course, thrillers are not always about a protagonist's labyrinthine consciousness and subconsciousness. Often the thriller protagonist is compelled to move through the twists and turns of external spaces—for example, a labyrinthine building from which, it seems, he or she may never be able to exit. Or the hero or heroine may be lost in the abstract convolutions of social structures—for example, the legal and governmental institutions that we assume will protect us. In thrillers, the supposed source of our sanity—our minds or our culture—may unaccountably plunge us into confusion and fear. Laws may be used against the innocent; government by and for the people may turn out to be a monstrous web of lies; our minds may fail to recognize deceit. The intensity of the extreme emotions set in play by these betrayals is agitating, but intensity is one of the thriller's main appeals, and its allure is the reason why there are more thrillers produced in the United States than any other kind of mass-entertainment movie.

Hitchcock is the director who towers over the history of the suspense thriller in a way that no one artist dominates any other film genre. Critic Charles Derry reminds us in his study *The Suspense Thriller: Films in the Shadow of Alfred Hitchcock* (1988) that all movies in this category are either indebted to or outclassed by "The Master," more likely both. Hitchcock's first solo flight as a director was a thriller, one of the earliest of the genre, *The Lodger: A Story of the London Fog* (1927). Produced while Hitchcock was still working in England, it is a silent film that tells the story of Joe (Malcolm Keene), a detective who suspects that an unnamed lodger (Ivor Novello) renting a room in the home of his girlfriend, Daisy (June Tripp), is a serial killer who is terrifying London. *The Lodger* begins Hitchcock's career by mapping the differences between the thriller and the detective or police film. Detective and police stories provide audience satisfaction through the discovery and arrest of a perpetrator. By contrast, *The Lodger*, while full of police and detective action, prefigures the thriller's larger, more sophisticated concerns as it creates the appearance that its story hinges on Joe's search for the murderer. In this narrative about how the detective and the public fail to deal with their fears of a handsome, strange, but innocent man, Hitchcock is actually out to demonstrate the dangers of what happens when a mob gets ensnared by its own hysteria.

The mob that rushes to kill "the lodger" at the end of the film is stopped only at the last moment by information that the actual murderer, never seen or even identified by name in the movie, has been caught. The lack of importance that Hitchcock gives to the capture of the real killer speaks volumes about his true concern: the mob's rush to judgment—and ours. By leading the audience to jump to the same conclusions as the detective and the crowd of angry citizens, Hitchcock creates for his viewers the experience of how ordinary people, like us, can suddenly turn murderous. His story provides us with an opportunity to look at what separates us from the criminal, or, to be more precise, to ponder the possibility of a demonic streak in all human nature, an eerie prospect that has increasingly come to define this complex and exciting genre.

By the time Hitchcock made *Rebecca*, his first American thriller, in 1940, he had endowed the genre with even more sophistication, by using a fluid camera to highlight the suspense of the plot, and by developing a cinematic vocabulary that even more piercingly demonstrates the fragility of the human mind under the pressure of intense feelings (a suggestion absent from detective and police films, with their confident reliance on the protagonist's skills and intelligence). And with his subsequent American films, he went on to evoke, ever more brilliantly, the process by which his protagonists become trapped by the slow buildup of uncontrolled (possibly uncontrollable) human evil. During his career, Hitchcock filmed a vast array of thrillers with such artistry and acute psychological insight that he raised to great heights the reputation of the genre, which had a certain cachet in Europe but was initially dismissed in America as a low form of entertainment.

Nevertheless, if most critics agree about Hitchcock's august standing, there is a great deal of uncertainty about the thriller, which presents an extreme overlap problem for genre study. Suspense, a defining characteristic of the thriller, is an aspect of *all* storytelling. Moreover, thrillers contain elements that are also plentiful in other genres: criminals, detectives, and policemen; crime stories; and shadows. Thrillers can even take place in settings that are normally thought of as definitively restricted to another genre, as, for example, a Western setting. Where do we draw the line around "the thriller"?

History

The cinematic thriller is a comparatively modern genre because the technology for producing suspenseful screen effects, like fluid point-of-view tracking shots, was not available in early cinema. Perhaps more important, there was less tolerance in the early twentieth century for the thriller's edgy, modern angst about what lies under the surface of ostensibly good society than there was in the 1940s and afterward. In fact, many of the silent and early sound films mistakenly identified in reviews and by movie renters as suspense thrillers are really mystery melodramas or detective films. For example, the movies in the Thin Man series (1934–1947), starring William Powell and Myrna Loy as Nick and Nora Charles, are witty and essentially comic detective movies but are often mislabeled as thrillers. Although Nick is officially a detective and Nora is not, she is eager to get into the mystery, despite Nick's objections, and this is the source of both the comedy and the suspense of their films. These films are essentially about a battle of the sexes and rarely if ever touch the deep-seated fears that the thriller targets. Among the few early American films that can credibly be distinguished as embryonic suspense thrillers is *The Most Dangerous Game* (1932). Based on a short story of the same name by Richard Connell, it shows Hollywood taking its first awkward steps toward the thriller genre. The hero, Bob Rainsford (Joel McCrea), is an attractive and famous hunter who begins the story as a lionized celebrity and who reveals in his casual remarks a streak of cruelty about the animals he hunts. Dismissing the feelings of the creatures he stalks, Rainsford thinks only of the excitement of conquest. The film's suspense turns on the problematic nature of the cruelty Rainsford epitomizes, for which society has made him a cultural hero.

The Most Dangerous Game **(1932)** In this frame, Bob Rainsford (Joel McCrea), manacled like an animal or a slave, has discovered Zaroff's (Leslie Banks) plans to hunt him for sport. The image displays the unsophisticated state of the thriller in early sound films, with its conventional placement of Rainsford and Zaroff center frame, its uninteresting lighting, and its unsubtle costuming of the hero in light clothing and the villain in dark.

When Rainsford is shipwrecked on an island ruled by a mysterious Count Zaroff (Leslie Banks), who is also an avid hunter, Rainsford learns uncomfortable truths about himself. Zaroff, bored with pursuing and killing animals, has taken to tracking and killing "the most dangerous game," human beings. After Rainsford becomes Zaroff's prey, he comes to feel at one with all the creatures he has unfeelingly killed and he repudiates his earlier attitudes. During the night of terror he spends struggling to escape Zaroff, the island becomes a maze of natural traps, limited by the surrounding ocean. As is typical of thrillers, civilization seems to give way as uncontrollable demons of passion and power unleashed by Zaroff's pursuit negate all the rules that keep men and women from slipping back to the law of the jungle. As is also typical of the thriller, in *The Most Dangerous Game*, we look into the psychology of the criminal with the same interest and emphasis that we look into the hero's. Parity between hero and antagonist is a curious feature of the thriller. In many crime and adventure fantasy films, the villain is reduced to a necessary stereotype of evil, his/her presence required only to give the hero a chance to demonstrate his courage or brains. In the thriller, the boundaries between the motives of the hero and the villain blur to some degree. In *The Most Dangerous Game*, Rainsford and Zaroff are both cruel hunters. However, Rainsford changes, providing a neat Hollywood ending. Later thrillers make the audience anxious about what might happen if the dark forces unleashed by the thriller plot cannot be restrained properly. But in 1932, Hollywood was not ready for that. Nor does *The Most Dangerous Game* fully encourage in the spectator the experience of the uncanny that later became the mark of the thriller. The audience watches Rainsford suffer from a comfortable distance.

The thrillers of the 1940s moved toward a heightened sense of peril. Because of the Hollywood Production Code, the majority of them retreated to comparative safety after giving the audience a glimpse of the bottomless pit of savagery into which people could sink, but there were a few groundbreaking films that refused to offer clichéd comfort. *Gaslight* (1944) is an example of the more conservative thrillers of the period. Although it is the story of Gregory Anton's (Charles Boyer) cruel determination to drive his new bride, Paula (Ingrid Bergman), into madness just to possess her aunt's jewels, *Gaslight* provides a generally happy ending. Anton is diabolically clever as he enfolds Paula in his convoluted lies—unnerving the audience in the process—but a kind policeman thwarts his plans and saves the day in the final scene. Similarly, in

Spellbound (1945), Constance Peterson (Ingrid Bergman), an attentive and brave psychiatrist, saves John Ballantine (Gregory Peck) from being sucked into a vortex of madness in a story of psychological manipulation that, as in *Gaslight*, is based on the lust for gain, and normality is restored. In *Keeper of the Flame* (1942), Christine Forrest (Katharine Hepburn) and Steven O'Malley (Spencer Tracy), a reporter, are lost in the labyrinthine coils of illusion created by Christine's late husband, Robert Forrest, about his political intentions. But their heroism eventually reveals the truth about Forrest's fascist organization and prevents it from taking over the United States. However, a new note is sounded in Hitchcock's *Rebecca* (1940). In this film, the nameless heroine (Joan Fontaine), who marries handsome, aristocratic Maxim de Winter (Laurence Olivier) after knowing him only a few days, must deal with the twists and turns of the dark legacy of his first wife, Rebecca. As the story progresses, the second Mrs. de Winter and Maxim achieve a kind of freedom from the memory of Rebecca, but Hitchcock makes it clear that she will never escape it entirely. Rebecca's evil will continue to haunt the second Mrs. de Winter even after she has gained a semblance of control over her marriage and her life.

Even more enduringly eerie is the pall cast over the life of Charlie (Teresa Wright), a small-town girl, in Hitchcock's *Shadow of a Doubt* (1943). Young Charlie, raised on conventional beliefs about the sanctity of the family and the essential goodness of the "normal" world, is permanently disillusioned by her adored Uncle Charlie (Joseph Cotten), who turns out to be a cold-blooded killer. Despite Charlie's ability to fight off her uncle's attempt to murder her when he becomes aware that she has guessed his terrible secret, and despite the romantic entrance into her life of a kind and courageous detective, she will never think about family and community in the same way again. In *Suspicion* (1941), Hitchcock takes the thriller further into the darkness, as Lina McLaidlaw (Joan Fontaine) is drawn into a tangle of truths and lies by her love for Johnnie Aysgarth (Cary Grant), who she comes to believe is an amoral killer. By threading the film with an impenetrable tangle of clues about Aysgarth's real nature, Hitchcock leaves open the possibility that poor Lina may be doomed. Johnnie's last-minute explanation of his actions sounds plausible, but the final image of his embrace of Lina resembles the coiling of a snake around a helpless rabbit. Lina may be about to die at the hands of the man who claims to love her. However, the thriller of this decade that pushes the envelope most radically is Orson Welles's

The Lady from Shanghai (1947), in which, under the erotic influence of the seductress Elsa Bannister (Rita Hayworth), Mike O'Hara (Orson Welles) finds himself inexplicably acting in a self-destructive (and illegal) manner. He finally manages to free himself from the vortex of hatred and murder into which Elsa has pulled him, but he does not emerge from his experience of the worst of human nature as a truly free man, but rather as a soul haunted by his part in an orgy of destruction.

Suspense thrillers evolved further in the 1950s because of the loosening of Hollywood's restrictive censorship rules after a major legal battle about "The Miracle," a segment of *L'Amore* (1948), an Italian anthology film. In "The Miracle," a modern-day Italian girl claims that, though pregnant, she is still a virgin. Religious authorities considered the film a blasphemous insult to the Virgin Mary, but eventually challenges to the Production Code Administration's attempts to censor "The Miracle" led to a 1952 Supreme Court decision that, for the first time, guaranteed First Amendment rights to movies. After that, suspense thrillers, along with many other film genres, were slowly liberated from PCA censorship and gradually began to treat subjects that had previously been taboo.

Nineteen-fifties thrillers like Hitchcock's *Strangers on a Train* (1951) and Charles Laughton's *The Night of the Hunter* (1955) embroil the protagonists and the audience in the convolutions of the minds of insane villains drawn with daring candor, carving out greater psychological depths for the genre. But if they evoke an inexplicable human darkness, these films still honor the venerable Hollywood convention of the happy ending. In the former film, Guy Haines (Farley Granger) meets the psychotic Bruno Anthony (Robert Walker) by chance on a train, only to find himself and his friends manipulated by Bruno's deranged attempts to frame Guy for the murder of his wife, a murder that Bruno actually commits. An accident of timing allows Guy to prove his innocence and marry his true love, but not before Bruno instigates nearly apocalyptic chaos at an amusement park. In *The Night of the Hunter*, Laughton creates a fanciful landscape of glowing stars, shining water, and small animals in which two children, John (Billy Chapin) and Pearl Harper (Sally Jane Bruce), are tormented by Harry Powell (Robert Mitchum), a homicidal drifter posing as an evangelical minister. Powell at first hoodwinks the small rural community in which the children live, which warmly welcomes him as the holy man he pretends to be. But, ultimately, when it is discovered that he has murdered John and Pearl's mother, Willa (Shelley Winters), recalling the mob scene in *The Lodger*, the townspeople

The Night of the Hunter **(1955)** The entire story of *The Night of the Hunter* (1955) is encapsulated in this wonderfully composed frame. The two innocent children, John (Billy Chapin) and Pearl (Sally Jane Bruce), look helplessly at the menacing double fist of Harry Powell (Robert Mitchum), who intends to bully them into telling him where their deceased father has hidden his money. In the tradition of the suspense thriller, the hiding place, Pearl's doll, is in plain sight and is well known to the audience, but not to the sinister villain, Harry. Just barely visible in this shot, though also well known to the audience are the words "Love" and "Hate" that Harry has tattooed on his right and left hands, respectively.

unnerve the spectator by matching Powell's savagery with their vengeful violence. In this strangely enchanted though in many ways grittily real backwoods world, the children are rescued by a chance meeting with the exceptional Rachel Cooper (Lillian Gish), an old woman with a much gentler religion than either Powell or the townspeople, who understands that life "is hard on little things."

With Robert Aldrich's *Kiss Me Deadly* (1955) and Hitchcock's *Vertigo*, the thriller ventures into the territory of featuring protagonists who are not "saved by the bell." In *Kiss Me Deadly*, Mike Hammer (Ralph Meeker) a hard-boiled detective, finds himself chasing shadows in a maze of clues that enable him to figure out what is behind the corruption of a group of powerful men but does not give him the power to prevent them from doing damage. In the final moments of the story, a mysterious suitcase he has been looking for blows up in a way that visually resembles a nuclear explosion, and the film does not make clear whether Mike and his secretary/girlfriend, Velda (Maxine Cooper), or anyone else in the vicinity, will survive the blast. *Vertigo* goes still further by reflecting doubts not only about the character of *some* powerful men but about the masculine ideal of entitlement that is so central to sexist gender mythologies.

At the heart of *Vertigo* is the fear that the feeling of entitlement characteristic of men of authority may pose immense dangers to our culture, although such men generally claim that social order depends on those entitlements. Gavin Elster, a wealthy businessman, presents himself to Scottie Ferguson as a kind and concerned husband, and a reasonable friend who wants to exert power over his wife, Madeleine, to keep her safe, but he is revealed to be an amoral person who intends to kill Madeleine and live on her money in Europe. His entitlements benefit him alone. Elster betrays the trust placed in him by manipulating all the symbols of power at his command to get away with murder. His prime weapon is Judy Barton, a woman whose appearance he has changed so that she resembles Madeleine. Elster has trained Judy to bring Scottie under her spell, understanding that Scottie, like all American men, has been socialized to desire the cool blonde, considered a trophy wife or a trophy mistress by influential leaders of American industry. Illusion rules Scottie's world the minute he agrees to help Elster. He and the audience glimpse the real Madeleine only once, and then very briefly, as she falls to her death. The only visible woman is the one Elster has created. As he explores this maze of sexually charged deception, Hitchcock identifies a frightening dynamic in our society that channels male sexual desire toward women packaged as commodities. There is nothing comforting in this film, which crowns with success Elster's plan to lure the normally honorable Scottie into becoming his accomplice. Worse, once Elster has absconded to Europe with his wife's fortune, he is never brought to justice, and the long-lasting effects of his villainy become manifest.

Scottie, devastated by his association with Elster, has a nervous breakdown. Even when he seems to recover, he is haunted by a longing for the woman he knew as Madeleine. When he runs into Judy, who has reverted to the way she looked before Elster transformed her, Scottie's obsessiveness takes a frightening turn. At first Scottie believes that Judy only resembles Madeleine, and, unaware that he is replicating the process by which Elster first transformed Judy, he compulsively builds a relationship with her, in which he forces her to reassume Madeleine's appearance. Even after Scottie realizes what Elster has done, there is no

***Vertigo* (1958)** This frame suggests the psychological complexity of this legendary suspense thriller. On the right of the image Scottie (James Stewart) clandestinely observes Judy/Madeleine (Kim Novak). What he does not know, however, is that she is posing for him, fully aware that he is looking at her. At the same time, although Scottie has placed himself so that he can keep her in sight without being seen, the tight frame of his eye by the door opening suggests how limited his sight really is. Similarly, that Judy/Madeleine appears as a mirror reflection here suggests the illusory quality of what Scottie observes. At the same time, while Judy believes she is only acting the part created for her by Gavin Elster, she will soon be genuinely in love with Scottie. There are nothing but twists and turns of events and passions illustrated in this moment.

release. Scottie and Judy helplessly reenact the death of Elster's wife. But this time it is Judy who falls to her death.

As the genre moves into the 1960s, it continues to peel away the security of both the protagonist and the audience, becoming less inclined to cushion the unnerving shocks it deals. Three thrillers of the 1960s vividly indicate this new trajectory: *Cape Fear*, *The Manchurian Candidate* (both 1962), and *Seven Days in May* (1964). Now, in response to the social upheaval of the period, a political aspect has been added to the genre. Also significant is that by this time the conventions of the genre had become established enough for Hollywood to produce a parody thriller: *Charade* (1963).

The epitome of the 1960s thriller is *Cape Fear*, in which the villain creates a feeling of helplessness and terror in the film's other characters and its spectators alike about the ability of the laws to protect us. The anxiety begins in the opening scene when the villain, Max Cady (Robert Mitchum), returns from jail to get even with the hero, Sam Bowden

(Gregory Peck), a kind and upstanding lawyer who helped convict Cady for the vicious rape of a sixteen-year-old girl, by serving as a witness in the court trial. Instead of directly attacking Bowden in a physically violent way, Cady, who has learned both patience and something about the law while serving his sentence, manipulates the virtuous Bowden into making himself a lawbreaker. Cady systematically overwhelms Bowden's usual restraint by playing on his baser emotions, which Cady understands very well, until Bowden becomes desperate enough to hire thugs to beat up his nemesis. Cady then turns the tables on Bowden, foiling the attackers and threatening Bowden with disbarment. Once the lawyer is on the wrong side of the law, Cady makes it clear that he intends to rape and torture Bowden's wife and daughter, releasing in Bowen his most primitive impulses.

Cady's dance of death with Bowden demonstrates that, given the right provocation, even the most cultivated people are only a step away from violence. The culmination of this war of nerves takes place on Bowden's boat, on the Cape Fear River, to which Cady has followed the

Cape Fear (1962) Here, Sam Bowden (Gregory Peck) is painfully aware of the presence of his relentless, terrifying nemesis, Max Cady (Robert Mitchum), behind him. The frame illustrates the ability of the thriller to create a sense of anxiety in the midst of the most ordinary setting, in this case a bowling alley, which is usually associated with wholesome family fun.

Bowden family. In this deserted place, the family has no legal defenses against Cady and must rely on their own courage and their willingness to protect themselves. When Bowden and Cady finally come to life-or-death hand-to-hand combat, Bowden, who wins the fight, must summon all his willpower to keep himself from killing Cady and making himself fully like his enemy. Since that would hand Cady the victory, Bowden deliberately decides that he will turn his tormentor over to the law.

But this is not the traditional Hollywood happy ending. Cady is in police custody, but the film has shown the loopholes in the law that enabled him to almost bring a decent man down to his level, thus leaving many doubts about how efficient the legal system will be in bringing Cady to justice again. Moreover, as the Bowdens return home from their ordeal, they do not give the appearance of people who have been victorious. Their quiet grimness suggests that they survived by the skin of their teeth and have seen aspects of themselves, and of the world, that will cast a shadow over the rest of their lives.

A similar doubt about the vulnerability of the law to manipulation plagues *The Manchurian Candidate*, which ends even more grimly. As this suspenseful film unfolds, the protagonist, Raymond Shaw (Laurence Harvey), discovers that while he was a prisoner of war in North Korea, he was brainwashed by the Communist enemies of the United States in collusion with his evil mother.

Ultimately, Shaw discovers that he has been primed to assassinate a popular U.S. presidential candidate, leaving the field clear for his stepfather, a sleeper Communist agent, to win the election. No longer confident that the law is up to the task of holding them all accountable, Shaw kills his mother, his stepfather, and himself. If we don't know whether Scottie can survive the awful events of his life at the conclusion of *Vertigo*, we do know that Shaw sees no option but suicide at the end of his story. His faith in himself and the world has been too compromised. *The Manchurian Candidate* preserves a semblance of optimism for the audience in a romantic subplot in which Major Bennett Marco (Frank Sinatra), one of the soldiers captured along with Shaw, not only survives the ordeal in the POW camp but finds true love. However, the film is not really optimistic that love is enough in a world so prone to corruption.

Seven Days in May, a mirror reflection of *The Manchurian Candidate*, is equally suspenseful. In contrast to *Candidate*'s vision of despicable and dangerous invading enemies, *Seven Days in May* tells a tale of democracy

***Seven Days in May* (1964)** In suspense thrillers, great oaks from little acorns grow. Here at the beginning of the film, Colonel Casey (Kirk Douglas) has what he believes to be a casual conversation with, office gossip, Lieutenant Dorsey Grayson (Jack Mullaney), unaware that he is hearing for the first time a small detail that will lead to his discovery of a plot within the military to overthrow the government.

attacked from within. Also a Cold War film that focuses on the tensions between the United States and the Communist world, *Seven Days in May* debunks the xenophobia of *The Manchurian Candidate* and its paranoid fears about Communists. In *Seven Days*, the danger lies in Americans infected by such paranoia.

The plot concerns a nuclear nonproliferation treaty with the Soviet Union negotiated by President Jordan Lyman (Fredric March) that has polarized opinion in the Congress and in the armed forces. General James Mattoon Scott (Burt Lancaster), a popular and charismatic figure, leads the charge against Lyman, who Scott believes is weakening the United States through his peace initiative. Slowly, Scott's personal assistant, Colonel Martin "Jiggs" Casey (Kirk Douglas), picks up clues that Scott, in his hysterical fear of Communism, is planning to overthrow the duly elected American government so that he can "save" it from a president who believes—foolishly, according to Scott—in diplomacy rather than military action. Casey reluctantly realizes that Scott, in his panic, has abandoned the Constitution and that he is the real danger to democracy. With difficulty, Casey is finally able to convince important politicians to join him in putting an end to Scott's plans. While presenting Scott as a brilliant soldier and a patriot, the film uses the suspense genre to illustrate the perils of powerful men driven by extremes of fear that lead them to ignore our most basic laws. The film ends with the country intact, but as a political thriller it effectively makes its case that the subversion of American democracy is more likely to come from within than from without, and from the Americans whom we least suspect, an anxiety-provoking suggestion.

Charade, a change of pace, plays comically with the thriller's conventional discovery of unsuspected destructive forces hidden within mundane circumstances. When Regina Lampert (Audrey Hepburn) returns to Paris from a vacation in Switzerland, she discovers, in true thriller fashion, that strange forces are at work in what she thought was her ordinary, upper-middle-class life. Her palatial apartment has been stripped of all her belongings, and her husband, Charles Lampert (who appears in the film only as a corpse), is not only dead but obviously was not the man she thought he was. In fact, no man in this film is as he presents himself to her. A devastatingly handsome stranger who introduces himself as Peter Joshua (Cary Grant) at the Swiss resort where she is staying changes his name and biography with each turn of the plot, at times seeming to be a criminal and possibly a killer. A man who introduces himself as Hamilton Bartholomew (Walter Matthau) and claims to be part of the CIA, calls Regina to his office to discuss the fortune her husband has stolen from the government, but it turns out that he has no office at the CIA and is not who he claims to be. These characters, all larger than life, and some cartoon-like thugs named Tex (James Coburn), Scobie (George Kennedy), and Leo (Ned Glass), turn Paris into a maze of clues, as Regina searches for the truth about her husband, the identity of the person who wants to kill her, and the location of the missing fortune. Regina's discovery of the instability of life, typical of the thriller, is played for laughs, as our heroine learns to go with the flow and finds love with a man with multiple identities. In time for the happy ending of *Charade*, the attractive Peter Joshua turns out to be Brian Cruikshank, a government agent, a safe man for Regina to marry, and capable of capturing the villain who killed Regina's husband and intends to kill her.

Charade projects the thriller protagonist's loss of control through a comic lens, ultimately concluding that it can be a good thing. As it reveals the plight of its hapless heroine, *Charade* suggests that the chaos that mystery has made of her life has improved her circumstances.

The film celebrates the importance of feeling at ease with letting go of things that give a false sense of stability; it is a perfect example of how satire and comedy define a genre by playing with what it is not. But the comic thriller is very much the exception to the rule in the history of the genre, which became increasingly dark and pessimistic in the period from the 1970s to the 1990s, leading to the virtually nihilistic visions in the twenty-first century. During the decades of the 1970s, '80s, and '90s, the social instability of a changing America dealing with the disastrous Vietnam War and reeling from the fallout of governmental conspiracies—the Watergate scandal during the Nixon administration and the Iran-Contra scandal during the Reagan administration—was reflected in such political thrillers as *Three Days of the Condor* (1975), as well as in *Jacob's Ladder* (1990), a remake of *Cape Fear* (1991), and *The Usual Suspects* (1995). Even more notorious thrillers of this period reflect on the women's liberation movement of those decades, including *Coma* and *The Eyes of Laura Mars* (both 1978), *Jagged Edge* (1985), *Fatal Attraction* (1987), *Sea of Love* (1989), and *Disclosure* (1994).

Three Days of the Condor and *Jacob's Ladder* both use thriller conventions to question whether there is a reason to have faith in democratic institutions. *Condor*, the more traditional political thriller of the two, begins with a CIA employee, Joe Turner (Robert Redford)—code name Condor—as he returns from a food run to the local deli. To his horror and confusion, he finds all his colleagues murdered, and he knows he's next. To save himself, he follows a tortuous trail of clues and discovers a secret organization within the CIA, unaccountable to any oversight or governance, dedicated to ensuring that the United States has a monopoly on the world's oil resources, and which is willing to do anything to keep their actions secret, even murder innocent CIA operatives. The film ends with Turner's meeting with one of his superiors on a street corner to tell him that he's given the *New York Times* evidence of corruption that he has unearthed, but whether the exposé will be printed or, if printed, call the guilty parties to account is not at all certain. Turner is left hanging, as is the United States, a man and a country both facing danger from a powerful, hidden enemy. Taking *Seven Days in May* to the next level of pessimism, *Three Days of the Condor* shows Joe Turner and the audience the possible death of democracy in the United States. In light of some Americans' willingness to trade civil liberties for security after the terrorist attacks of September 11, 2001, the dark fears of *Three Days of the Condor* have been given a renewed urgency.

Jacob's Ladder similarly expresses doubts about America's commitment to basic liberties when national security is threatened, but it takes a more innovative narrative approach. This film unfolds entirely in the mind of Jacob Singer (Tim Robbins), a Vietnam War veteran who is dying from wounds he suffered, not at the hands of the enemy but at the hands of other American soldiers. The suspense in this film is caused by a double layer of anxieties about Jacob's situation. Until the end of the film, the viewer doesn't know what is real and what is a figment of Jacob's imagination. The audience is uncertain about why Jacob's platoon turned on him, and Jacob appears to be chased by demons as he goes about his daily postwar life in New York. But when we discover that he never returned home from Vietnam, we realize that what he believes to be demons are all in his mind. The clues Jacob follows as he tries to figure out what is happening to him turn out to be messages from his subconscious that lead him through a circuitous mental dialogue between his desire to cling to life and his need to let go and accept death. The forces of death appear to him in demonic form until he resigns himself to his fate, at which point the demons disappear and the angelic form of his dead son arrives to escort him "upstairs."

If that much becomes clear, the film tantalizes us with the inconclusiveness of what Jacob believes he learns about the insane and fatal attack he suffered from fellow American soldiers. Some of the clues in Jacob's mental journey lead to his recognition of an illegal secret project conducted by the army to create more aggressive fighters by lacing the soldiers' food, without their knowledge or consent, with experimental drugs. The upshot of this violation of American fighting forces by their commanding officers is that the drugs deprive the soldiers of any civilized sense of restraint, leading to horrific fatal attacks on each other. The discovery of this vividly described experiment is both terrifying and confusing for the audience, as it plays on real-life rumors that such experiments were in fact carried out. However, the film undermines the credibility of the conspiracy when we discover that Jacob has remained within his own mind for the duration of the story. The suggested government abuse may be real, or it may be a phantom of Jacob's expiring brain. The film takes the destabilizing aspects of the thriller to a new level.

The 1991 remake of *Cape Fear* again brings up the question of the demonic aspect of humanity. Martin Scorsese's film retells the story of the original 1962 *Cape Fear*, but in Scorsese's version, unlike in the original, no one is innocent. The ex-convict Max Cady (Robert De Niro)

***Cape Fear* (1991)** In this scene, Martin Scorsese's version of Max Cady (Robert De Niro) is on the telephone with Sam Bowden's daughter, pretending to be her high school drama teacher. By inverting the frame, in which Cady is hanging upside down, Scorsese creates a defamiliarization of middle-class reality. The furniture behind Cady, seemingly on the ceiling, and Cady's distorted face give him the vampiric aura of a bat hanging from the rafters. Here we can see some of the changes that have taken place in the genre thirty years after the original *Cape Fear* was released. The banality of evil, visible in the framing of the 1962 film, has given way to a visual nihilism that negates all sense of the normal.

is corrupt, but so is lawyer Sam Bowden (Nick Nolte). In the remake, Cady returns for revenge because, even though Bowden was Cady's lawyer when he was on trial for torturing and raping a sixteen-year-old girl, Bowden was so repulsed by his client that he withheld information that might have turned the jury in Cady's favor. In Scorsese's version, Bowden also has a history of cheating on his wife and is engaged in a flirtation that could become an affair when the film begins. Thus, in Scorsese's film, the lines between Cady and Bowden are blurred from the first scene and, by the end of the film, when they do battle in a life-or-death struggle on the Cape Fear River, it is not the struggle between good and evil that we saw in the 1962 film. This Bowden does not keep Cady alive to be held accountable by the law, but kills him instead. The power of negative forces is very much alive at the end; the web Cady has woven to trap Bowden and his family has only revealed what was already present in them, leaving an uneasy sense that civilization is a fragile illusion.

Playing on fears about women's sexuality, the gender-specific thrillers of this period also tend toward the nihilistic. *Coma* is the most optimistic of these, responding to the anxieties stimulated by the women's movement by telling a feminist tale about the collapse of medical ethics under the pressure of a patriarchal emphasis on profit. Its feminist protagonist, Dr. Susan Wheeler (Geneviève Bujold), is beleaguered by the macho attitudes of her superiors and colleagues and the doubts of her lover, Dr. Mark Bellows (Michael Douglas), about whether she and her feminist aggressiveness are more trouble than she is worth. But it is Susan who discovers that there is a horrific conspiracy within the administration of the hospital. She notices that healthy, young patients are dying unaccountably in operating room number eight, and when she investigates, she learns that their organs are being secretly harvested by someone in the hospital who is reaping huge profits. Unclear about whom she can trust with her discovery when Mark fails to believe her, she picks the worst possible confidant, the head of the hospital, Dr. George Harris (Richard Widmark), who gives her the last piece of the puzzle. He is the power behind the conspiracy. In a final scene dependent on a last-minute rescue, Mark suddenly realizes that Susan is right and saves her while she is on the operating table under the knife of Dr. Harris. She leaves the operating room alive, as two policemen wait for Dr. Harris to emerge.

Coma is unusually sympathetic to liberated women, suggesting that if Susan is somewhat annoying in her assertion of her rights, she is also proud, strong, and able to see what no man in the hospital can see. By contrast, the majority of woman-centered thrillers of this period are part of a backlash against the women's movement. Some of these thrillers suggest that it is the women themselves who are filled with an evil that rages out of control when they are free of male authority. Others assert that the spectacle of a free woman brings out the worst in men, a situation for which the liberated woman is generally held responsible. Either way, in these films liberated women generate uncomfortable suspense.

A spectacular example of backlash thrillers about the evil of liberated women is the cult favorite *The Eyes of Laura Mars*, which dramatizes the beast released in men by powerful women and blames women for male weakness. *The Eyes of Laura Mars* portrays Laura (Faye Dunaway) as a kind, talented, successful, professional, whose fashion photographs reveal the violence of modern society. But Laura's insightful understanding of the subtleties of the world around her, good in itself, becomes problematic when it unbalances the man assigned to protect her, police detective John Neville (Tommy Lee Jones). Laura's erotic photographs bring to the surface the buried hatred Detective Neville feels for his negligent, selfish mother, which has caused him to develop a split personality. The law-abiding part of Neville admires, falls in love with, and wants to protect Laura. His submerged dark side hates her and wants to punish her by killing her friends and ultimately her. Laura takes the blame in this film for Neville's breakdown. The film implies that Neville would have been able to hold himself together were it not for Laura's uppity determination to be a successful career woman.

A new gender twist in a number of twenty-first-century thrillers suggests that, although America still has demonstrable problems with strong women in positions of power, the thriller genre has become fascinated by dark, hidden danger associated with men and the institutions created by patriarchy. The most fascinating examples of this group are the Bourne trilogy (2002–2007), *Syriana* and *A History of Violence* (both 2005), and *No Country for Old Men* (2007). *Syriana* and the Bourne trilogy each propose that the American government itself is a patriarchal conspiracy against the rights and lives of its citizens. *Syriana* depicts the discovery by Bob Barnes (George Clooney), a disillusioned CIA agent,

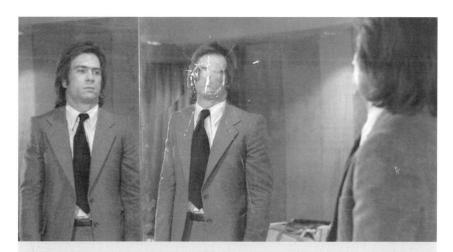

***The Eyes of Laura Mars* (1978)** One of the many spectacular mirror shots we find in suspense thrillers, this frame visualizes the split personality of John Neville (Tommy Lee Jones), a police detective and also a serial killer. The frame displays Neville's agonizing self-awareness of his schizoid condition as he looks in Laura Mars's mirror. In the foreground, the actor surveys a double mirror image. On the right, he sees his shattered pathological self where a stray bullet has hit the reflecting glass; on the left, he sees his horrified "normal" self. By giving Neville this moment in a mirror belonging to Laura Mars, the director complexly visualizes the film's presumption that strong, independent women damage men.

of the rot at the center of the American government. In a plot twist reminiscent of *Three Days of the Condor*, Barnes discovers a hidden cabal of very entitled men who are scheming to control oil resources no matter what the cost. The Bourne trilogy, arguably an updated version of *The Manchurian Candidate*, demonstrates the changes that have taken place in American culture since the Cold War. Like *The Manchurian Candidate*, the Bourne trilogy dramatizes the awakening of a man to governmental manipulation of his identity. Jason Bourne (Matt Damon) learns that the Kafkaesque government has programmed his individuality out of him through indoctrination and now threatens his life as well as his original identity, David Webb. But instead of locating Jason/David's afflictions in the evil mother and forces alien to America, the Bourne films depict women as the beleaguered agent's only natural allies, while painting a devastating picture of demonic forces inside militaristic American patriarchs that cause chaos in the name of national security.

The Coen brothers' *No Country for Old Men* also details the existence of pure male evil, for which neither the ethical man nor the pure woman is any match. Although set in the western United States, *No Country* is not a Western but rather a suspenseful thriller that traces the trail of death blazed by an unfathomably cold, motiveless killer, Anton Chigurh (Javier Bardem), and the desperate frustration of Sheriff Ed Tom Bell (Tommy Lee Jones), descended from a long line of heroic lawmen, at his inability to understand—let alone end—the reign of terror caused by his uncanny adversary. Chigurh is implacable, male aggression gone wild, and, like so many villains in suspense films, is seemingly impervious to pain, arguably a metaphor for the virtual indestructibility of human evil. Chigurh murders not only in self-defense and to aggressively pursue a goal but capriciously, according to his whims of the moment. Monstrous though he may be, however, Chigurh is chillingly characterized as completely human.

In creating a thriller with all the visual emblems of the Western, the Coen brothers are testing the limits of the thriller genre, a trend that is typical of more recent Hollywood productions. The film that has, so far, been the most extreme in its probing to see how far the thriller can go in constructing a frightening and disorienting maze is *Inception* (2010). The psychological labyrinth created by *Inception* is so dizzying that even after several viewings it may be impossible to follow all the leaps of internal and external experiences of time and space. The film is about Cobb (Leonardo DiCaprio) a man who, for enormous sums of money, uses his skill at manipulating the subconscious by creating mental landscapes and architecture that permit him to discover secrets and truths so deeply buried that his investigation's subjects themselves may not know of them, all for the purpose of industrial espionage. The case in this story concerns the request of an industrial magnate, Saito (Ken Watanabe), that Cobb infiltrate the subconscious of Robert Fischer (Cillian Murphy), the son of one of his competitors, not to discover secrets but to achieve something much more difficult and dangerous. Saito wants Cobb to plant a suggestion that will impel Fischer to come to a decision that Saito feels will be to his advantage. Complicating the situation is that Cobb's entrance into Fischer's inner mind injects into Fischer's secret life Cobb's own secret guilt about the death of his wife and his suffering at not being able to be with his children because of that guilt. If ever there were a thriller that robs us of confidence about the stability of our own minds, this is it.

At the same time, while all the thrillers we have previously discussed define a hero whose mind is at risk and a villain responsible for the disorientation, in *Inception,* there are no heroes and villains. Everyone

***Inception* (2010)** To audition Ariadne (Ellen Page), an "inception architect," as a possible member of his team for the job he has accepted from Saito, Cobb (Leonardo DiCaprio) has himself and Ariadne sedated to allow her to enter his dream. As the two of them "walk" around the landscape of Cobb's subconscious, Ariadne creates and uses mirrors that alter the dream she is sharing with her prospective boss. The look on Ariadne's face reveals her focus and determination. The look on Cobb's face reflects how impressed he is with Ariadne's skills. The infinite-regress image she creates through the positioning of parallel mirrors alerts the audience to the unsettling effects that manipulation of the subconscious can create.

is at some point placed into a dream state, and whatever Cobb may be doing, everyone, including Cobb, is menaced by the negative and terrifying forces inside the subconscious mind. Everyone is both victim and perpetrator of mind control. Cobb's mission on Saito's behalf has potentially positive and negative implications for Cobb, Saito, and Fischer. Moreover, Cobb's strategy for accomplishing his mission requires that he negotiate so many levels of the subconscious, in addition to the level of external reality, that at the film's end, the audience is unable to determine which, if any, of the concluding scenes are real and which are taking place on some dream level. Although Cobb's mission seems to be a success, and Fischer now thinks what Saito wants him to think, we never know in what ways Fischer's decision, as a result of Cobb's machinations, has hurt or helped Fischer and Saito. Moreover, although Cobb seems to have worked through his guilt and for the first time in a long time seems to be with his children, we never know if Cobb is alive, dead, or in a coma at the end of the film. With *Inception*, the questions endemic to the thriller about the nature of reality and evil reach such an extreme of inconclusiveness that the film poses threats to the coherence of the genre. The way forward, at least temporarily, seems to be backward, to old, more manageable recipes for thriller action. For example, *The Bourne Legacy* (2012) takes the thriller genre toward a retreat not only by using a retread of a familiar story but by constructing for its hero, Aaron Cross (Jeremy Renner, a pale copy of Jason Bourne/David Webb), a formulaic governmental maze, too familiar to provoke any real anxiety.

Typologies, Themes, and Theories

It is easier to chronicle the history of the thriller genre than to define it. It is also easier to define the suspense endemic to the genre than the genre itself. Hitchcock famously formulated the definitive statement on suspense in cinema when he differentiated it from surprise, noting that surprise produces the thrill of the sudden, unexpected occurrence, while suspense takes the strategy of informing the audience of exactly what is about to happen and forcing it to endure the anxiety of waiting for the inevitable. Hitchcock's most quoted example of this contrast is the difference between an explosion for which the spectator is unprepared and spectatorial knowledge of the existence of a bomb and the exact time it will explode. However, a suspenseful scene in which we know a bomb is about to explode but not how it can be stopped might occur in a detective film, a noir film, a melodrama, or an action-adventure film. What, then, is it that specifically defines the suspense of the thriller genre?

Critics have universally noted that the thriller keeps the audience emotionally on edge, a theory John McCarty painstakingly documents in *Thrillers: Seven Decades of Classic Film Suspense* (1992). Seeking a less vague and obvious definition of the genre, in *The Suspense Thriller: Films in the Shadow of Alfred Hitchcock*, Charles Derry proposes that the thriller is a "crime work which presents a violent and generally murderous antagonism in which the protagonist becomes an innocent victim or a nonprofessional criminal." According to Derry, the suspense thriller lacks the "traditional figure of detection in a central position." But this emphasis on the innocence of the protagonist and his nonprofessional status as he tries to understand his situation is insufficient. While generally applicable to some important films like *Suspicion*, *Strangers on a Train*, *The Manchurian Candidate*, and *Coma*, Derry's definition would eliminate at least 50 percent of the most celebrated thrillers, notably *Shadow of a Doubt*, *The Lady from Shanghai*, *Vertigo*, both versions of *Cape Fear*, *The Eyes of Laura Mars*, the Bourne trilogy, *From Hell* (2001), *Syriana*, *No Country for Old Men*, and *Inception*. In this group of films, the protagonists, far from innocent, are tinged by the same defects as the villain, and some of them contain a highly "traditional figure of detection" as the central figure.[1]

Canadian critic Northrop Frye and American critic John Cawelti both speak of the suspense genre as a form of romanticism, which emphasizes the marvelous for audiences stuck in the drudgery of ordinary life. But while heightened reality is often a part of the thriller, that definition alone would make it indistinguishable from a number of other genres, including the fantasy film, the musical, the science-fiction film, and the horror film. Alternatively, American critic Noël Carroll has described cinematic suspense as the creation of questions that the audience has an intense desire to answer. But that too describes a great many genres—for example, the detective story. We may intently wish to know who killed Mr. Ratchett (Richard Widmark) in *Murder on the Orient Express* (1974), but that film is a not a thriller because detective Hercule Poirot (Albert

---

[1] Charles Derry, *The Suspense Thriller: Films in the Shadow of Alfred Hitchcock* (Jefferson, NC: McFarland, 1988), 62–63.

Finney) provides answers that dispel all anxiety and confusion, the two characteristics that ultimately define the thriller. These common responses to the question of what defines a thriller overlook the generally unsuspected key to understanding this genre: its portrayal of the helplessness of reason in dealing with the crime at the center of the plot.

French critic Pascal Bonitzer's description of what he has named "partial vision" as the essential characteristic of both the medium of film and the experience of narrative suspense may be the most helpful critique we have for achieving a useful definition of the thriller, although Bonitzer is not writing about the thriller genre. Bonitzer's structural approach to film contains the key to the anxiety-ridden thriller genre, as he carefully explores the importance to film in general of the fact that we are always aware that we cannot see what is beyond the edges of the film frame. Interestingly, most film genres fight against this awareness, creating the illusion that we are seeing everything in the situation to give the audience a reassuring illusion of control. The thriller, however, aggressively reminds us of the partial vision of the film frame, which unnerves us, and therein lies the difference. The parodic *Charade* highlights how partial vision is a seminal condition of the thriller when it

***Charade* (1963)** A worried Regina Lampert (Audrey Hepburn) rushes in confusion through her stripped apartment. Behind her is a doorway through which she has exited a similarly empty room; before her is another doorway that will lead to another barren space. This frame is part of a montage particularly illustrative of the partial vision associated with suspense thrillers. The heroine wonders why she can't see beyond this mysterious manifestation of hidden forces threatening her life.

plays with the situation of its bewildered and frightened heroine. When Regina Lampert returns from her vacation, she finds her Paris apartment completely stripped of its contents: her clothes, her furniture, any trace of her husband. As she opens the doors to the different rooms, a rising expectation is created that something beyond this emptiness in the frame will emerge, but there is only more emptiness.

The centrality of partial vision in the thriller is especially prevalent in Hitchcock's films, which use suspense with a purity rarely achieved by other directors. In *Shadow of a Doubt*, we know the homicidal nature of Uncle Charlie before we watch young Charlie fall into his clutches, but as young Charlie points out at the end of the film, we can never pierce that darkness that motivates such a man. This is also true of the evil left behind by Maxim's first wife in *Rebecca*, and the evil in the soul of Gavin Elster in *Vertigo*. Unsolvable ambiguity, the sense that there is something about the situation we can't see, haunts us every time we see these films.

However, the most difficult generic line to draw is not between the thriller with its emphasis on irrationality and the detective film with its emphasis on rationality but between the thriller and film noir, both of which look into the irrational heart of darkness in human affairs. Both genres deal in the anxieties of modern life; both tend toward stylish, dark visuals. Neither suggests easy answers to the questions that plague their characters. One possible way to distinguish between the two is that film noir is the product of a specific historic period, right after World War II, while thrillers occur in all cinematic periods. Of course, there are also neo-noirs that began to appear in the 1980s, like *Body Heat* (1981), which might muddy the waters of this distinction. A more reliable differentiation emerges from the contrasts in their overall relationship to society. Thrillers tend to associate the flaws of the villain with the essential flaws in human nature and in the social structure, while noirs are more specific to their plot situation and the era in which they are set. *The Maltese Falcon* (1941), an early noir film, suggests the rot in the femme fatale Brigid O'Shaughnessy's (Mary Astor) soul and Sam Spade's (Humphrey Bogart) perverse erotic attraction to her as particular to them and to the period, not as an essential part of heterosexual relations. This contrasts with thrillers like *Vertigo*, which question the cultural construction of heterosexuality.

In other words, the thriller proposes a universal condition of instability. In his book *Thrillers* (1999), Martin Rubin points toward this central characteristic of the thriller when he opines that "suspense centrally involves the idea of suspension. We are suspended between question and answer, between anticipation and resolution, between alternative answers to the question posed, and sometimes between ambivalent emotions and sympathies that are aroused by a suspenseful situation."[2] Rubin insightfully suggests that a crucial moment in the thriller is the sudden experience of not being on solid ground, of hanging above it, a feeling compounded by the awful knowledge that a sense of well-being is a childish illusion one must learn to live without.

The relentless insecurity of the thriller landscape, particularly after 1950, results in the typical thriller's failure to restore balance to its fictional world, even in cases in which it seems to. Thrillers that seem to end "happily" somehow subvert what appears to be a satisfying resolution. For example, at the end of the first film of the Bourne trilogy, *The Bourne Identity* (2002), Jason Bourne seems to have found the perfect place to escape the government agents who are trying to kill him, in an idyllic hideaway by the sea with Marie (Franka Potente), the love of his life. But in *The Bourne Supremacy* (2004), the government persecution revives and claims Marie as its first victim. If the government appears to be trying to redeem itself by the end of *The Bourne Ultimatum* (2007) through an investigation of the secret cabal that indoctrinated Jason/David, based on evidence supplied by him, the protagonist himself is left at loose ends. A man without a country, with a history of violence, he is last seen swimming out of New York Harbor for parts unknown. Similarly, *Inception*, which seems to end with the happy reunion of Cobb and his children, may well be some form of hallucination. The rule is that the thriller protagonist winds up either dead, in peril of death, much sadder and somewhat wiser—or in some complicated limbo.

Another running characteristic of the thriller is its sense that the forces that afflict human beings, though much more overwhelming than we like to think, fall within the realm of the natural and the civilized. Unlike the horror film, in the thriller, although suffering sometimes seems to be the result of supernatural or demonic forces, it turns out to be caused by the all-too-human. While this may initially sound as if the thriller is tame in comparison to the monster movie, in many ways the thriller is more agitating. A monster can be disposed of by most

---

[2] Martin Rubin. *Thrillers* (Cambridge, UK: Cambridge University Press, 1999), 35.

viewers under the heading of the purely fictional. But what about the revelation of unsuspected dark places in human nature? Most people want to believe that their families and friends are understandable, comfortable, and familiar. We want to believe that criminals are fathomable and are guilty only of making mistakes or forced by circumstances to take a wrong turn. The thriller compromises that hope.

The list of mock supernatural elements in thrillers is long, but a few should suffice to suggest their omnipresence. In *Vertigo*, Judy/Madeleine's odd behavior is mendaciously explained by Elster as a case of supernatural possession by the ghost of Carlotta, Madeleine's supposedly demonic grandmother. However, the diabolical force at work is really Elster's greed and his macho sense of entitlement. In *Cape Fear*, *The Night of the Hunter*, and *No Country for Old Men*, the villains Max Cady, Harry Powell, and Anton Chigurh exhibit the kind of cold imperviousness to human suffering and even to their own pain that makes them seem like uncanny beings. But the films ultimately suggest that this is a sign of the depths of human depravity, not paranormal forces. In *Jacob's Ladder*, what at first seems to be a genuine demonic presence in New York City turns out to be images in the mind of Jacob, the film's protagonist. Finally, there is *The Usual Suspects*, a thriller that comes close to endorsing a supernatural presence. In fact, however, all that is documented about Verbal Kint/Keyser Söze (Kevin Spacey) is that he is cunning, merciless, and greedy, in the extreme. Since the entire story Kint tells Agent Kujan (Chazz Palminteri) is fictional, none of his statements connecting Söze with the devil are credible. Kint does say that the cleverest thing the devil ever did was to convince the world that he doesn't exist. But this could be a metaphorical statement about Kint's pose as a crippled, painfully self-conscious man, when in fact he has made himself invisible while committing numerous crimes. The allegation of supernatural hauntings in thrillers is part of the genre strategy that underlines the insecurity of human life.

Although some thriller protagonists, like Raymond Shaw in *The Manchurian Candidate*, are innocent victims of the thriller villain, the corruption of the thriller villain is often complicated by the presence of complementary flaws in thriller heroes. Mike O'Hara and the thriller seductress Elsa Bannister are equally sexually chaotic in *The Lady from Shanghai*. In *Shadow of a Doubt*, Young Charlie shares some of Uncle Charlie's longings for glamour and heightened existence, though, in the long

Strangers on a Train (1951) Employing Expressionistic imagery, including shadows, backlighting, and distorting angles, Alfred Hitchcock implies the collapse-in-progress of Guy Haines's (Farley Granger) sense of normality and security as the psychotic Bruno Anthony (Robert Walker), brandishing a gun, pursues him down the staircase in the Anthony mansion. This film is an important part of the foundation Hitchock built for later thrillers that would expand on the Master's use of the genre to express the modern sense of fear and hysteria.

run, she is able to temper them with a sense of brotherhood with other human beings in a way that he can not. Laura Mars and John Neville, in *The Eyes of Laura Mars*, are both attracted, albeit for different reasons, to the violent themes in Laura's fashion photography. If Max Cady is viciously heedless of civilized mores in both versions of *Cape Fear*, both Sam Bowdens sink to his level under pressure. In *The Most Dangerous Game*, Bob Rainsford acknowledges the cruelty in himself only when he sees it reflected in Count Zaroff. In the Bourne trilogy, Jason Bourne is, at least initially, as amoral as the government persecuting him. In *Strangers on a Train*, Bruno Anthony, the villain, is correct when he sees the homicidal streak in Guy Haines's desperation, though he misreads the power of social convention and restraint over him.

A corollary theme of the thriller is that the dark forces are contagious, moving with frightening ease from the villain to those characters who usually have their passions under control. Case in point: in the Bourne trilogy, Jason/David is finally forced to remember that he volunteered to become a killing machine. Although it is quite clear that he was lied to when he was told that his actions would save American lives, it remains true that he was willing to embrace the role of a merciless killer to serve what he thought were national ideals, not exactly an innocent beginning to his bloody and ultimately self-destructive career.

Iconography

The thriller genre is rich in iconic associations. The great Hitchcock has already been acknowledged as the dominant iconic director in the genre, and John Frankenheimer (*The Manchurian Candidate, Seven Days in May*) and Adrian Lyne (*Fatal Attraction, Jacob's Ladder*), although they have not attained Hitchcock's stature, have also come to be associated with the thriller. As far as actors are concerned, a number of the stars Hitchcock used repeatedly, for example, Cary Grant and James Stewart, have become icons of the genre. Ingrid Bergman, too, is associated with the suspense thriller, as a psychiatrist working her way through her patient's tormented memory in Hitchcock's *Spellbound* and as an undercover agent trapped in a maze of international intrigue in *Notorious* (1946), and also for her role as a wife whose husband intentionally tries to drive her mad in *Gaslight*. For his omnipresence in modern erotic thrillers, Michael Douglas has come to epitomize the man victimized by the labyrinth of desire forged by the powerful, sexual woman. The performances of Robert Mitchum in both the 1962 *Cape Fear* and *The Night of the Hunter* have become icons of the threat evoked by the thriller villain. Robert Walker's performance as Bruno in *Strangers on a Train*, a smiling thriller villain with a frightening ability to manipulate and twist circumstances, has also vividly marked the genre.

Another characteristic thriller icon is the presence of the woman widely spoken of as "the Hitchcock blonde." Among the blondes entangled in Hitchcock's suspense stories are the women played by Grace Kelly in *Dial M for Murder* and *Rear Window* (both 1954), and *To Catch a Thief* (1955); Doris Day in *The Man Who Knew Too Much* (1956); Kim Novak in *Vertigo*; Eva Marie Saint in *North by Northwest* (1959); and Tippi Hedren in *The Birds* (1963) and *Marnie* (1964). Blondes featured in thrillers created by other directors include Sharon Stone in *Basic Instinct* (1992); Glenn Close in *Jagged Edge* and *Fatal Attraction*; Joan Allen and Julia Styles in the Bourne trilogy; Maria Bello in *A History of Violence*; and Jessica Lange in the 1991 *Cape Fear*.

Of the images that iconically portray the sensation of entrapment and peril associated with thrillers, the main ones are the labyrinth, the spectacle of characters dangling precariously from high places, the shadowy figure, and point-of-view tracking shots through areas in which danger is patently lurking. All of these images appear in many genres when suspense is called for, but they are central to the thriller genre, appearing not for the purpose of invigorating a single sequence but as metaphorical embodiments of the film's basic premises and themes. The labyrinth (or maze) is in many ways the most perfect visual representation of the thriller. It incorporates in tangible form the protagonist's sensation that the world is closing in on him/her. In *Vertigo*, as Scottie Ferguson follows Judy/Madeleine, he is often led by her through a maze of winding streets, a physical manifestation of Elster's devious plans. At the beginning of *Shadow of a Doubt*, the villainous Uncle Charlie deviously leads a pair of policemen through turning and twisting streets as a visible sign of his evasive tactics for the rest of the film.

Charade's comic imitation of the genre's labyrinthine images appears in the maze of platforms and staircases in the Paris Métro through which Regina Lampert is chased, and also in the trap doors in the stage of a Paris theater that Brian Cruikshank must work his way through to save Regina. In both instances, the visual labyrinth stands for the convoluted situation in which the pair find themselves. Similarly, in *Coma*, Susan, caught in a web of bureaucratic evasions, finds herself crawling through their visual representation in a confusing tangle of hospital air-conditioning ducts to discover how Dr. Harris has arranged for carbon monoxide instead of oxygen to be administered during procedures in operating room number eight. The famous shadows through which Mike O'Hara is forced to travel in a fun house and his descent on a slide into the bafflement of the maze of mirrors at the end of *The Lady from Shanghai* similarly embodies the ordeal of his entire involvement with the Bannisters. The Bourne trilogy is a plum pudding of thriller iconography, as numerous houses, staircases, and government buildings turn into labyrinths, and a system of coordinated technology turns the entire world into maze through which Jason/David is hunted before foiling those in pursuit of him. And in *Three Days of the Condor*, the house in which Agent Joe Turner has his CIA office turns into a maze through which assassins move to murder everyone in his unit but him. In *Inception*, the forces of CGI are mobilized to visualize the maze of images that

***The Lady from Shanghai* (1947)** In this image, in the mirror maze of a fun house, Welles masterfully uses a mirror shot of Elsa (Rita Hayworth) and Mike (Orson Welles) to metaphorically visualize the mind in chaos, under the pressures of the plot's labyrinthine complications.

make up the different levels of the mind, which the protagonist Cobb must negotiate in his quest to fulfill his mission for Saito.

Helpless suspension over the abyss, a condition implied by the centrality of the theme of insecurity in the thriller, is embodied in thriller movies by numerous generic images of people hanging helplessly in space. Two of the most famous of these images occur in *Vertigo* and *North by Northwest*. In the first of these films, Scottie finds himself hanging from the gutter of a tall building in the opening sequence as a police chase over the roof ends horribly in the death of an officer with whom he is working, initiating his first experience of vertigo. Similarly, in *North by Northwest*, the hero, Roger O. Thornhill, and the heroine, Eve Kendall, are so precariously suspended from a presidential face carved into the stone of Mount Rushmore at the end of the film that it is hard to see how they will ever regain their balance and firm ground. In this tradition, in *The Bourne Identity*, Jason Bourne often dangles from the side of a building when he is running from government contract killers, and throughout the trilogy he must contend with heights from which he might fall. In *Rear Window*, hero L. B. "Jeff" Jefferies (James Stewart) hangs outside his window as the killer, Lars Thorwald (Raymond Burr), closes in, and in *Strangers on a Train*, a number of characters cling for dear life to the edge of a merry-go-round that is spinning out of control.

The fear-filled point-of-view tracking shot is ubiquitous in the thriller genre as protagonists attempt to figure out either where they are or the hiding place of something or someone they seek. An interesting example of the "Where am I?" tracking shot occurs often in *Jacob's Ladder*, in which Jacob often moves confusedly through unfamiliar hallways. Examples of the "Where are you?" tracking shot pepper *Basic Instinct*, as Detective Nick Curran (Michael Douglas) searches for Catherine Tramell (Sharon Stone). Similarly, in *Strangers on a Train*, we see through Guy Haines's eyes as he moves about the darkened mansion owned by Bruno's family, hoping to find Bruno's father to warn him of his son's desire to kill him. A variation of these shots occurs when we see through the eyes of the villain, as in the 1962 version of *Cape Fear*, in which we often see through the eyes of Max Cady as he stalks the Bowden family. And in a fascinating variation of the killer thriller point-of-view shot, in *The Eyes of Laura Mars*, Laura has recurring visions that allow her to see through the eyes of the murderer as he stalks her friends and ultimately her.

Finally, it is not unusual to see the thriller combining surprise with the distinct sense of foreboding endemic to suspense by allowing the villain to appear early and often in the film without revealing his identity. Whereas other genres might create mystery through an early visualization of the antagonist in clothes that hide or disguise, the thriller has evolved a technique that envelops a murderer with a sense of the supernatural or the not-quite-human—although he will eventually be revealed as quite human. This technique is particularly common in the erotic thriller. An example of this image occurs at the beginning of *Jagged Edge*, a film about Teddy Barnes (Glenn Close), a very successful lawyer who becomes sexually involved with Jack Forrester (Jeff Bridges), a client who may be a serial murderer. In the opening frames, the audience is confronted with a fully disguised person who ties a terrified woman to a bed. Is the person a man or a woman? Who is it? The mysterious figure is seen in darkness, wearing form-fitting tights and a long-sleeved black shirt, its head completely covered by a black mask. Brandishing a knife with a jagged edge, "it" is terrifying in "its" evocation of a minimally human form with no distinguishing traits, as if it were an as-yet-unfinished form animated by nothing but primitive urges. As Teddy continues her romance with Jack, the audience is encouraged to wonder if behind his handsome face and polished manner lurk terrible forces capable of inhuman savagery.

In sum, the thriller defamiliarizes human nature and the world, through its plot structure, its thematic concerns, and its iconic visual representations, and shows our species and our environment to us in an eerie, distorting mirror. More sensational than most genres, but also more audacious and unsparing in its insights into the human condition than many kinds of Hollywood films, the thriller can work as both heart-pounding entertainment and a thought-provoking journey into the heart of philosophical questions about the nature of life and the human condition. Suspense thrillers offer us all the benefits of encountering the dark side of life with none of the risks, and, arguably, they are part of the cultural resources that prepare us for discovering, as does the thriller protagonist, that things are not what we thought they were.

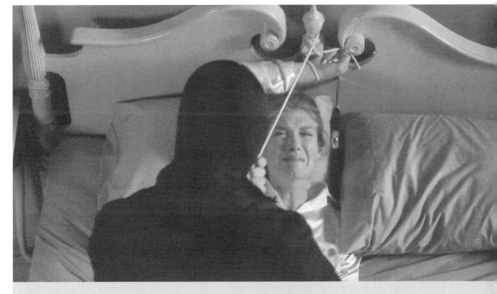

Jagged Edge (1985) The woman in this frame from the opening scene of *Jagged Edge* is Page Forrester (Maria Mayenzet), whose death is the catalyst for a traditional suspense story. Page's visual importance is that she occupies the position for which the heroine of the film, Teddy Barnes (Glenn Close), a lawyer, seems destined. The black, anonymous figure in this first image in the film is the equivalent of the bomb we know is in the room in Alfred Hitchcock's definition of suspense. Teddy is in harm's way, and it is only a matter of time before the killer attacks her. Of course, the identity of the killer is something of a surprise, but that revelation is only spice added to the continuous anxiety created about Teddy's safety. The pulse of *Jagged Edge* is suspense about whether Teddy will survive the attack, not whether it will come.

The Lady from Shanghai

The editing and frame compositions of the thriller support its thematic and visual concerns by using the language of cinema to produce feelings in the audience identical to those experienced by the characters, of being caught in a confusing space rendered obscure by an anxiety-filled partial vision. In *Vertigo*, for example, when Scottie Ferguson follows "Madeleine," we see San Francisco through the windshield of Scottie's car turn into a winding, confusing, and mysterious maze. Plunging the screen into darkness can produce a similarly eerie ocular limitation, as when, in *Strangers on a Train*, Guy Haines enters Bruno Anthony's home late at night hoping to tell Bruno's father about his son's madness. The deep shadow in the Anthony home is created by innovative use of the screen to create partial vision, which turns threatening indeed when it is Bruno and not his father who emerges from the darkness. But it is Orson Welles's thriller *The Lady from Shanghai* that pulls out all stops in its visual and aural evocations of the protagonist Mike O'Hara's near-fatal encounter with the disorientation caused by Elsa Bannister and her husband.

The Lady from Shanghai is the story of the experiences of Mike O'Hara, a sailor working as the bosun of a yacht owned by a famous defense attorney, Arthur Bannister (Everett Sloane), during a cruise Bannister takes through the Panama Canal and up the Mexican coast with his wife, Elsa, and his sleazy and peculiar business partner, George Grisby (Glenn Anders). Mike's passion for Elsa renders him blind to the full implications of her attempts to seduce him, her husband's wrath, and the sinister relationship between the Bannisters and Grisby. The victim of partial vision with a vengeance, Mike allows himself to be pulled by Grisby into a criminal conspiracy that no sane man would agree to. It almost immediately goes wrong, leaving Mike accused of murder, and the jealous Bannister acting as his lawyer, vengefully determined to see that Mike is found guilty and executed.

The film is filled with breathtaking, panoramic images of San Francisco, the ocean, Mexico, and the stunning Elsa Bannister, played by the screen goddess Rita Hayworth, so it would seem to be presenting us with a world in which everything of importance is in plain sight. But these appearances are deceiving. Mike's voice-over keeps reminding us that everything we have seen through his eyes is distorted, that he sees only what he wants to see while under the spell of the enchanting Elsa. Mike's claims of partial vision are supported by the numerous shocks he and the audience receive when there are sudden revelations of what has been hiding in plain sight.

The Lady from Shanghai begins with a high contrast between dark shadows and brilliant, sometimes glaring, light, suggesting the polarities of different kinds of obstructed sight and visibility. The light is so bright that it is as confounding to the eyes as the darkness. In fact, the first narratively significant moment in which we realize that something problematic lurks just beyond our field of vision occurs in dazzling sunlight on the Bannister yacht. After Bannister has briefly gone ashore, Mike is confronted by the spectacle of Elsa emerging from the water onto the yacht, a combination of mermaid and pinup girl, tantalizing and tempting him with a potpourri of bold seductive overtures and postures of quivering vulnerability. Welles frames this encounter in tightly focused shot–reverse shot close-ups of the pair, seemingly using cinematic language to create a world in which nothing exists but the powerful attraction between the two of them. The tight framing is especially evocative of the lovers' secret world when Elsa invites a kiss from Mike at the climax of this shot–reverse shot patterning, and, tempted beyond endurance, Mike leans in to kiss his employer's wife, erasing the space of propriety between them, and making the two a forbidden one. But what Welles is really doing is using close-ups to set up a moment that reveals Mike's partial vision. Suddenly, as Mike and Elsa move out of the kiss, their bliss is shattered by Grisby's broken, piercing voice, tearing into the frame with a sinister "So long, kiddies!" Grisby has been in a boat alongside the yacht all along. Unseen, but now revealed, he is a dangerous witness to their adulterous embrace. What else have we not seen?

The danger of partial vision erupts again as the plot thickens when Grisby makes his proposal to Mike, again in full sunlight, after the boat docks in Acapulco. Walking Mike away from the others, Grisby outlines a plan full of hidden implications that audiences are likely to miss initially because of the euphoric beauty of the landscape and the mesmerizing music on the sound track. However, those reading the visual language of this encounter will see that the images prefigure trouble. Grisby offers Mike $5,000 (equivalent today to about $51,000) to make it look as if Mike has killed him so that Grisby can disappear. Mike is appalled but tempted because the money, as he believes, would enable him to run away with Elsa. But what do the shot compositions say about his situation? The two men walk at the edge of a precipice that looks down on the famous beaches of Acapulco. They appear to walk at the limit of solid ground; a sense of the risk of slipping and falling permeates the scene. The dizzying spectacle suggests the danger both of them are in, the details of which we won't learn for a while. But it turns out that Grisby's proposal is riddled with lies. He claims that he wants to get away from his wife, but later Mike learns that Grisby was unmarried. He also claims that he wants to collect insurance once Mike has created the appearance of Grisby's death, but when Mike is no longer under Elsa's spell he realizes that Grisby can't collect insurance if the world thinks he's dead. What Grisby doesn't see is even worse. He's really about to be killed. And that too will have implications for Mike.

Images of Mike's walking into danger he cannot see abound in *The Lady from Shanghai*, and they become increasingly intense as the story unfolds. The next evening, Elsa, teasing Mike with the prospect of the two of them running away together, leads him through the maze-like twists and turns of an old neighborhood in Acapulco, filled with cramped, dark streets, peekaboo galleries of arches, and dead ends. Elsa is embroiled in a plot with Grisby to kill Bannister and may well have already decided that she will kill Grisby, and maybe Mike too, once she is free of her husband. But in the shadowy Acapulco maze, she limits Mike's sight to her charade of helpless bondage in an unhappy marriage.

Shadowy limits on sight are also invoked when Mike goes on trial after Grisby is actually murdered, and not by him. Bannister has insisted that he serve as Mike's lawyer, and his dark intentions to make sure Mike is convicted are telegraphed, as he and Elsa sit in the hallway of the courthouse, while Bannister meets and greets the shadows of the judge and the prosecuting attorney for Mike's trial. The men themselves are not visible onscreen.

The high point of the cinematic language of this thriller is reached when Mike realizes that Elsa herself is behind Grisby's murder. When Elsa's henchmen abduct him and leave him in the fun house of an amusement park closed for the season, he sees clearly that she is behind all his confusion. Welles's selection of an empty amusement park for Mike's realization that Elsa is his nemesis as well as his love allows him to portray Mike's awakening through an adaptation of the venerable European practice of misrule, an ancient tradition. During days of misrule, cities and towns became festivals in which all civilized order was turned on its head. Lower-class citizens impersonated those in authority and sometimes people in authority lived a day in the shoes of the people they normally ruled. Men and women might change roles. And violence and sexually charged behavior, normally restrained, were allowed into the open. In the fun-house scene, traditional social misrule is replaced by a modern psychological version of the shattering of normal order.

From the beginning of the film, Mike tells us that he was completely disoriented by Elsa's allure. We've seen him nearing the edge of a normal perception of reality throughout the film, and in the fun house he topples over the edge into the one of the most disorienting mazes in the history of the thriller genre, a topsy-turvy world of shadowy industrial beams and girders, and a cartoon-like cluster of images bearing the words "Stand Up or Give Up." As Mike stumbles around in confusion, he falls down a slide into darkness, through the mouth of a plaster-cast mythical beast into a room full of distorting mirrors and right in front of Elsa. The visual grammar of this progression of images establishes Elsa as the author of Mike's disorientation. Welles engineers the images so that we have no distance from Mike's ordeal. We wander, slip, and slide with him every step of the way.

In this moment of psychological misrule, it becomes clear to Mike that he has been living in a shadow world, unable to grasp the true danger Elsa poses. This realization frees Mike to acknowledge that if he does not take a stand against the chaos caused by the greed and corruption embodied in the Bannisters, his life will be meaningless and

**The Lady from Shanghai
(1947)** Mike (Orson Welles) enters a disorienting maze amidst shadows of beams and girders.

The Lady from Shanghai **(1947)** The maze continues into a fun house where Mike is confronted by the phrase, "Stand Up or Give Up." He then falls down a slide into darkness and is eventually confronted by Elsa (Rita Hayworth) at the end of his strange descent—indicating that she is at the core of Mike's hallucinatory experience.

hopeless. It isn't easy. Mike finds himself in the Hall of Mirrors with not only Elsa but also Bannister, who has followed them to the fun house, and this husband-and-wife pair have guns. The three are trapped inside self-generating illusions in which Elsa and Bannister endlessly reflect back at each other their selfishness and violence.

The hateful couple shatter the mirror maze as they shoot at each other, and they both die despite neither ever having a clear shot at the other among the many images of each in the mirrors. How do they manage to hit a real living body among so many deceptive reflections? It is this evil that Mike escapes as the Bannisters self-destruct, but, because Welles's film epitomizes Hollywood at its most sophisticated, there is no happy ending. Mike will never escape the wound he received at Elsa's hands. As he walks out of the disorienting fun house into the fresh open air, his voice-over tells us that it is very likely that he will always be her prisoner. "Maybe I'll live so long that I'll forget her," he says. "Maybe I'll die trying." If ever a film innovatively, challengingly, and vividly produced for the audience a visual engagement in the thriller's view of universal instability, it is *The Lady from Shanghai*.

Martha P. Nochimson

QUESTIONS FOR DISCUSSION

1. There has been much disagreement about the definition of the thriller. What is the most successful and helpful of the definitions of the suspense thriller genre described in this chapter?

2. Male bonding has traditionally been a source of security in Hollywood films. The partnership between the hero and his buddy or father often means the ability to solve a problem or bring a situation to a successful conclusion. Think of Obi-Wan Kenobi (Alec Guinness) and Luke Skywalker (Mark Hamill) in *Star Wars* (1977). Part of the insecurity that permeates the atmosphere of thrillers is a breakdown of male bonding. Which thrillers most clearly emphasize dangers that result from problems in crucial relationships between men?

3. *Seven Days in May, Three Days of the Condor, Jacob's Ladder*, the Bourne trilogy, and *Syriana* all use the form of the suspense thriller to make political statements. What makes the thriller a particularly powerful vehicle for political commentary?

4. The erotic thrillers of the 1970s, '80s, and '90s dramatize the national traumas set in motion by the success of the women's movement. Which thrillers of this period are feminist, which are antifeminist, and which are somewhere in between in their portraits of powerful and successful women?

5. In the comic *Charade* and the bleak and mind-bending *The Lady From Shanghai* and *Inception*, we see that the thriller can portray the chaos unleashed by great wealth and/or an inordinate desire for money. Discuss the ways in which these films link money and destabilization by means of the conventions of the thriller genre.

FOR FURTHER READING

Bonitzer, Pascal. "Partial Vision: Film and the Labyrinth." *Wide Angle* 4, no. 4 (1982), 56–63.

Cawelti, John G. *Mystery, Violence, and Popular Culture*. Madison: University of Wisconsin Press, 2004.

Derry, Charles. *The Suspense Thriller: Films in the Shadow of Alfred Hitchcock*. Jefferson, NC: McFarland, 1988.

Frye, Northrop. *Anatomy of Criticism: Four Essays*. Updated ed. Princeton, NJ: Princeton University Press, 2000.

Gottlieb, Sidney, ed. *Hitchcock on Hitchcock: Selected Writings and Interviews*. Berkeley: University of California Press, 1997.

Leitch, Thomas. *Crime Films*. New York: Cambridge University Press, 2002.

Leonard, Suzanne. *Fatal Attraction*. Malden, MA: Wiley-Blackwell, 2009.

Loker, Altan. *Film and Suspense*. Bloomington, IN: Trafford Publishing, 2006.

Martin, Nina K. *Sexy Thrills*. Urbana: University of Illinois Press, 2007.

McCarty, John. *Thrillers: Seven Decades of Classic Suspense*. Secaucus, NJ: Citadel Press, 1992.

Modleski, Tania. *The Women Who Knew Too Much: Hitchcock and Feminist Theory*. 2nd ed. New York: Routledge, 2005.

Rubin, Martin. *Thrillers*. New York: Cambridge University Press, 1999.

Truffaut, François, and Helen G. Scott. *Hitchcock*. Rev. ed. New York: Simon & Schuster, 1985.

PHOTO CREDITS

p. 10 The Ladd Company, Shaw Brothers, Warner Brothers Pictures 1982; **p. 12** A Rafran-San Marco Production 1968; **p. 15** Warner Brothers/Seven Arts 1967; **p. 17** Warner Brothers Pictures 1941; **p. 18** Paramount Pictures 1974; **p. 21** RSO, Paramount 1977; **p. 27** Bazmark Films/Warner Brothers 2013; **p. 32** Bettmann/Corbis; **p. 40** Charles Chaplin Productions 1925; **p. 57** Hal Roach Studios 1923; **p. 59** Universal Pictures/Zide-Perry Productions/Newmarket Capital Group/Summit Entertainment; **p. 60** Paramount Pictures/Jerry Lewis Enterprises 1963; **p. 61** Universal Pictures/Imagine Entertainment 1996; **p. 63** Buster Keaton Productions/Joseph M. Schenck Productions 1928; **p. 65** Paramount Pictures 1933; **p. 68** Hal Roach Studios 1932; **p. 70** New Line Cinema/ Dark Horse Entertainment 1994; **p. 72** Conquering Unicorn 1987; **p. 73** Conquering Unicorn 1987; **p. 74** Conquering Unicorn 1987; **p. 75** Conquering Unicorn 1987; **p. 77** Conquering Unicorn 1987; **p. 80** Universal Pictures/ Photofest; **p. 83** Paramount Pictures, Cruise/Wagner Productions 2006; **p. 85** Twentieth Century Fox/Paramount Pictures/Lightstorm Entertainment 1997; **p. 88** Charles Chaplin Productions 1921; **p. 90** RKO Radio Pictures 1933; **p. 92** Warner Brothers Pictures 1955; **p. 94** Universal International Pictures 1955; **p. 96** Monarch Pictures, Ufland, Universal Pictures 1998; **p. 99** Twentieth Century Fox/Jerry Wald Productions; **p. 102** Pickford Corporation 1926; **p. 103** Samuel Goldwyn Company 1937; **p. 106** Egg PicturesPolyGram Filmed Entertainment/Twentieth Century Fox 1994; **p. 107** Columbia Pictures/Cappa Productions 1993; **p. 111** Warner Brothers Pictures/ Lakeshore Entertainment/Malpaso Productions 2004; **p. 114** Warner Brothers Pictures/Lakeshore Entertainment/Malpaso Productions

2004; **p. 120** John Springer Collection/Corbis; **p. 122** Universal Pictures/Miramax Films /Bedford Falls Productions 1998; **p. 124** Paramount Pictures, Touchstone Pictures, Interscope Communications 1999; **p. 127** Famous Players-LaskyCorporation/ Paramount Pictures 1927; **p. 128** Columbia Pictures 1937; **p. 129** Paramount Pictures 1953; **p. 131** Castlerock Entertainment/Nelson Entertainment 1989; **p. 133a** Orion Pictures Corporation 1985; **p. 133b** Orion Pictures Corporation 1985; **137** Arwin Pictures, Universal International Pictures 1959; **p. 138** 40 Acres and a Mule Fileworks 2000; **p. 142** Fox 2000 Pictures/Dune Entertainment/Major Studios Partners 2006; **p. 147** Revolution Studios/Red Om Films/ Hughes Entertainment 2002; **p. 149** Columbia Pictures/Mirage 1995; **p. 151** Fox Searchlight Pictures/Watermark/Dune Entertainment III 2009; **p. 154** Fox Searchlight Pictures/Watermark/Dune Entertainment III 2009**; p. 160** Warner Brothers/HeyDay Films 2009; **p. 166** Hal Roach/MGM 1934; **p. 169** Twentieth Century Fox 1947; **p. 172** Orion Pictures Corporation 1985; **p. 175** Warner Brothers Pictures/ Paramount Pictures/Kennedy-Marshall Company 2008; **p. 179** Liberty Films 1946; **p. 183** Columbia Pictures/Ross Hunter Productions 1973; **p. 184** Universal international Pictures 1950; **p. 185** Twentieth Century Fox 1990; **p. 187** MGM 1939; **p. 189** RKO Radio Pictures 1933; **p. 190** MGM 1932; **p. 193** Orion Pictures Corporation 1985; **p. 196** Orion Pictures Corporation 1985; **p. 200** Mirisch-7 Arts/United Artists/The Kobal Collection; **p. 204** Warner Brothers/Vitaphone Corporation 1933; **p. 205** RKO Radio Pictures 1935; **p. 208** MGM/Loew's 1949; **p. 210** Columbia Pictures/Twentieth Century Fox 1979; **p. 214** Paramount Pictres 1932; **p. 215** Warner Brothers Pictures 1933; **p. 216** Universal Pictures/Bristol Bay Productions/Envil Films 2004; **p. 218** MGM/Loew's 1944; **p. 223** Twentieth Century Fox/Bazmark Films/Angel Studios 2001; **p. 227** Magna Theatre Corp/Rodgers & Hammerstein Productions 1955; **p. 229** Radio Pictures 1936; **p. 230** Loew's/MGM/RKO-Pathe Studios 1952; **p. 233** RSO, Paramount 1977; **p. 235** RSO, Paramount 1977; **p. 236** RSO, Paramount 1977; **p. 237** RSO, Paramount 1977; **p. 238** RSO, Paramount 1977; **p. 239** RSO, Paramount 1977; **p. 242** Bettmann/CORBIS; **p. 245** Edison Manufactoring Company 1903; **p. 247** William S. Hart Productions 1920; **p. 249** Walter Wagner Productions 1939; **p. 250** Produzioni Europee Associati/ Arturo González Producciones Cinematográficas, S.A/ Constantin Film

Produktion 1966; **p. 254** Warner Brothers/Seven Arts 1969; **p. 256** Tig Productions/Majestic Films International 1990; **p. 257** Paramount Pictures 1953; **p. 258** Warner Brothers/C.V. Whitney Pictures 1956; **p. 259** Columbia Pictures/Pax Enterprises 1966; **p. 261** Stanley Kramer Productions 1952; **p. 265** A Rafran-San Marco Production 1968; **p. 267** Charles K. Feldman Group/Monterey Productions 1948; **p. 269** Argosy Productions 1948; **p. 271a** Twentieth Century Fox 1946; **p. 271b** Twentieth Century Fox 1946; **p. 272a** Twentieth Century Fox 1946; **p. 272b** Twentieth Century Fox 1946; **p. 275** Twentieth Century Fox 1946; **p. 278** Dreamworks LLC/The Kobal Collection; **p. 282** Buster Keaton Productions/Joseph M. Schenck Productions 1926; **p. 283** TriStar Pictures/Freddie Fields Productions 1989; **p. 284** Warner Brothers 1941; **p. 287** Warner Brothers 1943; **p. 291** DreamWorks SKG/Warner Brothers/Anblin Entertainment 2006; **p. 293** Deputy Coroporation 195; **p. 294** EMI Films/Universal Pictures 1978; **p. 296** Zoetrope Studios 1979; **p. 299** Warner Brothers/ Village Roadshow Pictures/Village-A.M. Partnership 1999; **p. 302** Republic Pictures 1949; **p. 311** Paramount Famous Lasky Corporation 1927; **p. 312** Zoetrope Studios 1979; **p. 315** DreamWorks SKG/Warner Brothers/Anblin Entertainment 1998; **p. 318** DreamWorks SKG/ Warner Brothers/Anblin Entertainment 1998; **p. 324** Paramount Pictures/Photofest; **p. 331** Twentieth Century Fox 1951; **p. 334** APJAC Productions/Twentieth Century Fox 1968; **p. 337** Universal Pictures/ Anblin Entertainment 1982; **p. 339** Warner Brothers Pictures/Village Roadshow Pictures 1999; **p. 340** Anarchist's Convention Films/UCLA Film and Television Archive/A-Train Films 1984; **p. 343** Brandywine Productions/Twentieth Century Fox 1979; **p. 344** LucasFilms/ Twentieth Century Fox 1977; **p. 347** Paramount Pictures/Century Associates 1979; **p. 351** MGM 1956; **p. 352** Hemdale Film/Pacific Western/Euro Film Funding 1984; **p. 354** Orion Pictures Corporation 1987; **p. 355** MGM/Stanley Kubrick Productions 1968; **p. 359** The Ladd Company, Shaw Brothers, Warner Brothers Pictures 1982; **p. 360** The Ladd Company, Shaw Brothers, Warner Brothers Pictures 1982; **p. 361** The Ladd Company, Shaw Brothers, Warner Brothers Pictures 1982; **p. 362** The Ladd Company, Shaw Brothers, Warner Brothers Pictures 1982; **p. 364** The Ladd Company, Shaw Brothers, Warner Brothers Pictures 1982; **p. 365** The Ladd Company, Shaw Brothers, Warner Brothers Pictures 1982; **p. 368** The Kobal Collection/Warner Brothers; **p. 371** UniversalPictures 1925; **p. 372** Jofa-Atelier

Berlin-Johannisthal/Prana-Film GmbH 1922; **p. 373** Universal Pictures 1931; **p. 375** RKO Radio Pictures 1942; **p. 376** Friedman-Lewis Productions 1942; **p. 377** Shamley Productions 1963; **p. 378** Warner Brothers/Hoya Productions 1973; **p. 381** Amercent Films/American Entertainment Partners L.P./Davis Entertainment 1987; **p. 384** Strong Heart/Demme Production/Orion Pictures Corporation 1991; **p. 386** Casey Productions/Eldorado Films/D.L.N. Ventures Partnership 1973; **p. 389** Cruise/Wagner Productions/ Sociedad General de Cine (SOGECINE) S.A./Las Producciones del Escorpión S.L. 2001; **p. 391** Chessman Park Productions 1980; **p. 396** Celador Films/Northmen Productions/Pathé 2005; **p. 398** Compass International Pictures/Falcon International Productions 1978; **p. 400** Compass International Pictures/Falcon International Productions 1978; **p. 402** Evolution Entertainment/Saw Productions/Twisted Pictures 2004; **p. 403** Evolution Entertainment/Saw Productions/ Twisted Pictures 2004; **p. 404** RKO Radio Pictures 1945; **p. 406** United Artists/Photofest; **p. 412** First National Pictures 1931; **p. 413** Universal Pictures 1983; **p. 414** Warner Brothers Pictures 1931; **p. 418** Paramount Pictures/Alfran Productions 1972; **p. 420** Warner Brothers Pictures 1990; **p. 428** Universal Pictures 1983; **p. 429a** The Ladd Company/Embassy International Pictures/PSO International 1984; **p. 429b** Miramax Films, Initial Entertainment Group (IEG), Alberto Grimaldi Productions 2002; **p. 431** Circle Films, Twentieth Century Fox 1990; **p. 432** The Caddo Company 1932; **p. 433** Warner Brothers 1949; **p. 434** United Artists/Photofest; **p. 438** The Ladd Company/ Embassy International Pictures/PSO International 1984; **p. 440** The Ladd Company/Embassy International Pictures/PSO International 1984; **p. 443** The Ladd Company/Embassy International Pictures/ PSO International 1984; **p. 446** The Kobal Collection/Universal; **p. 448** Twentieth Century Fox 1947; **p. 451** Warner Brothers 1932; **p. 453** Twentieth Century Fox 1940; **p. 456** Independent Production Company (IPC)/Intl Union of Mine, Mill & Smelter Workers 1954; **p. 457** 40 Acres and a Mule Fileworks 1989; **p. 460** Tristar Pictures/ Clinica Estetico 1993; **p. 461** Mark Peterson/Corbis; **p. 462** Mirisch Corporation 1967; **p. 468** Havoc/Polygram Filmed Entertainment/ Working Title Films 1995; **p. 469** Stanley Kramer Productions 1959; **p. 471** Twentieth Century Fox 1979; **p. 472** Independent Moving Pictures Company of America 1913; **p. 476** Warner Brothers Pictures/ Industry Entertainment/Participant Productions 2005; **p. 479** Warner

Brothers Pictures/Industry Entertainment/Participant Productions 2005; **p. 484** Universal/The Kobal Collection; **p. 487** Paramount Pictures 1942; **p. 490** RKO Radio Pictures 1944; **p. 493** Paramount Pictures 1974; **p. 495** Mark Hellinger Productins/Universal Pictures 1946; **p. 496** Paramount Pictures 1944; **p. 498** Warner Brothers Picture 1945; **p. 499** Universal International Pictures 1949; **p. 502** Security Pictures/Theodora Productions 1955; **p. 505** Parklane Pictures Inc 1955; **p. 506** RKO Radio Pictures 1947; **p. 508** Twentieth Century Fox 1946; **p. 509** RKO Radio Pictures 1947; **p. 511** Parklane Pictures Inc 1955; **p. 512** Parklane Pictures Inc 1955; **p. 513** Parklane Pictures Inc 1955; **p. 514** Parklane Pictures Inc 1955; **p. 515** RKO Radio Pictures 1944; **p. 516** Security Pictures/Theodora Productions 1955; **p. 517** Security Pictures/Theodora Productions 1955; **p. 520** Paramount Pictures/Photofest; **p. 524** RKO Radio Pictures 1932; **p. 528** Paul Gregory Productions 1955; **p. 530** Paramount Pictures/ Alfred Hitchcock Productions 1958; **p. 531** Melville-Talbot Productions 1962; **p. 533** Seven Arts Productions/Joel Productions 1964; **p. 537** Amblin Entertainment/Cappa Films/Tribeca Productions 1991; **p. 539** Columbia Pictures 1978; **p. 541** Syncopy 2010; **p. 544** Universal/Stanley Donen Films 1963; **p. 548** Warner Brothers 1951; **p. 551** Columbia Pictures/Mercury Productions 1947; **p. 553** Columbia Pictures/Delphi IV Productions 1985; **p. 557** Columbia Pictures/Mercury Productions 1947; **p. 558a** Columbia Pictures/Mercury Productions 1947 **p. 558b** Columbia Pictures/ Mercury Productions 1947; **p. 558c** Columbia Pictures/Mercury Productions 1947.

INDEX

Allen, Joan, 549

Allen, Woody, 50, 56, 58, 60, 61, 67, 69, 96, 125, 130, 154, 171-73, 176, 193-97, 222

"All of Me," 148

All of Me (1984), 61, 140, 180

All Over the Guy (2001), 134

All Quiet on the Western Front (1930), 284

All That Heaven Allows (1955), 93, 94, 98

All That Jazz (1979), 210

Almira Gulch (character), 182

Almodóvar, Pedro, 103, 104

Alonzo the Armless (character), 370

Alraune (Hungarian 1918), 370

Alraune (German 1928), 370

Alraune (German 1930), 370

Alraune (German 1952), 370

Al Roberts (character), 485, 486

Altaira (character), 332

"Alter Ego," 228

Altman, Rick, 3, 26, 136, 212-13, 217-19, 224

Altman, Robert, 130, 210, 455, 492

Alton, John, 489, 502-3, 507, 517, 518

Alvy Singer (character), 69

Amadeus (1984), 216

Amanda (character), 401, 402

"Amapola," 439

Amazing Dr. Clitterhouse, The (1938), 415

Amazing Spider-Man, The (2012), 171

American Beauty (1999), 96, 178

American Cyborg (1993), 353

American Gangster (2007), 421, 427, 435

American Gun (2005), 459

American History X (1998), 449

American in Paris, An (1951), 202n.1, 207, 222

"American in Paris Ballet, An," 228

American International, 209

American Me (1992), 421, 435

American Pie (1999), 35, 52, 59, 64

American Pie series, 59

American soldiers, combat films' portrayal of, 304-5, 307-8

American Tragedy, An (1951), 454

American Werewolf in London, An (1981), 380

Amy Kane (character), 261, 262

Anaconda (1997), 393

Anatomy of Criticism (1957, Frye), 3

Anchorman (2004), 35

Anchors Aweigh (1945), 178, 228

Anders, Glenn, 554

Anderson, Bronco Billy, 246

Anderson, Paul Thomas, 53

Andrew Beckett (character), 460

Andrews, Dana, 499

Andrews, Julie, 220

Andromeda Strain, The (1971), 335

Angel and the Badman (1947), 261, 263

Angel Face (1952), 499

Angels with Dirty Faces (1938), 415, 435

Anger Management (2003), 53

animal comedies, 59

Animal Crackers (1930), 46, 67, 69, 211

animations

    fantasy, 163, 166-67

    science fiction, 335

    stop-motion, 164

Aniston, Jennifer, 132, 134, 155

Anna Dundee (character), 497, 499

Anna Karenina (1935), 89

Anna Karenina (Tolstoy), 96, 105

Anna Moore (character), 101

Ann Darrow (character), 164, 181-82

Annette (character), 234, 237, 238

Annie Get Your Gun (1950), 212, 224

Annie Hall (1977), 69, 122, 130

Annie Johnson (character), 101

Annie Reid (character), 136

À nous la liberté (1931), 41

Anthony Swafford (character), 298

anti-communist investigations, 454

Anton Chigurh (character), 540, 547

Apache (1954), 255

Apartment, The (1960), 136

Apatow, Judd, 55, 70, 154

Apocalypse Now (1979), 13, 294-96, 300, 312

Appaloosa (2008), 11, 251

Appointment with Danger (1951), 503

April in Paris (1952), 222

Apted, Michael, 458

Arachnophobia (1990), 380

Arbuckle, Fatty, 37, 41, 60

Archie Gates (character), 298

Ariel (character), 332

Aristophanes, 34, 121

Aristotle, 2

Arlen, Richard, 383

Armand (character), 105

Armstrong, Robert, 164

Arness, James, 332

Aronson, David, 419

Arquette, Rosanna, 133

art direction, in melodramas, 106

art films, horror and, 370

Arthur, Jean, 127, 152, 263

Arthur Bannister (character), 554-59

artificial intelligence, 346

Arzner, Dorothy, 90

As Good As It Gets (1997), 140, 148

Ashby, Hal, 130

Asian characters, in science fiction, 341

Asphalt Jungle, The (1950), 494

Assassination of Jesse James, The (2007), 251

Astaire, Fred, 35, 123, 192, 197, 201, 203–5, 207, 215, 217, 228, 229, 231, 233, 235, 238, 239, 469

Astaire-Rogers films, 204, 215, 231

"As Time Goes By," 156

Astor, Gertrude, 58

Astor, Mary, 545

Astounding Stories, 325

As You Like It (1908), 125

As You Like It (1912), 125

As You Like It (Shakespeare), 121, 139, 147

Atonement (2007), 96–97

Attack of the Giant Leeches (1959), 332

At the Movies, 75

audiences, 19–23

    changes in attitudes of, 22

    for contemporary combat films, 297

    expectations of, 4–5, 19

    meanings generated by, 5–7

    of melodramas, 81

    memories of, 8–9

    of science fiction, 347–48

Auguste Dupin (character), 488

Austen, Jane, 5

Autry, Gene, 206, 327

Avalon, Frankie, 209

Avenging Conscience, The (1914), 370

AVP: Alien vs. Predator series, 338, 347

Awful Truth, The (1937), 36, 126, 128

Aykroyd, Dan, 50, 52

B

Babes in Toyland (1934), 165–66, 180

Bacall, Lauren, 499, 510

backlash thrillers, 538–39

backstage stories (musical), 213–15

Back Street (1932), 89, 101

Back to Bataan (1945), 288

Back to the Future III (1990), 9

Backus, Jim, 92

Bad Girls (1994), 263

Badham, John, 239–40

Balanchine, George, 227

Ball, Lucille, 36

Ballad of Cable Hogue, The (1970), 251

Ball of Fire (1941), 128, 136, 212

Balzac, Honoré de, 82

Bambi (1942), 109, 167, 188

Bananas (1971), 60

Bancroft, George, 410

Bandido (1956), 253

Band Wagon, The (1953), 207, 217, 220, 225, 228, 230, 233, 234

Bank Dick, The (1940), 44

Bank Robbery, The (1908), 246

Banks, Leslie, 524, 525

Barber Shop, The (1933), 58

Barbie, 480

Bardem, Javier, 540

Barnes, Julian, 304

Barrymore, Drew, 132, 139

Barrymore, Lionel, 169

Barthelmess, Richard, 104

Basic Instinct (1992), 549, 552

Basinger, Jeanine, 286, 288, 310

Bassett, Angela, 341

Bataan (1943), 288

Bathing Beauty (1944), 215

Batman (1989), 171

Batman (character), 2, 190, 191

Batman Begins (2005), 171

Batman Forever (1995), 171

Batman movies, 171

Batman Returns (1992), 171

Battle at Elderbush Gulch, The (1913), 244

Battle Beyond the Stars (1980), 340

Battlestar Galactica, 178

Baum, L. Frank, 161, 163

"Be a Clown," 228

Bean, Sean, 480

Beast from 20,000 Fathoms, The (1953), 170, 381

Beatles, The, 15

Beatty, Warren, 130, 422

Beau Hunks (1931), 44

beauty, in romantic comedy, 140–43

Beauty and the Beast (1991), 167, 210

Bedlam (1946), 375

Bee Gees, 233, 234

Beetlejuice (1988), 162

Before Sunrise (1995), 135

Being John Malkovich (1999), 180

Belafonte, Harry, 339

Belasco, David, 84

Believers, The (1987), 394

Bell, Robert, 26

Bellamy, Ralph, 128, 152

Bell Boy, The (1918), 41

Bellboy, The (1960), 49

Burke, Billie, 187
Burke, Kathleen, 383
Burnett, W. R., 412
Burning Bed, The (1984), 457
Burns, Ken, 300
Burr, Raymond, 551
Burroughs, Edgar Rice, 163
Burton, Jeff, 334
Burton, Tim, 162, 170, 173, 174, 185, 333
Buscemi, Steve, 422
Buscombe, Edward, 3, 260n.2
Bush, George H. W., 175, 458
Busy Bodies (1933), 36, 44
Butch Cassidy and the Sundance Kid (1969), 254
Butcher Boy, The (1917), 60
"By Myself," 233, 234
Byrne, Gabriel, 407, 421, 431

C

Cabaret (1972), 210
Cabinet of Dr. Caligari, The (1920), 371, 395
Cabin in the Sky (1943), 206, 207
Caddyshack (1980), 53
Caesar Enrico Bandello (character), 412, 430, 434
Cage, Nicolas, 145
Cagney, James, 203, 204, 207, 217, 407, 412, 414–16, 435
Cahiers du Cinéma, 465
Cain, James M., 365, 488
Cali, Joseph, 237
Camelot (1967), 222
Camille (1936), 89, 105
Campbell, Eric, 55
"Can't Take My Eyes Off You," 156
Canutt, Yakima, 245–46
Cape Fear (1962), 492, 530–32, 543, 547–49, 552
Cape Fear (1991), 535, 536, 543, 549
Capone, Al, 413, 415, 416, 434, 435
Capra, Frank, 43, 53, 126, 179, 452
Captain America (character), 2
Captive City (1952), 486
Captive Women (1952), 330
Carell, Steve, 34, 58
Carlo, Yvonne De, 492
Carmela Soprano (character), 433
Carmen Jones (1954), 206
Caro, Niki, 474, 480, 481
Caron, Leslie, 207, 228
Carousel (1956), 209, 223
Carousel (musical), 227
Carpenter, John, 331, 378, 385, 398–401

Carrey, Jim, 34, 35, 54–56, 58, 63, 67, 69, 70
Carrie (1976), 390
Carrie (character), 141
Carroll, Noël, 116, 543
Carson, Diane, 144
Carvey, Dana, 52
Casablanca (1942), 9, 45, 154, 279
Casino (1995), 432, 435
Cassidy, Joanna, 357
casting, for romantic comedies, 154–56
Castle of Otranto, The (Walpole), 390
Casualties of War (1989), 294, 295, 305
Cat and the Canary, The (1927), 380
Catherine Tramell (character), 552
Catholic Church, 115
Catlin, George, 243–44, 260
Cat People (1942), 375, 403, 508
Cat-Women of the Moon (1953), 330
Cawelti, John, 254, 266, 543
Cazale, John, 295
Cecilia (character), 192–97
Celluloid Weapon, The, 464
censorship, 451, 453, 527
CGI, *See* computer-generated imagery
Chalky White (character), 427
Chan, Jackie, 55, 64, 70
Chandler, Raymond, 365, 486, 488, 490, 492, 506, 515
Chaney, Lon, 370, 371
Chaney, Lon, Jr., 373, 374
Changeling, The (1980), 391–92
Chapelle's Show, 190
Chapin, Billy, 527–28
Chaplin, Charlie, 33–36, 38–43, 47, 49, 52, 55–58, 63, 64, 70, 87, 88, 126
Charade (1963), 530, 534, 544–45, 550
Charisse, Cyd, 228, 231
Charles, Ray, 216
Charles Lampert (character), 534
Charles Pike (character), 138
Chase, Chevy, 52, 62
Chase, David, 421, 432
Chase, The (1946), 488, 500
"chase films," 37
Chato, 244
Cheadle, Don, 462
"Cheek to Cheek," 192, 231
Cher, 145, 461
Chevalier, Maurice, 201, 214
Chew (character), 363
Cheyenne Autumn (1964), 255
Cheyenne Social Club, The (1970), 262
Chicago (2002), 202n.1, 211

H

Haggis, Paul, 112
Hairspray (2007), 211
HAL 9000 (character), 335, 346, 349, 355
Hale, Jean, 433
Haley, Jack, 167, 187
Hall, Charles D., 390
Hall, Porter, 182
Hall and Oates, 156
Hallelujah! (1929), 206
Halloween (1978), 331, 378, 379, 385,
        398–401
Halloween (2007), 379
Hamburger Hill (1987), 294
Hamilton, Linda, 341
Hamilton, Margaret, 167, 182
Hamilton Bartholomew (character), 534
Hamlet (Shakespeare), 2
Hammer Films, 376
Hammerstein, Oscar, II, 208
Hammett, Dashiell, 365, 488
Hang 'Em High (1968), 251
Hank Aimes (character), 480
Hanks, Tom, 8, 136, 138, 303, 313, 314, 318,
        427, 460
Hannah, Daryl, 138, 357
Hannah and Her Sisters (1986), 96
Hannah Montana (character), 211
Hannibal Lecter (character), 369, 384–86
Han Solo (character), 344
Happy Gilmore (1996), 53, 58
"hard-boiled" crime fiction, 488
Hardwick, Gary, 134
Hardy, Babe, 43
Hardy, Oliver, 43, 44, 68, 165
Harlan County War (2000), 449
Harlem on the Prairie (1937), 206
Harlem Rides the Range (1939), 206
Harold Hill (character), 219
Harrelson, Woody, 474
Harryhausen, Ray, 162, 170
Harry Potter (character), 176, 192
Harry Potter and the Deathly Hallows: Part 2
        (2011), 160, 192
Harry Potter series, 161–62, 170, 171, 176,
        177, 192
Harry Powell (character), 527–28, 547
Hart, William S., 246, 247, 251, 263
Harum Scarum (1965), 222
Harvey (1950), 161, 170, 174, 183, 184
Harvey (character), 183
Harvey, Laurence, 532
Haskell, Molly, 62, 94

Hathaway, Anne, 132, 142
Hats Off (1927), 43
Hauer, Rutger, 357
Haunted Castle, The (1896), 370
Haunting, The (1963), 392
Haunting, The (1999), 392
Have Gun, Will Travel (1957–1963), 12
Havoc, June, 448
Hawke, Ethan, 151
Hawks, Howard, 7, 127, 128, 248, 331, 413,
        424–25, 466
Hawn, Goldie, 144
Haynes, Todd, 103, 104
Hays, Will, 451, 454, 463
Hays Office, 45
Hayworth, Rita, 527, 551, 554
Hazards of Helen, The (1914), 86
HBO, 457
"headliners," 447
Heart of Darkness (Conrad), 295
Heart of Maryland, The (1895), 84
Hearts in Dixie (1929), 206
Hearts of the World (1918), 306
Heathcliff (character), 100
"Heather on the Hill, The," 231
"Heav'n Heav'n," 46
Hedren, Tippi, 549
"Heigh Ho," 167
Heigl, Katherine, 59, 132
Heinlein, Robert A., 330
Helen Morgan Story, The (1957), 215
Helen Ramirez (character), 262
Hello, Dolly (1969), 202n.1
Hell's Hinges (1916), 246
Helmore, Tom, 521
Help, The (2011), 458, 465–66
Hemingway, Ernest, 177, 489
Henderson, Brian, 131
Henderson, Ray, 327
Henie, Sonja, 215
Henreid, Paul, 106
Henry (character), 384, 385
Henry, Charlotte, 165
Henry: Portrait of a Serial Killer (1986),
        384, 385
Henry Hill (character), 419–20, 426, 432,
        435–37
Henry Potter (character), 169, 182
Henson, Taraji P., 175
Hepburn, Audrey, 129, 141, 534, 544
Hepburn, Katharine, 36, 90, 127, 128, 136,
        204–5, 526
Herbert, Victor, 166

Jennings, Al, 246
Jenson, Lois, 474, 477–80
Jenson v. Eveleth Taconite Company, 474, 479
Jeremiah Johnson (1972), 253
Jerry the Mouse (character), 178, 228
Jesse James Meets Frankenstein's Daughter
    (1966), 381
Jezebel (1938), 89, 103, 105
Jheri Curl (character), 77
Jimmy Conway (character), 435
Jimmy Ringo (character), 254–55
Jim Stark (character), 92, 238
Joe Gillis (character), 496
Joe Kidd (1972), 251
Joe Turner (character), 535, 550
John, Elton, 223
John Ballantine (character), 526
John Baxter (character), 386
John Ford, 248–49
John Harper (character), 527–28
John M. Stryker (character), 288, 302, 303
John Neville (character), 538–39, 548
Johnnie Aysgarth (character), 526
Johnny Belinda (1948), 104
Johnny Case (character), 136
Johnny Guitar (1954), 262–63
Johnny Rocco (character), 422, 423
John Rawlins (character), 283
John Russell (character), 391
Johnson, Ben, 245–46, 264
Johnson, Nunnally, 453
Johnston, Eric, 454
Joke on the Joker, The (1912), 37
Jolson, Al, 202
Jolson Story, The (1946), 216
Jones, James Earl, 340
Jones, Shirley, 219, 226
Jones, Tommy Lee, 538, 540
Josey Aimes (character), 474–76, 478–80
Jourdan, Louis, 91
Judy Barton (character), 529
Julie (character), 105
Julius Kelp (character), 60
Jumping Jacks (1952), 62
Junger, Sebastian, 280
Junior Bonner (1972), 253
Juno (2007), 155
Jupiter Sharts (character), 283
Jurado, Katy, 12, 262
Jurassic Park (1993), 10
Jurassic Park films, 338, 347
Just Imagine (1930), 327

Just Like Heaven (2005), 136, 137
Just Married (2003), 146

K
Kael, Pauline, 466
Kalem, 125
Kane, Kathryn, 286
"Kansas City," 226
Karen Hill (character), 433, 436–37
Karen Walden (character), 298, 305
Karl Denham (character), 164
Karl Denholm (character), 181
Karloff, Boris, 373, 374, 392, 393
Karnick, Kristine, 62
Kasdan, Lawrence, 494
Kate and Leopold (2001), 148
Katharine Clifton (character), 105, 106
Kathie Moffat (character), 495, 499, 509
Kathy Selden (character), 1, 28
Kaufman, Geoff F., 117n.7
Kaufman, George S., 46
Kay Adams (character), 426, 432, 433
Kazan, Elia, 454
Keaton, Buster, 33–35, 41–43, 46, 49, 51,
    52, 55–57, 60, 62–64, 68, 70, 126,
    281, 282
Keaton, Diane, 426
Keegan, Rebecca, 470
Keel, Howard, 87
Keeler, Ruby, 204, 215
Keene, Malcolm, 522
Keeper of the Flame (1942), 526
Kefauver, Estes, 415
Kefauver Commission, 415
Kellner, Douglas, 457, 458
Kelly, Gene, 178, 207, 208, 217, 219, 227–31
Kelly, Grace, 261, 549
Kelly, Richard, 174–75
Kelly's Heroes (1970), 14
Kennedy, Arthur, 97, 99
Kennedy, George, 534
Kennedy, Jihmi, 283
Kennedy, John, 50
Ken Norton (character), 73
Kern, Jerome, 204, 208, 216
Kerr, Deborah, 100
Kerr-McGee, 461
Key Largo (1948), 422, 423, 492
Keyser Söze (character), 547
Keystone Film Company, 37, 38
Keystone Kops, 35, 38, 46, 50
Khouri, Callie, 468

Marvin's Room (1996), 95
Marx, Chico, 46, 58, 64, 65, 69
Marx, Groucho, 46, 50, 56, 58, 65, 67–69
Marx, Harpo, 46, 50, 56, 58, 68–69
Marx, Karl, 182
Marx Brothers, 34, 35, 46, 47, 50, 56, 58,
    63–65, 68, 70, 211, 222
Mary Brown (character), 58
Mary Jane Watson (character), 191
Mary Poppins (1964), 170, 202n.1, 209
Mary Poppins (character), 179
Mascot, 327
masculinity
    in combat films, 301–3
    ideals of, 320
    in science fiction, 339–40
M*A*S*H (1970), 279, 298
Mask, The (1994), 54, 70
"Masque of the Red Death" (Poe), 370
MasterCard, 15
Maté, Rudolph, 489
maternal melodramas, 89–91, 109–10
Matewan (1987), 447, 449
Matrimony's Speed Limit (1913), 125
Matrix, The (1999), 338, 339
Matrix effect, 338–39
Matrix trilogy, 341, 343, 347, 356
Matthau, Walter, 534
Mature, Victor, 274
Max Bercovicz (character), 419, 434, 441–43
Max Cady (character), 530–32, 536–37, 547,
    548, 552
Maxim de Winter (character), 526
Mayenzet, Maria, 553
Mayer, Louie, 452
Mayo, Virginia, 433
Maytime (1937), 213
Mazurki, Mike, 490
McAdam, Rachel, 177
McCabe and Mrs. Miller (1971), 13, 250,
    264–65
McCambridge, Mercedes, 262–63
McCarthy, Joseph, 416
McCarthy, Todd, 109
McCarty, William Henry, Jr. "Billy the
    Kid," 244
McConaughey, Matthew, 125, 132, 156
McCrea, Joel, 524
McDonald, Tamar, 139, 152
McDormand, Frances, 475
McGovern, Elizabeth, 434, 437, 438
McGregor, Ewan, 223
McIntosh, Burr, 101

McQueen, Steve, 257
meaning(s)
    cultural, 7–8
    generation of, 6–8
    and horror films, 387–88
    sources of, 5–6
Mean Streets (1973), 240
Mede (character), 73
Meeker, Ralph, 511, 512, 528
Meet Me in St. Louis (1944), 207, 216–18,
    223–24
Méliès, Georges, 37, 162–63, 326, 370
melodrama, 81–117
    "fallen woman" subgenre, 89
    "family," 91–93
    history of, 86–97
    iconography, 104–8
    maternal, 89–91, 109–10
    Million Dollar Baby, 108–17
    social-problem, 450
    in social-problem films, 459–61, 467,
        471–73, 477
    typologies, themes, and theories, 97–
        104
Melville, Jean-Pierre, 487
memories
    cultural, 14–16
    reconsolidation of, 14–16
men, in thrillers, 539–40
Men, The (1950), 461
Mendes, Sam, 96
Menges, Chris, 477
Mercury Theatre on the Air, The, 328
Merritt, Russell, 85
Mesa of Lost Women (1953), 330
Message in a Bottle (1999), 95
"message movies," 447
Messing, Debra, 135
Metalious, Grace, 99
Metropolis (1927), 326, 336–37, 357
Metropolitan Museum, 141
Meyers, Nancy, 133
MGM, 46, 164, 178, 180–81, 201, 206–9, 215,
    217, 230, 247, 374, 452
Michael Clayton (2007), 460, 462
Michael Corleone (character), 105, 417–19,
    426, 432–34
Michael Myers (character), 26, 385, 398–401
Michael Sullivan (character), 427
Micheaux, Oscar, 73, 450
Mickey Mouse (character), 167, 178, 187
Middleton, Charles, 328
Midler, Bette, 94

racism
in Civil War movies, 282–83
in combat films, 292
in fantasy films, 180–82
in science fiction, 341
in social-problem films, 449
Radcliffe, Daniel, 176
Raft, George, 412
Raiders of the Lost Ark (1981), 8
Railroaded (1947), 492, 502
Raisin in the Sun, A (1961), 455
Ralston, Jobyna, 42
Rambo (character), 78, 321
Rambo movies, 303
Ramos, Luis, 457
Randolph, Jane, 375
Random Harvest (1942), 100
Ransom Stoddard (character), 262
Raven, The (1935), 374
Raw Deal (1948), 492, 502
Ray (2004), 212, 216
Ray, Nicholas, 92
Raymond Shaw (character), 532, 547
Reagan, Ronald, 131, 295, 458, 535
realism, 14
in combat films, 280, 285, 295, 298, 299,
301, 309, 320
and fantasy, 178
in film noir, 502, 505
in gangster films, 428
in horror films, 378
and melodrama, 82, 87, 96, 98
and romantic comedy, 153
in slapstick, 76
in social-problem films, 447, 456, 459,
461, 471, 473–77
in video games, 297
reality, in thrillers, 543
Reality Bites (1994), 151
Rear Window (1954), 549, 551
Rebecca (1940), 523, 526, 545
Rebel Without a Cause (1955), 92, 105, 238
recognition, in melodramas, 100
recommendations to viewers, 26
Reconciliation Cause tradition (Civil War
movies), 281
reconsolidation of memories, 14–16
Recount (2008), 457
Red Cloud, 244
Redford, Robert, 109, 535
Red Kimona, The (1925), 451
Red River (1948), 248, 255, 259, 260, 267, 268

Red Rock West (1993), 494
Reeve, Christopher, 171
Reeves, Keanu, 339
Regan (character), 378, 384
Regeneration (1915), 409–10, 416, 427
Regina Lampert (character), 534, 544, 550
Reid, Wallace, 451
Reiner, Rob, 131
remarriage plot, in romantic comedy, 125
Remember the Night (1940), 128
Remington, Frederic, 244, 260
Renner, Jeremy, 475, 542
Rent (2005), 211, 222
repetition gags, in slapstick comedy, 67–69
Republic, 247, 327, 491
Republic Studios, 329
Rescued by Rover (1905), 86
Rescued from an Eagle's Nest (1908), 86
Reservoir Dogs (1992), 494
Restrepo (2010), 297
"Revolution" (Beatles), 15
Revueltas, Rosaura, 456
revues, 213
Rex Stetson (character), 137
Ribisi, Giovanni, 317
Rick Deckard (character), 357–65
Rickman, Alan, 149
Ride Lonesome (1959), 249
"Ride of the Valkyries" (Wagner), 295, 312
Riders of the Purple Sage (1925), 246
Ride the High Country (1962), 259, 262
Ringo Kid (character), 249
Rink, The (1916), 39
Rio Bravo (1959), 248
Rio Grande (1950), 255
Rio Lobo (1970), 248
Ripley (character), 341, 343
Rise and Fall of Legs Diamond, The (1960),
416, 435
Ritt, Martin, 458
rituals
genres as, 16–17
social function of, 16–17
Ritz, Al, 47
Ritz, Harry, 47
Ritz, Jimmy, 47
Ritz Brothers, 47
Rivera, Lance, 134
RKO, 201, 203, 247, 374, 491, 508
RKO Pictures, 374–75
Roach, Hal, 43
Road escapades, 211–12

—